WITHDRAWN

D1765868

University of Hertfordshire

Learning and Information Services

College Lane, Hatfield, Hertfordshire, AL10 9AB

For renewal of Standard and One Week Loans,
please visit the website: http://www.voyager.herts.ac.uk

This item must be returned or the loan renewed by the due date.
The University reserves the right to recall items from loan at any time.
A fine will be charged for the late return of items.

4827/KM/DS

EMERGING ISSUES IN TORT LAW

In this book, articles by leading tort scholars from Australia, Canada, Hong Kong, Israel, New Zealand, the United Kingdom and the United States deal with important theoretical and practical issues that are emerging in the law of torts. The articles analyse recent leading developments in areas such as economic negligence, causation, vicarious liability, non-delegable duty, breach of statutory duty, intentional torts, damages, and tort law in the family. They provide a foretaste of the issues that will face tort law in the near future and offer critical viewpoints that should not go unheeded. With its rich breadth of contributors and topics, *Emerging Issues in Tort Law* will be highly useful to lawyers, judges and academics across the common law world.

Emerging Issues in Tort Law

Edited by

**Jason W Neyers,
Erika Chamberlain** and
Stephen G A Pitel

·HART·
PUBLISHING

OXFORD AND PORTLAND, OREGON
2007

Published in North America (US and Canada) by
Hart Publishing
c/o International Specialized Book Services
920 NE 58th Avenue, Suite 300
Portland, OR 97213-3786
USA
Tel: +1 503 287 3093 or toll-free: (1) 800 944 6190
Fax: +1 503 280 8832
E-mail: orders@isbs.com
Website: www.isbs.com

© The editors and contributors severally, 2007

The editors and contributors have asserted their right under the Copyright, Designs and
Patents Act 1988, to be identified as the author of this work.

All rights reserved. No part of this publication may be reproduced, stored in a retrieval
system, or transmitted, in any form or by any means, without the prior permission of Hart
Publishing, or as expressly permitted by law or under the terms agreed with the appropriate
reprographic rights organisation. Enquiries concerning reproduction which may not be
covered by the above should be addressed to Hart Publishing at the address below.

Hart Publishing, 16C Worcester Place, OX1 2JW
Telephone: +44 (0)1865 517530 Fax: +44 (0)1865 510710
E-mail: mail@hartpub.co.uk
Website: http://www.hartpub.co.uk

British Library Cataloguing in Publication Data

Data Available

ISBN-13: 978-1-84113-707-0 (hardback)

Typeset by Columns Design Ltd, Reading
Printed and bound in Great Britain by
TJ International Ltd, Padstow, Cornwall

Foreword

The late Professor Albert Abel once observed wryly that legal analysis at its best combines overarching generality and tedious particularity. And so it is with the chapters in this volume. The authors take some of the seminal generalities in tort law—such as those of Lord Atkin, who reasoned 'The rule that you are to love your neighbour becomes in law, you must not injure your neighbour; and the lawyer's question, Who is my neighbour? receives a restricted reply,'[1] and Justice Benjamin Cardozo, who counselled against 'liability in an indeterminate amount for an indeterminate time to an indeterminate class,'[2]—as springboards into constellations of particularities. However, departing in this respect from Professor Abel's prescription, the articles in this volume are rarely tedious and at times are positively exhilarating.

While recognising that the application of generalities without particularity are difficult to predict, the authors show an awareness that particularities without generalities have little power to move the judicial mind, including (possibly) those of the several Chief Justices and other judicial figures who participated in the conference from which the content of this book is taken. One day soon, one expects, the authors' collective wisdom will be reflected in judgments of the courts thus represented and these in turn will become fodder for future such conferences. Thus does the common law advance.

Special mention should be made of the excellent chapter written by Professor Stephen Todd, who was honoured with the John Fleming Award for his contribution over the years to the law of torts. His analysis is a model of comparative scholarship.

The organisers of the *Emerging Issues in Tort Law* conference pulled together scholars, practitioners and judges from around the common law world and the Faculty of Law at the University of Western Ontario has done us all a great favour by publishing the results.

Justice Ian Binnie
Supreme Court of Canada
8 August 2006

---

[1] *Donoghue v Stevenson* [1932] AC 562 (HL) 580.
[2] *Ultramares Corporation v Touche* 174 NE 441 (NY 1931) 444.

Contents

Contributors

Elizabeth Adjin-Tettey, LLB, LLM, LLM, DJur, Associate Professor of Law, University of Victoria

Kumaralingam Amirthalingam, LLB, PhD, Associate Professor of Law, National University of Singapore

Peter Benson, AB, MSc, LLB, LLM, Professor of Law, University of Toronto

Vaughan Black, BA, MA, LLB, LLM, Professor of Law, Dalhousie University

Peter Cane, BA, LLB, DCL, Professor of Law, ANU College of Law, Australian National University

Erika Chamberlain, LLB, Assistant Professor of Law, University of Western Ontario

Israel Gilead, LLB, BA, LLD, Bora Laskin Professor of Law, Hebrew University of Jerusalem

Paula Giliker, BA, BCL, PhD, Reader in Comparative Law, University of Bristol

Rick Glofcheski, BA, LLB, LLM, Associate Professor of Law, University of Hong Kong

Lewis N Klar QC, BA, BCL, LLM, Professor of Law, University of Alberta

Michael A Jones, BA, LLM, PhD, Professor of Common Law, University of Liverpool

Richard Lewis, BA, MA, Professor of Law, Cardiff University

John Murphy, LLB, LLM, Reader in Law, University of Manchester

Jason W Neyers, BA, LLB, MSt, Associate Professor of Law, University of Western Ontario

Ken Oliphant, BA, BCL, City Solicitors' Educational Trust Reader in Tort, University of Bristol

David F Partlett, LLB, LLM, SJD, Dean and Asa Griggs Candler Professor of Law, Emory University School of Law

Stephen G A Pitel, BA, LLB, LLM, PhD, Associate Professor of Law, University of Western Ontario

Denise Réaume, BA, LLB, BCL, Professor of Law, University of Toronto

Robert H Stevens, BA, BCL, Lecturer in Law and Fellow and Tutor in Law at Lady Margaret Hall, University of Oxford

Andrew Tettenborn, MA, LLB, Bracton Professor of Law, University of Exeter

Stephen Todd, LLB, LLM, LLD, Professor of Law, University of Canterbury and Professor of Common Law, University of Nottingham

Shauna Van Praagh, BSc, LLB, LLM, JSD, Associate Professor of Law, McGill University

Stephen Waddams, BA, MA, PhD, LLB, LLM, SJD, FRSC, University Professor and Goodman/Schipper Professor of Law, University of Toronto

David R Wingfield, BA, MA, LLB, Partner, WeirFoulds LLP, Toronto

Richard W Wright, BS, JD, LLM, Professor of Law, Chicago-Kent College of Law, Illinois Institute of Technology

Introduction

JASON W NEYERS, ERIKA CHAMBERLAIN AND
STEPHEN G A PITEL*

THE ARTICLES IN this book arose from the *Emerging Issues in Tort Law* conference, held at the University of Western Ontario, Faculty of Law, on 9-10 June 2006. The conference brought together leading torts scholars, private law theorists, lawyers and judges from throughout the common law world, who gathered to discuss under-theorised and under-explored areas of tort law that are likely to be examined by appellate courts in the near future. For two days, this assembly of 'tortaholics' (as they were anointed by Justice Ian Binnie) was treated to a rich diet of scholarship, commentary, and informal exchange.

Despite the conference title, it was remarkable to hear several of the scholars begin their presentations with apologies for not addressing 'emerging' issues in tort law. It seems that we are accustomed to viewing tort law through the lens of history, and are cautious about proclaiming revolutionary developments. This is partly due to the common law nature of our subject, which mandates that the law develop in increments. It may also be attributable to the backlash that sometimes follows judicial attempts to rewrite or restate the law.[1] Yet perhaps it is an elemental characteristic of tort law that it cannot move forward without having one eye on the past. This tension between past and future emerges throughout the articles that follow.[2]

Peter Cane opens the book by proposing a distinction between the 'general' and 'specific' parts of tort law,[3] harking back to the same distinction initiated in criminal law by Glanville Williams.[4] He asks

---

* Each of the Faculty of Law, University of Western Ontario.
[1] One need only consider the fate of *Junior Books v Veitchi* [1983] 1 AC 520 (HL) to be suspicious of alleged revolutions in tort law.
[2] This tension manifests itself even in the most basic terminology: are tort victims 'plaintiffs' or 'claimants'? Given the international authorship of, and audience for, these articles, we have allowed the authors to make their own choices about which term to use. Several have chosen to use 'claimant' where the context is English law and 'plaintiff' where it is Canadian or Australian law.
[3] 'General and Special Tort Law: Uses (and Abuses) of Theory' ch 1.
[4] *Criminal Law: The General Part* (London, Stevens, 1953).

whether there is a general theory that defines tortious wrongs and responsibility, and if so, how its elucidation can contribute to our understanding and practice of tort law.

The chapters immediately following Cane's move to the 'special' part of tort law. The authors examine particular wrongs and types of damage that have been historically contentious, noting the constant evolution of tort law in conjunction with modern social conditions. Lewis Klar discusses the increasing role of statutory obligations in determining the tort liability of public authorities in Canada,[5] advocating an approach that accords with the decision in *The Queen v Saskatchewan Wheat Pool*.[6] Shauna Van Praagh[7] and Elizabeth Adjin-Tettey[8] critique tort law's understanding of modern intra-family relations, analysing respectively the range of responses to harms caused by children and the conventional arguments against recovery for involuntary parenthood. Rounding out the discussion of historically controversial claims, Michael Jones suggests a unifying principle for negligently inflicted psychiatric injury, an area that has been troubled by arbitrary categories and under-informed reasoning since its beginnings in the 19th century.[9]

The next group of chapters address the debate over recovery for economic loss, another historically contentious issue that continues to vex modern courts. Two of the chapters examine claims by contractual third parties, with Peter Benson looking particularly at the issue of disappointed legatees[10] and Stephen Waddams extending the discussion to contracts more generally.[11] Stephen Todd[12] and David Partlett[13] explore the notorious issue of defective structures, discussing the implications of denying recovery in both commercial and residential contexts. Tying all the above strands together, Israel Gilead examines the tools used by the courts to restrict the extent of liability, including relational and policy issues, indeterminacy and scope of risk.[14]

Moving from types of harm to other elements of liability, the next group of authors discuss the continuing evolution of the traditional doctrines of causation and vicarious liability. Richard Wright provides a theoretical perspective on the causal role of omissions.[15] Vaughan Black analyses the

---

[5] 'Breach of Statute and Tort Law' ch 2.

[6] [1983] 1 SCR 205.

[7] '"Sois Sage"—Responsibility for Childishness in the Law of Civil Wrongs' ch 3.

[8] 'Claims of Involuntary Parenthood: Why the Resistance?' ch 4.

[9] 'Liability for Psychiatric Damage: Searching for a Path between Pragmatism and Principle' ch 5.

[10] 'Should *White v Jones* Represent Canadian Law: A Return to First Principles' ch 6.

[11] 'Breaches of Contracts and Claims by Third Parties' ch 7.

[12] 'Policy Issues in Defective Property Cases' ch 8.

[13] 'Defective Structures and Economic Loss in the United States: Law and Policy' ch 9.

[14] 'Harm Screening Under Negligence Law' ch 10.

[15] 'Acts and Omissions as Positive and Negative Causes' ch 11.

unique problems raised by cases of 'decision causation', where it is impossible to know, for example, whether a consumer would have heeded a warning had one been provided by the manufacturer.[16] Robert Stevens explains the various instances of non-delegable duty with a view to showing that it is not a form of disguised vicarious liability.[17] John Murphy also discusses non-delegable duties, pointing out their often unclear justifications and proposing a general theory which could come to overtake vicarious liability in the future.[18] David Wingfield suggests that the term 'vicarious liability' should be replaced with 'strict liability', which more accurately describes its moral justifications and its application in modern cases of child sex abuse in institutional settings.[19] Completing the discussion, Paula Giliker examines the policy considerations involved in imposing vicarious liability for intentional wrongs, questioning how far the 'scope of employment' can be extended at the expense of employers and their insurers.[20]

The tension between past and future is further evident in the next group of chapters, which discuss new definitions of, and approaches to, seemingly well-entrenched tort law concepts. Andrew Tettenborn explores the elusive concept of loss[21] and Kumar Amirthanlingam foretells impending recovery for injuries engendered by the imposition of unconscionable risk or violation of autonomy.[22] Richard Lewis then examines the more contemporary issue of periodical payments, exposing the political motivations underlying recent reforms in the UK.[23]

The penultimate group of authors breathe new life into cases and principles that were becoming historical curiosities. Ken Oliphant revisits the age-old search for general principle in the law of intentional torts,[24] a quest which once occupied Pollock, Addison and Holmes, among others, and which continues to differentiate the common law from civilian systems. Similarly, Denise Réaume[25] describes how recent Canadian jurisprudence has rejuvenated the tort in *Wilkinson v Downton*,[26] even though

---

[16] 'Decision Causation: Pandora's Tool-Box' ch 12.

[17] 'Non-Delegable Duties and Vicarious Liability' ch 13.

[18] 'The Juridical Foundations of Common Law Non-Delegable Duties' ch 14.

[19] 'Perish Vicarious Liability?' ch 15.

[20] 'Comparative Perspectives on Vicarious Liability: Defining the Scope of Employment' ch 16.

[21] 'What is a Loss?' ch 17.

[22] 'The Changing Face of the Gist of Negligence' ch 18.

[23] 'Tort Law in Practice: Appearance and Reality in Reforming Periodical Payments of Damages' ch 19.

[24] 'The Structure of the Intentional Torts' ch 20.

[25] 'The Role of Intention in the Tort in *Wilkinson v Downton*' ch 21.

[26] [1897] 2 QB 57.

that tort was apparently rendered obsolete by the House of Lords' recent decision in *Wainwright v Home Office*.[27]

Finally, Rick Glofcheski provides a comparative perspective by surveying recent developments in the tort law of Hong Kong.[28] He argues that the emerging distinctiveness of Hong Kong tort law and its creative solutions to conventional problems commend it as a new, relevant source for courts and scholars in the more traditional common law world. A brief epilogue, courtesy of Stephen Todd, completes the book.

In all, the chapters in this book demonstrate that tort law continues to forge ahead, affording deference to the past where it is due but refusing to be bound by concepts that have lost their relevance, are incoherent, or have become unworkable. They provide a foretaste of the issues that will face tort law in the near future and offer critical viewpoints that should not go unheeded.

*   *   *

Both the conference and this book have benefited from generous support and assistance. We would like to thank the law firms who sponsored the conference: Bennett Best Burn LLP, Ledroit Beckett, Lerners LLP, McTague Law Firm LLP, Siskind, Cromarty, Ivey and Dowler LLP, Sutts, Strosberg LLP, and WeirFoulds LLP. We are also grateful for the financial support of the Social Sciences and Humanities Research Council of Canada, the Law Foundation of Ontario, and the Foundation for Legal Research, which, among other things, allowed us to have the editorial assistance of three talented law students: Daniel Dubois, Sean Flaherty, and Ryan Nielsen. We are indebted to the faculty, staff and students at Western Law, particularly Dean Ian Holloway and our conference coordinator, Michelle Bothwell, for their enthusiastic support of the conference. We are grateful to Justice Ian Binnie for penning the foreword. Finally, two of the editors, personally and on behalf of the authors, acknowledge the tireless efforts of Jason Neyers, who spent over a year planning, organising and promoting the conference. Jason has made the conference and this book possible.

We hope that you will enjoy these articles as much as we have. We are confident that they will benefit not only tortaholics but anyone interested in emerging issues in tort law.

---

[27] [2004] 2 AC 406.
[28] 'Where Principle Meets Pragmatism: Tort Law in Post-Colonial Hong Kong' ch 22.

1

General and Special Tort Law: Uses (and Abuses) of Theory

PETER CANE*

I. THE GENERAL/SPECIAL DISTINCTION

THE YEAR 1953 saw the publication of a major work by Glanville Williams entitled *Criminal Law: The General Part*.[1] The book's title alluded to a distinction—which Williams attributed to civil law systems—between the general and special parts of the criminal law. The author's declared motivation in adopting this distinction was practical: in the case of many crimes, the statutory provisions creating them have not, he observed, been the subject of judicial consideration. But there are certain general principles that apply to all crimes, an understanding of which would be useful to the practitioner confronted with a statutory provision as yet devoid of judicial interpretation. The topics covered in the book included mental states, attempts, the 'principle of legality', corporations, burden of proof, and so on. Various theorists of the criminal law have subsequently developed sophisticated 'philosophical' accounts of the general/special distinction. In recent years it has attracted more and more attention, to the point where it has recently been the subject of two substantial volumes of essays by leading scholars, one on the general part[2] and another on the special part.[3]

Another area in which the general/special distinction has made some impact is contract law. Here, the standard (student) texts tend to focus on general principles, detailed separate treatment of specific contracts such as bailment, construction, sale and so on being left to works written primarily

---

* ANU College of Law, Australian National University, Canberra ACT 0200, Australia.
[1] (Stevens, London, 1953).
[2] S Shute and AP Simester (eds), *Criminal Law Theory: Doctrines of the General Part* (Oxford, Oxford University Press, 2002).
[3] RA Duff and SP Green (eds), *Defining Crimes: Essays on the Special Part of the Criminal Law* (Oxford, Oxford University Press, 2005).

for practitioners, such as *Chitty on Contracts*.[4] But whereas civil law systems (following Roman law) tend to be structured primarily in terms of specific types of contract, common law systems start from general principles, developed through the action of *assumpsit*, and create categories of contracts by the implication of terms tailored to specific types of transaction.[5] Unlike criminal law theorists, contract law theorists have shown little interest in developing philosophical accounts of the general/special distinction. For this reason, and because contract law is outside my comfort zone, I will consider it no further in this chapter.

What about tort law? That, loosely put, is the question addressed in this chapter. At the outset, it is important to distinguish this from a different question, much discussed by writers on tort law in the late 19th and early 20th centuries when tort law was being created as a distinct legal category. This chapter is not concerned with the question of whether tort law (or some part of it, such as negligence law) is underpinned by a single liability-generating 'principle' such as 'the fault principle' or whether, on the contrary, tort law consists of various, more specific 'rules' of liability.[6] The concern, in other words, is not whether tort law can be described as what I have elsewhere called a 'loose federation of causes of action'[7] into one or another of which claimants must fit their case or whether, by contrast, it is for the defendant to give some good reason why a claim that falls within a broad principle of liability should, nevertheless, not succeed.[8] As we will see in more detail later, on no account of the general/special distinction in criminal law does the general part consist of one or more principles that generate the grounds of liability ('crimes') contained in the special part. Rather the general part deals with principles (or 'elements' or 'conditions') of liability that apply to offences contained in the special part. So, for instance, as commonly understood, the general part of the criminal law deals with culpability concepts such as intention and recklessness, and

---

[4] HG Beale (ed), *Chitty on Contracts*, 28th edn (London, Sweet & Maxwell, 1999), vol 1: General Principles and vol 2: Specific Contracts. Note the use of the plural 'contracts' in the title as opposed to the singular 'contract' used in the title of many student texts. Interestingly, although agency appears in general texts, it is dealt with in the second volume of *Chitty*. It has been argued that the idea that we have a law of contract, not contracts, has hindered the development of liability for unreasonable delay by insurers in settling claims: J Lowry and P Rawlings, 'Insurers, Claims and the Boundaries of Good Faith' (2005) 68 *MLR* 82.

[5] B Nicholas, 'Rules and Terms: Civil Law and Common Law' (1974) 48 *Tulane Law Review* 946, 948-52.

[6] A classic discussion is GL Williams, 'The Foundation of Tortious Liability' (1939-41) 7 *CLJ* 111.

[7] P Cane, *Tort Law and Economic Interests*, 2nd edn (Oxford, Oxford University Press, 1996) 447.

[8] This was the debate sparked by Lord Atkin's invention of the neighbour principle in *Donoghue v Stevenson* [1932] AC 562 (HL) and revived by Lord Wilberforce's recommendation of the two-stage approach (prima facie duty and countervailing policy considerations) in *Anns v Merton London Borough Council* [1978] AC 728 (HL).

with the concept of attempting a crime, while the special part tells us what sorts of conduct—what acts and omissions—are 'criminal': murder, theft, rape and so on.

The distinction between these two different questions can be framed in another way. Tort lawyers sometimes debate whether we have a law of *tort* or a law of *torts*. At one level, the answer seems obvious—we have a law of torts: trespass, nuisance, defamation, negligence, conspiracy and so on. In the same way (although the issue is undebated) we have a law of *crimes*—murder, rape, theft and so on—not a law of *crime*. But that conclusion tells us nothing about whether tort law has two parts—general and special—or whether we would do well to think about tort(s) law in this way, just as the fact that there are numerous 'crimes' has not prevented criminal law theorists from identifying two parts of the criminal law, and debating their respective nature and contents, and the utility of the distinction between them. So the puzzle is why tort lawyers and theorists have not identified tort law as a two-part affair, and the question is whether there would be any advantage in doing so.

Any attempt to solve the puzzle and answer the question requires us first to pay closer attention to the relevant debates in criminal law and criminal law theory. Having done that, I will briefly explore what tort theorists have made of the general/special distinction. There then follows a section which asks what benefits, if any, might be gained by reconstructing tort law along the lines of a general/special distinction. Finally, I express some concerns about the use of legal theory as illustrated by certain aspects of the debates around the general/special distinction.

II. A TWO-PART CRIMINAL LAW

The best place to start may be with Michael Moore, who has provided the most systematic and detailed account of and justification for the general/special distinction in criminal law.[9] According to Moore, citing George Fletcher in support,[10] the 'traditional' view is that the general part contains 'doctrines that *apply to all* crimes' and the special part 'doctrines that *define* particular crimes'.[11] Whereas Williams thought that the general/special distinction, thus drawn, had practical use, Moore thinks it useful

---

[9] M Moore, *Placing Blame: A General Theory of the Criminal Law* (Oxford, Clarendon Press, 1997) esp 30-35.

[10] Besides his major work in criminal law—GP Fletcher, *Rethinking Criminal Law* (Boston, Little Brown, 1978)—Fletcher is the author of an important contribution to the corrective justice strand of tort theorising: GP Fletcher, 'Fairness and Utility in Tort Theory' (1972) 85 *Harvard Law Review* 537. On the place of the corrective justice strand in tort theory more generally see P Cane, 'The Anatomy of Private Law Theory: A 25th Anniversary Essay' (2005) 25 *OJLS* 203.

[11] Moore, above n 9, at 30 (emphasis added).

pedagogically: since time is short, it is better to teach students those parts of the criminal law that have general application than to bother with the details of particular crimes. But he also thinks that the distinction, differently drawn, has theoretical significance. It reflects, he says, two kinds of 'moral' 'judgment' or 'theory': one about when we can say that a person has done something wrong and the other about when we can say that a person is (or ought to be held) responsible for his or her wrongdoing. The general part provides a theory of responsibility while the special part provides an account of wrongful action. Although he thinks that the two ways of drawing the general/special distinction will divide up criminal law doctrine in much the same way, Moore prefers the latter to the former because, in his opinion, the function of the criminal law is to 'attain retributive justice'. As he observes, 'Retributive justice demands that those [and only those] who deserve punishment get it.'[12] A person deserves punishment if he or she has done wrong culpably. The special part tells us what acts and omissions are wrong, and the general part provides an account of culpability.

For Moore, then, the general/special distinction is a theoretically useful, and incidentally a descriptively accurate, way of thinking about criminal law because the criminal law has a single goal, the attainment of which requires the satisfaction of two separate criteria (wrongdoing and responsibility). By contrast, he says, the general/special distinction is not a theoretically useful way of thinking about property law because (in his view) property law serves three goals, which he calls 'utility', 'fairness' and 'distributive justice', rather than one. It is also not useful because although property law might be said to have a special part—distinguishing between real property, personal property, intellectual property, and so on—in his opinion it lacks general criteria analogous to criteria of responsibility/culpability in criminal law governing the acquisition, use and transfer of the various kinds of property. So far as tort law is concerned, Moore's view is that the general/special distinction could be theoretically useful on the assumption that tort law can, by way of plausible description/explanation/interpretation, and should, by way of prescription, be understood in terms of (the single function of realising) 'corrective justice'.

Moore's ostensible aim is to provide an argument in favour of according the general/special distinction theoretical ('moral') significance and not just practical or educational significance. For him, the distinction is a necessary corollary of the proposition that the normative function of the criminal law is and should be the attainment of retributive justice by punishing, and punishing only, culpable wrongdoers. Nicola Lacey challenges Moore's view that the general/special distinction is in some sense intrinsic to

---

[12] *Ibid*, at 33.

criminal law by pointing out that the contrast between culpability and wrongdoing is relatively modern, and was much less sharply drawn in the 18th and 19th centuries.[13] While this criticism may cast doubt on any claim that Moore has discovered timeless or universal truths about criminal law, it does not obviously undermine his account of necessary conditions for a theoretically useful general/special distinction. Lacey also takes Moore to task for his views that (1) responsibility is a matter of fact[14] and a theory of responsibility is a metaphysical theory, whereas (2) in order to be 'interesting and useful' a theory of wrongdoing must be 'normative'.[15] The idea that the concepts of culpability and wrongdoing are of qualitatively different types strikes me as odd; but once again, this view seems incidental to Moore's argument about the usefulness of the general/special distinction.

Finally, Lacey questions whether the distinction between culpability and wrongdoing can be consistently drawn—by Moore, at least.[16] Her argument here seems to turn on a further distinction between consequentialist and non-consequentialist theories of wrongdoing. The so-called 'harm principle' forms the basis of a consequentialist theory of wrongdoing,[17] whereas Moore subscribes to what he calls 'non-exclusionary legal moralism' according to which the fact that a type of act or omission is ('morally') wrong always counts in favour of its criminalisation regardless of consequences—which is not to say, of course, that consequences should never be taken into account. Lacey apparently thinks that a theorist such as Moore, who adopts a non-consequentialist (or, as Moore refers to it, an 'agent-relative') theory of wrongdoing cannot tell us when and why 'killing', for instance, is wrong without taking account of the killer's culpability. In other words, in Lacey's view a non-consequentialist theory of wrongdoing cannot be independent of a theory of culpability, and so no clear distinction can be drawn between the general and special parts of the criminal law. This is a puzzling objection. For instance, a person might think that unjustified killing is wrong, because it shows disrespect for human life in general and the victim in particular, even if the killer does not, for some reason, deserve to be blamed or punished for the killing. Others may disagree, of course, but the view is not logically flawed.

---

[13] Book Review of *Placing Blame* (2000) 63 *MLR* 141. See also N Lacey, 'In Search of the Responsible Subject: History, Philosophy and Social Sciences in Criminal Law Theory' (2001) 64 *MLR* 350.

[14] Moore, above n 9, at 624.

[15] *Ibid*, at 66-67. See, similarly, J Gardner, 'Criminal Law and the Uses of Theory: A Reply to Laing' (1994) 14 *OJLS* 217, 220.

[16] Lacey, Book Review, above n 13, at 145-46.

[17] Famously expounded by HLA Hart in *Law Liberty and Morality* (Oxford, Oxford University Press, 1963), following JS Mill and followed by J Feinberg, *The Moral Limits of the Criminal Law* (Oxford, Oxford University Press, 1984-90). See also P Cane, 'Taking Law Seriously: Starting Points of the Hart-Devlin Debate' (2006) 10 *The Journal of Ethics* 21.

In fact, consequentialist accounts of wrongdoing actually support and, indeed, require some version (akin to Moore's) of the general/special distinction. Consequentialism about wrongdoing implies that the function of the criminal law is to prevent bad consequences in the future. There is no reason, *in principle*, to think that punishing a person responsible for some bad consequence in the past will contribute to the prevention of bad consequences of that type in the future, whether caused by that person or anyone else. If consequentialism governed allocation of criminal punishment as well as specification of criminal wrongfulness, the person rightly punished for any particular bad consequence would be the person judged to be in the best position to prevent consequences of that type in the future, whether caused by the person who caused the particular bad consequence or anyone else, and that person might or might not be the person who actually caused the bad consequence in question.

The point is familiar enough in the context of economic analysis of tort law. For instance, causation of harm in the past has no independent significance in the search for Calabresi's cheapest cost avoider.[18] As corrective justice theorists never tire of stressing, economic analysis cannot explain the bilateral structure of tort law: the basic (causal) link it forges between doing and suffering of harm. This was Hart's point, too, when he distinguished between the general justifying aim of the criminal law and principles for the distribution of punishment.[19] Pithily put, consequentialist theories of wrongdoing yield no independent theory of responsibility for past wrongs. In order to explain (and justify) the criminal law (and tort law) we actually have, the consequentialist theorist of wrongdoing needs a separate non-consequentialist theory of responsibility. So even if Lacey is right to say that the non-consequentialist theorist of wrongdoing will have trouble distinguishing clearly between his or her theory of wrongdoing and theory of culpability, the consequentialist theorist must be able to do so in order to produce a theory of the criminal law that has any pretensions at all to descriptive or explanatory validity. A fortiori, if the consequentialist wants to justify the sort of criminal law we actually have.

As I read it, Lacey's study of the history of criminal law theory[20] provides little support for her attack on Moore's account of the general/ special distinction. Moore derives that account from his views (1) that

---

[18]   G Calabresi, *The Costs of Accidents: A Legal and Economic Analysis* (New Haven, Yale University Press, 1970).

[19]   HLA Hart, *Punishment and Responsibility* (Oxford, Oxford University Press, 1968) ch 1.

[20]   Lacey, 'Responsible Subject', above n 13; N Lacey, 'Contingency, Coherence and Conceptualism: Reflections on the Encounter between "Critique" and "the Philosophy of the Criminal Law"' in A Duff (ed), *Philosophy and the Criminal Law: Principle and Critique* (Cambridge, Cambridge University Press, 1998).

criminal law has a function (is 'a functional kind', as he puts it);[21] (2) that unlike property law it has a single function that in case of conflict overrides all other functions it might serve; and (3) that its overriding function is to attain retributive justice. Lacey's account supports the conclusion that 18th and 19th century writers who made much less of the general part, as understood in modern criminal law theory, did not share Moore's vision of the criminal law. So it is not surprising that they did not adopt his approach to the general/special distinction. The fundamental basis of Lacey's disagreement with Moore about the possibility and utility of a general/special distinction is not historical but methodological, arising out of Moore's acceptance and Lacey's rejection of 'conceptualism' and a particular brand of philosophical realism—matters which, I suspect, were far from the minds of the older criminal law writers. From the 'critical', legal-realist perspective Lacey adopts, theoretical constructs such as the general/special distinction are at best contingent and at worst a misrepresentation of legal and social practices.

Despite the theoretical sophistication of Moore's account of the general part in terms of its subject-matter—the concept of responsibility/culpability as opposed to the concept of wrongfulness—most discussion of the general/special distinction builds on the 'traditional' understanding of the general part in terms of its breadth of application. Predictably, everyone seems to agree that the general part contains no norms that apply only to a single criminal offence. One view is that the general part contains only norms that apply to all criminal offences. Assessment of this approach requires a distinction to be drawn between descriptive and prescriptive theories of the general part. Take, for instance, the requirement of *mens rea*, which almost everyone includes in the general part. If the general part contains only norms that in fact apply to all criminal offences, *mens rea* should not be there because there are many crimes of negligence (objectively understood as breach of a standard of care) and strict liability. On the other hand, the *mens rea* requirement might certainly figure in a prescriptive theory of the general part, which sees it as setting limits on the criminalisation of conduct. On this basis, too, Douglas Husak argues that the general part should include the harm principle.[22]

Other theories of the general part are neither straightforwardly descriptive nor straightforwardly prescriptive. A common view is that the ideal criminal law would be 'coherent', 'rational' and 'principled', and that the general part makes an important contribution to the realisation of this

---

[21] This is a philosopher's shorthand for 'a kind of thing that is characterised by its function'. Similarly, a 'structural kind' is a kind of thing characterised by its structure, and a 'nominal kind' is a kind of thing characterised by its name.

[22] DN Husak, 'Limitations on Criminalization and the General Part of the Criminal Law' in Shute and Simester, above n 2.

ideal. But what do 'coherent', 'rational' and 'principled' mean? More particularly, what does the ideal, so expressed, tell us about the contents of the general part? It tells some people that a norm can be appropriately included in the general part even if it does not apply to all criminal offences, so long as it applies to a significant number of offences. Under this approach, for instance, the *mens rea* requirement would belong to the general part despite the existence of offences of negligence and strict liability. In that case, however, the general part might also need norms that 'rationally' and 'coherently' distribute offences (or elements of offences) amongst the categories of *mens rea*, negligence and strict liability.

John Gardner has argued for a smaller rather than a larger general part by questioning the link, implicit in the enthusiasm for larger versions, between rationality and generality.[23] The basic point (as I understand it) is simple enough: normative diversity may be rational and coherent, and more rational and coherent than uniformity, if it reflects significant differences between situations and circumstances. So, for example, it need not follow from inclusion of the *mens rea* principle in the general part that the demands of that principle (or, in other words, the definition of *mens rea*) must be invariant across all or most criminal offences. Gardner, in fact, argues against intention as a general paradigm of criminal responsibility by distinguishing between success in worthless activities (to which intention is central) and failure in worthwhile activities (to which it may not be). He argues that this explains why we might adopt intention as the paradigm requirement in homicide offences, but negligence as the paradigm requirement in motoring offences. In fact, Gardner's view seems to be that at least some aspects of the *mens rea* requirement are not elements of the general part.[24] He distinguishes between ascriptive and normative rules. For instance, the rule that children below a certain age cannot be held criminally liable is ascriptive, while rules specifying the 'mental element' of particular crimes are 'normative'. He allocates ascriptive rules to the general part, but normative rules to the special part because they are elements of definitions of crimes.

There is another strand in Gardner's argument about rationality and generality that deserves mention. The idea that the criminal law should be 'principled' appeals to a contrast between 'principle' and 'policy'. In this contrast, principle is identified with concepts of individual responsibility for conduct, while policy is associated with goals such as harm-prevention

---

[23] J Gardner, 'On the General Part of the Criminal Law' in Duff, above n 20. Gardner sees the link between generality and rationality as a manifestation of the decline of religion/authority-based value systems: 214-15.

[24] Gardner, above n 15. For background see J Gardner and H Jung, 'Making Sense of *Mens Rea*: Antony Duff's Account' (1991) 11 *OJLS* 559 and JA Laing, 'The Prospects of a Theory of Criminal Responsibility: *Mens Rea* and Methodological Doubt' (1994) 14 *OJLS* 57.

and security. In other words, principles are non-instrumental—or non-consequentialist in the terminology used earlier in this chapter—whereas policies are instrumental (or 'consequentialist'). Criminal liability should not depend on the consequences of conduct as opposed to the nature or quality of that conduct, so the argument goes, because criminal responsibility should track moral responsibility, and moral responsibility is a function of conduct, not of the consequences of conduct. For this reason, some would say, to the extent that negligence-based criminal liability and strict criminal liability are based on considerations of harm-prevention and social protection, they are unjustifiable. One of Gardner's aims is to develop a non-consequentialist—and, therefore, principled—account of what he calls 'regulatory offences', which can be committed without subjective *mens rea*. In this way he hopes to demonstrate that shrinking the general part by reducing the scope of operation of the *mens rea* principle need not lead to a less 'principled' criminal law. His strategy is to argue that moral responsibility is not only a matter of what we do, or fail to do, divorced from the consequences of our conduct. Rather, the realm of morality is the realm of 'wholehearted and successful pursuit of worthwhile activities':[25] the realm of achievement or failure—and, therefore, of consequences—as well as of action.

III. TRANSITIONAL STOCKTAKING

The time has come to draw together the strands of this rather discursive discussion of criminal law theory before moving on to tort law. The analysis so far enables us to identify various understandings of the general/special distinction:

- According to the **traditional account**, the distinction has two elements. First, the special part contains definitions of criminal offences, while the general part contains principles that apply[26] to crimes defined by the special part. Second, principles of the general part apply to all or a significant number of criminal offences.
- According to **Moore's account**, the special part is concerned with wrongdoing while the general part is concerned with responsibility and culpability.
- According to an account which Gardner ascribes to Ashworth ('**Ashworth's account**'),[27] the general part is a realm of non-instrumental *principle* whereas the special part is a realm of instrumental *policy*.

---

[25] Gardner, above n 15, at 220.
[26] Or, in another view, are capable of applying: RA Duff and SP Green, 'Introduction: The Special Part and its Problems' in Duff and Green, above n 3, at 3.
[27] Gardner, above n 23, at 209.

- In **Gardner's account**, the general part is 'ascriptive' whereas the special part is 'normative'. Similarly, in Moore's account, the general part's theory of responsibility is metaphysical (a matter of facts) whereas the special part's theory of criminalisation is 'normative'.

The criminal law literature also enables us to identify various suggested functions or uses of the general/special distinction:

- **Practical:** to enable lawyers to extrapolate from the known to the unknown.
- **Educational:** it makes pedagogical sense, so it is said, to focus on general principles of criminal liability as opposed to the details of particular offences.
- **Descriptive:** the idea here is that some version of the general/special distinction provides a reasonably accurate description of the criminal law as it actually is. This view may be more plausible in jurisdictions in which the criminal law has been codified than in common law jurisdictions, because a criminal code may contain general provisions separate from the definitions of particular crimes.
- **Explanatory/Analytical:** in relation to common-law jurisdictions, at least, it may be better to think of the general/special distinction as providing a way of explaining or analysing the law, as opposed to describing it.
- **Theoretical:** for Moore, the general/special distinction is a corollary of a theory of the criminal law as a 'functional kind' aspiring to attain retributive justice.
- **Prescriptive/Ideological:** by reason of the generality of its elements, the general part may be seen to serve 'rule of law' values[28] and to promote principled rationality in the criminal law. This function can appropriately be described as ideological because commitment to generality is sometimes associated with liberal individualism and attacked by critical theorists such as Alan Norrie.[29]
- **Supervisory:** this function has several aspects. The general part may be conceived as a way of constraining or disciplining the special part by imposing limits on the sorts of conduct that may be criminalised. The general part may, in common law jurisdictions at least, also be seen as enabling courts to supervise and constrain the legislature, where the formal power to create new criminal offences resides. So, for instance,

---

[28]   Eg Shute and Simester, above n 2, at 4. See also V Tadros, 'The System of the Criminal Law' (2002) 22 *Legal Studies* 448, 458: 'the desirability of generality determines whether an element is best considered as part of the General Part or the Special Part of a criminal code', and 467: 'There are some fundamental principles that help to determine whether a concept should evolve in the General Part.'

[29]   Eg A Norrie, *Crime, Reason and History* (London, Weidenfeld, 1993).

the *mens rea* requirement may be used as a principle of statutory interpretation to limit the creation of strict liability offences. In addition, many, if not all, contributors to the literature about the general/special distinction tend to treat it as raising 'theoretical' or 'philosophical' issues about criminal law. Some writers go so far as to speak of the general part in almost metaphysical terms, such as whether particular criminal law doctrines are 'properly ascribed' to the general part or 'rightly confined' to the special part.[30] Branding the general/special distinction in this way may be seen as an attempt by academic lawyers and philosophers to supervise and influence the development of the criminal law, both by courts and legislatures, in the name of some concept of metaphysical reality or objective value.

In distinguishing between these various accounts and functions of the general/special distinction, I do not mean to suggest that they are mutually exclusive or even necessarily in conflict with one another. I merely hope to convey the richness and complexity of debates around the distinction amongst criminal law theorists.

IV. TORT THEORY AND THE GENERAL/SPECIAL DISTINCTION

Tort law, as much as criminal law, has been affected—or afflicted, depending on one's predilections—by the late 20th-century craze for theorising and philosophising. Although Glanville Williams was a tort lawyer as well as a criminal lawyer, he appears not to have thought of tort law as having separate general and special parts. Nor have most subsequent tort theorists shown much interest in the general/special distinction. The closest to an explicit discussion of the distinction of which I am aware is found in quite a short passage in Jules Coleman's book *The Practice of Principle: In Defence of a Pragmatist Approach to Legal Theory*.[31] Because Coleman does not purport to be discussing the general/special distinction as such, I need to analyse this passage with some care in order to show how it bears on the topic of this chapter.

The main burden of Coleman's book up to the relevant point has been to demonstrate that corrective justice provides a better theory of tort law than economic analysis. As Coleman expounds it, the 'corrective justice' principle 'states that *individuals who are responsible for wrongful losses of*

---

[30] Eg AP Simester and S Shute, 'On the General Part of the Criminal Law' in Shute and Simester, above n 2, at 3. Victor Tadros speaks of analysis 'taking place in the General Part' and of the possibilities that there may be more than one or no definition of intention 'in the General Part' almost as if the General Part were a physical object or place: above n 28, at 451.

[31] (Oxford, Oxford University Press, 2001) 31-36.

others have a duty to repair the losses'.[32] By 'tort law' Coleman means 'the core of tort law' by which, in turn, he means 'a set of features (expressed at a certain level of generality) that forms part of our pretheoretic conception of [its] central elements'.[33] Those features are of two types: substantive and structural. The structural core of tort law is 'represented by case-by-case adjudication in which particular victims sue those they identify as responsible for the losses for which they seek redress', while tort law's substantive core is 'represented by its basic liability rules...fault and strict liability'.[34] In the passage we are focusing on, Coleman sets out to answer an objection that:

> corrective justice theory does not adequately explain tort law because it does not provide a theory of what counts as a wrong of the sort that gives rise to a duty of repair; nor, relatedly, does corrective justice tell us what the primary or first-order duties are that corrective justice enforces by imposing a second-order duty of repair.[35]

The answer he offers to this objection is complex.

Corrective justice, he says, pre-supposes an account of relevant first-order duties, but it does not 'pretend to provide' one because such duties are not duties of corrective justice. At the same time, he says:

> We cannot even make corrective justice intelligible as a principle of justice without identifying at least some first-order duties that might plausibly be said to give rise to duty of repair [sic].[36]

For this purpose, he identifies 'assault and battery against the person...together, perhaps, with some other, equally accessible paradigm cases'.[37] He claims that a 'set of paradigms suffices to make corrective justice an appropriately complete account of what it purports to explain'[38]—namely tort law. Moreover, he says, corrective justice imposes constraints on what can be recognised as first-order duties—although he does not attempt to spell out what those constraints might be.

Coleman draws what is, for our purposes, a pertinent analogy with retributive-justice explanations of criminal law. Retributivism, Coleman asserts, is a theory about the justification for punishing criminals, and does not provide an 'account of criminality'[39]; but no-one criticises it for that

---

[32] *Ibid*, at 15 (emphasis in original).
[33] *Ibid*, at 15 n 2.
[34] JL Coleman, 'Second Thoughts and Other First Impressions' in B Bix (ed), *Analyzing Law: New Essays in Legal Theory* (Oxford, Clarendon Press, 1998) 297.
[35] Coleman, above n 31, at 31-32.
[36] *Ibid*, at 32.
[37] *Ibid*. This must be read, of course, as meaning something like 'the duties of which assault and battery would constitute breaches'.
[38] *Ibid*. Later, at 34, Coleman drops the qualifier 'appropriately'.
[39] *Ibid*, at 33.

(or so he suggests). Nor, he continues, is a 'general theory of first-order duties from which we can derive them all systematically' required for 'an adequate account of tort practices'.[40] Indeed, he says:

> I am dubious about the prospects for such a theory…[because] much of the content of the first-order duties that are protected in tort law is created and formed piecemeal in the course of our manifold social and economic interactions.[41]

Although Coleman does not mention the general/special distinction in so many words, it seems fair to interpret this passage in those terms. His argument seems to be that the corrective justice principle provides a theory of the general part of tort law—its core substantive and structural features—but does not purport to provide a theory of the special part. Even so, it provides an 'adequate', or an 'appropriately complete', or a 'complete' theoretical account of tort law.

Coleman's account of corrective justice differs in significant respects from Ernest Weinrib's.[42] Coleman purports to offer a plausible account of a set of social practices whereas Weinrib presents a 'structural' or 'internal' account of a set of norms. Coleman offers corrective justice as a theory of tort law, whereas Weinrib presents it as a theory of 'private law'. Coleman thinks that the corrective justice principle explains strict tort liability as well as liability for fault, whereas Weinrib thinks that strict tort liability is ruled out by the concept of Kantian right which, in his theory, fills a space similar to that occupied in Coleman's theory by the 'substantive core of tort law'. Their respective approaches to the distinction between corrective justice and distributive justice also differ: whereas Weinrib thinks that the two forms of justice are 'categorically' distinct from one another, Coleman thinks they are 'connected… but independent'.[43] This, it seems, is why Coleman thinks that the corrective justice account of tort law 'presupposes' a set of first-order duties. Weinrib, by contrast, purports to expound corrective justice in terms of a metaphysical account of two-party human interactions.

Despite the differences, these two theorists do apparently share the view that while the corrective justice principle imposes certain constraints on the sorts of conduct that can count as tortious, it does not specify or provide an account of the 'grounds and bounds' of tort liability. Coleman seems to think that first-order duties are a product of 'piecemeal creation and formation', of which no 'systematic' theory would be possible, while Weinrib apparently thinks that 'tort-making' (the 'tortification' of conduct,

---

[40] *Ibid*, at 34.
[41] *Ibid*.
[42] EJ Weinrib, *The Idea of Private Law* (Cambridge, Mass, Harvard University Press, 1995).
[43] Coleman, above n 34, at 307.

we might say) is a political, not a legal matter. Coleman thinks that the corrective justice principle provides a better account of the core social practices of tort law than does economic analysis, while Weinrib thinks that no 'functional' account, whether economic or otherwise, of private law (including tort law) can explain what it really is.

V.   TORT THEORY THROUGH THE LENS OF CRIMINAL LAW THEORY

Now let us go back to criminal law theory. Recall that, in Moore's opinion, the general/special distinction will be useful in analysing an area of law if that area is thought of as having a single overriding function. Indeed for Moore, an 'area of the law' is precisely a set of legal norms that share a single overriding function. Thus for him, criminal law is the set of legal norms that share the function of realising retributive justice, and, he suggests, tort law may be understood as the set of legal norms that share the function of realising corrective justice. This not an entirely happy analogy. For one thing, at the very heart of Weinrib's theory is the idea that corrective justice provides not a functional account of tort law but a structural (formal) account, whereas Moore doubts the validity of at least certain types of structural accounts of law and favours functional accounts.[44] For another, whereas Moore's retributive-justice account is built on a judgment that realising retributive justice is good, Coleman expressly denies that his corrective justice account of tort law rests on 'the moral attractiveness of corrective justice'.[45]

Still, perhaps these differences are not of great significance. Even if neither Coleman nor Weinrib sees corrective justice as a single overriding function of tort law, both certainly see it as a unitary overriding explanation, and it is not difficult to interpret Coleman's and Weinrib's accounts in terms of Moore's distinction between responsibility and wrongfulness. Whereas retributive justice is concerned with punishment for wrongdoing, corrective justice is concerned with repairing the adverse consequences of wrongdoing. Whereas retributive justice requires that those, and only those, who deserve it should be punished, so corrective justice requires that those, and only those, who are responsible for adverse consequences should repair them. Despite their proponents' methodological differences, these propositions seem to me to be as consistent with Coleman's and Weinrib's accounts of tort law as they are with Moore's account of criminal law. In one respect, Weinrib's approach seems closer than Coleman's to Moore's account: Moore's general part is 'content-neutral' in the sense that

---

[44]   Moore, above n 9, at 22.
[45]   Coleman, above n 31, at 4-5.

it gives an account of responsibility that applies to any and all types of criminal wrongdoing,[46] whereas Coleman thinks that the idea of corrective justice has to refer to paradigm examples of wrongdoing to make any sense at all. However, it is hard to know precisely what Coleman means by this, so we can ignore it for present purposes.

Interpreting corrective justice accounts of tort law in terms of the general/special distinction is not only possible—it is also instructive. First, notice a stark contrast. Moore thinks that a theory of wrongdoing is an integral part of a retributive justice account of criminal law. Weinrib, by contrast, thinks that a theory of 'first-order duties' is not part of law at all but a matter of politics. Likewise, Coleman thinks that only a few paradigms of wrongdoing are needed to provide a complete account of the core of tort law, and that a systematic account of tort law's 'first-order duties' is probably unattainable. Second, recall that Moore's theory of wrongdoing is normative[47] and non-instrumental. By contrast, Coleman seems prepared to contemplate that a theory of tortiousness might be instrumental—he considers it worthwhile to assess the claim that economic efficiency might provide such a theory.[48] Weinrib's approach echoes Ashworth's distinction between non-instrumental principle and instrumental policy: tortiousness is a matter of politics, not law; distributive justice, not corrective justice; function, not form. Third, just as for Moore the general/special distinction is a theoretical corollary of his understanding of retributive justice, so for Weinrib the law/politics divide is a theoretical corollary of his understanding of corrective justice, based as it is on the abstract concept of Kantian right. Fourth, just as some criminal theorists think of the general part as supervising the special part, so Weinrib and Coleman think of the concept of corrective justice as imposing constraints on what may count as a tortious wrong.

Even if we accept that corrective justice theories of tort law, such as Coleman's and Weinrib's, are at least consistent with understanding tort law in terms of a general/special distinction, we might not think this a very interesting conclusion. After all, very few people who think seriously about tort law are formalists like Weinrib, and few are likely to be attracted to an approach, such as Coleman's, that purports to explain so little of the substance of tort law. Another worrying feature of much corrective justice theorising is its focus on tort claims—the idea that tort law is about 'cleaning up messes', to use Coleman's graphic phrase.[49] This limitation may be overcome, without throwing the baby out with the bathwater, by

---

[46] Moore, above n 9, at 32.
[47] He thinks that a descriptive account would be neither useful nor interesting.
[48] Coleman, above n 31, at 34-36.
[49] Coleman, above n 34, at 302. Similarly worrying is the focus on infliction of punishment in the retributive justice theory of criminal law.

thinking of tort law not only in terms of repairing certain wrongs but also in terms of norms of 'right' conduct: tort law tells us not only what happens when we do wrong but, more importantly, how we must behave in order to do right and avoid wrong. According to this approach,[50] tort law, like criminal law, is directed as much to the law-abiding as to the law-breaker: in Coleman's terms, it is as much about first-order as about second-order duties. But for many, this too is an unrealistic picture of tort law. Tort law, these people would say, is not about right and wrong conduct or about how we should behave in our dealings with each other. Rather, tort law is about compensation, risk-allocation, harm-prevention and loss-spreading. The best way—perhaps the only plausible way—of understanding tort law, such people would say, is in terms of the various social functions it serves.

If these objectors are right, it would follow, according to Moore, that tort law could not usefully be understood in terms of the version of the general/special distinction he prefers, which distinguishes between a theory of responsibility (in the general part) and a theory of wrongdoing (in the special part). It seems to me, however, that both the objectors and Moore are wrong. The objectors are wrong because in their functionalist enthusiasm they have jettisoned the sound core of corrective justice accounts, namely that tort doctrine organises social life in terms of bilateral interactions between individuals by establishing norms of behaviour, couched in terms of interpersonal rights and duties, and remedies for breaches of these norms. The various touted functions of tort law are precisely that—functions of *tort law*. In this sense, tort law is a means, not an end, and its inner logic is better described in terms of responsibility for wrongdoing than in terms of its social functions. However, Moore is also wrong because although the recruitment of tort law into various functionalist projects may damage the internal normative coherence of tort doctrine, it has not destroyed—and probably could not destroy—its basic normative structure. Indeed, in Australia in the last few years courts and legislatures have sought to re-emphasise the role of tort law as a set of norms of interpersonal responsibility at the expense of its social welfare and compensation functions.[51] At the same time, they have sought to adjust the balance of responsibility, as between doers and sufferers of harm, in favour of the former—but that is another story. My present point is not about how tort law allocates responsibility for risks and liability for harms on a bilateral basis, but only that it does so.

---

[50]   Which underpins my books *The Anatomy of Tort Law* (Oxford, Hart Publishing, 1997) and *Responsibility in Law and Morality* (Oxford, Hart Publishing, 2002).

[51]   P Cane, 'Reforming Tort Law in Australia: A Personal Perspective' (2003) 27 *Melbourne University Law Review* 649.

Although in this section I have been discussing the general/special distinction in Moore's preferred version, it is easy enough to map the traditional version of the distinction onto corrective justice tort theory: the structural feature of bilateralism is a universal feature of tort law and tort claims, and the substantive features of negligence-based and strict liability apply to more than one head of tort liability.

VI. A TWO-PART TORT LAW?

We could think about tort law in terms of some version of the general/special distinction. But would we gain anything by doing so? The easiest way to approach this issue might be to revisit the various uses to which, as we found earlier, the general/special distinction has been put in criminal law.

- **Practical**: interestingly, both of the leading English practitioner texts on tort law[52] begin with chapters on general topics before discussing particular torts. Matters discussed include capacity, causation, defences, vicarious liability, joint and several liability, damages and foreign torts. From an academic perspective, one can only assume that this arrangement meets a practical need. On the other hand, neither book contains, for instance, a general discussion of standards of conduct and liability—a topic which, in some form or another, would surely figure in any theoretically-informed account of the general part of tort law.

- **Educational**: my sense is that the typical student torts text begins with a relatively short general introduction dealing with matters such as the concept of a tort, the relationship between tort law and other areas of law, functions of tort law and alternatives to tort. Beyond that, it presents the law in terms of particular 'torts'. In the preface to the first edition of his famous text, John Fleming made a virtue of this arrangement:

  > I have preferred to cut loose from the traditional English order, which has always struck me as highly inconvenient and irrational for pedagogical purposes. Instead, I have adopted the plan of the American *Restatement* and plunged straightaway[53] into a discussion of specific torts, examining in turn the three bases on which every case of tort liability has to rest, viz intentional wrongdoing, negligence and strict liability.[54]

---

[52] A Grubb (ed), *The Law of Tort* (London, Butterworths, 2002) and AM Dugdale (ed), *Clerk and Lindsell on Torts*, 18th edn (London, Sweet & Maxwell, 2000).

[53] Actually, after a short introduction.

[54] JG Fleming, *The Law of Torts* (Sydney, Law Book Co, 1957) iii.

The 'traditional English order' can, perhaps, be seen in contemporary editions of *Salmond on Torts*[55] and *Winfield on Tort*,[56] which began with chapters on topics such as 'General Principles of Liability', 'Parties', 'Remedies', 'Joint Tortfeasors' and so on before getting to specific torts. William Prosser's famous text[57] also adopted the *Restatement* arrangement, which Prosser (the Reporter of the *Restatement (Second) of Torts*) himself traced to earlier authors such as Bohlen (the Reporter of the original *Restatement of Torts*). There is rich irony here. The intellectual lineage of the arrangement in terms of standards of liability is traceable to Oliver Wendell Holmes, who, in 'The Theory of Torts'[58] and the chapter on torts in *The Common Law*,[59] presented what is usually taken to be the first serious attempt at a general theory of tort liability.[60] It is noteworthy that none of the later text writers attempted to develop the standards-of-liability approach into anything more than an organisational framework.

My guess is that the typical first torts course (outside the US, anyway) focuses on the tort of negligence, and gives highly selective attention to other torts. 'Advanced' tort courses tend to focus on specific torts not covered in the first course—such as defamation and the 'intentional torts' (conspiracy, intimidation and so on). Study of tort law in terms of general concepts and theories seems to be relegated to courses on legal theory. There appears to be no pedagogical pressure to structure tort law along general/special lines. Whether there is a case for doing so is another matter.

- **Descriptive**: in the absence of codification of tort law, the general/special distinction is unlikely to have much descriptive salience.

---

[55] RFV Heuston (ed), *Salmond on Torts*, 11th edn (London, Sweet & Maxwell, 1953). The treatment of the first specific tort, trespass to land, began on page 227 (of 753). However, in the 12th edition (1957), it began on page 156 (of 776). In the Preface to the 12th edition (viii) Heuston wrote 'the substantive law of tort is now some eighty pages nearer the beginning as a result of transfer to the end of the chapters on judicial and non-judicial remedies. I had decided the make this change before reading the criticisms of English books on torts made by some academic jurists in North America, and more recently in this country, but I am glad to have my opinion on this matter confirmed.'

[56] T Ellis Lewis (ed), *Winfield on Tort*, 6th edn (London, Sweet & Maxwell, 1954). Note the plural 'torts' in the title of Salmond's book and the singular 'tort' in the title of Winfield's. The treatment of the first specific tort, trespass to the person, began at page 246 (of 813). However, in the 7th edition (1963) it began on page 144 (of 819). In the Preface to the 7th edition (v–vi), the new editor, JA Jolowicz, wrote, 'I have tried to find an arrangement which will not require the student too often to turn to a later part of the book in order to understand what he is currently reading.'

[57] WL Prosser, *Handbook of the Law of Torts* (St Paul, Minn, West Publishing Co, 1941). The second edition was published in 1955.

[58] (1873) 7 *American Law Review* 652.

[59] OW Holmes, *The Common Law* (Boston, Little, Brown & Co, 1881).

[60] For an excellent analysis see TC Grey, 'Accidental Torts' (2001) 54 *Vanderbilt Law Review* 1225.

- **Explanatory/analytical:** Coleman offers corrective justice as an analytical explanation of social practices that he calls 'the core of tort law'. This is the sort of project in which many tort theorists seem to be engaged: they seek a better understanding of what tort law is and how it works by developing accounts that are more abstract and general than the typical exposition of tort doctrine.

    In Moore's terms, corrective justice provides a theory of responsibility. As we have noted, Coleman denies the need for, and doubts the possibility of, a 'systematic' theory of tortious wrongfulness. Moore, by contrast, considers a normative theory of wrongdoing to be an integral part of his retributive-justice theory of criminal law. The reason is simple: in order to justify the imposition of criminal punishment, he says, we need to demonstrate not only that the accused was responsible for his or her conduct and its consequences, but also that what he or she was responsible for was *wrong*. The best explanation of criminal law will be one that shows how the law addresses both issues—responsibility and wrongdoing. On the other hand, Coleman apparently thinks that the best explanation of tort law need only tell us what the law says about responsibility, with the merest nod to the issue of wrongdoing. Over this difference, I side with Moore against Coleman. It seems to me that despite Coleman's argument to the contrary, his account of tort law in terms of corrective justice is too short by at least half. It is easy to explain the reason why this is so in terms of Coleman's own analysis.

    One of the grounds on which Coleman rejects economic analyses of tort law is that they are 'reductionist'—which means, roughly, that they interpret every rule and concept of tort law in terms of efficiency. Coleman explicitly cites the concept of duty of care as one that gets lost in economic analysis:[61] economic analysts, he says, explicate duty of care in terms of foreseeable risk.[62] The problem for Coleman is that duty of care also gets lost in his theory of corrective justice which, he insists, is a theory of the core of tort law—its bilateral structure and the concepts of negligence and strict liability. According to this definition, duty of care is not part of the core of tort law. It is not a structural feature of tort law, and it is not part of the concept of negligence. Rather it is what John Fleming many years ago called a 'control device'.[63] In more modern terms, it tells us how risks of negligent conduct and resulting harms are distributed by the law. It is a component of the part of tort law that Coleman refers to by the phrase

---

[61] Coleman, above n 31, at 23.

[62] *Ibid*, at 14.

[63] JG Fleming, 'Remoteness and Duty: The Control Devices in Liability for Negligence' (1953) 31 *Canadian Bar Review* 471.

'first-order duties'. No theory of the tort law we actually have could be complete or adequate without an illuminating account of duty of care. No other single rule or concept of tort law has received more attention in the legal literature on tort law (outside the US, anyway) in the past 40 years, but in most of the theoretical tort literature, whether instrumentalist or non-instrumentalist, consideration of duty of care is conspicuous by its absence.

It is in this respect, perhaps, that introducing the general/special distinction into our thinking about tort law might yield dividends. Consider the position in relation to criminal law. Increased reflection on the general/special distinction in recent years has stimulated criminal-law theorists to pay more attention to the special part and to realise that issues of criminalisation are of as much theoretical interest and importance as issues of responsibility. In many Western countries, legislative contributions to the 'war on terror' have given this topic fresh salience and urgency. Of course, such issues are not new. They formed the foundation of one of the most important jurisprudential debates of the 20th century—that between Patrick Devlin and Herbert Hart precipitated by proposed changes to the law of sexual offences. After the initial skirmishes, however, that debate was continued more by political theorists than by lawyers. A noteworthy feature of more recent theoretical work on the general/special distinction has been careful exploration of the relationship between theories of responsibility and theories of wrongdoing. Hart's influence may help to explain the earlier lack of interest in this topic: as is well known, he adopted a non-instrumental theory of responsibility but an instrumental theory of criminalisation. Moore's exposition of inter-related non-instrumental accounts of both parts of the criminal law may have provided a catalyst for newer, more integrated approaches.

The course of development of tort theory was significantly affected by the fact that pioneering economic analyses purported to offer complete accounts of tort law covering issues of both responsibility and wrongdoing. Because of their instrumental nature, such accounts are most obviously inadequate in their treatment of responsibility. Further, because non-instrumental theories of tort law were developed in reaction to economic analysis, they have tended to focus on responsibility. It is unclear to me why tort theorists have shown so little interest in developing non-instrumentalist, or even non-economic instrumentalist, accounts of tortious wrongdoing. It is also surprising that there is no counterpart, in relation to compensation (and reparation more generally), to the vast theoretical literature on punishment. Recent attempts by some senior English judges, such as Lord Hoffman and Lord Steyn, to draw attention to 'special part' issues in negligence cases in terms of the concept of 'distributive justice'[64] have attracted criticism and even scorn from academic commentators. Of course, the mere incantation of such a slogan is worth very little. But perhaps it shows an awareness of the need to get beyond the meaningless language of 'two and three stage tests' of duty, and empty slogans such as 'fair, just and reasonable',[65] and to think more substantively about how the various risks of social life ought to be distributed. Important work has already uncovered 'menus' of instrumental and non-instrumental principles and values relevant to duty of care in the tort of negligence.[66] But there is still much room for theoretical reflection.

Looking further afield, what contribution can legal theory make to thinking about questions such as whether invasion of privacy, breach of confidence, or harassment ought to be tortious? Or about the dense tangle of issues that arise in the various unplanned birth cases?[67] Or about when and whether liability for water pollution ought to be strict?[68] What is the relevance to tort law, and to civil law more generally, of debates about the proper limits of the criminal law?[69] Is Coleman right to say that there can be no viable economic account of first-order tort duties?[70] And should we follow him in thinking that in order to be worthwhile, a theory of first-order duties would need to be of the same 'systematic' quality as his corrective justice account of second-order duties? All these, and many other, questions about the special part of tort law seem to me to be worthy of theorists' attention. I do not mean to say that theorists' answers to questions, such as whether invasion of privacy ought to be a tort, are more deserving of attention than answers given by non-theorists. But theory may be able to help us approach such questions in a more thoughtful and systematic way.

- **Theoretical:** as explained earlier, the version of the general/special distinction preferred by Moore fits neatly with justice-based theories of tort law.
- **Prescriptive/Ideological:** 'rule of law' ideals such as predictability,

[64] P Cane, 'Distributive Justice and Tort Law' [2001] *New Zealand Law Review* 401, 410-12.
[65] For useful recent analysis of such approaches see C Witting, 'Duty of Care: An Analytical Approach' (2005) 25 *OJLS* 33.
[66] Eg J Stapleton, 'Duty of Care Factors: A Selection from the Judicial Menus' in P Cane and J Stapleton (eds), *The Law of Obligations: Essays in Celebration of John Fleming* (Oxford, Clarendon Press, 1998).
[67] For a brief account see P Cane, 'Taking Disagreement Seriously: Courts, Legislatures and the Reform of Tort Law' (2005) 25 *OJLS* 393, 396-400.
[68] For some background see P Cane, 'The Changing Fortunes of Rylands v Fletcher' (1994) 24 *University of Western Australian Law Review* 237.
[69] Cane, above n 17, at 41-44.
[70] Coleman, above n 31, at 35.

certainty and generality have commonly been thought less important in tort law than in criminal law or even contract law. This is because tort law is typically understood more in remedial than in regulatory terms. From a regulatory perspective, however, the relative advantages and disadvantages of various conduct standards are the subject of much debate[71] as, more generally, is the relationship between rule of law values and regulatory instrumentalism.[72] Insurers, we are told, dislike uncertainty and unpredictability, but it is not clear how serious a problem this is in relation to tort law, or that greater use of the general/special distinction would make tort law significantly more certain.

- **Supervisory:** despite the absence of the general/special part distinction in tort law, what Tony Weir has called 'The Staggering March of Negligence'[73] might be viewed as illustrating the supervisory effect of a general principle on the development of particular torts. The use by courts of the general part to supervise the creation of criminal offences by the legislature has no direct counterpart in tort law because creation of new torts is not a legislative prerogative. But an indirect analogy may be found in the role of the courts in deciding whether breaches of statutory duties are actionable in tort.[74] Whether the introduction of the general/special distinction into thinking about tort law would encourage the sort of intellectual elitism and strategic use of theory found in some criminal law theorising must be a matter for specula-tion. The perceived problem of over-criminalisation, which motivates some criminal law theorists, has no clear analogy in the tort arena. This is perhaps because academic tort lawyers tend to be imbued with a compensatory/regulatory mentality that favours progressive expan-sion of the boundaries of tort liability (so long as it exists), at least in relation to death and personal injury. Things may change if and when the philosophically-inclined turn their attention to the special part of tort law.

---

[71] P Cane, 'Tort Law and Regulation' (2002) 31 *Common Law World Review* 305, 313-15.

[72] L McDonald, 'The Rule of Law in the "New Regulatory State"' (2004) 33 *Common Law World Review* 197

[73] In Cane and Stapleton, above n 66.

[74] For background see P Cane, *Atiyah's Accidents, Compensation and the Law*, 6th edn (London, Butterworths, 1999) 78-81.

VII. CODA: THE LIMITS OF PHILOSOPHY

A. The (Dis)Unity of Tort Law

I have gone to considerable (some may say excessive) lengths to understand the general/special distinction as developed by criminal-law theorists and to explore how and with what effect it might be applied to tort law. Even so, I must admit to feeling some unease about the value of this project except, perhaps, as an exercise in the history and sociology of ideas. One cause for concern is whether tort law has the sort of internal unity—either conceptual or functional—that supports the understanding of criminal law in terms of a general/special distinction. I also wonder whether more 'philosophical' (and less pragmatic) versions of the general/special distinction make sense outside the theoretical framework of a sort of philosophical realism which invests 'areas of the law' and 'legal subjects' with metaphysical properties and existence. These related points deserve some elaboration.

As a category of legal thought, tort law was a product of the dismantling in the 19th century of the procedurally-oriented system of legal classification that had existed since the birth of the common law. Two figures loom large in this development, Frederick Pollock[75] and Oliver Wendell Holmes. Pollock's was probably the most influential of the pioneering torts textbooks of the period.[76] His understanding of torts as non-contractual, non-equitable wrongs remains the foundation of the modern torts text. In the US, according to Brian Simpson, the advent of realism in the early 20th century spelled the end of the (short) textbook tradition.[77] Be that as it may, realism did nothing to dislodge tort law as a category of legal thought alongside contract, property, criminal law and so on.

Although Pollock had a reputation as a philosopher as well as a lawyer, his work on tort law contained little theory. The first, and still most influential, modern theorist of tort law was Oliver Wendell Holmes. Holmes is the intellectual ancestor of those tort theorists of the late 20th century whose interest in tort law is primarily philosophical. Despite historical pretensions, Holmes' use of history is subordinated to a form of ahistorical conceptualism. According to Brian Simpson, Holmes failed to entertain 'the idea that the law is an evolving and untidy series of

---

[75] See N Duxbury, *Frederick Pollock and the English Juristic Tradition* (Oxford, Oxford University Press, 2004) esp ch 5.

[76] F Pollock, *The Law of Torts* (London and Boston, Stevens and Sons and CC Soule, 1887).

[77] AWB Simpson, 'The Rise and Fall of the Legal Treatise: Legal Principle and the Forms of Legal Literature' (1981) 48 *University of Chicago Law Review* 632.

compromises and accommodations between conflicting pressures'.[78] Thomas Grey describes Holmes as 'a philosophically-minded legal theoretician with deficiencies as a policy-maker'.[79] Grey finds no evidence in Holmes' writings that his theory was prompted by observation of the growing practical importance of tort law as a mechanism for compensating accident victims. Ironically, however, Grey also demonstrates that in order to generate a conceptually coherent theory of tort law Holmes was forced to focus on unintentional infliction of physical harm ('accident law' as some call it) at the expense of other non-contractual, non-equitable grounds of legal obligation and liability that developed through trespass and case and which ended up in treatises on tort law such as Pollock's. Holmes left unsolved the problem of how to develop a theoretically convincing account of a body of law—tort law—that consisted of a collection of legal obligations that originated in a system in which procedural affinity was the only way in which relationships between obligations and liabilities were understood.

Conceptualism, uninformed equally by the history of tort law and by facts about its social functioning, is the typical methodology of contemporary mainstream tort theorising. On the whole, contemporary tort theorists accept the established categories of legal thought, including tort law, as developed in the late 19th century. Such passive acceptance of received legal categories is most pronounced in the work of theorists who, in reaction to economic analysis, have attempted to construct non-instrumentalist (justice-based) theories. It is particularly problematic in relation to tort law. Theorists sensitive to the problem typically deal with it either by relegating parts of tort law that do not fit their theories to categorical limbo or by casting them into categorical hell. This involves an extreme exercise of what Roberto Unger calls 'revisionary power',[80] which must necessarily accompany attempts to rationalise bodies of law that result from the operation of pluralistic and (relatively) uncoordinated processes over long periods of time. The more abstract and universalistic in aspiration the rationalisation, the more radical the revision will need to be. Given the provenance of tort law, revision is an understandable strategy, but it risks circularity when the theorist presents the result of applying the strategy as the best theory of that part of tort law of which it is offered as a theory! As Coleman says in *The Practice of Principle*, even without a systematic account of first-order tort duties, corrective justice can provide a complete account 'of what it purports to explain'.[81]

---

[78] AWB Simpson, 'The Elusive Truth About Holmes' (1997) 95 *Michigan Law Review* 2027, 2034.
[79] Grey, above n 60, at 1281.
[80] RM Unger, *What Should Legal Analysis Become?* (London, Verso, 1996) 67.
[81] Coleman, above n 31, at 32 and 34.

One way to break out of the circle might be to treat tort law as what Moore calls 'a nominal kind'[82]—which means, in effect, that tort law is what people say it is. Unfortunately, there is little reason to think that tort law understood nominally is likely to be theoretically or philosophically interesting. For instance, the distinction between common law torts and equitable breaches of trust and fiduciary duty is, to some extent at least, based on institutional factors unrelated to either the structure or the substance of the various obligations involved. The idea of reparation for wrongs, which is central to Coleman's account of tort law, obviously provides no distinguishing feature. It is not surprising, then, that Weinrib offers corrective justice not as a theory of tort law but as a theory of private law, by which he seems to mean the law of obligations. The problem of defining a philosophically significant area of inquiry is not so acute for criminal law theorists, who have been able to use punishment and its associated stigma as boundary concepts, nor for contract theorists, for whom concepts such as promise and exchange can provide points of reference. The importance of this observation, for present purposes, is to warn us against according undue theoretical significance to conclusions cast in terms of 'tort law'. If, as many think,[83] tort is merely the residuum of the law of civil obligations left when other more specific categories, such as contract and trust, have been extracted, we would be well advised—for that reason if for none other—not to expect our study of its principles to yield high abstractions of much theoretical interest.[84] More particularly, if Moore is right to think that a legal category needs theoretical unity in order to be understandable in terms of the general/special distinction, some work remains to be done to show that tort law is suitable for such treatment.

B.   The Politics of Legal Philosophy

Finally, I want to express some concern about the political implications of some aspects of debates around the general/special distinction. I am thinking particularly of the idea that functions of the general part might include 'supervising' the special part or, even more problematically, 'controlling' the legislature. I am not suggesting that theory should not be used for prescriptive or ideological purposes, to encourage and persuade. The danger, I believe, comes from the transformation of the ideological into the

---

[82] See above n 9.
[83] Eg K Oliphant, 'The Nature of Tortious Liability' in A Grubb, above n 52, at [1.1]-[1.3].
[84] For a more generalised warning against investing legal categories with great theoretical significance see S Waddams, *Dimensions of Private Law: Categories and Concepts in Anglo-American Legal Reasoning* (Cambridge, Cambridge University Press, 2003).

'philosophical'. Some theorists, or so it seems to me, think that reflection on and analysis of legal issues deserves the name of 'theory' only if it rises to the level of 'philosophy' understood as a distinctive activity that provides access to a realm of reason as opposed to practical choice, or to a realm of 'pure' reason that contrasts with the legal realm of impure reason, contaminated by law's practical purposes and political engagement. In this guise, philosophy is the new natural law, a technique for generating concepts that are items of cosmic furniture. So understood, philosophy trumps even the best practices of democratic politics as a source of answers to the ultimate practical question of how we should live and to more immediate questions about what the law ought to be.[85]

In answering such questions it is important to distinguish between resolving disagreement on the one hand and managing disagreement on the other. When disagreement is resolved, the outcome is agreement. When disagreement is managed, the outcome is agreement to disagree. Law and politics play pivotal roles in the management of social disagreement by providing individuals with reasons to observe norms of behaviour and to follow courses of action with which they do not agree. The implicit aim of the sort of philosophy that causes me concern is the resolution of disagreement. Its motivating assumption seems to be that in its natural state the moral world is characterised by agreement and unity, not disagreement and plurality. Even if, in some universe, this assumption is justified, it flatly contradicts our lived experience. This contradiction casts serious doubt on the value of the assumption as a working hypothesis on which to base legal theory. To my mind, it is better and safer to think of philosophy as a distinctively rigorous way of expressing a point of view than as a route to the resolution of disagreement. By all means, if we can, let us use the general/special distinction as a tool to structure our thought, improve our understanding and promote our values. But let us avoid investing it with a metaphysical life of its own. Moderation in all things, including philosophy!

---

[85] Agreeing with Richard Posner, Jeremy Waldron makes a similar point: '"Ego-Bloated Hovel"' (2000) 94 *Northwestern University Law Review* 597. See also Unger, above n 80, at 72-73. The high priest of what Unger calls anti-democratic right-wing Hegelianism is Hayek: FA Hayek, *Law, Legislation and Liberty, vol 1: Rules and Order* (London, Routledge and Kegan Paul, 1982). But anti-democratic tendencies are intrinsic to much of the methodology of modern legal theory.

2

Breach of Statute and Tort Law

LEWIS N KLAR*

I. INTRODUCTION

IN 1983, THE SUPREME Court of Canada handed down its judgment in *The Queen v Saskatchewan Wheat Pool*,[1] apparently resolving one of the more difficult and important issues of contemporary tort law, namely, the relationship between statutory duties and the common law action in tort. As will be discussed shortly, the Supreme Court unequivocally asserted that the breach of a statutory duty did not in and of itself give rise to a private cause of action in tort by a party who had suffered damage as a result of that breach. The decision was important because of the proliferation of statutory duties which are imposed by legislators on persons in a wide range of settings. If a mere breach of a statutory duty, resulting in damage to another, gave rise to an action for damages, tort law would be considerably expanded and the penalty imposed on statute breakers would undoubtedly go far beyond that intended by the legislators in many cases.

It has been my impression that the Supreme Court of Canada's clear position on the interaction between statutes and tort law has been made considerably less certain by the tort law decisions of courts at all levels in the two decades plus since *Saskatchewan Wheat Pool*. It is thus timely to revisit the issue,[2] especially in view of recent Supreme Court of Canada

---

* Professor, Faculty of Law, University of Alberta. I would like to express my thanks to Professors Vaughan Black and Russ Brown for their helpful suggestions with respect to this chapter.

[1] [1983] 1 SCR 205 [*Saskatchewan Wheat Pool*].

[2] It is interesting to note that not much has been written about this issue, at least in Canada, since *Saskatchewan Wheat Pool* was decided. This contrasts with the considerable attention given to this issue prior to the judgment. Justice Allen Linden, in particular, wrote extensively on this problem, and his case comment on *Sterling Trusts Corporation v Postma* (1967) 45 *Canadian Bar Review* 121 was referred to by the Supreme Court in its judgment. For other articles written before 1983, see A Linden, *Canadian Tort Law*, 7th edn (Markham, Butterworths, 2001) ch 7 fn 1. I would suggest that most commentators think that this issue has been resolved by the Supreme Court in *Saskatchewan Wheat Pool*, making any additional

decisions involving public tort liability[3] and misfeasance in a public office.[4] The question that this chapter will focus on is whether the Supreme Court's admonition not to allow a breach of statutory duty to create a common law duty of care has been ignored in actions for negligence against statutory bodies. The same question will be raised in reference to the action for misfeasance in a public office, although an in-depth examination of this action will not be pursued in this chapter.

II. THE JUDGMENT IN *THE QUEEN V SASKATCHEWAN WHEAT POOL*

Mr Justice Dickson, who wrote the judgment for the Supreme Court, put the question of the relation of a breach of a statutory duty to a civil cause of action in precise terms:

> This case raises the difficult issue of the relation of a breach of a statutory duty to a civil cause of action. Where 'A' has breached a statutory duty causing injury to 'B', does 'B' have a civil cause of action against 'A'? If so, is 'A's' liability absolute, in the sense that it exists independently of fault, or is 'A' free from liability if the failure to perform the duty is through no fault of his?[5]

The plaintiff, the Canadian Wheat Board, was seeking to recover money from the defendant, the *Saskatchewan Wheat Pool*, which it had expended due to a breach of the Canada Grain Act[6] by the Wheat Pool. The Wheat Pool, which stored and shipped grain owned by the Board (as agent of the Federal Crown), loaded a quantity of grain from its elevator into a ship. It was later discovered that some of this grain was infested with rusty grain beetle larvae. As a consequence, the Board was required to divert the vessel, unload and fumigate the grain and the ship's holds, and reload the grain. This cost the Board nearly $100,000, which it sought to recover from the Wheat Pool.

The plaintiff did not allege negligence or any other specific cause of action in tort. It sued entirely based on the fact that the Pool had breached a section of the Canada Grain Act. This section specifically prohibited the delivery of infested grain out of a grain elevator. The trial judge had allowed the action since he found that the statutory duty was absolute, not being dependent upon evidence of a lack of reasonable care, and that civil

---

commentary unnecessary. An interesting recent article is C Forell, 'Statutes and Torts: Comparing the United States to Australia, Canada, and England' (2000) 36 *Willamette Law Review* 865.

[3] In particular *Cooper v Hobart* [2001] 3 SCR 537 [*Cooper*], and *Edwards v Law Society of Upper Canada* [2001] 3 SCR 562 [*Edwards*].

[4] *Odhavji Estate v Woodhouse* [2003] 3 SCR 263 [*Odhavji*].

[5] *Saskatchewan Wheat Pool*, above n 1, at 206.

[6] RSC 1970 c 7, s 86(c).

liability flowed from the breach to the damaged party.[7] The Federal Court of Appeal reversed the trial judgment.[8] Heald J decided that a breach of the Canada Grain Act did not grant a private right of action to a person who suffered damage as a result of that breach.

In agreeing with the Federal Court of Appeal, Dickson J made the following important points. First, Canadian law rejects a civil action for breach of statutory duty based solely on the breach of a statute causing damage to a plaintiff. Moreover, any approach which seeks to distinguish between those statutory breaches that give rise to a cause of action and those that do not based upon the presumed intention of the legislature is unacceptable in Canadian law. If the legislation itself did not provide for a civil cause of action, it is fair to conclude that the legislature did not have a civil action in mind when it passed the legislation, or that it had it in mind but deliberately rejected it. A court seeking to create a cause of action based on a breach of statutory duty, based on the presumed intention of the legislature, is engaged in judicial legislation.

Second, if a plaintiff seeks to utilise the fact that the defendant breached a non-industrial penal statute as evidence of the defendant's negligence, the plaintiff must first establish that a common law duty of care was owed.[9] As stated by Dickson J:

> Glanville Williams is of the opinion, with which I am in agreement, that where there is no duty of care at common law, breach of non-industrial penal legislation should not affect civil liability unless the statute provides for it.[10]

This is a critical statement. As will be elaborated upon later, common law duties of care do not exist merely because a person suffers foreseeable injury from another person's conduct, even if that conduct is negligent. If this point was not clear before, it certainly must now be in view of *Cooper v Hobart* and *Edwards v LSUC*.[11] One cannot create a common law duty of care based merely on the existence of a statutory duty. This would do exactly what Canadian law, as expressed by Dickson J in *Saskatchewan Wheat Pool*, has told us we cannot do.

Looking at *Saskatchewan Wheat Pool* from the perspective of duty, the Supreme Court did not address whether the defendant Wheat Pool's statutory duty not to allow infested wheat to be delivered out of its grain

---

[7] [1980] 1 FC 407.
[8] [1981] 2 FC 212.
[9] Dickson J accepted that special consideration is given to 'some industrial statutes' with respect to the imposition of absolute liability. This point was not relevant to the statute in issue in *Saskatchewan Wheat Pool* and no further elaboration was given. For the purposes of this chapter, I will leave aside this possible exception to the general Canadian approach to the interaction of breach of statute and tort law.
[10] *Saskatchewan Wheat Pool*, above n 1, at 223.
[11] Above n 3.

elevator gave rise to a common law duty of care toward the Canadian Wheat Board, extending to the Board's economic losses. The discussion seemed only to focus on whether an innocent breach of the statutory duty could be used as evidence of a breach of a common law duty, or whether more in the way of negligent conduct needed to be shown by the plaintiff.[12] I would suggest that, if one were to apply the more sophisticated duty analysis employed in *Cooper v Hobart* to *Saskatchewan Wheat Pool*, it might very well be that policy considerations could be raised to deny the existence of a common law duty of care in the first place, thereby eliminating the necessity of examining whether the breach of the Canada Grain Act was innocent or negligent.

Applying his approach to the facts of *Saskatchewan Wheat Pool*, Dickson J found that, in view of the absence of allegations that the infested grain had been either intentionally or negligently delivered out of the defendant's elevator, the mere fact that the delivery of the grain constituted a statutory breach did not give rise to a civil cause of action in favour of a party damaged by that breach.[13] The plaintiff's action was accordingly dismissed.

Saskatchewan Wheat Pool clarified Canadian law considerably, but because of its facts, did not deal with some important concerns. It is clear now that, with the possible exception of some penal, industrial legislation, a breach of a statute does not, in itself, constitute actionable conduct with respect to the law of tort. The breach may be used as evidence of negligent conduct within the context of a civil action for negligence. There is no presumption of negligent conduct merely because of the breach. The trier of fact may adopt the statutory standard as the specific standard that the defendant ought to have lived up to, if it so wishes, and if it does so, the defendant presumably has to explain why it failed to live up to the statutory requirement. Ultimately, therefore, as with the departure from a generally approved practice, a breach of a statutory standard can be added to the plaintiff's arsenal in order to prove that the defendant was negligent.

The Supreme Court implied that, had there been evidence that the defendant had negligently or intentionally breached the statute, the result in *Saskatchewan Wheat Pool* might very well have been different. Left unanswered, however, are questions relating to these situations. It can be implied from the judgment that a common law duty of care would have to be owed apart from a statutory duty in order to go down the route of negligence, but the elements of a common law duty were not discussed. An

---

[12]   Dickson J was concerned with the absence of evidence of the defendant's fault, and the harshness of imposing liability on the defendant in view of this. The reasoning behind recognising a common law duty relationship in the first place was not discussed.

[13]   In fact, the evidence supported the conclusion that the defendant had taken all reasonable care and had not been negligent.

intentional breach of the statute would seemingly be even more serious and, therefore, more likely to give rise to a successful claim, but what claim? A negligence action? Or some other actions? And if other actions, what more would need to be shown other than the fact that the statutory duty was intentionally breached? These, I would suggest, are the questions now vexing the courts.

III.   THE IMPACT OF *SASKATCHEWAN WHEAT POOL* ON CANADIAN LAW

What impact did *Saskatchewan Wheat Pool* have on Canadian tort law? Case commentaries were of the view that it dealt a serious, if not fatal, blow to the ability of courts to use statutes to create or even to extend common law duties. Some applauded this; others lamented it. Professor Fridman, for example, approved of this development.[14] His view was that the judgment:

> states categorically that in Canada there is no tort of statutory negligence or breach of statutory duty. Such a tort is not justified on principle or policy. [The judgment] rejects the notion that criminal statutes can impose civil liability, in the absence of any specific provision to that effect.[15]

According to Fridman, this rejection applied not only to innocent or even negligent breaches of statutory duties, but also to instances of deliberate statutory violations causing foreseeable harm to plaintiffs. Citing three important authorities that denied liability even for deliberate statutory breaches,[16] Fridman concluded:

> [A]t the present time the common law will not recognize as a wrong harm caused by the intentional, unjustifiable and inexcusable breach of a statute imposing criminal liability for its infringement.[17]

The principle enunciated in the Australian case of *Beaudesert Shire Council v Smith*[18] that an action for damages upon the case could be brought by a person who had suffered harm as the inevitable consequence of the unlawful, intentional and positive acts of another did not, according to Fridman, represent the current state of Canadian law.[19]

---

[14]   GHL Fridman, 'Civil Liability for Criminal Conduct' (1984) 16 *Ottawa Law Review* 34.

[15]   *Ibid*, at 61.

[16]   *Dunlop v Woollahra Municipal Council* [1981] 1 All ER 1202 (PC); *Lonrho Ltd v Shell Petroleum* [1982] AC 173 (HL); *Canada Cement Lafarge v BC Lightweight Aggregates* [1983] 1 SCR 452.

[17]   Above n 14, at 52.

[18]   (1966) 120 CLR 145 (HCA).

[19]   Above n 14, at 53-54.

Even those on the other side of the debate, who were more receptive to the use of statutory breaches to create civil liability, agreed that *Saskatchewan Wheat Pool* abolished the tort of breach of statutory duty and prevented courts from using statutory duties to extend the common law into areas such as nonfeasance. Professor Brudner, who had earlier argued that courts should be able to use statutes to create new common law duties if a statutory duty was for the protection of a right naturally inherent in persons,[20] conceded and lamented the fact that *Saskatchewan Wheat Pool* had put an end to that possibility.[21] According to Brudner:

> by submerging statutory tort in the law of negligence, the court has disarmed itself of a means by which to extend common law duties in the face of obsolete precedents without subjecting defendants to unfair surprise.[22]

The most that courts can now do, in light of *Saskatchewan Wheat Pool*, is to use the statutory standard as a useful standard of care within existing common law duty relationships.[23] Brudner also criticised the argument that *Saskatchewan Wheat Pool* still allows the courts to use statutes as an encouragement to advance the common law, even if it does not allow them to openly use the statutory duty to create new common law duties, as not of much value. He notes Chief Justice Laskin's warning in *Seneca College of Applied Arts and Technology v Bhadauria* that there is 'a narrow line between founding a civil cause of action at common law by reference to policies reflected in the statutes and standards fixed by the statute'.[24]

Was this optimism by those who favoured the Supreme Court's narrow approach, and the pessimism by those who did not, warranted? What has been the impact of the judgment on Canadian tort law? Have statutory breaches become less relevant in tort claims? I will answer these questions by focusing on the negligence action and dividing the subsequent case law into two categories: first, negligence actions based on clearly recognised

---

[20]   JRS Prichard and A Brudner, 'Tort Liability for Breach of Statute: A Natural Rights Perspective' (1983) 2 *Law and Philosophy* 89.

[21]   A Brudner, 'Case Comment on *Saskatchewan Wheat Pool*' (1984) 62 *Canadian Bar Review* 668.

[22]   *Ibid*, at 669. Brudner's argument was that courts should be able to use statutes to extend common law duties where there is a private law foundation for such an extension, based on a theory of natural rights, despite common law precedents to the contrary. This would justify using statutes that impose duties of affirmative action on parties to create civil liability for their failure to act in some cases. In their earlier article, Prichard and Brudner distinguish between a statute that enforces a natural right to be free from being subjected to the arbitrary will of others, and a statute that seeks to maximise social welfare in the aggregate. The court should extend the common law and impose civil liability for a breach in the case of the former statute, but not in the case of the latter.

[23]   The exception for penal industrial statutes is seen as insignificant by Brudner because most of these types of accidents have been removed from tort law in favour of workers compensation schemes.

[24]   [1981] 2 SCR 181, 188.

common law duties of care; and second, negligence actions where courts arguably are creating new duties of care, or extending existing ones, based on statutory duties. I will then briefly consider the action for misfeasance in a public office, although, as indicated above, elaboration of this will not be covered in this chapter.

A.   Statutory Standards Applied Within Existing Common Law Duty Relationships

Saskatchewan Wheat Pool clearly confirmed that statutory *standards of conduct* may be relevant in negligence actions where the parties are in a recognised common law duty relationship and the defendant's misconduct involved breaching a statutory standard of behaviour. This was uncontroversial. Where *Saskatchewan Wheat Pool* clarified the law, however, was in its finding that the breach of statute is not conclusive proof of negligent conduct, and nor does it create a presumption of negligence. It merely provides useful evidence of negligence, if a trier of fact chooses to use it as such.

One can illustrate this by pointing to the many cases decided since *Saskatchewan Wheat Pool* which used statutory breach in precisely this way. All automobile accident cases in which the plaintiff is able to point to a breach by the defendant of a provision of the applicable highway traffic act use the breach as evidence of negligence. There is no issue in these cases that there is a common law duty of care between the driver of a car and its occupants, occupants of other cars on the road, and pedestrians. When there is an accident and it is caused by a breach of the highway traffic act, there is a strong case that the defendant has been negligent.[25] Even here, however, the breach by the defendant driver is not conclusive evidence of negligence.[26]

One can find examples in other areas as well. A very recent one is the case of *Rudd v Hamiota Feed Lot*.[27] The plaintiff was a newly hired pen-rider at the defendant's feed lot. She was injured when the horse on which she was riding fell. The Manitoba Workplace Safety and Health

---

[25]   In fact, there is a statutory presumption that the accident was caused by the fault of the owner or driver where there is loss or damage sustained by a person in an automobile accident, subject to an exception for collisions between vehicles. See eg Highway Traffic Act RSO 1990 c H.8, s 193.

[26]   There are not many cases where the defendant has been able to escape a finding of fault after breaching a provision of the Act. The failure to wear a seatbelt is, perhaps, the best example of a breach of a statute that the courts may excuse in a negligence action. See also *Dubreuil v Sawyer* (1981) 12 MVR 206 (Ont HC), where a failure to maintain a car and its equipment in safe condition was excused.

[27]   2006 MBQB 22.

Act[28] imposes a number of duties on an employer with regard to ensuring the safety, health and welfare of its workers, including providing training and supervision. The court referred to these statutory duties, but noted also the well-recognised duty of an employer to its employees under common law. It was based on this latter, common law, duty and the breach thereof that the defendant was found liable to the plaintiff. The failure to properly instruct the plaintiff, train her, or supervise her were regarded by the court as negligent acts constituting a breach of the employer's common law duty of care.

In negligence actions against stockbrokers, breaches of legislation and regulations concerning their standards of conduct have been used to support plaintiffs' claims. In *Zraik v Levesque Securities*,[29] for example, the defendant broker breached his company's commodity trading policies and the regulatory standards governing commodity futures trading.[30] The court used these breaches as evidence of the defendant's negligence, but it did not use the statute as the basis of the parties' duty relationship. While the statutes, regulations and by-laws enacted to control commodity futures trading 'informed' the duty of care, they did not create it. The duty of care existed by virtue of the common law.[31]

Boulanger v Johnson & Johnson Corpn provides another example.[32] This was a class action brought against Johnson & Johnson for its alleged negligence in respect of a prescription drug it had manufactured. One of the allegations was that the defendant had breached provisions of the Food and Drugs Act[33] relating to the filings it prepared for the purpose of obtaining regulatory approval for the marketing of the drug in Canada. The Court of Appeal agreed with the motion judge's decision to strike out this portion of the claim, on the basis of *Saskatchewan Wheat Pool*, in so far as the pleadings simply alleged a nominate tort of breach of statute. Goudge JA stated that, while 'a statutory requirement can inform a common law duty of care, there is no cause of action in tort for breach of statute'.[34] Goudge JA also agreed that these pleadings could not support an action for negligent misrepresentation since there was no misrepresentation made by the defendant to the plaintiffs upon which the latter relied. Goudge JA was prepared, however, to let the claim proceed on the basis of a common law duty to design, formulate, test, manufacture, label, distribute, advertise, market and promote its drug with reasonable care. This

[28]   CCSM c W210, s 4.
[29]   (1999) 98 OTC 161 (SCJ).
[30]   The Commodity Futures Act RSO 1990 c C.20 and its regulations.
[31]   The Court referred to *Varcoe v Sterling* (1992) 7 OR (3d) 204 (CA) as the seminal case on this point.
[32]   (2003) 174 OAC 44 (CA) [*Boulanger*].
[33]   RSC 1985 c F-27.
[34]   *Boulanger*, above n 32, at [10].

common law duty might have been breached by the defendant's failure to take reasonable care in the filings it made in order to obtain regulatory approval to market the drug in Canada. The Court of Appeal concluded that it was not plain and obvious that a claim presented as such would fail and, thus, refused to strike it out.

The Supreme Court itself has reaffirmed this approach to *Saskatchewan Wheat Pool* in at least three relatively recent decisions. In *Stewart v Pettie*,[35] a commercial host was sued by an occupant of a car whose driver had been drinking at the defendant's establishment. Justice Major cited *Saskatchewan Wheat Pool* in noting that the fact that the defendant might have been in violation of a legislative provision forbidding the service of alcohol to a person who is intoxicated 'does not ground liability'.[36] The duty must be based on the common law's approach to this area of law, ie, the finding of a 'special relationship' between the parties which imposed a duty of affirmative action on the part of the commercial host for the protection of the patron and foreseeable others. In *Ryan v City of Victoria*,[37] Major J again reaffirmed Canadian law that 'a statutory breach does not automatically give rise to civil liability; it is merely some evidence of negligence'. Finally, in *Odhavji Estate v Woodhouse*,[38] Iacobucci J reiterated that there is no nominate tort of statutory breach in Canada. The fact that the defendant breached a statute is insufficient, by itself, to give rise to civil liability.

In short, it is clear and uncontroversial that breach of a statute can provide evidence of negligence in an action for negligence based upon a common law duty of care. There is no nominate tort of breach of statutory duty. These judgments would support the proposition that, while a statute can 'inform' a common law duty of care, it cannot, by itself, create a common law duty of care. Unfortunately, the difference between using a statute to inform, as opposed to create, a common law duty of care seems to be a subtle one, as the next category of cases discussed will illustrate.

B. The Use of Statutes in the Absence of a Common Law Duty Relationship

Much more problematic is the use of the breach of statutory duties in negligence actions where there arguably is no recognised common law duty relationship between the parties. Courts have approached these types of

---

[35] [1995] 1 SCR 131.

[36] Major J ultimately decided that there was no breach since the patron was in the company of two sober adults, and it was reasonable to assume that one of the sober people would be driving.

[37] [1999] 1 SCR 201, [29].

[38] Above n 4.

actions in different ways. One approach has been to follow the holding in *Saskatchewan Wheat Pool* that there is no nominate tort of breach of statute and to find that, in the absence of a common law duty of care, the plaintiff's action must be dismissed. The second approach has been to find the defendant liable for its breach of the statute despite the judgment in *Saskatchewan Wheat Pool*. The third approach has been to recognise that there is no nominate tort of breach of statute and to find the defendant liable based on the existence of a common law duty of care, but *one which the court essentially creates because of the statutory duty*. Let us examine some cases that illustrate these three approaches.

(i)   First Approach: no nominate tort of breach of statutory duty and, in absence of recognised common law duty of care, action is dismissed

The cases dealing with a defendant's failure to clear the snow from the public sidewalk abutting the defendant's property provide the best example of the first approach. By-laws provide that property owners are responsible for clearing the ice and snow from the public sidewalks abutting their properties, and provide fines for breaches of these provisions.[39] The by-laws do not expressly provide for a home owner's liability to pedestrians who fall on the sidewalk as a result of the home owner's failure to comply with the statutory duties. Most cases have made it clear that there is no common law duty imposed on home owners to ensure that the public sidewalks which abut their properties are kept in a reasonably safe condition for pedestrians who walk on them.[40] The courts reason that, since there is no common law duty of care, and (in view of the holding in *Saskatchewan Wheat Pool*) that there is no tort of breach of statutory duty,

---

[39]   See, for example, *Bongiardina v Corporation of the City of Vaughan* (2000) 49 OR (3d) 641 (CA) [*Bongiardina*], which dealt with Bylaw 300-93 of the City of Vaughan. It required owners of residential buildings to clear away snow and ice from the sidewalks on the highways in front of the land occupied by their buildings within 24 hours after a snow fall has ceased, and provided a penalty at the discretion of the convicting justice for breach of this statutory duty.

[40]   The reasons for rejecting a common law duty are invariably discussed superficially, if at all. In *Bongiardina*, *ibid*, for example, the Court of Appeal simply said:

although the 'neighbour' principle from *Donoghue v. Stevenson*, [1932] AC 562 (HL) has been expanded in recent years to cover a myriad of new relationships, it would stretch it too far if it was applied in . . .this case. A homeowner has a duty to ensure that his or her own property is maintained in a reasonable condition so that persons entering the property are not injured. If the homeowner complies with this duty, he or she should be free from liability for injuries resulting from failure to maintain municipally owned streets and sidewalks. The snow and ice accumulating on public sidewalks and the potholes on the street in front of the house are the legal responsibility of the municipality, not the adjacent property owner.

This is conclusory. There is no discussion of foreseeability, proximity, or policy. This sharply contrasts with other negligence cases based on statutory duties, where these matters are extensively explored, as I shall later discuss.

the actions are dismissed.[41] The fact that the breaches might have been, and in fact probably were, *intentional* breaches of duty, is not a factor raised in these judgments.[42]

Gould v Regina (East School Division No 77) is an educational malpractice case.[43] The plaintiff complained of the treatment she received at school from her teacher and alleged that her teacher as well as the Board of Education had failed to perform a number of the duties specified in the Education Act.[44] The court was of the view that, as a result of *Saskatchewan Wheat Pool*, the alleged statutory breaches could not, without more, provide the basis for the plaintiff's cause of action. It considered whether any torts might have been committed by the parties outside of their statutory breaches, such as assault, intentional infliction of mental suffering, or 'educational malpractice', and determined that none had been.

Beaton v Canada (Public Service Commission)[45] was an action brought by a plaintiff who complained that he had not been hired by the Canada Employment Centre due to a failure on the part of the Public Service Commission to abide by the hiring requirements of the Public Service Employment Act.[46] The court concluded that the Act had not been breached but added that, even if it had, the plaintiff would have to show 'some intentional or negligent breach of duty recognized in the general law of tort' in order to recover damages from the defendant.[47]

(ii) Second Approach: a breach of statute can form the basis of a private right of action in exceptional cases, despite the judgment in Saskatchewan Wheat Pool

A second approach that has been adopted, although infrequently, has been to find that, notwithstanding the judgment in *Saskatchewan Wheat Pool*, a breach of a statute still can form the basis of a private cause of action. In

---

[41] There are a number of cases. Aside from *Bongiardina, ibid*, see *Kluane v Chasse* (2001) 289 AR 226 (QB), aff'd (2003) 320 AR 376 (CA); and *Chong v Flynn* (1998) 233 AR 120 (QB), among others. Note that, in *Kluane v Chasse*, Lutz J, in an earlier application for a determination on a question of law, held that the bylaw did create a civil law duty on the part of the occupier—see [1998] AJ No 757 (QB) (QL).

[42] This is an interesting point for, as we shall see later, some have argued that the holding in *Saskatchewan Wheat Pool* does not apply to intentional statutory breaches. I think it is fair to assume that most homeowners who fail to comply with the bylaw do so intentionally.

[43] (1997) 32 CCLT (2d) 150 (Sask QB).

[44] RSS 1978 c E-1.

[45] (1984) 6 Admin LR 119 (FC) [*Beaton*].

[46] RSC 1970 c P-32, s 18.

[47] *Beaton*, above n 44, at 126. In *Cross v Sullivan* [2003] OTC 614 (SCJ), the plaintiff sued for an alleged breach of the National Defence Act RSC 1985 c N-5 (section not specified by the court). The court rejected the claim on the basis of *Saskatchewan Wheat Pool*. For other cases utilising this approach, see L Klar, *Tort Law*, 3rd edn (Toronto, Carswell, 2003) 327 n 146.

Whistler Cable Television Ltd v IPEC Canada Inc,[48] the plaintiff operated a cable distribution system. The defendant was operating its own unlicensed cable distribution system and was thereby cutting into the plaintiff's business. The plaintiff sued the defendant, alleging that the defendant was breaching a section of the Broadcasting Act which made it an offence to carry on broadcasting without a licence, and provided for a fine of up to $200,000 for each day that the offence continued.[49] The court made it clear that the gravamen in this case 'related to the common law action of the breach of statute and not the common law action of unlawful interference with a trade or business', since the question of intent to injure, 'which appears to be one of the essential elements of the tort of unlawful interference with a trade or business',[50] was not addressed by the parties. This is an important point. Had the action been framed as one of the business torts, with all of its constituent elements, breach of statute would clearly have been a relevant consideration.

Turning to the action based on breach of statute, Braidwood J reasoned that *Saskatchewan Wheat Pool* should be confined to actions based on breach of the duty of care within the context of negligence law, and that it should not be read as eliminating the tort of breach of statute where the right alleged to have been breached is a right 'specifically granted to the plaintiff by the statute by its very terms'.[51] In the case of actions brought by plaintiffs who are alleging that their statutory rights have been breached by the defendants, 'there remains a tort of statutory breach distinct from any issue of negligence'.[52] The only issue in this type of case is whether the plaintiff will be permitted the remedy of an injunction or damages as a consequence of the defendant's breach of its right.

The court held that, in this case, the exclusive right given to the plaintiff by the Broadcasting Act to operate a cable distribution system was breached by the defendant. Turning to the English jurisprudence on the tort of breach of statutory duty, Braidwood J applied the rule that, where it is apparent on the true construction of the Act that the obligation or prohibition was imposed for the benefit of a particular class of individuals or where an individual member suffers 'particular, direct and substantial' damage, other than and different from that which is common to the rest of the public in relation to the breach of a public right, a private right of

---

[48]   (1992) 75 BCLR (2d) 48 (SC) [*Whistler*].
[49]   SC 1991 c 11, s 32.
[50]   *Whistler*, above n 47, at 52.
[51]   *Ibid*, at 55.
[52]   *Ibid*.

action can be brought.[53] Braidwood J also referred to some Canadian judgments pre-*Saskatchewan Wheat Pool*. He examined the Broadcasting Act to determine:

(1) for whose benefit it was passed;
(2) whether it was passed in the interest of the public at large or for a particular class of persons or both;
(3) whether the plaintiff was within the class intended to be benefited;
(4) whether the damages suffered were the kind of damage the statute was intended to prevent;
(5) whether the penalties prescribed in the Act were adequate; and
(6) whether the Act set up a scheme designed exclusively to carry out the objects of the Act.

Braidwood J answered these questions favourably for the plaintiff and allowed the action to proceed to trial.

In my opinion, this approach is very problematic and resurrects the difficulties that the decision in *Saskatchewan Wheat Pool* was meant to resolve. It required the court to interpret the legislation to determine whether it was giving the plaintiff a specific right enforceable by way of a private action in tort. It ignored the argument that, had the legislator intended to confer a private right of action on the plaintiff, it would have expressly provided for it in the statute. It created what some have called judicial legislation, extending the penalty provided for in the statute, which in the case of the Broadcasting Act is quite extensive, by tacking on an additional financial penalty.

I do not believe that the reasoning and result of *Whistler Cable* can be reconciled with the reasoning of *Saskatchewan Wheat Pool* and most of the post-*Saskatchewan Wheat Pool* decisions. In a sense, all statutes which impose duties, the performance of which benefits other parties, can be said to be statutes which confer rights on other parties. For example, snow clearing by-laws arguably confer rights on pedestrians to walk in safety. The Canada Grain Act obligations at issue in *Saskatchewan Wheat Pool* can be said to have conferred rights on grain exporters to market grain which is free from harmful larvae. The search in statutory language for those parties who have 'exclusive rights,' for those parties who suffer 'particular, direct and substantial damage', or for those particular parties for whose benefit the statute was passed, engages the court in the type of interpretative process that the judgment in *Saskatchewan Wheat Pool* opposed.

[53] The court referred to the House of Lords' judgment in *Lonrho Ltd v Shell Petroleum Co Ltd (No 2)*, above n 16, at 185 for these propositions.

(iii)   Third Approach: ostensibly follow Saskatchewan Wheat Pool,
decide case based on negligence law principles, but create a common law
duty of care directly because of the statutory duty

The third approach is the one most frequently employed by courts. It
ostensibly follows *Saskatchewan Wheat Pool*, but bases the existence of
the common law duty of care in the negligence action upon the existence of
a statutory duty. In some of these cases, there is not even any discussion of
why there is a common law duty; one is simply assumed. Others consider
the existence or non-existence of a common law duty in situations where, I
would suggest, there would have been no common law duty had it not
been for the statutory duty.

The case of *YO v Belleville (City) Chief of Police*[54] provides a good
example of a court using a breach of a statute to create a private right of
action using the language of negligence law, even though, apart from the
statute, no common law duty of care would have existed. The police
breached a provision of the Young Offenders Act[55] by revealing the
plaintiff youth's criminal record to a potential employer. As a result, the
employer, the City of Belleville, decided not to hire the plaintiff. The
penalty for breaching that provision was criminal prosecution; no civil
remedy was statutorily provided to the victim of the breach. In fact, the
trial judge was inclined to the view that the legislature *did not intend there
to be a civil remedy*. Moreover, the trial judge referred to the judgment in
Saskatchewan Wheat Pool in asserting that there is no tort of breach of
statutory duty and, therefore, it would be incorrect to inquire into the
intention of the legislature. Relying on his interpretation of *Saskatchewan
Wheat Pool*, Byers J stated that the case before him had to be decided on
negligence principles, and that there had to be a duty of care, a breach and
damages for there to be liability.[56] He then found that 'all defendants had a
duty to the plaintiff to use reasonable care to keep his youth record
confidential'.[57] The defendants were careless and breached that duty.[58]
Liability thus was found. The problem with this reasoning is obvious. The
source of the common law duty not to reveal a youth offender's record was
the statute itself. Otherwise, there would have been no common law duty.
There was not even any discussion of why there was a common law duty.

---

[54]   (1991) 3 OR (3d) 261 (Gen Div) [*Belleville*].

[55]   RSC 1985 c 24 (2d Supp), s 34.

[56]   The plaintiff had not even pleaded negligence. The court, however, allowed the plaintiff
to request an amendment to his pleadings.

[57]   *Belleville*, above n 53, at 271.

[58]   In fact, the court found that the defendants were not even aware of the duty, or, if they
were, they flagrantly breached it.

In essence, the court created a private right of action based on breach of a statutory duty, despite recognising that there is no tort of breach of statutory duty in Canada.[59]

More difficult to analyse, and much more numerous, are those cases in which the courts purportedly use the common law to create a duty of care to exist independently of, but which in fact mirrors, the statutory duty that has been breached. By doing this, the courts are able to provide a private right of action to the claimant, for what was essentially a breach of the defendant's statutory duty, without seemingly running into conflict with the judgment in *Saskatchewan Wheat Pool*. Frequently, the judgments make no reference to *Saskatchewan Wheat Pool* at all, the courts apparently not aware of the fact that what they are doing might indeed contradict that judgment. The issue, however, which needs to be explored in all of these cases, is *whether there would have been a common law duty relationship between the parties at all, had it not been for the defendant's statutory duties*. If the answer to this question is 'no', it is my contention that the courts are essentially providing for civil liability for a breach of statutory duty, notwithstanding the use of common law duty of care language.

Two earlier Federal Court of Canada judgments in particular illustrate this problem. In *Brewer Brothers v Attorney General of Canada*[60] and *Devloo v Canada*,[61] the plaintiffs, who were grain producers, brought negligence actions against the Canada Grain Commission, alleging the Commission's negligence with respect to its statutory duties to regulate

[59] Based on *Odhavji*, one would think that this case would now be considered a case of misfeasance in a public office. The defendant police knowingly breached their statutory duty, where damage to the plaintiff was foreseeable and probable. Other similar cases are *JMF v Chappell* [1993] BCJ No 1281 (SC) (QL), and *LR v Nyp* (1995) 25 CCLT (2d) 309 (Ont Gen Div). In *Chappell*, a defendant newspaper published a sexual assault complainant's name, in breach of a publication ban order made pursuant to the Criminal Code. The judge found that the defendant owed the plaintiff a 'private law duty', which it breached, and allowed the action to proceed. There was no discussion as to why there was a private law duty aside from the existence of the publication ban itself. *Nyp* also involved the breach of a publication ban relating to a sexual assault complainant. The court considered the duty issue, finding that there was a relationship of proximity between the parties and no policy reasons to negate or limit the duty. This decision is more defensible in that it suggested that there is a general common law duty of care between newspapers and those who might be injured by what newspapers publish and thus the common law duty existed independently of the ban. Breach of the ban can then be used as evidence of the breach of this common law duty. The notion that newspapers have a duty to take reasonable care in reference to what they publish, and that an action for negligence, in addition to an action for defamation, can be brought against a newspaper warrants considerably more thought and discussion.

[60] (1990) 66 DLR (4th) 71 (TD), varied as to damages (1991) 80 DLR (4th) (CA) [*Brewer Brothers*].

[61] (1990) 33 FTR 1 [*Devloo*].

grain dealers under the Canada Grain Act.[62] Section 36(1)(c) of the Act provided that no grain dealer's licence:

> shall be issued unless the applicant establishes to the satisfaction of the Commission that... he is financially able to carry on the proposed [grain dealer's business] and has given security by bond, insurance or otherwise, sufficient to ensure that all obligations to holders of documents for the payment of money or delivery of grain issued by the applicant pursuant to this Act will be met.

The plaintiffs had lost money as a result of the insolvency of a dealer and were alleging that the Commission had failed in its duty. The Act provided one remedy for producers, namely, the right to realise on whatever security had been posted by the dealer, but it did not provide for the civil liability of the Commission.

Muldoon J, in his trial judgment in *Devloo*, approached this case from two perspectives. First, he considered whether the Canada Grain Act itself could be interpreted as conferring a private right of action on the producers, despite his own Court of Appeal's judgment, as well as the Supreme Court of Canada's decision in *Saskatchewan Wheat Pool*, that the Canada Grain Act was intended to regulate the grain industry and to protect the public interest, not the private interests of grain producers. Conceding that nowhere in the statutory provisions could the words 'cause of action', 'damages', 'tort,' 'liability', or 'claim' be found, Muldoon J concluded that the statutory duties imposed on the Commission were 'so specific' and 'so directly focused in the interests of grain producers' that 'there arises without difficulty an entirely plausible conclusion to the effect that Parliament ... did indeed provide in this statute the Commission's civil liability to producers for unsecured shortfall of payments'.[63]

If liability had been based on this reasoning, it would, in my view, have been in direct conflict with *Saskatchewan Wheat Pool*. Muldoon J seemed to recognise this and conceded that another, and 'perhaps the sounder course', would be to determine the case based on negligence law principles. Much of the discussion concerning the negligence action, however, revolved around the negligent conduct of the Commission with respect to the statutory duties it was required to perform, and the ways in which it failed to perform them. The important question from my perspective, however, was not whether the Commission negligently performed its statutory duties to regulate grain dealers, but whether the Commission *owed a common law duty of care to the grain producers in the first place*. In the absence of a common law duty of care between the parties, the Commission's negligence in performing its statutory duties would be irrelevant. Moreover, the recognition of a common law duty of care could

---

[62]   Above n 6.
[63]   *Devloo*, above n 60, at 11.

not be based solely on the fact that the Commission had statutory duties to regulate the grain industry and grain dealers. For if it were, the court would be doing exactly what *Saskatchewan Wheat Pool* had said is not permissible in Canadian law.

The discussion of the duty of care issue in this case was somewhat complicated, touching as it did on most of the 'hot button' duty issues. References were made to: the two-stage test created in *Anns v Merton London Borough Council*[64] and adopted by the Supreme Court of Canada in *City of Kamloops v Nielsen*,[65] which involved foreseeability of damage as the test of proximity at the first stage, followed by policy considerations at the second stage; the English rejection of the two-stage test in cases like *Peabody Fund v Sir L Parkinson*,[66] *Curran v NI Co-ownership Housing*,[67] and *Yuen Kun-Yeu v AG of Hong Kong*,[68] which expanded the first stage of proximity to include more than mere foreseeability; the Crown Liability Act;[69] the difference between nonfeasance and misfeasance; the policy/ operational dichotomy; and liability for pure economic losses. It is my submission that, all of this language aside, a common law duty of care was found because Muldoon J interpreted the Canada Grain Act as creating one. His conclusion rested on the following grounds: damage to the plaintiffs from a breach of the Commission's statutory duties was foreseeable; the statute created a special relationship between the parties in that the Commission's statutory duties were meant to protect the grain producers as a particular class; the breach of these statutory duties was a misfeasance; the breach of these duties did not involve policy decisions; and liability would not raise the spectre of indeterminate liability.

The Federal Court of Appeal affirmed the decision.[70] Stone JA made it clear, however, that, because of *Saskatchewan Wheat Pool*, it would not have been correct for Muldoon J to have found liability on the basis of the Canada Grain Act alone. According to Stone JA, 'the Act may be considered not as imposing liability *but as furnishing evidence of the existence of a private law duty of care in an appropriate case*'.[71] Following the lead of the Supreme Court of Canada in *Just v The Queen*[72] and the

---

[64] [1978] AC 728 (HL) [*Anns*]. Although *Anns* has been overruled in its country of origin, it remains good law in Canada. The *Anns* test was reaffirmed and explained by the Supreme Court in *Cooper*, above n 3, and *Odhavji*, above n 4.

[65] [1984] 2 SCR 2 [*Kamloops*].

[66] [1985] AC 210 (HL).

[67] [1987] AC 718 (HL).

[68] [1987] 2 All ER 705 (PC).

[69] RSC 1970 c C-38.

[70] (1991) 129 NR 39.

[71] *Ibid*, at 55 (emphasis added).

[72] [1989] 2 SCR 1228 [*Just*].

Federal Court in *Brewer Brothers*,[73] Stone JA used the following considerations to decide that a common law duty of care existed. He applied the two-stage test; interpreted the Act as protecting grain producers; asserted that the Act provided 'strong evidence of a private law duty of care';[74] found a relationship of proximity between the parties; found that there was no valid reason to exclude the duty; found that the Act was meant to protect producers from pure economic losses; found that the Act contained no exemption from liability; held that there was negligence in operations as opposed to policy; and held that the Commission's functions could not be considered as quasi-judicial or analogous to police functions.[75]

The judgments in the above cases illustrate the problem I am raising. Unfortunately, the approach the courts followed was, and still is, the common approach used in public tort liability cases in Canada. Courts agree that there is no tort of breach of statutory duty and that, for there to be liability, there must be a duty of care founded in the common law. They then proceed, however, to find the common law duty based entirely on the provisions of the statute, which they construe as creating one. One could characterise all of the leading Supreme Court of Canada cases on public tort liability, including *Kamloops*[76] and *Just*,[77] in this way. It thus might appear odd that I am raising this point now. After all, courts have been using breaches of statutory duties to impose civil liability on statutory authorities for decades, and as long as the normal hurdles are passed—for example, the courts are not questioning 'policy' decisions of public authorities, there will not be 'indeterminate liability', there is no statutory exemption from suit, or the impugned conduct does not fall into some other off-limits area such as being a judicial or legislative act—private causes of action based on statutory breaches have frequently been successful. So why am I raising this issue now?

The reason that I raise the point now is because of the Supreme Court of Canada's judgments in *Cooper* and *Edwards*.[78] For while these judgments do not explicitly refer to the subject of this chapter, namely the interaction

---

[73]   Above n 59.

[74]   Above n 69, at 56.

[75]   In *Brewer Brothers* one finds the same approach. The court recognises that civil liability cannot be based on the breach of statutory duty in the absence of a common law duty, but then creates the common law duty by arguing that the statute was meant to create one. Superficially, the reasoning in these cases seems defensible, in that they use the language of foreseeability, proximity, and policy to create the common law duty. However, in cases dealing with a defendant's failure to confer statutory benefits, common law duty principles, properly applied, should generally militate against the recognition of a duty. I will discuss this point more fully later in this chapter.

[76]   Above n 64.

[77]   Above n 71.

[78]   Above n 3.

between breaches of statute and tort law, they may have the effect, perhaps inadvertently, of steering Canadian tort law back onto the track laid down by *Saskatchewan Wheat Pool*.

Both *Cooper* and *Edwards* involved the alleged failure of statutorily created regulators to properly carry out their statutory functions, with consequent losses to the plaintiffs.[79] The issue for the courts was whether the regulators owed a private law duty of care to individual claimants, and the Supreme Court of Canada determined in each case that they did not. In arriving at its decision, the Supreme Court 'refined' the two-stage duty test developed in *Anns* by adding a 'proximity' element, apart from 'foreseeability', to the first stage of the test.[80] The Court decided that there was insufficient proximity between the parties to create a prima facie duty of care in both cases.

McLachlin CJ and Major J, who wrote the judgment of the Court in *Cooper*, openly acknowledged that, if a relationship of proximity existed between the parties sufficient to support the recognition of a prima facie duty of care, the factors giving rise to this proximity:

> must arise *from the statute* under which the Registrar is appointed. That statute is the only source of his duties, private or public. Apart from that statute, he is in no different position than the ordinary man or woman on the street. If a duty to investors with regulated mortgage brokers is to be found, *it must be in the statute*.[81]

The Court construed the statute and concluded that:

> *the statute does not impose a duty of care on the Registrar to investors* with mortgage brokers regulated by the Act. The Registrar's duty is rather to the public as a whole. Indeed, a duty to individual investors would potentially conflict with the Registrar's overarching duty to the public.[82]

---

[79] *Cooper* involved the Registrar of Mortgage Brokers and *Edwards* the Law Society of Upper Canada. The cases are actually very similar to the allegations raised in the earlier cases regarding the Canada Grain Commission's failure to regulate, although the Supreme Court of Canada viewed them as opening up a new 'category' of cases.

[80] There has been much written about this. See eg, L Klar, 'Foreseeability, Proximity and Policy' (2002) 25 *Advocates Quarterly* 360; SGA Pitel, 'Canada Remakes the *Anns* Test' [2002] 61 *CLJ* 252; N Rafferty, 'Developments in Contract and Tort Law: The 2001-2002 Term' (2002) 18 *Supreme Court Law Review* 153; B Feldthusen, 'The *Anns/Cooper* Approach to Duty of Care' (2002) 18 *Construction Law Review* 67; R Brown, 'Still Crazy After All These Years...' (2003) 36 *University of British Columbia Law Review* 159; J Neyers and U Gabie, 'Canadian Tort Law since *Cooper v Hobart* , Parts I and II' (2005) 13 *Torts Law Journal* 302, (2006) 14 *Torts Law Journal* 10; A Linden, *Canadian Tort Law*, 7th edn Supp (Markham, Butterworths, 2001), among others. I will not review the debate here.

[81] Above n 3, at [43] (emphasis added).

[82] *Ibid*, at [44] (emphasis added). At an earlier part of the judgment (see [34]), the Court recognised that 'proximity' involved the relationship that existed between the parties and involved looking at 'expectations, representations, reliance, and the property interests involved'. As I will discuss later, these factors are relevant to determining a common law duty of care and, had the Court followed through and examined whether or not there were

As has been commented upon, and lamented by Justice Allen Linden, the effect of *Cooper* and *Edwards* has been to stifle the development of negligence law, particularly in relation to negligent government conduct.[83] Many actions against government have been summarily dismissed because there was no proximity and, hence, no duty. Statutes have been increasingly interpreted as creating public duties, but not private law duties of care.

In *Deep v Ontario*,[84] for example, the plaintiff doctor sued the College of Physicians and Surgeons, among others, as a result of their decision to withhold his fees. The defendants maintained that the fees had been withheld as a result of the plaintiff's refusal to co-operate with a Medical Review Committee. The plaintiff alleged, among other things, that the defendants' actions were in breach of the Health Insurance Act.[85] The trial judge held that, in accordance with *Saskatchewan Wheat Pool*, any breach of statute must be considered in the context of a claim in negligence. Spence J, echoing the words of McLachlin CJ and Major J in *Cooper*, stated that:

> the statute is the only source of the Crown decision-maker's duties, private or public. Apart from the statute, a Crown decision-maker is in no different position from the ordinary man or woman on the street. *If a duty to the plaintiff is to be found, it must be in the pertinent statutory provisions. If the statute does not provide for a private law duty of care, no such duty exists and there can be no claim in negligence.*[86]

The judge found that 'the provisions of the Health Insurance Act do not in any way *evidence a legislative intent* to confer any private law duty of care upon the plaintiff'.[87]

---

representations, undertakings, or reliance between the parties sufficient to create a common law duty of care, I would have had no difficulty with the judgment. Unfortunately, the Court seemed to abandon this line of inquiry, focusing instead on construing the statute to determine whether the statutory provisions implied a private law duty of care.

[83]   See Linden, above n 79. Linden writes that 'it is becoming almost impossible nowadays to successfully attack negligent government conduct through tort law, despite the universal legislation indicating that governments are to be liable in the same way as if they were private persons and despite the fact that this same conduct may often be challenged through judicial review on administrative law or constitutional law grounds', at 12. Numerous failed cases are cited to support this contention.

[84]   [2004] OTC 541 (SCJ), aff'd (2005) 138 ACWS (3d) 572 (CA).

[85]   RSO 1990 c H.6.

[86]   Above n 83, at [57] (emphasis added).

[87]   *Ibid*, at [58]. The action was struck and the judgment was affirmed by the Ontario Court of Appeal. Similar reasoning with the same result is found in *Swift Current v Saskatchewan Power Corpn* (2005) 272 Sask R 160 (QB). The plaintiff city sued the Crown Investments Corporation, alleging, among other things, that it breached its statutory duties to supervise subsidiary Crown Corporations. The court held that there was no nominate tort of breach of statute and the action must be framed in negligence. Although utilising the language of *Anns* and *Cooper* to determine duty, the court looked to the statutory provisions to

The recently litigated cases in Ontario concerning the outbreak of SARS in that province are illustrative of a similar approach. A variety of plaintiffs, including patients, health care workers, and family members, sued the Federal and Provincial Crown and the City of Toronto for damages caused by the outbreak of SARS.[88] Cullity J's judgment in *Williams* focused on the issue of whether it was plain and obvious that the public body defendants who had been sued owed no duty of care to the claimants. While recognising that there is no tort of breach of statutory duty in Canada and that, if a duty of care is found, it must be based on the Anns test, as refined by *Cooper*, Cullity J asserted that the 'starting point' for determining proximity must be the statutes which govern the responsibilities and powers of the public authorities in question. In this respect, consideration must be given to things such as whether the legislation, 'expressly, or by implication, disclose *a legislative intention to confer – or to exclude – private law rights of compensation on individuals who suffered damages caused by the breach*';[89] and whether the duties were imposed in the interests of the public or of discrete classes which included the plaintiffs. Cullity J asserted that, although 'the issue of proximity is not dependent on finding a specific legislative intention to impose a private law duty of care owed to the plaintiffs' … 'if, on the construction of the statute, such an intention appears, *that will be the end of the inquiry*'.[90] Cullity J added that proximity could be found even if the statute were interpreted as creating only a public duty, in reference to the manner in which these

determine whether the legislature intended to impose a private law duty of care on the defendant vis-à-vis an individual person. The court decided it did not.

[88] There were several proceedings brought. The lead judgment is *Williams v Canada (Attorney-General)* (2005) 257 DLR (4th) 704 (Ont SCJ) [*Williams*]. It involved motions brought by the Federal and Provincial Crowns and the City of Toronto to strike out the statement of claim or portions of it. *Williams* was a class action brought by individuals who contracted SARS and their family members. *Laroza et al v Ontario* (2005) 257 DLR (4th) 761 (Ont SC) was an action brought by the family of a nurse who died. The nurse's son also contracted SARS. *Arbaquez v Ontario* (2005) 257 DLR (4th) 745 (Ont SC) was an action brought by nurses who contracted the disease. See also *Jamal Estate v Scarborough Hospital* (2005) 34 CCLT (3d) 271 (Ont SC); *Henry Estate v Scarborough Hospital* (2005) 34 CCLT (3d) 278 (Ont SC).

[89] *Williams*, above at [71]. Cullity J concedes at [71] that, 'in many cases, the search for an implication either way in the guise of an exercise in statutory interpretation will involve "looking for what is not there": *Sask. Wheat Pool*, at page 226, *but inferences may be drawn from the purpose and overall scheme of the legislation, Cooper* at para. 49' (emphasis added). With respect, this is my objection. No matter what the nature of the legislative scheme, the duty can only be based on the actual interaction which occurs between the parties as a result of the legislative scheme.

[90] *Ibid*, at [72].

public duties or powers were exercised. On this basis, Cullity J reviewed the statutory provisions and decided that they, by and large, did not create private law duties of care.[91]

It is my submission that, although the results of the above public tort liability cases are consistent with *Saskatchewan Wheat Pool*, their reasoning is not. Attempting to find the common law duty in the statutory provisions themselves is to create a common law tort of breach of statutory duty. Courts ought not to be interpreting the statutory scheme and provisions to determine whether the legislation intended a private law duty of care. By so doing, courts are searching for a non-existent legislative intention, a process condemned by Dickson J in *Saskatchewan Wheat Pool*. Statutes that are silent as to the existence of private rights of action for the breaches of statutory duties ought not to be construed so as to create civil remedies. If there is to be a duty owed by statutory bodies to private persons, *it is not to be found in the statutes; it is to be found in the common law*. Construing a statute to determine whether its provisions create a private law duty is to do exactly what *Saskatchewan Wheat Pool* advised against, no matter how the court answers this question.

C.   The Suggested Correct Approach to the Interaction Between Statutes and Negligence Actions

I would suggest that, in order to be consistent with the judgment in *Saskatchewan Wheat Pool*, courts ought to be utilising breaches of statutes in the following ways.

It is clear that, where there is a recognised common law duty relationship between the parties, breaches of statutes that provide standards of conduct in relation to that duty are relevant in determining the breach of duty issue. Thus, for example, as we have seen in some of the cases discussed above, the breach of the duty of care owed by drivers of cars to those who are foreseeable victims of negligent driving, or by employers to employees in relation to providing them with safe working conditions, can be established by providing evidence that specific statutory standards were not followed. There is no question in these types of cases that there is a common law duty of care that is not dependent upon the existence of a

---

[91]   In fairness to Cullity J, included in his list of factors were: what representations were made?, did the plaintiffs reasonably rely on them?, and what were the reasonable expectations of the parties?. These are relevant considerations in determining a common law duty. However, as in other cases, these factors seemed to be largely abandoned in favour of an examination of the statutory scheme in order to determine whether it created private law duties of care in addition to public duties. Cullity J does note the absence of reliance and a causal connection in determining that there was no proximity between the parties, but these comments are peripheral to his denial of a duty based on an examination of the statutory provisions themselves.

statutory duty. This type of use of statutory standards is quite common, and the statutes are invariably very helpful in establishing negligent behaviour.

The more challenging cases are those where the courts are dealing with parties whose very existence and functions derive from statutes. That is, unlike car drivers or employers, who do not drive cars or employ workers because they are statutorily required or empowered to do so, statutory bodies derive their raison d'etre, their responsibilities and their powers from statutes that created them. One can refer to many examples from the above discussion. The Canada Grain Commission, the Registrar of Mortgage Brokers, the Law Society of Upper Canada, the Board of Education, and the Ministry of Health, for example, are creatures of legislation, whose functions, powers, and responsibilities are to be found in statutes and regulations. *Saskatchewan Wheat Pool* tells us that, if the statutes under which these bodies operate impose public duties on them or authorise certain activities, but do not *expressly* provide for civil liability in the event that these duties are breached or these responsibilities are performed negligently, a private individual harmed by this misconduct cannot base a claim for compensation upon the statutory breach. The claim must be founded upon the common law negligence action. Does this mean, therefore, that these statutes are not relevant to the negligence action?

No, it does not mean that. The statutes are indeed relevant, but not because they contain within them an implied private law duty of care owed to certain individuals. They are relevant because they provide *the context and the factual environment* which brings the statutory actors and the alleged victims into contact with each other. And if the *common law* (not the statute) determines that *this type of interaction or relationship* warrants the imposition of a duty of care, the courts (not the legislature) will impose a duty.

The facts of an earlier case, *Gordonna Ltd v City of St John's*,[92] may illustrate the point I am trying to make. The plaintiffs were the owners and tenant of a building which was damaged by fire. They alleged that, because of an inadequate supply of water to fight the fire, more damage was done by the fire than should have been. They sued the City, whose statutory duty it was to supply and distribute water.[93]

The plaintiffs alleged both a breach of statutory duty and a breach of a common law duty. Steele J, relying on *Saskatchewan Wheat Pool*, held that there was no tort of breach of statutory duty and that the case could only

[92] (1986) 30 DLR (4th) 720 (Nfld SC).
[93] The statute was the City of St John's Act RSNL 1970 c 40, s 116.

succeed if a breach of a common law duty were established.[94] The statute, however, was not irrelevant to establishing the common law duty. As Steele J stated:

> If there was a breach of the statutory duty the civil consequences are to be subsumed in the law of negligence. I take it, however, that a common law duty of care may exist in the absence of proof of breach of a statutory duty. Where, as we have here, a statutory duty *it* [sic] helps *frame the relationship of proximity or neighbourhood existing between the parties and aids in determining whether in the reasonable contemplation of the defendant its carelessness would likely injure the plaintiffs.*[95]

In considering whether a common law duty relationship was created as a result of the statutory duty, Steele J considered the *Anns* and *Kamloops* tests and decided that there was not a sufficient relationship of proximity or neighbourhood between the parties. There were no reasons why the plaintiffs should reasonably have expected the City to have constructed the water distribution system to provide a more adequate supply of water to fight the fire at the building's location. There was no *reliance* by the plaintiffs upon the City's having done so. The City could not have reasonably contemplated that its failure to do so would likely injure the plaintiffs. As Steele J noted, had the city, through the *exercise* of its statutory powers, brought itself into a common law duty of care relationship with the plaintiffs, based on the 'dependency or reliance by the property owner and an awareness by the City no doubt that carelessness on its part would likely cause damage to the property owner', then a common law duty of care would have been owed.[96]

The objection I have to many of the judgments in the public tort liability area is that the courts frequently create a common law duty of care that is not justified based on common law principles as applied to the facts of those cases. The principal obstacle to the creation of a common law duty in many of these cases is the common law's refusal to impose a duty of

---

[94] Although Steele J did interpret the statutory provisions and decided that the statutory duty had not been breached.

[95] Above n 91, at 736 (emphasis added).

[96] An interesting judgment which seems to support this approach is *Exploits Valley Air Services Ltd v Bd of Governors of College of the North Atlantic* (2005) 258 DLR (4th) 66 (Nfld and Labrador CA), leave to appeal to SCC denied. The Court of Appeal held that a breach of the Public Tender Act RSNL 1990 c P-45 did not, of itself, ground liability in tort, citing *Saskatchewan Wheat Pool*. The plaintiff 'must establish a common law duty which corresponds to the statutory duty' (at [26]). Reference will be had to the 'reliance, expectations, representations and other circumstances that may have existed between the parties', citing *Cooper* (at [27]). The court considered the statutory provisions, and concluded that there was no proximity between the parties and, hence, no duty. It also took into account, however, the fact that there were no representations made and no reliance which could support a finding of proximity. It is my submission that it is these latter findings that are critical to a finding of no duty; not the nature of the statutory provisions.

affirmative action on one person for the protection of another person, in the absence of a 'special relationship' between the parties. Invariably the allegations in the public tort liability cases relate to a statutory body's negligence in failing to confer benefits; for example, its failure to regulate mortgage brokers for the protection of plaintiff investors, to regulate lawyers for the benefit of plaintiff clients, to regulate grain dealers for the benefit of plaintiff grain producers, to inspect construction for the benefit of plaintiff home owners, to monitor avalanche dangers for the benefit of plaintiff users of the road, to adequately protect the public against the spread of contagious diseases, and so on. The plaintiffs in these cases cannot claim that they have a contractual right to these protections or services, nor can they, because of *Saskatchewan Wheat Pool*, claim that they have a statutory right to them upon which a claim for compensation can be based. In the absence of a 'special relationship' or positive interaction with the statutory bodies, they also should not be able to claim that they have a right owed to them in tort. In the area of failure to confer benefits, mere foreseeability that harm will result if the benefits are not conferred cannot, by itself, support the creation of a duty.[97] Policy would negate the duty; that policy being the principle that tort law is not concerned with issues of conferring benefits, ie issues of distributive justice. Only the existence of a 'special relationship', which is an exception to the no-duty-to-assist principle, or an act that can be categorised as misfeasance, would justify the recognition of a duty.[98]

[97] It is usually foreseeable that a defendant's negligence or refusal to assist others will result in injury. This is clearly an insufficient element in recognising a duty. The argument that a failure to confer statutory benefits cannot, by itself, create tort liability, has been well articulated by the House of Lords in several important judgments. See *Stovin v Wise* [1996] AC 923; *X (Minors) v Bedfordshire County Council* [1995] 2 AC 633; and *Gorringe v Calderdale Metropolitan Borough Council* [2004] 1 WLR 1057. The Lords have made it clear that, unless the statute can be construed to have created a duty of care (which is permissible in English, but not Canadian, law), the statute cannot be used to generate a common law duty of care. The defendant's *conduct* (which was undertaken because of the statute) can give rise to a duty; but the statute, itself, cannot. See Lord Hoffman's words to this effect in *HM Commissioners of Customs and Excise v Barclay's Bank* [2006] UKHL 28, [39]. It is ironic that English courts, which do recognise the tort of breach of statutory duty, have held that a statute cannot be relied upon to generate a common law duty, whereas Canadian courts, which do not recognise the tort of breach of statutory duty, have used statutes to generate common law duties. Also see B Feldthusen, 'Failure To Confer Discretionary Public Benefits: The Case For Complete Negligence Immunity' (1997) 5 *Tort Law Review* 17.

[98] Canadian law's adherence to this principle was reaffirmed by the Supreme Court of Canada in its recently decided 'social host' liability judgment of *Childs v Desormeaux* [2006] SCC 18. The Court decided that, in the absence of a 'special link or proximity' between parties, a failure to act, even if it is negligent and injury is foreseeable, will not give rise to a duty to act. Three general situations where there is this link were identified: first, where the defendant actively created or controlled the risk, into which the defendant intentionally invited or attracted the plaintiff; second, where there is a relationship of supervision and control between the parties; third, where the defendant exercises public functions or engages in commercial enterprises which involve risks to the public. Although the latter category,

The factual context in which the parties operate can, in some cases, give rise to a common law duty. If the statutory defendant *acts* (as opposed to fails to confer a benefit) in a way which creates a foreseeable risk of harm to the plaintiff, there is a duty to take care (subject to policy reasons which might limit it). This explains why the 'operational' activities of statutory bodies subject the statutory actor to the same duty as is imposed upon the ordinary man or woman on the street. If the statutory actor *makes representations* upon which others reasonably rely, the statutory actor is subject to the same duty as is the non-statutory defendant to take reasonable care in making these representations. If the statutory actor *undertakes to provide a service, upon which undertaking others reasonably rely*, the statutory actor is subject to the same duty to reasonably carry through with these representations as would be the non-statutory defendant. If the statutory actor *creates a risk of harm by its positive conduct*, if it places itself in a *relationship of supervision or control*, or it otherwise creates a *special relationship* with others in circumstances in which, had a private individual done so, a duty would arise, the statutory actor is under a duty. In all of these cases, the reason the defendant has any interaction with the victim at all is because it has statutory responsibilities, but the reason it comes under a duty of care in tort must relate to the principles of the common law which would recognise a duty in this type of *interaction*.

In sum, mere foreseeability of injury is insufficient to impose a duty of care upon a statutory body where the allegations relate to a failure on the part of the statutory body to protect a private individual from harm. Moreover, to create a duty as a result of construing the relevant statute to determine whether the legislature intended that there be civil liability is to act contrary to the judgment in *Saskatchewan Wheat Pool*. A duty of care ought to be imposed only where it is supported by common law principles relating to duty. Thus, although I agree with the results of many of the recently decided public tort liability cases, I would argue that these results ought not to be justified by interpreting statutory provisions and concluding that the legislation was not intended to provide a civil remedy to aggrieved parties. They only can be justified on the basis that the nature of the interaction between the plaintiffs and defendants in these cases did not, based on common law principles, give rise to private law duties of care.

---

broadly interpreted, might implicate all statutory bodies, thus creating proximity based on breach of a statutory duty in general, the context for this category seemed to be restricted to public bodies that actively create risks and the public's legitimate expectation that these risks would be minimised. If it is interpreted more broadly than this, it would have to be reconciled with *Saskatchewan Wheat Pool*.

IV.   THE INTERACTION BETWEEN BREACHES OF STATUTORY DUTIES AND THE TORT OF MISFEASANCE IN A PUBLIC OFFICE

A very interesting development in the interaction between breach of statute and tort law is occurring with the recent extension of the tort of misfeasance in a public office. There are a number of elements to this tort; however, I will restrict myself to the breach of statutory duty issue.

In *Odhavji Estate v Toronto (Metropolitan Police Force)*,[99] the family of a man shot and killed by the police sued the police officers, alleging that they breached their statutory duties under the Police Services Act[100] to co-operate with a Special Investigations Unit assigned to investigate the shooting incident.[101] The tort of misfeasance in a public office, along with other causes of action, was raised.[102]

The intriguing part of this litigation for the purposes of this chapter was the use of a breach of a statutory duty to support the misfeasance tort. It raises questions concerning the application of Dickson J's judgment in *Saskatchewan Wheat Pool*. Where the breach of a statute is intentional, as opposed to negligent, does the judgment in *Saskatchewan Wheat Pool* apply? How does an intentional breach of statute that injures the plaintiff fit within the tort of misfeasance in a public office?

The defendants in *Odhavji* argued that the plaintiffs' claims relating to breach of statutory duty must be framed in negligence, relying upon *Saskatchewan Wheat Pool*. The plaintiffs submitted that *Saskatchewan Wheat Pool* did not preclude them from using a 'knowing breach of statutory duty' to support an intentional tort, in this case, the tort of misfeasance in a public office. Day J, the motions judge, stated that the 'law in this area is unsettled' and that:

> clarification on the issue of how intentional breaches ought to be treated, whether they are to be captured by *Saskatchewan Wheat Pool*, or whether they may be pleaded in separate torts, would be of great benefit.[103]

---

[99]   Above n 4.

[100]   RSO 1990 c P.15.

[101]   The action was brought against the police officers who committed the shooting, officers who witnessed it, the Chief of Police, the Police Services Board and the Province of Ontario. Negligence was claimed in addition to misfeasance in a public office. I will discuss only the misfeasance tort.

[102]   The plaintiffs were claiming that they had suffered 'mental distress, anger, depression and anxiety' as a result of the conduct of the police with respect to the post-shooting investigation. Iacobucci J stated that, although mere grief or emotional distress would not be sufficient to support a claim, sufficiently serious 'psychiatric damage' would be. This would be a matter to be determined at trial. In the recent case of *Watkins v Home Office* [2006] UKHL 17, the House of Lords decided that 'material damage' is a necessary element of the tort. Proof of anxiety or distress which falls short of physical or mental injury is insufficient.

[103]   [1998] OJ No 5426 (Gen Div) (QL) [29].

Since the plaintiffs had not alleged malice, which was an essential element of the tort of misfeasance in a public office, Day J held that the statement of claim should be struck out, with leave granted to the plaintiffs to plead misfeasance in a public office framed in malice.[104]

Borins JA, writing for the majority of the Ontario Court of Appeal, struck out the action with respect to the tort of misfeasance in a public office.[105] The gist of the judgment was the finding that the police officers, who refused to co-operate with the investigation, were not abusing an *executive or administrative power* which they had been given for their own private purposes. They were not, in fact, the recipients of such a power. The most that could be said of their behaviour was that they were in breach of a statutory duty. Borins JA referred extensively to Sadler, 'Liability for Misfeasance in a Public Office',[106] for the origin and history of the tort of misfeasance in a public office, noting in particular that:

> the central focus of the tort is a public officer who is invested with a power to act for the benefit of the public and who abuses the power by exceeding it, failing to exercise it, or, in some cases, purporting to exercise a power which he or she does not hold.[107]

The police officers in this case may have intentionally breached their statutory duties, but they did not, according to Borins JA, misuse their public office through the abuse of a statutory or prerogative power.[108]

Feldman JA dissented. According to Feldman JA, no distinction should be made between a public official who improperly exercises a power and one who deliberately breaches a statutory duty, where they know or are recklessly indifferent to the fact that injury to those in the position of the plaintiffs is likely to result. Thus the failure to carry out a statutory duty, the misuse of a power, or acting outside of one's powers can all constitute the tort, as long as this is done with either the intention of injuring the plaintiff or with knowledge that injury would be the natural and probable consequences of that act.

The issue for the Supreme Court of Canada was whether to adopt the majority of the Court of Appeal's narrow approach to the tort or the broad approach set out by the dissenting judge. Iacobucci J adopted the broad approach. He held that, while originally the tort might have been confined to the abuse of a power which a public official actually possessed,[109] it had

---

[104]   Day J also allowed a claim for breach of statutory duty to proceed.
[105]   (2000) 52 OR (3d) 181.
[106]   (1992) 14 *Sydney Law Review* 137.
[107]   Above n 104, at 195.
[108]   Borins JA also held that the motions judge erred in finding that the breach of the statutory duties gave rise to a cause of action, relying on *Saskatchewan Wheat Pool*.
[109]   Citing *Ashby v White* (1703) 92 ER 126.

been expanded in Canada by the Quebec case of *Roncarelli v Duplessis*.[110] Supported by this case, as well as by judgments from Australia,[111] New Zealand,[112] and Great Britain,[113] Iacobucci J held that the tort can be founded upon a 'broad range of misconduct' and is not limited to the 'unlawful exercise of a statutory or prerogative power actually held'. Any 'deliberate and unlawful conduct' by a 'public officer' which is engaged in either for the 'express purpose of harming the plaintiff',[114] or with the public officer's knowledge that the behaviour was both unlawful and 'likely to harm the plaintiff',[115] can constitute the tort. As stated by Iacobucci J, 'the tort involves the deliberate disregard of official duty coupled with knowledge that the misconduct is likely to injure the plaintiff'.[116]

The extension of the tort to public officials[117] who intentionally breach their statutory duties, not with the intention of harming any specific person, but where they should have known that their conduct was likely to harm individuals, is troubling, and in my opinion, comes perilously close to creating a tort of breach of statutory duty. It is a far cry from the situation where public officials deliberately abuse or exceed their powers[118] in order to injure specific individuals.

Let us consider a range of possible motives for deliberately breaching a statutory duty, but not with the intention to harm any specific person. As Iacobucci J himself concedes, if the breach was the result of budgetary constraints or other factors 'beyond the control' of the actor, the tort will not apply. As stated by Iacobucci J:

> the tort is not directed at a public officer who is <u>unable</u> to discharge his or her obligations because of factors beyond his or her control but, rather, at a public officer who <u>could</u> have discharged his or her public obligations, yet wilfully chose to do otherwise.[119]

---

110 [1959] SCR 121.
111 Notably, *Northern Territory of Australia v Mengel* (1995) 129 ALR 1 (HCA).
112 *Garrett v AG* [1997] 2 NZLR 332 (CA).
113 *Three Rivers District Council v Bank of England (No 3)* [2000] 2 WLR 15 (HL).
114 The so-called 'targeted malice' form of the tort.
115 The so-called 'untargeted malice' form of the tort.
116 *Odhavji*, above n 4, at 282.
117 The definition of 'public official or officer' may also be problematic. See, for example, the recent case of *Freeman-Maloy v Marsden* [2005] OJ No 1730 (SCJ) (QL), reversed (2006) 79 OR (3d) 401 (CA), as to whether the president of a university is a public officer for the purposes of the tort.
118 One can argue that all abuses of power are essentially acts which exceed powers. This, in my opinion, answers Iacobucci J's concern that, in *Roncarelli v Duplessis*, the court was not dealing with an abuse of power case because Duplessis did not actually *have* the power to revoke the plaintiff's liquor licence.
119 *Odhavji*, above n 4, at 284.

It is unclear, however, what might be considered to be 'beyond the control' of the defendant, and whether it would be the defendant's opinion or the court's opinion which would determine this matter.[120] Iacobucci J also concedes that a defendant can deliberately refuse to perform a statutory duty if it is in conflict with other statutory obligations or with his or her constitutionally protected rights, such as the right against self-incrimination. Not only is it difficult to envisage a statutory duty the execution of which would be unconstitutional,[121] but again the question as to who determines this matter is raised. Is it sufficient if the actor honestly believed that it was unconstitutional or beyond his or her control? Does this belief have to have been objectively reasonable? Is the defendant only liable if his or her belief was reckless? Is the test one of 'good faith'? What about other reasons for deliberately not carrying out a statutory duty? The officer, for example, might have believed that it would have been a bad idea from a public policy perspective to carry out that duty, that it would have been inhumane or insensitive in the circumstances to do so, or that other interests were more important. In all of these cases, the officer might have been aware that he or she would definitely be in breach, and that persons would likely be harmed, but the officer made the calculated decision that more harm would result if the duty was executed. Is the tort committed?

Unless the courts confine the tort of misfeasance in a public office to those officials who decide not to comply with their statutory duties because of bad faith, for example, a desire to injure someone, corruption, spite, or ill-will, its extension will in effect create an action for breach of statutory duty in Canada. In *Odhavji*, for example, it is my submission that the court that decides the case should have to determine whether the police officers' unwillingness to co-operate fully with the Special Investigations Unit was due to their desire to cause injury to the deceased's family, or for other ulterior motives, which go to malice. If the breach of the duty was not malicious, in addition to being intentional, I do not believe that the tort has been committed. The tort has already been extended from abuse of power to breaches of statutory duty. How much further it will be watered down remains to be seen.[122]

---

[120] Since the tort is an intentional tort, I presume that the defendant could only be liable if he or she knew that the duty could be performed, but refused to do so anyway. This, however, does not clarify what 'beyond the control' means. If, for example, a superior asks the employee not to perform his statutory duty, is it 'beyond the control' of the employee to perform it?

[121] I would argue that the scope of the duty itself would be defined by issues of legality and constitutionality.

[122] In *E(D) (Guardian ad litem of) v BC* (2005) 252 DLR (4th) 689 (BC CA), actions for misfeasance in a public office were brought against superintendents of hospitals that carried out sterilisations on mental patients pursuant to the provisions of the Sexual Sterilization Act SBC 1933 c 59. The allegation was that the superintendents knowingly exceeded their

V.   CONCLUSION

In *The Queen v Saskatchewan Wheat Pool*, the Supreme Court of Canada held that there is no nominate tort of breach of statutory duty in Canadian law. Despite this pronouncement, breaches of statutory duties and the failure of public authorities to carry out their statutory responsibilities with reasonable care have been important factors in the development of public tort liability in the past two decades. Recent jurisprudence stemming from *Cooper v Hobart*, however, indicates that the expansion of public tort liability has ended in Canada. Courts have been construing statutory provisions and concluding that they do not give rise to private law duties of care. While I agree with the results of many of these cases, I disagree with the reasoning that has been employed. Courts ought not to be interpreting statutory provisions to determine whether they give rise to private law duties. They ought instead to be examining the interaction between the parties to the dispute and applying common law principles to the parties' relationship. In the area of a failure to confer benefits, the common law refuses to impose a private law duty of care in the absence of a special relationship between the parties. This is the appropriate reason for the denial of a duty in many of the recent cases.

While the liability of public authorities based on negligence is being restricted, however, the action for misfeasance in a public office is being given new scope. Recent jurisprudence has allowed public authorities to be sued for breaching their statutory duties, even though they did not do so with the intention of injuring the plaintiffs. The restrictions on suing public authorities in negligence therefore threaten to be offset by the expanding tort of misfeasance in a public office.

authority under the Act by recommending sterilisations that could not be supported by the Act's provisions. The trial judge held that the plaintiffs failed to prove that the superintendents knowingly exceeded their authority. The Court of Appeal reversed this decision in so far as certain claimants were concerned and allowed the actions. There was no suggestion that the superintendents' intention was to abuse their powers in order to injure the claimants or that they were malicious, yet the claims succeeded. In another recent case, *Somwar v McDonald's Restaurants of Canada* (2006) 79 OR (3d) 172 (SCJ), the court considered whether a breach of the Consumer Reporting Act RSO 1990 c C.33, could support an action for breach of privacy. Following Iacobucci J's judgment in *Odhavji*, the judge held that, although there was no tort of breach of statutory duty, a breach of a statute can constitute an element of the tort of invasion of privacy. The action was allowed to proceed to trial.

UNIVERSITY OF HERTFORDSHIRE LRC

3

'Sois Sage'— Responsibility for Childishness in the Law of Civil Wrongs

SHAUNA VAN PRAAGH*

I. INTRODUCTION

A S I WAVE goodbye to my toddler, Ari, at the door of daycare in the French countryside, I call out 'Have fun!' Next to me, a mother bends down to her own child, Eloïse, for a last hug and whispers 'Sois sage!' The two messages coexist for these children, even at the age of one and a half. But they coexist awkwardly. On the one hand, we understand that very young children are at a stage of life full of learning, exploring and laughing; on the other, we see these children take their first steps towards responsibility for themselves and others. While it is fundamental that children act childishly, the 'sois sage' reminder seems to pull even a toddler into the sphere of careful and thoughtful behaviour expected of older children and adults.

The notion of being 'sage'—good, wise, careful, in line with rules and expectations—is reflected in the picture of the reasonable person in the private law of civil wrongs. 'Fun' is necessarily limited by 'sagesse'; self-fulfilment is necessarily shaped by the obligation not to hurt others. As children explore themselves and their surroundings, gradually becoming aware of others in their lives, they begin to move beyond the realm of

* Associate Professor, Faculty of Law and Institute of Comparative Law, McGill University. My appreciation goes to the Social Sciences and Humanities Research Council of Canada for its support of a research team project entitled 'Children, Family and State' and to my fellow researchers involved in that project. Thanks go to Beth Neelin-Robinson, Jennifer Poirier and Jacqueline Phillips, students at the Faculty of Law, McGill University, for their valuable assistance; to members of the Faculty of Law at Haifa University who provided helpful commentary on a preliminary presentation of the ideas expressed here; and to participants in the 2006 Emerging Issues in Tort Law conference at the University of Western Ontario.

'carefree' and into that of 'caring'. The obligation to care for others is slowly added throughout childhood to one's sense of self.

If we focus solely on the child in this picturesque moment, however, we risk missing that child's relationship with the parent delivering the message. As parents speak words of encouragement or caution to a child, their dual role comes into focus. On the one hand, they are expected to foster a child's sense of autonomy and self-fulfilment; on the other, they are meant to underline that same child's sense of responsibility for self and others. This too is reflected in the law of civil wrongs: while generally reticent to impose responsibility for the acts of others, the law does accept that parental behaviour can result in liability for the injuries inflicted by young people. Indeed, the harmful actions of a child may be assumed to arise out of failed supervision and direction on the part of a parent. Responsibility both for the child and on behalf of the child is placed—implicitly or explicitly—on the shoulders of the adults in children's lives.

Private law and public policy face a double challenge when dealing with the possibility of wrongdoing by children and the potential attribution of responsibility for the harms they cause. First, the rules related to individual wrongdoing require adjustment given the age of the actor, and, second, the general emphasis on liability for one's own behaviour shifts given the possibility of liability for the actions of others in our care. When we focus on the 'child as actor', we explore the standard of the reasonable person and the relevance of childhood to an analysis of potentially wrongful behaviour. When we focus on the 'child of parents', we examine the responsibility of parents for the injury-producing acts of their children.[1]

By combining the images of 'child actor' and 'child of parents', this discussion situates itself at the intersection of discovery, relationship and responsibility. This chapter thus aims to contribute to an area of law concerned with the relationship between wrongdoer and victim by investigating another relationship: that between young actors and their parents. Through sources, norms and narratives in the private law of civil wrongs (in both civil and common law traditions) and in children's literature, I suggest that the assumptions and rules regarding children's wrongdoing in private law are connected to assumptions and rules regarding children's relationships with the big people in their lives.[2]

---

[1]   Or, we might illustrate the 'child victim' by turning to contributory negligence and the extent of a child victim's responsibility for the injury incurred. While related to the discussion in this chapter, an analysis of the expectations placed on the young victim lies beyond its scope.

[2]   The emerging issues or methodologies explored in this essay can be expressed as follows: responsibility for another's actions; integration of sources across traditions and disciplines; and emphasis on the cultural study of law as opposed to instrumentalist or programmatic legal scholarship. See, eg, Paul W Kahn, *The Cultural Study of Law: Reconstructing Legal*

Case law, codes, legislation and doctrine, hand in hand with stories about and for children, provide narratives that combine development of individual responsibility with reliance on adult caregivers and rule enforcers. They provide sources for investigating the connection between developing capacity and responsibility of the individual young person and the picture of the relationship between parent and child. In particular, children's stories allow us to trace the ways in which law constructs responsible actors and the way in which it incorporates roles and relationships into that picture.[3] Various approaches to parental responsibility are identified and compared below in order to illustrate how the private law of civil wrongs both reflects and shapes the myths and realities of the transition, embodied in childhood, from 'fun' to 'sagesse'.

II.   LEARNING RESPONSIBILITY: CURIOUS GEORGE AND THE MAN WITH THE YELLOW HAT

Toddlers like Ari and Eloïse are nowhere near the age at which we expect adult sensibilities and responsibility. At this stage, as captured by Dr Seuss in *My Many-Colored Days*, feelings and actions seem all mixed up:

> Some days are yellow. Some are blue. On different days, I'm different too. You'd be surprised how many ways I change on different colored days.
> On bright red days how good it feels to be horse and kick my heels!
> On other days I'm other things. On bright blue days I flap my wings.
> Some days, of course, feel sort of brown. Then I feel slow and low, low down.
> Then comes a yellow day. And, wheeeeeee I am a busy, buzzy bee.
> ....
> Then come my black days. Mad. And loud. I howl. I growl at every cloud.
> Then comes a mixed-up day. And wham! I don't know who or what I am!
> But it all turns out all right, you see. And I go back to being...me.[4]

This is life and behaviour without any responsibility vis-à-vis others. The theme is self-discovery and self-acceptance. As children see bright pictures that evoke the mood of the words, they learn that 'being me' is alright, no matter what. Indeed, 'me', albeit transformed into different coloured animals, is the only character in the book.

Those same toddlers, however, live in a zone where discovery of oneself in relation to others and one's surroundings merges with the roots of

---

Scholarship (Chicago, University of Chicago Press, 1999); Roderick Alexander Macdonald, *Lessons of Everyday Law* (Montreal, McGill-Queen's University Press, 2002).

[3] See, as a related approach, an analysis of personal injury law as a reflection of American culture in Marshall S Shapo, *Tort Law and Culture* (Durham, Carolina Academic Press, 2003).

[4] Dr Seuss, *My Many-Colored Days* (New York, Alfred A Knopf, 1996) (no page numbers).

responsibility. They are having fun and, at the same time, beginning to understand how their words and actions have consequences with guidance from the 'big person' in the picture. Ari and Eloïse may not truly be able to translate 'sois sage' into anything particularly meaningful in their lives. But, as they move along the spectrum from discovery to responsibility, they begin to understand the instruction perfectly well, even if they find it difficult to turn comprehension into action.

Curious George, the creation of Margret and HA Rey,[5] acts as a bridge between the 'me' of *My Many-Colored Days* and the emerging lesson of responsibility. George is a 'good little monkey and always very curious'. In the original book, George explores a telephone for the first time. As he plays with the dial, he ends up calling the fire department by mistake. The 'naughty little monkey' is dragged off to jail by the firemen, one on each side. The transition from carefree curious monkey in the jungle to curious but responsible monkey in the city is the central theme of the Curious George stories.

Constantly drawn into trouble through his curiosity, George always seems to escape to the safety of his care-giver (and the person who took him from the jungle): the 'Man with the Yellow Hat'. Appropriately stern, always reliable, and consistently kind, the Man with the Yellow Hat is identified not by name but by recognisable sign. Bright, noticeable, tall, the hat and its wearer are the reference points for George as he returns again and again to the right path. The picture of George, curious and carefree, is only possible in the presence of the Man with the Yellow Hat. Someone is responsible for George—both in terms of caring for him and in terms of protecting others from his actions.

The story of Curious George captures the stage of life in which young people begin to learn responsibility. The lesson takes a very long time in reality, and is uneasily translated into legal language. We know that George, through repeated practice, slowly learns that there are consequences to his actions. The imposition of full obligation on George to watch out for others around him—as does the Man with the Yellow Hat—would be the stuff of real fiction. Instead, curiosity leads George into the kinds of interactions that call out for constant reminders of how to find and stick to the right path.

The role of principal adult in a young child's life is more likely to be played by 'mother' than by 'Man with the Yellow Hat'.[6] In *No David!*, a recent book by David Shannon, David's mother makes her first appearance

---

[5]   HA Rey, *Curious George* (Boston, Houghton Mifflin Company, 1941).

[6]   For discussion of the mother in the picture of civil responsibility of children, see Nathalie Des Rosiers, 'La responsabilité de la mère pour le préjudice causé par son enfant' (1995) 36 *Les Cahiers de Droit* 61.

on the title page.[7] She is faceless, drawn from chest down, from the perspective of a young child very aware of her hands-on-hips, toe-tapping stance. Indeed, she is primarily a voice, loudly repetitive in her 'No, David, no!' As young readers watch David try all kinds of 'no' behaviour, reaching for cookies, traipsing mud through the living room , and even jumping on the bed in cowboy boots, they join in the loud reproach: 'No, David!' And they are reassured when, at the end, a remorseful David is held tight by his mother who finally says 'Yes': 'Yes, David...I love you!' The mother is still faceless, but David is caught up in her arms, his head against the previously unyielding torso. The pain of learning seems to come with the warmth of not only love but also a sense that a parent—and perhaps particularly a mother—can put things right again. Both hard lessons and real protection accompany introduction to a world of rules and expectations.[8]

In Maurice Sendak's *Where the Wild Things Are*,[9] Max also moves from trouble-making, untamed child rebuked by his mother, to self-conscious returnee to the safety and domestication of home. As Desmond Manderson has shown, Max the wild thing accepts the weight of responsibility—and indeed welcomes it—as he leaves behind the rule-less world of wildness for his mother's hot supper (and rules) waiting for him in his room.[10] Like Curious George and devilish David, wild thing Max tries out 'naughtiness' and, when made aware of the consequences, begins to accept the inevitable taming that comes with growing up and accepting responsibility.[11] Of course, Max may set sail again the very next day for the land of the wild things. But he will always come back and, at some point, acting wild will start to carry real consequences.

Finally, the world of four year old Caillou is full of relationships that help the preschooler confront and solve everyday conflicts. With the encouragement and guidance of parents, grandparents and friends, Caillou learns essential lessons in the process of growing up. When Caillou breaks a flowerpot while racing around his backyard and blames the mess on his imaginary friend 'George', Caillou's Daddy makes a pointed effort to teach

---

[7] David Shannon, *No, David!* (New York, The Blue Sky Press, 1998).

[8] The role of parents in teaching children to understand obligation and consequence is illustrated in Robert Munsch's story, *A Promise is a Promise* (Toronto, Annick Press, 1988). Allashua, an Inuit child, is taught the value of a promise after putting herself and her family in a dangerous situation. Her parents teach her a lesson about promises, yet at the same time, they help to protect her from the consequences of her actions. It is the role of parents not only to teach and guide, but also to protect their children during the process.

[9] Maurice Sendak, *Where the Wild Things Are* (New York, HarperCollins, 1984).

[10] Desmond Manderson, 'From Hunger to Love: Myths of the Source, Interpretation, and Constitution of Law in Children's Literature' (2003) 15 *Law and Literature* 87.

[11] The final lines of *Olivia*, the story of a very rambunctious little girl pig, capture the dynamic: 'Olivia's mother gives her a kiss and says, "You know, you really wear me out. But I love you anyway." Olivia gives her a kiss back and says, "I love you anyway too."' Ian Falconer, *Olivia* (New York, Atheneum Books for Young Readers, 2000).

Caillou about taking responsibility for his own actions and repairing his mistakes.[12] When Caillou learns a bad word from an older child and uses it against his friend Clementine and hurts her feelings, Mom steps in to encourage Caillou to apologise for the hurt feelings he caused.[13] Here, parents are depicted not so much as direct supervisors of the young child's acts, but rather, as always-present supervisors of moral development and shapers of the child's moral compass.

Caillou's stories provide an environment for children to learn about the world around them and teach them that grown-ups are there to help them along the way. That environment is always cheerful and positive: no jail, no anger, no wild things. Here, the parental figure as authority and tutor patiently teaches the child to begin to accept responsibility for the destructive consequences of his actions. The fact that Caillou is constantly engaged in the negotiation and renegotiation of his relations with others around him illustrates the early roots of neighbourly behaviour. With his parents' help, Caillou begins to realise that he, too, can and should take care.[14] The process of becoming careful, of learning the consequences of making mistakes, is central to the stories.[15]

These particular examples of children's literature illustrate the stage of childhood that follows the self-discovery and fun of *My Many-Colored Days*. They are all about and for children not yet responsible but on the right path, and thus are clearly focused on curiosity, wildness, mistakes, and behaviour that elicits a loud 'no!' This stage of 'learning responsibility', captured by George and the others, moves beyond 'just me' to include the two new characters of victim and parent. The young child begins to see himself in a 'me and you' context that grounds personal responsibility toward others. At the same time, the voice of a parent figure not only finds a place in the child's head but begins to resonate in that child's actions and promises. Recognition of the potential victim of one's actions materialises through the child's relationship with a 'big person'—whether the Man with the Yellow Hat or the invisible mother. Even if relegated to the background, that big person helps the young child in the story take first steps towards responsibility. Learning responsibility appears to be a crucial prerequisite to accepting it.

---

[12] Eric Sevigny and Sarah Margaret Johanson, *Caillou: My Imaginary Friend*, Clubhouse Series (Montreal, Chouette Editions, 2004).

[13] PBS Kids, 'Caillou's Cross Word' from *Caillou at His Best* (USA, Warner Home Video, 2003).

[14] This is dramatically captured in Maurice Sendak's poem about little Pierre who didn't care. 'Pierre' in Sara and Stephen Corrin (eds), *Stories for Five Year Olds* (London, Faber and Faber, 1973) 60.

[15] In *Angela's Airplane*, by Robert Munsch, an unsupervised five year old makes a very big mistake in taking and flying (and destroying) an airplane. Her father re-enters the picture to ensure that his daughter postpones such activity to adulthood (Toronto, Annick Press, 1988).

If we are interested in the narratives told in law about responsibility for harmful actions by young people, then the lessons of children's stories explicitly centred on appropriate behaviour and modes of human interaction bring helpful insight. It should be obvious that children's literature does not derive value solely from its didactic quality;[16] further, lessons subtly gleaned from the best examples of children's literature may often have more impact on children's lives than those easily accessible in the stories selected for a discussion of the law of civil wrongs. But these particular stories do provide a source of norms that can be integrated with the more traditional sources associated with private law of civil wrongs. Such integration—of sources all of which take seriously childhood's 'developing care' character—produces a rich site for exploring assumptions about parent-child relationships and about responsibility for childish behaviour.[17]

As we try to grapple with the complex and, at times, ambiguous range of responses in private law to the question of responsibility for 'childish' harm, stories for children thus play an important role. Stories about the transition period between discovery and responsibility in children's lives provide a picture of the coexisting 'child as actor' and 'child of parents'. Together with stories of children in law, they illustrate the delicate balance between the legal responsibility of parents for the acts of their children and the sliding scale of that child's individual responsibility. Indeed, as sources of rules and myths, both the private law of civil wrongs and children's literary lessons mesh storytelling with law creation. And both combine reality or lived experience with fiction and the pedagogical character of narrative.

III.   RESPONSIBILITY FOR CHILDISH BEHAVIOUR

When a child on the seam or threshold of responsibility hurts another, what narratives are told in the law of civil wrongs, and what consequences flow? The answer is necessarily complicated and reveals a range of

---

[16] Examples of moralistic stories aimed at young children do exist, of course. See, eg, *Stories for Five Year Olds*, above n 14.

[17] James Boyd White describes why translation across sites of analysis is a fruitful pursuit: '[a] whole dimension of meaning [is] created whenever we speak, which I have called constitutive: who we are and become in our talking with each other. This is not only a central question for literature: it is a central concern for the law as well, for the law is not simply an instrument for achieving a certain distribution of items in the world, but a way of creating and sustaining a political and ethical community'. According to White, the texts are 'not coercive of their reader, but invitational: they offer an experience, not a message, and an experience that will not merely add to one's stock of information but change one's way of seeing and being, of talking and acting'. 'What can a Lawyer Learn from Literature?' (1989) 102 *Harvard Law Review* 2014, 2047. See also, Barbara Bennett Woodhouse, 'Hatching the Egg: A Child-Centred Perspective on Parents' Rights' (1993) 14 *Cardozo Law Review* 1747.

responses, indicating the difficulty of attributing wrongdoing to a young person who, by definition, is developing a sense of what it means to be careless, a bad neighbour, or an unreasonable person. That spectrum of responses, I will suggest, discloses assumptions about the normative relationship between children and the adults (generally parents) in their lives. Those assumptions, whether explicit or implicit, enrich our understanding not only of the responsibility of children but of the responsibility of adults with children in their care.

The central image of the wrongdoer in the law of civil wrongs is that of the unreasonable person. This is expressed in the *Civil Code of Quebec*[18] as a general and unified rule to abide by general rules of conduct: an obligation adhered to by the reasonable person, or traditionally 'bon père de famille'.[19] Action that fails to qualify as that of the reasonable person, described as 'une norme générale de conduite sociale imposant de se conduire en toutes circonstances avec prudence et diligence', constitutes a breach of the duty.[20] A parallel general rule of behaviour emerges from the duty of care in the tort of negligence, as expressed in Lord Atkin's neighbour principle in *Donoghue v Stevenson*.[21] The reasonable person is, by definition, not negligent.

The child has always posed a challenge to the reasonable person as objective standard. After all, it seems strange to substitute a child for the 'man on the Clapham omnibus'[22] and even more bizarre to imagine a child as the parental and authoritative figure of the 'bon père de famille'.[23] If the subjective characteristics and capacities of the wrongdoer are not part of the analysis, then a young child should be held to the reasonable person standard. But jurisprudence and doctrine related to children and wrongdoing reveals an alternate picture.[24]

---

[18] 'Every person has a duty to abide by the rules of conduct which lie upon him... Where he is endowed with reason and fails in his duty, he is responsible...'. RSQ 1991 c 64 art 1457.

[19] *Ibid*; *L'Oeuvre des Terrains de jeux de Québec c Cannon ès qual* [1940] 69 RJQ 112 (QB) 114.

[20] J Ghestin, G Viney and P Jourdain, *Traité de droit civil: les conditions de la responsabilité*, 2éd (Paris, LGDJ, 1998) [450].

[21] *Donoghue (or McAlister) v Stevenson* [1932] AC 562 (HL).

[22] Lord Bowen, quoted in *McQuire v Western Morning News Co* [1900-03] All ER 673 (CA) 675.

[23] Nicholas Kasirer examines the biases of an objective standard in the context of his exploration of responsibility of the young child in 'The infans as bon père de famille: "Objectively Wrongful Conduct" in the Civil Law Tradition' (1992) 40 *The American Journal of Comparative Law* 343, 370.

[24] For a brief history of the development of the common law of negligence and children, see Patrick Kelly, 'Infancy, Insanity, and Infirmity in the Law of Torts' (2003) 48 *American Journal of Jurisprudence* 179. See also John G Fleming, *The Law of Torts*, 9th edn (New South Wales, The Law Book Company Limited, 1998) 114; Lewis Klar, *Tort Law*, 3rd edn (Toronto, Thomson Carswell, 2003) 311-15.

A brief articulation of the approaches or tests identifiable in the law gives us a sense of the ambiguities imbedded in imposing blame on young people.[25] Let us take as our protagonist, a little boy à la Curious George, who, at the stage of developing responsibility,[26] throws stones and unintentionally hurts a little girl.[27] How does the law of civil wrongs understand and assess that behaviour, and articulate its consequences?

At one end of the spectrum, we might simply define childhood as incompatible with responsibility.[28] Here, the child as responsible actor fades away. Our harm-producing child is thus treated like an infant or toddler, incapable of taking care vis-à-vis others. As we have seen, the incongruence of admonishing a toddler to be 'sage' is striking.[29] It asks the impossible: that very young children control the 'me' of the moment, suppress the black or even the red, and project upon themselves the expectations and sensibilities of others, to which they are either oblivious or only partially aware. The law of civil wrongs generally accepts that incongruence and accepts that very young children cannot be held responsible for their actions.[30] Articulated as an exemption for children of tender years, the child's stage of development is acknowledged to prevent any possibility of sufficient intelligence, experience, or capacity to take on the responsibility for the consequences of childish behaviour.[31]

---

[25] See Marie-Christine Lebreton, *L'enfant et la responsabilité civile* (France, Publications de Rouen et du Havre, 1999). Lebreton canvasses numerous approaches to, and examples of, civil responsibility (or the lack of it) on the part of children.

[26] Anywhere between the ages of, roughly, 5 and 12 years old, as reflected in the jurisprudence.

[27] Much, of course, can be explored in the very choice of this image. The picture might be called paradigmatic in that it reflects real cases, most notably: *Ginn v Sisson* (1968) [1969] CS 585 [*Ginn*] (six years old) and *McHale v Watson* (1964) 111 CLR 384 (HCA) [*Watson*] (12 years old). And it is no mere coincidence that the 'wrongdoer' is a little boy. Little girls, I would suggest, are more often found as victims in tort law, and their actions are assessed in the context of contributory negligence (the failure to watch out for their own safety): see, for example, *Brisson v Potvin* [1948] BR 38 or *Saper v Calgary (City)* (1979) 21 AR 577 (QB) [*Saper*]. The gender dimension of responsibility and the 'taming' of the wild young boy-child is part of the narrative we find both in stories for children and in tort stories about children. See also Mayo Moran, *Rethinking the Reasonable Person* (New York, Oxford University Press, 2003) 58-91.

[28] For example, as found in Israel, a particular age could be defined as the age of responsibility, perhaps both for private (tort) law and public (criminal) law purposes.

[29] See *Tillander v Gosselin* [1967] 1 OR 203 (HC) 205 [*Tillander*]: 'Such an infant is considered to be lacking in sufficient judgment to exercise that reasonable care that is expected of one. His normal condition is one of recognised incompetency and he is devoid of ability to make effective use of such knowledge as he may have at that early age'.

[30] The exact age is not set in stone. Children ranging from three to nine years of age have been found to be of tender years for the purposes of the private law. See *Tillander*, above n 29; *Ledoux c Fortier-Aumond* (CQ, 1998-05-11), SOQUIJ AZ-98036305; Allen M Linden, *Canadian Tort Law*, 7th edn (Markham, Butterworths, 2001) 141.

[31] In *Saper*, above n 27, Mary Doe was deemed to be of a tender age on the basis of her naïve belief that, in carrying out the appropriate action—putting out her arm to cross

At the other end of the spectrum, we might hold the stone-thrower to the standard of the reasonable person: youth is held irrelevant. The child is pushed, alone, to the foreground of the image, directly into the lens of the law. According to this approach, the negligent young person is assumed capable and mature and is thus placed side-by-side with older adolescents and adults. The child is required to act with full 'sagesse' and to make amends for failing to meet obligations. This position can indeed be located in law, most clearly in what is known as the adult activity doctrine. That is, when children engage in so-called 'adult activities',[32] they may take on adult obligations.[33] In other words, when the child fails to behave as a child (which would imply staying away from activities reserved for adults), he or she exits childhood and takes on the full weight of responsibility.[34]

In the landscape that exists between these conflicting perspectives or book-ends, we find in the law's stories about children the very ambiguities that we can trace in the literature that introduces children to law in the form of behavioural norms. Those stories, reflected in the approaches sketched below, capture the extended stage of 'becoming responsible', the developmental context and reality of childhood, and the presence and role of responsible adults.

First, we can find the notion that our stone-throwing boy should be assessed against a picture of the 'average' child his age.[35] Problematic in its lack of any normative expectation or evaluation, this approach signals a 'boys will be boys' attitude. It indicates marked patience with youth through a reluctance to incorporate into our expectations of young people's behaviour the normative lessons imparted to children as they grow. It accepts that children will be curious and indeed wild, but that they will eventually get over it as they follow their peer group to adulthood.

As a second, intermediary alternative, we find a modified reasonable person test. Here the stone thrower's behaviour is assessed in light of how he *should* behave, given his age and stage of development. This age-appropriate standard of care, well-known and generally applied in Canadian common law, compares this child's comportment to that of a 'child of

---

traffic,—she would be protected from the ramifications of the dangerous act. She clearly did not connect the traffic lesson with the serious danger posed by cars and trucks in the street.

[32]   The most common 'adult activities' are driving an all-terrain vehicle, snowmobile, or car.

[33]   The following countries incorporate such an application of the adult standard: Australia (Fleming, above n 24); United States (*Restatement (Second) of Torts* (1965) §§281-503, §283 A(b) [*Restatement*]); Canada (Linden, above n 30, at 145-46).

[34]   Moran has suggested that the decision to apply the test or not hinges largely on the degree to which the activity is play-like, and the age of the defendant: above n 27, at 85. This is reflected in the decision in *Lutley (Guardian ad litem of) v Jarvis Estate* (1992) 113 NSR (2d) 201 (SC) [*Jarvis*].

[35]   As an example, see Kitto J in *Watson*, above n 27.

like age, intelligence and experience'.[36] Here, the law recognises that individual responsibility is learned over childhood, and thus assigns liability in an age-appropriate way. Young children like the two boys, aged six and nine, in *Strehlke v Camenzind*, who knew matches were dangerous but started a fire with them nonetheless, were found to lack the experience to understand fully that potential consequences included the burning down of a house.[37] The child's sense of responsibility, shaped by teaching, leadership and guidance, develops over time.

A third alternative, identifiable in Quebec civil law, combines attention to the individual child with a more objective assessment of the behaviour itself. The child's responsibility rests on a determination both of whether the act in question is 'fautif' in an objective sense, and of whether the child was able to discern right from wrong. If stone throwing can be considered to be objectively unreasonable behaviour, and if the little stone thrower knows that his behaviour would be grounds for punishment and, therefore, wrong, then even a six year old can be found liable.[38] In applying this two-pronged test, the law reflects and grapples with the obvious difficulty in assuming an exact connection between understanding and acting, knowing and doing. But it reveals a willingness to impose adult consequences on children who behave in ways clearly unreasonable in an adult world.

This array of approaches to the liability of children may seem messy and unsatisfying. Indeed, if we insist on articulating a clear rule to be applied to all young actors situated in the stage of learning responsibility that childhood represents, then the responses in the law of civil wrongs will necessarily be frustrating.[39] The difficulties in grappling with the young person who causes harm are tied to the very real difficulties of defining what we expect of children as they grow and develop, both in terms of their abilities and their appreciation of the impact of their actions. But they

---

[36] *McEllistrum Estate v Etches* [1956] SCR 787; *Heisler v Moke* [1972] 2 OR 446 (HC) 446. See also: *Restatement*, above n 33; Scottish Law Commission, *Legal Capacity and Responsibility of Minors and Pupils* (Edinburgh, The Commission, 1985) 238, which states '[t]he child will be liable if he has failed to show the care reasonably to be expected from someone of his age, intelligence and experience'; Linden, above n 30, at 126. The inconsistent application of this test is discussed at 143.

[37] *Strehlke v Camenzind et al* (1980) 27 AR 257 (QB) [25] [*Strehlke*]: 'I am satisfied that the boys knew it was wrong to play with matches but they had little understanding of why it was wrong and the possible consequences of playing with fire'.

[38] See *Ginn*, above n 27. For further discussion of the case and the approach, see Kasirer, above n 23.

[39] Students of tort law may express their frustration at the difficulties of sustaining an objective standard of care while trying to take into account the realities of children. They often offer a pragmatic response to the academic nature of the discussion by calling for a reality check grounded in the bank accounts and insurance policies of the parents of child wrongdoers. In turning to parents below, I aim to locate them in legal norms, rather than in practical realities related to who pays the bill.

are also tied to the insistence that we explore the various 'rules' regarding child actors by focusing on children all on their own. As we have already seen through samples of stories that capture the emergence of responsibility, children do not learn, develop, and modify their behaviour all by themselves. Learning responsibility is combined with obvious dependence.

An analysis of responsibility for childish behaviour that starts and stops with the child's own potential liability misses the parent as an important element of the picture painted by children's stories both in and beyond private law. Indeed, it fails to pay attention to the ways in which the law of civil wrongs, explicitly or implicitly, pulls the big person in the child's life into view. A recreation of the spectrum from the perspective of parental responsibility helps us integrate our understanding of individual wrongdoing with that of responsibility for the harmful acts of others in our care.

IV.   CHILDHOOD: WHERE THE PARENTS ARE

Parental presence may be theoretically explicit, as in a civil law approach that creates 'regimes' requiring one person to answer for the injury-producing actions and wrongdoing of others. It may be muted, as in a common law approach that insists on parallel links between victim and child on the one hand, and victim and parent on the other. Or, it may be blatantly imposed as policy embodied by parental responsibility legislation. Whatever its form, that presence underlines an expectation that parents teach their children well and play a series of age-appropriate roles in the child's life. We have seen examples of that expectation in children's literature touching on responsibility; here we see it in the law's stories of children.

Before canvassing the spectrum of sites at which parents can be found, it is helpful to illustrate the ways in which law sometimes makes failed assumptions about the relationship between harm-producing children and the adults in their lives. Such failure is most obvious at either end of childhood. That is, when children are very young, the law engages in mistaken myth when it puts parents aside. Similarly, the law creates problematic myth when it presumes responsibility on the part of parents of adolescents. Both instances of mythical constructions of the parent-child dynamic—the fiction of not seeing parents of the very young child and that of seeing parents only in the case of the adolescent—deserve our attention.

On the one hand, then, we have already seen that life for children in the 'me' stage of discovery is necessarily about play and adventure. Three-year old Éric Gabillet may well have imagined the stick in his hand to be a mighty sword, but when he accidentally poked his playmate in the eye while teetering on a broken seesaw, French law did not see childish fun. Instead, Éric's playing with the stick was found to breach his obligation to his friend to behave as a reasonable and 'sage' person should.[40] Putting aside the possibility that French preschoolers are particularly precocious, the three year old who finds himself saddled with civil liability for the outcome of his very 'pas sage' comportment is a mythical figure. He may be very real under the *Napoleonic Code*, in the sense that his patrimony is indeed indebted to the victim of his childish 'fun'. But the idea that he is truly responsible as a holder of an obligation to others around him is the stuff of fiction. It reminds us that the law's language of capacity and responsibility is not drawn from psychological reality.[41] It represents a decision to merge childhood fun and discovery with sagesse and responsibility from the earliest ages.[42] And it assumes that little Éric has nothing to learn from his parents and others around him.

On the other hand, we do expect young people who have moved beyond the stage of learning responsibility to answer for the consequences of their actions. While adolescence does not imply adult autonomy and behaviour,[43] we risk losing sight of the young person when we impose responsibility on the parents of teenagers. Recent parental responsibility legislation, particularly in Ontario, appears to run precisely that risk.[44] By imposing liability on parents for intentional property damage by their children, the Ontario Parental Responsibility Act's policy produces strange principle. The clear picture is of the delinquent property-damaging adolescent whose parent will pay the small claims court bill. Liability can be avoided only if the parents show that they adequately supervised the child at the time and that they tried to discourage the child from this kind of activity. The language of the legislation is that of presumption of parental liability;[45] the

---

[40]   *Gabillet c Noye*, Cass Ass Plén, 9 May 1984, Recueil Dalloz Sirey 1984, 529.

[41]   As Kasirer has pointed out, the idea that three year olds' behaviour is somehow 'wrongful' relies on a definition of that term that guts it of any real requirement of discernment. Above n 23, at 367.

[42]   French babies and toddlers may not be any more capable of grasping and directing the consequences of their behaviour, but it may indeed be the case that they are more likely to be subjected to a repetition of 'sois sage' reminders. And the fact that their parents pay 'assurance scolaire' for them from the age of two or three supports the otherwise mythical notion that their actions are imbued with obligation and potential liability. While 'assurance scholaire' for general activities is not yet obligatory in France, the majority of schools (and the French Minister of Education) strongly suggest parents take out civil responsibility insurance for their young children that covers injuries caused by, or suffered by, their children while at school. Such insurance is obligatory, however, for all extracurricular activities, such as field trips. F Terré, S Guincard and F Chapuisat (eds), *Pratique des assurances du particulier: personnes & biens* (Paris, Éditions du Juris-Classeur, 2003) §§054-28-054-29.

[43]   See Shauna Van Praagh, 'Adolescence, autonomy and Harry Potter: the child as decision-maker' (2005) 1 *International Journal of Law in Context* 335.

[44]   Parental Responsibility Act 2000 SO 2000 c 4.

[45]   The fault-based exculpatory phrase arguably makes this more properly a presumption of fault. The Act awkwardly attempts to bring together fault-based responsibility (linked to the tone of moral condemnation) with risk-based liability (linked to the same Act's ostensible goal of full compensation).

message seems to be that parents have children—and particularly teenagers—at their own risk. Here, in contrast to fictionalising an independent preschooler, the law conjures up the fictional presence of parents in all aspects of their adolescents' lives.

The two approaches canvassed above show mythical misconstructions of the role of parents with respect to the harmful behaviour of their children. The following discussion illustrates the law's capacity for a more sophisticated understanding of the complexities of evolving parent-child relations in the assessment of responsibility. Again, we take as our little protagonist the child at the age of learning responsibility. While the possibility of the child's liability may stand on its own, the law's response to injury inflicted by the tiny adventurer includes an element of parental responsibility. That is, the law may connect a parent to the young child who, by definition, is unable to shed childishness before outgrowing it.

The first and most obvious way in which parents are brought into the law's stories of children and their harmful behaviour is to provide for their direct responsibility. That is, parents may fail in their obligation to act with care towards the victim of their child's actions. The injury is thus seen to result from the parents' failure to supervise and control the activities of their children.[46] Such an action against a parent as a co-defendant with the child, or against the parent alone in the absence of a tort or fault on the part of the child, has always been possible in Anglo-Canadian common law.[47] Particularly in the absence of a responsible child tortfeasor, harm suffered by the victim may be connected to the failure of the parent to take appropriate precautions.[48]

Second, we might engage in a more obvious search for the responsible parent by turning immediately to the adult in light of a child's harmful behaviour. Thus, when a six year old throws stones and hurts another child, we might assume that the injury results from some failure in parenting. As an alternative to direct personal responsibility on the part of the parent, this assumption invites indirect strict liability. That is, the risk of parenting might simply include responsibility for the mistakes made by children. The law might demand that parents answer for the wrongs (or wrong-like actions) of their offspring. Such an approach would in effect

---

[46] *Taylor v King* (1993) 82 BCLR (2d) 108 (CA). The conduct of the parent is assessed according to the standard commonly accepted of parents generally in the community.

[47] This is also true in Quebec civil law. *Morissette c Allard* (2001) REJB 2001-23618, [2001] RRA 217 (CS). Here, the father was not found liable under the presumption of parental fault available in the Civil Code. Instead, the judge found that he was directly faulty as the facilitator of the dangerous situation.

[48] See, for example, *Michaud v Dupuis and Dupuis* (1977) 20 NBR (2d) 305 (QB) [11]: 'It seems to me that the defendant ought to have informed his children of the risk of danger which had specifically been brought to his attention and therefore his failure to do so makes him liable'.

remove the child as primary potential wrongdoer: liability would be attributed to parents, regardless of the quality of their supervision and upbringing.

Strict liability for the wrongful actions of others is well known to the law of civil wrongs, but is paradigmatically located in the context of the employer/employee relationship. In the event of a tortious action by the employee, the employer answers for that tort and thus bears the burden of compensating the victim. The general reticence of the common law in particular to hold people responsible for the actions of others gives way in the face of the particular dynamic of the relationship between employer and employee vis-à-vis victim.[49] It is that very dynamic that makes vicarious liability inappropriate in the parent-child context. While responsibility for the child is indeed central to the meaning of parenthood, simple control is not. The Man with the Yellow Hat does not control George; David's mother does not control her son. Unlike the employer who answers for the employee (and who takes on the consequences of enterprise risk), parents exercise their responsibility, in part, to develop the separate responsibility of the child. Given this particular and complex balance of identities, the strict liability alternative appears shallow and inappropriate.

Instead of presuming liability, the private law of civil wrongs is more likely to presume fault. The victim can bring an action against a parent without the burden of showing wrongful parental guidance and surveillance. When the stone thrower is of an age at which learning, rather than exercising, responsibility is front and centre, we thus presume that the parent has failed as teacher. This is the approach taken by the *Civil Code of Quebec* to the responsibility of parents for the harm-producing actions of their children. Those actions may or may not be 'faults' on the part of the young actors; that will depend on the assessment of the child. Regardless of whether the child in a particular case can answer for him or herself, the parent is presumed at fault. A reasonable person or, in traditional and context-appropriate terms, a 'bon père de famille', would not allow this to happen or, in other words, children do not misbehave and hurt others when the careful parent is on watch.

According to Article 1459, the parent is 'liable to reparation for injury caused to another by the act or fault of the minor ... unless he proves that he himself did not commit any fault with regard to the custody, supervision or education of the minor'.[50] If the parent shows reasonableness in bringing up the child and supervising day-to-day activities, then the child

---

[49]   The five factors considered in cases of strict vicarious liability are outlined in *Bazley v Curry* [1999] 2 SCR 534, [41]. The factors demonstrate the concern for these relationships. For further insight on the role of control in evaluating vicarious liability, see *Blackwater v Plint* [2005] 3 SCR 3, [20].

[50]   See above n 18, art 1459.

re-emerges in the picture. If capable of fault, the child may be liable; if not, then the harm-producing act simply turns into a non-compensable accident. As acknowledged by the *Civil Code of Quebec*, even children of good parents sometimes make mistakes.

Public policy in the form of legislation in some common law Canadian jurisdictions incorporates a similar focus on the parent.[51] The Ontario Parental Responsibility Act of 2000 modifies the traditional need in common law to establish direct negligence on the part of the parent.[52] Albeit badly drafted and therefore unclear,[53] section 10 appears to introduce a presumption of parental fault in tort actions stemming from a child's negligent infliction of personal or property damage. In such actions, 'the onus of establishing that the parent exercised reasonable supervision and control over the child rests with the parent'. The parent's failure to act reasonably thus becomes central in the law's response.

Turning to and focusing solely on the parent, and assuming that 'bad parenting' (or, in other words, less than reasonable upbringing and surveillance) leads to a child's harmful behaviour, fits easily within an approach that expects no real individual self-control and capacity for care on the part of the child. As discussed earlier in the context of the young child in the 'me' mode of discovery, denying the possibility of negligence or fault in the actions of a child of tender years is not only appropriate but easily merged with parental responsibility.[54] For children in a period of transition from discovery to responsibility, however, the relationship between child and parent is different. The six year old who throws stones may indeed hear a 'no' in his head. But six (or five or seven) is precisely the age at which we might expect children not to match action to understanding. Repetition—no, no, no—and gradual understanding of consequences are precisely the markers of this age.[55] As any parent knows, simply telling

---

[51] The following jurisdictions have legislation to this effect: British Columbia (Parental Responsibility Act SBC 2001 c 45); Ontario (see above n 44); Manitoba (Parental Responsibility Act CCSM 1996 c P8); Newfoundland and Labrador (Family Law Act RSNL 1990 c F-2, s 77). See further: Elizabeth Adjin-Tettey, 'Significance and Consequences of Parental Responsibility Legislation' (2002) 17 *Supreme Court Law Review* (2d) 221.

[52] Above n 44.

[53] Note the language of 'fault or neglect' rather than negligence, and, further, the lack of clarity related to causation. Ontario Parental Responsibility Act 2000, s 10(2).

[54] Seeing a child as a danger or risk is criticised by the British Columbia Court of Appeal in *Newton v Newton* 2003 BCCA 389, [10]: 'It seems to me that to say that there is a foreseeable risk of harm giving rise to a duty of care merely because children of age two years and three and a half months may be expected to engage in unpredictable behaviour and so unpredictability should be foreseeable as to impose a standard akin to a standard of absolute liability'.

[55] This is a reality acknowledged repeatedly in judgements concerning fires caused by young children. The problem, as the judges point out, is that these children, like Alexandra (*Promutuel Bagot c ING Groupe Commerce* (2001) REJB 2001-27672 (CS) [28]) or the young boys in *Strehlke* (above n 37, [31]) and in *Yorkton Agricultural and Industrial Exhibition Association Ltd v Morley et al* ((1968) 66 DLR (2d) 37 (Sask CA) 42) may have

children something once is not enough for them to make the leap from hearing to understanding, let alone knowing to doing. The child needs a big person (or many big persons) to help with the learning, and the big person needs to give the child a chance to practice over and over again.

Is it possible, then, to juxtapose the presumption of parental presence and even parental fault with the developing personal responsibility of the child? As we have seen, a child at the early stage of learning responsibility is assumed to be in the midst of an intensive process of figuring out how to behave, how to incorporate others into one's daily life, how to calm the potential for wildness. For any child, responsibility and reasonableness are gradually assumed; children learn about themselves and about how they should act toward others through constant interaction with people in their lives. By assuming that the parent's failure to teach, guide, and supervise results in injury inflicted by the young child, the law simply places particular emphasis on the responsibility of parents to play that role.

Shifting responsibility to a parent can coexist with an approach to children's harmful behaviour that accepts that behaviour as part of growing up. The stone might be thrown by the child, but the parent's failure to stop the throw is constructed as the reason for the injury and the source of responsibility. Our earlier articulation of a test based on the 'average' child noted the seeming lack of normative expectation: the emphasis is on how children 'do' act rather than on how they 'should' act. If we understand 'average' differently, in the sense that all children take time to develop the connection between their cognitive capacity and their actions, then a relationship-conscious look at this 'average' child can justify replacing the child's responsibility with that of the parent.

Article 1459 of the *Civil Code of Quebec* offers a model for capturing both the responsibility of the developing child actor and that of the parent. Its two part assessment of the child, in terms of individual discernment and the objective reasonableness of the activity, is combined with a presumption of fault on the part of the parent. This combination brings the parent into the picture automatically, but the evaluation of parenting is done hand-in-hand with an evaluation of the child's cognitive capacity and behaviour. A normative framework is thus created out of the relationship between what might be seen as primary and secondary defendants.

The explicit coexistence of the possibility of two agents of liability reflects the relationship between these two individuals, one big and one small. The approach of Article 1459 can be characterised as dynamic in its

---

been fully aware of the dangers of fire, but were unable to measure or comprehend the consequences and risks associated with the activity. This, however, is not consistent across all judgments. While the nine year old in *Strehlke* was free of blame, Roddy King, also nine, was held fully responsible for the fire that resulted from his playing with a candle. See above n 46.

ability to track the complexities of childhood. The reality of the relationship between child and parent can be captured in an inversely correlative attribution of responsibility. The classic Quebec case of Ginn v Sisson illustrates this dynamic. Howard, at six years old, injured his schoolmate, Willa, when he threw stones at the bus stop. His father was presumed at fault but, having taught Howard that such behaviour was wrong, was relieved of responsibility. Howard, himself, found to be aware of the consequences of his actions, took on individual liability.[56]

At the age of learning responsibility, a child like Howard is in the midst of a very long lesson with no obvious endpoint. Throughout this stage, he might know right from wrong, but that knowledge might not always translate into right behaviour. And yet, we know that throwing stones can cause considerable injury, regardless of whether we call it child's play or dangerous activity. The law translates that knowledge into responsibility on the part of the person whose role it is to prevent the stone-throwing in the first place. If the parent can show reasonableness in that role, characterised in the *Civil Code of Quebec* by the expectation of custody, supervision, and education, then the law is content that everything is unfolding as it should. That is, if parents are present in an appropriate way, then they move into the background.[57] At the same time, the child moves to the foreground of the image of wrongdoing, becoming more capable of assuming responsibility. Both parent and child are always potentially responsible to others. But it is the mutual responsibility—to teach and to learn, to guide and to grow—that is primarily significant in their lives.

When the law invests instead in a 'reasonable child approach'—thereby acknowledging childhood by modifying the reasonable person test to take age and experience into account—is it necessary to contemplate the role and responsibility of parents? Even in the absence of a presumption of parental fault, it might be argued that the law incorporates parents— invisibly but significantly—into its willingness to acknowledge the dependency of children and the fact that they grow into responsibility. The adult helps shape expectations on the part of children at each stage of their lives, and the law reflects those expectations. This implicit parent-child relationship can be integrated with a more explicit route to parental responsibility.

---

[56] *Ginn*, above n 27, at 588.

[57] Indeed, lots of wrongdoing and harming others might go on in a child's life without deserving the label of responsibility in private law. In determining how to assess the responsibility of a young child, the judge in *Jordan v Shofield and Kelly* (1996) 148 NSR (2d) 104 (SC) [12] referred to the following quotation from Fleming's *Law of Torts* (1987): 'This requires a weighing of the risks to others which the child's conduct involves against the competing need, to which the courts had been much alive, of giving those growing up sufficient scope to develop a sense of personal responsibility and reasonable latitude in pursuing forms of amusement and activity not necessarily restricted to those alone that are perfectly safe and harmless'.

Indeed, when the *Civil Code of Quebec* continues its presumption of parental fault throughout childhood, it seems at first glance to ignore the obvious differences between a young child just learning right from wrong and an adolescent insisting on autonomy. But the flexibility in the language of 'custody, supervision or education' allows for flexibility in assessing parenting behaviour. Parent and child are assumed always to be intimately connected through the presumption of fault, but that presumption can be countered in an age-appropriate way.

The recent legislated change to Ontario tort law looks like a similarly explicit nod to the possible coexistence of parent and child responsibility. A child may be assessed against an age-adjusted standard and, at the same time, parental negligence in 'supervision or control' might appear to be a source of liability. By placing the burden on the parent to show reasonable supervision, the Parental Responsibility Act highlights the supervisory responsibility of the big person in the picture.[58] Notably, education or upbringing is not included in the wording of the Act. This implies a literally 'hands-on' picture of parental responsibility, leaving no room for the flexibility that flows from the framing of the presumption of fault in the Quebec *Civil Code*.

The provocative and problematic starting point for the legislation is the misconception that pre-Act common law made no or inadequate provision for parental responsibility in the context of children's harmful and/or wrongful behaviour. The legislation puts parents on stage, but the central aim or premise—parental responsibility for intentional wrongdoing by their children—seems both crude and off-balance. As we have seen, parents were already in the picture. The role of parents is not only built into the analysis of the reasonableness of children but can be identified even when young people's actions are assessed according to a more stringent reasonable person standard. When the law imposes an objective standard of care on young people, it seems to overlook a development-based notion of responsibility, reliant on the relationship between children and parents. Thus, the adult activity 'test', applied by Canadian common law when the young person hurts someone through an activity reserved for adults, appears to make adults irrelevant. And yet, even here, a more careful look reveals the law's assumptions as to the whereabouts and behaviour of that parent: the very absence of the parent is judged, albeit indirectly, when tort law imposes responsibility on the child engaged in an 'adult activity'.[59]

---

[58] For an example of a supervision analysis under the Act, see: *Shannon v TW (Litigation Guardian of)* (2002) 12 CCLT (3d) 46 (SCJ).

[59] The law effectively says that the unacceptable comportment of the young person should have been supervised by the adult for whom the activity was reserved. It is in a decision not to apply the adult activity doctrine that this message is most clearly illustrated. Billy Joe Jarvis, 12, was driving a dirt bike on the highway when he collided with an oncoming truck. The judge did not hold this child—engaged in an apparently adult activity—to a reasonable

Contrary to what the Parental Responsibility Act suggests, then, parents are implicitly included in tort law's view of the young actor whose behaviour harms another. By examining the *Civil Code of Quebec*'s explicitly constructed equilibrium between parents and children, the ways in which that equilibrium belongs implicitly in Canadian common law comes into view. Both systems—and the traditions from which they derive—reveal assumptions about the relationship between children and the adults responsible for them. The stories they tell about children end up coinciding with the stories children learn as they navigate their way through the stage of learning responsibility and care for others.

This reading of the presence (and responsibility) of the parent indicates the potential for peaceful coexistence with a 'reasonable child' approach to harmful behaviour. Indeed, the reasonable child notion—evaluating a child's actions in light of what would reasonably be expected and tolerated by the child's peers—builds relationships in a child's life into the picture of that child found in law. Only through relationships with others, particularly those who influence and protect and guide and teach, can children learn what it means to be and act 6 or 10 or 16 years old. Perhaps combining parental responsibility with the responsibility of the reasonable child, as reflected in stories about children as they learn to be careful, is the most honest approach to capturing the development of responsible actors in the eyes of the law.

Importantly, however, that coexistence should not mask the fragile and partial nature of the relationship between parent and child. Just as the Man with the Yellow Hat is always hovering in the universe of Curious George, that same big person necessarily fades from the pages as we imagine George growing into the ability to control his curiosity. The parent slowly lets go while other relationships become central in the young person's life. During adolescence, the education received in early years becomes more significant than supervision. As parents fade, peers grow in importance. An adult, including a parent, may play some role in mediating peer relations, but, as the 'reasonable child' test indeed implies, that role is limited. The acceptance that one's actions may affect others may be underscored by peers rather than big people.

In *Madeline and the Bad Hat*,[60] it is Madeline—a very grown up little girl—who impresses upon the Spanish neighbour—a reckless and animal-teasing boy in a hat—that some kinds of comportment are simply unacceptable. As Pepito recovers in hospital from the injuries he brought upon himself, he tells Madeline:

---

person standard. Billy Joe's parents, the judge felt, had properly taught their son to use the bike, portrayed as a toy not an adult vehicle, in a safe manner. Billy Joe was held to be negligent, but not to 'as high a degree as if he were an adult': *Jarvis*, above n 34, at [75].

[60] Ludwig Bemelmans, *Madeline and the Bad Hat* (New York, The Viking Press, 1956).

'I've learned my lesson Please believe
I'm turning over a new leaf'.
'That's fine', she said. 'I hope you do.
We all will keep our eyes on you!'[61]

Here then, Madeline and her cohorts set the bar for proper behaviour. Pepito, the 'Bad Hat', learns to adjust to those norms. Indeed, he pays for the consequences of his actions on his own without the safety net of any adult in his life.[62]

This chapter has insisted throughout on the way in which the responsible child-self is constructed hand-in-hand with the responsible parent-self, whether in private law stories told about children or children's stories related to norms and rules of behaviour. But Madeline and Pepito, brought to our attention at the very end of the analysis, remind us that an insistence on the normative centrality of the parent in a child's developing responsibility may sometimes miss the point. Shifting responsibility to a parent without basing that shift on justifiable assumptions about the forms and meaning of a young person's own responsibility may be unconvincing. Public policy in the form of parental responsibility legislation must be careful to avoid that kind of failure. Unless a flexible dynamic between parent and child is built into such legislation, the development of the child and the ever-broadening sphere of influence in the child's life are left aside. The Ontario Act's blatant assignment of parental liability for intentional property damage by young people clearly distinguishes itself from the complex and subtle web of approaches balanced in the private law of civil wrongs.

V.   CONCLUSIONS

At the stage when children's responsibility begins to be formed, 'sois sage' and 'have fun' coincide. They coincide in children's lives, and they coincide in the messages that children receive from the big people always around them. Childishness is the antithesis of responsibility; but it is also the state in which we begin to look around us, practice the transition from wild to responsive and back again, and hear words that both express care and tell us how to behave. A study of the law of private wrongs inevitably requires some grappling with the question of responsibility on the part of young

---

[61] *Ibid*, at 43.

[62] Learning from peers is central to Marc Brown's *Arthur* series of books, published by Little Brown & Co (New York) and Random House (New York), which include stories about Arthur, an eight year old aardvark, and his group of animal friends as they navigate the adventures and challenges of growing up. Through socialisation and 'getting along', the characters of *Arthur* learn what it means to be a good friend, a good sibling and a good citizen of the world.

people. The array of approaches taken to children as wrongdoers reflects the assumption that the child develops in relationship to big people, part of whose role is to foster the child's own sense of responsibility.

Children become peers, friends, neighbours—in other words, able to watch out for others—through listening and learning, being cared for and guided. That appears to be the way in which children, and their evolving responsibility, are constructed through narratives, whether legal or literary. But parents are also constructed through the same narratives. Thus, the picture explored here is not of child actors on their own but rather, fundamentally, of those child actors in relation to the big people in their lives. In considering the possibility of parental responsibility for the harmful actions of children, we explore a picture of individual adult responsibility for others in our care. The assumed relationship between parents and children thus shapes the relationship between parents as potential defendants and corresponding potential plaintiffs. The responsible actor is assessed, as paradigmatically imagined in Quebec civil law tradition, as the reasonable parent or 'bon père de famille'. Responsibility for caring for children may carry with it parental responsibility vis-à-vis others who might be hurt by those children.

When parents call out 'Have fun!' and 'Sois sage!', they capture the necessary tensions in growing up and becoming responsible. They also take on the protection, teaching, encouragement, and guidance that parenting both demands and symbolises. Narratives—literary, legislative, codal and case law—continually construct that image and reality of parenting. They tell us stories about the individual subject, the relationships that shape that subject, and the contours of responsibility for 'childishness'.

4

Claims of Involuntary Parenthood: Why the Resistance?

ELIZABETH ADJIN-TETTEY*

I. INTRODUCTION

S HOULD PARENTS, who may actively have taken steps not to have a(nother) child, be able to recover reasonable costs of raising a child conceived and/or born due to the negligence of a health care professional(s)? Claims for damages consequent upon the birth of an unplanned child, to a large extent, have been determined based on policy considerations and have resulted in limited recovery that excludes damages for the cost of raising the unplanned child. This chapter examines the policy rationales underlying the limited recovery approach and the interests protected. Why is the law willing to countenance departure from the general negligence principles and the traditional understanding of corrective and distributive justice that underlie tort law when it comes to the protection of reproductive autonomy?[1] I argue that excluding damages for child-rearing is not gender-neutral. It is premised on gendered perceptions about women's reproductive capacities, socially constructed child care roles, and the family as an organising unit of society. Limited recovery also reflects a lack of appreciation of the effect on women's autonomy, security interests, bodily integrity and reproductive choice. I argue that both corrective and distributive justice support full recovery, based on the impact of childbirth and child care responsibilities on women's lives, including their participation in social, economic and political activities.

I have chosen to refer to these claims as involuntary parenthood or, more specifically, involuntary motherhood, as opposed to the often used terminology of 'wrongful birth'. The use of the term involuntary parenthood is

* Associate Professor, Faculty of Law, University of Victoria, British Columbia. This chapter is part of a research project partly funded by a Borden, Ladner, Gervais Summer Fellowship.
[1] Reproductive autonomy refers to the right to make decisions about procreation, including whether and when to bear children, and how many.

intended to, hopefully, avoid the philosophical difficulties associated with the term wrongful birth (which appears to characterise the birth of a child as unfortunate). Rather, the gist of involuntary parenthood claims is the recovery of costs to parents arising when the negligence of a health care professional frustrates their explicitly stated wishes regarding reproduction.

First, this chapter will examine current positions on recovery in claims of involuntary parenthood and how they represent a clear exception to the general principles of compensation. Next I will argue that, although the creation of this exception is allegedly justified on public policy grounds, policy does not necessarily support denial of these claims. Primarily, this exception has unavoidable gendered effects and undermines reproductive autonomy, which is a legally and socially accepted right. Instead, limited recovery seems arbitrary and premised on a moral revulsion stemming from an idealisation of the patriarchal family and a denial of the social, emotional and economic costs associated with parenthood. I will then illustrate some of the logical inconsistencies and erroneous assumptions in the rationales underlying resistance to compensation for such claims: the distributive justice rationale; the distaste at the seeming construction of the birth of a child as a legal injury; and fear of commodification of the child. In conclusion, this chapter links responses to claims of involuntary parenthood to the broader gendered treatment of issues affecting women's interests in tort law. Failure to respond to these claims undermines the importance of personal autonomy that is central to tort law and human dignity, and dismisses the physical, emotional and economic consequences of the infringement of reproductive autonomy on women's lives. This deprives women of equal protection under the law.

II.   OVERVIEW OF JUDICIAL AND LEGISLATIVE POSITIONS ON CLAIMS OF INVOLUNTARY PARENTHOOD

Claims of involuntary parenthood arise from the negligence of health care professionals in the form of negligent sterilisation, failed abortion procedures, misdiagnosis of pregnancy, misreading of test results, failure to detect pregnancy within a reasonable time so the mother could safely terminate the pregnancy, failure to adequately warn patients about the risks of pregnancy even after undergoing sterilisation procedures, etc.[2] At the heart of these claims is the violation of reproductive autonomy and the

---

[2]   However, claims that arise from the failure of a medical professional to advise the parent about genetic testing or to detect a disability at a time when the parents could have terminated the pregnancy raise bio-ethical complexities that are beyond the scope of this chapter. Thus, those issues are not explored here.

costs (financial and emotional) to the parents arising from interference with this autonomy. Claimants are, therefore, seeking vindication for the violation of their reproductive autonomy, which was caused by the defendant's negligence and has resulted in an outcome they have specifically sought to avoid. Viewed in this way, recovery of all the reasonably foreseeable costs to parents due to the birth of the unplanned child is necessary to vindicate the claimants' autonomy and dignity interests.

However, the law has failed to fully compensate parents for costs associated with the birth of the unplanned child. Parents are generally entitled to compensation for pecuniary and non-pecuniary losses associated with pregnancy and childbirth, but not the cost of raising the unplanned child. In addition, some jurisdictions allow recovery for additional costs associated with raising children born with disabilities following the negligence of a health care professional.[3] Limited recovery appears to be the predominant view,[4] now with a gloss of non-pecuniary damages for violation of parents' reproductive autonomy in some jurisdictions.[5] Under the limited recovery approach, parents are compensated for the financial and emotional costs associated with pregnancy and childbirth, but not for the cost of raising the child until the age of majority.

The common law of Australia recognises total recovery; parents are entitled to damages for the full costs of raising the unexpected child, with no deduction for the benefits parents may derive from the child's existence or their relationship with the child.[6] The common law position has been

---

[3] For examples, see the English position in *Parkinson v St James' and Seacroft University Hospital NHS Trust* [2001] 3 All ER 97 (CA) [*Parkinson*]; *Groom v Selby* [2001] EWCA Civ 1522. Legislation in Australian jurisdictions, where child-rearing costs are generally not recoverable, also permits recovery for additional costs associated with the child's disabilities. See Civil Liability Act 2002 (NSW) Pt II, s 71(2); Civil Liability Act 1936 (SA), s 67. The Queensland legislation also appears to incorporate the disability exception, albeit indirectly—Civil Liability Act 2003 (Qld) Pt 5, s 49A(2). Although I find the distinction between a healthy child and a child born with physical and mental disabilities problematic, I do not intend to address that issue in this chapter.

[4] See *McFarlane v Tayside Health Board* [2000] 2 AC 59 (HL) 114 [*McFarlane*].

[5] *Rees v Darlington Memorial Hospital NHS Trust* [2003] 4 All ER 987, [6], [8] [*Rees*]. The majority of the House of Lords acknowledged the wrong to parents from violation of their reproductive autonomy, and retreated from the *McFarlane* no-recovery approach in favour of awarding a conventional sum of £15,000 to all parents of children born through the negligence of a health care professional. The award is not intended to be compensatory. The British Columbia Supreme Court has adopted a similar position, although the quantum of damages is to be determined on an individualised basis: *Bevilacqua v Altenkirk* (2004) 242 DLR (4th) 338 [*Bevilacqua*]; *Roe v Dabbs* (2004) 31 BCLR (4th) 158 [*Roe*]. This is explored in further detail below.

[6] This position was adopted by a narrow majority of the High Court of Australia in *Cattanach v Melchior* (2003) 215 CLR 1 [*Cattanach*].

reversed by legislation in Queensland,[7] New South Wales[8] and South Australia.[9] Presumably, parents in these three states may still be entitled to recover the economic and non-economic costs associated with pregnancy and childbirth. However, given the limits on non-pecuniary losses, it is unlikely that parents can recover significant damages for this head.[10]

United States jurisprudence is equally mixed on damages for involuntary parenthood. Some states allow full recovery, including child-rearing costs, with or without offset. Nevertheless, most jurisdictions allow a limited recovery (damages for failed procedure, pregnancy and childbirth, but not child-rearing costs).[11]

In New Zealand, the law in relation to claims of involuntary parenthood and personal injury generally has been slow to evolve since the introduction of the no fault accident compensation scheme in 1972. Parents are beginning to seek common law damages for child-rearing expenses for children born due to medical negligence, because they cannot obtain compensation for such damages under the statutory scheme. The limited case law to date suggests that such claims are unlikely to succeed.[12]

Although the current Canadian position appears to be in a state of flux[13] (the Supreme Court of Canada has not had the opportunity to decide

---

[7] Civil Liability Act 2003 (Qld) Pt 5, s 49—no recovery for the economic costs ordinarily associated with rearing or maintaining a child born following a failed sterilisation procedure or negligent contraceptive advice.

[8] Civil Liability Act 2002 (NSW) Pt II, s 71—economic loss in relation to raising a child and loss of earnings by a claimant while raising the child are not recoverable. However, this does not preclude recovery for additional costs of maintaining a child with disabilities.

[9] Civil Liability Act 1936 (SA), s 67– prohibits recovery for the ordinary costs of raising a child born due to the negligence of a health care professional. Costs associated with the care of a child born with physical or mental disabilities are not excluded from recovery.

[10] In New South Wales, the Civil Liability Act 2002 specifically limits awards for non-economic loss. In addition to the cap, there is a minimum threshold for recovery. To be entitled to any damages, the severity of the loss must be at least 15% of a most extreme case (s 16).

[11] See generally, P Baugher, 'Fundamental Protection of a Fundamental Right: Full Recovery of Child-Rearing Damages for Wrongful Pregnancy' (2000) 75 *Washington Law Review* 1205; IJ Alvarez, 'A Critique of the Motivational Analysis in Wrongful Conception Cases' (2000) 41 *Boston College Law Review* 585; D Stretton, 'The Birth Torts: Damages for Wrongful Birth and Wrongful Life' (2005) 10 *Deakin Law Review* 319, 323-24.

[12] See *SGB v WDHB* [2002] NZAR 413 (HC Wellington); C Thomas, 'Claims for Wrongful Pregnancy and Damages for the Upbringing of the Child' (2003) 26 *University of New South Wales Law Journal* 125, 129-32.

[13] For an example of the range of responses to claims of involuntary parenthood in Canada, see *Colp v Ringrose* (1979) 3 *Legal Medical Quarterly* 72 (Alta SCTD) (no recovery); *Keats v Pearce* (1984) 48 Nfld & PEIR 102 (Nfld SCTD) (denied child-rearing costs on the basis of failure to mitigate (mother could have avoided the loss by terminating her relationship with the child through adoption)); *Roe* and *Bevilacqua*, above n 5 (limited recovery approach). In *Suite c Cooke* [1995] RJQ 2765, the Quebec Court of Appeal adopted the benefits/offset approach (parents were held entitled to recover costs of raising the unplanned child, subject to deductions for the emotional benefits the parents will derive from the child's existence).

whether child-rearing costs should be recoverable), the current weight of authority seems to favour the limited damages approach, which excludes recovery for child-rearing costs.[14]

Limited recovery is problematic because it draws an artificial distinction between the costs associated with pregnancy and childbirth and those associated with child-rearing.[15] An application of ordinary negligence principles supports compensation for reasonably foreseeable losses flowing from a defendant's negligence as part of restoring plaintiffs to their pre-tort position subject to remoteness. In this context, the consequences of the negligence of a medical professional, resulting in the birth of a(nother) child where the parent(s) have taken positive steps to avoid that very outcome, should result in compensation for (1) having their wishes frustrated, and (2) the costs in relation to the birth and care of the unexpected child. This would include recovery not only for the pecuniary and non-pecuniary costs associated with pregnancy and childbirth, but also for the emotional, social and reasonable financial costs of raising the child, at least to the age of majority, as foreseeable losses resulting from the defendant's negligence.[16] Such an outcome would be consistent with general principles of tort law and, in particular, the law relating to professional negligence (where a client seeks professional services or advice, changes his or her position in reliance on that advice, and suffers reasonably foreseeable consequences).[17] Plaintiffs are able to recover their reasonably foreseeable losses in such circumstances unless the claim raises the potential for indeterminacy.

III.   LIMITED RECOVERY: PARTIAL RECOGNITION OF REPRODUCTIVE AUTONOMY

In *Roe v Dabbs*,[18] Parrett J acknowledged the harm to parents arising from involuntary parenthood, and also stressed parents' entitlement to compensation for violation of their reproductive autonomy:

---

[14]   *Kealey v Berezowski* (1996) 136 DLR (4th) 708 (Ont Gen Div); *Roe*, above n 5; *Bevilacqua*, above n 5; *Mummery v Olsson* [2001] OTC 43 (SCJ); *MY v Boutros* (2002) 313 AR 1 (QB).

[15]   See S Todd, 'Wrongful Conception, Wrongful Birth, and Wrongful Life' (2005) 27 *Sydney Law Review* 525, 532.

[16]   See *Rees*, above n 5, at [6], [8]; *Cattanach*, above n 6, at [57] (McHugh and Gummow JJ).

[17]   See M Jones, 'Bringing up Baby' (2001) *Tort Law Review* 14, 16.

[18]   Above n 5.

[I]t is not rational to refuse compensation to a person who has made positive efforts to avoid the burden of another child and had those efforts frustrated by professional negligence. There is no rational basis for the law presuming that no harm results.[19]

Still, for public policy reasons, the court considered it inappropriate to compensate parents for the costs of raising an unplanned child.

The limited recovery approach creates an exception to the general principles of compensation in tort law.[20] This exception has been described as extraordinary, among other things, because it undermines the fundamental right to reproductive autonomy. The lack of an effective remedy to fully vindicate interference with reproductive autonomy renders this legally and socially accepted right of limited value.[21] It calls to mind Chief Justice Holt's memorable declaration in *Ashby v White*:

If the plaintiff has a right, [s]he must of necessity have a means to vindicate and maintain it, and a remedy if [s]he is injured in the exercise or enjoyment of it; and indeed it is a vain thing to imagine a right without a remedy; for want of right and want of remedy are reciprocal.[22]

As noted above, the predominant position in Canada and England favours limited recovery: parents are not entitled to recover damages for the cost of raising the unplanned child. The recent position in British Columbia appears similar to the revised English approach. Both jurisdictions recognise that the right to make reproductive choice is a fundamental human right and consistent with personal autonomy. Interference with this decision through the negligence of a health care professional violates the personal autonomy rights of parents, mostly mothers, with financial, personal and emotional consequences. Although not allowed child-rearing costs, parents are entitled to recover non-pecuniary damages for violation of the right to make personal decisions about the size of their families.[23] This is in addition to the pecuniary and non-pecuniary damages for pregnancy and childbirth. Unlike the English approach, which awards a conventional amount to all parents for involuntary parenthood (as per *Rees*), the British Columbia Supreme Court favours an individualised

---

[19]   *Ibid*, at [195]. See also *Bevilacqua*, above n 5, at [92]. In *MY v Boutros*, above n 14, the court noted *obiter* that, in appropriate cases, parents should be 'entitled to damages for the emotional impact of the unexpected child, the additional stress of the new responsibility and for the challenge of re-arranging their lives to accommodate the new child' (at [149]).

[20]   See *Rees* above n 5, at [98] (Lord Hutton).

[21]   See B Golder, 'From McFarlane to Melchior and Beyond: Love, Sex, Money and Commodification in the Anglo-Australian Law of Torts' (2004) *Torts Law Journal* 1, 60-61.

[22]   *Ashby v White* (1703) 2 Ld Raym 938 (KB), reversed (1704) 3 Ld Raym 320 (HL), 1 ER 417 (dealing with the right to vote in an election).

[23]   See *Rees*, *Bevilacqua*, and *Roe*, all above n 5.

assessment of damages.[24] The extent of the parents' loss has been assessed by considering their motives for the decision to limit the size of their family, and their actual circumstances at the time of sterilisation, pregnancy and childbirth, to determine the appropriate level of compensation.[25] The award is still problematic because it is considered non-pecuniary with no recognition of the financial and other losses resulting from the defendant's negligence, apart from those associated with the pregnancy and childbirth. Failure to compensate parents for the costs of raising the unplanned child is inconsistent with the recognition of the harm to parents arising from interference with their reproductive autonomy. It is also inconsistent with the compensatory goal of tort damages: to restore plaintiffs to the position they would have been in had the defendant's wrong not occurred.

Limited recovery is an exceptional approach to the assessment of damages in tort. It effectively confers immunity on members of the medical profession in respect of one particular type of wrong—breach of their duty of care resulting in violation of reproductive autonomy, something that has profound effects on women's lives. Claims of involuntary parenthood arise from medical malpractice. Generally, medical malpractice cases are extremely difficult to prove and also very costly. Cases can fail on a number of grounds, such as failure to prove that the defendant's conduct fell below the standard of care, lack of causation, or remoteness. The plaintiffs under consideration in this chapter are those who have successfully proved the elements of a negligence claim. There is therefore no doubt in these cases that the medical professional was negligent, and that the negligence caused the plaintiffs the very outcome they had sought to avoid.

There is no reason to confer immunity on health care professionals regarding the reasonably foreseeable consequences of their negligence in offering reproductive health services. Health care professionals enjoy no

---

[24] In *Bevilacqua*, Groberman J rejected the notion of a conventional award that is not intended to be compensatory as being contrary to principles governing the assessment of damages because the approach fails to consider the unique circumstances of individual plaintiffs. Above n 5, at [181]. See also N Priaulx, 'That's One Heck of an 'Unruly Horse'! Riding Roughshod over Autonomy in Wrongful Conception' (2004) 12 *Feminist Legal Studies* 317, 329-30, who rejects the one-size-fits-all English approach as being inconsistent with individual autonomy because it assumes that all parents are equally situated and would suffer undifferentiated harm from involuntary parenthood, regardless of social location and diversity among women.

[25] *Bevilacqua*, ibid; and *Roe*, above n 5. There was no mention of a possible distinction between cases involving the birth of healthy children and those born with disabilities. However, an earlier decision had awarded damages for raising a child with special needs until age 25 (when the child was expected to move into a group home or some assisted living arrangement with costs to be paid by the government) in addition to non-pecuniary damages for both parents and past income loss for the mother: *Jones v Rostvig* (2003) 17 CCLT (3d) 253 (BCSC). In *Roe*, the mother was awarded $55,000. In *Bevilacqua*, the mother received $30,000 while the father received $20,000.

such immunity in relation to the other services they offer. Indeed, it has been suggested that, given the importance of reproductive autonomy, claims for involuntary parenthood perhaps deserve to be treated more seriously than other medical malpractice cases,[26] especially because of the long-term physical, psychological, financial and social consequences that ensue from the negligence.[27]

Advancement in reproductive technology has made it possible for people to plan the size and timing of their families. It has also created legitimate expectations for those who choose to do so and submit to contraceptive procedures so that they can live their lives as they wish. The law should provide a remedy in the event of disappointment due to the negligence of medical professionals. Indeed, the medical profession should not be able to affect people's lives in such fundamental ways without assuming a corresponding responsibility when, because of their negligence, the expected benefits do not materialise.[28]

Failure to award the full costs of involuntary parenthood constitutes a limited recognition of the outcome-responsibility of the negligent party. Plaintiffs should be entitled to recover all reasonably foreseeable losses where the defendant's fault is not in issue.[29] It is not disputed that parents whose reproductive wishes have been frustrated through professional negligence will incur financial and other losses beyond those associated with pregnancy and childbirth. It is therefore arbitrary to recognise the violation of parents' autonomy rights and the harmful consequences flowing therefrom, while denying claims for financial losses and characterising the parents' loss as only non-pecuniary. This is a major setback for reproductive autonomy and women's well-being in general. The recognition of the wrong arising from the violation of reproductive autonomy, and the limited remedy vindicating this right, shows a tension between principle and policy and an attempt to limit the former based on the latter.

Although the negligence of health care professionals resulting in involuntary parenthood is not disputed, the decision whether to compensate parents for child-rearing costs largely depends on the legal construction of

---

[26]   See SJ LaCroix and LG Martin, 'Damages for Wrongful Pregnancy Tort Actions' in TR Ireland and JO Ward (eds), *Assessing Damages in Injuries and Deaths of Minor Children* (Tucson, Lawyers & Judges Publishing Co, 2002) 98; J Shaw, 'Wrongful Birth and the Politics of Reproduction: West German and English Law Considered' (1990) 4 *International Journal of Law & Family* 52, 62.

[27]   Similar reasoning underlies the seriousness attached to claims for sexual wrongdoing, which often leaves profound and long-term effects on its victims and therefore deserves to be taken seriously.

[28]   See N Priaulx, 'Joy to the World! A (Healthy) Child is Born! Reconceptualizing "Harm" in Wrongful Conception' (2004) 13 *Social & Legal Studies* 5, 5-6, 15-16.

[29]   See SR Perry, 'Loss, Agency, and Responsibility for Outcomes: Three Conceptions of Corrective Justice' in K Cooper-Stephenson and E Gibson (eds), *Tort Theory* (North York, Captus Press, 1993) 24, 44-45.

compensable harm. These claims are perceived by some as testing the limits of ordinary tort law principles and the underlying philosophy of corrective justice. Hence, it has been suggested that the issue is best resolved by reference to distributive justice and moral considerations as opposed to legal principles or legislation.[30] In *McFarlane v Tayside Health Board*, Lord Steyn conceded that principles of corrective justice support recovery for all the consequences of the birth of an unexpected child, including the costs of raising the child to adulthood.[31] However, he concluded that principles of distributive justice—the just distribution of burdens and benefits among members of society—compel denial of recovery.

The denial of child-rearing costs is premised on the idea that the existence of a child cannot be perceived as detrimental or in terms of cost to the family unit. Recovery has been rejected on grounds of public policy—that the uniqueness of the claim warrants different considerations than would be applicable in the run-of-the-mill tort cases. However, a policy-based approach does not necessarily support the denial of claims of involuntary parenthood.[32] If the policy-based approach is to reflect social reality (as it should), then it would actually support full recovery for the consequences of involuntary parenthood, given the importance of reproductive autonomy and the interests in safeguarding against its violation. As well, the practical effect of having a(nother) child on parents, especially mothers, supports recovery as a matter of gender, and to some extent, class equality, and consistency with the just distributions of burdens and benefits in society.

---

[30] Cane notes that the issue is morally charged, however one views it. Both recovery and non-recovery of child-rearing costs entail moral judgments about the value of the competing interests. He finds the majority decision in *Cattanach* (which allowed recovery for the upbringing of a child conceived as a result of a negligent sterilisation procedure) to be hypocritical for its failure to acknowledge the assumptions and values that informed the decision and for pretending it was an objective outcome based on application of ordinary tort law principles: P Cane, 'The Doctor, the Stork and the Court: A Modern Morality Play' (2004) 120 *LQR* 23, 23-24. Steel notes that failure to articulate the real reasons that influence judges' decisions is potentially dangerous because the underlying assumptions, which are based on gender stereotypes, remain unscrutinised and ultimately become transformed into accepted legal principles: J Steel, 'Scepticism and the Law of Negligence' [1993] *CLJ* 437, 466.

[31] *McFarlane*, above n 4, at 82-83.

[32] See Shaw, above n 26, at 56.

IV. DENIAL OF RECOVERY OF MAINTENANCE COSTS AS A MATTER OF DISTRIBUTIVE JUSTICE

The limited recovery approach has been justified, among other things, as a matter of distributive justice.[33] Utilitarian considerations regarding availability of health care funding to provide services to the general public or avoiding an insurance crisis (including high cost of insurance) are made to trump the right of individual parents for compensation. It is notable that the insurance crisis argument has often been deployed to justify shielding the medical profession from developments in tort law that are perceived to have the potential for increased liability.[34]

The distributive justice rationale, which underlies refusals to provide compensation for pecuniary and non-pecuniary costs of raising a child born due to medical negligence, is indefensible. In effect, it privatises the consequences of the defendant's negligence, which often involves disproportionate burdens for women. This outcome is hardly supportable as a just distribution of burdens among members of society. Departure from corrective justice in favour of distributive justice should be supportable only when it is necessary to vindicate fundamental rights,[35] or achieve substantive equality and social justice.[36] Invoking distributive justice

---

[33] See *McFarlane*, above n 4, at 82-83.

[34] For example, see *Snell v Farrell* [1990] 2 SCR 311 [*Snell*]. However, studies indicate that the current 'crisis' of rising malpractice insurance in the United States is not affected by tort claims, but rather, by market conditions. In addition, there is a lack of documented adverse effects of rising malpractice insurance rates on the number of physicians per capita. See LM Finley, 'The Hidden Victims of Tort Reform: Women, Children, and the Elderly' (2004) 53 *Emory Law Journal* 1263, 1270-74.

[35] When faced with difficult issues of causation, courts have sometimes relaxed the rules to ensure vindication of plaintiffs' fundamental rights. For example, in relation to failure to warn, see *Chappel v Hart* 1998 HCA 55; *Chester v Afshar* 2004 UKHL 41, [22]. In *Chester*, Lord Steyn referred to the modification of the rules of causation in *Fairchild v Glenhaven Funeral Services* [2003] 1 AC 32 (HL) that enabled the claimants to successfully establish causation notwithstanding the uncertainty whether the defendants' negligence caused their injuries as a principled approach, at [23]. See also Lord Walker, [101] and Lord Hope, [87]. Commentators also see these exceptions to regular principles as consistent with tort law's protection of the vulnerable and the plaintiff's right to autonomous decision-making in regard to his or her body. See P Cane, 'A Warning about Causation' (1999) 115 *LQR* 21, 24; A Grubb, 'Clinical Negligence: Informed Consent and Causation' (2002) 10 *Medical Law Review* 322, 323; T Honoré, 'Medical Non-Disclosure: Causation and Risk: *Chappel v Hart*' (1999) 7 *Torts Law Journal* 1, 20, 22; J Stapleton, 'Cause-In-Fact and the Scope of Liability for Consequences' (2003) 119 *LQR* 388, 420; M Stauch, 'Taking the Consequences for Failure to Warn of Medical Risks' (2000) 63 *MLR* 261, 267.

[36] Similarly, considerations of justice for plaintiffs have led courts to depart from conventional rules on causation when the plaintiff's injuries could have been caused by different factors, including the defendant's negligence. See for example, *Snell*, above n 34; *Fairchild*, above; *Barker v Saint Gobain Pipelines Plc* [2006] 2 WLR 1027 (CA). As well, exceptions are made by courts in the classic cases of overdetermination, such as *Cook v Lewis* [1952] 1 DLR 1 (SCC); and *Baker v Willoughby* [1970] AC 467 (HL). This is presumably because, as Stapleton explains, 'any concern for fairness to defendants is outweighed by a

considerations to support a stance that undermines the right to reproductive autonomy is detrimental to women's right to self-determination, bodily integrity, dignity and equality.

In *McFarlane*, although Lord Millett acknowledged the disproportionate cost of parenthood for mothers, he did not perceive this as justifying recovery for the cost of maintaining the child, preferring to describe it as simply the 'price of parenthood'.[37] Presumably, women have to pay a price for having a good thing (perhaps based on the adage 'no pain no gain'). Women are expected to bear this cost without compensation, whether they have chosen that situation or not. Such reasoning reflects gendered assumptions about women's care-giving role, while reinforcing heteronormativity and the nuclear family as ideal forms of social ordering and the basis for building lasting societies. Denial of the claim for child-rearing costs is influenced by notions of traditional patriarchal family forms with their emphasis on procreation as the major organising principle of society. Central to this view of women and their parental role is the stereotypical notion that links women's self-actualisation and fulfilment with motherhood. This is consistent with the view aptly described by Lord Denning:

> No matter how you dispute and argue, you cannot alter the fact that women are quite different from men. The principal task in the life of women is to bear and rear children . . . .. He is physically the stronger and she the weaker. He is temperamentally the more aggressive . . . . and she who responds. These diversities of function and temperament lead to differences of outlook which cannot be ignored.[38]

This reasoning is problematic because it implicitly renders invisible other family forms that are becoming increasingly common and accepted in society, such as childless couples (whether by choice or because of infertility), double career couples who start families later in life, same-sex couples, etc.[39] Even more disturbingly, it transforms the existence of women's reproductive capacity from their own benefit to that of a patriarchal society that controls women's reproductive autonomy and is perceived as being in a better position to make decisions about women's bodies. Within this paradigm, procreation is viewed as the primary role of women.

Denial of compensation for involuntary parenthood should not be premised on such paternalistic assumptions about reproductive freedom or, for that matter, women's childbirth and child-rearing roles. The denial of child-rearing costs:

---

concern that the law would be embarrassed if it were seen to treat the victim of multiple torts worse than the victim of one' (Stapleton, above, 413).

[37] *McFarlane*, above n 4, at 114.

[38] Lord Denning, *The Due Process of Law* (London, Butterworths, 1980) 194.

[39] See *Cattanach* above n 6, at [164] (Kirby J); Golder, above n 21, at 60-61.

is arbitrary and unjust ... [and] could even be said to be discriminatory, given that it involves a denial of the application of ordinary compensatory principles in the particular circumstances of child-birth and child-rearing, circumstances that biologically and socially pertain to the female experience and traditionally fall within the domain of women.[40]

It disregards the costs that women incur in their everyday lives due to their child care responsibilities, and the fact that these costs are exacerbated by women's unequal access to societal resources. The skewed distribution of burdens associated with care-giving is even more pronounced given the precarious social citizenship of women in the neo-liberal state, with few and diminishing social programmes to cushion the impact of women's reproductive and care-giving responsibilities.

In spite of the growing perception, and perhaps expectations, of egalitarian parenting between men and women, the reality is that women continue to bear a disproportionate burden of child care and domestic responsibilities.[41] The gendered and unequal division of child care and other domestic responsibilities does not stem so much from women's biological role in reproduction, but is mostly due to their socially constructed primary care-giving role and the patriarchal family structure that sustains the gendered division of labour within the home.[42]

The reality for many women is that the gendered organisation of domestic life limits their participation in social, economic and political life. Specifically, it limits their educational opportunities and participation in the waged labour force. It also continues to negatively affect their overall economic condition, including their dependence on others, usually men.[43] Although there has been a steady increase in the participation rates of women in higher education and the waged labour force, the percentage of working women continues to trail that of men.[44] Women's work patterns

---

[40]   *Cattanach*, above n 6, at [162] (Kirby J).

[41]   See Statistics Canada, *Women in Canada: A Gender-Based Statistical Report*, 5th edn (2006) (Catalogue No 89-503-XIE) [*Women in Canada, 2006*]; R Graycar and J Morgan, *The Hidden Gender of Law*, 2nd edn (Sydney, Federation Press, 2002) 88-89; L Turnbull, *Double Jeopardy: Motherwork and the Law* (Toronto, Sumac Press, 2001) ch 1.

[42]   See Shaw, above n 26, at 57-58; Golder, above n 21, at 58-59.

[43]   See *Women in Canada, 2006*, above n 41, at 109-110; E Gibson, 'The Gendered Wage Dilemma in Personal Injury Claims' in K Cooper-Stephenson and E Gibson, (eds), *Tort Theory* (North York, Captus Press, 1993) 199-200; Turnbull, above n 41, at chs 1 and 3; R Graycar, 'Judicial Activism or Traditional Negligence Law? Conception, Pregnancy, and Denial of Reproductive Choice' in I Freckelton and K Petersen (eds), *Disputes and Dilemmas in Health Law* (Annandale, Federation Press, 2006), making references to the impact of child-rearing on women's earning potential, including J Beggs and B Chapman, 'The Foregone Earnings from Child-Rearing in Australia' *Centre for Economic Policy Research Discussion Paper 190* (Canberra, Australian National University, 1988); M Gray and B Chapman, 'Foregone Earnings from Child Rearing' (2001) 58 *Family Matters* 4.

[44]   See *Women in Canada, 2006*, above n 41, at 105-7.

continue to be influenced, among other things, by their child care responsibilities.[45] The lower participation rate of women is particularly noticeable among women in prime child-bearing years and those with very young children (preschoolers). Women in this group tend to work part time because of child care and other family responsibilities.[46] In addition, the increasingly precarious social security system, influenced mostly by notions of individual responsibility, limits expectations of reliance on that system for financial and other assistance to meet women's child care needs.

The disproportionate burden of the limited recovery approach on women is inconsistent with the compensatory and loss spreading philosophies underlying modern tort law. It is also contrary to the corrective and distributive justice models that underlie modern tort law.[47] Interests protected in the distributive justice calculus appear to promote the well-being of others, leaving the innocent victims, mostly women, to bear the burden of involuntary parenthood. Given that the victims, women, are a disadvantaged group, this further undermines their equality because of the limitations imposed by their parental roles.

At a minimum, meaningful remedies for involuntary parenthood are 'necessary to protect important individual and societal interests in procreative autonomy...[and] attempts to [limit such] claims severely threaten these interests'.[48] Graycar notes that the non-recovery position constitutes judicial activism, and should be avoided.[49] More importantly, this activism is legally and socially regressive because its practical effect is to promote sex inequality by reinforcing the social construction of women based on their reproductive capacities. This activism implicates the state and, more specifically, the law, in creating and reinforcing patriarchal family forms and women's socially constructed roles within the family unit.[50]

---

[45] In 2004, 34% of women between the ages of 25 and 44 worked part-time because of their child care responsibilities. As well, women are more likely than men to miss work because of family reasons. See *Women in Canada, 2006*, above n 41, at 109-110; Graycar and Morgan, above n 41, at 90.

[46] *Women in Canada, 2006*, above n 41, at 109.

[47] See K Cooper-Stephenson, 'Corrective Justice, Substantive Equality and Tort Law' in K Cooper-Stephenson and E Gibson (eds), *Tort Theory* (North York, Captus Press, 1993) 48. See also references on complementarity of corrective and distributive justice in modern tort law in E Adjin-Tettey, 'Replicating and Perpetuating Inequalities in Personal Injury Claims through Female Specific Contingencies' (2004) 49 *McGill Law Journal* 309, 343.

[48] Anon, 'Wrongful Birth Actions: The Case against Legislative Curtailment' (1987) 100 *Harvard Law Review* 2017, 2034.

[49] Graycar, above n 43. See also US cases, such as *Ochs v Borelli* 455 A 2d 883 (Conn 1982) 885, referred to in Graycar, where the court explicitly refused to create such an exception.

[50] See Shaw, above n 26, at 58; Golder, above n 21, at 36.

V.   CONSTRUCTION OF LEGAL INJURY OR COMPENSABLE HARM

It is considered contrary to public policy to compensate parents for the costs of raising a child born through the negligence of medical profession-als because the birth of a child, regardless of how it came about, is perceived to be a good thing. Hence, it cannot be the basis of a legal wrong. It is also argued that, although parenthood entails benefits/advantages and burdens/disadvantages, the two are inseparable and the net balance is beneficial. Individuals may be entitled to perceive the net results of parenthood as unfavourable and take positive steps to avoid experienc-ing the pleasures and burdens of parenthood. However, society must take the net result of the existence of a child as beneficial. It is therefore morally repugnant to consider a child to be more trouble that it is worth.[51]

One thing that all societies share is the interest in procreation and maintenance of the species. In the context of damages for involuntary parenthood, this utilitarian view of the birth of a child appears to override women's autonomous decision-making regarding reproduction and the size of their family, as well as the right to have that choice respected. However, the legitimacy/legality of family planning mechanisms, including abortion, is evidence that legislatures and courts recognise that these communal benefits must be balanced with women's right to control their reproductive capacity in order to fully participate in society. Even if society thinks human life is always a good thing, individuals who have to meet the daily needs of children are perfectly entitled to abstain from this otherwise good thing or limit how many children they want to have. As pointed out in *Cattanach*, it is the parent-child relationship that is being avoided, as opposed to human life itself.[52] The declining birth rates[53] and smaller family sizes[54] in almost all industrialised countries are evidence of the widespread and implicit acceptability of reproductive choices or control of one's fertility.

---

[51]   *McFarlane*, above n 4, at 113-14 (Lord Millett).

[52]   *Cattanach*, above n 6, at 3 (Gleeson CJ).

[53]   For examples of the steady decline in birth rates in selected industrialised countries, see Information Please Database (Pearson Education Inc, 2006), source: United Nations Monthly Bulletin of Statistics, June 1997 and the US Census Bureau, International Database. See <http://www.infoplease.com/ipa/A0004395.html> (date accessed: 23 August 2006). Accord-ing to Statistics Canada, the crude birth rate in Canada fell to an all-time low in 2002, down to 10.5 live births for every 1,000 people. This is the lowest birth rate since vital statistics began to be produced nationally in 1921. Statistics Canada, 'Births' *The Daily* (19 April 2004). See <http://www.statcan.ca/Daily/English/040419/d040419b.htm> (date accessed: 23 August 2006).

[54]   The average family size in Canada was 3.1 in the 1991 and 1996 censuses. This figure was down to 3.0 according to the 2001 census. Statistics Canada, Nation Series, Catalogue No 93F0022XDB96008. See <http://www.statcan.ca/english/census96/oct14/fam1.htm> (date accessed: 23 August 2006). By way of comparison, the average family size in Canada was 3.7

Denial of recovery for child-rearing costs brings into question what constitutes a legal injury or the circumstances in which legal protection will be extended to a new type of claim. Women's reproductive choice is now a legally protected right. Violation of a legally protected right/interest constitutes a legal injury.[55] Hence, negligent conduct that results in violation of a woman's reproductive choice and the resulting infringement of her freedom to determine the size of her family and her lifestyle constitute a violation of her personal autonomy and human dignity.

The consequences of having one's autonomy and human dignity violated in this manner are well known—parents will incur personal, financial and emotional costs.[56] These costs can detrimentally affect the economic stability and emotional wellbeing of the family unit. To the extent that a person's economic and emotional stability are legally protected interests, interference with them through the negligence of another by an unexpected addition to the family satisfies the definition of a legal wrong or injury.[57]

Denial of child maintenance costs is grounded in a particular view of legal or compensable injury as a bad or unfortunate event. The purpose of tort damages is to restore victims to their pre-tort position, free of the unfortunate event that has altered their lives either temporarily or permanently. According to this view, the birth of a child cannot be considered a legal harm because it is not an 'unfortunate' event. This analysis is flawed, because, among other things, it posits a restrictive vision of autonomy by making availability of a remedy contingent upon tangible injury. It undermines the right to determine one's own destiny whether other people think well of it or not. It also undermines the plaintiff's capacity to make decisions about reproduction by suggesting that, when the net result of frustrating the person's reasoned decision happens to be something that society considers beneficial, then this cannot be considered a loss even if it is contrary to the person's stated wishes.

What gets lost in this position is the parent's choice or deliberate efforts to specifically avoid this outcome, and the fact that she sought the defendant's professional services specifically to further this choice. The legitimacy of a person's decision to take positive steps to avoid having children, to limit the number of children or delay the timing of children is not questioned. It is also consistent with the inherent right to bodily security, self-determination and autonomy. Failure of tort law to give full

---

in 1971. Natural Resources Canada Website, The Atlas of Canada: http://atlas.nrcan.gc.ca/site/english/maps/peopleandsociety/family/family1996/1 (date accessed: 23 August 2006).

[55] See *Black's Law Dictionary*, 8th edn (Minnesota, West Publishing, 2004) 801.

[56] See *McFarlane*, above n 4, at 107 (Lord Millett); *Parkinson*, above n 3, at 114-17 (Hale LJ); T Weir, 'The Unwanted Child' (2000) 59 *CLJ* 238, 239.

[57] See *Roe*, above n 5, at 195. See also *Bevilacqua*, above n 5, at [92].

effect to the power of autonomous decision-making relating to reproduction not only undermines deterrence and harm reduction, but may also be a regressive use of tort law.

The law does not take such a position in relation to other violations of personal autonomy, including medical battery. The law readily compensates those whose fundamental right to bodily and mental security and autonomy over their bodies have been violated even though no tangible harm results, such as the remedy provided by the trespassory torts—assault, battery and false imprisonment. In addition, the law provides a remedy based on respect for autonomy in cases of medical battery, which may entail incalculable benefits for the 'victim', such as the opportunity to continue living, when the treatment is administered against the patient's wishes.[58]

The sanctity of life justification to deny recovery of child-rearing costs is flawed in light of legal developments in relation to, for example, the legality of abortion,[59] respect for an individual's decision to refuse or discontinue life-saving medical treatment when the decision will clearly end the patient's life,[60] and the decriminalisation of suicide and attempted suicide. As Professor Ronald Dworkin explains:

> Recognizing an individual right of autonomy makes self-creation possible. It allows each of us to be responsible for shaping our lives according to our own coherent or incoherent—but, in any case, distinctive—personality. It allows us to lead our lives rather than be led along them, so that each of us can be, to the extent a scheme of rights can make this possible, what we have made of ourselves. We allow someone to choose death over radical amputation or a blood transfusion, if that is his informed wish, because we acknowledge his right to a life structured by his own values.[61]

There is no reason to treat the harm arising from involuntary parenthood through the negligence of medical professionals any differently from other claims that respect personal autonomy and dignity.

Denial of damages for the full cost of involuntary parenthood trivialises the harm to women arising from the defendant's negligence, and is inconsistent with the importance of reproductive autonomy in promoting human dignity.[62] It is incongruous to say that women have the right to make decisions about reproduction and at the same time have that decision-making ability usurped by abstract notions of morality, the place

---

[58]   For example, see *Malette v Shulman* (1990) 67 DLR (4th) 321 (Ont CA).
[59]   See *R v Morgentaler* [1988] 1 SCR 30.
[60]   See *Nancy B v Hôtel-Dieu de Québec* (1992) 86 DLR (4th) 385 (Que SC).
[61]   R Dworkin, *Life's Dominion: An Argument about Abortion and Euthanasia* (New York, Knopf, 1993) 224.
[62]   Priaulx, above n 24, at 329.

of the family in society, or unarticulated and contested religious beliefs about the sanctity of life in an increasingly secularised world.[63]

More importantly, it is questionable whether the state has any moral authority to make such claims, given the increasing privatisation of child care, which leaves parents, mostly mothers, to care for their children. This, coupled with the unequal distribution of societal resources, mostly to the detriment of women and other marginalised groups, entrenches poverty of women and children.[64] It is easy for the state to pretend to be the guardian of morality and protector of the public interests in relation to the value of children, when in fact it can abdicate responsibility for ensuring that the needs of those children are being met. The state can unilaterally withdraw services that benefit children and it has consistently done so in recent times. In making policy decisions about when tort law should provide a remedy, Fleming notes that one of the considerations might be the availability of effective social security schemes to meet the needs of potential claimants.[65] Denying costs of care for children born with disabilities for the period when the plaintiffs are expected to be in state care is premised on similar reasoning.[66] The pattern of retrenchment in social services makes it unrealistic for parents to expect meaningful assistance from the state in meeting some of the costs of having a child thrust on them. This could make the consequences of involuntary parenthood more onerous than the child as a blessing stance will admit. This reality must equally inform policy considerations underlying decisions regarding recoverability of the costs of bringing up an unexpected child conceived and/or born through medical negligence.

As already noted, the injury to women from medical malpractice resulting in frustration of their decisions regarding reproduction is not disputed. It is also clear that the loss to the mother is not limited to the discomfort and inconvenience of pregnancy and childbirth. More importantly, women experience a profound sense of loss in being robbed of the right to proceed through life the way they have chosen, a decision they are free to make both as a matter of law and morality.[67] It is this sense of loss that remains at the heart of involuntary parenthood claims. The harm to women arises from having their right to determine how they want to live

---

[63] See *Harriton v Stephens* [2006] HCA 15, [13], [110] [*Harriton*] (Kirby J, dissenting). Although *Harriton* was a claim for 'wrongful life', the caution about not being influenced by religious or moral convictions in such cases is equally applicable in parents' claims for the costs of raising a child born due to the negligence of a health care professional, because similar arguments about the sanctity of life have been advanced to justify the denial of claims.

[64] See Priaulx, above n 24, at 328-29. In *Moge v Moge*, the Supreme Court of Canada acknowledged that the feminisation of poverty is an entrenched social reality: (1992) 99 DLR (4th) 456, 482.

[65] JG Fleming, *The American Tort Process* (Oxford, Clarendon Press, 1988) 26-27.

[66] For example, see *Krangle (Guardian ad litem of) v Brisco* [2002] 1 SCR 205.

[67] See Lord Bingham's admission of this fact in *Rees*, above n 5, at 8.

their lives frustrated, the responsibilities thrust on them in their role as mothers, and the limitations on their lives resulting from their care-giving role.[68] Recovery of child-rearing costs entails recognition of the consequences of the negligence of medical professionals, even if the plaintiff ends up with something society considers priceless.

To perceive the birth of a child mostly in terms of the benefits/joys/ blessings is to have a romantic view of childbirth and parenting based on the supposed desirability of parenthood, moral notions of the sanctity of life, the family as a social unit and women's reproductive and care-giving roles. Although this is an issue that affects all parents of children conceived after improper sterilisation and/or abortion procedures, it predominantly affects women because they are often the primary care-givers, even in dual parent families. Limited recovery does not seem to appreciate women's personal autonomy and security interests, and the long-term effects on parents and their relationships with others, including the 'unplanned' child's sibling(s).

The rising incidence of lone parent families[69] headed mostly by women[70] and the constraints on women's lives arising from their care-giving roles is further evidence that forced parenthood predominantly affects women's autonomy and dignity interests, as well as their social and economic conditions. Although there has been a significant increase in the employment rates of women generally and of those with young children in particular, female lone parents have a lower participation rate in paid employment than women in two-parent families.[71] Commenting on how childbirth and childcare responsibilities impoverish women, McKinnon notes:

---

[68] See Priaulx, above n 28, at 10.

[69] The 1991 census data indicated that there were 953,640 lone parents in Canada. This figure rose to 1,137,510 in the 1996 census. Statistics Canada, *Census Families in Private Households by Family Structure* (2001): <http://www.statcan.ca/english/census96/oct14/fam1.htm> (date accessed: 23 August 2006); *Women in Canada, 2006*, above n 41, at 38.

[70] Out of the 1,311,190 lone parent families in Canada in 2001, 1,065,360 were headed by women. Statistics Canada, 2001 Census Catalogue No 95F0487XCB2001001. See <http://www12.statcan.ca/english/census01/products/standard/profiles/RetrieveProfile. cfm?Temporal=2001&PID=56146&APATH=1&RL=3&IPS=95F0487XCB2001001> (date accessed: 23 August 2006). In 2001, 20% of all families with children in Canada were headed by female lone parents. The number of female lone parents in Canada has doubled since 1971. See *Women in Canada, 2006* above n 41, at 38. Factors accounting for the increasing number of female lone parent families include the high rate of marriage breakdowns and the fact that mothers often get the custody of children. *Women in Canada, 2006*, above n 41, at 37, 40.

[71] See *Women in Canada, 2006*, above n 41, at 103-7.

When a single parent is impoverished as a result of childbearing, usually the parent is female. When someone must care for the children, it is almost always a woman who does it, without her work being valued in terms of money or social status.[72]

For women or families already living on the edge, whose decision to limit the size of their family may have been influenced by financial considerations, recovery for child-rearing costs would make a difference between a life of dignity and a life of financial hardship for all family members. Thus, as Justice Bablitch notes in *Marciniak v Lundborg*, recovery of child-rearing costs can actually enhance the unplanned child's life.[73] Hence, determination of such claims should be informed by pragmatic considerations of the reality for those affected, and not bound up in philosophical arguments about the value of human life or the morality underlying such claims.

VI.   COMMODIFICATION RATIONALE FOR DENYING CHILD MAINTENANCE COSTS

Denial of recovery is also premised on an assumption (based on the child as a blessing stance) that exhorts parenthood and perceives parents as obtaining undeniable benefits from their parental role. Hence, claims for the costs of raising the unexpected child born due to medical negligence are seen as reflecting an unnatural rejection of parenthood, more specifically motherhood, and thereby causing a moral panic. The current anti-recovery and even revulsion climate invokes ideologies of good and bad mothers and stigmatises those who seek recovery for the consequences of the conception and/or birth of a(nother) child, an outcome the mothers have specifically sought to avoid.

Characterising the birth of a child as a tortious injury is perceived to be contrary to public policy, morality and human dignity because it inappropriately commodifies children through the assessment of the tangible and intangible costs of their membership in a family unit. It requires the assessment of the benefits and costs to the plaintiff(s) arising from the birth of the child to arrive at the net loss that should form the basis of compensation. This process entails the risk of parents denying their joy in the birth of a child and its developments through the various stages in life. It also gives rise to difficulties in quantification of both the costs and benefits from the life of a particular child. As well, there is a risk of

[72]   CA MacKinnon, *Women's Lives, Men's Laws* (Cambridge Mass, Belknap Press, 2005) 137.
[73]   450 NW 2d 243 (Wis 1990) 246. See also *Cattanach*, above n 6, at 56; *Harriton*, above n 63, at 131 (Kirby J, dissenting).

exaggerating the costs or negative contingencies associated with the life of a child in order for parents to obtain greater financial gain for a loss that is more theoretical than real.[74] This process is seen as undesirable and something that should be discouraged because it is potentially detrimental to family dynamics and intra-family relations.[75] Further, recovery of child-rearing costs is perceived as inconsistent with the human dignity of the child because it leads to its commodification and, as such, should not be permitted.[76]

However, this commodification anxiety is based on a particular world view that has been increasingly challenged, rather than on a pre-existing reality. As well, this anxiety about the costs of child-rearing is inconsistent with developments in other areas where similar concerns were once expressed. Even within claims of involuntary parenthood, moral arguments against recovery of child-rearing costs only begin after the child has been born—compensation for emotional and financial costs associated with pregnancy and childbirth are not perceived as giving rise to similar moral dilemmas, the potential to corrupt the proper domain of tort law, or family dynamics. Many people do have great joy in discovering they are pregnant, although pregnancy also entails some responsibilities such as proper pre-natal care and limitations on lifestyle. Yet compensation for emotional, social and financial costs associated even with a 'normal' pregnancy is not considered morally repugnant.[77]

Concerns about commodification generally stem from a bifurcated worldview with separate spheres and hostile worlds.[78] According to this view, there is 'a sharp divide...between intimate social relations and economic transactions, marking any contact between the two spheres as moral contamination'.[79] Within this paradigm, the private sphere of family

---

[74] See *Roe*, above n 5, at [198]–[199]; *Cattanach*, above n 6, at [25] (Gleeson CJ, dissenting).

[75] *Roe*, above n 5, at [201].

[76] See *Cattanach*, above n 6, at [261] (Hayne J, dissenting).

[77] In *Roe*, Parrett J noted that the distinction between losses incurred before and after a child is born following another's negligence is artificial and illogical. Above n 5, at 205. Similarly, in *Bevilacqua*, the court noted that it is artificial to attempt to separate pregnancy and childbirth from the human life created as a result of these events and the subsequent need to care for the child. Above n 5, at [162]-[164]. See also *McFarlane*, above n 4, at 114, where Lord Millett notes that the claim in respect of pain and distress in relation to pregnancy and childbirth is no different from the costs of raising the unplanned child. However, his solution was to deny both types of claims because the same reasoning underlies these heads of damages.

[78] Traditional Western liberal thought is premised on a dualistic view of the world—the public/private distinction. See J Locke, *Two Treatises of Government* (New York, New American Library, 1965) (ed P Laslett); JB Elshtain, *Public Man, Private Woman: Women in Social and Political Thought* (New Jersey, Princeton University Press, 1981) 116-27.

[79] JC Williams and V Zelizer, 'To Commodify or Not to Commodify: That is *Not* the Question' in MM Ertman and JC Williams (eds), *Rethinking Commodification: Cases and Readings in Law and Culture* (New York, New York University Press, 2005) 364.

and home is the appropriate domain for values that are central to humanity and human dignity, such as morality, spiritual values, emotions, etc. Biological reproduction, child care and family relations are also perceived to be within the private sphere. These interests, values and relations risk being corrupted and destroyed when they are brought within the commercial sphere.[80]

Denial of child-rearing costs partly stems from the perception that the assessment of damages in this context entails intermingling dichotomous spheres—intimacy and sentiments of family life on the one hand, and the market on the other. This is a distorted view of human and social relations, as no relationship or activity can be neatly packaged into one particular sphere. As Williams and Zelizer note, 'people participate in dense networks of social relations that intertwine the intimate and economic dimensions of life'.[81] Thus, social reality contradicts the supposed dichotomy between emotional or family life and the market.[82] Feminists have challenged the

---

[80]   See N Taub and E Schneider, 'Women's Subordination and the Role of Law' in D Kairys (ed), *The Politics of Law: A Progressive Critique* (New York, Pantheon Books, 1990) 151, 155; F Olsen, 'The Family and the Market: A Study of Ideology and Legal Reform' (1983) 96 *Harvard Law Review* 1497, 1499; K O' Donovan, *Sexual Divisions in Law* (London, Weidenfield and Nicolson, 1985) 5, 109; C Dalton, 'An Essay in the Deconstruction of Contract Doctrine' (1985) 94 *Yale Law Journal* 997, 1113. See also *Balfour v Balfour* [1919] 2 KB 571 (CA).

[81]   Williams and Zelizer, above n 78, at 366.

[82]   Contract law was premised on classical liberal philosophy, which relied on a dichotomy between private and public, reason and passion, knowledge and desire. See JS Mill, *On Liberty* (London, Dent, 1910) 9; R Unger, *Knowledge and Politics* (New York, Free Press, 1975); S Lukes, *Individualism* (Oxford, Blackwell, 1973) 62. This led to the perception that the law was not concerned with relationships, emotion and morality. *Addis v Gramophone Co Ltd* [1909] AC 488 (HL) is the leading case confirming that contract law was not concerned with compensation for emotional or intangible injuries. See also *Hamlin v Great Northern Railway Co* (1856) 1 H & N 408, 156 ER 1261 (Ex) and *Hobbs v London & Southwestern Railway Co* (1875) LR 10 QB 111. However, in recent years, courts have recognised non-pecuniary losses flowing from breach of contract in several cases. See, for example, *Farley v Skinner* [2002] 2 AC 732 (HL); *Fidler v Sun Life Co. of Canada* [2006] 2 SCR 3; *Newell v Canadian Pacific Airlines Ltd* (1977) 14 OR (2d) 752 (Co Ct); *Jarvis v Swan Tours Ltd* [1973] 1 QB 233 (CA); *Weinberg et al v Connors* (1994) 21 OR (3d) 62 (Gen Div); *Mason v Westside Cemeteries Ltd* (1996) 135 DLR (4th) 361 (Ont Gen Div). Commentators argue that morality has always been part of contracts in the commercial context. See JA Manwaring, 'Unconscionability: Contested Values, Competing Theories and Choice of Rule in Contract Law' (1993) 25 *Ottawa Law Review* 235; M Romanin, 'Good Faith and Contracts: Principles, Doctrines, and Other Considerations' (2002) *The Law Society of Upper Canada Special Lectures 2002 Real Property Law.* In *LAC Minerals Ltd v International Corona Resources Ltd* (1989) 61 DLR (4th) 14 (SCC) 44, La Forest J stated bluntly that '[i]t is simply not the case that business and accepted morality are mutually exclusive domains'. In addition, he stressed that this concept was not new. 'Texts from as early as 1903 refer to the obligation of "good faith by partners in their dealings with each other extend[ing] to negotiations culminating in the partnership, although in advance of its actual creation" (Lindley, *A Treatise on the American Law Relating to Mines and Mineral Lands* (reprint of 2nd edn 1983).' Even in purely commercial settings, the reality is that the formation of a contract often initiates a long-term relationship between the contracting parties. See I Macneil, *The New Social Contract* (New Haven, Yale University Press, 1980).

public/private distinction as central to women's oppression, both ideologically and materially. The distinction marginalises issues that uniquely affect women by perceiving them as inappropriate for legal regulation or market rationalisation.

Recovery for the financial and emotional consequences of interference with one's reproductive autonomy does not undermine the notion of human life as priceless. Rather, it serves a limited purpose—valuing the human right that has been interfered with. This is not related to the value of life created as a result of that interference,[83] nor does it diminish the child's membership in the family unit, or for that matter, the value of human life. As Silbaugh notes, it is possible to have multiple understandings or meanings from a single activity.[84] Hence, it is not inconsistent to attempt to compute the financial and non-economic costs of interference with reproductive autonomy, bodily integrity and human dignity, while simultaneously recognising that human life, or specifically the life of the particular child at the centre of the claim, is still priceless.

For example, no one would suggest that a rape victim who subsequently becomes pregnant, gives birth to a child and does not put the child up for adoption cannot complain about the circumstances that gave rise to the conception because she was blessed with the priceless gift of life in the existence of her child. On the contrary, the birth of a child arising from sexual wrongdoing is considered an injury and victims in some jurisdictions may be entitled to recover the cost of maintaining the child under victims of crime legislation.[85] Similarly, the joys of being blessed with a child do not obviate the need or legal requirement of a non-custodial parent to make child support payments even if the custodial parent is seen as enjoying the pleasure of the child's company.[86] Taken to its logical conclusion, the commodification argument would also condemn parents, usually mothers, who demand child support payments, for turning their children into 'gold mines'. On the contrary, the law and society in general condemns 'dead beat dads' for neglecting their children.[87]

---

[83]   See K Silbaugh, 'Commodification and Women's Household Labor' in MM Ertman and JC Williams (eds), *Rethinking Commodification: Cases and Readings in Law and Culture* (New York, New York University Press, 2005) 298.

[84]   *Ibid*, at 297.

[85]   See eg, Crime Victim Assistance Act SBC 2001 c 38, s 4(1)(k); Compensation for Victims of Crime Act RSO 1990 c 24, s 7.1(e); Compensation for Victims of Crime Act RSNS 1989 c 83, s 9.1(e).

[86]   For example, see *Curle v Lowe* [2004] OTC 794 (SCJ).

[87]   Fathers are sometimes threatened with imprisonment for non-payment of child support. Lone parents, usually mothers, are therefore not only supported in their claim for child support payments, but can even be required in some instances to claim them, without the suggestion that they are commodifying their children. In fact, receipt of child support payments is accepted as being essential in preventing child poverty and improving the social and material conditions of children. A federal office has been established to assist and support the provinces and territories in their enforcement activities by searching for debtor addresses,

The commodification argument against recovery is akin to the public's response to the idea of life insurance in the first part of the 19th century, which was one of revulsion at the thought that human life could be valued in monetary terms.[88] Yet today, life insurance is not only widespread but actually encouraged. As well, tort law routinely asks questions about the value of human life, evaluates human suffering (both physical and mental), loss of limbs, and privacy interests.[89] Specifically, non-pecuniary damages for pain and suffering, loss of enjoyment of life and loss of expectation of life,[90] and compensation for wrongful death of close family members are maintainable without having the effect of or being perceived as commodifying human life.

It is worth noting that actions for wrongful death are prohibited at common law for similar reasons as those advanced to deny recovery for involuntary parenthood: the sanctity of life and a supposed aversion of placing monetary value on something as sacred and invaluable as human life underlie the bar to recovery.[91] The common law position has been

---

garnishing designated federal monies such as income tax refunds, and denying passports and specified federal licences to certain support payers who are in persistent arrears. Department of Justice Canada, *Overview of the Canadian System of Support Enforcement*: <http://www.justice.gc.ca/en/ps/sup/enforcement/enforcement_overview.html> (date accessed: 23 August 2006). For similar programs in the provinces and territories, see British Columbia Maintenance Enforcement Program, *What we do/How we do it*: <http://www.fmep.gov.bc.ca/about-the-fmep/what-we-do-how-we-do-it/> (date accessed: 23 August 2006); Ontario Ministry of Community and Social Services News, 'McGuinty government takes action to help families get the support they are entitled' (6 February 2004). See http://ogov.newswire.ca/ontario/GPOE/2004/02/06/c7357.html?lmatch=&lang=_e.html (date accessed: 23 August 2006); Kids Canada, *Child Maintenance Enforcement/Services, Provinces and Territories* <http://www.cprn.com/en/kids/28209.pdf> (date accessed: 23 August 2006).

[88] See eg, VR Zelizer, *Morals and Markets: The Development of Life Insurance in the United States* (New York, Columbia University Press, 1979), as cited in Silbaugh, above n 83, at 298.

[89] Personality and publicity interests are protected in the Canadian common law provinces through the tort of appropriation of personality. The tort is premised on an economic value of the person who alleges appropriation of his or her personality, in particular, that the image of celebrities is a 'commodity' with a market value that can be sold and bought in the market. For a discussion of the tort of appropriation of personality and its theoretical foundations, see RG Howell, 'Publicity Rights in the Common Law Provinces of Canada' (1998) 18 *Loyola of Los Angeles Entertainment Law Journal* 487.

[90] Recovery under this head of damages, in cases of catastrophic injuries, includes compensation for the losses suffered due to the victim's shortened life span. See *McGarry v Canada West Coal Co* (1909) 11 WLR 597 (Alta CA); *Flint v Lovell* [1935] 1 KB 354 (CA). The Law Reform (Miscellaneous Provisions) Act 1934 c 41 (UK), permitted recovery of damages for loss of expectation of life in a survival suit; *Rose v Ford* [1937] AC 826, 58 Ll L Rep 213 (HL) 218 (Lord Atkin), 220 (Lord Russell of Killowen) [cited to Ll L Rep]. *Rose* was followed in Canada, but legislatures in many Canadian jurisdictions have sought to reverse it. See K Cooper-Stephenson, *Personal Injury Damages in Canada*, 2d edn (Toronto, Carswell, 1995) 742.

[91] At common law, surviving family members had no right of action in tort for their own losses resulting from the death of another on the basis that the death of a human being cannot be complained of as an injury—*Baker v Bolton* (1808) 170 ER 1033 (KB); *Monaghan v Horn*

reversed by statute.[92] Today, tort law provides monetary compensation for fatal and personal injuries (including loss of limbs and loss of enjoyment or expectation of life). Wrongful death claims are premised on an understanding that the deceased's life was of value to the claimant or eligible family members, and that value is a legally protected interest.[93] Yet, this has not led society to believe that human life or body parts are worth a certain amount in the market.

These valuations are simply for the purposes of providing remedies for the claimants' loss arising from the wrongful death of a family member, and do not commodify the interests at stake. Similarly, compensating parents for the pecuniary and non-pecuniary costs associated with caring for a child conceived and/or born due to the negligence of a medical professional should not be perceived as involving commodification of the child's life. Rather, recovery entails a recognition of the consequences of the defendant's negligence on the plaintiff's life, costs that the parent had specifically sought the defendant's professional services to avoid.

Arguments against recovery of child maintenance costs are also similar to the resistance to recognising the economic value of women's work in the home, and a corresponding failure to award compensation for loss of homemaking capacity in personal injury claims. At best, loss of homemaking was considered part of non-pecuniary damages.[94] Women are now entitled to compensation for impaired homemaking capacity as part of their pecuniary losses in personal injury claims, standing on the same footing as their claim for impaired earning capacity.[95] There is no indication that this has resulted in the devaluation of women. On the contrary, it has reinforced women's claim that homemaking is productive work and should be valued in the same way as work performed in the labour market. Recognition of the claim is acknowledgment that one may derive satisfaction from something without necessarily compromising its economic value.

(1882) 7 SCR 409; *Pilford v Skog Estate* (1989) 64 DLR (4th) 186 (BCCA). See also WS Holdsworth, 'The Origin of the Rule in *Baker v. Bolton*' (1916) 32 *LQR* 431.

[92] Lord Campbell's Act – An Act for Compensating the Families of Persons Killed by Accidents 1846, as rep. by Fatal Accidents Act 1976 (UK). All Canadian jurisdictions now have fatal injury legislation. See eg: Family Compensation Act RSBC 1996 c 126; Fatal Accident Act RSA 2000 c F-8; Fatal Accidents Act CCSM c F-50; Fatal Accidents Act RSNL 1990 F-6; Fatal Accidents Act RSNWT 1988 c F-3; Family Law Act RSO 1990 c F.3.

[93] See WS Malone, 'The Genesis of Wrongful Death' (1964-65) 17 *Stanford Law Review* 1043, 1044, 1052.

[94] See Graycar and Morgan, above n 41, at 126-31.

[95] See *Fobel v Dean* (1991) 83 DLR (4th) 385 (Sask CA); *McLaren v Schwalbe* (1994) 148 AR 1 (QB); Cooper-Stephenson, above n 90, at 312-22; E Adjin-Tettey, 'Contemporary Approaches to Compensating Female Tort Victims for Incapacity to Work' (2000) 38 *Alberta Law Review* 504, 527-34.

Recognition of the full range of economic and non-economic consequences of involuntary parenthood not only reflects the reality for those affected, but also promotes the human dignity of members of the family unit, including the unplanned child. As Golder notes:

> in a practical sense, the conceptual notion of children's rights (as compelling a denial of child rearing damages) serves only to cheat [some] individual children of much needed money to pay for their food, clothes and future education and to subordinate the economic interests of mothers (who in reality suffer the greatest loss) to the interests of negligent tortfeasors ... for by privileging a nostalgic legal and social ideal of the family, it is real families which suffer.[96]

The commodification argument against recovery privatises the costs involved in caring for one's own children and renders it invisible. The 'pricelessness' of human life justification to deny recovery ignores the practical reality entailed in parenthood, which disproportionately falls on women. Commodification arguments tend to be invoked in response to women's claims for compensation for things traditionally perceived to be invaluable and, hence, expected to be altruistically offered. For instance, society has no difficulty paying for the care of children when provided by non-family members in the market, even though the caregivers may also receive intangible rewards for caring for society's children.[97] Although it is now possible for extended family members to be paid to care for relatives, they receive less than foster care rates, and must often prove financial need in order to be compensated.[98] This reflects fundamental uneasiness in claiming compensation for looking after one's family members. This stems from the perception that care work is something that families, or more appropriately, women, just do or should do. Seen in this light, claims for compensation for interference with reproductive autonomy, including the financial and emotional losses associated with parenting, challenge cultural, albeit gendered, understandings of motherhood or care work.[99]

VII. CONCLUSION

Responses to claims of involuntary parenthood can be seen as part of the broader gendered treatment of issues affecting women's interests in tort law. For instance, although the law now provides redress for sexual

[96] Golder, above n 21, at 56-57.
[97] However, the feminisation of child care influences the low valuation of child care services.
[98] Relatives caring for a child in British Columbia can be reimbursed for their costs pursuant to a kith and kin agreement under the Child, Family and Community Service Act 1996 RSBC c 46, s 8; or through a child in home of a relative (CIHR) under the Employment and Assistance Regulation BC Reg 263/2002, s 6..
[99] See *Roe*, above n 5, at 201.

wrongdoing (victims are overwhelmingly female), the quantum of damages is often low compared to damages in other areas. Part of the difficulty relates to the inability of courts to fully appreciate the seriousness of harm arising from sexual violation. The growing trend of caps on non-economic loss also disproportionately affects women because non-economic losses make up the majority of compensation for highly gendered types of injuries, such as sexual wrongdoing or gynaecological malpractice.[100] The realities of women's lives in their socially constructed role of parenting also continue to influence assessment of damages when their earning capacity has been impaired by another's wrongdoing, usually through negative female contingency deductions.[101]

As MacKinnon notes, women's reproductive role is a major source of their social inequality and subordination.[102] This view is confirmed by social science data that show a net negative effect of reproduction on labour force participation and, hence, women's lifetime earnings. The detrimental impact of reproduction on women's labour force participation appears to be exacerbated by unplanned childbirth.[103]

The importance of personal and reproductive autonomy as well as the physical, emotional and financial consequences of parenthood demands that a plaintiff be entitled to compensation for involuntary parenthood. Given the deeply moral, ideological, ethical and sometimes religious convictions implicated in decisions to terminate pregnancy and/or give a child up for adoption, the law is wise not to require a duty to mitigate in claims of involuntary parenthood.

Concerns over an indeterminate amount of damages for child-rearing costs could be addressed by limiting pecuniary damages to the parent's legal obligations in a parent-child relationship, based on governmental estimates of the average costs of raising a child. In any event, such a limit would be less arbitrary than the current limit to pregnancy and childbirth related costs. The reality is that the birth of a child entails both benefits and burdens. There is no reason that this could not be seen as an issue of collateral benefits. However, there are exceptions to the collateral benefits rule: not all collateral benefits are deductible from damages awards. The charitable gifts exception allows a plaintiff to obtain full compensation without a set-off for gratuitous benefits received due to the injury at issue.[104] Future benefits that parents may derive from the child should also be considered an exception to the collateral source rule. Among other

---

[100]   Finley, above n 34, at 1312.
[101]   See E Adjin-Tettey, 'Replicating and Perpetuating Inequalities in Personal Injury Claims through Female Specific Contingencies' (2004) 49 *McGill Law Journal* 309, 343.
[102]   MacKinnon, above n 72, at 134.
[103]   See LaCroix and Martin, above n 26, at 109-11.
[104]   See *Cunningham v Wheeler* [1994] 1 SCR 359.

reasons, the alleged benefits are in the future, uncertain and, hence, speculative. Also, any benefits that accrue to parents will most likely be intangible, and should not be used to offset the tangible costs of raising the child.[105]

The failure to recognise the full range of effects on women's lives in their role as parents fails to give meaning to their reproductive autonomy and dignity. Ignoring the pragmatic effect on the parent and the child in favour of an abstract, idealised view of human life and family has the effect of denying real-life families solace, and in some cases, given the retrenchment of governmental support and feminisation of poverty, even a life of dignity. Since it is mostly women who are affected by the no-recovery position, failure to recognise the harms entailed in involuntary parenthood constitutes gender-based discrimination because it deprives women of equal protection of the law and subordinates their interests to seemingly utilitarian goals. This confirms the observation that women are always the losers in clashes between the law and women's lives/bodies.[106] The law should not reinforce women's inequality in this way.

---

[105] See *Cattanach*, above n 6, at 167-75 (Kirby J).
[106] *Women's Lives, Men's Laws*, above n 72, at 32-33.

5

Liability for Psychiatric Damage: Searching for a Path between Pragmatism and Principle

MICHAEL A JONES*

I. INTRODUCTION

THE RULES ON the recovery of compensation for negligently inflicted psychiatric harm are widely regarded as some of the silliest and most arbitrary in the law of torts. They draw distinctions between claimants that are almost impossible to justify by reference to other rules applied in the sphere of personal injury claims or by reference to medical understanding of the causal mechanisms of psychiatric harm. Despite their supposedly 'pragmatic' basis, they fail to provide a 'bright line' rule by which practitioners can give clear legal advice to their clients. In *White v Chief Constable of South Yorkshire*, Lord Hoffmann almost despaired of reaching sensible conclusions when he declared that 'the search for principle was called off in *Alcock*'.[1] English law has at least four, and possibly more, categories of victim whose entitlement to compensation depends upon the precise context in which they happen to sustain their psychiatric harm. The practical result is that the law is both too restrictive and too generous in the way it responds to claimants who have sustained psychiatric harm, depending upon the category into which they happen to fall.

How did this situation come about, and is there anything that can be done about it? The courts have a somewhat 'schizophrenic' attitude to liability for psychiatric harm. This is attributable, on the one hand, to genuine concern about the uncertainty surrounding psychiatric diagnoses

* Professor of Common Law, Liverpool Law School. I would like to thank Fiona Beveridge, Paula Case, Tony Dugdale and Keith Stanton for their helpful comments on an earlier draft of this chapter. Any remaining errors are, of course, entirely my responsibility.
[1] [1999] 2 AC 455 (HL) 511 [*White*].

and the causal assumptions adopted by psychiatry—historically, the courts have demonstrated a generally sceptical attitude towards the discipline of psychiatry, a scepticism that to some extent remains significant today.[2] An initial perception that symptoms were easy to fake and would lead to numerous false claims, and subsequently the realisation that psychiatric reactions were much more widespread than had been appreciated, which could lead to numerous genuine claims, has led the courts to adopt a restrictive approach to compensating this type of harm. On the other hand, with greater understanding and acceptance of psychiatric conditions and the recognition that not only can psychiatric harm be seriously disabling but it may not even be possible, scientifically, to separate it from physical harm, the courts have flirted with the idea that this form of loss should be assimilated into the mainstream liability rules for compensating personal injury.

It is arguable that whatever the scientific arguments for treating psychiatric harm as simply a form of physical injury, the courts are right to maintain the Cartesian mind/body dichotomy. Notwithstanding that psychiatric damage can be as disabling as physical injury, it is sensible to treat it as a different type of damage. That is how it is conceived of by lay people, and the common law should pragmatically reflect the understanding of the common man or woman, appropriately informed by expert opinion. Nonetheless, it is possible by pragmatically maintaining that distinction to take a more principled approach to the recovery of compensation for psychiatric harm. This would involve changing the rules applied *both* to cases of 'pure' psychiatric damage (that is, psychiatric harm sustained in the absence of physical injury to the claimant) *and* to cases of psychiatric damage arising from physical injury. The test for liability in respect of psychiatric harm *in both cases* should be foreseeability of psychiatric damage. Fault liability requires foreseeability of harm as a fundamental requirement of attributing *responsibility* for that harm to a *culpable* defendant. This proposition may seem trite, but it is one that is sometimes hidden behind other policy objectives in the realm of compensation for personal injuries. An appropriate application of the test would involve: (1) a recognition that the 'thin skull rule' should not apply to cases of physical injury in order to 'passport' the claimant to recovery of compensation for psychiatric harm; and (2) the arbitrary rules applied to the recovery of pure psychiatric harm being replaced by a foreseeability test. In order to meet the objection that this would involve opening the

---

[2] Though note Professor Wessely's comment that the Law Commission's approach to causation in its Consultation Paper no 137, *Liability for Psychiatric Illness* (1995) implied 'greater confidence about our knowledge of the aetiology of psychiatric disorders than is justified': S Wessely, 'Liability for Psychiatric Illness' (1995) 39 *Journal of Psychosomatic Research* 659, 667.

floodgates, the foreseeability test should be based not on the foresight of medical experts but on the foresight of the reasonable man or woman, as guided by medical evidence and interpreted by the court.

II.   CATEGORIES OF CLAIMANT

In very broad terms, the English law on recovery for psychiatric harm is based on four categories of claimant. First, a distinction is drawn between claimants who suffer physical injury as a result of the defendant's negligence and then develop psychiatric sequelae and claimants who sustain 'pure' psychiatric harm. Second, within claims for 'pure' psychiatric harm, English law divides claims arising from participation in or observation of a single traumatic event from those where the claimant falls outside the traditional 'nervous shock' paradigm of a sudden traumatic event. Finally, for claimants who suffer psychiatric harm arising out of a single traumatic event, there is a further division into so-called 'primary' victims and 'secondary' victims. Some of these categories are fluid. Claimants who might at first sight seem to be simply witnesses of a sudden shocking event causing harm to others, and therefore categorised as 'secondary' victims, may find that the 'nervous shock' paradigm does not apply. They can thus claim the status of being a 'primary' victim, with all the implications that attach to that label in terms of making the duty of care easier to establish, even though, were they within the 'nervous shock' paradigm, they would not satisfy the criteria for being a 'primary' victim.

The Australian and Canadian courts have, sensibly, not been tempted into adopting these artificial categories of claimant in cases of pure psychiatric damage. In Canada the test is simply 'reasonable foresight of nervous shock to the plaintiff',[3] and the manner in which the foresight test is applied allows the courts scope to reject claims from especially sensitive plaintiffs.[4] The Australian courts have explicitly rejected the categorisations developed by the House of Lords in recent years,[5] but have retained

---

[3] *Bechard v Haliburton Estate* (1991) 5 OR (3d) 512 (CA) 518 (Griffiths JA); *Duwyn v Kaprielian* (1978) 22 OR (2d) 736 (CA) 747 [*Duwyn*] (Morden JA): the 'test of liability for nervous shock is the foreseeability of nervous shock'. See also *Rhodes v Canadian National Railway* (1990) 75 DLR (4th) 248 (BCCA).

[4] *Duwyn*, above n 3; *Vanek v Great Atlantic & Pacific Co of Canada* (1999) 48 OR (3d) 228 (CA).

[5] *Tame v New South Wales* (2002) 211 CLR 317 (HCA) [*Tame*]; *Annetts v Australian Stations Pty Ltd* (2002) 211 CLR 317 (HCA) [*Annetts*]; *Gifford v Strang Patrick* (2003) 214 CLR 269 (HCA) [*Gifford*]; *Cubbon v Roads and Traffic Authority of New South Wales* [2004] Aust Torts Reports 81-761 (NSWCA).

sufficient flexibility in a foreseeability test to allow claims by relatives told about the death of a loved one who did not witness the event or its aftermath,[6] which would be denied in English law, but reject those of the abnormally sensitive.[7] Much of what follows, then, focuses on English law, though there would appear to be little difference in courts' reactions to claimants who have suffered physical injury and then develop a psychiatric condition in the different jurisdictions.[8]

A.   Psychiatric Harm Following Physical Injury to the Claimant

Just as claims in respect of economic loss following physical injury to person or property are not regarded as giving rise to conceptual problems for recovery of the financial loss, subject to the rules on causation and remoteness, so also claims for psychiatric harm following physical injury to the claimant are generally treated as non-problematic. If a claimant suffers physical injury and subsequent psychiatric harm, assuming that breach of duty can be established, everything turns on establishing the causal link between the negligence and the damage. So if the claimant's physical injuries result in clinical depression, the defendant is liable for the depression and the foreseeable consequences of the depression.[9] If the claimant develops a personality disorder as a result of the injury, the defendant must compensate for the consequences of that disorder.[10] I will argue, however, that this category of case *is* problematic in so far as the thin skull rule applies to these claims. The effect is that, subject to proof of the causal connection, a claimant who suffers minor, even trivial, physical harm may recover for psychiatric harm that is totally unforeseeable.

---

[6]   As in *Annetts*, above n 5 and *Gifford*, above n 5.

[7]   As in *Tame*, above n 5, where the police made an erroneous recording of the plaintiff's blood alcohol level in a road traffic accident report, but the error was soon spotted and corrected.

[8]   See the decision of the High Court of Australia in *Shorey v PT Ltd (as trustee for McNamara Australia Property Trust)* (2003) 197 ALR 410 (HCA).

[9]   Including the victim's suicide: *Pigney v Pointer's Transport Services Ltd* [1957] 1 WLR 1121 [*Pigney*]; *Corr v IBC Vehicles* [2006] 2 All ER 929 (CA), where the Court of Appeal accepted that the judge had reached the correct conclusion in *Pigney*, though for what would now be regarded as the wrong reasons.

[10]   Including, in *Meah v McCreamer* [1985] 1 All ER 367 (QB) [*Meah*], the consequences of being sent to prison, where brain damage produced a personality change which led the claimant to commit violent attacks on women for which he was subsequently convicted. In *Clunis v Camden & Islington Health Authority* [1998] QB 978 the Court of Appeal expressed some doubt whether the decision of Woolf J in *Meah* was correct.

B. Claims for Pure Psychiatric Harm in the Paradigm 'Nervous Shock' Action[11] Involving Participation in or Observation of a Traumatic Event

These cases have always been regarded as problematic. The starting point was to reject such claims altogether.[12] The first breach in the wall of non-liability emerged in *Dulieu v White* where the claimant succeeded for psychiatric harm sustained as a result of being put in fear for her own safety by the defendant's negligence,[13] and this was extended to 'ricochet' victims in *Hambrook v Stokes Bros*, where the claimant recovered for psychiatric harm as a result of being put in fear for her children's safety by the defendant's negligence.[14] The House of Lords came close to adopting a test for the duty of care based simply on foreseeability of psychiatric harm in *McLoughlin v O'Brian*,[15] but in *Alcock v Chief Constable of the South Yorkshire Police* their Lordships came down firmly in favour of some specific restrictions on claims by ricochet victims, even where the damage was foreseeable.[16] In *Alcock* Lord Oliver drew a distinction between 'primary' victims and 'secondary' victims, a distinction that has created its own body of litigation as claimants have sought to place themselves in the more favourable 'primary' victim category.

(i) Primary Victims

According to Lord Oliver a primary victim is a claimant who was involved, either mediately or immediately, as a participant in the event created by the defendant's negligence. This includes someone who: (1) was actually exposed to the risk of physical injury, even though no physical injury occurred;[17] or (2) reasonably believed himself or herself to be at risk of physical injury;[18] or (3) who, as a result of the defendant's negligence, reasonably believed that he or she had been the cause of injury to someone else. Here the defendant's negligent conduct had foreseeably put the

---

[11] The term 'nervous shock' originally had some medical significance, though its use in clinical medicine has long been abandoned. Lawyers have used the term to refer both to the circumstances in which a potential claim for psychiatric damage arising out of a single event could arise, and the psychiatric harm itself. It has been described as a 'misleading and inaccurate expression': Attia v British Gas [1988] QB 304, 317 (CA) (Bingham LJ).

[12] *Victorian Railway Commissioners v Coultas* (1888) 13 App Cas 222 (PC).

[13] [1901] 2 KB 669 [*Dulieu*].

[14] [1925] 1 KB 141 (CA).

[15] [1983] 1 AC 410 (HL) [*McLoughlin*].

[16] [1992] 1 AC 310 (HL) [*Alcock*].

[17] As in *Dulieu*, above n 13.

[18] The claimant's genuine but unreasonable belief that he or she was at risk of physical injury is not sufficient: *McFarlane v EE Caledonia Ltd* [1994] 2 All ER 1 (CA) and *Hegarty v EE Caledonia Ltd* [1997] 2 Lloyd's Rep 259 (CA) 271.

claimant in the position of being an unwilling participant in the event.[19] In the case of a primary victim foreseeability of the damage was sufficient to establish responsibility, assuming that breach of duty and causation were established.

The position was complicated by the decision of their Lordships in *Page v Smith* where a majority of the House of Lords held that in the case of primary victims the test was whether the defendant could reasonably foresee that his or her conduct would expose the claimant to the risk of personal injury, *whether physical or psychiatric*.[20] If the answer was yes, it was irrelevant that physical injury did not occur or that the psychiatric injury was unforeseeable because the claimant had an 'eggshell personality'. The defendant had to take the victim as found. Mr Page was involved in a minor road traffic accident which resulted in no physical harm to the occupants of the two vehicles but did produce a recrudescence of his myalgic encephalomyelitis from which the claimant had suffered for about 20 years but which was then in remission. The defendant admitted that he had been negligent but argued that the psychiatric injury was unforeseeable and therefore irrecoverable as a head of damage. Their Lordships disagreed.[21] The consequence was that following a relatively trivial accident in which no one suffered any physical injury the defendant's insurers had to compensate Mr Page for, inter alia, his loss of earnings for the rest of his life.[22]

Page made the position of a primary victim particularly favourable in terms of establishing liability. In effect, a primary victim is treated *as if* he had sustained physical injury and is then dealt with on the same basis as a claimant who suffers consequential psychiatric harm, even if the psychiatric harm was entirely unforeseeable. The justification for this was a laudable attempt to have legal principle reflect medical understanding:

> In an age when medical knowledge is expanding fast, and psychiatric knowledge with it, it would not be sensible to commit the law to a distinction between physical and psychiatric injury, which may already seem somewhat artificial, and may soon be altogether outmoded. Nothing will be gained by treating them as different 'kinds' of personal injury, so as to require the application of different tests in law.[23]

---

[19]   See *Dooley v Cammell Laird & Co Ltd* [1951] 1 Lloyd's Rep 271; *Hunter v British Coal Corp* [1998] 2 All ER 97 (CA).

[20]   [1996] AC 155 (HL) [*Page*].

[21]   Though Lords Keith and Jauncey gave trenchant dissenting speeches.

[22]   Although the trial judge discounted the damages award to reflect the probability that the claimant would, even without the collision, have continued to suffer symptoms associated with his condition from time to time: see *Page v Smith (No 2)* [1996] 1 WLR 855 (CA) 857 [*Page (No 2)*].

[23]   *Page*, above n 20, at 188 (Lord Lloyd).

Unfortunately, *Page* does not fit with medical understanding of the causes of psychiatric harm. The mere fact that minor or trivial physical injury has occurred—let alone has not occurred but was simply foreseeable—is not an indicator for developing a psychiatric reaction. Minor contact on the forearm, for example, producing a slight cut and some bruising would not in itself make a psychiatric reaction foreseeable to a doctor. The circumstances in which the injury was sustained might do so, but the injury itself would be incidental.

Page was given a further twist by their Lordships in *White*, where it was held that not only was exposure to the risk of foreseeable physical injury a *sufficient* condition for a claimant to qualify as a 'primary' victim, it was also a *necessary* condition.[24] *White* involved claims by police officers who acted as rescuers or 'quasi-rescuers' of the victims at the Hillsborough stadium disaster, in which 96 football fans died and over 400 were injured. A claim for psychiatric damage based on their employment relationship, given that the Chief Constable was vicariously liable for the negligent decision to permit football fans outside the stadium to crowd into a confined area, was upheld in the Court of Appeal but overturned in the House of Lords. This was because it seemed unjust that the police officers should succeed in their claims for psychiatric damage arising from what they had witnessed when the claims of the relatives of the same dead and injured victims had been rejected by their Lordships in *Alcock*. The effect of *White* is that if the claimant does not fall within the zone of physical danger, either as someone who was actually exposed to the foreseeable risk of physical injury or who reasonably believed that he or she was exposed to such a risk, he or she does not qualify as a primary victim.

(ii)   Secondary Victims

In *Alcock* Lord Oliver characterised a secondary victim as a claimant who was simply a passive and unwilling witness of injury caused to others. Secondary victims have a number of hurdles to jump:

- The circumstances must be such that psychiatric injury was foreseeable in a person of 'customary phlegm'.[25] This rule does not apply to primary victims.
- There must be a relationship between the accident victim and the claimant which involves close ties of love and affection.
- The claimant must either be present at the scene of the accident or come upon its immediate aftermath. This involves physical proximity, which must be close, in both time and space.

---

[24]   Above n 1.
[25]   *Bourhill v Young* [1943] AC 92 (HL) 110 [*Bourhill*].

- The psychiatric injury must have been the product of what the claimant perceived with his or her own unaided senses. There is no action in respect of harm sustained as a result of what the claimant was told by others.
- The manner in which the psychiatric illness was caused must involve a sudden assault on the nervous system—a sudden appreciation by sight or sound of a horrifying event, which violently agitates the mind.[26]

This list of qualifying criteria is likely to be fulfilled quite rarely. It is designed to exclude the ordinary bystander who witnesses a traumatic event,[27] since he or she will not normally have a relationship of love and affection with the person injured or killed by the defendant's negligence, and to exclude loved ones who were not present at the scene of the accident unless they can bring themselves within the concept of the 'immediate aftermath'.[28]

C.   Claims for Pure Psychiatric Harm where the Claimant Falls Outside the 'Nervous Shock' Paradigm of Sudden Traumatic Events

The fourth category of claimant involves an action where there was no physical injury to the claimant, but the circumstances in which the psychiatric harm was sustained do not fall into the 'nervous shock' paradigm of a sudden shocking event. This category is typified by: (1) a relatively gradual onset of the psychiatric condition; and (2) a relationship of some sort between claimant and defendant other than that arising out of the tort itself (that is, the parties tend not to be strangers). The cases include: (a) the liability of an employer for psychiatric harm in respect of occupational stress;[29] (b) the liability of a professional person for foreseeable psychiatric harm to a client arising out of professional negligence;[30] (c) the liability of a prison authority to a prisoner who is known to be at

---

[26]   *Alcock*, above n 16, at 401 (Lord Ackner).

[27]   As in *Bourhill*, above n 25.

[28]   In *McLoughlin*, above n 15, seeing the accident victims at the hospital two hours after the event, but before they had been properly attended to by medical staff, fell within the 'immediate aftermath'. Cf *Alcock*, above n 16, where identifying a victim's body at a mortuary some eight or nine hours after death did not. See also *Jaensch v Coffey* (1984) 155 CLR 549 (HCA) [*Jaensch*].

[29]   *Walker v Northumberland County Council* [1995] 1 All ER 737 (QB) [*Walker*]; *Hatton v Sutherland* [2002] 2 All ER 1 (CA) [*Hatton*]; *Barber v Somerset County Council* [2004] 1 WLR 1089 (HL) [*Barber*]; *Hartman v South Essex Mental Health and Community Care NHS Trust* [2005] ICR 782 (CA) [*Hartman*].

[30]   *Landau v Werner* (1961) 105 SJ 257 (QB), affd (1961) 105 SJ 1008 (CA) (psychiatrist); *McLoughlin v Jones* [2002] 2 WLR 1279 (CA) (lawyer).

risk of developing a psychiatric condition;[31] and (d) mental harm due to distressing knowledge, such as anxiety at the prospect of illness or disability caused by the defendant's negligence,[32] or being informed by a medical professional, wrongly, that one's young child had died,[33] or believing oneself responsible for creating the circumstances in which one's children were sexually abused.[34] In some of these cases the language of primary and secondary victims has surfaced, despite the fact that these labels were formulated to deal with very different circumstances. Employees claiming in respect of occupational stress have been described as primary victims, for example,[35] even though this label adds nothing to the analysis of the employer's obligations—indeed it is potentially confusing since it is clear that in order to be actionable any psychiatric harm to an employee arising from stress must be foreseeable to the defendant employer,[36] whereas primary victims do not necessarily have to demonstrate that the psychiatric harm was foreseeable. In some cases involving the negligent communication of false information the claimant is said to be a primary victim, because there is no other 'victim' of the defendant's negligence,[37] and in others the claimants are said not to be primary victims because to classify them as such would open up the range of potential claims to a wide class of individuals.[38]

[31] *Butchart v Home Office* [2006] 1 WLR 1155 (CA) where the claimant alleged that the defendants knew that he was psychiatrically vulnerable in that he had been in a depressed and unstable condition, but had nonetheless been incarcerated with another remand prisoner who was known to be a suicide risk and who did in fact commit suicide. The Court of Appeal characterised a claimant's action with regard to his own psychiatric harm as a claim in respect of breach of a primary duty of care, so that he or she did not have to satisfy the control mechanisms applied to secondary victims.

[32] *CJD Litigation: Group B Plaintiffs v Medical Research Council* [2000] Lloyd's Rep Med 161 [*CJD Litigation*], in which the claimants developed a psychiatric condition as a result of negligently being exposed to the risk of developing Creutzfeldt-Jakob Disease at some point in the future; *APQ v Commonwealth Serum Laboratories Ltd* [1999] 3 VR 633 (SC). See now, however, *Grieves v FT Everard & Sons* (2006) Times, 31 January where the English Court of Appeal held that a defendant who negligently exposed a claimant to the risk of contracting a disease was not liable for free-standing psychiatric injury (depression) caused by the fear of contracting the disease.

[33] *Allin v City & Hackney Health Authority* [1996] 7 Med LR 167 [*Allin*]; *Farrell v Avon Health Authority* [2001] Lloyd's Rep Med 458 [*Farrell*].

[34] *W v Essex County Council* [2001] 2 AC 592 (HL).

[35] *Hatton*, above n 29; *Barber*, above n 29.

[36] See *Hartman*, above n 29.

[37] *Farrell*, above n 33, at 471 (Bursell J).

[38] *CJD Litigation*, above n 32, at 165 (Morland J). See J O'Sullivan, 'Liability for Fear of the onset of future Medical Conditions' (1999) 15 Professional Negligence 96.

III.   CONSEQUENCES OF THESE CATEGORISATIONS IN RELATION TO PURE PSYCHIATRIC DAMAGE

Psychiatric harm stands out as the one form of personal injury to which special, restrictive rules apply. This is despite a general acknowledgement, even amongst the judiciary, that psychiatric harm can be just as disabling, sometimes more so, than physical injury.[39] The most obvious consequence of the rules is their arbitrary effects as between different claimants sustaining psychiatric harm, let alone as between those claimants sustaining psychiatric harm and those suffering physical injury. A brief selection of some, but by no means all, of those arbitrary effects will serve to illustrate the point.

First, although the majority decision in *Page* was intended to reflect the view that the law should minimise the differences between physical and mental harm,[40] the effect of the decision has been to privilege certain categories of claimant who do not even have to prove that their psychiatric harm was foreseeable. Provided physical harm was foreseeable, even if it did not occur, unforeseeable psychiatric harm may be recovered by a primary victim. On one view, this could mean that all forms of personal injury are to be regarded as the same 'type' of damage, and provided one form was foreseeable the claimant can recover for any other unforeseeable form of personal injury. Indeed, if there is to be no distinction between *physical* injury and *psychiatric* injury, there is little obvious justification for distinguishing between different types of *physical* injury, at least in the case of personal injuries. However, if all forms of personal injury are to be treated on the same basis, the position of secondary victims, who are subject to highly restrictive rules, looks particularly anomalous.

Second, in *White* Lord Goff pointed out the problem arising from two rescuers at a major disaster, both of whom developed a psychiatric reaction as a result of witnessing the scenes of death and injury.[41] If the first was working in a part of the disaster where there was a continuing risk of physical injury (but did not suffer any physical injury) and the second was not, the first would qualify as a primary victim and recover compensation for the psychiatric reaction, but the second would be a secondary victim and would in all likelihood fail to satisfy the requirements for a successful claim. As Professor Trimble has put it, commenting on the law's categorisations, 'Some get splattered with blood, others with money.'[42] The whole

---

[39] See *Bourhill*, above n 25, at 103 (Lord Macmillan); NJ Mullany and PR Handford, *Tort Liability for Psychiatric Damage: the law of 'Nervous Shock'* (Sydney, Law Book Co, 1993) 309.

[40] Above n 20.

[41] Above n 1, at 487.

[42] M Trimble, 'Medicine and the Law: Conflict or Debate' (1995) 39 *Journal of Psychosomatic Research* 671.

question of who qualifies as a primary victim leads to the drawing of distinctions that make the calculation of the number of angels on the head of pin seem like an entirely rational exercise. Thus, if there is no secondary victim, the claimant 'must be' a primary victim.[43] But if the classification of the claimant as a primary victim could theoretically result in a large number of claims by individuals in analogous circumstances, then it may be better not to classify the claimant at all.[44] At one time rescuers probably fell into the category of primary victim, reflecting the traditionally generous view that the common law takes of rescuers injured in the course of their rescue attempt. However, this view was overturned by the House of Lords in *White* because to some it seemed unjust to compensate a rescuer while not compensating secondary victims for their psychiatric illness arising out of the death of a loved one. Moreover, the categories of primary and secondary victim can simply break down under close scrutiny. For example in *W v Essex County Council* the House of Lords held that it was at least arguable that the parents of children abused by a boy placed with them as a foster child by the local authority might establish that they were primary victims, on the basis that they had suffered psychiatric damage as a consequence of feeling that they were indirectly responsible for their children's sexual abuse, having brought the boy into their home as a result of the defendants' failure to warn them about his previous history of abuse.[45] Clearly the parents themselves were not at risk of any physical harm or in the 'zone of danger' and though they could satisfy some of the criteria for a secondary victim, they had not witnessed the events with their own unaided senses.

Third, as is well-known, the most arbitrary effects of the categorisations are in relation to secondary victims:

- The requirement that the claimant be proximate in time and space to the event causing injury to a loved one or to the immediate aftermath of the event gives rise to fine distinctions between relatives who were at or close to the scene, and those who were a little further away and could not get to the hospital in time.[46] Should liability depend upon a race with the ambulance?[47]

---

[43] *Farrell*, above n 33, at 471.

[44] *CJD Litigation*, above n 32, at 165.

[45] Above n 34.

[46] Compare *McLoughlin*, above n 15, where the claimant got to the hospital within two hours of the accident to her family, with the relatives in *Alcock*, above n 16, who arrived at the mortuary some eight or nine hours after death. Even if the identification could be described as part of the 'aftermath', it could not be described as part of the 'immediate aftermath', 405 (Lord Ackner). H Teff, 'Liability for Psychiatric Illness after Hillsborough' (1992) 12 *OJLS* 440, 446 comments that 'Invidious distinctions are inevitable when the "immediate" aftermath is treated in isolation, as a crude notion of temporal proximity.'

[47] See the comment by Brennan J in *Jaensch*, above n 28, at 439.

- The requirement that a claimant's psychiatric illness be the product of sudden shock—a sudden appreciation by sight or sound of a horrifying event, which violently agitates the mind—excludes claims where the onset of symptoms is gradual. This leads to the bizarre proposition that psychiatric harm resulting from watching one's child slowly die is excluded from compensation, whereas witnessing his or her sudden demise fits the bill for compensation.[48] It leads to the drawing of capricious distinctions.[49] A single event can be sudden, but drawn out over a period of more than 24 hours.[50] Moreover, the approach to the claimant who has a gradual onset of psychiatric problems depends on the causal context. If it is a gradual reaction to a specific traumatic event, the claim is excluded, yet if it is a gradual reaction to a series of events it may be allowed, for example in the context of the employer-employee relationship where the claim is in respect of occupational stress.[51]

- Secondary victims cannot recover for being informed about the event, but in some situations which do not fit the conventional 'nervous shock' paradigm a primary victim can recover for what he or she is told. This can produce a situation in which a mother told about the death of her child who has been killed by the negligence of the defendant cannot recover for her resulting psychiatric harm, whereas a

---

[48] See *Sion v Hampstead Health Authority* [1994] 5 Med LR 170 where a father watched his son deteriorate in hospital over a period of 14 days. This was held not to be a sudden shocking event, but an 'expected' event. Commenting on the very different case of *King v Phillips* [1953] 1 QB 429 (CA) [*King*], Professor Goodhart in 'Emotional Shock and the Unimaginative Taxicab Driver' (1953) 69 *LQR* 347, 352-53 observed that 'it is not immediately obvious why a mother should receive less of a shock when she sees her child being slowly run over than when it is done rapidly. The length of time consumed would seem at first sight to increase rather than to lessen the effect of such a shock.'

[49] And for this reason it has been widely criticised. See H Teff, 'The Requirement of "Sudden Shock" in Liability for Negligently Inflicted Psychiatric Damage' (1996) 4 *The Tort Law Review* 44 for cogent criticism of the 'sudden shock' requirement. The English Law Commission recommended that the 'sudden shock' requirement should be removed for both primary and secondary victims: *Liability for Psychiatric Illness*, Law Com No 249 (1998) [5.33].

[50] *Walters v North Glamorgan NHS Trust* [2003] Lloyd's Rep Med 49 (CA).

[51] Though such claimants are now categorised as primary victims. The employment relationship is not per se the basis of the employer's potential liability, since the House of Lords held in *White*, above n 1, that where the employer's negligence produces a single traumatic event employees who suffer a psychiatric reaction must satisfy the secondary victim criteria. This produces the result that an employer's general duty to take reasonable care to protect the health and safety of employees, although extending to their psychiatric health: *Hatton*, above n 29, will more readily provide a remedy where the employee has developed a psychiatric condition over a period of time than when the employee's psychiatric state is a response to a sudden, traumatic event, which is almost the reverse of the situation where there is no employment relationship.

mother negligently informed that her child has died, when it has not, can recover for the resulting psychiatric harm.[52]

IV.   PSYCHIATRIC HARM FOLLOWING PHYSICAL INJURY TO THE CLAIMANT

Claims involving psychiatric harm following physical injury to the claimant can also be arbitrary in their consequences. This is a result of the way in which the courts apply the 'thin skull rule' to claims involving psychiatric harm and a causation test that makes it very difficult for expert witnesses to conclude that there was no causal connection, given modern understanding of the aetiology of many psychiatric conditions.

A.   The Thin Skull Rule

The basic principle is that a defendant must take the claimant as found, so that if injury to the claimant is more extensive than might have been foreseen due to some inherent weakness or predisposition in the claimant the defendant remains responsible. The rule applies, for example, to a fragile skull,[53] a weak heart,[54] a weak back,[55] haemophilia,[56] and even an 'eggshell personality'.[57] There is a strong element of policy involved in the thin skull rule. As Professor Fleming put it, 'Human bodies are too fragile and life too precarious to permit a defendant nicely to calculate how much injury he might inflict.'[58] There is, however, a countervailing policy judgment to be made which is linked to the whole basis of fault liability. This is that fault liability looks to a defendant's *culpability* as the reason for concluding that the defendant *ought* to be held responsible and therefore *ought* to pay compensation for the claimant's harm. Culpability involves foresight of harm, and, it is argued, the defendant's foresight should relate to the harm that the claimant has actually suffered, not merely foresight of *any* damage that might have been caused by the defendant's conduct. As Viscount Simonds put it in *The Wagon Mound*:

> It is not the act but the consequences on which tortious liability is founded. Just as . . . there is no such thing as negligence in the air, so there is no such thing as

[52]   *Allin*, above n 33; *Farrell*, above n 33. The distinction does not apply in Australia, given the rulings of the High Court in *Annetts*, above n 5 and *Gifford*, above n 5.

[53]   *Owens v Liverpool Corporation* [1939] 1 KB 394 (CA) 401.

[54]   *Love v Port of London* [1959] 2 Lloyd's Rep 541 (QB).

[55]   *Athey v Leonati* [1996] 3 SCR 458.

[56]   *Bishop v Arts & Letters Club of Toronto* (1978) 18 OR (2d) 471 (HCJ).

[57]   *Malcolm v Broadhurst* [1970] 3 All ER 508 (QB). *Page*, above n 20, can be taken as the classic example of this principle at work in the context of psychiatric harm.

[58]   JG Fleming, *The Law of Torts*, 9th edn (North Ryde, LBC Information Services, 1998) 235.

liability in the air . . . . [T]he only liability that is in question is the liability for damage by fire. It is vain to isolate the liability from its context and to say that [the defendant] is or is not liable, and then to ask for what damage he is liable. For his liability is in respect of that damage and no other. If, as admittedly it is, [the defendant's] liability (culpability) depends on the reasonable foreseeability of the consequent damage, how is that to be determined except by the foreseeability of the damage which in fact happened—the damage in suit? And, if that damage is unforeseeable so as to displace liability at large, how can the liability be restored so as to make compensation payable?[59]

Since *The Wagon Mound* the rules on remoteness of damage have involved an uneasy compromise between an insistence on foreseeability of the damage that has occurred and a rule that permits the claimant to recover all the direct consequences of the defendant's negligence, under the guise of the thin skull rule.[60] The court must determine precisely what it is that has to be foreseen. The question is usually framed in terms of whether the damage that has occurred was of the *same type* as the damage that was foreseeable: if so the damage is not too remote; if it is of a different type it is unforeseeable. On the other hand, provided that the type or kind of damage could have been foreseen, it does not matter that its extent or the precise manner of its occurrence could not have been foreseen.[61]

There has been no categorical statement as to how one is meant to determine what constitutes a *type* of damage, and certainly no statement that all forms of personal injury constitute a single type of damage so that if personal injury of any kind is foreseeable then any resulting personal injury is recoverable. That view can be inferred from *Page*: if the claimant was exposed to the foreseeable risk of physical harm, he or she can recover for completely unforeseeable psychiatric harm, even though no physical harm has occurred. In *Page* Lord Lloyd was explicit about treating psychiatric harm and physical harm as equivalent forms of damage:

> There is no justification for regarding physical and psychiatric injury as different 'kinds' of injury. Once it is established that the defendant is under a duty of care to avoid causing personal injury to the plaintiff, it matters not whether the injury in fact sustained is physical, psychiatric or both.[62]

This was in contrast to their Lordships' approach just three years earlier in *Alcock* where Lord Ackner stated:

---

[59] *Overseas Tankship (UK) Ltd v Morts Dock and Engineering Co Ltd (The Wagon Mound)* [1961] AC 388 (HL) 425 [*The Wagon Mound*].

[60] The clearest example of the latter element is the decision of Lord Parker CJ in *Smith v Leech Brain & Co Ltd* [1962] 2 QB 405 (QB), where the defendants were liable for causing a burn to the claimant's lip and also held responsible for the claimant's death from cancer when the burn triggered a pre-malignant condition.

[61] *Hughes v Lord Advocate* [1963] AC 837 (HL).

[62] Above n 20, at 190.

It is now generally accepted that an analysis of the reported cases of nervous shock establishes that it is a type of claim in a category of its own. Shock is no longer a variant of physical injury but a separate kind of damage.[63]

Leaving aside for a moment the question of who is right on this issue in the context of 'nervous shock' cases, *Page* was a case concerned with the extent of a defendant's duty of care, not remoteness of damage.[64] It is difficult to think of two more different types of personal injury than physical harm and psychiatric harm.

The policy judgment underpinning Professor Fleming's aphorism is clear and understandable. But in reality it is a principle that rarely has to be invoked in relation to physical injuries. But this is not the case for psychiatric reactions. As Professor Wessely has observed, 'in practice eggshell skulls themselves are few and far between. The same is not true of eggshell personalities.'[65] The courts are dealing daily with cases in which the claimant sustains very minor physical injury but then develops a psychiatric condition which may be totally disabling, due essentially to a constitutional predisposition to psychiatric harm. The injury caused by the defendant's negligence may have triggered the psychiatric condition to which the claimant was predisposed as a result of several factors.[66] It could have been anything that triggered the reaction, but it happened to be a tort. In a system of fault-based liability should the defendant be saddled with the financial consequences of the claimant's unforeseeable psychiatric reaction? Why should the defendant be held responsible (culpable) for a condition that was almost entirely to do with the claimant's make-up or constitution—a combination of the individual's personality and history—and had virtually nothing to do with the defendant's negligence? If the thin skull rule applies, then the defendant must take a claimant's psychological makeup as he or she finds it. But if psychiatric damage and physical injury are discrete forms of damage, should the thin skull rule apply?

Courts at the highest level in both the UK and Australia have held that it should. Provided that a causal connection can be demonstrated between the physical injury and the psychiatric condition, defendants have been held liable in full for the psychiatric consequences, no matter how unforeseeable. For example, in *Shorey v PT Ltd (as trustee for McNamara Australia Property Trust)* the High Court of Australia held that where the

---

[63] Above n 16, at 400. Though, curiously, in a short speech, Lord Ackner agreed with Lord Lloyd in *Page*, above n 20.

[64] In *R v Croydon Health Authority* [1998] PIQR Q26 (CA) 32-33 Kennedy LJ rejected the suggestion that *Page* had removed the distinction between physical injury and psychiatric injury for the purposes of remoteness of damage, but his Lordship did not give any reasons for his view.

[65] Wessely, above n 2, at 667.

[66] The medical literature indicates that the causes of psychiatric conditions are often multifactorial. See the discussion below.

defendant's negligence had resulted in the claimant suffering a fall, the claimant was entitled to recover for the consequences of a conversion disorder which resulted in paraplegia for which there was no organic cause.[67] The physical effects of the fall were probably resolved within about 12 months, but the fall was held to be the cause of 'bizarre symptoms', because it was the trigger or 'sentinel event'. The basis for this was the thin skull rule:

> The principle of law is that a negligent defendant must take its victim as it finds her and must pay damages accordingly. It is not to the point to complain that the injury, in the form of the fall, was trivial in itself and that it would be unfair to burden the [defendants] with the obligation to bear costs consequent upon the fact that the [claimant] was peculiarly susceptible to developing bizarre symptoms inherent in a conversion disorder. If such symptoms were genuine and a consequence of the subject trauma, the apparent disproportion between cause and effect is not an exculpation for the negligent party. It does not render the damage 'unforeseeable' or otherwise outside the scope of the damages that may be recovered.[68]

Thus, the defendant was held responsible for the claimant's bizarre disabling symptoms when there was evidence that she had had serious back problems in the past (for which she had undergone surgery), and that she had significant psychiatric problems arising from feelings of guilt following the death of her husband, for which she felt partly responsible, some time after her fall and subsequent worries about losing her home in a family dispute. Kirby J acknowledged that there were multiple causes of the claimant's conversion disorder, and that the fall simply operated as a 'trigger' event, but criticised the New South Wales Court of Appeal for apparently looking for a 'single cause' of the disability.

Yet maybe one factor which the Court of Appeal considered significant, and which was clearly important for Callinan J's dissent in the High Court, was the timeline of events. The fall occurred in April 1988. Three weeks after the accident the claimant was able to walk, do housework, drive a car and go shopping, all without the aid of a walking stick. Over a period of years she consulted orthopaedic specialists and psychiatrists. She started to use a walking stick. By July 1992 she was using a walking frame and in early 1993 she started to use a wheelchair. There was evidence that she had a complicated or unresolved bereavement. She had failed to give a full and accurate history of significant events to the psychiatric expert witnesses. Still, despite all this and the experts' admission that it can be extremely difficult to determine the aetiology of a conversion disorder, the trial judge and the majority of the High Court accepted that the fall was the 'trigger'.

---

[67]   Above n 8 [*Shorey*].
[68]   *Ibid*, at [44] (Kirby J) (citation omitted).

In *Simmons v British Steel* the claimant sustained an accidental blow to the head at work, which caused swelling, headaches and minor physical symptoms that lasted several weeks.[69] He then suffered an exacerbation of a pre-existing skin condition, psoriasis, and developed personality change resulting in depression. He was unable to return to work. The conditions were genuine but the first change, the psoriasis, had occurred several weeks after the accident. The trial judge found that none of these conditions—the exacerbation of the psoriasis, the personality change and the depression— were caused by the accident. He considered that the exacerbation of the psoriasis had probably occurred as a result of the claimant's anger at his post-accident treatment by his employers (he believed that they should have shown a little more concern) although there was also anger at the fact that the accident had happened. The deterioration in his mental state occurred after the recurrence of the psoriasis. The psychiatric evidence was that the accident could be said to have materially contributed to the claimant's mental state. The House of Lords held that a causal connection was established between the claimant's anger following the accident and his psychiatric reaction,[70] and since he was a 'primary victim' because he had actually sustained physical injury, unlike the claimant in *Page*, it was not necessary to demonstrate that his psychiatric reaction was foreseeable. The defendants had to take their victim as they found him. It was irrelevant whether a psychologically more robust individual would have recovered from the accident.[71]

Such cases are not rare. On the contrary, they are commonplace. A typical example arises when a claimant sustains a minor injury to the back, but goes on to display a great deal of overt pain behaviour on examination. This could include guarding, bracing, grimacing, sighing, exclaiming, collapsing and hyperventilating, together with non-organic and behavioural responses such as low back pain being reported on axial loading and simulated rotation of the spine, tests which are not an organic cause of pain. It could also include widespread non-anatomical tenderness, improvement in lumbar flexion and straight leg raising with distraction, and generalised giving way of multiple muscle groups in the legs.[72] Such

---

[69] [2004] ICR 585 (HL) [*Simmons*].

[70] Lord Hope commented, *ibid*, [26], that 'there were several causes of the pursuer's anger. It was enough that one of them arose from the fault of the defenders. The pursuer did not need to prove that that cause would of itself have been enough to cause the anger which produced the exacerbation. He was entitled to succeed if it made a material contribution to it.' Lord Hope applied *Bonnington Castings Ltd v Wardlaw*, [1956] AC 613 (HL) [*Bonnington*] and *McGhee v National Coal Board* [1973] 1 WLR 1 (HL).

[71] *Ibid*, at [56] (Lord Rodger).

[72] See *McWhinnie v British Coal Corporation* 1993 SLT 467 (Court of Session: Outer House). See also *Burke v Royal Infirmary of Edinburgh NHS Trust* 1999 SLT 539 (Court of Session: Outer House) and *Burns v Harper Collins Ltd* 1997 SLT 607 (Court of Session: Outer House) for further examples.

behaviour may be characterised by an expert witness for the claimant as an entirely genuine and unconscious 'abnormal illness behaviour', whereas an expert for the defendant will typically conclude that the claimant is grossly exaggerating these symptoms. The trial judge then has to resolve this conflict in the evidence. So commonplace is this type of case that they are scarcely considered to give rise to a significant legal issue, other than the evidential problems of trying to assess whether the claimant's condition is a genuine psychiatric illness or a deliberate exaggeration of the extent of the injuries or even malingering.[73]

There are, of course, many occasions when granting compensation for psychiatric harm following physical injury is entirely appropriate, the most common probably being a claimant's depression arising from a permanent disability. The problem stems from those cases where the claimant sustains minor, often trivial, physical injury, which resolves quite quickly, but then develops what most ordinary individuals would consider to be an entirely unforeseeable psychiatric condition. The concept of fault liability, responsibility for harm based on the defendant's culpability, struggles to justify compensating such claimants. In the words of Viscount Simonds, 'If... [the defendant's] liability (culpability) depends on the reasonable foreseeability of the consequent damage, how is that to be determined except by the foreseeability of the damage which in fact happened—the damage in suit?'[74]

V.   THE MEDICAL CONTEXT

The traditional explanation, which carries much force, for how the English common law got itself into such an unprincipled position in relation to claims for pure psychiatric harm[75] is that the judges have sought to avoid opening the floodgates, particularly where it is alleged that the harm has resulted from injury to others. Indeed, the Law Commission considered that the floodgates argument still justified some restrictions on liability for psychiatric harm beyond a simple foreseeability test.[76] To some extent these concerns are intertwined with competing perceptions about the nature of psychiatry and psychiatric illness in general. Psychiatry and

---

[73] For a fascinating case which illustrates the blurred edges between genuine psychiatric conditions (such as total body pain or somatisation disorder), exaggeration, and malingering following minor physical injury see *Bridges (also known as Giblett) v P & NE Murray Ltd* (1999) Times, 25 May (CA), discussed in MA Jones, 'Law, lies and videotape: malingering as a legal phenomenon' in PW Halligan, C Bass and D Oakley (eds), *Malingering and Illness Deception* (New York, Oxford University Press, 2003) 218-19.

[74] *The Wagon Mound*, above n 59, at 425.

[75] 'No one can pretend that the existing law, which your Lordships have to accept, is founded upon principle': Lord Hoffmann in *White*, above n 1, at 511.

[76] Law Commission, above n 49, at [6.8].

psychiatric diagnoses can be surrounded by uncertainty, subject to dispute even within psychiatry, stigmatising for the patient, and poorly understood by the general public. They can also often involve normative judgments.[77] For all these reasons they can be controversial. As Lord Bridge commented in *McLoughlin*, 'earlier generations of judges have regarded psychiatry and psychiatrists with suspicion, if not hostility'.[78] In fairness, the last quarter of the 20th century saw a greater willingness by the judiciary to engage with psychiatry as a discipline,[79] and there is a wider recognition that psychiatric harm can be seriously disabling. Yet some of the courts' language and categorisations appear to treat psychiatric harm as less deserving of our attention in terms of compensation; as 'secondary' to physical injury. That ambivalence can also be seen in the courts' reaction to what it means to suffer psychiatric injury. In *Page*, for example, Lord Lloyd acknowledged that it may not even be possible, scientifically, to separate psychiatric harm from physical harm.[80]

The English Law Commission suggested that 'any discussion of the possible future development of the law in this area should only be undertaken in the light of current medical knowledge'.[81] Although it might seem that any attempt to have the law reflect medical understanding is to be commended, there are potential pitfalls in this process. Lawyers rely heavily on the classifications of psychiatrists in identifying psychiatric conditions, particularly those contained in the American Psychiatric Association's *Diagnostic and Statistical Manual of Mental Disorders* and the World Health Organisation's *International Classification of Mental and Behavioural Disorders*—known as 'DSM-IV' and 'ICD 10' respectively. The Law Commission report was no exception. One problem was that, initially at least, the Law Commission concentrated on post-traumatic stress disorder (PTSD). Thus, as Professor Simon Wessely, a distinguished psychiatrist and incidentally an expert witness for the claimant in *Page*, observed, nearly all of the psychiatric research literature quoted by the Law Commission in its consultation paper concerned PTSD.[82] Although he acknowledges that the Commission was aware of some of the problems with the term—'more so than some psychiatrists who use the

---

[77] See Wessely, above n 2; Trimble, above n 42, at 672.

[78] Above n 15, at 433.

[79] In *Mount Isa Mines Ltd v Pusey* (1970) 125 CLR 383 (HCA) 395 [*Mount Isa Mines*] Windeyer J famously said that in 'nervous shock' cases, he could observe 'Law, marching with medicine, but in the rear and limping a little.'

[80] *Page*, above n 20, at 188. See also the comments of Lord Browne-Wilkinson at 182-83.

[81] Law Commission, above n 49, at [3.1].

[82] Wessely, above n 2. The final report of the Law Commission made some effort to address this point and acknowledged that it was preferable not to concentrate exclusively on PTSD: [3.3]. Moreover, the medical evidence was that PTSD was not necessarily the most prevalent diagnosis following trauma, and PTSD has a high level of comorbidity.

diagnosis'[83]—the report sometimes gave 'too high a credence to psychiatric nosology and classification, and too little attention to the ambiguity of psychiatric diagnosis'.[84]

PTSD was a diagnosis 'created' by a section of the American mental health community in response to the experience of veterans after the Vietnam War.[85] DSM and ICD assume that the diagnoses they contain exist as independent entities in the world, a condition that a patient can somehow acquire independently of the diagnostic category. But 'this may not accurately reflect how diagnoses are created in psychiatry, nor the value judgments involved'.[86] PTSD was not a diagnostic category in DSM-II, and first made an appearance in DSM-III in 1980. DSM-III-R required that for a diagnosis of PTSD the 'stressor' be 'a psychologically traumatic event that is generally outside the range of usual human experience'.[87] This was dropped for DSM-IV, with the consequence that the diagnosis of PTSD has 'come to be associated with a growing list of relatively commonplace events'.[88]

It might be said that the point here for the lawyer is simply to be cautious about using psychiatric diagnoses, and allow for the inherent uncertainty of the patient's diagnosis. It is of wider significance, however, than simply casting a critical eye over any given psychiatric report. The very categories of psychiatric disorder are themselves fluid. At its most general the process of categorisation involves identifying a set of symptoms and attaching a label to that set, which then constitutes a diagnostic category or psychiatric condition. That, in essence, is the model of DSM-IV. The label, or category, is then often regarded as having explanatory power. So a patient who displays the symptoms of schizophrenia, say, has those symptoms *because* he is schizophrenic. By the same token, a patient suffering from symptoms of PTSD is regarded as having the

---

[83]   Wessely, above n 2, at 660.

[84]   Wessely, above n 2, at 661. Even the distinction between mere 'mental distress' and a 'recognisable psychiatric condition', which is crucial for what counts as compensable damage, is not clear: Law Commission, above n 49, at [3.27], referring to the Introduction to DSM-IV where it is said that 'it must be admitted that no definition adequately specifies precise boundaries for the concept of "mental disorder."' Thus, classifications 'remain arbitrary with an overlap between categories and without clear justifications for distinctions between normality and mental disorder': R Mayou, 'Psychological, Quality of Life and Legal Consequences of Road Traffic Accident Injury' [1995] *Journal of Personal Injury Law* 277, 280, cited in Law Commission, above n 49, at [3.27].

[85]   Wessely, above n 2, at 661-62; D Summerfield, 'The invention of post-traumatic stress disorder and the social usefulness of a psychiatric category' (2001) 322 *British Medical Journal* 95.

[86]   Wessely, above n 2, at 662.

[87]   Law Commission, above n 49, at [3.9], note 29.

[88]   Summerfield, above n 85, at 96.

symptoms *because* he was exposed to a traumatic event.[89] But the symptoms that count and the psychiatric categories themselves often change over a period of time, suggesting that we are not dealing with fixed phenomena. This is unlike most physical conditions; a broken leg is a broken leg is a broken leg, even if the technical means of diagnosing the fracture and its subsequent treatment may change over time with improved knowledge. DSM IV-TR (2000) lists 395 psychiatric conditions, although some are attributable to different degrees of severity for a single condition. There were only 106 conditions in DSM-I in 1952.[90] It is a truism in medicine, but poorly recognised by lawyers, that psychiatry is a culturally determined practice and there are undoubtedly fashions in diagnosis. Thus there is evidence that as psychiatric criteria for diagnosis change, patients adapt their descriptions of symptoms in order to fit the criteria.[91] It would be naïve to think that changing fashions in psychiatric diagnosis have no effect on popular imagination or the inclination to litigate. The example of the Australian epidemic of repetitive strain injury in the 1980s is well-documented.[92] PTSD could be regarded as another example of that process, and occupational stress claims have seen a significant increase in frequency in the UK since the first reported successful claim.[93] These concerns are not simply the reaction of a sceptical lawyer to psychiatric diagnoses. Some psychiatric diagnoses, including PTSD,[94] remain highly controversial within the medical profession.[95]

---

[89] But as Wessely observed, above n 2, at 661, epidemiological studies have found that PTSD is associated with a history of childhood behavioural problems, parental divorce, physical abuse, current unemployment, and even a genetic predisposition. Some patients have all the features of PTSD without any exposure to trauma.

[90] D Double, 'The limits of psychiatry' (2002) 324 *British Medical Journal* 900, 902.

[91] 'The constructs of "psychology" or "mental health" are social products. Collectively held beliefs about particular negative experiences are not just potent influences but carry an element of self fulfilling prophecy; individuals will largely organise what they feel, say, do and expect to fit prevailing expectations and categories': Summerfield, above n 85, at 96.

[92] W Hall and L Morrow, '"Repetition Strain Injury": An Australian Epidemic of Upper Limb Pain' (1988) 27 *Social Science and Medicine* 645; P Brooks, 'Repetitive Strain Injury' (1993) 307 *British Medical Journal* 1298. An epidemic of RSI in Australia has been attributed to the interaction of an ill-defined syndrome, conflicting medical opinions, alarmist media publicity and a compensation system that was too easy to access. When the scope of compensation was reduced, the episode ended: Wessely, above n 2, at 665.

[93] *Walker*, above n 29.

[94] 'In Western societies the conflation of distress with "trauma" increasingly has a naturalistic feel; it has become part of everyday descriptions of life's vicissitudes. The profile of post-traumatic stress disorder has risen spectacularly, and it has become the means by which people seek victim status—and its associated moral high ground—in pursuit of recognition and compensation': Summerfield, above n 85, at 96.

[95] The classic example is myalgic encephalomyelitis (ME), also known as chronic fatigue syndrome, and at one time popularly described as the 'yuppie flu'. There is considerable dispute as to whether the condition even exists, although it is generally accepted that individuals diagnosed with the condition do not have inflammation of the brain (encephalomyelitis).

The English Law Commission noted that there was an emphasis in negligence claims on PTSD, rather than other forms of psychiatric harm, which may stem from the courts' requirement that a claimant prove he or she is suffering from a shock-induced, medically recognised, psychiatric condition. The definition of PTSD includes a causal relationship between the claimant's psychiatric condition and a traumatic 'stressor', and therefore causation is virtually built into the diagnosis. It is unsurprising, then, that claimants' lawyers look for a diagnosis of PTSD. Indeed, PTSD is the only diagnostic category in DSM-IV to contain an attribution of causation, either because there is uncertainty about the causal process for many psychiatric conditions or because there is explicit recognition that causes are commonly multifactorial.[96] On the other hand, many people do not develop PTSD in response to even a very serious traumatic event.[97] The medical uncertainty of causal attribution is rendered irrelevant, however, by the application of a legal principle designed to overcome claimants' problems in establishing causation in the very different context of industrial disease.

VI.   CAUSATION

DSM-IV was not designed for lawyers, who nonetheless look to it for guidance on the identification of harm—what counts as 'psychiatric damage'—and an elucidation of causation for the purpose of attributing legal responsibility. But the medical evidence is that even PTSD, which apparently builds in the causation requirement to the diagnosis (*post-traumatic*), is recognised as having multifactorial causes. The same traumatic event will have widely different psychiatric consequences for different people depending on their personal history, their individual circumstances, subsequent events, and their psychological make-up.

But rules taken from the different context of industrial disease claims tell us that we do not have to identify a single, or even a substantial, cause of the claimant's damage. The claimant merely has to demonstrate that the defendant's negligence was a material contribution to the damage, and

---

[96] 'The entire canon of diagnostic categories in DSM-IV is phenomenological and descriptive, bar post-traumatic stress disorder. Aetiology is not included in definitions because it is invariably multifactorial. Only post-traumatic stress disorder supposes a single cause... What makes the disorder preferred to other potential diagnoses is the term "post-traumatic" in its name, which seems to "prove" a direct aetiological link between the present and an index event in the past that excludes other factors. This is scientifically and clinically dubious. Studies of those exposed to a range of manmade and natural events have consistently found that factors before the event account for more of the variance in symptoms of the disorder than do characteristics of the event': Summerfield, above n 85, at 97.

[97] Law Commission, above n 49, at [3.7].

anything that exceeds a *de minimis* contribution will count.[98] This is hardly an onerous test in the context of psychiatric harm. When the scientific evidence is that many psychiatric conditions, including PTSD, have multifactorial causes, it is difficult for an expert witness to rule out one potential cause (the accident) as having *no* effect, even if there are numerous other factors predisposing the claimant to the psychiatric reaction. Mr Page had suffered, on and off, from his myalgic encephalo-myelitis for 20 years before the accident involving Mr Smith, the most recent episode occurring only four months prior to the accident, yet the accident was still considered to have contributed to the condition. In theory, if psychiatric symptoms are attributable to several different causes, of which the tort is merely one, then it would be logical to attempt to apportion liability accordingly.[99] In practice, however, it seems that this has rarely been done since the principle that the claimant establishes causation if it is proved that the defendant's negligence has materially contributed to the damage has been understood to mean that the claimant succeeds in full. This was the view expressed in *Simmons*[100] and *Shorey*,[101] for example, though the Court of Appeal[102] and more recently the House of Lords now appear to be more willing to apportion responsibility in relation to claims for industrial disease.[103]

VII.   HOW SHOULD LAWYERS RESPOND TO CLAIMS INVOLVING PSYCHIATRIC HARM?

There have, broadly, been two responses to the incoherence represented by the present state of the law on psychiatric harm. The first is to suggest that liability for pure psychiatric harm should be abolished altogether.[104] The second is to argue that the test for liability in respect of psychiatric damage should be foreseeability of psychiatric injury.[105] The English Law Commission considered, but rejected, the first option. It did not favour removal of all controls, but did seek to widen the scope of recovery by secondary victims by removing the need for them to be present at the scene of the

---

[98]   *Bonnington*, above n 70. This test has been applied to psychiatric conditions: see *Page (No 2)*, above n 22. See also *Vernon v Bosley (No 1)* [1997] 1 All ER 577 (CA).

[99]   *Hatton*, above n 29, at [41] (Hale LJ).

[100]   Above n 69.

[101]   Above n 8.

[102]   *Holtby v Brigham & Cowan (Hull) Ltd* [2000] 3 All ER 421 (CA).

[103]   *Barker v Corus (UK) plc* [2006] 2 WLR 1027 (HL). In any event, the trial judge in *Page* had discounted the damages award to reflect the possibility that Mr Page would have had a recurrence of his psychiatric condition in the future.

[104]   See J Stapleton, 'In Restraint of Tort' in P Birks (ed), *Frontiers of Liability* (New York, Oxford University Press, 1994).

[105]   Mullany and Handford, above n 39.

event or its aftermath and abolishing the requirement for a sudden shocking event. These changes would bring English law broadly into line with Australian law.

Fifty years ago Denning LJ was able to assert confidently that 'the test of liability for shock is foreseeability of injury by shock',[106] a dictum approved by the Privy Council in *The Wagon Mound*.[107] Professor Goodhart agreed that 'foreseeability of physical injury to the plaintiff ought to be irrelevant in cases of emotional shock'.[108] But in *Page* Lord Lloyd considered that Denning LJ's dictum was wrong, because it was 'both too wide and too narrow'.[109] It was too wide where the claimant was a secondary victim, but too narrow where the claimant was a primary victim. Of course, as a description of the current state of English law, Denning LJ's dictum clearly is wrong. However, that does not address the more fundamental question of whether the principle underlying it was correct.

Apart from the floodgates argument, the other objection to a foreseeability test is the uncertainty of its application. As Denning LJ recognised in *King v Phillips*, much rests on the powers of observation of a hypothetical 'reasonable man' and the scope of his or her imagination: 'One judge may credit him with more foresight than another. One judge may think that he should have foreseen the shock. Another may not.'[110] But this problem is not unique to claims involving psychiatric damage. It is inherent in all claims for negligence where reasonable foresight plays such a significant role. It is not suggested that for that reason we should adopt arbitrary rules to curb potential claims, on the basis that judges cannot assess the foresight of the reasonable person. Whilst recognising the importance of a medical perspective in cases involving psychiatric harm, there must also be some scope for the exercise of common sense judgments about what falls within the scope of a defendant's obligations, and so about what is and what is not culpable.[111]

Thus, much would depend upon how a foreseeability test was applied in practice, although neither the Canadian courts nor the Australian courts seem to have much difficulty in applying the test and reaching, on the

---

[106] *King*, above n 48, at 441.

[107] *The Wagon Mound*, above n 59, at 426. See also *Mount Isa Mines*, above n 79, at 402 where Windeyer J observed: 'We have at least one "fixed and definite line." Liability for nervous shock depends on foreseeability of nervous shock. That, not some other form of harm, must have been a foreseeable result of the conduct complained of. The particular pathological condition which the shock produced need not have been foreseeable. It is enough that it is a "recognisable psychiatric illness."'

[108] Goodhart, above n 48, at 352.

[109] Above n 20, at 193.

[110] Above n 48, at 441.

[111] See, eg, the speech of Lord Jauncey in *Page*, above n 20, at 178.

whole, sensible conclusions. The question of what is foreseeable is normally assessed ex post facto, on the basis of what a hypothetical reasonable person would say it was proper to foresee.[112] The judgment as to what is foreseeable is a matter for the court, not expert psychiatrists, but this should be done on the basis of 'informed judicial opinion'.[113] But—and this is an important caveat—the judges need to be much more aware of the controversies about possible psychiatric diagnoses not just within medicine (it is relatively easy to find an orthopaedic surgeon to disagree with a psychiatrist) but within psychiatry itself. DSM-IV is a *diagnostic* manual intended for therapeutic and research purposes. The psychiatric conditions described in it are invariably provisional and fluid—the symptoms and criteria for a specific diagnosis can change over quite short time periods.[114] Moreover, psychiatric thinking about causal relationships does not easily map onto legal concepts of causation.

A test based on foreseeability of psychiatric harm would provide a more principled approach, and at the same time it would both expand the range of potential claimants and reduce the range of potential claimants. It would expand the range of potential claimants by removing the artificial barriers to recovery applied to secondary victims. It would narrow the range of potential claimants by requiring primary victims *and* claimants who sustain physical injury to demonstrate that psychiatric harm was foreseeable in the circumstances. In other words, *all* claimants should be required to show the 'customary phlegm', even where they had sustained physical injury, thus excluding from compensation the unforeseeable psychiatric reactions of claimants who currently benefit from an extremely relaxed application of the thin skull rule. The pragmatism involved in this solution would be to ignore the scientific possibility that psychiatric harm is merely a manifestation of physical harm, and to treat physical and psychiatric harm as entirely separate heads of damage. The argument that psychiatric harm is simply a form of physical harm may have some basis in science. Drugs can alter physical states in the brain, which can alter mental states. There is a sense in which we are all simply a collection of nerves and synapses, with electrical impulses coursing around our bodies. The problem is that, whatever explanatory power this model may have for science, it provides precious little guidance for lawyers when making judgments about culpability and compensation. Whatever the scientific arguments for treating psychiatric harm as simply a form of physical injury, the law is

---

[112]   *Bourhill*, above n 25, at 110.

[113]   *McLoughlin*, above n 15, at 433 (Lord Bridge).

[114]   'With each new edition [of the DSM] some disorders are classified for the first time (where were they before?) and others disappear (where did they go?). This is a reminder that a psychiatric diagnosis is primarily a way of seeing, a style of reasoning, and (in compensation suits or other claims) a means of persuasion: it is not at all times a disease with a life of its own': Summerfield, above n 85, at 97.

right to hold fast to the Cartesian mind/body dichotomy when it comes to our thinking about legal responsibility for harm, and what that harm involves. Cartesian dualism is embedded in much of lawyers' thinking about the law and legal responsibility.[115] It is probably how the man or woman on the Clapham omnibus conceptualises the world. Whatever the science tells us about the link between physical and mental states, the distinction between physical and mental harm still has a significant role to play in the legal process. Over-reliance on medical categories can be just as misleading as fixed legal categories.

In *White* Lord Steyn commented that:

> Courts of law must act on the best medical insight of the day.... [But] [i]t would, however, be an altogether different proposition to say that no distinction is made *or ought to be made* between principles governing the recovery of damages in tort for physical injury and psychiatric harm. The contours of tort law are profoundly affected by distinctions between different kinds of damage or harm.[116]

That statement was made in the context of claims for pure psychiatric harm, but it applies with equal force to claims where the individual has sustained physical injury. So in *Corr v IBC Vehicles*, for example, a case where an employee sustained physical injury in an industrial accident, subsequently developed depression, and committed suicide six years later, Ward LJ commented that:

> The need for reasonable foresight at once imports a value judgment which is no doubt based upon a general public sentiment of moral wrongdoing for which the offender must pay: per Lord Atkin in *Donoghue v Stevenson*. Eventually the answer to this case, as in other areas of the law of tort, must depend upon whether it is fair, just and reasonable to hold the defendant responsible for Mr Corr's death. It is a policy decision.[117]

His Lordship held that the suicide was unforeseeable, on the basis that the legal issue was not whether the kind of damage was 'logically foreseeable' but whether it was 'reasonably foreseeable'.[118] This was a dissenting judgment, however, with Sedley and Wilson LJ holding that the employers were liable for their employee's death.

It is apparent that Ward LJ was using the phrase 'reasonably foreseeable' to encompass a policy judgment about whether the defendant ought to have been held responsible for the employee's death, rather than an

---

[115] Not least in the context of the criminal law. Much of the criminal law is built on the assumption that it makes sense to talk about *mens rea* (the guilty mind), which is discrete from the *physical* actions (the *actus reus*) of the defendant.

[116] Above n 1, at 492.

[117] Above n 9, at [61].

[118] *Ibid*, at [56].

assessment of the probabilities of a particular chain of causation. His Lordship considered that the self-induced nature of the damage ought to be relevant to that judgment, though acknowledging that one's response 'may be more visceral than cerebral'.[119]

Arguably, our response to claims in respect of psychiatric harm needs a more visceral basis. With all the emphasis on categorisation of claimants we have lost sight of notions of *fault* and *culpability*. Rather than focusing on the category into which the claimant falls, as if that somehow provided the rationale for a conclusion of 'liability' or 'no liability', we should return to an emphasis on the defendant's *fault*, which in turn would take us back to the concept of foreseeability.

[119] *Ibid*, at [60].

6

Should White v Jones *Represent Canadian Law: A Return to First Principles*

A TESTATOR, wishing to leave a gift to a third party, employs a solicitor to prepare and execute a will to give effect to his or her testamentary intentions. The intended beneficiary, we assume, is not a party to the contract between the testator and solicitor, knows nothing of the testator's intentions, and has no other dealings with the solicitor. Due to the solicitor's failure to exercise reasonable care, the will is not properly done or not done at all and, upon the testator's death, probate of the invalid will is refused. As a result, the third party is not entitled to the intended benefit. Instead the benefit is distributed to others under intestacy provisions or a prior will, depending upon the particular facts of the case. The simple question is whether the third party should have standing to bring an action against the solicitor for the lost benefit.

In the influential case of *White v Jones*,[1] the House of Lords answered this question in the affirmative, recognising the third party's standing to sue the solicitor in negligence for the lost benefit. At this time, the Supreme Court of Canada has yet to give its own answer to this question. Should the Supreme Court endorse the tort analysis in *White v Jones*? To shed light on this issue, I want to examine whether the analysis proposed by the House of Lords, and more particularly by the leading speech of Lord Goff, rests upon a solid intellectual base. Lord Goff's discussion of tort liability goes to first principles and raises the question of whether *any* negligence-based claim to recovery can be juridically cogent. It requires that we clarify the essential and most basic features of liability in negligence. I will address

* Professor, Faculty of Law, University of Toronto. My thanks to Fredrick Schumann for his excellent and helpful research assistance.
[1] [1995] 2 AC 207 (HL).

this question not only in general terms but also with reference to the Supreme Court of Canada's recent important consideration of the structure of negligence in *Cooper v Hobart*.[2] If, as I argue, a third party should have no claim in negligence against the solicitor, then there is the further question of whether there is any other, intellectually defensible basis upon which the third party can claim the lost benefit against the solicitor. It is widely thought that injustice will result unless the third party can recover against the solicitor and that therefore some basis must be found to give the third party standing to sue. By way of conclusion, I shall suggest a solution that attempts to ensure justice between the parties in a manner consistent with widely accepted principles of private law in general and with Canadian common law in particular. It is this approach, I submit, which should be taken by the Supreme Court of Canada.

Throughout this chapter, I make the following three assumptions. The first is an assumption of fact. Because, *ex hypothesi*, the third party is completely unaware of the testator's intention to benefit him or her under the will, he or she has done nothing in reliance upon the expectation of this benefit. The third party has not changed position to his or her detriment by forgoing opportunities or incurring expenses in reliance upon an expectation of receipt of the benefit. Similarly, the third party has been given no representations of any kind by the solicitor. There has simply been no interaction at all between the third party on the one hand and the testator or solicitor on the other hand with respect to this transaction. The question of the third party's claim against the solicitor is determined in the complete absence of such representations or reliance.

Second, given these facts, I suppose as an assumption of law that the *only* legal basis upon which the third party can claim a protected interest with respect to the intended benefit is the will itself which, if valid, confers upon the third party a *spes successionis* of an ambulatory character upon the death of the testator. Absent a valid will, the third party has no existing protected interest in the benefit cognisable in law: the third party's 'interest' is just the content of the testator's intention and it has failed to receive legal effect and reality as a separate interest attributable to the third party. The disappointed beneficiary never becomes legally entitled to the benefit.[3] At the same time, this failure results directly and solely from the

---

[2]   [2001] 3 SCR 537 [*Cooper*].

[3]   The view that the beneficiary does not have a legally protected interest in the absence of a will is widely shared by judges and academic writers. Lord Goff takes it to be one of the conceptual difficulties with *Ross v Caunters*, below n 4. Rarely has there been any judicial attempt to specify just what such a right would be. Exceptionally, in *Hill and Associates v Van Erp* (1997) 188 CLR 159 (HCA) 197, Gaudron J suggests that the third party *does* have a present existing legal right which she characterises as 'a right to have the testator's estate properly administered in accordance with the terms of the will'. According to Gaudron J, the testator intends the third party to have this legal right. More would have to be said by her to

solicitor's want of due care. The testator dies with the crystallised and unchangeable intent to confer this benefit and thinks, mistakenly, that this intent has been given satisfactory legal form and effect. But for the solicitor's carelessness, his or her intention would have received legal form and effect and the third party would have been entitled to the benefit.

Third, and finally, I suppose throughout my argument an assumption of principle that questions of justice between the parties are determined solely by reference to their legally recognised rights *inter se*. A claim of justice must be made by one party against another and must be rooted in a relation of right and correlative duty between them. Apart from this, no issue of justice arises. For the purposes of the following discussion, there is no such thing as 'justice in the air'.

I. THE TWO ROUTES TO LIABILITY CONSIDERED IN *WHITE v JONES*

The central question that I address in this chapter is whether a third party should have his own direct and free-standing claim in negligence as against the solicitor for the loss of the intended benefit. In *White v Jones,* Lord Goff identifies two generally recognised bases of liability for negligence upon which the plaintiff might try to rest his or her claim and rejects both. The first, adopted by Megarry V-C in *Ross v Caunters*,[4] would construe the plaintiff's claim in terms analogous to traditional claims in negligence for injury to person or property—the 'physical loss' model—despite the fact that the claim is for pure economic loss. The second would view the plaintiff's claim as analogous to the kind of action for pure economic loss that can be brought under *Hedley Byrne*.[5] Implicit in his speech (as well as in those of the dissenting Law Lords) is the view that these two routes are the *only* two possible bases in negligence that can ground the third party's claim against the solicitor. What are the main features of these two approaches and do they exhaust the possible bases for liability in negligence in these circumstances?

---

explain what this right is and how it qualifies as a recognisable protected interest. I have difficulty distinguishing it from either a right to the solicitor's performance of the promised service or a right to the intended benefit that would result from performance of the service. But the former belongs to the testator alone; the latter is not a right at all in the absence of a valid will. I should add that if indeed the disappointed beneficiary has a present legal entitlement to the benefit despite the absence of a valid will, the case for negligence becomes straightforward. Although the protected interest may be financial, the action is analogous to one for injury to person or property governed by ordinary principles of negligence. In such cases, the fact that the plaintiff's property or person is injured by conduct that is performed under contract with another does not bar the plaintiff from having a free-standing tort action for the injury he or she sustains.

[4] [1980] 1 Ch 297 [*Ross*].

[5] *Hedley Byrne &Co Ltd v Heller & Partners Ltd* [1963] AC 465 (HL) [*Hedley Byrne*].

My answer has two steps. To begin, in this section, I consider the two approaches as they are presented and discussed by Lord Goff. This preliminary treatment will set the stage for a more in-depth discussion in the next section where I suggest how they should be understood as first principles of negligence and see whether they exhaust the fundamental categories of duty-relation in negligence.

As I have just indicated, the first approach which Lord Goff identifies is modeled on the principle governing liability for so-called physical loss and would hold the defendant solicitor liable in negligence merely for foreseeably causing the beneficiary to be deprived of the intended legacy. The fact that this deprivation is the foreseeable and direct consequence of the solicitor's carelessness is sufficient to establish a prima facie duty on the part of the solicitor to avoid causing the deprivation. This conclusion of prima facie duty might further be limited or negated by policy considerations, such as a concern about the possible imposition of indeterminate liability. In *Ross*, Megarry V-C refers to this approach as the 'pure *Donoghue v Stevenson* principle'.

It is important to highlight the structure of relations giving rise to liability under this approach. The solicitor is contractually bound to his or her client to provide a service to the client. If this service is performed without reasonable care, the testator can undoubtedly sue the solicitor for breach of contract and concurrently in negligence. Clearly, the third party will not in fact become entitled to receive under a valid testamentary disposition. The third party's loss results then from the solicitor's failure to perform as promised. Megarry V-C underlines the fact that the third party need not have relied in any way upon the solicitor's representations or skill. Nor need the solicitor have made any representations or undertakings of responsibility to the third party. That would bring the *Hedley Byrne* principle into play. Even in the absence of these factors, the third party's loss is actionable in negligence so long as it is foreseeable. Here then we have a third party, C, with an actionable claim in negligence against a solicitor, B, simply on the basis that C's loss *foreseeably* results from B's act or omission which constitutes a breach of promise or obligation owed to A, the testator. This analysis supposes that foreseeability alone is a sufficient foundation of a relation of duty in negligence.

Treating foreseeability as the decisive factor in establishing a relation of duty might arguably be justified if the defendant solicitor's act or omission directly threatens to injure the property or person of others—that is, in general, if this is a case of 'physical' or property loss.[6] Here, however, the defendant provides a service which is to be used by the testator or others

---

[6] The Supreme Court of Canada has made this point most recently in *Childs v Desormeaux* 2006 SCC 18, [31] [*Childs*] (McLachlin CJC).

and any threat to their interests follows immediately or indirectly *only* from their decision to make use of—in other words, to rely upon—that service. Independently of such reliance, the careless execution of the service does not endanger anyone's existing legal interests. In the case of the intended beneficiary, there are simply no existing protected interests to be interfered with. Moreover, the loss is purely economic and certainly since *Murphy v Brentwood District Council*,[7] English law has reaffirmed that there must be something more than mere foreseeability to establish a duty relation with respect to such loss. What is puzzling about the first approach is that it applies a model that simply ignores these features.

It is on basis of such 'conceptual problems'[8] that Lord Goff, as well as the dissenting Law Lords, reject the approach taken in *Ross*. Since it is Lord Goff who sets out these difficulties most carefully, it is important to highlight the central problems as he sees them.

Lord Goff begins with the well-established general proposition that a solicitor acting on behalf of a client owes a duty only to his or her client. This point may be stated in either contractual or tortious terms: there is privity of contract between solicitor and client and there is an assumption of responsibility in tort by the solicitor toward his or her client, but to no one else. A solicitor, acting on behalf and for the sake of a client, need not, therefore, consider the impact of acts, omissions, or representations made in that capacity upon the interests of third parties. Specifically, in terms of the law of negligence, the starting point of analysis is that there is no relation of duty between solicitor and third parties despite the fact that the solicitor's acts or omissions may foreseeably affect their interests and irrespective of whether the solicitor's representations to his or her client induce reliance on the part of third parties.

In the absence of either direct interaction between the solicitor and intended beneficiary or representations made by the former to the latter, the only factor that might relevantly distinguish the intended beneficiary case from others is that here the testator *intends* to benefit the third party and the solicitor is engaged to give legal effect to that intention. But this intention, taken by itself and before it is embodied in a valid will, cannot give the third party a right as against the solicitor: not in contract, because this would be to ignore the doctrine of privity; not in negligence, because the intention alone, in the absence of a legally effective will, does not give the third party a proprietary or personal right which, if negligently affected, can possibly give rise to a claim. The difficulty here is that the 'loss' suffered by the disappointed beneficiary cannot be construed as a loss in the legal sense but only as a failure to obtain a benefit: 'All that has

---

[7] *Murphy v Brentwood District Council* [1991] 1 AC 398 (HL) [*Murphy*].
[8] This is Lord Goff's phrase in *White v Jones*, above n 1, at 260.

happened is that what is sometimes called a *spes successionis* has failed to come to fruition.'[9] This leads to a final 'objection of a conceptual nature'. Not only is it difficult to construe the disappointed beneficiary's claim as a loss, but, in addition, the solicitor need not have *done* anything and as a general rule, Lord Goff points out, there is no liability in negligence for an omission in the absence of some special relationship between the parties. Lord Goff contends that because the approach taken by Megarry V-C in *Ross* does not meet any of these difficulties, it should be rejected as inappropriate.

What about the second line of analysis, founded upon the *Hedley Byrne* principle? As Lord Goff understands that principle, it applies only where there has been interaction between the parties constituted by representations on the one side and reliance upon those representations on the other side. Interaction of this kind is necessary to the existence of a special relation between the parties in the sense required by the principle. Without explaining how or why, Lord Goff asserts that the conceptual problems that vex the first approach do *not* pose a difficulty for a *Hedley Byrne* analysis. Presumably, the existence of a special relationship allows the law of negligence to impose liability for pure financial loss without running afoul these conceptual difficulties. How this might be so is a question of the first importance for our understanding of the principle. I will take it up in the next section. For Lord Goff, in agreement with the dissenting Law Lords, the difficulty with applying the *Hedley Byrne* principle to the plaintiff's claim in *White v Jones* is simply that the proper factual basis for its application is lacking. Given the absence of representation and reliance, *Hedley Byrne* liability cannot be imposed.

The upshot of Lord Goff's analysis is that it is not possible to establish a relation of duty between the parties on either of the recognised principles of negligence. Since Lord Goff appears to treat these two principles as exhaustive of the possible bases of liability in negligence—he does not refer to any other fundamental principle of liability that might possibly apply— his conclusion seems to be that there cannot be a relation of duty in negligence in the circumstances of *White v Jones*. As I now wish to explain, this conclusion, if warranted, has important implications for Canadian common law.

In its substantial clarification of the *Anns* test for negligence in *Cooper*,[10] the Supreme Court of Canada emphasises that the first stage of analysis, by which the existence of a relation of duty is determined, refers only to considerations intrinsic to the relationship between the parties— such as the parties' 'expectations, representations, reliance, and property or

---

[9]   *White v Jones*, above n 1, at 257.
[10] Above n 2.

other interests involved'.[11] These are considerations that pertain to the 'closeness' or proximity of the relationship between plaintiff and defendant and allow courts to determine whether it is just and fair, in light of this relationship, to impose a duty of care upon one party toward the other. The court emphasises that whether a relation of proximity obtains between the parties is not reducible to the sole consideration of the foreseeability of harm. Indeed, the court distinguishes proximity from reasonable foreseeability of harm: both proximity and reasonable foreseeability are required for a duty of care to arise.

Moreover, sufficiently proximate relationships, the court says, are to be identified through the use of categories. Although the categories are not closed, generally proximity is established by reference to such categories. Certain categories of cases represent clear instances where a relation of proximity has been recognised. Where, for instance, the defendant's act foreseeably causes *physical* harm to the plaintiff's person or property, there is proximity giving rise to a duty of care in negligence. Another recognised category is the analysis of liability for negligent misstatement found in *Hedley Byrne*. However, pure economic loss to the plaintiff that results from interference with or injury to something in which the plaintiff does not have a proprietary or possessory interest—so-called relational economic loss—is not recoverable (apart from general average cases or situations of joint venture) because here there is no relation of proximity and no duty arises.[12]

According to the Supreme Court, it is the first stage in the *Anns* analysis of negligence that determines the existence of a duty relation between the parties. It does so by exploring the normativity of the relation between the parties. All the positive work in the analysis takes place at this first stage. In the second stage, the court considers, negatively, whether there are reasons external to the relationship between the parties which might justify qualifying, limiting, or negating the prima facie duty posited at the first stage. One such consideration, according to the court, is the risk of imposing indeterminate liability upon a defendant for causing pure economic loss. But unless a duty has been found at the first stage, there is simply nothing to limit at the second.

How does the relation between an intended beneficiary and solicitor fit within the recognised categories of duty? If we provisionally accept the reason Lord Goff rejects the approach taken in *Ross* and his conclusion that the *Hedley Byrne* principle does not apply, the plaintiff's claim does not seem to meet the requirements of any of the recognised categories of

[11] Above n 2, at 552.
[12] Above n 2, at 553.

duty noted in *Cooper*. The plaintiff's claim is that the solicitor's careless-ness has foreseeably prevented the creation of a protected interest in the plaintiff. It is definitely not a case of physical loss and there has been no interference with any existing right or legally protected interest belonging to the intended beneficiary. Reasonable reliance by the plaintiff is absent. There would appear to be no recognised category of proximity to explain the existence of a relation of duty between the parties. Indeed, cases of relational economic loss in which *no* duty arises seem to be, by analogy, the closest to the situation of the disappointed beneficiary: in both the plaintiff lacks a proprietary or possessory interest which has been affected by the defendant's negligence and in both the 'loss' is merely the foreseeable consequence of a breach of duty owed to another. Although the question of a solicitor's liability to an intended beneficiary in the absence of reliance might be viewed as novel, in a deeper sense it can be understood as already coming within a category of relation—one which does *not* give rise to a duty of care.

There is no difference between the dissenting Law Lords and Lord Goff with respect to the analysis of duty which they think must underpin an intended beneficiary's claim for it to be actionable in negligence. It must fail unless it can be rationalised on the basis of either the physical loss model or *Hedley Byrne*. Despite this conclusion, Lord Goff grants recovery simply and solely to prevent a lacuna in the law which, he contends, exists if the beneficiary cannot succeed. The lacuna necessitates a remedy, even in the absence of a recognised basis for a relation of duty. Whether or not non-recovery by the intended beneficiary results in a lacuna in the way suggested by Lord Goff is a crucial question that deserves careful treat-ment. I will do this in section three.

Thus far I have provisionally accepted the view, implicit in Lord Goff's (as well as the dissenting Law Lords') analysis of duty, that the intended beneficiary's claim has to be founded upon the model of liability for physical loss or upon *Hedley Byrne* if it is to be actionable in negligence. Expressed in the terms of *Cooper*, there does not seem to be any established category of proximity within which to fit the plaintiff's claim. I now want to explore this provisional conclusion and see if it is justified. The question is whether, in addition to the two approaches represented by *Donoghue v Stevenson* and *Hedley Byrne*, there is a third fundamental yet distinct conception of relation which can establish a free-standing duty of care on the part of the solicitor toward the intended beneficiary. This would also be necessary to satisfy the first stage of the *Anns* test as presented by the Supreme Court of Canada in *Cooper*: Is there a hitherto unrecognised category of relation of proximity that establishes a duty relation in these circumstances? To see whether there is, or even can be, a third fundamental category of relation, we should first clarify the essential features of the two recognised categories. In doing so, it will be important to consider more carefully the conceptual difficulties identified by Lord Goff.

II. THE FUNDAMENTAL CATEGORIES OF DUTY RELATIONS IN NEGLIGENCE

A. The Three Elements of Duty and Liability for Physical Loss

I begin with the first approach which the *Ross* case calls the 'pure *Donoghue v Stevenson* principle'. It incorporates 'ordinary principles of negligence governing so-called physical loss, that is, harm to person or property. What are the essential features of the duty relation as specified by it? My discussion draws upon the foundational judgments of Lord Atkin in *Donoghue (or McAlister) v Stevenson*[13] and of Cardozo J in *Palsgraf v Long Island Railroad Co*[14] as well as important clarifications in later decisions.

The first requirement for a duty relation is that it must be possible to construe the outcome of the defendant's act or omission *as an injury to an existing legally protected interest which rightfully belongs to the plaintiff as against the defendant*. The religious and ethical command to love your neighbour becomes in law the prohibition against injuring your neighbour. To be actionable, negligence must involve the invasion of a right or legally protected interest. In general terms, the common law of negligence recognises two categories of protected interests: integrity of the person (and whatever this entails) as well as proprietary or possessory interests in a broad sense.[15] Thus, it is not enough that the defendant merely fails to confer a benefit upon the plaintiff or that the defendant deprives the plaintiff of something to which the latter did not have a present existing right as against the defendant. The fact that a plaintiff may have enjoyed the use of something until the defendant deprived him or her of it can be an injury for the purposes of negligence if, and only if, the plaintiff had a right to such use exclusive as against the defendant. This requirement may be styled as the principle that there is no liability for nonfeasance. In this context, it is important to underline that for something to count as a legally protected interest here, as elsewhere in the law, it must not be *sui generis*. Instead it must be an interest that can be generally recognised whenever applicable and that shares essential characteristics in common with other recognised protected interests in negligence. One cannot create

---

[13] [1932] AC 562 (HL).
[14] 162 NE 99 (NY CA 1928) [*Palsgraf*].
[15] A typical statement of this is found in *Allen v Flood* [1898] 1 AC 1 (HL) 29 (Cave J).

protected interests ad hoc for the purpose of imposing a liability which is justified on some other independent basis. The requirement of threatened injury to a protected interest is the first step toward carving out a direct and free-standing relation of correlative right and duty just as between the two parties.

Second, the plaintiff must count, in Lord Atkin's terms, as the defendant's neighbour. This is where the idea of proximity, understood in a narrow sense,[16] enters the analysis of the duty relation as a further element or requirement. The plaintiff must be someone who is *so closely and directly* affected by the defendant's act or omission that the defendant must reasonably have the plaintiff in mind as being so affected when the defendant is deciding upon the act or omission. This second element builds upon the first because 'affecting' the plaintiff means the misfeasance of injuring the plaintiff's legally protected interest. What is the normative contribution of proximity to the analysis of duty? I would suggest, tentatively, that the requirement of closeness and directness pertains to an idea of intention that is appropriate to negligence and that marks the action as fault. A consequence (viz affecting someone) that is close and direct is something that reasonably can be part of your intention and therefore can be imputed to you when you cause it. While, in the circumstances of negligence, you do not consciously intend the consequence, it is something to which you could have averted and which you could have avoided when exercising intention. As such, it can be imputed to you as a responsible agent.

The third and final element that is necessary to establish a relation of duty between the parties is foreseeability: there is a duty of care if one's acts or omissions are such that one can reasonably foresee that they would be likely to injure one's neighbour. Foreseeability applies to a class of injuries that I might cause someone who is directly and closely affected by my act or omission. Unless there is such a class, there is nothing that I could have chosen to avoid and so no basis for imposing a duty of care. The foreseeability requirement is constitutive of the duty relation: in the

---

[16] In *Cooper*, above n 2, at [32]-[34], the Supreme Court of Canada refers to 'proximity' not only in the narrow sense of 'close and direct' but also in a wide sense as encompassing the features of the relation between plaintiff and defendant that make it fair and reasonable to impose a duty of care upon the latter toward the former. This wider sense of proximity incorporates the three elements that I have identified as necessary conditions of a duty relation in negligence. Use of the term 'proximity' in this double sense is widely found in the case law, particularly during the last few decades. There is nothing wrong about this, so long as we are aware of it and keep track of it in argument. Interestingly, the classic formulations of proximity by Lord Atkin and Justice Cardozo take it in the narrow sense.

words of Cardozo J, 'The risk reasonably to be perceived defines the duty to be obeyed, and risk imports relation; it is risk to another or to others within the range of apprehension.'[17]

All three requirements, taken together, are necessary to specify fully a relation of correlative right and duty in negligence, assuming that such a relation has to do with a defendant's acts or omissions that injure the plaintiff's legally recognised interests in a way that, morally, can be imputed to the defendant. The fact that the defendant affects the plaintiff's protected interest without the latter's consent shows that the defendant may have injured the plaintiff and not merely failed to confer a benefit. Liability is imposed for misfeasance only.[18] But this does not yet establish that the causing of this consequence is the violation of any duty. Only conduct exercising choice and intention comes under the idea of duty. To establish this, the causing of injury must satisfy the further requirements of proximity and foreseeability. Both are necessary. It would surely be inadequate to require only foreseeability without the proximity require-ment of having to keep in mind only those who are directly and closely affected by my acts or omissions. It is theoretically foreseeable that any act might affect someone or something almost anywhere. Taking foreseeability alone as the standard of conduct would empty the idea of responsibility of any practical meaning.

Where these three requirements are met, there will be a relation of duty in negligence between the parties. In a case of so-called 'physical loss' where, say, a defendant carelessly collides with and damages the plaintiff's car, if the plaintiff can establish that the defendant foreseeably imposed damage, a duty relation has typically been made out. It might seem that at least in these cases mere foreseeability of harm is sufficient to establish a duty relation. This is not so. What may make it appear to be true is that often, in such scenarios, the requirement of closeness and directness is clearly satisfied or the foreseeability requirement itself is applied in a way that incorporates the requirement of directness and closeness, so that the question of the reasonable foreseeability of the harm becomes the principal object of focus. Each of the three elements—the requisite protected interest, proximity in the sense of closeness and directness, and foreseeability—is always required.[19]

---

[17] *Palsgraf*, above n 14, at 100.

[18] By misfeasance, I do not mean act as opposed to omission. Rather it refers to any conduct (act or omission) that injures another's legally protected interest. Clear judicial statements of the misfeasance/nonfeasance distinction are those of Cardozo J in *H R Moch Co Inc v Rensselaer Water Co* 159 NE 896 (NY CA 1928) 898 [*Moch*] and Lord Diplock's speech in *Dorset Yacht Co Ltd v Home Office* [1970] AC 1004 (HL) 1027.

[19] In *Childs*, above n 6, at [31], McLachlin CJC suggests that 'foreseeability without more *may* establish a duty of care', and illustrates this with the case 'where an *overt act of the defendant* has *directly caused foreseeable physical harm* to the plaintiff'. Note that the

Although *Cooper* identifies proximity and foreseeability as the two main elements necessary to establish a duty of care in negligence, it is not inconsistent with the view that I have just suggested. The Supreme Court of Canada uses 'proximity' to mean not only 'close and direct' but also more broadly to connote the kind of relationship between plaintiff and defendant in which it is just and fair, having regard to that relationship, to impose a duty of care in negligence upon the defendant.[20] When it holds that mere foreseeability is not ordinarily sufficient and that proximity is also necessary, it is referring to the latter in this broad sense. Taken in this way, proximity includes the required element of injury to protected interest.[21] Moreover, as I have already alluded to earlier, the central category of proximity to which the Supreme Court refers, the causing of so-called physical loss, makes explicit the requirement that the negligence must interfere with the plaintiff's person or property and the central case in which proximity is said to be absent, relational economic loss, fails precisely for want of the requisite possessory or proprietary interest.

'Physical' loss or harm to person or property is widely viewed as the central category of duty relation and as representing 'ordinary principles of negligence'. It is the 'pure *Donoghue v Stevenson* principle' of *Ross*. The characterisation as *physical* loss can, however, be misleading. The fact that loss is non-physical does not necessarily exclude it from this category and, conversely, not all actionable physical loss comes under this category. For example, physical loss may in given circumstances be actionable in negligence only under a reliance analysis modelled on the *Hedley Byrne* principle. What feature or features make this a distinct and unified category? To answer this, we must specify the way the three elements of the duty relation apply in it.

I want to suggest that the crucial factor that marks this category as distinct and basic is how the first prerequisite of the duty relation—viz that the defendant has injured the plaintiff's protected interest (whatever its particular content)—is established. Let me elaborate.

As a general matter in negligence, the plaintiff establishes the element of injury to a protected interest simply by showing that he has a right to something as against the defendant and that the defendant has affected the thing without his consent. In all cases of so-called physical loss, the *origin* of the plaintiff's right is *wholly independent of the conduct that establishes a duty relation between the parties*. The plaintiff must *already* have this right prior to and independently of the defendant's conduct, and the

---

example incorporates the elements of injury to a protected interest ('causing physical harm') and proximity ('directly') in addition to foreseeability. This is quite typical of judicial statements to this effect.

[20] See above n 16 and accompanying text.
[21] See above n 19 and accompanying text.

defendant brings about a duty relation, not through any interaction with the plaintiff, but rather by affecting or acting upon the plaintiff's interest. By 'interaction', I mean a two-sided relation constituted by the mutually related acts of both parties. Injury is an act or omission that is incompatible with a protected interest that arises in this way. In determining whether 'loss' represents an injury and not merely the failure to receive a gain, we refer only to the meaning and scope of the plaintiff's right to exclude and ask whether it has been complied with. There is no reference at all to any interaction between the parties. The further requirements of proximity and foreseeability are similarly specified in relation to this protected interest and what it entails. In cases of 'physical' loss, the analysis of duty does not root any of the constituent elements of the duty relation in any interaction between the parties. Defendant and plaintiff are represented solely as active and passive respectively, with the first affecting or impacting upon the second.

Not all exclusionary private law rights and duty relations originate in this way. Some require, and indeed are constituted by, interaction between the parties. The chief instance of this is contract where the duty relation is constituted by mutual and identical acts of assent on both sides. Indeed, in contract, the parties' protected interests are *wholly* constituted in and through their interaction and are no sense acquired independently of or prior to the interaction. It is because their rights are explicitly and thoroughly transactional that they are contractual.[22] The question is whether there is a second category of negligence in addition to that of so-called physical loss. To be part of negligence, it would have to incorporate the three requirements of threatened injury to protected interest, proximity, and foreseeability, as already set out. To be a distinct, second basic category of negligence, it would have to make *some* reference to interaction between the parties as constitutive of the fundamental requirements of their relation. It would not be a matter just of one party foreseeably affecting or acting upon the protected interests of the other. The mutually related acts of *both* parties would be relevant. However, to be distinct from contract, this second category of negligence could not make the parties' interaction *wholly* constitutive of the duty relation. Does tort law already recognise a category of negligence that meets these desiderata? I wish to show that it does and that, properly understood, the *Hedley Byrne* principle is this second fundamental category.

Consider a typical case of so-called relational economic loss. The plaintiff, we shall suppose, has been enjoying the use of a facility without having a right to this use as against the defendant. The plaintiff has neither

---

[22] While I believe this point is relatively straightforward, I have presented it more fully in 'The Philosophy of Property' in J Coleman and S Shapiro (eds), *The Oxford Handbook of Jurisprudence and Philosophy of Law* (Oxford, Oxford University Press, 2002) 777-99.

a proprietary or possessory interest in the facility nor a contractual right against the defendant to its use. The plaintiff may simply have the liberty to do this or, alternatively, may have been given a contractual right to use it by a third party. Expecting to enjoy the continued use of the facility, the plaintiff has, in connection with this use, expended money and forgone other opportunities which, in the absence of this expectation, the plaintiff would, respectively, either have not made or have not given up. We also suppose that if the plaintiff is deprived of the use of the facility, his or her expenditures will be wasted and the pursuit of the forgone opportunities will be more costly. In addition, the plaintiff will not make certain profits which he or she would have earned through the continued use of the facility. In this situation, the defendant—a complete stranger to the plaintiff— damages the facility, thereby depriving the plaintiff of its use and causing him or her loss in the form of increased costs, wasted expenditures and lost profits.

The common law of negligence in England, Canada, and the United States clearly holds that while the owner of the facility may recover damages in negligence from the defendant, the plaintiff's claim for these financial losses must fail: there is no duty relation between the parties to found the action. Viewed in light of the three elements of the duty relation, the reason the plaintiff's claim must fail is that while his or her claim depends upon having a protected interest in the present and continued use of the facility, the plaintiff lacks the requisite protected interest therein: there is a complete absence of exclusive right on the side of the plaintiff as against the defendant with respect to such use. With no protected interest, the loss caused cannot count as injury and there has been no wrong done, only nonfeasance. In accordance with the analysis of the duty relation suggested above, the claim must fail even if the defendant can reasonably view the plaintiff as 'closely and directly affected' by his act and despite the fact that the plaintiff's loss may be perfectly foreseeable. In the terms of *Cooper*, there is an absence of proximate relation between the parties at the first stage of the analysis. To impose liability in these circumstances on a *Ross* approach immediately leads to the conceptual difficulties noted by Lord Goff and discussed earlier. All these difficulties stem from the basic problem that the first prerequisite of a duty relation has not been met.

On the above facts, the plaintiff relied on the continuing availability of the facility for his purposes. As against the defendant, this reliance was not rooted in any right. Nor was there any interaction between them which might make the plaintiff's reliance reasonable and justified vis-à-vis the defendant. In relation to the defendant, the plaintiff relied at his or her own risk. Suppose that we change the facts and say that the plaintiff's reliance upon the continuing use of the facility is *invited or induced* by the defendant. Now there is interaction between them: an invitation to rely on the one side and actual reliance in response on the other side. Can this interaction make a difference to the analysis of the duty relation and more particularly to the determination of the three elements that constitute that relation?

B.   A Second Category of Negligence: the Reliance Model

Our question is: what role, if any, might interaction between the parties involving invited reliance have in shaping, and enshrining, the analysis of the duty relation between them? To answer this question, I shall consider two very different models that have been applied to situations of reliance, each of which may be found in decided cases and legal scholarship. My contention is that only one of these can possibly establish a relation of duty with its three prerequisites and it is this model that qualifies as a second basic category of negligence. In fact, it is only the second of the models discussed that makes reliance pertinent to the analysis of negligence. I also conclude that, in conceptual terms, the two basic categories of negligence—viz the duty analysis for so-called physical harm and the duty analysis for reliance, properly understood—necessarily exhaust the elementary forms of negligence. This conclusion, we will see, has immediate and important implications for our assessment of the *White v Jones* case and for the rational development of Canadian tort law.

The first model that is sometimes applied to reliance situations is illustrated and explained by the often-cited Supreme Court of California decision in *Biakanja v Irving*.[23] In that case, the defendant, a notary public but not an attorney, agreed to prepare and supervise the execution of a valid will for the testator, his client. If the will were valid, the testator's sister, the plaintiff, would have received the whole of the testator's estate. The facts referred to by the court do not indicate one way or another whether the plaintiff knew about the intended benefit or relied upon the expectation of receiving it. The defendant failed to warn either the testator or the witnesses to the will that the witnesses had to sign in the presence of each other and the testator. The will was declared invalid because of the defendant's negligence in failing to have it properly attested. As a consequence, the plaintiff received only one-eighth of the estate instead of the whole of it. The plaintiff brought an action in negligence for the difference. The court held that, despite the absence of privity between the defendant and plaintiff, the former owed the latter a duty of care in negligence and was liable for the loss caused by his want of due care.

The court reached this conclusion in the following way. It began by noting what it referred to as 'the leading case' of *Glanzer v*

[23]   320 P 2d 16 (Cal Sup Ct 1958) [*Biakanja*].

Shepard[24](decided by Justice Cardozo) in which a purchaser of beans overpaid the vendor in reliance upon an erroneous certificate negligently furnished by the defendant, a public weigher, employed and paid by the vendor under contract to perform this service. The *Biakanja* court highlighted Cardozo J's statement that the purchaser's use of the certificate was, to the defendant weigher's knowledge, the 'end and aim' of the transaction—that is, the contracted-for service of weighing the beans and sending the certificate to the purchaser who foreseeably relied upon it. The court further noted that recovery was denied in other cases where the 'potential advantage' to the plaintiff was merely a collateral consideration of the contract or where the loss of that advantage was not foreseeable. On the basis of these precedents, the court held that whether or not a defendant should be liable in negligence to third parties in these circumstances was to be decided as 'a matter of policy and involves the balancing of various factors'.[25] Among these factors, the court noted the following as relevant:

> [the] extent to which the transaction was intended to affect the plaintiff, the foreseeability of harm to him, the degree of certainty that the plaintiff suffered injury, the closeness of the connection between the defendant's conduct and the injury suffered, the moral blame attached to the defendant's conduct, and the policy of preventing future harm.[26]

The court found the defendant liable on the basis that passing the testator's estate to the plaintiff was, quoting *Glanzer*, the 'end and aim' of the transaction. Moreover, the defendant reasonably must have been aware from the terms of the will itself that, if faulty attestation of the will made it invalid, the plaintiff would suffer the very loss which occurred. Since the testator died without revoking his will, the plaintiff would have received the whole of the estate, but for the defendant's want of due care. The court noted, in conclusion, that the defendant would be improperly immune from civil liability if the plaintiff, 'the only person who suffered a loss, were denied a right of action'.[27]

What is striking about the reasoning in *Biakanja* is that the factor of reliance, which figures centrally in the *Glanzer* opinion, is not even mentioned either in the court's general statement of principle or in its application of that principle to the facts before it. In *Glanzer*, Cardozo J refers to *the plaintiff's use of and reliance upon the defendant's service* as being, to the knowledge of the defendant, the 'end and aim' of the

---

[24]   135 NE 275 (NY CA 1922) [*Glanzer*]. *Glanzer* is the source of my second model of reliance and I discuss it in detail below.
[25]   Above n 23, at 19.
[26]   *Ibid.*
[27]   *Ibid.*

agreement with the vendor.[28] The purchaser, relying upon the accuracy of the certificate, makes an expenditure on that basis. Although the *Biakanja* court cites this fact situation as the central example of a prospective benefit to the plaintiff that is *not* a collateral consideration of the transaction, its formulation of the first factor in its test, namely—'the extent to which the transaction was intended to affect the plaintiff'—does not make clear whether the intention to affect must be directed toward reliance by the plaintiff upon the defendant. Indeed, if anything, the court seems to hold the contrary view. This is evident when it actually decides the issue of liability on the facts before it. Citing *Glanzer* one more time, the court holds that, looking at the content of the will, it is clear that the passing of the estate to the plaintiff is the 'end and aim of the transaction'. In other words, the end and aim of the transaction is simply the testator's intention, as embodied in his instructions to the defendant, and not the plaintiff's reliance, if any, upon the defendant. The test can be satisfied whether or not there has been reliance and without referring to it if it exists. In short, the factor of reliance makes no difference to the analysis.

What the court in *Biakanja* emphasises are just the elements of proximity ('degree of certainty' and 'the closeness of the connection between the defendant's conduct and the injury suffered') and foreseeability. While we have seen that these are indeed essential elements in establishing a duty relation, they are not sufficient. The plaintiff also needs to show that the defendant's negligent conduct threatens to injure something that belongs to the plaintiff as a legally protected interest, as a matter of exclusive right. Indeed, this is, conceptually, the first requirement of duty and the other requirements of proximity and foreseeability are specified in relation to it. But all that the plaintiff can assert here against the defendant is that he or she has been deprived of something that existed as a purpose in the mind, and instructions, of the testator—ie nothing that is generally recognised as a legally protected interest.

The view taken in *Biakanja* entails, then, the very same difficulties identified by Lord Goff with the *Ross* case. These difficulties, which Lord Goff rightly terms 'conceptual' stem from the failure to include the first essential element, a suitably specified protected interest. There may be *damnum* but it is *absque injuria*. *Biakanja* is a case of nonfeasance. The *Biakanja* approach roots everything in the intention of the testator, on the one hand, and in the proximity and foreseeability of the loss: it does not explain how the plaintiff is entitled to assert a free-standing and independent claim to this loss against the defendant. Generalised as a principle of negligence, it would imply recovery by a plaintiff who sustains relational

---

[28] Above n 24, at 275. I discuss this point, which is of the highest importance, in my presentation of *Glanzer*.

economic loss as a result of the defendant interfering with something to which the plaintiff does not have a possessory, proprietary, or any other right exclusive as against the defendant. For this reason alone, *Biakanja* cannot satisfy the first stage of the *Anns* test, as clarified in *Cooper*.

Let me now turn to a second model which, in sharp contrast with *Biakanja*, establishes a relation of duty on the basis of interaction involving reliance. Here, reliance makes all the difference, from a legal point of view. This model, I shall argue, meets all the requirements of a duty relation and is vulnerable to none of the conceptual difficulties noted by Lord Goff. I will suggest that the principle of liability which this model embodies provides the most reasonable interpretation and elucidation of the analysis of assumption of responsibility and special relationship as developed in *Hedley Byrne*. Indeed, the *Hedley Byrne* principle, viewed as a distinct but fundamental form of duty relationship, is, and must be, identical with this second model if it is to make sense within tort law. This, at least, is what I shall argue. This conclusion, we shall see, has decisive implications for the intellectual viability of the solution proposed by *White v Jones* as well as for the rational development of Canadian common law in the light of *Cooper*.

To set out in a preliminary way the second model, I draw upon the leading decision of *Glanzer* which, along with the *Hedley Byrne* case, is certainly the most influential judgment in this part of tort law. Indeed, in my view, despite its brevity, Cardozo J's judgment elucidates more clearly than any other decision the fundamental basis of liability relating to undertakings.

As I already mentioned briefly in connection with *Biakanja*, the facts in *Glanzer* were that the plaintiffs purchased beans from a third party and they agreed that the beans were to be paid in accordance with weight sheets certified by the defendants, public weighers. The seller wrote the defendants, informing them that the beans had been sold to the plaintiffs and requesting that they weigh the beans and send copies of the certificates of weight to both themselves and the purchasers. The sellers informed the defendants that the purpose of the weighing was to determine the price the purchasers would pay the vendor. The defendants performed the service pursuant to a contract with the vendor who remunerated them. The plaintiffs paid the sellers for the beans on the faith of the certificates. When the plaintiffs later attempted a resale, they discovered that the actual weight of the beans was less than the weight as certified and that they had overpaid the sellers. They brought suit against the defendants for the amount overpaid. Writing for the New York Court of Appeal, Cardozo J affirmed the decision of the Appellate Division ordering judgment for the plaintiffs.

In holding that the defendants were under a duty of care in negligence toward the plaintiffs as well as to the sellers, Justice Cardozo underlined the following crucial features of their situation. First, it was reasonably apparent and indeed known to the defendants that the main purpose of the service of weighing was that the plaintiffs would use the certificates to determine what they paid the sellers. As a result of the seller's communications to them, the defendants knew that the beans had been sold and that in reliance on the certificates issued by them payment would be made. The defendants also reasonably knew that the plaintiffs would be aware that the defendants had been so informed by the seller and that the plaintiffs, knowing the defendants to be public weighers employed by the seller, would view the defendants as acting, not casually, but in the pursuit of their independent calling. In these circumstances, the defendants sent a copy of the certificates directly to the plaintiff for their use.

Viewing the defendants' action in its setting, the defendants may reasonably be seen as 'intend[ing] to sway [plaintiffs'] conduct'.[29] Cardozo J characterises the defendants' action as 'directed toward the governance of conduct' rather than 'directed toward the person of another or his property'.[30] The question is how proximately or remotely does governance of the conduct of another figure in the 'thought and purpose' of the defendant. It is clearly *not* the seller's intention but rather the *defendants'* intention, reasonably construed, which specifies 'the end and aim' of the transaction. The transaction is the service—the act—of weighing the beans and recording the outcome in a certificate, all to be done by the defendants under contract with the sellers. Here, Cardozo finds that the very end and aim of the transaction is *to induce action on the part of one who relies.*

Glanzer suggests the following analysis: a defendant will be under a duty of care in negligence toward a plaintiff when he or she may reasonably be viewed by the plaintiff as inducing or inviting the plaintiff to do or omit to do something in reliance upon the defendant's reasonable performance of a service or reasonable making of a representation. We are now in a position to see how the two elements of proximity and foreseeability are specified here in terms of interaction constituted by an invitation or inducement to rely on the one side and induced reliance on the other side. It is this interaction that frames and shapes the application of 'close and direct'— this is reflected in the characterisation of the plaintiff's use as the 'end and aim of the transaction—as well as the criterion of foreseeability. But what about the requirement that the defendant must threaten injury to a legally protected interest of the plaintiff's? Following the general line of argument I am suggesting, we should expect that it too is specified in and through the interaction of invited reliance. Cardozo J does not bring out and explain this aspect explicitly. We must now try to do this.

---

[29] *Glanzer*, above n 24, at 276.
[30] *Ibid.*

The key to understanding this aspect is to be clear, right from the start, that the protected interest cannot be in the defendant's performance or the content of his or her representation. The plaintiff has no right to these or to their value. Such a right can only be acquired by contract and can be directly enforceable only by an action for breach of contract, whether for specific performance or for expectation damages. Indeed, this is the principal defect with the *Biakanja* model—namely, that it confers upon the plaintiff a right that can only be grounded in contract—and with this defect come the conceptual difficulties noted by Lord Goff. The plaintiff's right and protected interest must be with respect to something other than the performance or representation.[31] Stated more abstractly, to be irreducible to a contractual right, the protected interest must be in something that does not originate in the parties' interaction; but, at the same time, if this interest is to be shaped by the parties' interaction, it must be in some way constituted by the invitation to rely followed by reliance. What might this be?

Apart from the performance or representation itself, the only other salient factor in these situations is that the plaintiff may have given up some actual or potential benefit or may have made some expenditure, all in reliance upon the defendant's performance or representation. In *Glanzer*, for example, the plaintiffs made an expenditure (over-payment) in reliance upon the defendants' proper performance of the service of weighing. This is something the plaintiffs would not have done had they not relied and had the defendants weighed carefully. It is the amount of over-payment that Cardozo treats as the measure of recovery. And this measure of recovery implies the following protected interest: the plaintiffs are treated as having a protected interest in the condition they would have been in if they had not made an over-payment. In other words, they have a protected interest in having the amount of their money represented by over-payment not being used (wasted) in this way. This is the pre-reliance asset that they assert against the defendants. It is the baseline that must not be impaired by the defendants' negligence.

It follows from this that the wrong is not primarily in depriving the plaintiff of the performance (weighing) as such or of the state of affairs represented (by the certificate) but in causing the plaintiff to change position to his or her detriment.[32] So long as the defendant enables the plaintiff who has relied to regain his or her pre-reliance position, no wrong

---

[31] Warren Seavey makes this point clearly in his important article 'Reliance upon Gratuitous Promises or Other Conduct' (1951) 64 *Harvard Law Review* 913, 925.

[32] As Seavey, above n 32 noted: '[T]he wrong is not primarily in depriving the plaintiff of the promised reward but in causing the plaintiff to change position to his detriment.'

is done, despite the fact that the service is unperformed and notwithstanding the failure to fulfill the representation.[33] Of course, if it turns out that upon full performance of the service or after the fulfillment of the representation, the plaintiff receives less than what he or she would have had if he or she had not relied, this cannot be imputed to the defendant as an injury but must be viewed as self-imposed by the plaintiff.

Now although this pre-reliance asset can be construed as originating prior to and independent of the parties' interaction—more specifically the defendant's invitation to rely—and so, to this extent, it appears to be the kind of protected interest required by tort law in contrast to contract law, there immediately arise the following related difficulties. First, the defendants did *not* in fact literally destroy or injure the plaintiffs' asset. Rather, the plaintiffs themselves made the over-payment. Their loss could not have occurred without their decision to make the over-payment. Why should the defendants be held responsible for the choice of others? Unless this is so, the plaintiffs cannot show that the *defendants injured* anything. Moreover, it might very well be that the plaintiffs never *actually* had an asset prior to the tortious interaction. For example, it might be the case that plaintiffs *could* have pursued some beneficial, opportunity but did not, in reliance upon the defendant. How can a *potential* benefit which a plaintiff never possessed count as an asset that exists prior to the tortious interaction? And in any case, at the point of negligence, the plaintiffs no longer have this asset and so, the argument goes, they do not have a present protected interest that can be injured.

If correct, these objections must be fatal to the plaintiff's action since it would follow from them that the first requirement of duty in negligence, viz that there be threatened injury to a protected interest, would not be satisfied. We would not have shown how reliance-based liability can be misfeasance and therefore how it can be a category of tort liability at all. The fact of invited reliance answers these objections. Because the defendants *induced* the plaintiffs to rely upon their service by making the payment on that basis, it does not lie in their mouth to deny responsibility for the reasonably foreseeable and unavoidable consequences of this reliance. As a matter of fairness and reasonableness between the parties, the defendants must be taken to have assumed responsibility for the consequences of the plaintiffs' reliance because of their own decision to invite the plaintiffs to rely. The plaintiffs' reliance, although their act, was invited: the consequences are imputed to the defendants and are not at the plaintiffs' risk. The same reasoning holds for the question of protected interest. The reason the plaintiffs either did not obtain, or gave up, the

---

[33] In another important decision, *Imperator Realty Co v Tull* 127 NE 263 (NY CA 1920), Justice Cardozo makes this point explicitly.

pre-reliance asset was that they responded reasonably to the defendants' invitation to rely upon their representations of performance. The plaintiffs, we suppose as a matter of fact, can show that they *could and would* have obtained or retained the benefit had they not been induced to forego it at the inducement of the defendants. In other words, they could and would have made it their own independent of their interaction with the defendants. Had they done so, it could and would have constituted a protected interest in the ordinary way as against the defendants. Once again, as a matter of reasonableness and fairness between the parties, the defendants are estopped from asserting that this foregone or lost opportunity is not a present, pre-existing asset which they must take reasonable care not to impair or damage. In light of their inducement to rely, the defendants must treat the foregone or lost opportunity as a present, pre-existing asset that functions as a protected baseline for the purposes of adjudicating the parties' interaction.

We can now appreciate the role that reliance plays in this analysis. For the defendant's conduct to constitute negligence, it must impair, injure or otherwise adversely affect some interest which the plaintiff can assert by rights as against the defendant. There is no such thing as negligence in the air. Apart from a plaintiff's reliance in the form of giving up a potential or actual benefit that otherwise could and would have been enjoyed, there is nothing but the defendant's performance or representation itself that can be the object of the protected interest which the plaintiff must have to bring an action in negligence. But a plaintiff can acquire a right to the performance or representation itself only on the basis of a contract between him or her and the defendant. It follows, therefore, that, in these circumstances, the plaintiff's reliance, in the sense of changing position to his or her detriment, is a *necessary* condition of the plaintiff having a legally protected interest for the purposes of negligence. This is essential to the plaintiff being able to claim for misfeasance.[34] Moreover, it is only insofar as this reliance *has been invited or induced* by the defendant that the consequences of the plaintiff's reliance can reasonably be imputed to the defendant and that the plaintiff's reliance can provide the basis of the *kind* of pre-existing protected interest that tort requires *against the defendant*. The assertion of a protected interest (of the kind required by the law of negligence), and the claim that the defendant has injured that interest, are worked out in light of the interaction between the parties, where this interaction is constituted by an inducement or invitation to rely on the one side and by reliance in response to such inducement on the other side. The requirement of injury to a protected interest is specified

---

[34] For an interesting and careful recent judicial discussion of the role of reliance in a different context in connection with the misfeasance/nonfeasance distinction, see *Childs*, above n 6, in particular at [31]-[48].

through this bilateral interaction. This is nowhere expressed more clearly than in Lush J's remarkable opinion in *Seale v Perry*, where he writes:

> In the negligent misrepresentation cases it may perhaps be said that a right arises in the plaintiff out of the facts of reliance by the plaintiff on the misrepresentation and an acceptance of responsibility by the defendant for the advice contained in the misrepresentation, a right which arises out of a relation of 'proximity', a para-contractual right.[35]

It is essential, I have argued, that the plaintiff's reliance be invited. In the absence of invitation, the reliance is not reasonable and, to that extent, the plaintiff can rightly claim neither a protected interest nor injury by the defendant. The standard by which the presence and extent of such invitation are determined is objective: how would the defendant's words and actions reasonably appear to the plaintiff as a reasonable person in the circumstances of their interaction? The plaintiff must be able reasonably to infer that the defendant has invited the plaintiff—not someone else—to rely in the way the plaintiff does rely. This entails that the plaintiff be able reasonably to infer that the defendant would himself or herself reasonably know that, by his or her words or actions, he or she would be so viewed by the plaintiff. In this sense, the plaintiff must reasonably be able to impute to the defendant an *intention* that the plaintiff rely upon him or her.[36] Whether a plaintiff can reasonably infer this can, of course, be decided only in light of the particular facts of the particular interaction between the parties.

In light of this discussion of invitation and reliance, I wish to deal with a related point that requires treatment because it is, in my view, too often misunderstood in a way that affects the fundamental analysis of liability in reliance situations. I am referring to the relevance of indeterminate liability.[37]

Supposing that the imposition of liability on a defendant would result in making him or her liable 'in an indeterminate amount for an indeterminate time to an indeterminate class,' to use the influential words of Cardozo J in *Ultramares v Touche*,[38] the question is: what is the relevance, if any, of this consideration to the analysis of negligence? The overwhelmingly prevailing

---

[35] [1982] VR 193 (SC) 202.

[36] See my discussions of this in 'The Basis for Excluding Liability for Pure Economic Loss in Tort Law' in D Owen (ed), *The Philosophical Foundations of Tort Law: A Collection of Essays* (New York, Oxford University Press, 1995) 450-54 and 'The Unity of Contract Law' in P Benson (ed), *The Theory of Contract Law: New Essays* (Cambridge, Cambridge University Press, 2001) 174 ff. My understanding of invitation and intention in the reliance context agrees with Stephen Perry's analysis in 'Protected Interests and Undertakings in the Law of Negligence' (1992) 42 *University of Toronto Law Journal* 247, 281-85.

[37] I have discussed this question in 'Pure Economic Loss,' above n 36, at 433-34 and more specifically Cardozo's view in n 19, above.

[38] 174 NE 441 (NY CA 1931) [*Ultramares*].

view—the view, for example, of the majority judgments in *White v Jones* and *Hill v Van Erp* as well as of the court in *Cooper*—is that this is a policy consideration that serves to limit or negate a prima facie finding of duty at a first stage of analysis. In the past, this view went hand in hand with an approach to negligence that founded a prima facie duty of care on foreseeability alone. When 'proximity' is equated with foreseeability and a prima facie duty is imposed for causing relational economic loss just so long as it is foreseeable, the defendant may be subject to liability for extensive and indeterminate economic losses that arise through the complex interdependence of commercial interests in any modern society. This is viewed as unfair to defendants who may have been momentarily careless in relatively trivial ways. As well, such liability may be excessive from a social point of view. As a result, courts may limit or negate the finding of a duty when doing so is necessary to avoid the imposition of indeterminate liability.[39] Once this equation between duty and mere foreseeability is rejected, as it has been by the Supreme Court of Canada in *Cooper* and by the House of Lords in *Murphy* and other important decisions, it now becomes a fresh question as to whether this understanding of the significance of indeterminate liability is satisfactory. Although *Cooper* continues to endorse it,[40] it is by no means clear that it fits with the Supreme Court's new approach to proximity.

What is striking, to say the least, is that the very judgment which continues to be cited by all subsequent decisions and scholarly discussions as *the* modern statement of this view about indeterminate liability—the *Ultramares* case—does *not* in fact take it but rather understands its relevance *as part of the analysis of duty.* Cardozo J is very clear and explicit on this point: if the imposition of a duty toward the plaintiff would *eo ipso* expose the defendants to indeterminate liability to an indeterminate class, this must 'enkindle doubt whether a flaw may not exist in the implication of a duty that exposes to these consequences'.[41] Quoting his earlier decision in *HR Moch Co v Rensselaer Water Co*,[42] Justice Cardozo writes that as a result, '[t]he assumption of one relation will mean the involuntary assumption of a series of new relations, inescapably hooked together'.[43] His point may be put as follows. The central question in these situations is whether or not a defendant may reasonably be taken to have

---

[39] F James Jr, 'Limitations on Liability for Economic Loss Caused by Negligence: A Pragmatic Appraisal' (1972) 25 *Vanderbilt Law Review* 43.

[40] Above n 2, at [37].

[41] *Ultramares*, above n 38, at 444.

[42] Above n 18, at 899. In *Moch*, the plaintiff's action in negligence was denied despite the fact that he relied upon the defendant's undertaking to the city and to the public in general to supply water. The plaintiff could not reasonably view the defendant as having invited this reliance.

[43] Above n 18, at 899.

intended that a plaintiff rely upon his or her work or representation which was done at the immediate request of and for another under a contract between the defendant and this other person. If, in the particular circumstances, an affirmative conclusion would entail a similar assumption of responsibility of indefinite extent to indefinite others, it would prima facie be unreasonable to impute this intention (or assumption of responsibility) to the defendant even with respect to the plaintiff. It is not reasonably to be assumed that a person would take on a responsibility that cannot be measured and limited in advance. There would have to be clear evidence, in the face of the presumptive unreasonableness of this implication, that the defendant did in fact *undertake* a responsibility of this kind.

On this alternative view, the significance of the concern about indeterminate liability lies in its being a concern about imputing a certain kind of intention and assumption of responsibility to the defendant, which is the essential basis of the duty relation with the plaintiff. It is directly relevant to ascertaining the existence and the extent of an invitation to rely in given circumstances. It thus clearly pertains to the determination of duty. This conclusion is further supported by the fact that, to my knowledge, Justice Cardozo only refers to this consideration in the context of negligent *undertakings*. He does not treat it as a free-standing policy concern that can be deployed generally in negligence cases. Interestingly, in contract law cases such as *Kerr SS Co Inc v RCA*,[44] Cardozo treats the prospect of indeterminate liability in an identical way when determining what is clearly the same basic issue in a contract setting, namely, whether a defendant has assumed responsibility for the consequences of breach under the doctrine of *Hadley v Baxendale*.[45] Understood as relevant to the determination of a duty relation in reliance cases, the concern about indeterminate liability belongs therefore to the *first* stage of the *Anns* test as clarified in *Cooper.*

C.   The Two Fundamental Categories of Negligence: Comparisons and Conclusions

I want now to gather together the main conclusions that have emerged from the foregoing discussion of the duty relation in negligence. I have suggested two distinct categories of duty relation which nonetheless share the three common elements of, first, the idea of injury to a protected interest, next proximity (in the sense of closeness and directness), and finally foreseeability.

In the first category, the parties' relation is constituted by the defendant being active and the plaintiff being passive. The plaintiff merely asserts a

---

[44]   157 NE 140 (NY CA 1927).
[45]   (1854) 9 Ex 341, 156 ER 145 [*Hadley*].

right to exclude the defendant from something, does nothing, and seeks to be left alone. The defendant chooses a course of conduct which affects the plaintiff's protected interest, resulting in loss. Here, assuming that the plaintiff seeks redress for loss caused to his person or property, the central questions will be: was the plaintiff someone who would be closely and directly affected by the defendant's act and second, was injury to the plaintiff's interest reasonably foreseeable? For a duty to arise between the parties, all three elements must be satisfied. These are cases of so-called 'physical loss'.

In the second category of relation, the three elements are satisfied by an interaction in which both parties actively participate: the defendant invites the plaintiff to rely and the plaintiff, in turn, relies by changing position to his detriment. In the circumstances of these cases, this interaction is a necessary condition for the satisfaction of the three elements of the duty relation. It is only if the plaintiff has actually changed position in response to the defendant's invitation that he can possibly have a protected interest in tort (as opposed to contract) and the defendant's act or omission can be taken to be an injury to that interest. Absent reliance by the plaintiff upon the defendant, there is simply no pre-existing asset which can be affected by the defendant's act or omission. Absent the defendant's invitation to rely, the fact that the plaintiff does not pursue or no longer has this asset will be the consequence of *his or her,* not the defendant's, decision and so at the plaintiff's risk. Resulting loss will be the plaintiff's misfortune, not the defendant's responsibility. It will be *damnum absque injuria.* Just as there cannot be negligence in the air, so there cannot be closeness and directness or foreseeability in the air. These have application only as specified with respect to a protected interest of the requisite kind. For instance, with respect to the meaning of closeness and directness, the plaintiff counts as a 'neighbour' if, but only if, it was the intention, reasonably construed, of the defendant to invite reliance, such that the plaintiff's reliance was not collateral or incidental but rather the very end and aim of the invitation. Invited reliance is thus the lynch-pin of this second form of duty relation.

These two categories are mutually distinct. What is more, they represent a way in which the possible elementary forms of duty relations in negligence can be completely and exhaustively differentiated. This follows from the fact that they are contraries with respect to a basic aspect under which persons are viewed for the purposes of the analysis of negligence: whether the parties have interacted and therefore have done something or not. In the one case, only the defendant has acted; in the other, both parties have. To establish a duty relation in negligence, the parties' interaction must be amenable to an analysis in terms of either the physical loss model or the reliance-based model.

Let me return to *White v Jones*. Clearly, the way Lord Goff and the dissenting Law Lords present the *Hedley Byrne* principle, it is most consistent with the reliance-based model. They, correctly in my view, understand that *Hedley Byrne* treats the factor of reliance as an essential ingredient in the action and that it requires that such reliance must be reasonable as between the parties. While *Hedley Byrne* is a case of negligent misstatement, the principle it articulates is clearly not so limited but encompasses any interaction that is constituted by invited reliance. This is reflected in the Law Lords' endorsement of *Glanzer* and other cases involving negligent performance of a service as earlier statements of the principle. Indeed, so long as there is the requisite interaction of invited reliance, with the plaintiff changing position to his or her detriment, it makes no difference whether the loss is purely financial or physical: either is recoverable. It is perhaps Lord Mustill who brings out most fully the interactional basis of duty under this principle. That is why they agree that the *Hedley Byrne* principle cannot apply to the situation in *White v Jones* where, *ex hypothesi*, the plaintiffs do not rely in any way on the defendant and the plaintiffs cannot reasonably view the defendant as having assumed responsibility toward them. The plaintiffs have not changed position to their detriment. The sort of interaction which *Hedley Byrne* requires is simply absent.

In light of the foregoing analysis of the categories of duty relation in negligence, we must conclude that the defendant solicitor does not wrong the plaintiffs in negligence by failing to use due care in preparing the will for the testator. To apply the physical loss model, the plaintiffs must establish that they have an existing protected interest that can be injured by the non-completion of the will. But, as all the Law Lords agree, they have no such interest. Unless the plaintiffs have relied to their detriment at the invitation of the solicitor, they cannot satisfy the second category of liability. In the absence of a factual basis to support reliance-based liability, there can be no liability *whatsoever* in negligence. The plaintiffs lack *any* protected interest that might be opposable against the solicitor. The solicitor has not injured anything belonging to the plaintiffs that the law views as a protected interest. It is a case of nonfeasance. On the analysis proposed here, Lord Goff correctly rejects the approach taken in *Ross* which, I have suggested, is indistinguishable from, and therefore subject to the very same difficulties as, *Biakanja*.

This same conclusion holds from the standpoint of *Cooper*. The Supreme Court of Canada lists, among the established categories of proximity, the categories of physical loss and of liability for negligent misstatement. I suggest that the two kinds of duty relations in negligence that I have presented in this chapter should be taken to underpin these well-established categories. There are no other categories listed by the Supreme Court that provide a basis for finding a relation of proximity between private individuals in a situation where there is nothing analogous to physical harm to property or person and where there is a complete absence of jjreliance, by the plaintiff upon the defendant. To the contrary, liability is denied in circumstances of relational economic loss where an appropriate protected interest is lacking. In light of my account of the two fundamental categories of negligence, the Supreme Court should not treat the question of a solicitor's liability to an intended beneficiary for a failed bequest in the absence of reliance as requiring a novel category of proximity. Rather, it should take the view that recognised principles of negligence already settle the question and that like cases of relational economic loss, liability should be denied. The requisite conditions of duty—which include more than mere foreseeability—have not been met at the first stage of the *Anns* test.

III.   THE REQUIREMENTS OF JUSTICE AND A PROPOSED SOLUTION

No differently than the dissenting Law Lords, Lord Goff holds that the plaintiffs' claim can neither be brought within the *Hedley Byrne* principle nor sustained as an 'ordinary action in tortious negligence' (that is, as a 'physical loss' case). He implicitly treats these two routes as exhaustive, insofar as he does not propose a third possible basis of duty between the parties. Thus far, I have tried to show that Lord Goff's analysis and conclusions are supportable at the level of first principles. But this is not the end of the story. Lord Goff's focus shifts from the basis of duty and liability to the need for a remedy. However, in deciding whether or not to grant a remedy in negligence, he treats these two matters as completely separate and unconnected. His discussion of the appropriateness of a remedy is free-standing and is independent of his analysis of duty. It is only in this way that he is able to come to his decision to grant the plaintiff a direct remedy in negligence. In order to fashion an effective remedy to achieve practical justice, Lord Goff extends to the disappointed beneficiary a remedy under the *Hedley Byrne* principle by holding that the assumption of responsibility by the solicitor towards his client should be held in law to extend to the beneficiary who may be foreseeably deprived of the intended legacy as a result of the solicitor's carelessness. He concludes that as a result of this extension of the *Hedley Byrne* principle, imposing liability on the solicitor in these circumstances does not entail the conceptual difficulties that beset *Ross*: 'In the result, *all* the conceptual problems...can be seen to fade innocuously away.'[46]

I want to begin my discussion of Lord Goff's reasons for extending this remedy by considering the last point. We saw that the difficulties with the

---

[46] *White v Jones*, above n 1, at 269 (emphasis added).

Ross approach are genuinely conceptual, in that it fails to satisfy certain essential prerequisites of the duty relation and it seems clearly to be in tension with the exclusionary rule for relational economic loss. The *Hedley Byrne* principle is not subject to these difficulties because, but *only* because, it is reliance-based in the manner I have explained. But Lord Goff himself concludes that reliance-based liability is inapplicable to the facts of *White v Jones* and he therefore holds that, so understood, the analysis of duty in *Hedley Byrne* does not sustain the plaintiff's action. Nevertheless, he holds that the assumption of responsibility by solicitor to client, which arises through invited reliance, can be 'held in law to extend' to the beneficiary who has not relied and not been invited to rely. How can an 'extension' of the remedy under *Hedley Byrne* unmoored from its analysis of duty resolve any of the conceptual difficulties? It is submitted that it cannot .

Despite this conclusion, we must still consider the 'reasons of justice'[47] which lead Lord Goff, like the majority of judges and academic writers, to conclude that some remedy must be available to the disappointed beneficiary in at least certain circumstances. As I already noted, Lord Goff holds that the remedy under *Hedley Byrne* must be given 'to fill a lacuna in the law and so prevent the injustice which would otherwise occur on the facts of cases such as the present'.[48] Not only is this contention of a lacuna the single crucial point which separates Lord Goff from the dissenting Law Lords. In addition, Canadian courts that endorse Lord Goff's justification, such as *Graham v Bonnycastle*, make this the basis of recovery and treat it as a limiting condition to recovery.[49] What exactly, according to Lord Goff, is this lacuna and how does it arise?

Although the solicitor has breached his or her contract with the testator and, in addition, has failed to discharge an assumption of responsibility in negligence toward the testator under the principle of *Hedley Byrne*, the loss resulting from these breaches of duty is sustained not by the testator but rather by the intended beneficiary. Neither the testator nor the estate has sustained any financial detriment. Because neither the testator nor his or her estate has suffered a loss, neither will have a remedy against the solicitor. At most, they can recover nominal damages. The beneficiary, by contrast, *has* sustained a loss: the beneficiary has lost the benefit intended by the testator. But for the solicitor's breach of duty, the beneficiary would have received it. However, the beneficiary has an action neither in contract (being a third party beneficiary) nor in negligence (in the absence of reliance). Consequently—this, according to Lord Goff, is the lacuna in the law—the only person who may have a valid claim (the testator or estate)

---

[47]   The phrase is used by Lord Goff, *White v Jones*, above n 1, at 259.
[48]   *Ibid*, at 268.
[49]   (2004) 354 AR 266 (CA).

cannot recover and the only person who has suffered a loss (the beneficiary) has no claim. The solicitor's duty turns out to be meaningless. To fill
this lacuna and therefore to ensure 'practical justice', Lord Goff extends
the remedy under *Hedley Byrne* to the beneficiary, who now has a
free-standing claim against the solicitor.

At first blush, the claim that there is a lacuna seems puzzling. On the one
hand, if, as Lord Goff holds, a duty owed to the beneficiary cannot be
rooted in widely accepted principles of negligence, then, in the absence of
some hitherto unrecognised principled basis that can be coherently integrated into negligence law, the beneficiary's claim must fail. Since no duty
has been found to exist, it would therefore be a *requirement* of the law that
the beneficiary be non-suited for failing to state a cause of action in
negligence. Lord Goff does not propose a new principle but instead is
concerned, as he explains, to fashion 'an effective remedy for the solicitor's
breach of his professional duty to his client'.[50] On the other hand, if, as
Lord Goff contends, neither the testator nor the estate has suffered a loss in
contract law or tort law—in other words, if it is the case that the estate
should only receive nominal damages if it were to bring an action against
the solicitor for breach of contract—this result is also *required* as a matter
of law. Here, then, we have two required legal outcomes in the apparently
correct analysis of two distinct and separate sets of relation. Neither
outcome, being required, represents a lacuna in the law. Nor can taking
them together possibly result in a lacuna. Supposing this analysis of the
parties' claims in contract and negligence to be correct, there cannot be a
lacuna.

Despite this conclusion, it is striking that the great majority of judges
and academic writers who have considered the question of whether a
disappointed beneficiary should have recourse to a remedy have answered
in the affirmative. The remedy has taken different forms. But a remedy has
been given. Lord Goff refers to the 'reasons of justice' that prompt judges
and writers to reach this conclusion. I do not think it would be reasonable
to ignore or dismiss the sense, so widespread, that justice requires some
remedy. But what exactly is the injustice that needs correction and what is
the appropriate remedy to do this? These are the two main questions that I
address in the remainder of this chapter. In answering them, I shall suppose
throughout that there is no such thing as justice-in-the-air but that
questions of justice between parties are determined solely by reference to
their legally recognised rights *inter se*. A claim of justice must be made by
one party against another and must be rooted in a relation of right and
correlative duty between them. Moreover, I suppose that for a remedy to

---

[50]   *White v Jones*, above n 1, at 260.

be appropriate it must cohere with, and not distort or obfuscate, established principles of tort and contract law.

At different points in his speech, Lord Goff refers to the injustice to the disappointed beneficiary as well as to the testator that results if the solicitor is not liable in damages for his carelessness. As we have seen, Lord Goff presupposes that while the solicitor has breached his contract with the testator, neither the testator nor the estate is entitled to anything more than nominal damages. And while the disappointed beneficiary has not received the intended legacy, this is at most *damnum absque injuria* since he is only a third party and has not relied. Just as there does not seem to be a lacuna in the law here (because the result that no substantial damages can be awarded is required by principles of contract and tort), so there does not seem to be any injustice here, (because the only violation of rights that has occurred is corrected in accordance with legal principle). Yet it is precisely the fact that 'neither the testator's estate nor the disappointed beneficiary will have a claim for the loss' which Lord Goff identifies as '*the* injustice which...the judges of this country should address by recognising that cases such as these call for an appropriate remedy'.[51]

The legally required outcome of no damages for the estate and no claim by the disappointed beneficiary must now become our focus. Thus far, I have simply assumed, with Lord Goff, that this conclusion is indeed required by legal principles. But is it? To set the stage for this discussion, I wish to contrast the idea of a lacuna, as Lord Goff understands it, with the so-called 'black hole' cases.

In what is perhaps the most often cited black hole case reference in English law, *GUS Property Manage*ment *Ltd v Littlewoods Mail Order Stores Ltd*,[52] the defendants negligently damaged a building which at the time was owned by R. Shortly thereafter, R transferred title to the building to the plaintiffs, a newly created, wholly owned subsidiary company. The agreed-upon price was set, in an internal group transaction and for accounting purposes only, without any reference to the true market value of the building. Some time after ownership was transferred, R assigned to the plaintiffs any rights it had as against the defendants arising out of their negligence. By this assignment, the plaintiffs were entitled to claim recovery of any loss suffered by R. But it had to be R's loss, not their own. While the plaintiffs, as new owners, had repaired the building at their own

---

[51] *White v Jones*, above n 1, at 269 (emphasis added). Lord Goff refers to other secondary 'reasons of justice', at 259-60. These include the importance of legacies in modern society, the point that a solicitor cannot complain if liability is imposed one way or another for unreasonably defeating his or her client's testamentary intentions, and the fact that the public relies on solicitors to prepare wills. It seems to be Lord Goff's view that while these points reinforce and supplement his central concern, they would not, by themselves, require that a remedy be fashioned.

[52] 1982 SC HL 157.

expense, R had not made any such expenditures. The defendants argued that by transferring title to the plaintiffs for consideration, R had lost any claim for damages against the defendants. Any loss sustained was by the plaintiffs, not R. Thus, the plaintiff acquired no claim to damages through R's subsequent assignment to them.

At the House of Lords, Lord Keith of Kinkel, with whom the other Law Lords agreed, rejected the defendants' argument, writing that it 'is absurd to suggest that in such circumstances the claim to damages would disappear … into some legal black hole, so that the wrongdoer escaped scot-free'.[53] R's claim crystallised when its building was damaged through the defendants' negligence. R did not lose its title and interest to pursue this claim simply by parting with its property to another. Its claim did not disappear into a legal black hole, with the consequence that neither R nor anyone who stood in its place was entitled to recover the loss. Moreover, the fact that R received consideration in return for the transfer of its building was relevant only insofar as it established that R obtained some value for the property. It went to a claim for damages measured by diminution in value. The question remained as to what R would have received had the building not been damaged. The fact that repairs were made and paid for by the plaintiffs and not R does not show that R had not suffered a loss. The cost of repairs incurred by the plaintiffs were relevant as also indicating the scale of expenditure which it was likely that R would have had to incur if it had continued to own the building. As such, it could have evidential value for the purpose of estimating the loss suffered by R, depending upon which measure of recovery—diminution of value or cost of repairs—was determined to be appropriate.

When Lord Keith speaks of a legal black hole, he is referring, I think, to the possibility that a valid legal claim to substantial damages can simply disappear, not because it has been satisfied or waived, but by operation of a rule that is has nothing to do with the merits of the claim, with the result that the duty is effectively unenforceable. Notice that what disappears is a *valid legal claim* for *substantial damages*. This is different than Lord Goff's lacuna where, according to him, the valid claim (the estate's) is *not* for any damages and the loss (the beneficiary's) is *not* actionable as a valid claim. I want to pursue the idea that the problem with non-recovery in *White v Jones* is analogous to the black hole. To see it in this way, it is essential to identify in at least one of the parties a valid claim for substantial damages that arises from the defendant's wrong. So far as the beneficiary is concerned, the central argument of this chapter is that no such right exists in negligence. Nor does it exist in contract, since the beneficiary is not a party to the contract with the solicitor. Against this, one might point to the

---

[53] *Ibid*, at 177.

fact that a number of jurisdictions recognise a limited 'contractual' remedy in certain circumstances for third party beneficiaries. While the availability of this remedy is well-established and its basis merits careful consideration—which I will take up shortly when I set out a proposed solution—none of these jurisdictions treats the beneficiary as having in law a full, free-standing contractual right. The claim is subject to conditions, qualifications, and defences that are incompatible with its being such. If there is a valid claim for substantial damages, it must belong to the testator or his estate.

Here we must take on the view, often asserted without any argument, that while the testator or his estate can certainly sue the solicitor for breach of contract, the estate can recover only nominal damages for the breach. I shall try to show that this conclusion is wrong in principle and that is not required by authority.

All agree that where a testator discovers before his or her death that the solicitor has failed to prepare a will in accordance with his or her instructions, the testator can, if necessary, sue the solicitor for breach of contract and recover, by way of damages, any costs or losses associated with having a proper will prepared. Such substantial damages, whether small or large, ensure that the testator receives by way of damages the performance owed him or her by the solicitor. Now suppose that the testator dies before discovering any deficiency or defect in the will or finds out when he or she is no longer able to make a will and his or her testamentary intentions are frustrated. The legacy goes, not to the intended beneficiary, but to someone else. The breach of the testator's contractual right, which survives his or her death, produces the following further consequential loss: the solicitor in effect directs the testator's assets toward the wrong person, thereby vitiating the testator's power to dispose of his or her assets in the way he or she sees fit and has sole authority to decide. To vindicate the testator's valid and continuing contractual right, this consequential loss has to be remedied. The fact that the testator is dead or otherwise not in a position to make a will should not cause his or her claim to a remedy for consequential loss to disappear in a legal black hole of nominal damages.

Such consequential loss is in principle recoverable under the first branch of *Hadley*. To meet this test, it will be recalled, a plaintiff must establish that the loss was reasonably contemplated by the parties at the time of contract formation as something that would likely result from the breach in the usual course of events. More particularly, the testator or the estate must show that it was reasonably apparent to the solicitor at the time of contract formation that a main or principal purpose of the testator in requesting the solicitor's service was to confer the benefit upon the third party. By contracting on this basis, the solicitor may reasonably be taken to have assumed responsibility for the foreseeable effects of his or her breach upon this intended use. In *White*, for example, it seems clear that the estate could satisfy this test. Where, however, a breach affects third parties in a way that does not frustrate a reasonably apparent purpose of this kind, there should not be liability under this test, even if the loss is " foreseeable". Being extrinsic to such purposes, the loss is indeterminate in relation to the transaction. But it cannot be reasonable to impute to the defendant an intention to assume responsibility for such loss. This analysis also applies if the defendant is sued in tort by third parties under the *Hedley Byrne* principle. Absent direct interaction between the defendant and third parties affected by the negligent performance, the latter have to show that their reliance is part of the testator's end and aim in requesting the defendant's service. The kind of loss that was denied in *Ultramares* would also fail the *Hadley* test.

Supposing that on the facts of *White* the estate can sue the solicitor for consequential loss under *Hadley*, the question is how to measure it. General principles dictate that the consequential loss is measured by what it costs to transfer the intended asset to the beneficiary: nothing more but also nothing less. Since the asset, we suppose, is irretrievably gone as a matter of law and fact, the measure of this cost is essentially the value of the intended asset. This value is what the defendant solicitor owes the testator or his or her representative by way of damages. However, while the defendant owes the estate this value, the estate is not entitled to keep it for itself. This is because the entire basis of its claim to such damages is that they represent the cost of transferring the asset to the third party, in keeping with the crystallised and unalterable intention of the deceased testator. This is the loss suffered by the testator: not the depletion of his or her holdings but the vitiation of his or her power to dispose of his or her assets in a particular way. For the estate to keep the value of the asset for itself would be to recover an uncovenanted profit at the defendant's expense. The damages represent the value of the injury or wrong to the testator's contractual right. But, on this analysis, the right to performance is vested with, and the injury is suffered by, the testator (or his or her representative) *only*. Because the only right and loss in question here are those of the promisee alone, no issue of privity arises.

From this legal perspective, an agreement with you for consideration to deliver my horse to a third party or to deliver your horse to the third party would be essentially the same as the above transaction. It is true that in these transactions, you are obliged directly to transfer the horse to the third party as part of your contractual performance and that it is part of my right against you that you transfer the horse in accordance with the agreed-upon terms. But the only difference this makes is that the right to substantial damages representing the value of the transfer would now be a simple application of the expectation remedy rather than a claim to damages for consequential loss under *Hadley*. Otherwise, the analysis would be identical. What in both cases I contract for is not an asset for myself but rather your *service of conferring, directly or consequentially, a benefit on a third party*, not privy to our agreement. If damages are merely nominal, you are entitled to keep the consideration and do nothing in return. This clearly deprives me of the whole consideration promised. It turns your obligation into an illusory and unenforceable duty and denies the whole end and aim of the transaction. Without question, nominal damages would be completely inadequate.

The claim that a plaintiff can have a contractual right to substantial damages for breach of a duty to perform a service that directly or consequentially benefits a third party is consistent with authority and well-reasoned judicial opinions. Where the defendant's contractual duty is directly to confer a benefit upon a third party, the important case of *Beswick v Beswick* establishes without any doubt that nominal damages would be grossly inadequate and that, where reasonable and possible, the defendant will be ordered to specifically perform the promised service, even where the service is transferring money.[54] In that case, both at the Court of Appeal and in the House of Lords, all the judges rejected the defendant's argument that the deceased party's personal representative could recover only nominal damages because the breach did not cause the estate a financial loss.

While *Beswick* involves a contractual obligation to transfer a benefit directly to a third party and the remedy given is specific performance, the same reasoning animates a number of recent decisions and judicial opinions which show that it applies equally to circumstances where the benefit is conferred as a consequence of the service and where damages rather than specific performance are granted. There is the body of decisions led by *Radford v De Froberville*[55] and *Ruxley Electronics and Construction Ltd v Forsyth*[56] as well as the important judicial opinions (which have received wide academic discussion and endorsement) of Lord Griffiths in *St Martins Property Corporation Ltd v Sir Robert McAlpine Ltd*[57] and of Lords Goff and Millett in *Alfred McAlpine Construction Ltd v Panatown Ltd*,[58] to mention the most influential recent instances.[59]

---

[54]   [1968] AC 58 (HL) [*Beswick*].
[55]   [1977] 1 WLR 1262 (Ch) [*Radford*] (Oliver J).
[56]   [1996] AC 344 (HL) [*Ruxley*].
[57]   [1994] 1 AC 85 (HL) [*St Martins*].
[58]   [2001] 1 AC 518 (HL) [*Panatown*].
[59]   Of course there are others. See for example, Lord Scarman's speech in *Woodar Investment Development Ltd v Wimpey Construction UK Ltd* [1980] 1 WLR 277 (HL) 300-1 (quoted with approval by Lord Millett in *Panatown*, at 589) or Lord Nicholls' statement: 'The law recognizes that a party to a contract may have an interest in performance which is not readily measurable in terms of money. On breach the innocent party suffers a loss. He fails to obtain the benefit promised by the other party to the contract.' (see *A-G v Blake* [2001] 1 AC 268 (HL) 282).

The upshot of these decisions and opinions is the simple proposition that a contracting party is not limited to nominal damages but, to the contrary, can be entitled to substantial damages for breach of contract even where the defendant's obligation is to perform a service that is reasonably intended or understood by both parties to confer a financial benefit, not on the contracting party, but rather on a third party. The measure of the contracting party's damages may be cost of performance or diminution of value, depending on the contract and surrounding circumstances. The proposition is presented and understood as based upon 'classical contract theory'[60] and as reflecting the general and ruling principle of contract damages that the aim of contract remedies is to give the plaintiff the value of the promised performance in fulfilment of his or her reasonable contractual expectations. In this way, the plaintiff's performance or expectation interest is sufficiently protected.[61] Recognition of the plaintiff's right as promisee to substantial damages does not raise an issue of privity.

Perhaps the most perspicuous discussions of this proposition are those found in the speeches of Lords Goff and Millett in *Panatown*. Both are clear and emphatic that the issue at hand is determining the plaintiff's, and not the third party's, loss from the breach of contract and that the only loss which the plaintiff is entitled to claim for the purposes of damages is his or her own.[62] Both reject limiting the scope of such loss to the 'diminution in [the promisee's] overall financial position resulting from the breach'.[63] Instead, the plaintiff's loss consists in her not receiving the bargain for which he or she contracts—whether the performance of the bargain financially benefits the plaintiff or a third party.[64] And both see the requirement that a plaintiff must not keep the damages for his or her own benefit but rather must dispose of them consistently with the terms of the agreed-upon performance as ensuring that the plaintiff's remedy is reasonably required to compensate for the loss caused without giving the plaintiff an uncovenanted profit at the defendant's expense.[65] This does not mean that the plaintiff is accountable for the damages to the third party.[66] It implies no relation of rights between them. It is the plaintiff's loss and his alone that is being compensated. No issue of privity is raised. Nor does the plaintiff's claim to substantial damages representing the cost of performance depend upon the plaintiff actually being out-of-pocket for this

---

[60] *Darlington Borough Council v Wiltshier Northern Ltd* [1995] 1 WLR 68 (CA) 80 (Steyn LJ).
[61] *Panatown,* above n 58, at 546 (Lord Goff).
[62] See, eg, *Panatown,* above n 58, at 580 (Lord Millett).
[63] *Panatown,* above n 58, at 588 (Lord Millett).
[64] *Ibid,* at 547-48 (Lord Goff).
[65] *Ibid,* at 556 (Lord Goff) and 593 (Lord Millett).
[66] *Ibid,* at 594 (Lord Millett).

amount.[67] As already indicated, all that the plaintiff must show is that this measure of damages quantifies the value of performance for which he gave consideration, subject always to the proviso that the damages recovered be used for the purpose of performance.[68]

Six years after *White v Jones*, in *Panatown*, Lord Goff works out the consequences of this view. In one of his hypothetical illustrations,[69] Lord Goff instances a contract made by a father who wishes to help his daughter by making improvements to her house at his expense and as a gift to her so that she can then put her house up for sale. He enters into a contract with a builder that contains a liquidated damages clause. The sum specified in the clause is intended to reflect the economic circumstances prevailing at the time and the enhancement in the value of the house when the work is done on time and in accordance with the contract. The question is whether, supposing the building work is delayed in breach of contract, the father

---

[67] *Ibid*, at 547 (Lord Goff).

[68] This 'proviso', as I have called it, applies as well to the *White v Jones* scenario inasmuch as the estate is not entitled to retain for itself the damages recovered which must go instead to the third party. Drawing on the important remarks of Oliver J in *Radford*, Lord Lloyd in *Ruxley* and Lord Goff in *Panatown* see this proviso as ensuring that the basis of the plaintiff's claim—which is that the defendant has failed to perform a particular service for the benefit of the plaintiff himself or for a third party—is reasonably carried through at the remedial stage, no less but also no more. The plaintiff should not use a remedy to recover an uncovenanted profit or to impose on the defendant an uncovenanted burden. This view can be elaborated as follows. Where, for example, a plaintiff claims the kind of interest in performance that may justify the more onerous measure of cost of performance instead of diminution in value, the court wants to ensure that this higher measure is genuinely necessary to remedy the breach and that it truly reflects a loss that the plaintiff has genuinely suffered. In this regard, cost of performance is equivalent in damages to specific performance. A plaintiff may only obtain specific performance if a less onerous damage award is inadequate to protect his or her contractual interest. When the plaintiff is granted specific performance, the plaintiff does not receive money damages which can be used to purchase other things; what he or she obtains is just the performance of the terms. When, in given circumstances, damages measuring cost of performance (repairs, reinstatement) are higher than the diminution in value caused by a breach, a court may similarly require the plaintiff to justify the need for the more onerous measure of damages. Cost of performance aims to approximate specific performance, albeit through an award of damages. Hence, in the words of Lord Griffiths, a court 'will of course wish to be satisfied that the repairs have been or are likely to be carried out'. (*St Martins*, above n 57, at 97). If, to the contrary, the plaintiff treats the cost of performance damage award as a means of purchasing other things rather than to accomplish the performance promised, the plaintiff's interest in performance is no longer as claimed. It is now an interest in value and diminution in value is adequate to repair the loss. I think that something like this rationale animates Lord Lloyd's discussion of this issue in *Ruxley*, above n 56, at 372, which he concludes with the following illustration. 'Suppose in the present case Mr Forsyth had died and the action had been continued by his executors. Is it to be supposed that they would be able to recover the cost of reinstatement, even though they intended to put the property on the market without delay?' For other discussions of this issue, see B Coote, 'Contract Damages, *Ruxley*, and the Performance Interest' [1997] 56 *CLJ* 537, 559-70; S Smith, *Contract Theory* (Oxford, Oxford University Press, 2004) 422; C Webb, 'Performance and Compensation: An Analysis of Contract Damages and Contractual Obligation' (2006) 26 *OJLS* 41, 62-65.

[69] *Panatown*, above n 58, at 555.

cannot enforce the clause on the ground that it is not, and cannot be, a genuine pre-estimate of *his* loss. Here is Lord Goff's answer:

> The whole purpose of the father in placing the contract at his own expense is to ensure that his daughter is in a position to reap the benefit of that enhancement; and I do not see why the sum so specified should not constitute a genuine pre-estimate of the damage suffered by him by reason of the delay in receiving the benefit of the building work. Indeed, he will then be in a position to make good the gift which he intended to make to his daughter, by handing the damages over to her; and he will, if necessary, have no difficulty in satisfying a court of his intention to do so. If that is not right, it is difficult to see how there could be an effective liquidated damages clause in such a contract, although such clauses are a manifest convenience to both parties in building contracts.[70]

What is remarkable about this answer is how far Lord Goff carries the logic of protecting a contracting party's expectation interest even with respect to a subsidiary clause the benefit of which is intended to, and can, be enjoyed solely by the third party. What the defendant promises the father is a service (improvements made to his daughter's house) at a certain time and the fact that it is delayed, although it cannot affect his interests, constitutes a *loss suffered by him*; and the measure of *his* loss is set by a clause whose *sole* purpose is to benefit his daughter. The defendant's delay presumably postpones the sale of the house and results in the daughter not having the benefit of the sale money from the house when she should have, had the defendant performed on time. This is her father's loss because he is unable to give her the kind of gift that would have been possible if the defendant performed as promised. The particular kind of loss in question here is *consequential* loss that would ordinarily have to satisfy the test in *Hadley*.[71]

This same analysis, as Lord Goff himself presents and explains it, applies to the testator-intended beneficiary scenario. The testator employs the defendant to perform a service which, if performed as promised, will result in the intended beneficiary receiving an entitlement to the intended benefit. The testator's loss is that he or she is unable to give the beneficiary the gift he or she intends. The means of accomplishing this aim is the defendant's promise and the defendant's breach of contract makes it impossible for the testator to accomplish his or her goal. Giving the third party this benefit is the *use* which the testator makes of the defendant's promised performance. It comes squarely within the purview of *Hadley* as a form of consequential

---

[70]   *Ibid.*

[71]   For an excellent discussion of this issue, see Coote, above n 68, at 552. Lord Goff expressly approves Coote's argument that such consequential damages may be recoverable by the plaintiff even in a three-person context. See, *Panatown*, above n 58, at 556. Interestingly, Coote suggests that this analysis also applies to a *White v Jones* scenario. Is it unreasonable to think that Lord Goff himself must surely agree, given what he says in *Panatown* and in light of his express endorsement of Coote's view?

loss. The measure of damages must be that which is necessary to repair this loss. Where the intended benefit is transferred to the wrong person as a result of the defendant's breach and the estate cannot recover it, the estate can do nothing more to mitigate this loss. The defendant must provide damages equivalent to the value of the intended benefit. The court must be satisfied that the damages will be transferred to the third party in accordance with the testator's intention. Otherwise, the remedy is unnecessary to vindicate the plaintiff's contractual interest.

In my view, this analysis is not only consistent with but is indeed required by fundamental principles of contract law. The defendant solicitor's breach of contract gives the testator's personal representative a claim to substantial damages reflecting the loss caused. Now, if this is correct, the lacuna which Lord Goff asserts in *White v Jones* does *not* exist: the person with a valid claim *can* have a right to more than merely nominal damages. It is critically important, however, to keep in mind that, on the foregoing analysis, there is *only* one loss—the testator's. That the third party will benefit from performance and therefore is deprived of this benefit by breach is a matter of fact, not rights: there is no right to this benefit or any injury suffered through its deprivation. The only legal relation is that between testator and solicitor. The analysis does not challenge the doctrine of privity. The fact that the third party would have received a benefit or obtained a right had there been no breach of contract or negligence in relation to the testator does not make this benefit or potential entitlement a protected interest belonging to the third party. All that it establishes is a causal relation of fact between the defendant's conduct and the outcome. Similarly, the fact that I sustain injury because you do not rescue me from risk which you have not imposed does not establish that, as against you, I have a protected interest in the condition of being free from this harm and that you interfere with a protected interest by failing to help. Whether something is a protected interest is a question of right, not fact.[72] The very concept of injury in tort or contract presupposes the possibility of *damnum absque injuria*.

Thus far, I have tried to establish the proposition that the testator or his or her representative can have by ordinary contract principle a contractual

---

[72] Gaudron J fails to make this distinction in *Hill v Van Erp*, above n 3, at 197 when she writes: 'Once it is accepted...that but for negligence on the part of a solicitor, a person would have benefited under the will of a testator, the would-be beneficiary's loss is not properly treated as the loss of a mere *spes successionis*. To determine what has been lost, it is necessary to look to the situation as it would have been had there been no negligence. And when viewed in that way, it is apparent that the intended beneficiary has lost a legal right, namely, the right to have the testator's estate properly administered in accordance with the terms of the will.' McHugh J (dissenting) does not make this mistake (see 211-13). On the contrary, his opinion stands almost alone in the High Court in taking seriously and understanding the conceptual difficulties set out by Lord Goff.

claim to substantial damages equaling the value of the gift he or she intended to confer upon the third party. The testator's representative should have a right to sue for substantial damages because in breach of contract the defendant has caused the testator's intended gift to go to the wrong person, thereby vitiating the testator's power to dispose of his or her goods after death. The fact that this breach does not affect the net wealth of the estate is irrelevant. At this point, however, we must take into account the fact peculiar to *White v Jones* and other such cases, namely, that it is an *estate*, governed by the law of intestacy and wills, which is suing. What consequences follow from this? There are, at bottom, two different views.

The first is that the estate, no differently than the testator or his or her personal representative, can recover for breach of contract damages equaling the intended but failed gift. Supposing this view to be correct, the question arises: what if the estate, for its own valid reasons, declines to bring an action against the defendant? Since the estate does not stand to be benefited in a pecuniary sense from enforcement of the deceased testator's right, the motive to enforce that right may be lacking. Here there *does* appear to be a lacuna. There is a potential gap between the testator and the estate that is unavoidable given the divergent interests between them. The lacuna lies in the fact that the representative of one who has a valid claim for substantial damages may not have an incentive to enforce it. As a result of this divergence, the testator's contractual interest may not be fulfilled and the defendant's duty may become unenforceable, giving rise to unjust enrichment by the defendant at the testator's expense. The absence of incentive on the part of the estate has nothing to do with the justice of the claim. And that is the problem. While the testator's claim does not, strictly speaking, disappear into a legal black hole because the estate has standing to sue for substantial damages and may choose to exercise this right, this outcome—and therefore the justice that is owed the testator—is by no means assured.

The second view is this. The estate is governed by the laws respecting wills and intestacy. Suppose, for example, that the estate has been distributed under a valid will, albeit not the one intended by the testator. This second view treats the law of wills as *superseding* the contractual claim for breach and holds that the estate has *not* been injured by the unintended distribution. It is not just that the estate is not worse off financially as a result of the breach. By operation of the law of wills, the estate has no grounds for complaint. If this view is accepted,[73] there *is* indeed a problem of a legal black hole in the strict sense: the operation of

---

[73] Although by no means clear, both Lord Mustill (278) and Lord Goff (266) make remarks in *White v Jones*, above n 1, that appear to reflect this view.

the *law* of wills causes the contractual claim to substantial damages to disappear without satisfying it or showing it to be invalid.

On either view, it must be emphasised that the problem does not arise from tort or contract law. I have tried to show how these provide a complete and plausible account of the duty relations between the parties and of the modes of enforcing those duties. The common law of contract does not require an unduly narrow conception of loss that defeats the parties' expectations and leads to injustice. Rather, the problem lies solely either in the possible divergence of interests between the testator and his estate or the fact that the law of wills is treated as superseding the testator's valid contractual claim. On either view, the outcome is unjust. The testator's contractual right turns out to be worthless and illusory and the defendant's contractual duty to be unenforceable. From a legal point of view, this is intolerable. This brings me to the final question of whether the law can provide any means to avoid this. I will only present the most essential points.

Clearly, in the absence of a legislative solution, a judicial solution will give standing to sue to someone other than the estate. Given the argument of this chapter, however, it is essential that any such solution must respect the following two interrelated conditions. First, the solution must operate *only* at the remedial stage and must not presuppose the creation of any new rights or obligations at the duty stage.[74] It must in no way change or add to the analysis of rights and duties between the parties, whether in contract or in tort. It is crucial therefore that the solution, though giving the party a right of action against the solicitor, *not* base it upon a true free-standing and non-derivative right as against the defendant. There is no relation of right and duty between them. Second, the solution must not only be consistent with but must also fulfill the testator's contractual intention. In other words, it must embody the very same claim that the testator (or his or her personal representative) is entitled to assert and ensure the very same remedy that the testator (or his or her personal representative) should receive. Whoever has standing and however his or her standing is understood, the solution must put him or her in the exact position that the contracting party would occupy if it sued the defendant for breach of contract.

This approach stands in sharp contrast to the tortious solution in *White v Jones*. Lord Goff's extension of the *Hedley Byrne* principle requires that courts find a direct and free-standing relation of duty between solicitor and intended beneficiary. What is more, they must do so on a basis that lacks the very features of interaction required by that principle. Although Lord

---

[74] The solution provides, quite literally, 'an effective remedy for the solicitor's breach of his professional duty to his client'. See *White v Jones* [1993] 3 All ER 481 (CA) 489 (Nicholls V-C).

Goff himself frames the legal challenge as one of fashioning a suitable remedy, the solution he proposes encompasses the duty stage and imposes an ad hoc conclusion respecting duty detached from any recognised analysis of that concept.

Notice that the kind of remedial solution that I am proposing gives effect to the testator's *contractual* claim. This is the route favoured by most jurisdictions and writers.[75] Focusing on the testator's contractual interest seems natural and appropriate. Given that the relationship between a solicitor and his client is nearly always contractual, the contract provides the most explicit and complete legal ordering of the parties' interaction. Focusing upon the contractual relation gives primacy to the testator's intention to benefit the third party. This reflects the most significant legal feature of the situation. Even for Lord Goff, what takes the wills cases out of the general rule that a solicitor acting on behalf of a client owes a duty of care only to his or her client and not to third parties is that the third party's loss results from the solicitor's failure to give effect to the testator's intention. In the absence of invited reliance by the third party upon the solicitor, the only factor that brings the third party into the picture is the testator's intention. By contrast, a *tort* analysis based upon the *Hedley Byrne* principle focuses upon the *defendant's* intent to invite the plaintiff's reliance, not the testator's intention.

There are a variety of legal methods of achieving this solution. I will briefly touch on two, which appear offhand to be the most promising: subrogation[76] and a third party beneficiary action.

For present purposes, the notion of subrogation that is pertinent is the one that views it as an equitable remedy, not a cause of action, against a party who would otherwise be unjustly enriched.[77] As such, it is part of the

---

[75] Interestingly, this is also the view taken by the English Law Commission in its report on Privity of Contract (1996). See Report No 242, *Privity of Contract: Contracts for the Benefit of Third Parties* (London, the Stationary Office, 1996), at [7.27]: '[A]t a theoretical level we prefer the view that the right of the prospective beneficiaries *more properly belongs within the realm of contract than tort*....Had *White v Jones* been decided against the potential beneficiaries, we would have seriously contemplated a separate provision...giving [them] a right to sue the negligent solicitor for breach of contract. The primary basis of such a provision would have been that a right of action for the beneficiaries is *the only way to ensure that the promisee's expectations engendered by the solicitor's binding promise are fulfilled.*' (emphasis added) This statement is quoted by Stephen Waddams in his interesting chapter in this collection, 'Breaches of Contract and Claims by Third Parties'. It is thanks to his chapter that I became aware of it.

[76] This is the solution discussed by Waddams, above.

[77] Here I follow Lord Hoffman's classification and discussion of subrogation in *Banque Financière de la Cité v Parc (Battersea) Ltd* [1999] 1 AC 221 (HL) 236 *et seq* [*Banque Financière*]. Other discussions are *Boscawen v Bajwa* [1995] 4 All ER 769 (CA) 777 (Lord Millett) and Goff and Jones, *The Law of Restitution*, 6th edn (London, Sweet & Maxwell, 2002) ch 3.

law of restitution, not contract.[78] The categories of restitutionary subrogation, as it may be called, are not closed and the remedy is available in a variety of different factual situations to prevent unjust enrichment. Moreover, since the plaintiff is subrogated to the rights of another, there is no danger of confusion by attributing to the plaintiff a free-standing claim against the defendant. In the disappointed beneficiary scenario, the beneficiary would be subrogated to the testator's contractual claim against the solicitor and would bring an action in that capacity against the solicitor as defendant.

If subrogation can be understood very broadly as an equitable mechanism to enforce a remedy that would otherwise be defeated by 'accident'[79] and if it is plausible to view the lacuna or the legal black hole, discussed earlier, as such an accident, the basis for subrogation might be arguable.

On the other hand, if subrogation is in reality a mechanism to reverse unjust enrichment at the plaintiff's expense, it is not so clear that it can be applied without distorting its basis. In general terms, unless the third party has, as against the testator or the solicitor, some legally protected interest which they can affect either jointly or individually, I do not see how it is possible for either of them to be enriched at the expense of the third party. The third party must have as a matter of exclusive legal right something of his or her own that can be affected, used, or retained in some way (in connection with the breach or the claim for damages) by the solicitor or the estate for their benefit and at the third party's expense. This presupposes a relation of rights between the third party and these others (at least one of them). But there is no such relation. That is why the third party's claim fails in negligence. That is also why the third party cannot establish that anyone has been enriched at his or her expense. If subrogation is a remedy for unjust enrichment, then it is not available to the disappointed beneficiary.[80]

To conclude, I want to suggest that even a more appropriate route to a remedial solution would be to give the disappointed beneficiary standing to

---

[78] Subrogation also can be contractual. As such, it is a contractual arrangement for the transfer of rights against third parties and is founded upon the common intention of the parties. In Lord Hoffman's words, the contractual and restitutionary notions of subrogation represent 'radically different institutions.' *Banque Financière,* above n 77, at 231. Since there is no express or implied contract between the testator and the intended beneficiary, this contractual notion of subrogation does not apply.

[79] This is the rationale given by Turner LJ in *Jenner v Morris* (1861) 3 De GF & J 45, 45 ER 795. This reference is taken from Waddams, above n 75.

[80] I note that in Waddams, above n 75, he writes that in cases where subrogation is appropriate as a requirement of justice, 'the interests of the two potential claimants are closely aligned, and...the defendant would be unjustly enriched at the expense of the two potential claimants jointly if there were no liability to either.' While I agree that the defendant would in some sense be unjustly enriched at the estate's expense, I am questioning whether this would also be true in relation to the disappointed beneficiary.

sue as a third party beneficiary. In one form or another, this solution has been adopted and worked out in detail in a number of jurisdictions, most importantly in American common law and European civil law, and there is a large and rich body of academic writing to interpret and explain it. While not free from difficulties and wrong turns, it represents, to date, the most stable and workable solution which is 'in accordance with principle and also does practical justice between the parties, without leaving too great a legacy of problems for the future'.[81] For present purposes, I will highlight only the main features of the solution. But before doing so, it is essential that I make certain preliminary remarks to prevent misunderstanding.

This solution does not challenge or qualify the doctrine of privity, properly understood. The core idea at the heart of privity is that *only* persons who *participate in the interaction required to give rise to contractual rights and duties acquire such rights or are subject to such duties.* Supposing that a duty relation in contract must be constituted by mutually related manifestations of assent of the requisite kind,[82] only one who interacts in this way acquires a direct and free-standing *contractual* right and that right is, and must be, only as against the other party to the interaction. Understood in this way, the doctrine of privity is simply a manifestation of the core idea of private law which is: relations of rights and duties arise through and apply to conduct *inter se* and only those who engage in this way are related through such rights and duties. Each part of private law has—and must have—its own suitably specified idea of privity. For example, it is clearly the central organising idea that animates Justice Cardozo's great judgment in *Palsgraf*.[83] Similarly, under the *Hedley Byrne* principle, one who does not participate in the interaction of invited reliance cannot be subject to a duty of care or have the corresponding right to care. There can be no question of qualifying or 'making an exception to' the doctrine so understood, whether all at once or incrementally. Certainly, this cannot be done within the domain of contract law or negligence by courts whose task is to expound and develop private law.

---

[81] These are Lord Goff's words used in a different context in *Panatown*, above n 58, at 546.

[82] As a matter of positive law, this interaction must take the form of offer and acceptance and promise for consideration. I discuss this more fully in 'The Unity of Contract Law', above n 36.

[83] 'The plaintiff sues in her own right for a wrong personal to her, and not as the vicarious beneficiary of a breach of duty to another... .The passenger far away, if the victim of a wrong at all, has a cause of action, not derivative, but original and primary. His claim [is] to be protected against invasion of his bodily security ... What a plaintiff must show is "a wrong" to herself; i.e. a violation of her own right, and not merely a wrong to some one else, nor conduct "wrongful" because unsocial... Negligence, like risk, is thus a term of relation.... If the harm was not willful, he must show that the act as to him had possibilities of danger so many and apparent as to entitle him to be protected against the doing of it... The victim does not sue derivatively, or by right of subrogation, to vindicate an interest invaded in the person of another... He sues for breach of a duty owing to himself.' (*Palsgraf*, above n 14, at 100-1).

On this view of contractual privity, one who does not participate in the interaction required to form a contract cannot have a true contractual right. At the same time, privity of contract does not preclude a stranger to the contract from having a right in negligence against one or both of the contracting parties, so long as the requirements for tort liability are satisfied. Where, for example, one of the parties has invited the third party's reliance and the latter has in response changed position to his detriment, there certainly can be a direct duty relation between them under the *Hedley Byrne* principle.[84]

It follows that the intended beneficiary cannot have a true contractual right. Assuming that there has been no interaction of invited reliance between the beneficiary and the solicitor, the beneficiary can have no right under *Hedley Byrne*. And supposing that the third party has no legally protected interest in the intended benefit given the absence of a valid will, there can be no right against the solicitor in negligence.

The proposed solution of giving standing to the third party to sue must respect these limits. Everything turns, therefore, on the way this standing is framed and explained. What is needed is a conception of third party standing that, negatively, does not depend upon third party reliance on the solicitor and does not recognise in the third party a *contractual* right as against the solicitor, and positively, does nothing more or less than 'ensure that the *promisee's* [ie testator's] expectations engendered by the solicitor's binding promise are fulfilled'.[85] In addition, it should be a conception that, within reasonable limits, coheres with the case law in those jurisdictions where third party can sue on the contract and that resolves the main third party scenarios, including of course the disappointed beneficiary cases. To my knowledge, the most carefully and fully worked-out conception that satisfies these criteria, at least for a common law jurisdiction, is Melvin Eisenberg's 'third- party-beneficiary principle'.[86]

Eisenberg begins with the well-established premise of law that a third party will never have standing to sue with respect to the contractual performance owed between others where this would conflict with the contractual interests and expectations of the contracting parties. Based upon this premise, there is the rule, supported by the cases and endorsed by the *Restatement (Second)*, that, in the absence of invited reliance by the

---

[84] The damages awarded for such a claim should equal the foreseeable loss suffered by the third party as a result of his reliance. This might ordinarily coincide with the value of the promisee's performance, but not necessarily. This action is *not derivative* but original and free-standing, sounding in negligence. In my view, § 90 of the American *Restatement (Second) of the Law of Contracts* (1979) is best viewed as embodying such a claim, as Seavey, above n 31, argued much earlier.

[85] English Law Commission, above n 75, at [7.27] (emphasis added).

[86] MA Eisenberg, 'Third-Party Beneficiaries' (1992) 92 *Columbia Law Review* 1358. He states, discusses and applies this principle from 1385 and ff.

third party on the promisor, the promisor can raise against the third party any defence he or she would have had against the promisee. Similarly, the contracting parties are free to modify or rescind their contract except to the extent that the third party reasonably relies on it before the modification or rescission. As Williston noted in his 1920 Treatise, these limits on the third party's action are inconsistent with the beneficiary having 'a direct right of his own' because 'it ought not to be extinguished without his consent.'[87]

Eisenberg takes this fundamental premise, which is framed in negative terms, as the positive basis of the governing principle which 'determine[s] whether *any given* third-party beneficiary should have the power to enforce a contract'.[88] Under the first branch of this principle, the third party has standing to sue for performance if, but only if, 'allowing the beneficiary to enforce the contract is a necessary or important means of effectuating the contracting parties' performance objectives, as manifested in the contract read in the light of surrounding circumstances'.[89] As Eisenberg makes clear, the purpose of allowing the third party to sue is *not* to ensure that he or she obtains a benefit but simply to effectuate the contracting parties' performance objectives. A third party recognised under this principle has 'a power, not a right, and the power is derivative, not direct'.[90] This power is meant only to ensure that the contractual interests of the contracting parties are fulfilled. Hence, Eisenberg emphasises more than once, under this principle, the law of third-party beneficiaries is 'conceived as *remedial* rather than substantive'[91]: it is 'an apt remedial device to further the contracting parties' performance objectives'.[92] And by 'performance objectives', he understands the objectives of the *enterprise* embodied in the contract and these encompass all the objectives and interests that are relevant to determining claims for expectation damages or specific performance as well as damages for consequential loss under *Hadley*. As such, the content and scope of these objectives are ascertained objectively by reference to the contract itself read in the light of surrounding circumstances, as what the parties knew or should have known at the time the contract was made. Precisely because the principle is anchored in the parties' performance objectives, it does not give the third party standing to sue for merely indirect or collateral loss that would not be

---

[87] S Williston, *Contracts* (New York, Baker, Voorhis & Co, 1920) § 396. Quoted in Eisenberg, above n 86, at 1417.

[88] Eisenberg, above n 86, at 1385.

[89] Eisenberg, above n 86, at 1385. The second branch reads: 'or, (II) allowing the beneficiary to enforce the contract is supported by reasons of policy or morality independent of law and would not conflict with the contracting parties' performance objectives'. For the purposes of this chapter, the first will be taken as the relevant branch.

[90] Eisenberg, above n 86, at 1426.

[91] *Ibid*, at 1386.

[92] *Ibid*, at 1430.

actionable under the first branch of *Hadley* and that does not fall within the end and aim of their transaction.[93]

As I have already mentioned, Eisenberg argues that all the principal scenarios in which American common law has recognised a third party action are readily explained by this principle. While I find his discussion subtle and persuasive, this is not the place to consider it. Suffice it to say, that Eisenberg shows how the principle explains the cases in which 'would-be legatees' are given standing to sue on the contract between testator and solicitor.[94] According the disappointed legatee third party standing would be an important and efficient, if not the only, way to effectuate the testator's crystallised intention where the estate has no incentive or interest in suing.

In my view, adoption of this or a similar principle by the Supreme Court of Canada would not only be consistent with its jurisprudence concerning third-party beneficiaries but would clarify it. At present, while continuing to uphold the doctrine of privity, the court admits what it refers to as incremental changes that reflect the emerging needs and values of Canadian society.[95] Wholesale change must be left to the legislature. This is not satisfactory as a framework for justification. The distinctions it makes are quantitative, not qualitative, and these are not explained on the basis of first principles.

What is needed is an approach that clarifies and takes seriously the rational basis and role of privity, the reasonable and consistent articulation of relations of rights and duties between parties in three-way scenarios, and the difference between claims in contract and tort. This is what recommends something like Eisenberg's principle.

Apart from the well-established 'exceptions' to the 'privity rule' (eg assignment, trust, agency, collateral contract, and so forth) and in the absence of a reliance-based claim by the third party, it should be unambiguously recognised that the third party has *no right against the promisor* that must be recognised by giving him or her standing to sue. No injustice is done to the third party, absent reliance. The injustice, if any, is against the promisee, whose contractual interests are not fulfilled. Therefore, where, by fact or law, the promisee's interests would be defeated for reasons that have nothing to do with either with the merits of his or her claim or with his or her decision to compromise or waive the claim, a remedial device is justified to secure those expectations. In such circumstances, where the remedy, damages or specific performance, which the promisee should receive must go to the third party in order to fulfill the

---

[93]   *Ibid*, at 1374-76.
[94]   *Ibid*, at 1393-96.
[95]   *London Drugs Ltd v Kuehne & Nagel International Ltd* [1992] 3 SCR 299, 438 [*London Drugs*] (Iacobucci J).

promisee's enforceable contractual interest, the third party should be able to bring an action to enforce that interest in such a way that the defendant's liability is not enlarged beyond what is owed the promisee. This solution, I submit, is of general application to all three-party scenarios. No new rights are created. Because it preserves privity as a permanent and essential feature of private law analysis, it respects the bounds of incremental development which the Supreme Court of Canada has demarcated.[96] It is not only consistent with principles of contract and tort, but demonstrates the law has the resources to ensure that the very rights it recognises are upheld and the very duties it imposes are discharged. Since this is accomplished in a way that does not require a court to conjure up new rights and wrongs or to extend well-established principles in a manner that ignores their most basic requirements, the court, by recognising the third party's standing to sue, does not exceed its legitimate role and inherent jurisdiction.

In *Beswick*, Lord Reid—clearly considering the possibility that, in different circumstances, an administrator might not have an interest in suing with the result that the defendant might end up keeping the business without paying the price he agreed to pay—famously warned: 'If one had to contemplate a further long period of Parliamentary procrastination, this House might find it necessary to deal with this matter.'[97] Now, almost

---

[96] Moreover, there is no obvious conflict between the proposed analysis and recent Supreme Court of Canada decisions such as *London Drugs*, *ibid*, where the Court has 'relaxed' privity. To the contrary, these decisions are explicable in light of Eisenberg's principle or on the reliance-based *Hedley Byrne* principle. In *London Drugs*, the Court allowed employees to use a limitation clause as a shield against actions brought by a customer despite the fact that the clause was contained in a contract between the customer and the employer. Assuming that the contract limitation clause expressly or by necessary implication is reasonably intended by the contracting parties to include the employees, one can see this protection as a benefit which the employer wishes to confer upon the employees. If the customer attempts to circumvent this protection by suing the employees and so would frustrate the contractual intention to confer this 'gift', granting the employees the power to use this clause as a defence may be an important and efficient, if not a necessary, way to effectuate this contractual intention. On this analysis, which ignores the possibility of reliance by the employees on the clause, the employees' power to use the defence would be justified under the first branch of Eisenberg's principle. If, on the facts, we conclude that there is reliance by the employees, they would have a limited but certainly free-standing right to reasonable care in negligence as against the customer. There can be actual or presumed reliance in these circumstances if the limitation clause should reasonably be construed as including the employees and if, therefore, the employees may reasonably view themselves as being invited by the customer to do the work on the assumption that the customer assumes the risk of loss. On this analysis, there is a *Hedley Byrne* duty relation between the customer and the employees when the latter actually rely, that is, when they enter upon the work. Because it is a direct and non-derivative duty relation, it can no longer be modified or negated at will by the contracting parties. Any change must reasonably ensure that the employees do not suffer a loss through their reliance. That the facts in *London Drugs* may lend themselves to this sort of reliance-based analysis seems arguable and appears to fit with Iacobucci J's remarks at 445-46.

[97] *Beswick*, above n 54, at 72

forty years later, it must be open to a highest appellate court to take the purely remedial step of giving a third party standing to sue where otherwise *the contracting party's right against the defendant* would be unenforced, not because such non-enforcement reflects the contracting party's intentions but for reasons entirely unconnected with those intentions.

7

Breaches of Contracts and Claims by Third Parties

STEPHEN WADDAMS*

T
HE CASE OF *White v Jones*,[1] involving a lawyer's liability to the disappointed beneficiary of an ineffective will, has been found difficult to classify, and has indeed been described by Sir Guenter Treitel as *sui generis*, that is, unclassifiable.[2] But there are several other kinds of case in which liability has been imposed for breach of contract in favour of a claimant who is not a contracting party. Instances are not uncommon in which the defendant is in breach of contract, but the primary interest in performance of the contract lies in a person who is not a party to it. Such instances include cases of assignment, contracts for the benefit of third parties, contracts for the carriage of goods where the goods are consigned to a third person, building contract cases where the building is owned by a person not a party to the contract, and product liability cases where the claim is for deficient value of the product. These are all cases in which the plaintiff complains, in substance, of non-performance by the defendant of a contractual obligation owed primarily to someone else. Anglo-Canadian law has had difficulty with these cases because the claimant is not a party to the contract, and therefore the imposition of liability appears to contravene a generally accepted principle, namely that of privity of contract. Attempts to resolve this difficulty by resort to tort law, however, have created further conceptual and practical problems, because the cases do not fit the usual tort pattern of a wrongful act that damages a prior right of the claimant. It is worth reconsidering , therefore, whether, after all, these cases might not be better resolved in a contractual framework of thought.

---

* University Professor and the holder of the Goodman/Schipper chair at the Faculty of Law, University of Toronto.
[1] [1995] 2 AC 207 (HL) [*White*].
[2] GH Treitel, *The Law of Contract*, 10th edn (London, Sweet & Maxwell, 1999) 569.

In its report on privity of contract in 1996, the English Law Commission, though excluding cases of negligent will-drafting from its proposed reform, expressed the view that such cases should preferably be resolved in a contractual framework:

> [A]t a theoretical level we prefer the view that the right of the prospective beneficiaries more properly belongs within the realm of contract than tort. It is very difficult to explain the basis of the claim, which deals with an omission and pure economic loss, as being other than one to enforce the promise of the solicitor (albeit by a party who was not intended to have that right). Had *White v Jones* been decided against the potential beneficiaries, we would have seriously contemplated a separate provision—outside our general reform—giving prospective beneficiaries a right to sue the negligent solicitor for breach of contract. The primary basis of such a provision would have been that a right of action for the beneficiaries is the only way to ensure that the promisee's expectations engendered by the solicitor's binding promise are fulfilled.[3]

The Commission thought that, in view of the actual result in *White v Jones,* there was no urgent need for reform on this point. Nevertheless, as Peter Benson demonstrates in chapter 6 of this book, the tort lines of reasoning in *White v Jones* have serious weaknesses, and therefore the contractual framework deserves further consideration.

Lord Goff, in his speech in *White v Jones* also indicated that he was initially attracted by a contractual approach, but he thought that the doctrine of privity of contract prevented its adoption:

> It may be suggested that, in cases such as the present, the simplest course would be to solve the problem by making available to the disappointed beneficiary, by some means or another, the benefit of the contractual rights (such as they are) of the testator or his estate against the negligent solicitor, as is for example done under the German principle of Vertrag mit Schutzwirkung fur Dritte. Indeed that course has been urged upon us by Professor Markesinis, 103 LQR 354, 396-97, echoing a view expressed by Professor Fleming in (1986) 4 OJLS 235, 241. Attractive though this solution is, there is unfortunately a serious difficulty in its way. The doctrine of consideration still forms part of our law of contract, as does the doctrine of privity of contract which is considered to exclude the recognition of a jus quaesitum tertio. To proceed as Professor Markesinis has suggested may be acceptable in German law, but in this country could be open to criticism as an illegitimate circumvention of these long established doctrines.[4]

I would suggest that the strength of these objections to a contractual framework of thought is not overwhelming. The doctrine of privity of

---

[3] Law Commission, 'Privity of Contract: Contracts for the Benefit of Third Parties' (Law Com No 242, 1996) [7.27].

[4] Above n 1, at 266.

contract is not precisely defined in any authoritative source. Many exceptions have been recognised, both at law and in equity, including assignment, subrogation, trust, agency, and collateral contract. The Supreme Court of Canada has recognised broad exceptions where considerations of justice and commercial convenience require them.[5] Moreover, Lord Goff's argument must be looked at in the context of his decision in *White v Jones* itself, imposing tortious liability on the solicitor mainly because the absence of contractual liability created what he identified as a lacuna in the law. The idea that a contract gives rise to tortious duties to third parties is potentially a far greater 'circumvention' of the concept of privity than a limited contractual exception. Is there not something deeply perverse about an argument that contractual liability is impossible because the principle of privity must not be circumvented, and that therefore a (potentially far more extensive) tortious liablity is desirable and necessary? Truly, as Maitland said, the forms of action still rule us from their graves.[6]

The common law refused to enforce assignment of choses in action, such as debts, but where the assignee had paid value equity did recognise and enforce assignments. One reason for the intervention of equity was that it was unjust for an assignee who had paid value to be left empty-handed while the debtor escaped liability for a valid obligation. In substance the debtor would, in that case, be unjustly enriched at the expense of the assignee. The enforcement of assignments is now so well accepted that we have forgotten that it was in origin an equitable exception to the idea of privity. The effect of the equitable doctrine was to protect the assignee's legitimate interest without enlarging the obligation of the debtor, which remained an obligation defined and limited by the original contract under which it arose, and subject to any just defences (equities) that the debtor might have against the assignor.

Cases of contracts for the benefit of third parties have given rise to much difficulty in English law. In the old case of *Dutton v Poole*, a father, wishing to give money to his daughter and proposing to cut down trees to raise the money, agreed with his son and heir that he would refrain from cutting down the trees if the son would pay the daughter a sum of money.[7] The son inherited the land with the timber intact, but refused to honour his promise. The promise was held to be enforceable. Until *Tweddle v Atkinson* it was generally accepted that *Dutton* was rightly decided, though it was evidently an exception to the idea of privity of contract.[8] The

---

[5] *London Drugs Ltd v Kuehne & Nagel International Ltd* [1992] 3 SCR 299; *Fraser River Pile and Dredge Ltd v Can-Dive Services Ltd* [1999] 3 SCR 108.

[6] FW Maitland, *Equity, also The Forms of Action at Common Law* (Cambridge, Cambridge University Press, 1910) 296.

[7] (1678) 2 Lev 210, 83 ER 523 (KB), affd Raym T 302, 83 ER 156 [*Dutton* cited to ER].

[8] (1861) 1 B & S 393, 121 ER 762 (QB).

reason for the conclusion in *Dutton* plainly has something to do with general considerations of justice, including unjust enrichment. As the report put it, 'the son hath the benefit by having of the wood, and the daughter hath lost her portion by this means'.[9] Plainer language could scarcely have been found to express the thought that the son had been unjustly enriched at the expense of the daughter. In a parallel modern case, *Beswick v Beswick*, an uncle transferred a coal business to his nephew in exchange for the nephew's promise to pay an annuity to the uncle's widow. The promise was held to be enforceable, but only because the widow happened to be the administratrix of the uncle's estate, and so entitled, in the opinion of the House of Lords, to a decree of specific performance. Again it is plain that general considerations of justice were in play. Lord Reid described the possibility of there being no remedy as 'grossly unjust.'[10]

In *White v Jones* Lord Goff identified a 'lacuna',[11] that it was necessary for the court to fill in order to achieve 'practical justice', a phrase that occurs seven times.[12] In several other cases the House of Lords has spoken of a 'black hole', again to support the conclusion that the imposition of liability was necessary, despite the absence of privity of contract.[13] On the face of it, the implication of these metaphors (lacuna and black hole) might seem to be that there should be no liability: if there is no principle capable of articulation that justifies the imposition of liability, the natural conclusion would seem to be that the plaintiff has no cause to complain if the action is dismissed. But, of course, the implication of these metaphors was precisely the opposite. A 'lacuna' or a 'black hole' was something that ought not to exist, and the need to avoid these gaps was taken to justify the court in imposing liability. Overriding considerations of 'practical justice' prevailed in these cases over conceptual difficulties. It is part of the task of the commentator to suggest what these overriding considerations of justice were, and how they might be articulated in a form that is recognisably principled.

In *Junior Books Ltd v Veitchi Co Ltd* the House of Lords held that the installer of a defective, but not dangerous, floor was liable in delict, or tort, to the owner of the building, even thought there was no contract between the installer and the owner.[14] In succeeding cases, culminating just eight

---

[9]   *Dutton*, above n 7, at 524.
[10]   [1968] AC 58 (HL) 73.
[11]   Above n 1, at 265, 268.
[12]   *Ibid*, at 259, 260, 263, 264, 265, 268 and 269.
[13]   *GUS Property Management Ltd v Littlewoods Mail Order Stores Ltd* 1982 SC 157 (HL) 177; *Linden Gardens Trust Ltd v Lenesta Sludge Disposals Ltd* [1994] 1 AC 85 (HL) 109; *Alfred McAlpine Construction Ltd v Panatown Ltd* [2001] 1 AC 518 (HL) 534, 568, 574 and 575.
[14]   [1983] 1 AC 520 (HL) [*Junior Books*].

years later in *Murphy v Brentwood District Council*, the House of Lords retreated dramatically.[15] I would suggest that *Junior Books* and its aftermath show that we have been walking up a blind alley in seeking to force cases of this sort into a tortious framework. The installation of cheap but non-dangerous flooring is not a tort, and does not become one because of the possibility that someone may at some time pay someone else more than its value. Installation of cheap flooring is only a wrong insofar as it constitutes a breach of contract. Ordinarily an action for breach of contract lies only in the other contracting party: to this extent the idea of privity has force. But there are circumstances in which overriding considerations of justice justify an action by one who is not a contracting party. This is where the primary interest in performance of the contract rests, not in the other contracting party, but in a third party, and where the defendant would be unjustly enriched at the expense of the two potential claimants jointly if he or she escaped liability to both of them.

The reasoning in the building cases has run into difficulties because of attempts to force it into a tortious framework. The advantages of a contractual framework of thought are several. On the one hand, the claimant would not need to prove negligence (only a breach of contract, which does not necessarily involve negligence); on the other hand, the scope of the defendant's obligation would be defined by the contract, including the required quality of materials and workmanship (or, in the case of a solicitor, the scope of the retainer), and any valid agreed limitations of liability, or arbitration clauses, or valid post-dispute settlements. There would be no theoretical difficulties in respect of liability for omissions, or for purely economic loss, or for loss of mere expectation of a gift. The two potential claimants, considering their interests jointly, would receive a precisely appropriate remedy for the breach of contract, and the defendant would be liable to precisely the extent (no more and no less) that he or she had reason to expect as the consequence of the contractual breach. Several of these points were made by John Fleming, in the article referred to by Lord Goff in *White v Jones*. '[S]hould we not ask ourselves', Fleming wrote, 'whether it is wise to let tort intrude into so complex a relationship as that of the various participants in a building project under the umbrella of long-tested standard contracts?'[16]

A mechanism would be required for joining the interests of the two potential claimants, in order to ensure that the defendant's liability was not enlarged and in order to supply a framework for resolving possible disputes between the potential claimants. Several devices are available for

---

[15] [1991] 1 AC 398 (HL).

[16] JG Fleming, 'Comparative Law of Torts' (1984) 4 *OJLS* 235, 241. See also W Jones, 'Economic Losses Caused by Construction Deficiencies: the Competing Regimes of Contract and Tort' (1991) 59 *University of Cincinnati Law Review* 1051.

this purpose. It could be required that the action be in the name of the contracting party, or in the joint names of the two potential claimants, with the proceeds to be held on trust for the third party, or the cause of action could be held on trust for the third party, or there could be an imputed assignment of the contractual rights. In other words, a framework is required that permits a fusion of the rights of the contracting party with the interest of the non-contracting party, and a transfer of the benefits of the resulting obligation to the latter.

Something very similar was effected by equitable subrogation. This is not a technical or narrow doctrine. There are many statements to the effect that subrogation is a broad equitable remedy, not confined to particular categories, and available wherever justice and equity require it.[17] In *Jenner v Morris* Turner LJ said, quoting from Redesdale's *Treatise on Pleading*:

> 'Cases frequently occur in which the principles by which the ordinary Courts are guided in their administration of justice give a right, but from accident, or fraud, or defect in their mode of proceeding, those Courts can afford no remedy, or cannot give the most complete remedy; and sometimes the effect of a remedy attempted to be given by a Court of ordinary jurisdiction is defeated by fraud or accident. In such cases Courts of Equity will interpose to give those remedies which the ordinary Courts would give if their powers were equal to the purpose, or their mode of administering justice could reach the evil; and also to enforce remedies attempted to be given by those Courts when their effect is so defeated.'
> It is therefore an ancient head of the jurisdiction of this Court to interpose in cases in which the principle of the law gives a right but the forms of the law do not give a remedy.[18]

This was said in the context of payments to a deserted wife for the purchase of necessaries. The payer was permitted to be subrogated to the rights of the tradespeople who had supplied the necessaries, who if they had been unpaid would have had an action against the husband at common law. The words are also very apt in the present context. It can truly be said, in all the cases under consideration, that 'the principle of the law gives a right but the forms of the law do not give a remedy'.[19] I would suggest that the equitable device of subrogation may offer a workable and

---

[17]   *Orakpo v Manson Investments Ltd* [1978] AC 95 (HL) 110 (Lord Salmon), 112 (Lord Edmund-Davies); *Boscawen v Bajwa* [1996] 1 WLR 328 (CA) 335 (Millett LJ); R Goff and G Jones, *The Law of Restitution*, 6th edn (London, Sweet & Maxwell, 2002) 3-011, 3-018.

[18]   (1861) 3 De GF & J 45, 45 ER 795 (Ch) 799 [*Jenner* cited to ER]. Lord Campbell LC, at 797-98, characterised the legal problem as lack of privity, but this was not a reason for withholding the remedy of subrogation; on the contrary it was the very reason why an equitable remedy was necessary. He also explained the result on the basis of imputed assignment: 'it may possibly be that equity considers that the tradespeople have for valuable consideration assigned to the party who advanced the money the legal debt which would be due to them from the husband on furnishing the necessaries, and that, although a chose in action cannot be assigned at law, a Court of Equity recognises the right of the assignee'.

[19]   *Jenner*, above n 18.

principled solution. A general principle might be formulated along these lines: where a contractual obligation is owed to one person, but the primary interest in performance of the contract is in another person, the latter is, where justice requires it, subrogated to the contractual rights of the former. This formulation retains some flexibility with the phrase 'where justice requires it,' appropriately, it is suggested, since it is not possible to foresee all cases, but the principle is not empty of content. In the classes of case mentioned justice has often been seen to require a remedy. These are typically cases where the interests of the two potential claimants are closely aligned, and where the defendant would be unjustly enriched at the expense of the two potential claimants jointly if there were no liability to either.

It may be said, by way of objection to the analogy with subrogation, that the claimant in *White v Jones* sought to assert a right different from that held by the testator or the estate. Three answers to this point may be suggested. First, it was often the effect of equitable subrogation to enforce a right not actually held by the person to whom the claimant was subrogated, as, for example, in *Jenner*, where the claimant was permitted to assert the rights that the tradespeople never actually held but which they *would have had if unpaid*. Second, it is arguable that the testator in *White v Jones* did, at a point of time before his death when it had become impossible for him to make a will, have a right to recover damages against the solicitor, the damages to be measured by the full value of the property lost, just as he would have had in a case where the solicitor irretrievably caused the loss of property intended to be transferred inter vivos.[20] Third, it may be emphasised that equitable subrogation was not a narrow or technical doctrine, and could be extended by analogy to do equity, or 'practical justice' as Lord Goff repeatedly called it. The court in *Jenner* did not in fact use the word 'subrogation', and it is not necessary to force every case into a precise definition.

Equitable subrogation is not a species, genus, or category of legal obligation. It is a device for enabling the court to transfer the benefit of an obligation from one person to another. It is closely related, as has been suggested at several points in this chapter, to unjust enrichment. Insofar as it rests on an acceptable principle and describes past cases generally thought to have been rightly decided it has a certain explanatory, justificatory, and persuasive power, and passes as valid currency in legal discourse. But the object of this chapter is not to prove that equitable subrogation is the only approach, or even the best approach to the cases under discussion. The same result could be attained by what might be called implied

---

[20] Lord Goff said: 'had a gift been similarly misdirected during the testator's lifetime, he would either have been able to recover it from the recipient or, if not, he could have recovered the full amount from the negligent solicitor as damages'. *White*, above n 1, at 265.

assignment, or a trust of contractual rights, or a special equity or simply a transfer of obligations where necessary for a modern court to do justice to both parties. My purpose has not been to establish a nomenclature but to suggest that, where the defendant's obligation is derived from contract with a person other than the claimant, a framework of thought is needed that gives due recognition to the contractual dimensions of the obligation.

8

Policy Issues in Defective Property Cases

STEPHEN TODD*

I. INTRODUCTION

LET US TAKE a simple set of facts. A, a builder, constructs a house for B. A fails to follow approved building practice and builds the house on inadequate foundations. No one is aware of the problem, and one year later B sells the house to C. The contract of sale excludes any possible liability of the vendor in respect of the state or quality of the building. Shortly afterwards the house starts to subside. C engages an engineer, who reports that it will cost $100,000 to fix the foundations. Can C recover this loss from A? The answer to this question has divided the courts in the common law world. In England, the answer originally was yes but then changed to an emphatic no. By contrast, in Canada, Australia and New Zealand, the courts have allowed and have continued to allow the owner's claim. Yet recent decisions show at least some doubts and uncertainties about the potential ambit of the builder's duty, and these certainly need to be confronted because they have the capacity to destabilise the core principle of liability.

We need at the outset to identify the nature of the problem posed by C's claim. A court asked to award damages to a subsequent owner of defective property must decide whether or how the negligence remedy can operate in a setting where the task assumed, and the terms upon which it is assumed, are matters of contractual negotiation between the builder and the original owner. Of course, in *Donoghue v Stevenson*,[1] the House of Lords exploded the so-called 'privity fallacy'—the view that a person performing a task pursuant to a contract could incur obligations only in contract, and

* Professor of Law, University of Canterbury; Professor of Common Law, University of Nottingham. I would like to thank Professor John Burrows for his very helpful comments on a draft of this chapter.
[1] [1932] AC 562 (HL) [*Donoghue*].

accordingly that a claim by anyone other than the contracting party was barred by the privity doctrine.[2] Rather, where negligence by A in performing a contract with B caused damage to C, then A could owe a duty in tort to C to take care, founded not on the contract with B but on the foreseeability of harm to C and the closeness of the connection or relationship between A and C. But *Donoghue v Stevenson* concerned a claim for negligence by a manufacturer allegedly causing the plaintiff to suffer physical injury. The question here is whether a duty of care can arise where the claim is not in respect of physical injury or physical damage done to other property, but for the cost of putting right the property containing the defect. If we express the distinction in the context of the facts of *Donoghue v Stevenson*, the action is equivalent to the purchaser of the bottle of adulterated ginger beer suing the manufacturer not for injury caused by drinking the contents, but for the money wasted in buying or replacing it.[3] A claim of this kind is for economic loss. The building or chattel has never existed except in its defective state and in this sense it has not been *damaged* by the defendant, although sometimes a defect has physical consequences on the property itself. Accordingly, our concern is whether, or the extent to which, the law of negligence ought to allow an action by a subsequent owner against a builder, engineer, manufacturer or other person who has contributed to a defect in property that has diminished the value of the property but has not damaged anything else.[4]

The question certainly is controversial, for reasons which are discussed at length in the cases, to which we now turn. We need to traverse briefly some well-trodden ground and then to examine what the latest decisions have to say.

II.   AN OVERVIEW OF THE CASES

A.   England

The whole debate about the property owner's action in tort started with the decision of the English Court of Appeal in 1972 in *Dutton v Bognor*

---

[2] As to which view see *Winterbottom v Wright* (1842) 10 M & W 109, 152 ER 402.

[3] In *Donoghue v Stevenson*, it was Mrs Donoghue's friend, rather than Mrs Donoghue herself, who purchased the ginger beer.

[4] In many of the cases considered below, the defendant is a local authority whose building engineer has allegedly been negligent in approving building plans or whose inspector has allegedly failed properly to carry out checks during construction of the building. Any policy concerns that apply in claims against those who have actually created a defect must apply equally in claims against a local authority, which has merely failed to prevent a building with a defect from being erected. Further concerns, which apply only to claims against a local authority or other regulatory body, are considered briefly later on.

Regis Urban District Council,[5] upholding an owner's claim against the defendant council for negligence in inspecting the foundations of her house and failing to detect that it had been built on a filled-in rubbish dump. Lord Denning MR specifically rejected the argument that the damage was irrecoverable as amounting to pure economic loss. He said that if this were right it would mean that, if the house collapsed and injured a person, the council would be liable, but if the owner discovered the defect in time to repair it, the council would not be liable. This, he thought, was an impossible distinction. The council was liable in either case. The damage was not solely economic loss but physical damage to the house. Five years later, in *Anns v London Borough of Merton,*[6] the decision was affirmed by the House of Lords, although on rather different grounds. Their Lordships held there that a local authority owed a duty to owners or occupiers who might suffer injury to health caused by defective foundations to take care in inspecting the foundations. Lord Wilberforce thought that the damage sustained by the plaintiff was 'material, physical damage'.[7] What was recoverable was the amount of expenditure necessary to restore the dwelling to a condition in which there was no longer a present or imminent danger to the health or safety of persons occupying it.

In *Junior Books Ltd v Veitchi Co Ltd,*[8] the House of Lords was prepared to extend the *Anns* principle and hold that subcontractors who had built a defective floor in the plaintiff's factory were liable for the cost of repairing the floor, notwithstanding that the defect posed no injury to health. The claim was recognised as being for a financial loss, yet it was recoverable because of the close proximity between the parties. However, doubts about this developing line of authority were quickly expressed,[9] leading to its partial rejection in *D & F Estates Ltd v Church Commissioners for England*[10] and, soon afterwards, its total rejection in *Murphy v Brentwood District Council.*[11]

In *D & F Estates,* the House of Lords held that builders could not be liable to the lessees of a flat in respect of the financial loss they incurred in renewing plaster work incorrectly applied by subcontractors. To recognise a duty would be to impose on the builders for the benefit of those with whom they had no contractual relationship the obligation of one who

---

[5] [1972] 1 QB 373 (CA) [*Dutton*].
[6] [1978] AC 728 (HL) [*Anns*].
[7] *Ibid*, at 759.
[8] [1983] 1 AC 520 (HL).
[9] *Governors of the Peabody Donation Fund v Sir Lindsay Parkinson & Co Ltd* [1985] AC 210 (HL) [*Peabody*]; *Leigh and Sillavan Ltd v Aliakmon Shipping Co Ltd (The Aliakmon)* [1986] AC 785 (HL) [*Aliakmon*]; *Muirhead v Industrial Tank Specialities Ltd* [1986] QB 507 (CA); *Simaan General Contracting Co v Pilkington Glass Ltd (No 2)* [1988] QB 758 (CA).
[10] [1989] AC 177 (HL) [*D & F Estates*].
[11] [1991] 1 AC 398 (HL) [*Murphy*].

warranted the quality of the plaster as regards materials, workmanship and fitness for purpose. A claim based on breach of a warranty of quality could only be maintained by one contracting party against the other. However, two lines of argument were left open. First, their Lordships did not decide whether there could still be recovery where a defect posed a danger to health. Second, they recognised the possibility that one element of a complex structure could be regarded as distinct from another element, so that damage to one part caused by a hidden defect in another part might qualify as physical damage to 'other property'. The recoverable damages might then include the cost of making good the defect, as essential to the repair of the property that had been damaged by it.

Both questions were subsequently examined in *Murphy*. The defendant council had approved a faulty design for the foundations of a house, with the result that the house was built with defective foundations. It later subsided and the owner, instead of repairing it, sold it for less than half its market value in an undamaged state. The owner sought to recover from the council the amount of the diminution in value and other losses and expenses. The English Court of Appeal upheld the claim, on the ground that the defect posed a danger to health. But the House of Lords held unanimously that the claim should fail and that *Anns* should be overruled. The owner's claim was for pure economic loss and, if allowed, would open up a very wide field of claims involving the introduction of something like an indefinitely transmissible warranty of quality. These would not be limited to buildings, but would include a mass of product liability claims which the law had not previously entertained. In so deciding, their Lordships declined to draw a distinction between a mere defect of quality and a dangerous defect. In both cases, the owner suffered a diminution in value of property, not injury to health. Again, the description of the damage as physical or material did not withstand analysis. The manifestations of the defective nature of the structure by some physical symptoms were merely the outward signs of a deterioration resulting from the inherently defective condition in which the building had been brought into being, and could not properly be described as 'damage' caused to the building in any accepted use of the word. As for the 'complex structure' theory, this was accepted in principle but held not to apply on the facts. Lord Bridge said that if, for example, a negligently defective central heating boiler explodes and damages a house, the owner could recover damages from the manufacturer on *Donoghue v Stevenson* principles. But where inadequate foundations lead to differential settlement and cracking, the structure as a whole is seen to be defective and, as it deteriorates, will only damage itself.

Since *Murphy*, then, the law in England has been reasonably clear. There has been some limited discussion about complex structures and the circumstances in which one part of a structure may be seen as having damaged another.[12] But otherwise a tort action for repair costs brought by a subsequent owner cannot be maintained. Even so, the owner may not be remediless.[13] Under the National House Building Council's warranty scheme, successive owners of new residential buildings are protected against defects in materials and workmanship for a two year period and against structural defects for another eight years. The builder is obliged to insure against liabilities arising under the scheme. In addition, there is, by statute, a six year warranty of quality and habitability imposed on builders of private dwellings for the benefit of subsequent owners.[14]

B. Australia

Following *D & F Estates* and *Murphy*, the question naturally arose whether a similar view would be taken elsewhere. It soon became apparent that it would not, and that other common law courts of high authority preferred to retain a remedy for the disappointed purchaser. In *Bryan v Maloney*,[15] the High Court of Australia held that the builder of a house who had negligently installed inadequate footings causing damage to the fabric owed a duty of care to a subsequent purchaser, who was entitled to recover the consequential loss measured by the decrease in the value of the house. The duty arose out of the relationship of close proximity between a builder and a first owner, which could be equated with that between the builder and a subsequent owner. Although their only connection was the house itself, it was a substantial connection. Economic loss to a subsequent owner was obviously foreseeable, for the house was a permanent structure to be used indefinitely and likely to represent a major investment for the owner. Their relationship was characterised both by an assumption of responsibility on the part of the builder and by reliance on the part of the owner. The existence of a duty also was supported by analogy with the duty owed to those suffering physical injury to person or property by reason of the defect. It could hardly be right to differentiate between

---

[12] See *Bellefield Computer Services Ltd v E Turner & Sons Ltd* [2000] BLR 97 (CA) (builder who constructed insufficient internal fire wall separating a storage area from the rest of a factory, allowing a subsequent fire to pass over the top, was liable for damage to the owner's plant and equipment outside the storage area but not for damage to the fabric of the building itself); *Baxall & Norbain v Sheard Wilshaw Partnership* [2002] BLR 100 (CA) (architects not liable for damage by flooding caused by a poorly-designed gutter, because the defect was latent and the claimants' own surveyors should have discovered it by the exercise of reasonable care and skill).

[13] See generally *Winfield and Jolowicz on Tort*, 17th edn (London, Sweet & Maxwell Ltd, 2006) [9.37]-[9.38].

[14] Defective Premises Act 1972 (Eng).

[15] (1995) 182 CLR 609 (HCA) [*Bryan*].

circumstances of liability and no liability according to whether remedial work was done in time to avert any physical damage.

Bryan v Maloney was criticised both in academic commentary[16] and in judicial decision-making[17] for creating a number of imponderables and promoting widespread uncertainty. A major concern was whether the same principle should apply to commercial buildings or to buildings with mixed commercial and residential purposes, and the first of these questions was in issue in *Woolcock St Investments Pty Ltd v CDG Pty Ltd*.[18] An engineer designed a warehouse for a developer who later sold it to a new owner. One year later, it became apparent that the building was suffering substantial structural distress, and the owner brought proceedings in negligence against the engineer. The High Court of Australia held by a majority that the engineer owed no duty of care to the owner.

The joint majority judgment of Gleeson CJ, Gummow, Hayne and Heydon JJ doubted whether the decision in *Bryan* should be understood as depending upon drawing a bright line between cases concerning the construction of dwellings and cases concerning the construction of other buildings. They thought that any such line would be far from bright, straight, clearly defined or even clearly definable. Their Honours also noted that the decision depended upon the view that proximity represented the 'conceptual determinant' of the categories of case in which the common law recognised the existence of a duty to take care; yet subsequent decisions revealed that proximity was no longer seen as the conceptual determinant in this area. In any event, the reasoning in *Bryan* did not support a duty in the instant case and that there was good reason for denying it.

Unlike *Bryan*, here no duty was owed to the original owner. The engineer obtained a quotation for geotechnical investigations, but the owner refused to pay for it and instead, it was alleged, directed the adoption of particular footing sizes. So this was a relationship in which the original owner asserted control over the engineer's work. There was not an identified element of known reliance or any assumption of responsibility. Accordingly, in the absence of any binding authority, the question arose whether in these different circumstances a duty ought to be recognised. Their Honours were satisfied that it should not, primarily because the new owner was not vulnerable to the economic consequences of negligence by the engineer. The facts alleged did not show that the owner could not have

---

[16] Hon Justice R Brooking, '*Bryan v Maloney*: Its Scope and Future' in NJ Mullany and the Hon Justice AM Linden (eds), *Torts Tomorrow: A Tribute to John Fleming* (Sydney, Law Book Co, 1998).

[17] *Zumpano v Montagnese* [1997] 2 VR 525 (CA), 528-36 [*Zumpano*].

[18] (2005) 216 CLR 515 (HCA) [*Woolcock*].

protected itself from the economic consequences of the defendant's negligence, either by obtaining a warranty from the vendor against defects in the building or by an assignment of any rights of the vendor against third parties. Whether doubt should be cast on *Bryan v Maloney* was left for another day. The actual decision had been overtaken to a significant extent by various statutory forms of protection,[19] and neither the principles applied in *Bryan* itself or in subsequent cases supported the contention that the engineer owed to the owner a duty of care to avoid the economic loss which it alleged it suffered.

McHugh J and Callinan J delivered concurring judgments. But Kirby J, in a dissenting opinion, was satisfied that there was an arguable claim. The argument of the appellant owner, if upheld, not only would redress a wrong which arguably arose as a foreseeable consequence of the respondent engineer's acquiescence in the erection of the building without the structural tests that the engineer had proposed. It would also instil proper standards of professional engineering conduct. It would sanction unsafe building practices. It would encourage better building design and supervision and protect life, property and investments from the kind of unsafe conduct that was alleged in this case. And his Honour considered also that the approach to the duty issue taken by the Court in earlier decisions justified allowing the case to proceed.[20] Thus, the loss was not only reasonably foreseeable but actually foreseen; the extent of the respondents' potential liability was limited to the class of future owners and users; the respondents were already under a clear duty of care to the original owner, and there was no undue interference with their commercial autonomy; the appellant was vulnerable because it had no reasonable intermediate opportunity of discovering and protecting itself against the latent defect of which it now complained; and the respondents knew or should have known of the risk and the consequences of it occurring. In all the circumstances, the appellant should have the opportunity at trial, by evidence and argument, to establish that there was a duty and that it was breached. No principled barrier could exist because the appellant was a corporation or because its investment was a commercial building.

The reasoning of the joint majority judgment in *Woolcock* can hardly be read as a ringing affirmation of *Bryan v Maloney*. Perhaps their Honours would be receptive to arguments directly challenging it, but for the time being, the decision stands. At the least it is not going to be extended to personal property. *Bryan* left open the question whether a duty might be

---

[19] Their Honours referred to the judgment of Callinan J, who noted that the appellant chose to seek an inspection and report by the local authority under the Building Act 1975 (Qld), s 53.

[20] Kirby J relied particularly on *Bryan*, above n 15; *Perre v Apand Pty Ltd* (1999) 198 CLR 180 (HCA) and *Sullivan v Moody* (2001) 207 CLR 562 (HCA).

owed by a manufacturer to a purchaser of a defective chattel,[21] but claims of this kind have been firmly rejected in state courts.[22]

C. Canada

Supreme Court of Canada decisions pre-*Murphy* favoured the *Anns* duty,[23] and post-*Murphy* this stance has been maintained. The leading decision is *Winnipeg Condominium Corporation No 36 v Bird Construction Co*.[24] In this case the subsequent owner of a 94-unit apartment building sued the building contractor after a large piece of concrete cladding fell from the building, necessitating the removal and replacement of the entire cladding. The question was whether the builder could be liable to the owner for the cost of making the repairs.

La Forest J, delivering the judgment of the court, regarded the degree of danger to persons and other property created by the negligent construction of a building as a critical consideration. In his view, where a contractor was negligent in planning or constructing a building, leading to the creation of defects that posed a real and substantial danger to the occupants, the reasonable cost of repairing the defects and putting the building back into a non-dangerous state were recoverable in tort by the occupants. A duty of this kind in tort arose independently of the terms of the contract pursuant to which the building was erected. What was undertaken by the contract would indicate the nature of the relationship that gave rise to the common law duty of care, but the nature and scope of the duty of care should not depend on specific obligations or duties created by the specific terms of the contract. The duty in contract with respect to materials and workmanship flowed from the terms of the contract between the contractor and the home owner. The duty in tort with respect to materials and workmanship flowed from the contractor's duty to meet reasonable and safe standards of construction, and the bounds of that duty were not defined by reference to the original contract. Certainly, a contractor who made a contract with the original owner to use high-grade material or special ornamental features would not be liable to subsequent purchasers if the building did not meet these special contractual standards. But the contract could not absolve the contractor from the duty in tort to subsequent owners to construct the building according to reasonable standards.

---

[21] *Woolcock*, above n 18, at 630.

[22] For example, *Minchillo v Ford Motor Co of Australia Ltd* [1995] 2 VR 594 (CA); *CBD Investments Pty Ltd v Ace Ceramics Pty Ltd* (1995) Aust Torts Reports 81-359 (NSWSC).

[23] *City of Kamlooops v Nielsen* [1984] 2 SCR 2 [*Kamloops*]; *Rothfield v Manalokos* [1989] 2 SCR 1259.

[24] [1995] 1 SCR 85 [*Winnipeg*].

La Forest J also thought that there were strong policy justifications for imposing liability in cases where a building was dangerous. If a contractor could be liable where a building caused actual damage to persons or property, then the contractor should also be liable where the defect was discovered and the owner mitigated the danger by fixing the defect. In both cases, the duty in tort served to protect the bodily integrity and property interests of the inhabitants of the building. Furthermore, applying *D & F Estates* and *Murphy*, the plaintiff who moved quickly and responsibly to fix a defect had to do so at his or her own expense, whereas a plaintiff who allowed a defect to develop into an accident might benefit at law from the costly and potentially tragic consequences. Maintaining a bar against recoverability provided no incentive for plaintiffs to mitigate potential losses and tended to encourage economically inefficient behaviour. Accordingly, cases involving dangerous defects were properly distinguishable from cases where workmanship was merely shoddy or substandard and which brought into play the questions of quality of workmanship and fitness for purpose. So in the instant case, if the contractor was found negligent at trial, the owner would be entitled to recover the reasonable cost of putting the building into a non-dangerous state, but not the cost of any repairs that would serve merely to improve the quality, and not the safety, of the building.

Interestingly, the decision in *Winnipeg* does not give any particular significance to the commercial context in which the duty question arose. So builders creating potentially dangerous defects can owe a duty to commercial claimants in the same way as to private owners living in their dwellings. The decision leaves open the question whether contractors should be liable for the cost of repairing non-dangerous defects,[25] and later determinations of lower courts have given varied answers where the element of dangerousness has been in issue.[26] Some courts have allowed a claim, or at least have refused a striking out application, where the defect was not dangerous.[27] But others have insisted that real and substantial danger be shown,[28] although not that the danger should be imminent.[29] Again, on similar reasoning, liability has been imposed on manufacturers

---

[25] *Ibid*, at [41].

[26] See the study commissioned by the Insurance Bureau of Canada by C Brown, SGA Pitel and JW Neyers, *The Impact of Recent legal Developments on Liability Insurance* (University of Western Ontario, August 2005) 98.

[27] *Del Harder v Denny Andrews Ford Sales Inc* (1995) 173 AR 23 (QB); *Condominium Plan No 9421710 v Christenson* (2001) 298 AR 55 (QB).

[28] *Blacklaws v 470433 Alberta Ltd* (2000) 84 Alta LR (3d) 270 (CA); *Brett-Young Seeds Ltd v Assié Industries Ltd* (2002) 166 Man R (2d) 33 (CA).

[29] *Roy v Thiessen* (2005) 257 Sask R 239 (CA).

for the cost of remedying or replacing dangerously defective chattels.[30] In this latter context, it has been held that a defect inducing reliance and a false sense of safety and security could qualify, even though the defect was not dangerous in itself.[31]

D. New Zealand

In *Bowen v Paramount Builders (Hamilton) Ltd*,[32] decided just before *Anns*, the Court of Appeal held that a builder who put up a house on inadequate foundations owed a duty of care to a subsequent purchaser of the building. Liability was founded on the builder having negligently created a hidden defect that was a source of danger to persons whom he or she could reasonably foresee were likely to suffer damage in the form of personal injuries or damage to property. As in *Dutton*, the claim was seen as being primarily for physical damage to the structure of the house. However, in later cases, the reasoning was different. In particular, in *Stieller v Porirua CC*,[33] the Court of Appeal held that a builder's or an inspecting council's obligations were not confined to defects affecting health and safety, nor to defects damaging or threatening to damage other parts of the structure. It was enough that they reduced the value of the premises.

Then came the decision of the House of Lords in *Murphy*, and for five years it was undecided whether the remedy of the homeowner in New Zealand would also come to be abandoned. The question eventually was determined in *Invercargill CC v Hamlin*,[34] where the Court of Appeal upheld the duty and the Privy Council decided that there was no good reason for it to intervene. In the Court of Appeal, little was said about the reasoning in *Murphy*, and the judgments concentrated instead on local conditions. In brief, community standards and expectations were seen as requiring the imposition of a duty, Parliament had had the opportunity to change the law in the Building Act 1991 (NZ) but had chosen not to do so, the principles of liability were well established, and to change the law at this stage would require a wide-ranging analysis and assessment of all the economic and social implications. In the Privy Council, Lord Lloyd was sympathetic to this approach. Applying the test in *Australian Consolidated*

---

[30] *Privest Properties Ltd v Foundation Co of Canada* (1995) 128 DLR (4th) 577 (BCSC) affd (1997) 143 DLR (4th) 635 (CA); *M Hasegawa & Co v Pepsi Bottling Group (Canada) Ltd* (2002) 1 BCLR (4th) 209 (CA).

[31] *Hughes v Sunbeam Corporation (Canada) Ltd* (2003) 219 DLR (4th) 467, where the Ontario Court of Appeal refused to strike out a claim against the manufacturer for economic loss suffered by the plaintiff, who purchased a defective smoke detector from a retailer.

[32] [1977] 1 NZLR 394 (CA) [*Bowen*].

[33] [1986] 1 NZLR 84 (CA) [*Stieller*].

[34] [1994] 3 NZLR 513 (CA), affd [1996] 1 NZLR 513 (PC) [*Hamlin*].

Press Ltd v Uren,[35] it could not be said that the Court's decision was reached by a process of faulty reasoning, or that the decision was based on some misconception. Rather, the perception in the Court of Appeal was that conditions in New Zealand were different to those in England, and that the duty of care on local authorities and builders alike to ensure compliance with local bylaws, upheld in a succession of cases over a 20 year period, ought to be maintained. New Zealand judges were in a much better position to decide on such matters than the Board. It would be rash for their Lordships to ignore these views and, accordingly, the decision of the Court of Appeal should not be disturbed.

Hamlin did not decide whether a duty ought to be recognised in the case of commercial property. In the Court of Appeal, Cooke P left the question open,[36] and certainly the 'local' factors mentioned in that decision are hardly relevant to commercial buildings. Recently, in *Rolls Royce New Zealand Ltd v Carter Holt Harvey Ltd*,[37] the question required an answer. Carter Holt Harvey (CHH) contracted with the Electricity Corporation of New Zealand (ECNZ) and another to procure the design, manufacture, construction, purchase and installation of an industrial plant at CHH's Mill (the Cogeneration Contract). Shortly afterwards, ECNZ entered into an agreement with Rolls Royce (RR) to design, construct and commission the plant (the Turnkey Contract). There was no direct contractual relationship between CHH and RR, although the Cogeneration Contract had been entered into on the basis that RR would be the subcontractor. CHH claimed that the plant built by RR was defective and did not conform to the contractual specifications. It alleged that RR owed and was in breach of a duty to take reasonable care to ensure the plant was constructed in accordance with the Turnkey Contract, free from defects and in accordance with good engineering practice. It also claimed, on the basis of the *Hedley Byrne* principle, that RR owed and was in breach of a duty to take care in making statements and giving advice about the plant. RR sought to strike out the former claim, although it accepted that the *Hedley Byrne* claim could not be determined on a strike out application.

Glazebrook J, delivering the judgment of the court, was satisfied that, in these circumstances, there was no duty to take care. First, the contractual context pointed clearly against any duty being recognised. The parties were sophisticated commercial parties with equal bargaining power, and CHH for its own reasons chose not to enter a direct contract with RR. Second, the terms of the main contract and of the subcontract differed in various respects and both contained limitation clauses. As regards the Cogeneration Contract, CHH had only paid for what was to be provided under that

[35] [1969] 1 AC 590 (PC) 644.
[36] *Hamlin*, above n 34, at 524.
[37] [2005] 1 NZLR 324 (CA) [*Rolls Royce*].

contract and should not be able to improve on its bargain by direct suit. As for the Turnkey Contract, a limitation clause could impact upon CHH even though it was not a party. The presence of a limitation clause in a contract between a head contractor and a subcontractor could signify clearly, if known to the owner, the subcontractor's unwillingness to do the job otherwise than subject to the limitation. Third, the difficulty in setting quality standards in cases involving contractual specifications had long been a reason for not imposing a duty of care in the kind of case under consideration. The problem was not so serious in the case of buildings or products destined for private individuals, but it was acute in commercial construction contracts for specialist plants with detailed specifications. Last, there was the need for commercial certainty. Commercial parties were normally entitled to expect that the risk allocation that they had negotiated and paid for would not be disturbed by the courts. It was also to be expected that commercial parties were capable of looking after their own interests, including the risk of insolvency of an intermediate party. By contrast, private individuals might not necessarily be in a position to protect themselves, and this could justify a difference in treatment.

In *Rolls Royce*, then, the commercial context pointed away from a duty, both as a matter of CHH's choice in structuring its relationship with ECNZ and RR, and as a matter of policy in leaving CHH to safeguard its own interests by way of contractual negotiation. At the same time the *Hamlin* principle remains undisturbed. Indeed, legal protection for the house owner has recently been bolstered by statutory intervention. The Building Act 2004 (NZ) lays down mandatory statutory warranties in all contracts for building work for 'household units'[38] and contracts of sale of household units made by a 'residential property developer'.[39] The warranties require, broadly, that all building work be done with reasonable care, properly and competently and in accordance with the plans and building consents; that materials used will be suitable and, unless otherwise stated, new; that household units intended to be occupied on completion of the work will be suitable for occupation; and if the contract specifies the particular purpose for which the work is required, that the work and materials will be reasonably fit for that purpose.[40] A right of action for breach of any of these warranties is not confined to the other contracting purchaser. A subsequent owner may take proceedings 'as if' the owner

---

[38]   A household unit is a building or part of a building that is used or intended to be used only or mainly for residential purposes and occupied or intended to be occupied by a single household, and does not include a hostel, boardinghouse, or other specialised accommodation: Building Act 2004 (NZ), s 7.

[39]   A residential property developer is a person who, in trade, builds the household unit or arranges for it to be built or acquires it from a person who built it or arranged for it to be built, for the purpose of selling it: Building Act 2004 (NZ), s 7.

[40]   Building Act 2004 (NZ), ss 396, 397.

were a party to the contract.[41] Seemingly, then, the action is subject to any contractual controls, including the operation of the relevant limitation period. The orthodox view is that the six year period runs from the date of the breach of contract.[42] So a subsequent owner will inherit the balance of the period, if any.

Whether there can be an action equivalent to that in *Hamlin* for negligence in the manufacture of a chattel has not been finally determined, but the limited authority considering the question is not in favour of such an action.[43] Furthermore, in 1993, Parliament introduced a statutory remedy for consumers against manufacturers or importers of defective goods, covering both wasted expenditure and consequential losses.[44] Any wider tort action covering commercial claimants could be seen as operating inconsistently with the limits imposed by the legislature on the statutory remedy. Accordingly, it is unlikely that a manufacturer of goods owes any duty of care with respect to financial loss suffered by a later purchaser of the goods.

III.   LEGAL PRINCIPLE

A core reason for denying a duty of care in negligence, articulated most clearly by the House of Lords in *D & F Estates* and *Murphy*, is the contention that an owner's claim is in the nature of an action for breach of a warranty of quality, which in its very nature ought to be maintained in contract. And on one interpretation at least, Lord Bridge's judgment in *Murphy* decides that the primary right to which the claimant needed to appeal could come into existence only through agreement.[45] On this view, as a matter of legal principle, the law of negligence can have no part to play in claims by owners seeking compensation simply in respect of property which is defective or otherwise of poor quality.

In weighing up this argument we should remember that the law of torts does not stand still. Litigation constantly tests the limits of existing principle. The core areas of liability naturally are reasonably well established, but claims on the boundaries are always arising and provide fertile sources for disputation. When a court is asked to adjudicate on a novel claim, the starting point is the accumulated wisdom and experience of

---

[41]   *Ibid*, s 398(1).

[42]   *Rabadan v Gale* [1996] 3 NZLR 220 (HC); *Stuart v Australian Guarantee Corporation (NZ) Ltd* (2002) 16 PRNZ 139 (HC).

[43]   See especially *New Zealand Food Group (1992) Ltd v Amcor Trading (NZ) Ltd* (1999) 9 TCLR 184 (HC).

[44]   Consumer Guarantees Act 1993 (NZ), s 27.

[45]   A Beever, 'A Rights-Based Approach to the Recovery of Economic Loss in Negligence' (2004) 4 *Oxford University Commonwealth Law Journal* 25, 38.

earlier courts in reaching decisions which help throw light on the question in issue. The courts usually prefer to proceed cautiously and to emphasise the need for incremental development of the law. Yet this approach can only take a court part of the way. Decisions extending existing principle ultimately rest on policy considerations, sometimes express, sometimes implicit. Policy necessarily guides the courts in deciding whether to create new areas of tortious liability or to refuse to build upon existing limits.

Sometimes, of course, courts debate whether to create new torts. But disputes more commonly are about the boundaries of existing torts, and negligence no doubt is the pre-eminent example. Existing limits represent policy choices. So a decision of policy was required in *Donoghue v Stevenson* itself. A majority of their Lordships decided that the basis for recovery by a person suffering injury caused by a defective chattel should be broadened, from a category by category approach to a general rule of liability based upon foreseeability of injury to one's neighbour. Another major development came with the decision of the House of Lords in *Hedley Byrne & Co Ltd v Heller & Partners Ltd*,[46] recognising for the first time that there may be a cause of action for negligence in words which causes a person who is induced to rely upon the words to suffer a financial loss. The *Hedley Byrne* principle came to be accepted in other common law jurisdictions including, in particular, Canada,[47] Australia[48] and New Zealand,[49] and all debate has been about how far economic loss caused by negligence ought to be recoverable, not about whether it ought to be recoverable at all. Certainly there are many instances where a duty has been denied,[50] but so also there are many where a duty has been upheld. In well known examples, solicitors alleged to have been negligent in relation to the drawing up of a client's will owed a duty of care to disappointed legatees;[51] the writer of a reference to be given to a prospective employer owed a duty to the person who was the subject of the reference;[52] and a surveyor preparing a report about the condition of a house for a building society was liable to purchasers who relied on the report in deciding to buy

---

[46] [1964] AC 465 (HL) [*Hedley Byrne*].

[47] *Haig v Bamford* [1977] 1 SCR 466; *Hercules Managements Ltd v Ernst & Young* [1997] 2 SCR 165 [*Hercules*].

[48] *Esanda Finance Corporation Ltd v Peat Marwick Hungerfords* (1997) 188 CLR 241 (HCA) [*Esanda*].

[49] *Scott Group Ltd v McFarlane* [1978] 1 NZLR 553 (CA); *Boyd Knight v Purdue* [1999] 2 NZLR 278 (CA) [*Boyd Knight*].

[50] Eg, *BDC Ltd v Hofstrand Farms Ltd* [1986] 1 SCR 228 (negligent courier); *South Pacific Manufacturing Co Ltd v NZ Security Consultants and Investigations Ltd* [1992] 2 NZLR 282 (CA) [*South Pacific Manufacturing*] (negligent insurance assessor); *Downsview Nominees Ltd v First City Corporation Ltd* [1993] AC 295 (PC) (negligent receiver).

[51] *Gartside v Sheffield Young & Ellis* [1983] NZLR 37 (CA); *White v Jones* [1995] 2 AC 207 (HL); *Hill v Van Erp* (1997) 188 CLR 159 (HCA) [*Hill*].

[52] *Spring v Guardian Assurance Plc* [1995] 2 AC 296 (HL).

the house.[53] This last case in particular should prompt us to ask why, in England, a surveyor of a defective building can be liable to a purchaser but the builder cannot.

The various cases demonstrate that no special mystery attaches to claims for financial loss. The nature of the loss is no reason in itself for denying a duty. It may be a reason for caution, and it has been said to weigh against a duty,[54] but this is because there is a greater likelihood that claims seeking recovery of financial rather than physical loss will involve policy concerns pointing away from a duty, not because there is an intrinsic objection to such claims. In each case, there needs to be an analysis of the proximity or relationship between the parties, together with any matters or concerns outside that relationship.[55] Viewed in this way, there can be no objection of principle to the claim by a subsequent purchaser of property. The High Court of Australia certainly thought this in *Bryan*, where *D & F Estates* and *Murphy* were dismissed as resting upon a narrower view of the scope of the modern law of negligence and a more rigid compartmentalisation of contract and tort than was acceptable in Australian law. Rather, the question for Australia and elsewhere is whether the claim can be justified as a matter of desirable policy.

IV.   POLICY CONCERNS

We have seen that leading decisions in England, Australia, Canada and New Zealand have come to differing conclusions in determining whether or how far the common law can fashion a remedy for the owner of defective property. This is not in itself a cause for concern. In *Invercargill City Council v Hamlin*,[56] the Privy Council recognised that the ability of the common law to adapt itself to the differing circumstances of the countries in which it has taken root is one of its great strengths. It would not otherwise have flourished as it has, with all the common law countries learning from each other. And the Judicial Committee considered that the question whether a subsequent owner ought to be able to sue for his or her financial loss was especially unsuited for the imposition of a single monolithic solution. Accordingly, the judges in the New Zealand Court of Appeal were entitled to depart from English case law, on the ground that conditions in New Zealand were different.

Some policy factors will operate in the same way across the different jurisdictions. But some may not. In particular, the social and economic

---

[53]   *Smith v Eric S Bush* [1990] 1 AC 831 (HL) [*Eric S Bush*].
[54]   *South Pacific Manufacturing*, above n 50, 295 (Cooke P).
[55]   For an overview of the duty inquiry see S Todd, 'A Methodology of Duty' in P Cane (ed), *Centenary Essays for the High Court of Australia* (Sydney, Butterworths, 2004) 221.
[56]   Above n 34.

background to the owner's claim, the statutory context, the need for a cause of action in negligence in light of any alternative actions or remedies that may be available, and any recognition given by Parliament or the courts to a 'consumer' ethos, may well point in different directions. So, where appropriate, the relevant concerns of policy need to be assessed in light of local conditions.

A.   Promoting Professional Accountability

Imposing a duty of care on builders, engineers, architects and the like in respect of defects in property may be justified on the ground that negligent professionals ought to be held accountable for the consequences of their negligence. Yet the argument, while unexceptional, cannot take us very far. It is little removed from the notion that for every wrong there ought to be a remedy. But the law of negligence is full of cases where there may have been a wrong but, for good reasons of policy, there was no remedy. This is what the duty debate is all about. Even so, the idea that professionals should be accountable outside contract to persons who suffer damage caused by their negligence has been gaining ground. One of the themes of the decision of the House of Lords in *Arthur JS Hall & Co v Simons*[57] was that professional persons normally may be held liable for negligence, and that barristerial immunity was an anomalous exception to ordinary principle. The New Zealand Supreme Court has taken a similar view,[58] whereas the High Court of Australia has upheld the immunity only on finality and relitigation arguments.[59] Again, and closer to the matter in issue, we can see examples of successful *Hedley Byrne* actions where information or advice has been given to another and then passed on to and relied on by the person now bringing the action.[60]

The idea of promoting accountability for negligence can give a degree of support to the owner's action but certainly cannot be decisive on its own. Other, arguably weightier, policy concerns must be considered in determining whether an action ought to lie.

B.   Imposing a Proportionate Burden of Liability

A duty of care is likely to be limited or denied altogether where its recognition would tend towards the imposition on the defendant of a

---

[57] [2002] 1 AC 615 (HL).
[58] *Chamberlains v Lai* [2006] NZSC 70 (SC).
[59] *D'Orta-Ekenaike v Victoria Legal Aid* (2005) 223 CLR 1 (HCA).
[60] *Eric S Bush*, above n 53; *Edgeworth Construction Ltd v ND Lea & Associates Ltd* [1993] 3 SCR 206.

potentially indeterminate liability. The justification is not simply one of practicality. Rather, it is the perception that the burden of liability would be a disproportionate response to the defendant's wrongdoing. So it is a conclusion of policy founded ultimately on a broad notion of fairness. In Australia, for example, in *Tame v NSW: Annetts v Australian Stations Pty Ltd*,[61] Gleeson CJ observed that the law is concerned not only with the compensation of injured plaintiffs but also with the imposition of liability upon defendants, and the effect of such liability upon the freedom and security with which people may conduct their ordinary affairs. Again, in New Zealand, in the *Rolls Royce* case,[62] Glazebrook J referred to a balancing of the plaintiff's moral claim to compensation for avoidable harm and the defendant's moral claim to be protected from undue restrictions on its freedom of action and from an undue burden of legal responsibility.

A major reason why claims in negligence for financial loss receive especially close scrutiny is the potential for such claims to lead to virtually limitless liability. The danger is acute in the case of financial loss caused by words, for in the nature of things, 'words are more volatile than deeds, they travel fast and far a field. They are used without being expended.'[63] Accordingly, the duty of care in making statements is hedged with various restrictions that are aimed, very generally, at imposing a suitably proportionate duty.[64] But, as has been emphasised in a number of the cases,[65] there is no similar fear where a property owner seeks to recover the cost of repairing defective property. Indeed, the defendant's burden of liability may be far heavier in physical damage cases. Where a defect in property causes physical injury or physical damage to other property, there is no inherent limit or control on the amount of the damages the defendant may be liable to pay. Where the owner sues for his or her financial loss, the maximum amount of the damages is the value of the property or cost of repair, together with, perhaps, loss of use during replacement or repair. And even if the concern is simply with the risk of creating a cause of action for a large number of claims, the evidence suggests that it can be discounted. In *Woolcock*,[66] McHugh J noted that, in New Zealand, Canada and Australia, the courts had not apparently been flooded by tort claims for economic loss arising out of defective premises.

---

[61] (2003) 211 CLR 317 (HCA) 329.
[62] Above, n 37, at [60]; and see *South Pacific Manufacturing*, above n 50, at 306 (Richardson P).
[63] *Hedley Byrne*, above n 46, at 534 (Lord Pearce).
[64] See generally *Caparo Industries plc v Dickman* [1990] 2 AC 605 (HL); *Hercules*, above n 47; *Esanda*, above n 48; *Boyd Knight*, above n 49.
[65] See especially *Winnipeg*, above n 24, at [48]-[50].
[66] Above n 18, at [97].

A fear that a duty owed by a builder to a house owner will give rise to indeterminate liability really expresses two different, although interrelated, fears—that a negligence duty will take over substantial parts of the law that are traditionally the preserve of the law of contract, and that any duty cannot be confined to the construction of houses but must extend to cover all persons who contribute to the creation of defects in any property which may be sold or otherwise passed on to a new owner, including commercial buildings and chattels. We will be inquiring into both of these concerns.

C.   Maintaining Contractual Certainty

While acceptable as a matter of legal principle, the negligence action may yet be thought undesirable as a matter of policy by reason of its impact on the law of contract. Some possible objections, in brief, are: that well-established boundaries between the provinces of tort and contract should not be disturbed; that the tort action has a tendency to cut across and upset contractual negotiation; that parties negotiating for building contracts need to be able to plan with a reasonable degree of certainty about future liabilities; that the content of any obligations imposed in tort are irredeemably uncertain; and that builders and others who take on duties of limited obligation or exclude their liability, and who are paid accordingly, should not be at risk of action by third parties not in contractual privity who allege breach of a wider obligation in negligence or of an obligation untrammelled by limiting or excluding clauses.

In order to assess these various objections, we need to consider two key questions. The first asks whether or how the courts can set a standard of care for the builder that can operate independently of the terms of the contract pursuant to which the work was carried out. And assuming an appropriate standard can be determined, the second asks whether or how far any contractual modifications of that standard can affect or limit a claim by a subsequent purchaser of the property.

(i)   Ascertaining the Standard of Care

It is clear that the standard of care expected of the builder, engineer or architect must be objectively ascertainable, and that it cannot depend for its existence on the particular terms of a contract pursuant to which a building was constructed. A mere complaint about quality without more cannot be enough, for the content of an obligation of quality must vary in accordance with what the builder has undertaken with the other contracting party to do and the price that other party has agreed to pay. The builder may have agreed to do a cheap job at a minimal price, or to adhere to the highest possible standards of building construction using the most expensive materials, or to do the work at some intermediate standard. So some external touchstone is needed.

In Canada, of course, in the *Winnipeg* case, the duty of the builder was founded upon the defect being dangerous. In New Zealand, in the *Rolls Royce* decision, Glazebrook J recognised that the danger posed by a defect was a possible test, but pointed to difficulties in its application and to its rejection in earlier decisions of the New Zealand courts.[67] Undeniably, there are likely to be deserving cases involving serious defects where the element of danger is by no means clear-cut.[68] And a building with a defect may not initially be dangerous, so the owner has no right of action, but the defect may gradually get worse and become dangerous and, at that time, will cost far more to fix. An underlying objection is that the potential damage giving rise to the duty is not the damage that the owner has in fact suffered. In particular, where the owner sues in respect of danger to him or herself or to another, the damages do not represent the injury that has been averted. Indeed, the non-owning occupant of a dangerous building cannot sue unless he or she is actually injured. The plaintiff necessarily is the owner, and the loss he or she suffers is the cost of putting the property in a state that is commensurate with the taking of reasonable care in its construction.

An arguably workable test is that put forward by the New Zealand Court of Appeal in *Stieller v Porirua CC*.[69] It was held there that the standard of the builder's duty did not depend on the element of danger, but extended to an obligation to take care to build a reasonably sound structure, using good materials and workmanlike practices. Perhaps the notion of reasonable habitability for dwellings or reasonable useability for other buildings also can assist. Indeed, the obligation to build a habitable dwelling is long established as a matter of contract. In the case of a contract for the sale of a house to be built, there is an implied warranty that the builder will do the work in a good and workmanlike manner and will supply good and proper materials, and that the house will be reasonably fit for human habitation.[70] Seemingly the content of an equivalent obligation in tort is no more difficult to determine. Both require the court to decide whether a dwelling is reasonably habitable, the

---

[67] See *Stieller*, above n 33; *Brown v Heathcote CC* [1986] 1 NZLR 76 (CA) (subsequently affd [1987] 1 NZLR 720 (PC)).

[68] In *Stieller*, above n 33, the plaintiff complained of warped weather-boards and stormwater drains which were not connected to any outlet. The Court of Appeal decided that danger to safety or health did not have to be shown, but that, in any event, it might exist in an extreme case where the weather-boards let water into the house.

[69] *Ibid.*

[70] *Perry v Sharon Development Ltd* [1937] 4 All ER 390 (CA); *McKey v Rorison* [1953] NZLR 498 (CA).

difference being that the contractual duty is strict and the tort duty is to take care. So, in contract, the builder warrants that the materials are good and proper, whereas in tort, the builder must take care to use good materials, and is not liable if, without personal fault, they unexpectedly turn out to be defective. In other respects, of course, the tort duty goes a good deal further. In particular, in the case of a house already complete before sale, there is at common law no implied warranty as to its state or fitness.[71] So here tort has filled an anachronistic gap in the law of contract and, at the same time, has extended a right of action to subsequent purchasers.[72]

External standards also may assist in setting a standard of care. The common practices of skilled and experienced builders or other professionals and any legislative or regulatory standards are all relevant to, although not determinative of, the common law standard of reasonable care. In particular, in *Askin v Knox*,[73] Cooke P recognised that the provisions of building bylaws and whether due care has been taken to comply with them are important in considering allegations of negligence.

Too much can be made of any difficulty in determining the standard of care that a builder might reasonably be expected to attain. Identifying a breach of duty may be a matter of impression and degree, yet the judiciary should be able to forge a recognisable distinction between minor problems and normal wear and tear, for which a property owner has no redress, and serious deficiencies affecting the habitability or fitness or useability of a building, to which a duty should apply.[74] However, setting an objective standard in the case of the manufacture of goods may be harder. A core expectation is that buildings should be reasonably durable so that they can be lived in or occupied or used. Chattels have widely variable purposes, which are not necessarily related to durability or structural integrity. There is a difficulty also if a duty is said to depend upon the element of danger. In *Winnipeg*, La Forest J rejected the argument put by Lord Keith in *Murphy* (that danger posed by an article could be avoided by discarding the article), on the ground that the owner of a home with a value far outweighing the cost of repair of a dangerous defect did not in reality have the option of avoiding the danger by discarding the home instead of repairing the

---

[71] *Stieller*, above n 33.

[72] Vendors and lessors formerly were immune from suit (*Robbins v Jones* (1863) 15 CB(NS) 221, 148 ER 768 (CP); *Bottomley v Bannister* [1932] 1 KB 458 (CA)), but more recent decisions have held that a builder can owe a duty of care to a purchaser or a third party irrespective of whether the builder was also the vendor: *Anns*, above n 6, at 759; *Mt Albert BC v Johnson* [1979] 2 NZLR 234 (CA); *Rimmer v Liverpool CC* [1985] QB 1 (CA).

[73] [1989] 1 NZLR 248 (CA) 253.

[74] See further E Quill, 'Consumer Protection In Respect Of Defective Buildings' (2006) 14 *Tort Law Review* 105, 112-13.

defect.[75] But an owner may well be able to exercise a real option by discarding a dangerous chattel.[76] So this is one possible reason why defective chattels could be treated differently from defective buildings.[77]

(ii)   Modifying the Standard of Care

We must consider now how the terms of a contract may affect a claim in tort by or against a third party. In the latter case, the third party may gain the benefit of a contract by a particular application of the principle of notice. A person can, of course, limit or exclude his or her liability for negligence by way of notice to another. For example, as held in *Hedley Byrne*, if advice is given subject to a stipulation disclaiming liability for it, the recipient is bound. He or she cannot accept the advice yet at the same time reject the stipulation.[78] A similar principle can apply where an excluding notice protecting A is given in a contract between B and C. In *Smith v Eric S Bush*,[79] the purchaser of a house applied for a mortgage to a building society, who instructed valuers to carry out a mortgage valuation. The mortgage application form contained a disclaimer of liability for the accuracy of the report, covering both the building society and the valuer. The House of Lords held that the exclusion notice provided the valuer with a defence at common law to an action for negligence by the purchaser.[80] Again, in the *Rolls Royce* case,[81] the limitation on the defendant's liability contained in the contract between the owner and the main contractor was known to and accepted by the owner, which accordingly was bound. There are other decisions that can be explained broadly on the basis that the defendant gave notice in a contract between the plaintiff and another that the defendant's liability was excluded.[82]

In addition, in some jurisdictions, there is legislation modifying the privity rule and allowing a designated third party who is intended to have

---

[75]   Above n 24, at [39]-[40].

[76]   See JW Neyers and U Gabie, 'Canadian Tort Law since *Cooper v Hobart*: Part I' (2005) 13 *Torts Law Journal* 302, 320-21, commenting on *Hughes v Sunbeam* Corporation (Canada) Ltd (2003) 219 DLR (4th) 467 (Ont CA).

[77]   For others, see below nn 102-104 and accompanying text.

[78]   *Hedley Byrne*, above n 46, at 504.

[79]   Above n 53.

[80]   However, the valuer could not rely on the notice because it failed to satisfy the requirement of reasonableness in s 2(2) of the Unfair Contract Terms Act 1977 (Eng).

[81]   Above n 37, at [109].

[82]   *Norwich City Council v Harvey* [1989] 1 WLR 828 (CA) (held not just and reasonable to exclude a subcontractor from the protection of a provision in a contract between an owner and a contractor which put the risk of damage to the building on the owner); *Pacific Associates Inc v Baxter* [1990] 1 QB 993 (CA) (engineer able to rely on a clause in a contract between a contractor and an owner which excluded the engineer's liability to the contractor); cf *McKinlay Hendry Ltd v Tonkin & Taylor Ltd* NZCA 81/04, 9 December 2005, [29]-[31] (new owner could not rely on engineer's site report stated to be prepared solely for benefit of client).

enforceable rights to enforce a benefit, including the benefit of an exclusion clause, in a contract between other persons.[83] Indeed, developments in the common law in Canada cover this case and allow the third party to take advantage of such a clause. The Supreme Court of Canada has extended the benefit of an exclusion clause to a third party in circumstances where the contracting parties intended this and the activities performed by the third party were the very activities contemplated as coming within the scope of the contract or of the particular provision in the contract.[84]

Let us take now the case where the parties to a contract purport to place the *burden* of an exclusion clause on a third party. Normally A and B cannot simply rely on their agreement by contract that one or both of them are not liable to the plaintiff.[85] As a general rule, it is not possible to place the burden of a contract on a non-consenting third party. However, a contractual exclusion of this kind may bind the third party if he or she acted in such a way as to indicate acceptance of the stipulation.[86] In the *Rolls Royce* case,[87] Glazebrook J said that the presence of a limitation clause in a contract between a head contractor and a subcontractor signifies clearly, if known to the owner, the subcontractor's unwillingness to do the job otherwise than subject to the limitation. The owner's acquiescence can then be deemed an acceptance of the terms under which alone the subcontractor is prepared to enter into a relationship defining its duty to the owner. A plaintiff should not be allowed to circumvent either a contractual bargain between the plaintiff and the defendant or even a non-contractual but clear understanding between parties as to where the risk should lie.

Some authority goes further in suggesting that an exclusion or limitation provision in a contract between a builder and an original purchaser may operate to limit or exclude the builder's tortious liability to a subsequent purchaser, by treating the builder as having assumed no responsibility to the purchaser.[88] In *Woolcock*, in a passage referred to with approval in the *Rolls Royce* case,[89] the joint majority judgment accepted that the provisions of a building contract can affect the standard of care required of a builder in an action by a third party, by defining the task that the builder or engineer undertook to do.[90] Their Honours thought that there would be

---

[83] See the Contracts (Privity) Act 1982 (NZ); Contracts (Rights of Third Parties) Act 1999 (UK).

[84] *London Drugs Ltd v Kuehne & Nagel International Ltd* [1992] 3 SCR 299; *Fraser River Pile & Dredge Ltd v Can-Dive Services Ltd* [1999] 3 SCR 108.

[85] *Bowen*, above n 32, at 407, 419; *Aliakmon*, above n 9, at 817.

[86] *Morris v CW Martin & Sons Ltd* [1966] 1 QB 716 (CA).

[87] Above n 37, at [110]-[113].

[88] For example *Council of the Municipality of Woollahra v Sved* (1996) Aust Torts Reports 81-398 (NSWCA); *Zumpano, above n* 17.

[89] Above n 37, at [68].

[90] *Woolcock*, above n 18, at [28]; and see *Bryan*, above n 15, at 624-25.

evident difficulty in holding that a builder owed a subsequent owner a duty of care to avoid economic loss if performance of that duty would have required the builder to do more or different work than the contract with the original owner required or permitted. But there is no deemed acquiescence in this kind of case, the subsequent purchaser having no choice in the matter. Accordingly, if this principle is accepted, it would appear that the builder can modify the duty he or she owes to a subsequent purchaser irrespective of any question of reasonable notice to the purchaser or of the purchaser's consent. On similar reasoning, it is at least arguable that the builder should be able to limit his or her liability or exclude it altogether. Yet this clearly is contrary to the rule that contractual burdens cannot bind non-consenting third parties.

We do not allow contractual limitations to protect defendants who cause physical harm to third parties. There is no justification for taking a different view where the loss is financial. Once it is accepted that the builder owes a duty of care to the purchaser, the standard of care must be determined objectively and there can be no room for unilateral modifications or exclusions of the duty. Suggestions that the builder has assumed no responsibility, or has taken on only a limited obligation, or has taken on no obligation at all, ought to be rejected. Suppose indeed that a builder knowingly creates a serious fault by failing to use proper materials, on the owner's instructions in the interests of saving money. The owner has no action, but it is hardly tenable to argue that a third party ought to be bound. It is difficult to understand why a builder should not be liable for, say, obviously inadequate foundations, simply because the builder agreed with a prior owner to build them inadequately.

D.   Responding to Need

In determining whether a duty of care is owed, the seriousness of the foreseeable consequences can be an important factor in the balancing exercise.[91] In the present context, the nature of the injury which is inflicted, involving the creation and likely covering up of defects in property that is intended for long-term use, often by successive owners, suggests that a remedy in tort is clearly necessary. In the case of houses, there is the importance of giving a remedy in respect of a purchase which for most people is likely to be the most significant of their lifetime. Recent events in New Zealand provide a graphic illustration. A major problem in the building industry has emerged concerning the adoption of flawed building techniques which have allowed water to leak into and cause substantial damage to large numbers of new houses. In many cases, the law of contract

[91] *South Pacific Manufacturing*, above n 50, 295 (Cooke P (CA)).

alone cannot provide a remedy. And with more buildings found to be leaking, the problem is getting worse. The New Zealand Department of Building and Housing estimates that there are 15,000 affected houses and that the cost of repairs may amount to NZ$1 billion. Industry sources suggest that the true number may be 40,000 houses, with a repair bill nearer NZ$5 billion.[92]

The need for a remedy in tort may be tempered by any alternative claim or right of action for the owner that might be available. We have seen already that homeowners in England have a right to claim for compensation under the National House Building Council's warranty scheme and also a right to sue under statute.[93] Certainly, the decision in *Murphy* would have had a lesser practical impact in England than a similar decision in other jurisdictions. In New Zealand, substantial protection is now given pursuant to the provisions of the Building Act 2004,[94] but these cannot help in respect of defects predating the coming into force of the Act (30 November 2004), or where the six year limitation period in contract has expired.[95] In another example, in Ontario there is warranty protection for owners of dwellings and their successors, up to a maximum period of seven years in the case of structural defects.[96] So a tort action may not be necessarily the only available option, yet in each of Canada, Australia and New Zealand it remains of central concern at least to many house owners.

What of the position of commercial owners? Seemingly a direct claim would be possible in the case of a negligent statement, under the *Hedley Byrne* principle. But there could be a remedy via an action by the promisee to a building contract, who might be able to sue for the benefit of the third party purchaser. In *Linden Gardens Trust Ltd v Lenesta Sludge Disposals Ltd*,[97] the House of Lords, applying the rule in *The Albazero*,[98] held that,

---

[92]   See G Cumming, 'But wait, there's more' *New Zealand Herald* (13 May 2006) <http://www.nzherald.co.nz/author/story.cfm?a_id=88&ObjectID=10381550> (date accessed: 23 August 2006); and see generally PJ May, 'Performance-Based Regulation and Regulatory Regimes: The Saga of Leaky Buildings' (2003) 25 *Law and Policy* 381.

[93]   Above n 13 and accompanying text.

[94]   Above nn 38-41 and accompanying text.

[95]   There is also a private scheme of limited scope operated by the New Zealand Master Builders' Federation.

[96]   Ontario New Home Warranties Plan Act RSO 1990 c 0.31.

[97]   [1994] 1 AC 85 (HL); and see *Darlington Borough Council v Wiltshier Northern Ltd* [1995] 1 WLR 68 (CA).

[98]   [1977] AC 774 (HL). It was held here, confirming the decision of the House of Lords in *Dunlop v Lambert* (1839) 2 Cl & F 600, 7 ER 824, that in a commercial contract concerning goods, where it is in the contemplation of the parties that the proprietary interest in the goods may be transferred to another before any breach causing damage to the goods, an original party to the contract is to be treated as having entered into the contract for the benefit of the other person and may recover the actual loss suffered by that person. See generally N Palmer and G Tolhurst, 'Compensatory and Extra-compensatory Damages: The Role of *The Albazero* in Modern Damages Claims' (1998) 12 *Journal of Contract Law* 1, 97; B Coote, '*Dunlop v Lambert*: The Search for a Rationale' (1998) 13 *Journal of Contract Law* 91.

where a building development was, to the knowledge of the parties, likely to be acquired by third parties, who would foreseeably suffer loss from defective performance of the contract but who would be unable personally to sue on the contract, the contracting party could recover in respect of the third party's loss. Of course, this remedy depends upon the promisee deciding to sue; the third party cannot force the promisee to take action. It also is subject to any contractual limitations negotiated by the defendant builder, over which the new purchaser has or may have no control. A further limitation was identified in *Alfred McAlpine Construction Ltd v Panatown Ltd*,[99] where their Lordships held that there was no justification for applying the *Linden Gardens* exception to the privity rule if the third party had a direct remedy against a party to the contract. So one party had no claim against the other for negligence in building an office block in circumstances where the block was owned by a third party, and the builder had entered a duty of care deed accepting liability to the third party for negligence.[100] Accordingly, the promisee's action operates simply as a back-up, to fill a gap if the new owner has no other right of action. Arguably it is not needed if, conceivably, the owner can take advantage of a statutory modification of the privity rule, and sue as an identified third party who is intended to be able to enforce the building contract.[101] But here, again, the first owner can negotiate away third party rights. Contractually agreed shoddy building practices or limiting or exclusion clauses will bind the third party beneficiary. If the third party owner has a right of action in tort, then, in accordance with the preceding discussion, the problem disappears.

Accordingly, there are available to commercial owners at most only limited alternative rights of action. Assessed in terms of need, a remedy in negligence deserves to be supported. And, in accordance with the preceding discussion, any such action does not operate inconsistently with the contractual context.

In the case of defective chattels, the position is different. In Canada, an action against the manufacturer lies where the chattel is dangerous, but the clear trend elsewhere is not to allow it. Certainly there is a lesser need for a remedy in tort in respect of a defective chattel as opposed to a defective building. Manufactured goods normally will reach the ultimate purchaser via a chain of contracts made between all or any of the manufacturer,

---

[99] [2001] 1 AC 518 (HL); B Coote, 'The Performance Interest, *Panatown*, and the Problem of Loss' (2001) 117 *LQR* 81.

[100] More controversial is the view of Lord Griffiths in *Linden Gardens*, which would allow recovery by the promisee for its own loss in not receiving the bargain for which it had contracted. In *Panatown*, their Lordships were divided on whether the promisee would be bound to provide the benefit to the third party.

[101] Eg, under the Contracts (Privity) Act 1982 (NZ) or the Contracts (Rights of Third Parties) Act 1999 (Eng).

distributor, wholesaler, retailer and purchaser. Where loss is suffered by the purchaser because of a defect in the goods, he or she may be able to sue the retailer for breach of the express terms of the contract, if any are applicable, or for breach of terms as to correspondence with description, fitness and merchantability that are implied into the contract by legislation governing the sale of goods.[102] There may also be consumer legislation providing an alternative (and non-excludable) remedy.[103] So normally, purchasers from business vendors have perfectly adequate contractual protection. And sometimes purchasers of consumer goods have additional rights of action against the manufacturer.[104]

An inquiry into the need for a remedy in tort tends to overlap with an inquiry into whether the action can operate consistently with any relevant statutes. As regards buildings, the argument can cut both ways. Where there has been statutory intervention to protect owners of dwellings, then on the one hand, the implication might be drawn that the courts should go no further in developing a remedy for commercial owners. But on the other hand, the implication could also be that Parliament intended to leave the question of a remedy in commercial cases to the common law. In *Rolls Royce*,[105] Glazebrook J regarded the statutory context as favouring a duty of care with respect to domestic construction but as neutral as regards commercial construction. By contrast, as regards chattels, the statutory context in each of the countries under review very arguably points away from any common law action.

---

[102] The whole scheme originally laid down in the Sale of Goods Act 1893 (UK), including the regime of implied terms, was adopted throughout the states and territories of Australia, the provinces and territories of Canada (except in Quebec) and in New Zealand, and (with varying degrees of amendment) continues to apply.

[103] In Canada, for example, see the Consumer Protection Acts in Manitoba (RSM 1987 c C200, s 58), the Northwest Territories (RSNWT 1988 c C-17, s 70), Yukon (RSY 2002 c 30, s 58), and Nova Scotia (RSNS 1989 c 92, s 26). In Australia, see the Trade Practices Act 1974 (CW) Pts IVA, V, VA; and see also the Fair Trading Act 1987 (NSW); Fair Trading Act 1999 (Vic); Fair Trading Act 1989 (Qld); Fair Trading Act 1987 (SA); Fair Trading Act 1987 (WA); Fair Trading Act 1990 (Tas); Fair Trading Act 1992 (ACT); Consumer Affairs and Fair Trading Act 1990 (NT). In New Zealand, see the Consumer Guarantees Act 1993 Pts I, II. In England, various reforms were introduced in the Sale of Goods Act 1979 and the Sale and Supply of Goods Act 1994 aimed at giving greater legal protection to consumers. See further below n 106.

[104] In Canada, see the Consumer Products Warranties Act 1977 (Sask). In Australia, see the Trade Practices Act 1974 Pt V Div 2A; and see also the Sale of Goods Act 1923 (NSW) Pt 8; Manufacturers' Warranties Act 1974 (SA), ss 3, 4; Law Reform (Manufacturers' Warranties) Act 1977 (ACT), ss 3, 4. In New Zealand, see the Consumer Guarantees Act 1993, s 27.

[105] Above n 37, at [115]-[116].

E. Protecting the Vulnerable

We will turn now to consider whether an owner should reasonably be expected to take his or her own steps to guard against the risk of suffering loss. Recent decisions show the courts becoming increasingly concerned to protect persons who are vulnerable to suffering harm and who have no reasonably available means of protecting themselves. It might be seen as a form of 'consumer' protection at common law, and to this extent it reflects legislative developments in many common law jurisdictions during the later part of the 20th century.[106] On the other hand, a duty may be denied if a plaintiff could reasonably have been expected to take self-protective measures and, in that way, to look after his or her own interests. Of course, this idea already underlies various defences to liability—notably that the plaintiff failed to take reasonable steps in mitigation of a loss, that he or she assumed the risk, or that he or she was guilty of contributory negligence—but it also has a role to play in the duty inquiry.[107] In particular, in certain commercial cases, the principle can bring into account the plaintiff's bargaining power and the market structure, by asking whether self-protective measures could reasonably have been expected or bargained for or whether the market reality was that contractual or other forms of protection could not reasonably have been obtained. Seemingly, then, it can be tied in with notions of distributive justice and economic efficiency.

Some examples will show both limbs of the principle in operation. In *Smith v Eric S Bush*,[108] the House of Lords held that a surveyor of a house reporting to a building society owed a duty of care to the prospective purchaser of the house, and influential factors were that the value of the house was modest, the plaintiff was likely to rely on the one survey, and the surveyor knew this. Again, in *Hill v Van Erp*,[109] an intended beneficiary of a will depended upon the testator's solicitor performing the client's retainer with care, and could do nothing to ensure that this was done. By

---

[106] This of course is a vast topic. Instances are given in nn 103-104, above. For overviews of the position in England, see *Benjamin's Sale of Goods*, 6th edn (London, Sweet & Maxwell Ltd, 2002) ch 14; PS Atiyah, *The Sale of Goods*, 10th edn (Harlow, Longman, 2001) (by JN Adams and H McQueen) Pt II, especially ch 15. In Canada, see GHL Fridman, *The Sale of Goods*, 5th edn (Toronto, Carswell, 2004) ch 8, especially at 201-3. In Australia, see C Turner, *Australian Commercial Law*, 24th edn (Sydney, Law Book Co, 2003) ch 17. In New Zealand, see C Hawes (ed), *Butterworths Commercial Law in New Zealand* (Wellington, LexisNexis NZ Ltd, 2005) chs 9, 18.

[107] J Stapleton, 'Duty of Care and Economic Loss: A Wider Agenda' (1991) 107 *LQR* 249, 265-66.

[108] Above n 53.

[109] Above n 51.

contrast, in *Esanda Finance Corporation Ltd v Peat Marwick Hunger-fords*,[110] a financier lending money to a company could have made inquiries about the financial position of the company rather than depend upon the auditor's certification of the accounts. McHugh J remarked that, if the liability of auditors were extended to third parties in these circumstances, the common law would be conferring rights on a sophisticated group who had the means in most cases to take steps to avoid the risk of loss.[111] So also, in *Brownie Wills v Shrimpton*,[112] solicitors retained by a bank who failed to carry out instructions to give advice to a director about the implications of guaranteeing a loan from the bank to the director's company owed no duty to the director, who was not totally dependent upon the defendants and could easily have sought advice for himself.

Whether a plaintiff has adopted sensible commercial practices by way of self-protection has also emerged in the debate about recovery for 'relational' financial loss caused by damage to the property of another. La Forest J has pointed out that a significant reason for denying a duty in this type of case, at least as a general rule, is that such denial channels to the property owner both potential liability to the plaintiff, who can contract with the owner for compensation for loss of use of the property, and the right of recovery against the tortfeasor.[113] In *The Aliakmon*,[114] for example, no duty was owed to buyers of goods that were damaged by the defendants when in transit and at a time when the risk but not the ownership had passed to the buyers. One reason was that the buyers could have protected their interests in a contract with the sellers, by inserting a term that the sellers should sue on the buyers' account or should assign to the buyers the right to sue.

As we have seen, a similar theme has emerged in the defective property cases, where increasing emphasis has been put on the element of vulnerability. Some see this as a good reason for denying the owner's claim altogether. In *Woolcock*,[115] Callinan J questioned the correctness of *Bryan* and maintained that a purchaser of any premises, whether a dwelling or otherwise, was not especially vulnerable. His Honour pointed out that a purchaser had several means of protecting itself, including insistence on a warranty or condition of fitness or soundness, or the seeking of an inspection and report by an expert, who will become liable if negligent in not discovering and reporting relevant defects. Certainly these are possible options: but in many cases they may not count for much.

---

[110]   Above n 48.
[111]   Above n 48, at 284.
[112]   [1998] 2 NZLR 320 (CA).
[113]   *Canadian National Railway Co v Norsk Pacific Steamship Co Ltd* [1992] 1 SCR 1021, 1052.
[114]   Above n 9.
[115]   Above n 18, at [211]-[213].

The first possibility is the opportunity for negotiating for a warranty of soundness with the vendor. In the case of houses, usually purchasers *are* vulnerable. On the sale of a dwelling house, the principle of caveat emptor normally prevails and is likely to be non-negotiable, thereby barring a remedy against the vendor. Denying a duty on the part of the builder thus will hardly promote self-help, and in many cases the purchaser will be left with no remedy at all. By contrast, it can be argued that the owner of a commercial building should be confined to a remedy in contract against the vendor, on the grounds that the network of contractual relationships will normally provide appropriate and sufficient avenues of redress without any supervening tort duties.[116] The parties at least are more likely to be able to bargain about the matter on relatively equal terms and to agree on an appropriate allocation of the risk.

The second possibility is for the purchaser to engage his or her own expert. It is certainly true that purchasers of houses can do this, but many do not. Indeed, at least where a building is new or nearly new, it is arguably unreasonable to place the onus on a purchaser to check that it is sound. Why should the purchaser not be able to expect that the builder has taken care? And even accepting that an independent check would be prudent, the reality is that ignorance of the risk and social and economic constraints may operate to inhibit many purchasers from taking this kind of precaution. Furthermore, a properly conducted inspection may not reveal the problem, which only becomes reasonably detectable at a later date. On the other hand, as McHugh J in *Woolcock*[117] and Glazebrook J in *Rolls Royce*[118] particularly emphasised, parties to commercial dealings normally have better means of protecting themselves than purchasers of houses. So, on this view, commercial purchasers must look after themselves and negotiate in contract for the right to a remedy or take other self-protective steps.

But if there is to be no duty in 'commercial' cases, the courts must decide where to draw the line. It should not depend simply on whether property is commercial or residential. The view expressed in the majority judgment in *Woolcock*, that any such line could not be clearly defined and might be indefinable, must be correct. An obvious instance of difficulty would be where a building has both commercial and residential purposes.[119] Or a commercial plaintiff may be the owner of a small business and in a highly vulnerable position, whereas a residential plaintiff complaining of defects in a multi-million dollar mansion may be very well able to look after his or

---

[116] *Hamlin*, above n 34, at 520 (Cooke P).
[117] Above n 18, at [80]-[86].
[118] Above n 37, at [60]-[61], [118], [123].
[119] See, eg, *Three Meade Street Ltd v Rotorua District Council* [2005] 1 NZLR 504 (HC) (defects in motel: duty denied).

her own interests. Seemingly the question would have to be whether the builder (or architect, or engineer) should foresee harm to a vulnerable plaintiff who could not reasonably be expected to protect him or herself from economic loss in acquiring a defective building. Yet this would mean that the question would be at large in every case. Whether the particular plaintiff was or could be expected to be vulnerable could be argued in relation to a residence, an office, a factory, a corner dairy or any other building. And the answer could hardly turn on whether the particular plaintiff happened to be rich or poor.

For a principle of vulnerability to work properly, we need to be able to point to a *category* of claim where plaintiffs can be treated as vulnerable and as being unable to take steps to protect their financial interests. A good example arguably is that of the disappointed legatee mentioned above, who can be seen as a member of a vulnerable class. Again, in a *Hedley Byrne* action, the notion that a commercial concern contemplating the takeover of a company should reasonably be expected to consult its own advisers provides at least a workable test. So also purchasers of defective chattels can be hived off into a class of their own, on the basis that there is no special need for a remedy in tort. But if we allow a claim by the owner of a defective building, there is no good stopping point in distinguishing between different kinds of buildings. Seemingly it is all or nothing. Either we allow such claims or we reject them entirely.

The solution ought to be to allow them. This indeed was the view of Kirby J in *Woolcock*, whose arguments are very persuasive. Financial loss to a subsequent owner certainly is a reasonably foreseeable consequence of a builder's failure to take care. There is a public interest in discouraging the putting up of defective buildings, of whatever kind, and tort law can respond by giving a remedy to the owner. This compensates for a wrong and at the same time helps to maintain proper professional standards in the engineering and building industry. Subsequent purchasers of new or fairly new buildings, whether private or commercial, in many cases will have no other adequate remedy, and are vulnerable to the risk of harm in the sense that they are acquiring property which misleadingly appears to be sound. Indeed, they can reasonably expect at least a minimum level of durability and soundness, and to this extent they should not be deprived of a legal remedy merely because they could have engaged an expert prior to a purchase. Furthermore, defects usually are latent and may not be easily discoverable even if an expert is in fact called in to make a report.

More generally, imposing a duty of care on a builder in a commercial context does not interfere with commercial autonomy or freedom of contractual negotiation. Parties to contractual matrices are free to accept restrictions on their taking tort actions, but subsequent non-consenting purchasers are not and should not be bound. There is no danger of multiple claims or loss of an indeterminate amount, and potentially liable builders or engineers can seemingly insure against liability in respect of a broadly quantifiable risk. Indeed, a builder who is simply performing a contract pursuant to its terms may be able to obtain an indemnity from the original contracting party. Taking these various factors into account, the commercial building owner, like the house owner, has a strong claim for redress.

V.   NEGLIGENT INSPECTIONS

The focus of the debate in the preceding pages has been on whether a duty of care is or ought to be owed by those who create defects in property to those who later acquire the property. A further complication arises in cases where the defendant has not created the defect but has failed to intervene to prevent another from creating it. In the present context, the question is whether local authority inspectors or other regulatory bodies may also be held to owe a duty to the owner. This introduces the whole question of duty in relation to omissions, the full consideration of which is outside the scope of this article. However, a few brief points will be made.

Duties of positive action commonly arise out of an assumption of control over or responsibility for an activity. Local councils assume responsibility by instituting and requiring adherence to building and planning regulations and exercise control over the work of the builder. Building by-laws commonly require notification to and approval by the council of building work at particular stages, creating a continuing supervisory role for that body. This has been seen as providing the foundation for a duty to take care to inspect the building work.[120] It arises because the council has taken on the task of ensuring that the work has been done properly. A duty also has been seen as consistent with the statutory context in which building inspectors work.[121] But pre-*Murphy*, the House of Lords rejected a claim for negligent inspection, partly on the ground that the recovery by owners of financial loss was outside the purpose of the statutory powers of inspection.[122]

Whether an inspecting authority ought to come under a duty to take care no doubt can be debated, particularly in light of the propensity of negligent builders to go out of business and the use of sham companies. Local authorities very frequently will have to carry the burden of negligent wrongdoing by others. At all events, even if the negligent inspector can be liable, it is unlikely that a body with general regulatory powers over the

---

[120] *Dutton*, above n 5, at 392; *Hamlin*, above n 34, at 519, 525-26, 530 (CA), 516, 518 (PC).

[121] *Kamloops*, above n 23; Stieller, above n 33.

[122] *Peabody*, above n 9.

building industry in relation to the public at large can be similarly liable. In *A-G v Body Corporate No 200200*,[123] the New Zealand Court of Appeal held that the New Zealand Building Industry Authority (BIA) owed no duty to building owners to exercise its powers under the Building Act 1991 (NZ) and the Building Code by taking steps to warn about and prevent poor building practices leading to leaky building syndrome. There was insufficient proximity between the BIA and property owners; responsibility rested far more directly on developers, designers, builders and certifiers; the BIA exercised quasi-legislative or quasi-judicial functions where no duty of care could arise; a duty of general superintendence would require the courts to review the reasonableness of resources allocated to the BIA; and the policy of the 1991 Act was not to produce official over-vigilance but to place responsibility on building certifiers.

VI.   LIMITATION OF ACTIONS

Building defects sometimes will be concealed and lie undiscovered for many years. In these cases, there will be a long delay following the building work before an owner brings an action, which could cause hardship to the builder. The problem of delay normally is dealt with by a statutory limitation period, commonly six years from the date when the cause of action accrued. In England, the House of Lords held initially that time in a defective property case ran from the date of physical damage to the property. So a claim against engineers in respect of the negligent design of a chimney was barred in circumstances where the action was brought more than six years after the date that cracking in the chimney started, even though the cracking was not discovered until a much later date.[124] But this decision overlooked the true nature of the damage. In *Invercargill City Council v Hamlin*, Lord Lloyd said that, once it was appreciated that the owner suffered a financial loss, the difficulties surrounding the limitation question fell away. The plaintiff's loss occurred when the market value of the house was depreciated by reason of the defective foundations. If an owner resold the house at full value before the defect was discovered, he or she suffered no loss. Thus in the common case the occurrence of the loss and the discovery of the loss would coincide. And the plaintiff could not postpone the start of the limitation period by shutting his or her eyes to the obvious. The cause of action accrued when the cracks become so bad, or the defects so obvious, that any reasonable homeowner would call in an expert. Accordingly, in this type of case, the date of discoverability is also the date of the damage.

---

[123] [2007] 1 NZLR 95 (CA).
[124] *Pirelli General Cable Works Ltd v Oscar Faber & Partners* [1983] 2 AC 1 (HL).

A discoverability rule also has been adopted in Canada[125] and Australia.[126] So the way is open for claims to be made against builders long after their work has been completed. The courts cannot easily deal with this problem for they cannot impose limitation periods of their own. Even so, as time passes, plaintiffs may find it increasingly difficult to prove who, if anyone, originally was negligent or caused the loss. This might be thought to be an inadequate control, and a more satisfactory solution is a long-stop limitation period imposed by statute.[127]

VII. CONCLUSION

Whether a builder, or an engineer, or a sub-contractor, or a manufacturer, or anyone else who has contributed to the construction or manufacture of defective property should be held to owe a duty of care to a subsequent purchaser of the property involves a weighing of relevant considerations of policy. In the case of buildings, these point in favour of a duty. The owner's loss certainly is foreseeable and the likelihood in many cases is that it will also be very serious, yet at the same time there is no danger of opening the floodgates to an indeterminate number of claimants suffering losses that are indeterminate in amount. House purchasers may have special need for a remedy, yet commercial purchasers cannot sensibly be treated differently, and all are vulnerable to suffering loss through acquiring structures for long-term use but with hidden defects. The objection that a tort claim trespasses impermissibly into an area of law which is the proper preserve of the law of contract, sometimes seen as an objection of principle, is not convincing. Judges need not throw up their hands and say that tort cannot help. Rather, the action simply holds negligent professionals accountable for their wrongdoing. However, in the case of defective chattels, the relationship is different, it is more difficult to determine the content of the manufacturer's obligation to the ultimate owner independently of the terms of a contract, and there is no similar need for a tort remedy, both because the loss is likely to be much less serious and because there is a far greater likelihood of an efficacious remedy in contract.

The builder's duty of care to a first purchaser perhaps can be founded on both contract and tort, and certainly the negligence duty outflanks the old law denying that there can be an implied warranty on the sale of a completed house. Some possible implications of recognising the duty will

---

[125] *Kamloops*, above n 23; *Central Trust Co v Rafuse* [1986] 2 SCR 147.

[126] *Hawkins v Clayton* (1988) 164 CLR 539 (HCA) 600-1; *Bryan*, above n 15, at 627.

[127] In New Zealand, see the Building Act 2004, s 393(2) (re-enacting the Building Act 1991, s 91(2)) (civil proceedings relating to any building work may not be brought against any person after 10 years or more from the date of the act or omission on which the proceedings are based); and see *Johnson v Watson* [2003] 1 NZLR 626 (CA).

need to be considered. One particular question might be whether an owner/vendor can, exceptionally, be liable—where, for example, the owner knowingly conspires with the builder to build a sub-standard house. There are existing questions, mentioned above, concerning the ambit of liability for negligent inspection and the limitation issue. But there is no reason to suppose that these and other difficulties cannot be satisfactorily resolved.

9

Defective Structures and Economic Loss in the United States: Law and Policy

DAVID F PARTLETT*

I. INTRODUCTION

I N THIS SHORT contribution to the book, I offer a chapter in two parts. In the first part, I undertake to summarise the United States law pertaining to the issue of negligence liability for defective structures and its changing face. In the second, I suggest a policy perspective beyond those identified by Professor Todd in his insightful and persuasive chapter. Professor Todd, in this volume, examines the liability of professionals, builders and public authorities for losses arising to beleaguered purchasers of premises rendered defective by the negligence of those actors. He describes the conflicting law in England, Australia, Canada and New Zealand. That case law offers significant insights to American lawyers and policy makers facing the same issues of the scope of negligence liability. Many of the judicial opinions are carefully and closely considered, and should be brought to American jurisprudence. At the same time, the American law is strikingly absent from Commonwealth law, and unusually so considering that American tort law has played a significant part in the evolution of Commonwealth tort law.[1]

---

* Dean and Asa Griggs Candler Professor of Law, Emory University School of Law. The author thanks John Appelbaum, Washington and Lee Class of 2008, and Laura Huffman, Emory University Class of 2008, for valuable research assistance on this chapter.
[1] Consider the use of *MacPherson v Buick Motor Co*, 217 NY 382 (1916) in *Donoghue v Stevenson* [1932] AC 562 (HL) 577, 598, 617; or *Ultramares v Touche, Niven & Co* 255 NY 170 (1931) [*Ultramares*] in *Hedley Byrne v Heller & Partners* [1964] AC 465 (HL) 471, 487-88, 537.

One common characteristic can be found in both bodies of law: doctrinal uncertainty. It is another legal dog's breakfast.[2] When a construction defect does not result in personal injury or damage to other property, the same empty slogans are on display—allowing recovery will 'open the flood-gates',[3] or will lead contract to 'drown in a sea of tort'.[4] The label 'economic loss', like a mystical invocation, convinces a majority of courts that the only possible outcome is to deny liability. Other courts, bending to the tide of modern negligence law, allow recovery based on the nature of the buyer, foreseeability, or likelihood of physical harm.[5]

II. LAW, LEGISLATION AND BEHAVIOUR

A. An Overview of United States Case Law

United States common law in construction defect cases varies widely by jurisdiction, and is changing in some places toward offering more protection to unsophisticated buyers.[6] Whether the economic loss rule, preventing recovery in tort for loss that is purely financial rather than damage to person or property, should apply at all in construction defect cases leads to lively discussion in both opinions and commentary.[7] Most jurisdictions apply the economic loss rule to primary commercial construction transactions, reasoning that commercial buyers are sophisticated enough to protect themselves in contract.[8] The few cases between builders and

---

[2] Here I allude to AWB Simpson: 'The position in modern tort law is similar—since all questions about liability for negligence are supposed to turn on the doctrine of the duty of care, one must expect the duty of care to be something of a dog's breakfast too. It is.' *A History of the Common Law of Contract: The Rise of the Action of Assumpsit* (Oxford, Clarendon Press, 1975) 325.

[3] *Jimenez v Superior Court* 29 Cal 4th 473 (2002) 481.

[4] *East River Steamship Corp v Transamerica Delaval, Inc* 476 US 858 (1986) 866 [*East River*] citing G Gilmore, *The Death of Contract* (Columbus, Ohio State University Press, 1974) 87-94.

[5] *Rousseau v KN Construction Co* 727 A 2d 190 (RI 1999) 193 (the economic loss doctrine does not apply to consumer transactions when the consumer lacks privity of contract with the offending party); *Sewell v Gregory* 179 W Va 585 (1988) 588 [*Sewell*] (foreseeable that there would be subsequent owners of a home); *Council of Co-Owners Atlantis Condominium, Inc v Whiting-Turner Contracting Co* 308 Md 18 (1986) 35 (permitting recovery of economic loss to repair construction defects imposing a 'clear danger of death or personal injury', but not merely a 'risk to general health, welfare or comfort').

[6] PH Thompson and C Dean, 'Continued Erosion of the Economic Loss Rule in Construction Litigation By and Against Owners' (Fall 2005) 25 *The Construction Lawyer* 36.

[7] Eg: *Linden v Cascade Stone Company, Inc* 283 Wis 2d 606 (2005) 628-38 [*Linden*] (Bradley, Butler JJ and Abrahamson CJ dissenting); *Moransais v Heathman* 744 So 2d 973 (Fla 1999) 980-82 [*Moransais*]; PL Bruner and PJ O'Connor, Jr, *Bruner and O'Connor on Construction Law* § 19:13 (West 2006).

[8] Thompson, above n 6, at 40.

subsequent commercial purchasers take the same position.[9] Some jurisdictions, such as New York, make no distinction based on the experience of the buyer, holding that the economic loss rule applies to all transactions.[10]

However, many jurisdictions allow negligence actions by subsequent buyers of residential properties.[11] Beyond the courts, state legislatures are acting to protect both home buyers and the construction industry. Several states have enacted new home warranty laws requiring builders to provide a warranty against certain defects and construction practices that do not meet specified standards.[12] This provides a contractual remedy to residential buyers, and the warranty is transmissible to subsequent purchasers. California and Nevada are prime examples of the effect of notice and right to repair statutes and associated rights of action. The courts of Colorado and South Carolina have found that builders have a duty in tort to act without negligence in construction of residences, thereby precluding application of the economic loss rule.[13]

B. Defective Buildings, Products Liability, and the United States Supreme Court

Defective buildings do not fit comfortably into traditional definitions because they are rarely considered products. The principle that an owner can recover for a defective product in tort only if it causes personal injury or injury to other property is well established.[14] *The Restatement (Third) of Torts: Products Liability* defines three situations where builders may be treated as product sellers: 1) when the building has attachments (such as appliances or other manufactured equipment); 2) when the building is prefabricated or manufactured at another location and then moved to its

---

[9] *Hayden Bus Ctr Condominiums Assoc v Pegasus Development Corp* 209 Ariz 511 (App Div 1 2005); *Boston Investment Property #1 State v EW Burman, Inc* 658 A 2d 515 (RI 1995).

[10] *Corporex Development & Construction Management, Inc v Shook, Inc* 106 Ohio St 3d 412 (2005); *Linden*, above n 7; *Prendiville v Contemporary Home, Inc* 32 Kan App 2d 435 (App 2004) [*Prendiville*]; *Carstens v City of Phoenix* 206 Ariz 123 (App Div 1 2003); *Ofsowitz v Georgie Boy Manufacturing, Inc* 231 AD 2d 858 (NY App Div 4th Dept 1996).

[11] *The Milton Co v Council of Unit Owners of Bentley Place Condominium* 121 Md App 100 (Spec App 1998); *George B Gilmore Co v Jimmy E Garrett* 582 So 2d 387 (Miss 1991); *Floraday v Don Galloway Homes* 340 NC 223 (1995); *Cosmopolitan Homes, Inc v Weller* 663 P 2d 1041 (Col 1983) [*Cosmopolitan Homes*]; *Sewell*, above n 5.

[12] Those states are: Connecticut, Indiana, Louisiana, Maryland, Minnesota, Mississippi, New Jersey, New York, and Virginia. R Sutton, 'Validity, Construction and Application of New Home Warranty Acts' (2006) 101 *American Law Reports Annotated*, 5th Series 447, 459.

[13] *AC Excavating v Yacht Club II Homeowner's Assoc Inc* 114 P 3d 862 (Colo 2005) [*AC Excavating*]; *RJ Griffin v Beach Club II Homeowners Assoc Inc* 384 F 3d 157 (4th Cir 157) [*RJ Griffin*].

[14] *Restatement (Third) of Torts: Products Liability* (1998) § 21.

final destination; or 3) when dwellings are built on a major scale (in which case strict liability attaches).[15] Much debate in defective building cases revolves around whether the building is considered 'other property' or not.[16]

While the United States Supreme Court has never considered a defective building case, in its definitive products liability case, *East River Steamship Corpn v Transamerica Delaval, Inc*, the Court held that economic loss was not recoverable in a situation where defective turbines made steamships unavailable.[17] The respondent turbine manufacturer had contracted with the petitioners' parent company to design, manufacture and supervise installation of turbines on four supertankers.[18] After each ship was completed, the parent company chartered it to one of the petitioners.[19] Each charterer assumed responsibility for the cost of any repairs required to the ship.[20] After the petitioners put the ships into service, they found the turbines on three of the ships were defective, and the turbine on the fourth ship was installed improperly.[21] The petitioners claimed $8 million damages for the cost of repairing the ships and the income lost while the ships were out of service.[22]

The Court held that a manufacturer in a commercial relationship has no duty in either negligence or strict products liability to prevent a product from injuring itself.[23] The Court found that, when there is no personal injury involved, the commercial user can insure itself against increased costs, or loss of value of the product.[24] The Court rejected intermediate approaches that turned on the nature of the defect, the type of risk, and the manner in which the injury occurred, as too indeterminate for manufacturers to plan their business behaviour, and as infringements on the core concerns of contract law.[25]

A few years later, in *Saratoga Fishing Co v JM Martinac & Co*, the Court allowed a subsequent owner of a fishing vessel to recover the cost of equipment added by a previous owner when the vessel sank due to a defectively designed hydraulic system, reasoning that the added equipment was 'other property', which could be recovered under traditional product

---

[15]   *Ibid*, at § 19.
[16]   *Linden*, above n 7, 625; *Prendiville*, above n 10, at 446; *Mt Lebanon Personal Care Home, Inc v Hoover Universal, Inc* 276 F 3d 845 (6th Cir 2002) 850-51 [*Mt Lebanon*]; *Gunkel v Renovations, Inc* 822 NE 2d 150 (Ind 2005).
[17]   Above n 4, at 875.
[18]   *Ibid*, at 859.
[19]   *Ibid*, at 860.
[20]   *Ibid*.
[21]   *Ibid*, at 860-61.
[22]   *Ibid*, at 861.
[23]   *Ibid*, at 871.
[24]   *Ibid*.
[25]   *Ibid*, at 870.

liability rules.[26] The Court found that *East River* reasoning did not work in the context of resale after an initial use, because the subsequent user does not contract directly with the manufacturer.[27] In dissent, Justice Scalia opined that the Court should have applied *East River* reasoning because the petitioner was a commercial entity, and further suggested that the *East River* rule applied only to commercial, not consumer, transactions.[28] Nevertheless, most state courts rely on *East River* when analysing defective building claims to find no duty to either a commercial or residential subsequent buyer.[29]

C. The Economic Loss Doctrine Always Applies: New York

The course of law in New York has shown the appellate courts' continuing adherence to the economic loss rule and a refusal to carve out an exception for tort claims involving construction defects. In 1987, in *Lake Placid Club Attached Lodges v Elizabethtown Builders*,[30] a New York Appellate Division court held that condominium owners, who purchased their homes from a developer, could not recover in tort from builder and architects for the cost of repairing alleged construction defects.[31] The plaintiff's damages were limited to 'failure of the products of the construction (the dwelling units) themselves, and thus were held to constitute economic loss, for which there can be no recovery on the basis of negligence'.[32] However, the court appeared to base its decision at least partly on the fact that the plaintiffs submitted no evidence that the construction defects posed a risk of accidental injury to 'persons or property'—suggesting that liability in negligence might be imposed on builders who create dangerous defects.[33]

The court further denied recovery to condominium owners on contractual grounds, holding that breaches of the construction contract would only be actionable, in the absence of privity, if the subsequent purchasers were the 'intended' third-party beneficiaries of the contract between the developer and builder/architect.[34] Unsurprisingly, the court found no evidence that the developer in fact intended to provide this benefit to

---

[26] 520 US 875 (1997) 877 (majority).
[27] *Ibid*, at 882.
[28] *Ibid*, at 889 (Scalia and Thomas JJ, dissenting).
[29] *Calloway v City of Reno* 116 Nev 250 (2000) 258 (majority) [*Calloway*]; *Mt Lebanon*, above n 16, at 848; *Prendiville*, above n 10, at 438.
[30] 131 AD 2d 159 (NY App Div 3d Dept 1987) [*Lake Placid*].
[31] *Ibid*, at 161.
[32] *Ibid*.
[33] *Ibid*.
[34] *Ibid*.

subsequent purchasers, and accordingly, found no liability on the part of the builder and the architects involved in the construction project.[35]

Another Appellate Division court affirmed its willingness to apply economic loss principles to construction defects in 1988, affirming that there is no reason to distinguish 'between the liability of one who supplies a chattel and one who erects a structure'.[36] An owner could not recover his losses from an architect and an engineering firm, as he had suffered purely economic damages, thus precluding recovery in tort.[37] In denying summary judgment on contractual grounds, the court affirmed that there was no contractual recovery without privity.[38]

Yet a third Appellate Division court joined the fray in 1993. Columbia University was denied recovery in strict liability for defects in one of its dormitory buildings—despite the fact that the defects allegedly caused the façade of the building to collapse. The construction company and construction manager were deemed to perform a service of construction, and not to manufacture a product.[39] However, echoing *Lake Placid*, the court decided to allow recovery in negligence on the grounds of extraordinary dangerousness, holding that 'the particular project... is so affected with the public interest that the failure to perform completely could have had catastrophic consequences'.[40] According to the court, builders did have an independent duty in tort to exercise reasonable care to avoid creating a catastrophic danger to the public, regardless of the economic nature of the actual harm suffered.

However, this exception to the economic loss rule was rejected by New York's highest court in *Bocre v General Motors*.[41] The judges decided that allowing recovery in tort even for an 'unduly dangerous' product, when only economic damages occur, would impermissibly blur the line between contract and tort and inject uncertainty into the law.[42] The same Appellate Division court, which earlier decided *Columbia*, would later affirm in *7 World Trade Center v Westinghouse*, that in light of the *Bocre* decision, purely economic losses stemming from dangerous defects were simply not compensable in tort.[43]

As confirmed by recent decisions of the Appellate Division courts in *Amin v K&R Construction*,[44] and *Weiss v Polymer Plastics*,[45] recovery in

---

[35] *Ibid*.

[36] *Key Intl Mfg v Morse/Diesel, Inc* 142 AD 2d 448 (NY App Div 2d Dept 1988) 452.

[37] *Ibid*.

[38] *Ibid*, at 453-54.

[39] *Columbia University v Gwathmey Siegel* 192 AD 2d 151(NY App Div 1st Dept 1993) 154.

[40] *Ibid*.

[41] 645 NE 2d 1195 (NY 1995).

[42] *Ibid*, at 1198.

[43] 256 AD 2d 263 (NY App Div 1st Dept 1998).

[44] 100 NY 2d 515 (App Div 1st Dept 2003).

negligence or strict liability continues to be unavailable in New York in construction defect cases that involve purely economic damages.

However, purchasers of defective homes in New York are not left without a remedy. While the courts were foreclosing recovery in tort for economic damages from construction defects, the judges also came to recognise an implied warranty assumed by a builder in constructing a new home. In *Caecci v Di Canio Construction Corpn*,[46] the New York Court of Appeals adopted an implied warranty theory to allow a homeowner to recover from the builder the expense of repairing a kitchen floor laid upon a defective foundation. In New York, there now was:

> an implied term in the express contract between the builder-vendor and purchasers that the house to be constructed would be done in a skillful manner free from material defects.[47]

While this judicially recognised warranty initially seemed to benefit only the purchasers of new homes, the New York legislature subsequently stepped in to extend implied warranty protection for subsequent purchasers—as long as the subsequent purchase occurs within a certain time limit. As recently affirmed by the court in *Lupien v Bartolomeo*,[48] the common law warranty enforced by the Court of Appeals in *Caecci* has now been superseded by a statutory housing merchant warranty, codified in New York General Business Law Article 36-B.[49] According to the statute, a housing merchant warranty gives recourse to an 'owner' of a 'new home'.[50] Subsequent purchasers are explicitly protected, as the 'owner' is defined as the 'first person to whom the home is sold and, during the unexpired portion of the warranty period, each successor in title to the home and any mortgagee in possession'. However, this protection is strictly circumscribed by the time limits and other conditions of a statutory warranty remedy.[51]

D.   Statutory Causes of Action: California and Nevada

In some states where the economic loss rule had been applied to residential construction defects, state legislatures intervened to provide homeowners with a cause of action. In *Aas v Superior Court*, the Supreme Court of California applied the economic loss rule to a negligence action by

---

[45]   21 AD 3d 1095 (NY App Div 1st Dept 2005).
[46]   526 NE 2d 266 (NY 1988) 270.
[47]   *Ibid*, at 267.
[48]   5 Misc 3d 1025A (NY Sup 2004).
[49]   *NY CLS Gen Bus § 777 et seq* (2006).
[50]   *Ibid.*
[51]   *Ibid. Ibid.*

homeowners where the construction defects had not caused personal injury or property damage.[52] After California homeowners (and voters) expressed concern about the decision that 'defects must cause actual damage prior to being actionable in tort', the California legislature passed a bill establishing detailed and specific liability standards for newly constructed housing, but also putting in place a pre-litigation process aimed at encouraging settlements rather than litigation.[53] In a recent case, the California Court of Appeals held that the cause of action for construction defects did not accrue until the defects were discovered, so the subsequent owners of two houses could maintain negligence claims against the builder.[54]

In *Calloway v City of Reno*, owners of Nevada townhomes brought a class action against the developer, contractor, subcontractors and inspectors of their townhomes, alleging defects in roofing, siding, framing, plumbing and heating and air conditioning.[55] The claims against the developer and general contractor were settled.[56] The Supreme Court of Nevada held the economic loss doctrine applied in all construction defect cases.[57] In dissent, Chief Justice Rose argued that, to avoid leaving home purchasers with no remedy, the economic loss doctrine should not apply in construction defect cases.[58] The Nevada legislature enacted a statute (after the *Calloway* causes of action accrued) that made contractors liable for construction defects made by them or their agents, employees or subcontractors.[59] In *Olson v Richard*, an action commenced after the statute was enacted, a homeowner brought a negligence action against a stucco finish subcontractor, claiming that inappropriate application of stucco caused water intrusion and could lead to future surface deterioration.[60] The Supreme Court of Nevada interpreted the statute to mean that the legislature did not intend the economic loss rule to apply in construction defect cases, and allowed the action to proceed.[61] In yet another vigorous dissent brought on by interpretations of the economic loss doctrine, Justice Becker accused the majority of finding a cause of action contrary to the plain language of the statute.[62] Justice Becker agreed that homeowners should not be left without a remedy, but argued that, because in the instant

---

[52]   24 Cal 4th 627 (2000).

[53]   *Rosen v State Farm General Insurance Company* 30 Cal 4th 1070 (2003) 1079 citing Cal Civ Code Ann § 895 (West 2006).

[54]   *Siegel v Anderson Homes, Inc* 118 Cal App 4th 994 (Cal App 5th Dist 2004) 996.

[55]   Above n 29, at 254 (majority).

[56]   *Ibid*, at 255.

[57]   *Ibid*, at 261.

[58]   *Ibid*, at 281 (Rose CJ, dissenting).

[59]   89 P 3d 31 (Nev 2004) 33 (majority) quoting NRS 40.640.

[60]   *Ibid*, at 32.

[61]   *Ibid*, at 33.

[62]   *Ibid*, at 34 (Becker J, dissenting).

case the homeowners had claims in breach of contract and warranty, it was not necessary to extend a claim in negligence as well.[63]

E. Duty to Construct Without Negligence: Colorado and South Carolina

Courts in some states have found that builders have a duty, running to both initial and subsequent buyers, to construct dwellings without negligence.[64] Colorado allows negligence claims for economic loss by subsequent residential buyers. In *Cosmopolitan Homes, Inc v Weller*, the fourth owners of a house claimed negligent design and construction after the foundation of the house cracked due to settling.[65] The district court found that the builder did not owe a duty of care to subsequent owners because of lack of privity.[66] The Court of Appeals reversed, holding that the purchaser of a used home may recover for property damage caused by the negligence of the builder, and the Colorado Supreme Court affirmed.[67] Justice Rovira in dissent stated that, while the builder might owe a duty to a subsequent buyer, it should be in contract and not in tort.[68] Justice Rovira felt the decision of whether to allow tort claims by subsequent purchasers was better left to the legislature.[69]

The debate in Colorado about the economic loss rule continues from that decision in 1987 to today. In *AC Excavating v Yacht Club II Homeowners Association, Inc*, the homeowners association alleged a host of construction defects against the subcontractors who built the condominium complex.[70] The association originally included the general contractor and developer in the action, but settled with them before trial.[71] The Colorado Supreme Court held that the economic loss rule had no application because subcontractors owe homeowners a duty of care, independent of any contractual obligations, to act without negligence in the construction of homes.[72] In dissent, Justice Kourlis argued that, because the

---

[63] *Ibid*, at 35.
[64] *Kennedy v Columbia Lumber & Mfg Co* 299 SC 335 (1989) 347 [*Kennedy*]; *AC Excavating*, above n 13; *RJ Griffin*, above n 13.
[65] Above n 11 (majority).
[66] *Ibid*, at 1042.
[67] *Ibid*.
[68] *Ibid*, at 1048 (Rovira J, dissenting).
[69] *Ibid*, at 1051.
[70] Above n 13, at 864. The defects included improperly installed windows, roofs, chimneys, and doors; improperly braced roof trusses; improperly graded soils, reverse sloping driveways, and improper draining systems. The resulting impact included water penetration, heaving front porches, heaving and cracking basement floors, damaged drywall, and water-stained sills, walls, carpets, and baseboards.
[71] Above n 13, at 864.
[72] *Ibid*, at 870.

homeowners association had already recovered from the general contractor and the developer, the economic loss rule should apply to the subcontractors.[73] He warned that the majority's decision would only increase the cost of homebuilding because subcontractors would have to insure against the same risk that general contractors already assumed.[74]

Like Colorado, South Carolina has recognised an independent common law duty of care by builders to construct homes without negligence, thus eliminating the application of the economic loss rule. In 1989, the Supreme Court of South Carolina found in *Kennedy v Columbia Lumber & Mfg Co* that builders had a legal duty to avoid negligence. The court found that failure to meet a building code or an industry standard violated a legal duty for which a builder can be held liable in tort for proximately caused losses even if they are only economic.[75] If no building code or industry standard applies, the builder has a legal duty to refrain from construction that it knows or should know would pose serious risk of physical harm. If the builder violates this duty, it may be liable in both contract and tort.[76] South Carolina continues to use this standard, holding in *RJ Griffin & Co v Beach Club II Homeowners Assoc, Inc,* that the homeowners association could sue its contractor in tort for construction defects discovered during an inspection prompted by water leaking through exterior walls.[77] While South Carolina has not yet had an opportunity to consider a subsequent buyer construction defect case, based on current case law it is likely that it would be allowed.

F.   Comparative Policy Considerations Between the United States and England, Australia, Canada and New Zealand

So various and inconsistent is the United States case law on defective property that the approaches taken in England, Australia, Canada and New Zealand can all be found somewhere in the kaleidoscope. Many jurisdictions impose a duty of care on builders and other professionals outside contract to promote professional accountability. Florida recognises professional malpractice as an exception to the economic loss doctrine, and has applied it specifically to inspection engineers who were not in privity with the homeowner.[78]

The liveliest debate over applying the economic loss doctrine to construction defect cases is around the proportionate burden of liability. Here

---

[73]   *Ibid*, at 874 (Kourlis and Coats JJ, dissenting).
[74]   *Ibid*.
[75]   Above n 65, at 347.
[76]   *Ibid*, at 345-46.
[77]   Above n 13, at 163.
[78]   *Moransais*, above n 7, at 983-84 (majority).

the dissenting opinions run fast and furious. In *Moransais v Heathman*, where the economic loss rule was not applied in Florida to negligence by inspection engineers, the dissenting opinion warned that the majority decision would lead to an increase in malpractice insurance and resulting increased costs of all types of professional services to consumers.[79] The dissenting justice claimed that the majority had obliterated the distinction between contract and tort.[80] In contrast, in *Linden v Cascade Stone*, where the economic loss doctrine was applied in Wisconsin to negligence by subcontractors, the dissenting opinion warned that the majority was frustrating the homeowner at every turn.[81] The dissenting justice claimed the majority view that the homeowners should have allocated the risk with the subcontractor was 'long on philosophy but short on reality'.[82] The observation by Justice McHugh in *Woolcock Street Investments Pty Ltd v CDG Pty Ltd* that courts in New Zealand, Canada and Australia have not been overwhelmed with tort claims for economic loss from defective premises is instructive in predicting what might happen if more United States jurisdictions moved in that direction.[83]

G. What's a Builder To Do? Insurance and Risk Mitigation Cost and Availability of Insurance

Although many courts reason that defective property is the proper concern of contract law because participants can insure themselves against losses, several standard insurance carriers have stopped covering the construction industry, and new carriers are not coming in to take their place.[84] Those that continue to cover the construction industry focus on commercial contractors because the liability risk for construction defects is too high in the residential market.[85] Premiums and deductibles for homebuilders have risen significantly.[86] The National Association of Homebuilders (NAHB) claims liability insurance fees add $15,000 to the cost of a home in

---

[79] *Ibid*, at 985 (Overton J, dissenting).
[80] *Ibid*.
[81] Above n 7 (Bradley and Butler JJ and Abrahamson CJ, dissenting).
[82] *Ibid*, at 631.
[83] (2005) 216 CLR 515 (HCA) [97].
[84] 'Sizing Up the Construction Market' (2 Jan 2006) *Insurance Journal* 14.
[85] *Ibid*.
[86] S Sclafane, 'Danger Lurks in Construction Defect Market' (2004) 108(37) *National Underwriter Property & Casualty* 13, 17. Two examples of the recent pricing trends: a builder in California (one of the most difficult markets) who had paid $60,000/year for liability insurance would pay $1,000,000/year; in the calmer market of South Carolina, a subcontractor with $1.8M revenue and a spotless record who had paid $6,000/year in the late nineties paid $20,000/year in 2004 for a policy with a $250,000 deductible.

Arizona, California and Nevada.[87] The higher cost of insurance is passed on to home and building owners in both higher prices and construction shortages.[88]

Three recent decisions highlight why builders are concerned about insurance coverage of construction defects.[89] The question turns on whether inadvertent construction defects are considered 'occurrences', which invoke both coverage and the duty to defend. The Supreme Court of Wisconsin held that construction defects may be considered occurrences, and the exclusions of each individual policy must be reviewed to determine whether coverage applies.[90] Builders in Wisconsin have both the protection of the economic loss doctrine applied in residential and commercial settings, and potential insurance coverage for construction defects. The Supreme Courts of Nebraska and South Carolina held that only construction defects that cause damage to other property must be considered occurrences, finding that faulty workmanship, standing alone, is not an accident and therefore not an occurrence.[91] Builders in Nebraska have the protection of the economic loss doctrine,[92] but may or may not have insurance coverage. Builders in South Carolina have a duty to construct without negligence measured by adherence to building codes, as discussed previously, and do not have insurance coverage for faulty workmanship standing alone.

H.   Risk Management Strategies

(i)   Statutes

The NAHB views notice and opportunity to repair statutes as an approach to solving the general liability insurance crisis by giving builders the opportunity to settle a claim with a homeowner before going to court.[93] At least half the states have enacted these statutes, and other states are considering them.[94] A typical statute applies to a residence or dwelling,

[87]   S Zurrier, 'Repair in Progress' (1 Aug 2005) 29(10) *Builder* 51.

[88]   Sizing Up, above n 84.

[89]   CJ Shapiro, 'The Good, the Bad and the Ugly: New State Supreme Court Decisions Address Whether an Inadvertent Construction Defect is an 'Occurrence' Under CGL Policies' (2005) 25 *The Construction Lawyer* 9.

[90]   *Am Family Mut Ins Co v American Girl, Inc* 673 NW 2d 65 (Wis 2004).

[91]   *Auto-Owners Ins Co v Home Pride Companies, Inc* 268 Neb 528 (2004); *L-J Inc v Bituminous Fire & Marine Ins Co* 366 SC 117 (2005).

[92]   *Moglia v McNeil Co, Inc* 270 Neb 241 (2005).

[93]   Zurrier, above n 87.

[94]   DT Allen, 'Construction Defects Litigation and the "Right to Cure" Revolution' CONBRIEF NO 2006-3, 1 (Mar 2006). The following states have notice and opportunity to repair construction defect statutes: Alaska, Arizona, California, Colorado, Florida, Georgia,

although there are exceptions.[95] It may cover new construction, additions, improvements and repairs, and it may apply to architects, subdivision owners and developers, builders, contractors, subcontractors, engineers and inspectors.[96]

Critics of notice and opportunity to repair statutes argue that they place an undue burden on homeowners because the procedures can be complicated.[97] Any failure to comply with a single procedural requirement can restart the waiting period, and homeowners often need a lawyer to help them interpret their responsibilities.[98]

The efficacy of these statutes is much in doubt. They seem to apply a layer of procedure much like the tort reform statutes requiring pre-litigation arbitration and conciliation prior to recourse to the courts. In the tort reform arena, statutes have not achieved their purpose of dampening tort litigation.[99] They may, however, send a signal to the courts that liability does have an impact in the construction industry, and thereby encourage more restrictive liability. On the other hand, they may be seen as a concession of the legitimacy of liability.

(ii) Self-insurance

Builders that have been unable to find affordable liability insurance have turned to self-insurance through a captive company.[100] The builder pays an annual premium designed to more than cover claims plus operating expenses.[101] Any capital that remains after expenses and claims are covered can either be reinvested to lower future premiums or kept as a hedge against unexpected losses.[102] Large builders are most likely to be able to afford to form a captive company.[103] In New York, the parent company must have a net worth of at least $100 million to form a captive

---

Hawaii, Idaho, Indiana, Iowa, Kansas, Kentucky, Minnesota, Missouri, Montana, Nevada, New Hampshire, New Jersey, Ohio, Pennsylvania, South Carolina, Tennessee, Texas, Washington and West Virginia.

[95] *Ibid.* The Tennessee statute does not apply to residential property (defined as a 'dwelling unit intended as a residence of a person or family').

[96] *Ibid.*

[97] *Ibid.*

[98] *Ibid.*

[99] PM Danzon, *Medical Malpractice: Theory, Evidence and Public Policy* (Cambridge, Mass, Harvard University Press, 1985) 202-4.

[100] M Power, 'Self Insurance; "Captive" Plans Offer a Viable Alternative to Traditional Coverage' (2004) 27(9) *Builder* 68.

[101] *Ibid.*

[102] *Ibid.*

[103] Sclafane, above n 86. A contractor doing $10 to $25 million in sales volume is too small to form a captive insurance company for itself, but could join other companies.

company, but this is a higher threshold than other domiciles.[104] Builders that are not big enough to form a captive company on their own can join with others to form a captive or risk retention group.[105]

(iii)   Other Risk Management Techniques

In a way that is reassuring about the efficacy of liability rules, insurance companies are working with the building industry to reduce the number of construction defects.[106] Insurance carriers require a third party risk assessment as a condition of coverage to give the insurance carrier a high degree of confidence that the construction professional is working to minimise risk.[107] Insurance carriers are also requiring third party inspections of homes during the course of construction to prevent problems from occurring.[108] Such measures are music to the ears of those lawyers/ economists who search for liability rules inculcating risk reducing behaviour.[109]

Another approach to risk management for larger builders is to combine an extended warranty with a captive insurance company.[110] This fits the California market well, where the notice and opportunity to repair statute creates strict liability for many defects.[111] The homebuyer pays $500-$1,000 for the extended warranty.[112] The builder can then use the aggregated payments to fund a captive insurance company, avoiding tax liability and creating capital to fund future repairs if needed.[113]

III.   POLICY

As Professor Todd's chapter shows, the courts have invoked various policy factors of negligence law to calibrate the scope of liability. The American authorities employ a similar array, although American jurisprudence has

---

[104] 'U.S. Captives, RRGs (Risk Reduction Groups) Still On the Grow' (2006) 110(9) *National Underwriter Property & Casualty* 12. The New York Insurance Department is trying to reduce the threshold of parent company net worth to $25 million, but has not been able to pass legislation. As a result, New York loses business to other domiciles like Vermont and South Carolina.

[105] Zurrier, above n 87.

[106] M Strech, 'California Residential Construction Efforts Reduce Risk of Defect Litigation' (2 Jan 2006) *Insurance Journal*.

[107] *Ibid*.

[108] *Ibid*.

[109] RA Posner, *Economic Analysis of Law*, 5th edn (New York, Aspen, 1998) 179-83.

[110] S Sclafane, 'Alternative Markets Ease Construction Woes' (2004) 108(37) *National Underwriter, Property & Casualty/Risk & Benefits Management Edition* 14.

[111] *Ibid*.

[112] *Ibid*.

[113] *Ibid*.

not gone to the defining precision of the Commonwealth courts. I agree with Professor Stapleton[114] that pragmatic, case by case development is likely to produce a more stable body of law than a theory not attentive to the factual distinctions in the classes of 'economic loss' cases.

The telling factor in the defective structure cases, as in the classic *Robins* cases,[115] is that loss occurs within a web of contractual relationships. If this pragmatic factor is accounted for, a policy not referenced by the Commonwealth Courts or Professor Todd is put into relief. In this instance, the liability rule ought to aid the forming of wealth-maximising cooperative arrangements.[116] In construction contracts, as McNeal and others show, the law of contract is designed not to anticipate efficient breach, but to consolidate the relations between the parties.[117] These are the classic relational contracts.[118] Thus, engineers will wish to assure their head contractors of the quality of their work by agreeing to the implied term supplied by a liability rule that the work will be done to the level of the ordinary competent engineer. Such a term acts as a bond enhancing the consummation of the contract that must subsist over time. In other words, the liability rule ought to mimic the arrangement that would have been reached through explicit bargaining. To the extent that the liability lowers agency costs in these complex arrangements, it will promote the consummation of cooperative relationships.[119]

Too often, the cases view tort and contract in conflict. Thus, we have 'contract drowning in a sea of tort'.[120] But, in the best sense, they should be consonant. Take, for example, the famous set of cases on negligently drawn wills and disappointed beneficiaries.[121] The courts have struggled mightily to find that the attorney should owe a duty of care to the disappointed beneficiary.[122] The root of the problem in establishing a duty

---

[114] J Stapleton, 'Comparative Economic Loss: Lessons From Case-Law-Focused "Middle Theory"' 50 *UCLA Law Review* 531.

[115] Eg, *Robins Dry Dock & Repair Co v Flint* 275 US 303 (1927); *Leigh and Sullivan Ltd v Aliakmon Shipping Co Ltd (The Aliakmon)* [1986] AC 785 (HL).

[116] RA Posner, 'Wealth Maximization and Tort Law: A Philosophical Inquiry' in DG Owen (ed), *Philosophical Foundations of Tort Law* (Oxford, Clarendon Press, 1995) 99-111. See also DG Baird, RH Gertner and RC Picker, *Game Theory and the Law* (Cambridge, Mass, Harvard University Press, 1994). Game theory explains the choice of legal liability rule by reallocating payoffs based on strategic interaction.

[117] I Macneil, *The Relational Theory of Contract: Selected Works of Ian Macneil* (London, Sweet & Maxwell, 2001).

[118] RE Scott and JE Kraus, *Contract Law and Theory*, 3rd edn (Newark, Matthew Bender & Co, Inc, 2002) 313-15.

[119] DF Partlett, *Professional Negligence* (Sydney, Law Book Co, 1985). This reader covers the foundational details of cooperative relationships in law. See also E Posner, *Law and Social Norms* (Cambridge, Mass, Harvard University Press, 2000) 148-66.

[120] *East River*, above n 4.

[121] Eg, *Biakanja v Irving* 320 P 2d 16 (Cal 1958); *Auric v Continental Cas Co* 331 NW 2d 325 (Wisc 1983); *White v Jones* [1995] 2 AC 207 (HL).

[122] Cf P Benson, 'Should *White v Jones* Represent Canadian Law?' ch 6.

has been that the usual indicia of a duty, assumption of responsibility and reliance, are absent. The will cases, however, are not a usual case of *Hedley Byrne* liability, requiring reliance and voluntary assumption of responsibility. Here tort comes to the rescue of contract. The attorney is interested to bond his work. In the absence of the duty to the beneficiary, attorneys would be systematically faced with a sub-optimal level of deterrence; they could draft wills negligently without recourse. Putative testators would then be less than optimally sure of the due diligence of the attorney. Thus, a solution, among others, is to provide a duty of care owed by the attorney to the beneficiary. This is the bond that the attorney would provide to reduce agency costs.[123]

In the construction context, one finds a rich tapestry of interwoven relationships. Many obligations are not reflected in law but in norms built on an iterated prisoner's dilemma.[124] Thus, where commercial parties are involved, liability rules have a subdued role. Repeat players are more likely to bond performance and cure defects through private ordering outside a liability rule. For example, a reputation for sound work is hard won and assiduously maintained where information is freely available.

It should be noted that I do not assert that a commercial party will have an enhanced ability to uncover a latent defect. Construction defects are invisible to both commercial and residential buyers. Furthermore, it may be the case that a builder or construction professional is in the better position to take precautions regardless of whether the subsequent buyer is commercial or residential. The commercial buyer, however, has a clear ability to assess the assignment of risk in a normal commercial way, laying off the risk through pricing and spreading the risk through a portfolio of investments.[125] The longevity of structures creates an uncertainty in accounting for risks in the distant future that may have a high claim value. The administrative costs of contingent claims are substantial.[126]

On the other hand, the residential consumer contract is radically different. Home buyers are engaged in an arrangement in frequency and

---

[123] Other mechanisms may be available. Professor Waddams finds liability through the interrelation of wrongdoing and entitlement. S Waddams, *Dimensions of Private Law: Categories and Concepts in Anglo-American Legal Reasoning* (Cambridge, Cambridge University Press, 2003) 52-56. See also H Luntz, 'Solicitors' Liability to Third Parties' (1983) 3 *OJLS* 284, suggesting reform of the law of wills to overcome the lacuna. Note that the courts often innovate when faced with a systematic underdeterrence. *Herskovits v Group Health Cooperative of Puget Sound* 99 Wash 2d 609 (1983). The 'loss of chance' doctrine performs a similar function. See *Chappel v Hart* [1998] 195 CLR 232 (HCA); *McKellips v St Francis Hosp, Inc* 741 P 2d 467 (Okla 1987) 471; *Pipe v Hamilton* 274 Kan 905 (2002).

[124] R Ellickson, *Order without Law* (Cambridge, Mass, Harvard University Press, 1991) 156-66.

[125] HM Markowitz, 'Foundations of Portfolio Theory' (1991) 46 *The Journal of Finance* 469, 469-77.

[126] GL Priest, 'The Current Insurance Crisis and Modern Tort Law' 96 *Yale Law Journal* 1521.

magnitude that is unique for them. They will be vulnerable in the way modern English and Australian judicial authorities articulate as a factor in establishing a duty of care. This is mitigated somewhat by the frequency of legal representation of the consumer in these transactions. Moreover, as for the commercial buyer, the defects are latent and the builder or profession-als are in a better position to take precautions, the ability for express exclusion signalling that no duty may be implied, open and available.[127] The true distinction is the relative inability of the residential buyer to spread risk, and the strong appeal, now reflected in legal doctrine, to give succour through a liability rule to those vulnerable persons suffering disproportionate loss.

The policy concerns traditionally associated with the economic loss doctrine can be addressed in latent construction defect cases by focusing on whether the buyer is a sophisticated participant who could be expected to protect him or herself in contract, or a vulnerable participant who merits the additional protection of tort law. Using the approach of the United States jurisdictions that find a builder has a duty to construct buildings without negligence, there is no 'liability in an indeterminate amount for an indeterminate time to an indeterminate class'.[128] Liability to the initial and subsequent owners of the building is based on appropriate building codes and industry standard practices. Concerns about making the liability rule workable are alleviated by recognising the true nature of the loss as economic. Thus, the limitation period begins to run when the latent defect becomes apparent, that is, when the economic loss arises.[129]

Such are the stakes in terms of potential liability that the legislature will play a significant role in shaping liability. Courts should, however, engage in their time-honoured capacity in channelling the debate and formulating a default liability rule that places the burden of liability on builders and construction professionals for premises bought by residential purchasers. It would behove American courts and policy makers to pay close attention to the crystallising law found in the Commonwealth. In this debate my claim is humble. It is that the contractual context be noted and that the liability rule be seen, not as a mechanism for compensation or corrective justice, but rather, as a mechanism to reduce agency costs among those actors contracting for the construction, and subsequent sales of, structures.

---

[127] But cf B Codd, R Hinchy and V Nase, 'An Alternative View of Woolcock Street Investments' (2004) 12 *Torts Law Journal* 194.

[128] *Ultramares*, above n 1, at 179.

[129] *Pirelli General Cables Works Ltd v Oscar Faber & Partners* [1983] 2 AC 1 (HL); *Sparham-Souter v Town and Country Developments (Essex) Ltd* [1976] 1 QB 858; Partlett, above n 119, at 353-64.

10

Harm Screening Under Negligence Law

ISRAEL GILEAD[*]

I. INTRODUCTION

THE LAW OF negligence has always faced two basic challenges. The first is how to determine whether the conduct of an actor was undesirable, or careless, at the time it occurred, namely whether the actor was at fault. Did the risks that were generated by the conduct render it faulty ex ante? The second challenge is to determine ex post the scope of liability for any given faulty conduct. Specifically, for which harms caused in fact by faulty conduct is the actor liable and for which is he or she not? This is the screening challenge.[1]

Screening, which is the subject of this chapter, raises two central and interrelated sets of questions. First, once it is established that the actor's conduct was faulty, and that it was the cause-in-fact of the plaintiff's harm,[2] what are the justifications, and what should the criteria be, for excluding certain harms from the scope of liability? The second set of questions has to do not with substance but rather with form. Which 'legal devices' are best designed or best suited to perform the screening task given its justifications and criteria?

---

[*] Bora Laskin Professor of Law, The Hebrew University of Jerusalem. I wish to thank David Enoch, Alon Hare, and Ehud Guttel for useful comments on earlier drafts of this chapter.

[1] The harm screening question is also referred to as the question of the 'appropriate scope of liability for consequences': J Stapleton, 'Cause in Fact and the Scope of Liability for Consequences' (2003) 119 *LQR* 388.

[2] The following discussion of the scope of liability for harms presupposes that factual causation exists between harms and the faulty conduct and, furthermore, that the conduct also increased the risk of the harm being inflicted. For the requirement of increased risk see *Restatement (Third) of the Law of Torts: Liability for Physical Harm–Proposed Final Draft no 1* (2005) at §30. For factual causation see RW Wright, 'Once More into the Bramble Bush: Duty, Causal Contribution, and the Extent of Legal Responsibility' (2001) 54 *Vanderbilt Law Review* 1071.

The prevailing answer to the first set of questions regarding justifications and criteria for harm screening seems to be that there are two cumulative criteria and justifications and, accordingly, two kinds of screening: 'relational screening' on the one hand and policy-based 'liability-watch' screening on the other hand. Relational screening is a concept according to which tort liability for harms factually caused by faulty conduct should be imposed only for those harms which are sufficiently related to the faulty conduct. As a rule, and subject to exceptions, harms are considered to be related to the faulty conduct when they originate in risks that rendered the conduct faulty in the first place—when they were 'fault-factors'.[3] Ex post liability, then, should, as a rule, correspond with the reasons that ex ante rendered the conduct faulty and be restricted accordingly. This rule of relation, which insists upon a sufficient correlation between the tortious nature of the ex ante risks and ex post harms, is known as the 'scope-of-risk' rule or the 'risk standard'. A rigorous and influential expression of this rule of risk-related screening can now be found in the *Restatement (Third) of the Law of Torts: Liability for Physical Harm–Proposed Final Draft No 1*. Under the title 'Limitation of Liability for Tortious Conduct', §29 provides that 'An actor's liability is limited to those physical harms that result from the risks that made the actor's conduct tortious'.[4] Liability, as a rule, is limited to those harms that result from the tortious risks (harms-within-risk) and denied for harms that do not result from such risks (out-of-risk harms). The second type of screening—policy-based, 'liability-watch' screening—screens harms, including harms-within-risk, because of concerns that liability for certain harms may lead to undesirable consequences that should be avoided. These undesirable consequences include over-deterrence (using terms like 'chilling effect' and 'crushing liability'), a costly flood of claims that may overload the courts (the 'floodgate' argument), interference with other branches of private law (the notion of the tort elephant smashing the rose gardens of contract law), and

---

[3] 'Normally the law limits liability to those consequences which are attributable to that which made the act wrongful': Lord Hoffmann in *SAAMCO v York Montague* [1996] 3 All ER 365 (HL) 371. Cf Fleming: 'Limitations on legal responsibility inevitably reflect a policy of keeping a rough correlation between what made the defendant's conduct culpable and what consequences he should be answerable for': JG Fleming, *The Law of Torts*, 9th edn (Sydney, LBC Information Service, 1998) 232. See also DB Dobbs, *The Law of Torts* (St Paul, West Group, 2000) 443-47, 458-60.

[4] Above n 2. In their notes to comment (d) of §29, the reporters introduce a very long list of cases and academic writings that have supported risk-related screening for over a century (610-14). Notably, a similar risk-related screening concept is now proposed with regard to pure non-pecuniary loss by in the *Restatement (Third) of the Law of Torts: Economic Loss and Related Torts—Preliminary Draft no 2* (2006) §16. For those unfamiliar with the process, the American Law Institute is proceeding with the *Restatement (Third) of the Law of Torts* as a series of separate projects. To date two parts have been completed: *Restatement (Third) of the Law of Torts: Products Liability* (1998) and *Restatement (Third) of the Law of Torts: Apportionment of Liability* (2000).

unfair consequences. The aim and justification of liability-watch screening is to prevent such undesirable consequences by exerting effective control over the scope of liability.

As to the second question, regarding which 'legal devices' are best suited to perform the screening tasks, Anglo-American law has traditionally employed two basic screening devices: 'duty' and 'legal causation', the latter usually termed 'proximate cause' in the US and 'remoteness' in England. The proposed *Third Restatement on Physical Harm*, however, deviates from this tradition. As noted, it embraces the 'scope-of-risk' rule as the major tool for relational screening, and declares that this 'risk standard' is supposed to succeed proximate cause and limit the screening role of duty.[5]

These two aspects of the screening challenge have always been a source of contention and confusion. Risk-related screening was recently criticised for being incoherent and undesirable.[6] Ex post harms, it was argued, cannot be grouped into ex ante risks in a manner that distinguishes between harms that originate in tortious risks (unscreened) and those that do not (screened). As to liability-watch screening, differences exist regarding the adequate scope of such screening, differences that reflect contentions about the weight that should be attached to concerns about over-deterrence, increased litigation and the like. Confusion and contention also dominate the 'screening devices' query. Duty and legal causation are complex, amorphous, and multi-faceted concepts[7] that as screening devices are often used interchangeably. Indeed, the problem of open-ended 'screening devices' that exchange roles and overlap connects the old debate in *Palsgraf v Long Island RR Co* [8] as to whether unforeseeable harm to an unforeseeable plaintiff is a question of duty or of legal causation with the recent debate on the structure of negligence in the *Third Restatement on Physical Harm*.[9]

Against this background, the following discussion reconsiders some of the basic issues of screening. Part two re-examines the notion of 'risk' and copes with the attack against the rule of risk-related screening. It maintains

---

[5] *Restatement (Third)*, at §29. In a 'Special Note on Proximate Cause' the reporters express the hope that the concept of 'proximate cause' would gradually disappear (above n 2, at 574-75). In comment (f) to §29 they explain why and how the screening role of duty is restricted (586-88).

[6] HM Hurd and MS Moore, 'Negligence in the Air' (2002) 3 *Theoretical Inquiries in Law* 333, 411.

[7] J Stapleton, for example, identifies 24 aspects of duty: 'Duty of Care Factors: A Selection from Judicial Menus' in P Cane and J Stapleton (eds), *The Law of Obligations: Essays in Celebration of John Fleming* (Oxford, Clarendon Press, 1998) 59. JCP Goldberg and BC Zipursky introduce four meanings of duty in 'The *Restatement (Third)* and the Place of Duty in Negligence Law' (2001) 54 *Vanderbilt Law Review* 657.

[8] 248 NY 339 (CA) (1928) [*Palsgraf*].

[9] See the symposium on negligence in vol 54 of the *Vanderbilt Law Review* (2001).

that there are four aspects to the notion of risk in the context of relational screening—the person harmed, the type of harm, the manner of its infliction and its extent—and that all four aspects must be taken into account not only in the ex ante stage, where the faultiness of particular conduct is examined, but also in ex post screening. It further argues that with regard to the extent aspect of risk, a distinction should be drawn between the magnitude of the primary harm, on the one hand, and of secondary harms that evolve from the primary harm, on the other. The discussion then tackles the contention that due to the different levels of generalisation of risk description, it is impossible to differentiate between harms-within-risks and out-of-risk harms because there are no defensible ways to describe a risk. In response, part two maintains that (a) this 'description problem' is a not just a problem of risk-related screening but rather of negligence law as a whole; (b) levels of generalisation of risk description are not arbitrary; and (c) the distinction between the different aspects of risk contributes to the accuracy of the description. However, the discussion acknowledges a related problem. The distinct harms/benefits analysis required for each risk, in order to classify it as tortious or non-tortious, faces difficulties whenever specific harms that particular conduct generates cannot be associated with specific benefits to form a distinctive and classifiable risk. Nevertheless, the discussion concludes that through the use of common sense and the ability to distinguish between the different aspects of risk, this 'harms/benefits correlation problem' may have sensible contextual solutions, namely that the distinction between tortious and non-tortious risks and consequently between harms-within-risks and out-of-risk harms is a workable one. The discussion shows how the description of risks and their classification for the purposes of risk-related screening contribute to the fairness of liability and to the avoidance of undesirable over-deterrence

Part three examines *unforeseeable* harms and exceptions to risk-related screening. Unforeseeable harms are not 'fault-factors' as they are not taken into account when the faultiness of a given conduct or risk is determined ex ante. Yet, where these ex post unforeseeable harms ensue from risks that are tortious because of other harms that are foreseeable, the case for their screening is weak. They can be considered as being sufficiently related to the faulty conduct despite their unforeseeability, as an exception to risk-related screening. The discussion first offers a justification for the rule that sanctions the screening of unforeseeable harms. Arguably, this rule is justified by the need to offset the conduct's externalised benefits against its externalised harms, an offset that promotes fairness and efficiency. The discussion then proceeds to the exceptions to this rule. After differentiating between the different kinds of unforeseeability with the help of the distinction between the different aspects of risk, the major exceptions to the risk-related screening that allow liability in negligence for unforesee-able harms are briefly examined, with a focus on the exceptions that allow for liability in the event of unforeseeable *extent* of harm.

Harms that pass the test of relational screening (risk-related screening and its exceptions) are still subject to policy-based 'liability-watch' screen-ing. The question whether the underlying concerns, namely that liability may lead to undesirable consequences such as over-deterrence, increased litigation and so on, are real and acute or whether they serve to excuse and disguise judicial conservatism exceeds the scope of this chapter. It is important, however, to understand that this kind of screening also operates through the different aspects of risk. Liability may be denied with regard to certain kinds of actors or activity, with regard to certain kinds of harmed persons, with regard to types of harm, or with regard to the extent of harm. The discussion of these issues in part four attributes the increased complexity of this kind of screening to the expansion of tort liability into the realm of 'pure' losses, an expansion that necessitates a more sophisti-cated screening process which tends to become less categorical and closer to the facts of each case.

Part five discusses the 'screening devices' of relational screening and liability-watch screening and suggests that the confusion surrounding the common law screening devices of duty and legal causation (proximate cause/remoteness) can be cleared up, at least to some extent. Most importantly, one should bear in mind that each of these concepts has two distinct screening roles—relational screening on the one hand and liability-watch screening on the other hand—and therefore two different meanings. Despite the common label 'duty', relational duty and liability-watch duty are two separate concepts, and the same is true for relational legal causation and liability-watch legal causation. In addition, the distinction between the different aspects of risk provides a basis for a better 'division of labour' between the different screening concepts, in that each concept can be linked with a various aspect of the risk. For example, the concept of legal causation can be perceived as 'specialising' in the causal chain of events that links the negligent conduct with the harm and not as a general screen, and such 'specialisation' allows us to draw clearer dividing lines between the screening roles of duty and legal causation. Such a 'division of labour' may well be preferable to the 'revolutionary' attempt of the *Third Restatement on Physical Harm* to dispense with relational duty and legal causation and to replace them by the 'risk standard'. However, the *extent* of harm aspect calls for a specialising screening concept other than legal causation and duty.

Following a short summary in part six of the major points made, part seven concludes with two notes. The first underlies the importance of the court clarifying whether liability for an unforeseeable harm is denied because the conduct is not negligent or because the harm is not related to the negligent conduct. The second note questions Ernest Weinrib's assertion that the screening concepts of legal causation and duty support his claim that negligence law is a law of corrective justice which excludes considerations of efficiency and distributive justice.

II.   RELATIONAL SCREENING: THE-SCOPE-OF-RISK RULE

Relational screening seeks to exclude from the scope of liability harms that are not sufficiently related to the faulty conduct. As a rule, harms are considered as being related to the faulty conduct when they result from risks that made the actor's conduct faulty: when they are 'fault-factors'. This rule of risk-related-screening (the scope-of-risk rule or the risk standard) seeks to make the scope of ex post liability consistent with its ex ante reasons. The opening question, then, is what risks render particular conduct faulty.

A.   What Makes Conduct Faulty and a Risk Tortious?

For the purposes of screening analysis, faulty conduct can be characterised in its broad and widely-accepted sense. Conduct is faulty when its foreseeable and avoidable harms render it undesirable at the time it takes place. Foreseeable harms render conduct undesirable ex ante if they outweigh the foreseeable benefits of the conduct, or if such harms can be avoided or reduced for a lesser reduction in the corresponding benefits. Conduct is faulty if its net harms/benefits evaluation, when compared with the same evaluation of alternative conduct, is negative.[10] The foreseeable harms that are taken into account at the negative side of the equation are accordingly 'fault-factors'.

This harms/benefit evaluation, conducted by a judge or jury, involves various normative judgements: which harms or benefits should be considered, what their relative weights should be, and how should they be balanced against one another. Different theories of tort law—efficiency, corrective justice, distributive justice, or any combination of them—may

---

[10] Arguably, conduct may be characterised as faulty regardless of its foreseeable outcomes and only on the basis of being wrong per se. Breaching a statute or a moral code may serve as an example. Yet, it is difficult to separate the allegedly inherent wrongfulness from its foreseeable negative consequences. The latter may well be the reason behind the former: see H Hurd, 'The Deontology of Negligence' (1996) 76 *Boston University Law Review* 249, arguing that negligence law cannot be explained in deontological terms. Subjective awareness of the faultiness of the conduct, however, does affect the scope of liability: see below part III.C.

well lead to various outcomes.[11] This normative debate, however, should not concern us here, because relational screening takes as a given any normative judgments made at the stage of ex ante harms/benefits evaluation, and applies them in the ex post screening stage. For example, if conduct is faulty because it creates risks of inefficient harms, risk-related screening should screen efficient harms. Additionally, if it is faulty because it harms the unprivileged, harms to the privileged should be screened.

Given that faulty conduct is characterised by a negative net harms/benefits balance, the major assumption behind risk-related screening is that the overall harms and benefits of particular conduct can be grouped or divided into distinct and describable risks, and that these risks can be classified into tortious (unreasonable) risks on the one hand and non-tortious (reasonable) risks on the other hand. Liability is to be imposed, subject to 'liability-watch' screening, only for those harms that are the realisation of tortious risks and therefore harms-within-risk, but not for harms that ensue from non-tortiuos risks. The latter should be screened because they are out-of-risks harms. But what exactly do we mean by 'risk'?

B. The Four Aspects of Risk

When actors reason about the risks that their conduct generates, they think of four aspects of risk. The first aspect relates to the causal chains of events that the conduct can trigger. Speeding, for example, may trigger different chains of events: crashing into another car, running over a pedestrian or overturning on a sharp curve. The second aspect is associated with the various collections of persons likely to suffer harm; a negligent misstatement may mislead very different audiences. The third aspect is the type of harms that may be inflicted on a given person; the same malpractice may cause bodily injury, property damage, 'pure' economic losses, or non-pecuniary losses. The fourth aspect is the extent of each potential harm. Arguably the extent of harm, which is usually perceived as raising one issue, actually raises two distinct issues. The first is the magnitude of the primary harms. A primary harm is a harm caused by the original and distinct causal chain of events triggered by the faulty conduct. The magnitude of such a primary harm may vary. For instance, a person involved in a particular road accident may be slightly injured or may die, and the damage to property in such an accident may be small or large, depending on the value of the car and its damaged cargo. The second issue

---

[11] On the different perspectives on the harms/benefits evaluation see the symposiums on negligence in vol 54 of the *Vanderbilt Law Review* (2001) and vols 3(2) and 4(1) of *Theoretical Inquiries in Law* (2001-02).

is the evolution of primary harms, through distinct causal chains of events, into additional, secondary harm or harms. A person injured in an accident can become depressed and later commit suicide. The primary harm (bodily injury) evolves through a distinct chain of events (depression and suicidal act) into the secondary harm (death).

All of these four aspects of risk should in principle be taken into account, not just for the ex ante harms/benefits evaluation that determines the faultiness of the conduct, but also for the ex post relational screening phase. Of special importance is the causal chain of events aspect, which is a major factor at the ex ante stage. After all, the probability of harm, which is a major factor of any risk (P in the Hand Formula), depends on the different manner in which it can be inflicted. Moreover, the causal chain of events very often determines who will be harmed, by what type of harm and to what extent. This is well illustrated by *Palsgraf*,[12] in which a chain of events different than what was expected led to different types of harm to different kinds of people.[13]

Although all aspects of risk should in principle be taken into account in the screening process, the risk-related screening of some aspects, mainly the extent aspect, may be less rigorous and thereby form exceptions to risk-related screening. These exceptions are discussed in part three.

C.   The 'Description Problem' and the Attack on Relational Risk-Related Screening

A few years ago, Heidi Hurd and Michael Moore launched a fierce attack on risk-related screening and argued that harm-within-risk screening (HWR) 'is conceptually incoherent, normatively undesirable, and it gives an inaccurate description of the decided cases'.[14] The attack, introduced as one which aims 'to explode entirely the risk analysis'[15] is based on an alleged 'description problem' and on an 'all-inclusiveness problem'.[16]

The 'description problem' argument threatens to undermine the ability to distinguish between tortious risks and non-tortious risks in order to screen harms that correspond with non-tortious risks (out-of risk harms). Such a distinction can be made only if the different risks that particular

---

[12]   Above n 8.

[13]   By being allegedly negligent in helping a passenger onto a moving train, the railroad employees created risks that involved foreseeable chains of events such as the passenger falling or the contents of the carried package breaking. However, a different causal chain of events ensued. Fireworks in the package exploded, and the shock of the explosion caused scales at the other end of the platform to fall, injuring the plaintiff. It is the unforeseeability of the causal chain of events that made the plaintiff and her harm unforeseeable.

[14]   Above n 6, at 411.

[15]   *Ibid*, at 333.

[16]   For discussion of the 'all-inclusiveness problem' see below n 27.

conduct generates can be described in a meaningful and defensible way. Alas, claim the authors, 'there is no right answer to the question of how one ought to describe the types of harm risked.... all levels of description of the harm risked can be equally accurate; it would thus appear that any choice of a description is inherently arbitrary. And this makes the HWR test inherently arbitrary'.[17] According to their view, there is no defensible way to describe risks.

However, although risk description is a problem that exists in negligence law, this problem neither 'explodes' HWR relational screening nor does it undermine its major role in making the scope of liability consistent with its rationale. The crux of the authors' argument is that risks in the sense of future harmful events can be described differently at various levels of generalisation, ranging from the general to the most particular, and that none of human psychology, morality, or the law provide 'a source of determinate answers concerning how the risks generated by a defendant's conduct ought to be described'.[18] In their view this renders relational screening 'entirely vacuous' and arbitrary.[19] The problem with this argument is that it identifies the risk description problem with risk-related screening. The impression created is that if risk-related screening is abandoned, the description problem will disappear. But it will not. Describing the risk is first and foremost an integral part of the preliminary stage at which the conduct's faultiness is examined ex ante. To perform the harms/benefits evaluation of the particular conduct, courts should ascertain the foreseeable harms, and to that end they must identify and describe the risks of harms. It is at this stage that courts should decide on the level of generalisation for risk description. Different levels of generalisation would identify different harms as foreseeable, thereby affecting the outcome of the harms/benefits evaluation. If the authors are correct and risk descriptions are arbitrary, then courts' findings regarding the faultiness of any conduct are also arbitrary, and negligence law as a whole is arbitrary as well. To the extent that risk description is a problem, it is a problem of negligence law and not only of risk-related screening, although the problem does often surface at the screening stage.

At any rate, the authors exaggerate in their argument that all risk descriptions are arbitrary. It is widely accepted that the question of whether a reasonable risk was foreseeable refers not to specific, concrete descriptions of risk but rather to a generalised description that conforms to

---

[17] Hurd and Moore, above n 6, at 375. The authors also claim that 'Absent a source of determinative answers concerning how the risks generated by the defendant's conduct ought to be described, the question of whether the harm caused by a defendant is within the risk(s) that make(s) the defendant negligent is an empty one' (380).

[18] Hurd and Moore, above n 6, at 380.

[19] *Ibid*, at 376.

the level of generality and abstraction by which reasonable people perceive risks.[20] Indeed, reasonable actors may have different perceptions regarding the level of risk abstraction, a diversity which creates a *range* of reasonable generalisations of risk descriptions. This variety may cause uncertainty, especially when judges 'manoeuvre' between different levels of abstraction in order to reach desired results.[21] However, this 'manoeuvrability' is limited to the range of what is reasonable, and it can equally be found in other aspects of negligence law.[22]

It should also be noted that the authors themselves contribute to the alleged 'description problem'. In their view a risk is described for HWR screening either by a 'weak version' which refers only to one aspect of the risk (who may be harmed) or by a 'strong version' which refers to two aspects of the risk (who may be harmed and the type of harm).[23] However, risk, as we have seen, has two additional aspects that are integral to its description: the different causal chains of events that may be triggered by the faulty conduct and the extent of the potential harms.[24] The authors, though, appear to exclude these aspects from the description of risk,[25] and thereby artificially weaken the ability to classify risks in the flexible,

---

[20] See C Morris, 'Duty, Negligence and Causation' (1952) 101 *University of Pennsylvania Law Review* 189; *Bradford v Robinson Rentals* [1967] 1 WLR 337, 344-45; HLA Hart and T Honoré, *Causation in the Law*, 2nd edn (Oxford, Clarendon Press, 1985) 80; SP Perry, 'Responsibility for Outcomes, Risk, and the Law of Torts' in GJ Postema (ed), *Philosophy and the Law of Torts* (Cambridge, Cambridge University Press, 2001) 97-101. See also Dobbs, above n 3, at 466-68.

[21] Usually, under a higher level of generalisation more harms are considered foreseeable and the scope of liability is extended. This is exemplified by an Israeli case in which the question was whether a dentist was liable for unprecedented, permanent, and severe neurological damage caused by a dental local anaesthesia, where the expected damage was temporary dizziness and fatigue. Some of the justices argued that the notion of damage in this case could be generalised to include all kinds of negative effects of such an anaesthetic on the brain and that therefore even the unprecedented severe damage should be considered 'foreseeable'. The other justices argued that the slight and the severe harms were different kinds of damage and not different magnitudes of the same foreseeable damage. See *Mosheh v Kliford* (2003) 57(4) PD 721 [*Kliford*]. For the 'right' level of generalisation where foreseeability of the causal chain of events is concerned see *Hughes v Lord Advocate* [1963] AC 837 (HL) and *Jolley v Sutton LBC* [2000] 3 All ER 409 (HL).

[22] As the authors themselves skilfully summarise, 'negligence calculus should be limited to those risks that reasonable persons, subject to common cognitive constraints and limited research possibilities, would anticipate and deliberate in the time available to them': above n 6, at 381-82. For the appropriate range of generalisation, see also Fleming, above n 3, at 243.

[23] Above n 6, at 334-35.

[24] See P Cane, 'Fault and Strict Liability for Harm in Tort Law' in G Jones and W Swaddling (eds), *The Search for Principle—Essays in Honour of Lord Goff of Chieveley* (Oxford, Oxford University Press, 1999) 193.

[25] As to the manner of infliction, they argue that 'the relevant risks are types of harms, not including the routes or instrumentalities by which such harms are produced': above n 6, at 407. For the exclusion of the extent of harm from the risk description see the discussion at 407-11.

sophisticated manner needed for relational risk-related harm screening.[26] The conclusion is that there are sensible solutions to the 'degree of generalisation problem' and therefore to the 'description problem' as raised by the authors.

The above analysis, however, encounters a different kind of 'description problem' that risk-related screening faces. This problem has to do with another factor that describes the risk and affects its classification as tortious or non-tortious, namely the benefits generated by faulty conduct. This problem is discussed below.

D. The 'Harms/Benefits Correlation Problem'

Risk-related screening, as noted, is based on the assumption that a net harms/benefits evaluation can be conducted not only to determine the faultiness of the conduct, given the entirety of its harms and benefits, but also to determine whether each risk is tortious or non-tortious. Such classification requires a distinct harms/benefits analysis for each single risk. Thus courts must identify the harms and the benefits belonging to the same risk in order to associate given harms with given benefits. Sometimes it is clear which benefits are associated with which harms. In such situations, there is a clear one-to-one relationship between specified benefits and specified harms of a given risk. There are situations, however, in which there is no clear one-to-one relationship between specific benefits and specific harms, and the same benefits can be associated with different harms. Such situations create the 'harms/benefits correlation problem' or risk evaluation problem. In absence of well-founded guidelines as to which benefits should be associated with which harms, how can risks be characterised as tortious or non-tortious?[27]

---

[26] Arguably, this unexplained failure to include the manner of harm infliction and the harm extent in the description of risk undermines the authors' argument that risk-related analysis fails to account for existing rules of causation such as intervening causes, 'thin skull' issues and spatio-temporal remoteness (403-11). It 'fails' to do so because the authors artificially exclude the causal aspects from the risk description.

[27] In their criticism on risk related screening, Hurd and Moore, above n 6, seem to hold the view that the harms and benefits that particular conduct generates cannot be grouped into distinct risks that are classified as tortious or non-tortious. In their view all these harms together constitute the negative aspect of the conduct and all these benefits together constitute its positive aspect. Therefore, if total harms exceed total benefits all harms should be considered as 'fault-factors'. In their words, 'But if *all* harms, discounted by their probability, are to be included in the calculus of risk, then it would appear that any harm that happens as the result of a defendant's unjustified conduct is within the risks that make the defendant's conduct unjustified': *ibid*, at 365 (emphasis added). This allegedly leads to the absurd outcome that 'all defendants are responsible for all harms that they cause to all persons': *ibid*. Yet this alleged 'all-inclusiveness problem'(*ibid*, at 365-74) seems far-fetched. Unforeseeable

This is illustrated by the following example. A cholesterol-reducing drug is expected to cause headaches. Given its unusual effectiveness in bringing about cholesterol reduction and the resultant benefits to the user's health, the harms of a headache to each consumer are outweighed by the benefits of reduced cholesterol. However, it was also reasonably foreseeable that the drug will cause liver problems to a percentage of its consumers. If the combined effect of liver problems and headaches outweighs the benefits of reduced cholesterol, this renders the conduct of marketing such a drug faulty, assuming that such design defect cases are governed by negligence law rather than by strict liability. The problem here is that there are two sets of risks (liver problems and headaches) but only one set of benefits (reduced cholesterol). With which set of harms should the one set of benefits be associated for the purpose of harms/benefits analysis? Should all the headaches be screened? Or just the headaches of consumers who benefit from the drug? Or the liver problems? Or should no harms be screened?

This hypothetical situation exemplifies the 'harms/benefits correlation problem'. In the absence of clear guidelines as to which benefits should be associated with which harms, risk-related screening seems to fail to provide convincing criteria for distinguishing between tortious and non-tortious risks and thereby between harms-within-risk and out-of-risk harms.

Can this problem be solved? Before we reach the answer let us first examine the rationale of risk-related screening.

E.   Rationale and Justifications for Risk-Related Screening of Foreseeable Harms

Why should liability be restricted ex post only to those harms that originate in ex ante tortious risks? It may be argued, plainly and simply, that once the conduct is found to be faulty, fairness requires that the actor should in principle be held liable for *all* of its consequences, subject only to practical considerations such as administrative costs. Moreover, unscreened liability for all harms caused in fact by this conduct would increase the deterrent effect of liability, creating stronger incentives not to behave in a negligent manner.[28]

Indeed, it appears that the reporters of the *Third Restatement on Physical Harm*, while embracing risk-related screening, struggle to justify

harms are usually not considered 'fault-factors', and therefore do not fall into the all-inclusiveness 'trap', and the same applies to some foreseeable harms that are offset by specific benefits: see below part III, and part II.F.

[28] Fleming observes that neither logic nor policy compel the conclusion that the reasons for creating liability should also delimit it: above n 3, at 238.

the risk standard.[29] As for deterrence, they concede that 'for negligence-based torts, scope-of-liability limitations are difficult to justify from a pure deterrence stand-point .... imposing liability, regardless of the connection to the harm, can only improve deterrence'.[30] They also concede that 'there is a mildly uncomfortable conclusory aspect to the common justification' that the reasons for creating liability should limit it and that the standard is indeterminate.[31] Yet they nevertheless endorse risk-related screening on the following grounds: its relative simplicity, its flexibility and adaptability to different circumstances, its appeal to intuitive notions of fairness and proportionality that perceive liability for unrelated harms as an arbitrary and unjust penalty, the avoidance of administrative costs involved in determining liability for out-of-risk harms, concerns that the combination of uncertainty regarding the level of due care and the threat of extended liability for out-of-risk harms may lead to over-deterrence, and, finally, that despite all its weaknesses it is a better screening concept than the rival 'direct consequences' test.

Notably, the reporters make no distinction between the two kinds of screened harms: *foreseeable* harms that are nevertheless screened because they are associated with non-tortious risks and *unforeseeable* harms that are screened even when they are associated with tortious risks. As the case for screening is stronger for the former, let us focus first on the screening of *foreseeable* harms.

As for questions of fairness, it is obviously unfair to impose liability for foreseeable harms which are associated with a reasonable, non-tortious, risk (namely, where the benefits of the risk outweigh its harms) just because the same conduct triggers another risk which is unreasonable and tortious. Let us assume, for example, that a specific medical treatment has a net positive effect on the blood system (good risk) but a net negative effect on the immune system (bad risk), that the two cannot be separated, and that the latter outweighs the former so that the treatment is negligent. It is obviously unfair to impose liability for the harms of the good risk to the blood system just because there is another bad risk to the immune system. In such cases there is a strong feeling of unfair 'free-ride' as the plaintiff benefits from the coincidental existence of other risks, and of unfair punishment as the defendant is forced to pay for the positive aspects of his or her conduct. As society approves of and even encourages the

---

[29] See comment (e) to §29, above n 2, at 585-86 and Reporters Notes to comment (e), above n 2, at 615-16.

[30] *Third Restatement on Physical Harm*, at 615.

[31] *Ibid.*

creation of such risks,[32] it seems wrong to 'punish' those who created them just because the same conduct generates other risks that render the conduct faulty in other respects.

As for questions of deterrence, concerns of over-deterrence are much more acute where liability is imposed on harms that originate in reasonable, non-tortious, risks only because the same conduct creates tortious risks as well. On the practical level, potential actors that fail to realise that liability was imposed on a 'good' risk just because of the accompanying 'bad' risks may avoid desirable activities that generate 'good' risks even in the absence of 'bad' risks. On the more theoretical level, risk-related screening can be justified on the ground that it plays a major role in the internalisation of *externalised* benefits. Recall that from the economic perspective, deterrence is tort law's response to the externalities problem. Whenever an actor externalises the harms that his or her conduct may cause to others, the private costs to that actor are less than the social cost, and this gap distorts resource allocation. The actor's conduct may generate too many harms. Tort liability for the externalised harms rectifies this distortion by internalising the externalised harms to the actor, thereby closing the gap between the private and social costs of the actor's activity.[33] The need for internalisation, however, applies not only to externalised harms but also to externalised benefits.[34] These benefits may open an opposite gap where the private cost of the activity to the actor exceeds the social cost. Externalised benefits should therefore be internalised by the actor. Tort law, however, unlike unjust enrichment law, cannot internalise such benefits directly but rather only indirectly by offsetting externalised benefits against externalised harms. Failure to do so creates or exacerbates the problem of *excessive liability* and *excessive damages*, which is obviously the case when actors have to pay for the creation of reasonable and socially desirable risks. Excessive liability and excessive damages are problematic because they can lead to over-deterrence by inducing actors to either avoid or to curtail socially desirable activities.[35] Risk-related screening provides a partial solution to this internalisation problem. By grouping foreseeable harms into distinct risks, evaluating the harms/benefits balance of each risk, and excluding from the scope of liability reasonable risks

---

[32] Stapleton refers to such a risk as 'one that a reasonable person would not have done more to avoid': above n 1, at 418.

[33] I Gilead, 'Tort Law and Internalization: The Gap between Private Loss and Social Cost' (1997) 17 *International Review of Law & Economics* 589.

[34] *Ibid.* On the importance of externalised benefits for the determination of efficient resource allocation see KN Hylton, 'The Theory of Tort Doctrine and the *Restatement (Third) of Torts*' (2001) 54 *Vanderbilt Law Review* 1413, 1420-23.

[35] See in this regard s 1 of the Compensation Act 2006 that under the title of 'Deterrent effect of potential liability' politely asks the court to consider whether negligence liability may negatively affect desirable activities.

whose benefits outweigh corresponding harms, risk-related screening may effectively offset externalised benefits against corresponding harms, thereby reducing the probability of excessive liability and excessive damages and the ensuing over-deterrence.

The conclusion, then, is that risk-related screening of foreseeable harms that originate in non-tortious risks can convincingly be based on considerations of fairness and deterrence. Moreover, the extent to which the benefits of the conduct are externalised by the actor—in other words, enjoyed by the plaintiff or by third parties—can serve as a relevant screening criterion. So greater externalisation may justify enhanced screening, especially where the plaintiff is the beneficiary.

Given the above conclusion, we can return to the 'harms/benefits correlation problem'.

F. Tackling the 'Harms/Benefits Correlation Problem'

Remember that the 'harms/benefits correlation problem' is the problem of how to relate the benefits of a given conduct to its harms in order to determine, for the purpose of risk-related screening, which risks are tortious and which are non-tortious. The problem was exemplified above using the cholesterol-reducing drug that causes headache and liver problems. The following numerical values highlight the problem. The drug is used by 10,000 consumers. Each consumer enjoys a cholesterol reduction valued as 10, and suffers from a headache valued as 3. There are 1,000 consumers that will suffer liver problems (group A) valued as 80 for each consumer. The other 9,000 consumers (group B) suffer only headaches. Overall, the conduct is faulty because its total risks (110,000) outweigh its total benefits (100,000). But which risks are tortious and which are non-tortious? Which harms, if any, should be screened? Notably, both the liver problems and the headaches are 'fault-factor' harms. Without any of them the conduct becomes non-faulty.

One possible answer is that both risks should be considered tortious and accordingly no harm should be screened. Another way of looking at this problem is to associate the benefits of the drug with one of the risks at a first stage and then to associate the remaining benefits with the other risk. This may lead to different outcomes depending both on the order of association and on whether it is carried out on the collective level or the personal level. If, for example, the benefits are first associated with the risk of headaches, then this risk would be considered non-tortious, both on the collective level (100,000>30,000) and on the personal level (10>3). Liability for headaches will be screened for groups A and B but imposed for the liver harms (80,000>70,000). If, in contrast, the benefits are first associated with the liver problems, they become non-tortious on the collective level (100,000>80,000), but remain tortious on the personal level for each member of group A (80>10). The headaches, under this order of association, are tortious on the collective level (30,000>20,000), but on the personal level they are tortious for members of group A (no benefits 'left') but non-tortious for members of group B (10>3). Yet another way to approach this harms/benefits relation question is to somehow split the benefits between the different risks, and this may also lead to different outcomes.

The above discussion of the justifications for relational screening shows that considerations of fairness and efficiency can provide reasonable solutions in ways which are not arbitrary. Arguably, in this case the risk of headache to all consumers should be considered non-tortious. Members of group B suffered no liver harms and enjoyed a benefit of 10, compared to a harm of only 3. These consumers are the beneficiaries of the drug and compensating them for harms suffered by group A is clearly an unfair 'free-ride'. Why should they benefit from the existence of other risks to others that render the conduct faulty?[36] As for members of group A, once they are compensated for their liver harms they also become beneficiaries of the drug and compensation for their headaches would be a 'free-ride' on their other harm. Moreover, making the producer liable for the headaches of group A but not for the headaches of group B may appear to be unequal treatment of the same harms. As for the producers, assuming that all the benefits of 100,000 are externalised alongside the costs of 110,000, the net externalities are 10,000 and it therefore appears that the liability of 80,000 rather than of 110,000 is fairer and less likely to induce over-deterrence. Common sense tells us as well that the tortious risk is the liver problems.

The 'harms/benefits correlation problem', to sum up, can be solved with the help of considerations of fairness and efficiency as well as with common sense. Adequate harms/benefits relation choices may be reached under risk-related screening in ways that are conceptually and practically sensible and defensible. Solutions, however, have to be adjusted to the circumstances of the case and may change accordingly. In this regard, the suggestion that risk should be described for risk-related screening through its four aspects provides the necessary flexibility. The risk in the above hypothetical, for example, can be described according to the *type* of harm (headaches versus liver problems) or according to who is harmed (group A

---

[36] In Justice Cardozo's words, they should sue for a wrong aimed at them 'and not as the vicarious beneficiary of a breach of duty to another': *Palsgraf*, above n 8, at 342.

versus group B). Indeed, different descriptions may lead to different results and that may create indeterminacy, but indeterminacy is not arbitrariness: 'it can be understood as a virtue'.[37]

An interesting conclusion that emerges from the discussion is that harms that are 'fault-factors', like the headaches in the above hypothetical, may nevertheless be screened. This may appear puzzling. If a given harm is necessary to render conduct faulty, how can it later be excluded from the scope of liability as being unrelated to it? The answer is, and this is precisely the point, that the subject of risk-related screening is not stand-alone harms but rather harms associated with benefits under the risk concept. A given harm is screened, even if it is a fault-factor, because it originates in non-tortious risk.

III.   UNFORESEEABLE RISKS AND EXCEPTIONS TO RISK-RELATED SCREENING

The risks that render conduct faulty are risks of foreseeable harms. Unforeseeable harms are not 'fault-factors' as they are not taken into account when the faultiness of particular conduct or risk is determined. The rule of risk-related screening therefore screens unforeseeable harms. The imposition of liability for such out-of-risk harms constitutes an exception to risk-related screening. It implies that these harms are per-ceived as being related to the faulty conduct although they are not related to it by risk. Liability for unforeseeable harms, then, creates a divergence between the general idea of relational screening and its major expression in the risk standard. What justifies the rule that screens unforeseeable harms? And what justifies its exceptions?

A.   Screening Unforeseeable Harms: Justifications

The screening of unforeseeable harms that result from *non-tortious* risks is self evident. The considerations of fairness and deterrence that justify the screening of *foreseeable* harms that result from such risks obviously justify the screening of the unforeseeable harms. But when unforeseeable harms result from risks that are *tortious* because of other foreseeable harms, their screening is not self-evident. Although they are not 'fault-factors' and were not taken ex ante into account when the risk was classified as tortious,

---

[37] *Third Restatement on Physical Harm*, above n 2, at 585. It is argued there, in this regard, that 'The risk standard can be employed to do justice in a wide range of cases in which the particular facts require careful consideration and thereby resists any rule-like formulation': comment (e) to §29.

policy considerations may support their ex post characterisation as being sufficiently related to the tortious risk. As to fairness, given that these unforeseeable harms are in fact caused by the realisation of a tortious risk, is it not fair, ex post, to channel them as well to those who created these risks, regardless of why these risks were considered tortious ex ante? As to deterrence, concerns of over-deterrence are convincing when liability is imposed for the creation of desirable, non-tortious risks, but such concerns seem less convincing when liability is imposed on the results, although unforeseeable, of tortious risks. After all, we do want to prevent such risks. Indeed, we have seen that the reporters of the *Third Restatement on Physical Harm* struggle to justify risk-related screening of such unforesee-able harms.[38]

It is suggested that support for the rule that screens unforeseeable harms can be found, in terms of fairness and deterrence, in the above discussion of externalised benefits. As for fairness, it seems unfair to count unforesee-able harms against the actor while disregarding unforeseeable benefits. If a drug, for example, has two unforeseeable side-effects, one positive and one negative, it may be unfair to hold the producer liable for harms caused by the negative side-effect while disregarding the positive side-effect. Imposing liability for unforeseeable harms is a deviation from a major characteristic of negligence law, namely that liability should not be decided upon the wisdom of hindsight. If hindsight is allowed, fairness requires that it should be allowed in both directions. Hindsight, however, may lead to peculiar results. It may, for example, transform ex ante undesirable conduct into ex post desirable conduct because of unforeseeable ex post benefits. As for deterrence, where it is known in advance that liability will be imposed for unforeseeable harms but will not be mitigated by unfore-seeable benefits, this may enhance over-deterrence due to the indeterminate and unbalanced nature of such liability.

The conclusion, then, is that although the rule that screens unforeseeable harms is justified, exceptions to this rule that allow liability for unforesee-able harms when resulting from tortious risks may also be justified. Before turning to these exceptions, we should first consider the different kinds of unforeseeability.

B.   The Different Kinds of Unforeseeability

That some unforeseeable harms are screened (under the rule of risk-related screening) while other are not (under exceptions) implies that there are different kinds or different 'degrees' of unforeseeability. This variation corresponds with the earlier distinction between the different aspects of

---

[38]   See the text accompanying n 29 above.

risk. A particular harm may be unforeseeable because of the kind of person harmed, the type of harm, the kind of causal chain of events or the extent of the harm. These different aspects of unforeseeabilities may accumulate. Harm may be unforeseeable in just one or in all four aspects. One could claim that the 'degree' of unforeseeability increases with the number of the unforeseeable aspects. Arguably, this 'degree' of unforeseeability may serve as a factor in the decision to allow or disallow liability for unforeseeable harm.

The distinction between the different aspects of risk bears on the decision whether to impose liability for unforeseeable harms in another important way. It appears that the exceptions to the rule which sanctions the screening of unforeseeable harms are more prevalent with regard to some aspects of risk and less prevalent with regard to others. They are less prevalent with regard to unforeseeable kinds of plaintiffs. When the plaintiff is unforeseeable the case for screening is the strongest because the basic relationship between the parties is not established. In contrast, these exceptions are much more prevalent where the unforeseeable aspect is the extent of harm. Here the case for screening is the weakest and the exceptions actually overshadow the rule.[39] The case for screening on type of harm and on causal chains of events that link the harm to faulty conduct seems to lie somewhere in between. For example, regarding the screening of unforeseeable causal chains of events, one can find the 'common wisdom' of courts that 'the manner in which the harm occurs is irrelevant to the scope of liability as long as the harm is foreseeable',[40] and in contrast, decisions and statements that support such screening.[41]

---

[39] See below part III.C.

[40] *Third Restatement on Physical Harm*, above n 2, notes to comment (o) to §29, at 601. The *Restatement (Second) of Torts* (1965) provides that an actor is liable only where there is 'no rule of law relieving the actor from liability because of the manner in which his negligence has resulted in the harm': §431(b). Such rules are stated in §§ 435-61. See also ML Wells, who argues that where the magnitude of the harm was foreseeable, liability should be imposed regardless of whether the type of harm or the causal chain of events that led to it were foreseeable: 'Proximate Cause and the American Law Institute: The False Choice between the Direct-Consequences Test and the Risk Standard' (2003) 37 *University of Richmond Law Review* 389.

[41] Fleming notes that liability is to be denied where foreseeable harm is brought about by an unforeseeable chain of events: above n 3, at 242. An Israeli case exemplifies such screening. A decision not to perform a Caesarean section was found to be negligent because it was ex ante foreseeable that the baby's excessive weight could cause complications in vaginal delivery. Ex post the baby was damaged at birth by unforeseeable rare complications that had nothing to do with excessive weight, but that would have been avoided had a Caesarean section been performed. The Israeli Supreme Court noted that as the harm was realised in an unforeseeable manner—the ex post harm was not the result of the risk that rendered the conduct negligent ex ante—liability may well be denied: *Plonit v Bnei-Zion Medical Center, Haifa* (2003) 58(1) PD 516.

Given the different kinds of unforeseeable risks, we should now look briefly at the actual exceptions to the rule that screens unforeseeable harms and at their justifications.

C.   Unscreened Unforeseeable Harms: Undeserving Actors, Deserving Plaintiffs and the Extent of Harm

Liability for unforeseeable harms may be justified either because the actor's conduct is so anti-social or immoral that it should be discouraged and punished by extended liability, or because the plaintiff's conduct is so commendable that it should be encouraged by the provision of extended protection against his or her unforeseeable harms. The *Third Restatement on Physical Harm* provides such examples. Intentional and reckless tortfeasors are held liable for physical harms factually caused by such conduct, even where such harms were unforeseeable.[42] Conversely, liability to rescuers who suffered physical harm extends to include 'abnormal efforts' to rescue and ensuing harms which may be unforeseeable.[43]

The distinction between the different aspects of risk and accordingly between the different kinds of unforeseeable harms illuminates the major exception to risk-related screening: the imposition of liability for the unforeseeable *extent* of harm. Courts tend to impose liability for unforeseeable harms whenever the only unforeseeable aspect is the extent of harm. Indeed, once it is established that a foreseeable plaintiff suffered a foreseeable type of harm caused in a foreseeable manner by faulty conduct, it appears fair that the risk of greater unforeseeable extent should be born by the faulty defendant rather than by the innocent plaintiff. After all, it is the defendant that may benefit from reduced liability for harms that are unforeseeably of a small extent. This fairness-in-harm-allocation argument is most appealing when the unforeseeable extent of harm was caused by unforeseeable pre-existing physical and mental conditions of the victim. Defendants should take the victim as found, for better or for worse.

These intuitions of fairness are indeed embodied in the law governing unforeseeable extent. The perception that defendants should take the

---

[42] Above n 2, at §33. For a similar extension see P Cane, 'Responsibility and Fault: A Relational and Functional Approach to Responsibility' in P Cane and J Gardner (eds), *Relating to Responsibility: Essays for Tony Honoré on His Eightieth Birthday* (Oxford, Hart Publishing, 2001).

[43] Above n 2, at §32. The provision limits the scope of liability to harms that arise 'from a risk that inheres in the effort to provide aid'. Although English law has not yet recognised liability to unforeseeable rescuers—see *White v Chief Constable of South Yorkshire* [1999] 2 AC 455 [*White*]—Fleming notes that in rescue cases 'the law has sympathetically stretched foreseeability to a transparent fiction': above n 3, at 248.

victim as found is well reflected by the 'thin skull' exception,[44] which has also been applied to property damage.[45] Moreover, the perception that the extent of harm is the actor's problem led to a more comprehensive non-screening exception, a blanket exception that allows unrestricted liability for the unforeseeable magnitude of primary harms.[46] But has the law gone too far in allowing liability for unforeseeable extent? In this regard it is helpful to use the above distinction between the magnitude of the *primary* harms caused by the original causal chains of events that the faulty conduct triggers and the *secondary* harms that evolve from primary harms through subsequent and distinct causal chains of events.[47]

As to the *magnitude of the primary harm*, although the 'thin skull' exception is justified, one should bear in mind that it applies in principle to the extent of the original primary harm and not to its type or to the causal chain of events leading to it. For example, someone who insults another or pushes another slightly is not liable if the latter's rare emotional instability or severe heart disease cause a heart attack.[48] This explains why the overruling of *Re Polemis and Furness, Withy & Co* by the *The Wagon Mound (No 1)* did not affect the 'thin skull' exception.[49] Although the borderline between the type of the primary harm and its magnitude (extent) is not always clear,[50] it must be drawn to keep the 'thin skull' exception within its rationale.[51] It is questionable, however, whether the

---

[44]   Fleming, above n 3, at 234.

[45]   *Ibid*, at 236; *Third Restatement on Physical Harm*, above n 2, comment (d) to §31, at 643.

[46]   See T Weir, *Tort Law* (Oxford, Oxford University Press, 2002) 78; Fleming, above n 3, at 240-41; *Third Restatement on Physical Harm, ibid*, comment (p) to §29, at 602 and the Note on §31, at 646; Dobbs, above n 3, at 464.

[47]   For this distinction see above part II.B. Arguably a distinct chain of events is triggered by human acts or natural causes which, in terms of probability and human experience, or because of remoteness in time and space, are not an integral part or direct consequence of the original chain of events.

[48]   See Tony Weir's criticism of *Page v Smith* [1996] 1 AC 155 (HL), where the thin skull was applied to the type of the primary loss and not to its magnitude: above n 46, at 82. Dobbs similarly comments that the rule does not require the defendant to exercise special care for an unforeseeable vulnerable plaintiff: above n 3, at 465.

[49]   See *Smith v Leech Brain* [1962] 2 QB 405, discussing *Overseas Tankship (UK) Ltd v Morts Dock & Engineering Co; The Wagon Mound (No 1)* [1961] AC 388 (PC). Arguably, *Re Polemis* [1921] 3 KB 560, where a plank dropped negligently ignited benzene fumes and destroyed the whole ship, was not a thin-skull case as neither the causal chain of events that led to the primary harm nor its type were reasonably foreseeable.

[50]   See, eg, *Kliford*, above n 21. As noted earlier, in this Israeli case the justices differed as to whether dizziness and fatigue on the one hand and unprecedented permanent neurological damage on the other hand, when caused by a local anesthesia at a dental clinic, are different *types* of harm or different *extents* of the same type of harm.

[51]   Interestingly, the proposed *Third Restatement on Physical Harm* applies the thin skull exception to harm that 'is of greater magnitude *or different type* than might reasonably be expected' (§31, emphasis added). The application of the exception to the *type* of the primary harm and not just its *extent* seems to involve a substantial and, arguably, problematic expansion of the 'thin skull' exception.

broader exception of blanket liability for unforeseeable magnitude of primary harms is justified. The reporters of the *Third Restatement on Physical Harm* rightly question the fairness of this exception, which allows disparity between the degree of culpability and extent of liability.[52] They nevertheless justify the exception on grounds of 'administrative convenience' in avoiding inquiry into the foreseeability of the magnitude of harms in this 'modestly-sized class of cases'.[53] Still, it appears that this blanket exception goes too far. Courts should preserve their discretion to screen unforeseeable magnitude of harm where they find such liability unjustified, and therefore should not bind themselves by such a blanket exception.[54] After all, the different levels of risk description and the 'thin skull' exception provide sufficient discretion in this regard.

With regard to *secondary harms*, the argument that extent is the actor's problem seems to lose some of its vigour. Recall that secondary harms are additional harms that evolve from primary harms through subsequent, distinct causal chains of events. A road-accident injury to the claimant's arm may evolve years later into a broken leg when she falls from a ladder because of sudden pain in the injured arm. Years later, the injured leg may cause a ski accident, and so forth. As the sequence of distinct causal chains gets longer, the ensuing secondary harms become more and more remote, in causal terms, from the faulty conduct. True, there may be situations in which fairness requires the inclusion of unforeseeable secondary harms in the scope of liability even when they are not 'thin skull' cases. 'Enhanced harm due to efforts to render medical or other aid' is an example provided by the *Third Restatement on Physical Harm*.[55] Still, fairness requires that liability should not be stretched too far towards the remote end of the chain of events. Such a limitation applies not just to unforeseeable secondary harms but also to such foreseeable harms.[56]

IV.   LIABILITY-WATCH SCREENING: JUSTIFICATIONS, METHODS AND INCREASING COMPLEXITY

The discussion thus far has focused on relational screening, which examines whether a given harm is sufficiently related to the faulty conduct. The

---

[52] Comment (o) to §29, above n 2, at 602.

[53] *Ibid.*

[54] Fleming suggests that the blanket exception should not apply to unforeseeable plaintiffs: above n 3, at 237. This, however, is not a real limitation as the blanket exception usually applies to foreseeable plaintiffs.

[55] Above n 2, at §35. Still, the provision limits the scope of liability to rescuers only to harms that arise 'from a risk that inheres in the effort to render aid': see above n 43.

[56] Fleming, above n 3, at 250: 'liability does not reach into infinity in time'.

other major kind of screening, liability-watch screening, screens liability for related harms on the ground that imposing liability may lead to undesirable outcomes.

A major consideration behind liability-watch screening is concerns regarding the undesirable consequences of *indeterminate* liability. Indeterminacy here lies not in the unforeseeability of harms,[57] but in the open-ended nature of liability to a very large number of potential plaintiffs and for numerous harms. This kind of indeterminacy is often associated with the phenomena of the *ripple effect* (one harm leading to others) and harms by *ricochet* (harms to one person negatively affecting others as well: relational loses) that characterise 'pure' economic and 'pure' emotional harms. Such indeterminacy raises various concerns.[58] One concern is over-deterrence. Given the indeterminacy of potential liability, actors may overestimate the potential legal risk involved in their intended activities and this may negatively affect desirable activities. A second indeterminacy-related concern is a costly flood of claims that may overload the courts and consume precious societal resources.[59] A third indeterminacy concern is that liability will impose upon a few defendants a heavy burden, composed of many small harms, that are otherwise spread out, as in the famous 'cable cases'.[60] A fourth concern that calls for the restriction of liability, especially indeterminate liability, is the unfairness of imposing a heavy burden on an actor who acted bona fide but was nevertheless negligent under the demanding reasonable person standard. The discrepancy between the degree of fault and the ensuing sanction may be too disturbing. A fifth consideration is that it may be unfair to differentiate between different groups that suffered the same type of loss. Liability to one group may be denied just because it was denied to the other group.[61] A sixth liability restricting concern, also magnified by indeterminacy, is the prospect of vexatious or unfounded claims for alleged harms that are difficult to deny such as 'pure' emotional harms. Examples of more specific policy-based screening considerations are concerns that tort liability in negligence may interfere with the operation of the other branches of law

---

[57] See above part III.A.

[58] These concerns are emphasised by the *Third Restatement on Economic Loss and Related Torts*, above n 4. It states, in various contexts, that duty is to be denied where liability would be indeterminate: see §§ 9(3)(a), 12(1)(c), 20(2)(b) and 21(d) and accompanying comments and notes.

[59] For discussion of the politics that affected the use of the duty concept as a 'gatekeeper' in both directions see D Owen, 'Duty Rules' (2001) 54 *Vanderbilt Law Review* 767, 774-79.

[60] See the cable cases studies in M Bussani and VV Palmer (eds), *Pure Economic Loss in Europe* (Cambridge, Cambridge University Press, 2003) 171-221.

[61] In *White* it was argued that if bereaved relatives of victims are denied compensation for their psychiatric damage, it is wrong to award compensation to policemen who suffered such damage: above n 43, at 510 (Lord Hoffman).

that apply to the same harms, and that it may disturb the separation of powers if imposed on policy decisions made by governmental authorities.[62]

There are differing views regarding the scope of liability-watch screening that is justified by the above concerns and by other policy considerations. In general, it appears that, in the long run, the scope of liability-watch screening tends to diminish as the boundaries of negligence liability expand. In this regard, two basic characteristics of liability-watch screening should be highlighted.

The first characteristic has to do with the different aspects of liability-watch screening. Notably, the distinction between the different aspects of risk is useful in this regard just as in relational screening. Undesirable liability can be denied through liability-watch screening with regard to kinds of plaintiffs (such as where there are no 'special relations' or reliance), with regard to types of harm (such as 'pure' economic or emotional losses), with regard to kinds of activity (such as 'pure' omissions[63] or discretional acts of governmental authorities) and with regard to the extent of harm or even to the manner of its infliction.

The second, and related, characteristic of liability-watch screening is that it tends to become more complex with the gradual expansion of negligence liability. In the past, liability could have been effectively screened through only one screening aspect. A prominent example is the 'exclusionary rule' which through the 'type of harm' aspect screened liability for 'pure' economic losses from the scope of negligence liability. With the gradual expansion of liability through a growing number of exceptions to the exclusionary rule, screening harms only because of their 'type' had become too aggressive and courts then had to introduce additional requirements for screening, employing other aspects of risk such as who is harmed (requiring 'justifiable reliance'), who inflicted the harm (requiring 'assumption of responsibility'), or a combination of the two (requiring 'special relations').

---

[62] See D Fairgrieve, M Andenas and J Bell (eds), *Tort Liability of Public Authorities in Comparative Perspective* (London, British Institute for International and Comparative Law, 2002).

[63] A 'pure' omission is the defendant's failure to protect the plaintiff from a risk generated by a third person or occurrence and not by the defendant: see §37 of the *Third Restatement on Physical Harm*, above n 2.

V. THE SCREENING DEVICES AND THE 'DIVISION OF LABOUR' BETWEEN THEM

A. Screening Concepts: The Confusion

To cope with the complicated screening mission of relational screening and liability-watch screening and to achieve its goals, courts need to design adequate screening devices. To this end, Anglo-American law has tradition-ally employed as 'screening devices' the two framework concepts of 'duty' and 'legal causation', the latter usually termed 'proximate cause' in the US and 'remoteness' in England. A major problem with these concepts is that none have really acquired a distinct, specialised role in the screening process: they have often been used interchangeably.[64] The lack of 'division of labour' between these major screening devices and of a specialised role for each has produced great confusion.[65]

The *Third Restatement on Physical Harm*'s stance on screening may even add to that confusion. Under the title 'scope of liability', §§29-36 introduce a 'revolutionary' approach to the screening devices. The report-ers openly suggest that proximate cause, the major expression of legal causation, should in principle be abandoned.[66] They also limit the screen-ing role of the duty concept, arguing that it should not screen liability 'on factors specific to an individual case', but only 'when a court can promulgate relatively clear, categorical, bright-line rules of law'.[67] As a substitute, the 'risk standard', the rule of risk-related screening, is intro-duced in §29. It provides that 'An actor's liability is limited to those physical harms that result from the risks that made the actor's conduct tortious'.[68] This rule, which screens out-of-risk harms, is accompanied by

---

[64] With regard to duty and remoteness in England, John Davis notes that 'duty and remoteness issues become indistinguishable', 'Tort Law' in P Birks (ed), *English Private Law vol II* (Oxford, Oxford University Press, 2000) 432, n 117, and Fleming comments that 'both concepts serve precisely the same function of marking the outer boundaries of recovery': above n 3, at 243. Lord Denning accordingly suggested that 'time has come to discard those tests which have proved so elusive': *Spartan Steel & Alloys v Martin & Co* [1973] QB 27 (CA) 37. Tony Weir notes that the concept of duty has perhaps been overstrained in being applied to all the elements of liability: above n 46, at 30. With regard to duty and proximate cause in the US, GE White observes that 'A robust use of the duty element...tends to result in a reduced role for the causation element in its "legal" capacity'.: *Tort Law in America: An Intellectual History* expanded edn (Oxford, Oxford University Press, 2003) 319.

[65] Yet another problem is that legal causation has been perceived as caught up with questions of factual causation. For a discussion of the need to 'unpack causation' see J Stapleton, above n 1, and below part V.E.

[66] In a 'Special Note on Proximate Cause' the reporters, on behalf of the American Law Institute, express a hope that the words 'proximate cause' will disappear from the *Restatement (Fourth) of Torts*: see above n 5.

[67] Comment (a) to §7, at 91. See also comment (c) to §29, above n 5.

[68] Above n 4, at §29.

specified exceptions that allow liability for out-of-risk unforeseeable harms: the 'thin skull' exception, rescuers, intentional or reckless wrong-doing, and aid-receiving situations.[69]

Can this confusion be cleared up, at least to some extent? The following paragraphs try to cope with this challenge.

B.   Distinguishing between Relational and Liability-Watch Screening Devices

The first step toward clearing away the confusion is creating a distinction between devices of relational screening on the one hand and devices of liability-watch screening on the other hand. Relational screening devices should specialise in harms that are unrelated to the tortious conduct, mainly out-of-risk harms. Liability-watch screening devices should special-ise in related harms that are nevertheless excluded from the scope of liability because of the undesirable effects of liability. This proposition is obviously in line with the *Third Restatement on Physical Harm* which distinguishes between the screening devices of relational, 'scope of liability' screening (the risk standard and its exceptions) and those of liability-watch screening (duty).[70] The distinction can also be found in the draft of the *Third Restatement on Economic Loss and Related Torts.*[71]

The next step is to examine a more adequate way to cope with the confusion that has accompanied the traditional screening devices for so long. One way is to follow the *Third Restatement on Physical Harm*'s 'revolutionary' restructuring of the screening devices, which dispenses with legal causation and restricts duty. The other way is to stick to the traditional concepts of legal causation and duty, but to sharpen and tighten them in ways that create a much clearer division of labour between their screening roles and better explain their interrelations.

C.   The Pros and Cons of the *Third Restatement*'s Screening 'Revolution'

As noted, relational screening is marked by confusion regarding the roles of legal causation and duty as screening devices and their interrelations. Against this background, the bold position taken by the *Third Restatement on Physical Harm*, to dispose of legal causation (proximate cause) and to

---

[69]   See above part III.C.

[70]   'There are two different legal doctrines to withhold liability: no-duty rules and scope of liability doctrines': above n 2, comment (a) to §7, at 91.

[71]   Above n 4.

restrict the role of duty, is appealing. It seems to have many advantages: avoiding the nebulous concept of legal causation with its many changing faces, employing a relational screening concept—the risk standard—which already lies at the core of relational screening, limiting the role of duty to liability-watch screening and thereby significantly reducing the confusion around it, and drawing a clearer line between devices of relational screening and those of liability-watch screening.

These advantages, however, are accompanied by difficulties that may render the *Third Restatement on Physical Harm*'s way of coping with the screening-devices problem less attractive. A major difficulty is that the risk standard, if used as the only principled concept of relational screening, may be too wide in some respects and too narrow in other respects. It may be too wide because the general statement that 'the harm is not within the risk' does not provide much guidance regarding relational screening and may even seem arbitrary.[72] The risk standard, for example, does not distinguish between the different aspects of risk but rather refers to risk as a package. Given the importance of this distinction to relational screening, this package needs 'unpacking'. In contrast, the risk standard may prove to be too narrow because it does not cover the whole range of relational screening in a principled manner. Exceptions to the rule of risk-related screening allow liability for unforeseeable out-of-risk harms which are related to the faulty conduct but not by the risk standard.[73] These exceptions require a conceptual framework that accommodates them, and while such a framework is provided by the traditional concepts of duty and legal causation, it can hardly be found in the *Third Restatement on Physical Harm*'s approach.[74]

Another difficulty lies with the *Third Restatement on Physical Harm*'s claim that relational screening (scope of liability) is to be decided by factors specific to the individual case, whereas liability-watch (duty) screening is categorical and applicable only to a general class of cases.[75] As to the alleged general nature of no-duty findings, it was noted that liability-watch screening tends to become more complex with the expansion of liability, so that it now requires fine-tuning which is less categorical and closer to the

---

[72] Stapleton observes that the question of the appropriate scope of liability for consequences is neither acknowledged, let alone resolved, by crude slogans that the consequences must be within the scope-of-risk: above n 1, at 411.

[73] See above part III.C.

[74] Interestingly, whereas the *Third Restatement on Physical Harm* enumerates the specific exceptions to the risk standard (§§31-33, 35), the *Third Restatement on Economic Loss and Related Torts* states vaguely that the risk standard only applies 'generally' (§16(2)) and that 'The scope of liability may be determined by standards and rules other than the risk standard', referring, inter alia, to public policies and rules of damage quantification: comment (d) to §16, above n 4, at 226-28.

[75] See above n 67.

facts of the case.[76] Tony Weir notes, accordingly, that it is now difficult to 'strike out' a claim on grounds of 'no duty' without ascertaining its facts.[77] It appears that no-duty findings regarding affirmative duties and 'pure' non-physical losses may become even more contextual in the future, as indeed envisaged by the draft of the *Third Restatement on Economic Loss and Related Torts*.[78] As to the alleged contextual nature of relational screening, it appears that some exceptions to the risk standard, such as the 'thin skull' exception, are of a categorical nature.

One can also question the assertion that liability-watch screening (duty) is a question of law for a judge while relational screening (scope of liability) is a question of fact for a jury.[79] Arguably, relational screening does involve questions of law for the judge.[80]

Finally, the concept of legal causation and the role of duty in relational screening are so deeply entrenched in the minds of judges, academics, and lawyers that it is questionable whether these deeply-rooted concepts can simply disappear with time as the American Law Institute 'fervently hopes'.[81] Indeed, the 'demotion' of the duty concept has triggered a loud clamour and attracted much criticism.[82] Defenders of legal causation have also voiced their objections to its replacement by the risk standard.[83] Moreover, if this aspiration is met and these concepts disappear from the legal discourse in the US, other common law jurisdictions may not follow suit, and this may negatively affect the dialogue between major common law jurisdictions.

[76] See above part IV, in the last paragraph.

[77] Weir observes that after the Strasbourg Court's decision in *Osman v United Kingdom* (1999) 29 EHRR 245, UK courts 'now say that the question of "duty or no duty" cannot properly be decided until the actual facts are known': above n 46, at 31. While Weir expresses concern that this development may 'destroy the utility of the duty concept', the above analysis indicates that it is an inevitable response to the need to refine the screening devices in order to cope with expanding boundaries of negligence liability: see above part IV, in the last paragraph.

[78] The draft is actually based on a concept of a series of duty rules 'of increasing specificity with each rule giving way to a more specific rule': above n 4, Reporter's Memorandum, iii.

[79] Comment (f) to §29, above n 2, at 587. See also Dobbs, above n 3, at 449-50.

[80] See PJ Kelly who argues that courts 'decided proximate cause questions, more often that not, as matters of law, leaving few proximate cause issues for the jury': 'Restating Duty, Breach, and Proximate Cause in Negligence Law: Descriptive Theory and the Rule of Law' (2001) 54 *Vanderbilt Law Review* 1039, 1062.

[81] Being aware that limitations on liability are associated with the concept of proximate cause, the reporters included the term in a parenthetical following the 'scope of liability' title, hoping 'that the Restatement Fourth of Tort will not find that parenthetical necessary': see above n 5.

[82] Goldberg and Zipursky refer to the academic aspiration to eliminate duty from negligence and to 'duty scepticism' as an unfounded 'gut instinct': above n 7, at 662. They accuse the reporters of the *Third Restatement on Physical Harm* of an 'effort to reinvent negligence law without duty under the guise of restatement' (698).

[83] See Hurd and Moore, above n 6.

Given all these complexities, we should now examine the alternative to the *Third Restatement on Physical Harm*'s 'revolution', one that preserves the traditional screening devices of duty and legal causation.

D. 'Division of Labour' between Duty and Legal Causation: An Illustration

The other way to reduce the confusion that envelops the existing screening devices is to establish a 'division of labour' between them. Such a 'division of labour' would attach specified screening roles to each concept in a manner that clarifies their distinct tasks, their interrelations, and their overlap. Arguably, such a 'division of labour' can be achieved without deviating from the traditional ways in which these concepts have been perceived and applied by courts.

The first necessary step would be to realise that each of the two concepts, duty and legal causation, has two distinct screening roles and therefore two distinct meanings. Relational duty is one screening device and liability-watch duty is another distinct screening device, despite their common 'duty' title.[84] The same applies to legal causation: relational legal causation is one screening device and liability-watch legal causation is another. The two relational screening devices screen unrelated harms, while the two liability-watch screening devices screen related harms whenever liability for these harms is undesirable. Once this duality is acknowledged, much of the confusion surrounding the screening devices can be cleared away.[85]

---

[84] In contrast, as mentioned, the *Third Restatement on Physical Harm* takes the opposite view that there should be only one kind of duty, liability-watch duty. The notion of relational duty is criticised also by Jane Stapleton who argues that 'owing a duty to act carefully in relation to only one foreseeable risk' is incoherent, and even circular and awkward: 'Legal Cause: Cause in Fact and the Scope of Liability for Consequences' (2001) 54 *Vanderbilt Law Review* 941, 994-96. In her view, duty is one and indivisible: to act like a reasonable person in the circumstances. But can it be disputed that a major role of the duty concept has always been to distinguish between the different risks and harms of the same conduct?

[85] Duty is often perceived not just as a screening concept that limits the scope of liability for given faulty conduct, but as a *constitutive element* of liability. According to this view, duty, in the sense of an obligation established by law not to carelessly inflict a specified type of harm upon a specified type of person, is the source, the engine, of fault-based liability. This concept of 'duty' as a specific primary obligation underlies Goldberg and Zipursky's criticism of the proposed *Third Restatement on Physical Harm*: see above n 7 and n 82. Their major complaint is that the proposal refers only to duty in its exemption (screening) sense and fails to relate to it as a specific primary obligation. Yet the concept of duty as a specific primary obligation makes sense only where there is no 'negative duty of very great generality' owed by the entire world to the entire world not to endanger others carelessly: OW Holmes, 'The Theory of Torts' (1873) 7 *American Law Review* 652, 662. Where such a general obligation is recognised there is no need for the duty concept to establish specific primary duties, as these specific duties are 'overtaken' by the general obligation. Where a general obligation is

Given that two screening devices (relational duty and relational legal causation) are responsible for relational screening, and that two other screening devices (liability-watch duty and liability-watch legal causation) are responsible for liability-watch screening, different 'divisions of labour' may apply within each pair. The following provides an illustration, based on the preceding discussion, of such a possible division.

The general idea behind this instance of a 'divisions of labour' is that different screening devices should be adapted to different aspects of the risk, and that this can be done by sharpening and tightening the definitions of the traditional concepts. More specifically, legal causation can and should be understood in its literal meaning, namely as specialising in the causal chain of events that links the negligent conduct with the ensuing harm, and as focusing on the manner in which the harm was inflicted. This association of legal causation with just one aspect of risk may seem questionable. After all, legal causation has often been perceived as applying to all aspects of risk: who is harmed, type of harm, and its extent. But this can be easily explained. Legal causation does in fact screen liability for other aspects of risk but it does so *indirectly*, since it is the causal chain of events that often determines who is harmed *(Palsgraf)*, the type of harm

---

recognised, the role of the duty concept is only to restrict and monitor the liability that the general obligation generates. In the formative years of negligence law no general legal obligations to avoid careless conduct were recognised and the duty concept was rightly perceived as the source of specific primary obligations protecting limited kinds of interests against careless conduct. With the gradual expansion of fault-based liability, however, general obligations not to act carelessly have emerged, and the duty concept has accordingly been gradually transformed from a 'generator' of liability into a 'screener' of liability. So while there are different views as to whether a general obligation had been recognised in the past (see Wright, above n 2, at 1086-96 and White, above n 64, at 305-7, 318-19), the proposed *Third Restatement on Physical Harm* (§7) clearly recognises the existence of a general obligation not to endanger others carelessly where risks of physical harms are involved. In this regard the duty concept is rightly perceived as a 'screener' rather than a 'generator', so that Goldberg and Zipursky's criticism is unfounded. Interestingly, one can discern a similar trend even with regard to pure economic losses. While the first *Restatement (Third) on the Law of Tort: Economic Loss and Related Torts— Preliminary Draft* (2005) opened with a declaration of 'no general duty' (§8), the second draft (above n 4) now opens with a recognition of two general duties: one is based on an invitation to rely (§9(2)) and the other is an open-ended general duty (§9(4)). Indeed, these general duties are significantly restricted by policy considerations (§9(3)) and by the following specific duties (§§ 10-14, 19-21) but this is exactly the point—on the background of general obligations each of the specific duties now functions not just as a 'generator' but also as a 'screener'. As to pure omissions and stand-alone emotional disturbances, the reporters of the *Third Restatements* seem to hold the view that a general obligation does not yet exist, so that specific primary duties are required: see §§ 37-44 of the final draft on physical harm (pure omissions) and §§ 45-47 of Preliminary Draft No 5 of 29 August 2005 (emotional disturbance). It may be argued, however, that even in these regards the developing exceptions already overshadow the no-general-obligation rule so that 'de facto' general primary obligations begin to emerge. In any case, for our purposes, even duty as a specific primary obligation can be considered a screening concept in the sense that it limits the scope of liability for negligent conduct.

(*Wagon Mound (No 1)*) and the extent of harm.[86] Unrelated causation may often lead to the result that the plaintiff, and/or the type of harm, and/or the extent of the harm, are also unrelated. But where the causal chain of events is sufficiently related, screening of plaintiffs, types of harm and the extent of the harm is not a causal-based screening, and a screening device other than legal causation can be employed.

Under this exemplary 'division of labour', the role of relational legal causation is to directly screen out unrelated (usually out-of-risk) causal chains of events and to indirectly screen out plaintiffs, types of harm, and extent of harm that are unrelated because the causal chain of events is unrelated. The role of relational duty is accordingly to directly screen not just unrelated plaintiffs, but also unrelated types of harm and extent of harm. Indeed, the duty concept in its relational screening role is usually identified with the screening of unrelated plaintiffs and not with the screening of unrelated types of harm and extent of harm. Still, such screening does take place. For example, in cases where a defendant's liability for negligent misstatement is based on his or her 'assumption of responsibility' or 'invitation to rely',[87] and a particular extent of harm is excluded from the scope of the assumed responsibility or the invitation, liability for the excluded extent would usually be denied on grounds of no duty rather than on grounds of lack of legal causation.[88]

As to liability-watch screening, the view that legal causation specialises in the causal chain of events that links harm with conduct leads to the conclusion that legal causation is in principle irrelevant for liability-watch screening. It is irrelevant because undesirable liability is usually screened through the other aspects of the risk and only rarely through the screening of the causal chain of events.[89] In our example, then, liability-watch screening lies in the domain of liability-watch duty.[90] Obviously, the duty

---

[86] For the screening aspects of *Palsgraf* see above nn 8 and 13. In *Wagon Mound (No 1)*, oil discharged into the water by the defendants was ignited by an unforeseeable chain of events that led to an unforeseeable *type* of harm, namely the burning of the plaintiff's dock, rather than to its pollution: above n 49.

[87] See the draft of the *Third Restatement on Economic Loss and Related Torts*, above n 4, at §9(2).

[88] For 'assumption of responsibility' as a duty-related concept see WVH Rogers, *Winfield & Jolowicz on Tort*, 9th edn (London, Sweet & Maxwell, 2002) 145-47; S Deakin, A Johnston and B Markesinis, *Tort Law*, 5th edn (Oxford, Clarendon Press, 2003) 115-24.

[89] See C Radé and L Bloch, who comment, for France, that 'the doctrine of causation appears to be an arbitrary means by which to make reparations determinations....it is difficult rationally to explain why one kind of loss is considered too remote but that another can be compensated': 'Compensation for Pure Economic Loss Under French Law' in WH van Boom, H Koziol and CA Witting (eds), *Pure Economic Loss* (Wien, Springer, 2004) 45.

[90] That legal causation has often been used by common law courts for liability-watch screening of extent, types of harm and even types of plaintiffs can be attributed to the absence of a clear distinction between relational screening, where legal causation does play a major role, and liability-watch screening.

concept is well equipped to function as a general liability-watch screening device. As it operates through all the aspects of risk, it can deny liability for types of plaintiffs, types of harm and their extent,[91] types of activities and actors and, most importantly, with regard to any combination of these aspects. These combinations provide the fine tuning that the gradually expanding liability needs.

The above illustration shows how the combined effect of the distinction between relational screening and liability-watch screening, the distinction between the different aspects of risk, and the sharpening and the tightening of the traditional screening concepts in accordance with these distinctions can remove at least some of the confusion that surrounds harm screening, thereby providing an adequate alternative to the *Third Restatement on Physical Harm*'s screening 'revolution'.

E.   Three Observations

The preceding discussion leads to three interesting observations. The first is that not just the duty concept, but also its components, may have two different meanings. Indeed, it appears that the notion of 'proximity' does have two such different meanings: relational proximity and liability-watch proximity. The lack of relational proximity usually means that the plaintiff is an out-of-risk plaintiff (unforeseeable or undeserving). By contrast, the lack of liability-watch proximity means that the plaintiff, although being within-the-risk (foreseeable and deserving), does not belong to a sufficiently limited class of persons so that liability to him or her is denied in order to avoid concerns like over-deterrence or increased litigation.[92]

---

[91] I fail to see why the reporters of the *Third Restatement on Physical Harm* find it awkward to state that an actor has no duty to avoid causing a type of harm: above n 2, comment (f) to §29, at 588.

[92] The victims of crime are often foreseeable and deserving, and their injuries can be clearly related to the fault of the police in failing to apprehend criminals. These harms would not, therefore, be excluded by relational proximity. Still, they may be excluded by liability-watch proximity where the class of potential victims is too large. In *Home Office v Dorset Yacht Co Ltd* [1970] AC 1004 (HL) proximity was recognised where the class of potential victims was limited by geographical proximity. It was denied, by contrast, in *Hill v Chief Constable* [1989] AC 53 (HL), where the class of potential victims was too large. This distinction between the two meanings of proximity solves the problem raised by Lord Goff regarding the meaning of proximity when it is no longer treated as a relationship based on foreseeability: see *Leigh & Sillivan v Aliakmon Shipping Co* [1985] QB 350 (CA), 395. Another example of the different meanings of proximity has been recently provided by the Supreme Court of Canada in *Childs v Desormeaux* 2006 SCC 18 [*Childs*]. It held that social hosts of parties where alcohol was consumed did not owe a duty of care to public users of highways injured by a drunken guest because the proximity necessary to meet the first stage of the *Anns* test (from *Anns v Merton London Borough Council* [1978] AC 728 (HL)) had not been established. Why not? One reason was that the injury was not reasonably foreseeable on the established facts. This refers to lack of proximity in its relational screening

The second observation is that the concept of 'legal causation' as a relational screening device may be preserved. The call to 'unpack' causation so that the term refers only to factual causation[93] stems from the view that the concept of 'legal cause' is misleading and indeterminate.[94] Under the above illustration of the 'division of labour', however, the term applies not to all of the aspects of risk but rather specialises in the causal chain of events that links negligent conduct with ensuing harms, which is the subject matter of factual causation as well. With this common subject matter, factual causation and legal causation have rightly been perceived as different aspects of the same issue and their coexistence within the causation package is justified.

The third observation is that the screening of the *extent* aspect deserves a distinct device of harm screening. This screening, as we have seen, is unique in many respects:[95] the distinction between the magnitude of primary harms and evolving secondary harms, exceptions to risk-related screening that allow liability for an unforeseeable extent (such as the 'thin skull' exception and the criticised 'blanket exception'), and denial of liability for foreseeable secondary harms when the chain of causation is too long. This uniqueness originates in special considerations that apply to the extent aspect and to the allocation of its risks. All of this requires special awareness and special treatment, but these can hardly be achieved by the general concepts of duty and legal causation which have to deal with the

---

role. The victim was an out-of-risk victim. Another reason was that even if foreseeability were established, proximity was nevertheless absent because a host is entitled to respect the autonomy of a guest and should not be made to bear the costs of the guest's personal choice unless the host's conduct implicates him or her in the creation or exacerbation of the risk. This clearly refers to lack of proximity in its liability-watch screening role. Notably, the no-liability determination in this case can also be explained not on no-duty grounds but rather on the ground that the hosts' conduct was reasonable in the circumstances: see below n 97.

Notably, it is questionable whether the judicial distinction between proximity and the other element of the duty concept, either under *Anns* or the test in *Caparo Industries plc v Dickman* [1990] 2 AC 605 (HL) [*Caparo*] is a useful one. Lord Oliver noted that these are 'merely facets of the same thing' (*Caparo*, 633) and Nicholls VC observed that the different elements of duty under *Caparo*–proximity and the 'fair, just and reasonable' element–'are no more than two labels under which the court examines the pros and cons of imposing liability in negligence': *White v Jones* [1995] 2 AC 207 (CA) 221, aff'd [1995] 2 AC 207 (HL). See also Fleming, above n 3, at 153, who remarked that proximity is 'a convenient screen for not disclosing any specific reasons behind a decision for or against a finding of duty' and Stevenson J of the Supreme Court of Canada who noted that 'proximity expresses a conclusion, a judgment, a result, rather than a principle... The concept of proximity is incapable of providing a principled basis for drawing the line on the issue of liability': *Canadian National Railway Co v Norsk Pacific Steamship Co* [1992] 1 SCR 1021, 1178.

[93]   In a series of articles, Jane Stapleton has called for the 'unpacking of causation'. In her view, causation should mean only factual causation, while the question of legal causation should be relegated to the general question of 'the scope of liability for consequences': above n 84, at 957-69.

[94]   Above n 84, at 978.

[95]   See above part III.C.

other aspects of the risk. Such a special treatment can be found in Israeli law, where a statutory provision has been construed by the courts as specialising in the screening of the extent aspect.[96] This provision accommodates the 'thin skull' exception and other doctrines that cope with the uniqueness of the extent aspect, including the 'mitigation of loss' rule.

VI.   A SHORT SUMMARY

The following summarises the major points made in the above discussion:

- Liability for harms caused in fact by negligent conduct is monitored by two different kinds of harm screening: relational screening, which screens harms on the ground that they are not sufficiently related to the negligent conduct, and liability-watch screening, which screens related harms on the ground that liability for such harms is undesirable.

- At the core of relational screening lies the concept of risk-related screening (the risk standard) which screens harms that do not result from tortious risks (out-of-risk harms). Despite an alleged 'description problem' caused by the different levels of risk description, there are meaningful and defensible ways to describe risks.

- The classification of risks into tortious and non-tortious risks, however, raises a 'harms/benefits correlation problem' whenever specific harms that particular conduct generates cannot be associated with specific benefits in order to form a distinctive and classifiable risk. This problem, which complicates the classification of risks, can be solved on a contextual basis.

- Risk-related screening of foreseeable and unforeseeable harms is justified, as a rule, on grounds of fairness and deterrence. It is supported by the need to offset the benefits of faulty conduct against its harms and to internalise benefits that the actor externalises.

- Exceptions to the rule of risk-related screening, which allow liability for unforeseeable harms, are justified when such harms, although out-of risk, are sufficiently related to the negligent conduct because of deserving plaintiffs, undeserving defendants, or considerations of fair allocation of harms.

- The notion of 'risk' has different aspects: actors and activities, causal chains of events, persons harmed, types of harms, and extent of harms. The distinction between these aspects, and their interrelationships provide useful tools and important insights regarding the description

---

[96] Civil Wrong Ordinance, s 76(1).

of risks and their classification, the scope and nature of the exceptions to risk-related screening, and their justifications.

- Liability-watch screening tends to become more complex and more contextual with the gradual expansion of liability and the decrease in the scope of this policy-based screening. The distinction between the different aspects of risks adds to the flexibility and the sophistication that liability-watch screening requires.

- The confusion that envelops the operation of the major screening devices—duty and legal causation—can be cleared up, at least to some extent, by two steps. The first step is to recognise that each of these major screening devices has a relational screening role and a liability-watch screening role, and accordingly two different meanings. The second step is to achieve a better and a clearer 'division of labour' between the four screening devices by sharpening and tightening their respective roles with the help of the distinction between the different aspects of risks. Identifying legal causation with the screening of the causal chain of events and not with the other aspects of risk is an example of a confusion-clearing 'division of labour', which is an alternative, and possibly a preferable one, to the *Third Restatement on Physical Harm*'s 'revolutionary' attempt to replace legal causation and relational duty with the risk standard.

- Given its unique features, the 'extent of harm' aspect of risk deserves a specialising screening device that should distinguish between primary harms and secondary harms.

VII. TWO CONCLUDING NOTES: UNFORESEEABILITY AND CORRECTIVE JUSTICE

The above analysis highlights the different effects and aspects of the unforeseeability of harm. Unforseeability of harm may lead to a result of no liability on two different grounds: that the conduct is not faulty ex ante, or that while the conduct is faulty the harm ex post is not related to it. It is therefore important that courts specify the ground for denying liability in order to send a clear message as to whether the conduct is faulty or not, unless for some reason they prefer to avoid such a clear message.[97] In contrast, the unforeseeability of harm would in principal play no role in

---

[97] One gets the impression that this was indeed the case in *Childs*, above n 92. Finding that the harm to the person injured by the driving of the drunken guest was unforeseeable, the court could have avoided the duty and the proximity analysis by stating that hosts acted reasonably when they did not prevent the guest from driving. Yet the court preferred to deny liability on the ground of unforeseeability by the finding of no duty (no proximity) rather than by the finding of reasonable conduct.

liability-watch screening, which usually applies to foreseeable harms that have already passed relational screening.[98]

Finally, the above analysis does not support Ernest Weinrib's argument that the concepts of 'duty' and 'legal causation' substantiate his 'corrective justice claim', namely that in the correcting of the injustice caused by the doer to the sufferer through the interaction between them, considerations that are 'external' to this bilateral interaction, such as efficiency and distributive justice, should be excluded.[99] Although 'duty' and 'legal causation', as relational screening devices, do create a strong linkage between the tortious risks created by the doer and the harms incurred by the sufferer, they are actually indifferent to the reasons and considerations that render the ex ante creation of risks tortious. If a given conduct or risk is characterised ex ante as tortious because it is inefficient or unjust in the distributive sense, relational screening, being an ex post adjustment mechanism, would screen harms that are efficient or just in distributive terms.[100] Relational screening per se does not exclude any normative considerations for being 'external' to the doer/sufferer relationship. As to liability-watch screening through the duty concept, Weinrib concedes that considerations of efficiency and public policy do play a major role in this kind of screening. He laments that this has led to the 'disintegration of the duty concept'.[101] However, we have seen that this 'disintegration' is actually an inevitable and desirable development of the duty concept that has become more complex, refined and contextual as it copes with the challenges of monitoring expanding liability.[102]

---

[98] The proposed *Third Restatement on Physical Harm*, which recognises only liability-watch duty and not relational duty, states accordingly that 'Despite frequent use of foreseeability in no-duty determinations, this Restatement disapproves that practice': above n 2, at 98.

[99] EJ Weinrib, *The Idea of Private Law* (Cambridge, Mass, Harvard University Press, 1995) 145-70.

[100] See above part II.A.

[101] EJ Weinrib, 'The Disintegration of Duty' in MS Madden (ed), *Exploring Tort Law* (Cambridge, Cambridge University Press, 2006) 143.

[102] See above part IV.

11

Acts and Omissions as Positive and Negative Causes

RICHARD W WRIGHT[*]

I. INTRODUCTION

INDIVIDUAL MORAL OR legal responsibility for an actual or potential state of affairs does not exist unless one's conduct (possibly) was a cause of that state of affairs.[1] Conduct includes omissions as well as acts. In this chapter, the terms 'act', 'omission', and 'cause' are used in their core factual senses, unburdened by the normative factors that are often loaded onto or confused with them. An act is simply a volitional physical movement or exertion of a part of one's body, while an omission is a volitional *failure* to move or exert a part of one's body in a specific way.[2] A

---

[*] Professor of Law, Chicago-Kent College of Law, Illinois Institute of Technology. Permission is hereby granted to copy for noncommercial purposes as long as appropriate citation is made to this publication.

[1] I focus here on interactive justice rather than distributive justice. See Richard W Wright, 'The Grounds and Extent of Legal Responsibility' (2003) 40 *University of San Diego Law Review* 1425, 1429-34; Richard W Wright, 'The Principles of Justice' (2000) 75 *Notre Dame Law Review* 1859, 1883-92.

[2] An omission or 'negative act' rarely involves a complete lack of motion or exertion, contrary to what was literally stated but probably not intended by Jeremy Bentham:

> [Acts] may be distinguished . . . into *positive* and *negative*. By positive are meant such as consist in motion or exertion: by negative, such as consist in keeping at rest; that is, in forbearing to move or exert oneself in such and such circumstances. Thus to strike is a positive act: not to strike on a certain occasion, a negative one. Positive acts are styled also acts of commission, negative, acts of omission or forbearance.

Jeremy Bentham, *An Introduction to the Principles of Morals and Legislation* (1823) (New York, Hafner Press, 1948) ch VII s VIII, 72. Bentham assumed that acts and omissions are volitional, but he was not concerned with providing a precise account of the nature of the required volition. *Ibid*, at 72 fn 1. For the purpose of this chapter, I also do not need a precise account, but I think it is helpful to note, as suggested by my colleague, Richard Warner, that the movements or exertions (or lack thereof) need not be *consciously* controlled by one's will. For example, moving one's arms or standing completely still while lecturing is conduct, regardless of whether one is consciously aware of one's doing so, but movements or failures to move are not conduct if they are the result of a pure muscular reflex or the application of external force or if they occur while one is unconscious or soundly asleep. The volition

cause is a condition that contributed, from a purely factual, scientific standpoint, to some result.[3]

Omissions raise difficulties for both theoretical and 'commonsense' accounts of causation. Although from a commonsense, intuitive perspective, lawyers and lay persons often identify omissions—such as the failure to water a plant or to pay attention when driving—as causes of losses or harms, some philosophers have trouble with the idea that an omission—the absence of something—can cause anything. As John Stuart Mill stated, 'From nothing, from a mere negation, no consequences can proceed'.[4]

Conversely, from a commonsense, intuitive perspective, lawyers and lay persons often fail to identify omissions as causes in situations in which, from a theoretical or more carefully considered practical perspective, they are seen to be causes. For example, legal texts and cases routinely treat the failure to build a dam to a sufficient height or to properly maintain its spillways to prevent flooding during ordinary storms as not being a cause of the dam's overflow during an extraordinary storm that would have produced the overflow even if the dam were built to a proper height and its spillways were properly maintained.[5] As I have previously explained, these dam overflow cases are instances of causal overdetermination, which present philosophical and analytical difficulties even when acts rather than omissions are the source of the causal overdetermination.[6]

The greatest difficulties seem to exist when multiple omissions overdetermine a causal process. An often cited example is the *Saunders* case, in

---

requirement applies only to the alleged act or omission itself, not to its consequences. My activating my muscles to take a step is volitional, even if I am unaware and have no reason to foresee that my doing so will set off a hidden trigger for an explosive. On the other hand, my being pushed by someone else onto the trigger or falling onto it due to an epileptic seizure does not involve any act or omission by me and, thus, does not constitute conduct on my part.

[3] Considerable confusion exists due to the use of causal language to refer to not merely the issue of factual causation but also the issue of normative responsibility. See Richard W Wright, 'Causation, Responsibility, Risk, Probability, Naked Statistics, and Proof: Pruning the Bramble Bush by Clarifying the Concepts' (1988) 73 *Iowa Law Review* 1001, 1004-14. Additional confusion results from the use of the word 'cause' to refer to conditions that *would* have been but were not actually causes since their potential causal efficacy was preempted by the actual cause. This is the case with Hart and Honoré's 'additional cause' and 'alternative cause' categories and David Fischer's 'multiple sufficient cause', 'successive cause', and 'dependently sufficient cause' idioms. See HLA Hart and Tony Honoré, *Causation in the Law*, 2nd edn (Oxford, Oxford University Press, 1985) 235–53; David A Fischer, 'Causation in Fact in Omission Cases' (1992) *Utah Law Review* 1335, 1337 fn 5, 1349-50; David A Fischer, 'Successive Causes and the Enigma of Duplicated Harm' (1999) 66 *Tennessee Law Review* 1127, 1127-30; David A Fischer, 'Insufficient Causes' (2006) 94 *University of Kentucky Law Review* 277, 279, 281.

[4] John Stuart Mill, *A System of Logic: Ratiocinative and Inductive*, 8th edn (London, Longmans, Green & Co, 1872) bk III ch V s 3.

[5] Eg, *Restatement (Second) of Torts* (1965) § 432, comment b and illustration 2 [*Restatement Second*].

[6] Richard W Wright, 'Causation in Tort Law' (1985) 73 *California Law Review* 1735, 1799-1800; Wright, Legal Responsibility, above n 1, at 1437-40; see pt III below.

which a collision occurred when a motorist driving a rental car allegedly did not attempt to brake until it was too late to avoid the collision, but the brakes allegedly were defective due to a lack of proper inspection and maintenance by the rental car company and therefore would not have stopped the car in time even if the driver had applied them earlier.[7] In this and other cases involving a failure to attempt to use (in a timely, proper manner) a missing or inadequate safeguard (a safety device or warning), courts routinely hold that the fact that the safeguard was missing or inadequate was not a cause of the unavoided injury—unless there was no attempt to use the safeguard because it was known that the safeguard did not exist or was inadequate, in which case the failure to provide an adequate safeguard was a necessary condition for, and hence clearly a cause of, the injury.[8] In those cases in which the courts discuss the causal status of the failure to attempt to use the safeguard, they hold that it was a cause of the injury.[9] At least one of the omissions must have been a cause, since, considered together, they were a necessary condition for the occurrence of the injury. However, intuitive evaluations of causation in these types of situations reportedly are mixed,[10] and their proper theoretical resolution is controversial. Indeed, some have argued that it is impossible to resolve the causal issue in these cases, or any overdetermined-causation case, through a purely factual, non-normative account of causation, and that this impossibility undermines the very idea of such an account.[11]

I have argued that there is a purely factual, non-normative concept of causation that underlies and is embodied in the NESS (necessary element of a sufficient set) test for singular instances of causation, which—given sufficient information about the particular factual situation and the possibly applicable causal laws—can be used to resolve any causal issue,

---

[7] *Saunders System Birmingham Co v Adams* 117 So 72 (Ala 1928) [*Saunders*].

[8] Eg, *Saunders*, above n 7; *Rouleau v Blotner* 152 A 916 (NH 1931) (alleged failure of driver to signal prior to left turn, but driver of oncoming car was not looking forward); *Weeks v McNulty* 48 SW 809 (Tenn 1898) (failure to provide fire escape, which hotel guest did not check for or attempt to use); *Safeco Insurance Co v Baker* 515 So 2d 655 (La App 3d Cir 1987) (inadequate instructions, which however were not read); *McWilliams v Sir William Arrol & Co* [1962] 1 All ER 623 (HL) (failure to supply safety belt, which would not have been used if it had been supplied).

[9] Fischer, Omission Cases, above n 3, at 1354.

[10] Fischer, Insufficient Causes, above n 3, at 314-17.

[11] Eg, Fischer, Omission Cases, above n 3, at 1335, 1344-60; Fischer, Insufficient Causes, above n 3, at 288-89; Jane Stapleton, 'Perspectives on Causation' in Jeremy Horder (ed), *Oxford Essays in Jurisprudence, Fourth Series* (Oxford, Oxford University Press, 2000) 61-66, 77, 79-80, 81-84; Jane Stapleton, 'Legal Cause: Cause-in-Fact and the Scope of Liability for Consequences' (2001) 54 *Vanderbilt Law Review* 941, 957 fn 38, 966-67, fns 60-61.

including the most difficult multiple omission cases.[12] In this chapter I
retrace and elaborate that argument, emphasising the importance of
understanding the sense of sufficiency in the NESS test and the differences
between positive causation and negative causation while building toward a
discussion of overdetermination by multiple negative conditions.

II.   POSITIVE AND NEGATIVE CAUSATION

How can an omission—an absence of something—cause anything? Mill
himself provides the answer, wrapped around his seemingly contrary
statement that '[f]rom nothing, from a mere negation, no consequences can
proceed':

> [A sentry's] being off his post was no producing cause [of the army's being
> surprised by the enemy], but the mere absence of a preventing cause: it was
> simply equivalent to his non-existence. From nothing, from a mere negation, no
> consequences can proceed. All effects are connected, by the law of causation,
> with some set of *positive* conditions; negative ones, it is true, being almost
> always required in addition. In other words, every fact or phenomenon which
> has a beginning invariably arises when some certain combination of positive
> facts exists, provided certain other positive facts do not exist . . ..
> The cause, then, philosophically speaking, is the sum total of the conditions
> positive and negative taken together; the whole of the contingencies of every
> description, which being realised, the consequent invariably follows. The nega-
> tive conditions, however, of any phenomenon, a special enumeration of which
> would generally be very prolix, may be all summed up under one head, namely,
> the absence of preventing or countervailing causes.[13]

Several different causal processes are at issue in Mill's example. The army's
being surprised will occur through a causal process that includes the
enemy's stealthy approach unless, through a different causal process, some
preventing cause intervenes. A preventing cause prevents the successful
completion of the prevented causal process by eliminating one or more of
its necessary positive conditions. One possible preventing cause of the
enemy's attempted surprise of the army is the army's being forewarned by
its sentry. Going one level deeper in the causal analysis, the question is why
this forewarning did not occur. It failed due to the absence of the sentry,
since the sentry's presence is a necessary positive condition for the
successful completion of the forewarning causal process. The sentry's
absence prevented the forewarning causal process from occurring, and

---

[12] See Wright, above n 6, at 1788-813; Wright, above n 3, at 1018-42; Richard W Wright,
'Once More Into the Bramble Bush: Duty, Causal Contribution, and the Extent of Legal
Responsibility' (2001) 54 *Vanderbilt Law Review* 1071, 1101-9, 1123-31; Wright, Legal
Responsibility, above n 1, at 1440-50.

[13] Above n 4, at bk III ch V s 3.

thus, along with the absence of other possible preventing causes, ensured the successful completion of the surprise causal process. A condition (eg, the sentry's absence) that causes the failure of a possible preventing cause (forewarning by the sentry), by negating a necessary positive condition for the occurrence of the preventing cause, is a *negative cause* of the consequence of the unprevented causal process (the army's being surprised by the enemy).

As Mill notes, for any particular causal process there is a multitude of possible preventing causes that will prevent the successful completion of the causal process by preventing the existence of one of its necessary positive conditions. Mill's omnibus negative condition—the absence of any preventing cause—encompasses all the many different possibilities. If the necessary positive conditions for the causal process were fully specified in complete detail, there would be no need to specify the absence of any preventing cause, since the satisfaction of all the necessary positive conditions would be inconsistent with the existence of any preventing cause. However, since such a complete, detailed listing of all the necessary positive conditions is rarely if ever possible in practice, Mill's omnibus negative condition fills the descriptive void, while also emphasising the importance of always considering the possible existence of preventing causes. Moreover, in many situations—for example, the death of a plant or animal due to a lack of food or water—an attempt to describe the cause by listing all the necessary positive conditions without mentioning the critical negative condition would, at the least, be unilluminating.

Omissions generally operate as negative causes of some consequence, by precluding the occurrence of a possible preventing cause. However, omissions can and often do operate as positive causes, when a sentient being's observation of an omission affects that being's conduct. For example, a military officer's noticing a private's failure to salute may cause the officer to reprimand or otherwise discipline the private, an umpire's noticing a ballplayer's failure to touch a base will cause the umpire to call the player out, and a mother's noticing a child's failure to brush her teeth may cause the mother to instruct the child to do so.

In the analysis of causation, it is the distinction between positive causation and negative causation that is significant, rather than the distinction between acts and omissions. The philosophical and analytical difficulties posed by omissions as negative causes are posed also by acts when those acts similarly give rise to negative causation—the failure of some preventing or counteracting cause. For example, the act of removing a safety device or damaging it so that it no longer works results in a situation identical to that which exists if there had been no safety device in the first place. The act of removing the top X feet from a dam or filling its spillways with debris results in a situation identical to that which exists if the dam initially lacks those X feet of extra height or if its spillways fill with debris due to a lack of proper maintenance. The act of taking away a child's food results in a situation identical to not supplying food in the first place or to the child's failure to eat supplied food.

III.   OVERDETERMINED POSITIVE CAUSATION

It is commonly recognised that the usual legal test for causation—the necessary condition ('but for' or *sine qua non*) test—fails to reach the proper result in situations involving causal overdetermination—that is, when there is (or may be) more than one condition that would have been sufficient (in conjunction with other existing conditions) for the occurrence of the consequence on the particular occasion. A frequently mentioned situation involves two fires, each of which was sufficient by itself to destroy some property, which merge and destroy the property. Since neither fire—nor any possible alternative condition—was necessary given the existence of the other fire, the necessary condition test would result in the clearly erroneous conclusion that neither fire was a cause of the destruction of the property, which rather somehow mysteriously occurred without any cause.

To reach the correct result in situations involving causal overdetermination, some test other than the necessary-condition test must be used.[14] In these situations the courts usually state that a condition was a cause if it was a 'substantial factor', made a 'material contribution', or simply 'contributed'.[15] The words 'factor' and 'contribute' in each of these formulations merely restate the causal question without providing any test for resolving it. In the absence of any workable test, the unqualified contribution question—best posed as 'did it contribute, in even the most minimal way'—is an improvement on asking whether the condition was 'a cause' or 'the cause', since these latter formulations, especially the last,

---

[14]   An aggregate necessary-condition test would treat the two fires as a group as a cause, but it is over-inclusive. It would designate both fires as a cause even if one arrived first and preempted the other, and it would recognise causally irrelevant conditions as causes by including them with the two fires in the group being tested. A modified necessary-condition test, which asks whether the condition at issue was necessary for the occurrence of the consequence *at the time that it occurred*, would not be over-inclusive and would correctly identify more causes than the usual necessary-condition test. However, in many situations (including our two-fires case), it might be difficult to determine whether the condition at issue had any effect on the timing of the consequence, and the condition might still be a cause even if it had no effect on the timing. See Wright, Once More, above n 12, at 1114.

[15]   Eg, *March v E & MH Stramare Pty Ltd* (1991) 99 ALR 423 (HCA) (material contribution); *Athey v Leonati* [1996] 3 SCR 458 (materially contributed); *Sew Hoy & Sons Ltd v Coopers & Lybrand* (1996) 1 NZLR 392 (CA) (material contribution); *Fairchild v Glenhaven Funeral Services Ltd* (2002) [2003] 1 AC 32 (HL) (material contribution); *Kingston v Chicago & Northwestern Ry Co* 211 NW 913 (Wis 1927) (substantial factor); *Mitchell v Gonzales* 819 P 2d 872 (Cal 1991) (substantial factor).

commonly lead people to focus on only one of many contributing conditions—the most important one given their particular purpose or perspective—and thus import normative considerations into what should be a purely factual analysis. The 'substantial factor' and 'material contribution' formulations explicitly bring (unelaborated and unspecified) quantitative, qualitative, and normative considerations into the causal analysis, by requiring not merely a causal contribution but also that the contribution be 'substantial' or 'material'. They thereby confound the factual issue of causal contribution with the normative issue of the extent of legal responsibility for tortiously caused consequences—a nonfactual policy issue that should be clearly recognised and analysed as such, rather than as an issue regarding factual causation.[16]

What test do people implicitly employ to reach the correct conclusion regarding causation in the situation involving two independently sufficient fires that merge and destroy the property? The answer is stated in the question: a test of sufficiency rather than necessity. Not sufficiency in the strict sense of the condition's being sufficient by itself (it is doubtful that this is ever true), nor sufficiency in the trivial weak sense of merely being part of a set of conditions that is sufficient (this would treat anything as a cause, no matter how irrelevant it was to the sufficiency of the set), but rather sufficiency in the strong sense of being part of the complete instantiation of a set of conditions the specification of which includes only those conditions that are necessary for the sufficiency of the set.[17] In causal analysis, the relevant set is the antecedent ('if' part) of a causal law. A causal law is a statement that describes an empirically derived relation between a set of conditions (called the antecedent) and a condition (called the consequent) such that the complete instantiation of all the conditions in the antecedent on a particular occasion is sufficient for the instantiation of the consequent, the instantiation of which occurs subsequent to (or perhaps simultaneously with) the instantiation of all the conditions in the antecedent.[18] Thus, a condition was a cause of some consequence if and

---

[16] Wright, above n 6, at 1742-50, 1781-84; Wright, above n 3, at 1012-14; Wright, Once More, above n 12, at 1073-80. This is true even if 'material' and 'substantial' are interpreted in a purely quantitative manner. Preclusion of liability is inappropriate when the contributing condition, although *de minimis*, was a necessary or independently sufficient condition, or when all the other contributing conditions also were *de minimis*. See *Restatement (Third) of Torts: Liability for Physical Harm (Proposed Final Draft No 1)* (2005) § 36 and comments a & b [*Draft Restatement Third*]; Wright, Legal Responsibility, above n 1, at 1449-50, fn 84.

[17] Wright, above n 3, at 1020-21.

[18] Causal laws have a direction or order of succession. The conditions specified in the antecedent of the causal law, when fully instantiated, are a cause of the occurrence of the condition specified in the consequent, but not vice versa. This directionality is incorporated in the proper sense of sufficiency: (being part of) the complete instantiation of the antecedent of the relevant causal law. It precludes supposed problems such as being able to treat the length of a shadow 'cast' by a flagpole as the cause of the flagpole's height, on the ground that knowing the length of the shadow and the angle of the sun is sufficient to calculate the height

only if it was part of the complete instantiation of the antecedent of a causal law that specifies, as Mill stated, 'the sum total of the conditions positive and negative taken together; the whole of the contingencies of every description, which being realised, the consequent invariably follows'.[19]

Our knowledge of 'the sum total of the conditions' in the antecedent of the causal law is based on experience and empirical investigation. To determine whether a condition really is part of a causal law—whether it is necessary for the sufficiency of the set of antecedent conditions in the causal law—scientists employ Mill's Difference Method in carefully designed experiments to see if removing the condition makes a difference in the occurrence of the consequent.[20] Our knowledge of causal laws often is incomplete, and even when it is complete we rarely refer to completely specified causal laws. We rather employ causal generalisations, which are incompletely specified causal laws that have only as much specificity as is possible and needed to resolve the causal issue in the particular situation. For example, we usually refer to the causal generalisation that specifies that bringing a flame into contact with combustible material causes that material to burn, without referring to other necessary antecedent conditions such as the presence of oxygen or the absence of a soaking rain—unless the latter expected conditions did not exist in the particular situation or, conversely, existed but were not expected.

This conception of causation underlies the NESS (necessary element of a sufficient set) test for singular instances of causation that was first articulated by Herbert Hart and Tony Honoré,[21] which I have refined, extended, and defended in several articles. Under the NESS test, a condition contributed to some consequence if and only if it was necessary for the sufficiency of a set of existing antecedent conditions that was

---

of the flagpole. See Richard Fumerton and Ken Kress, 'Causation and the Law: Preemption, Lawful Sufficiency, and Causal Sufficiency' (2001) 64(4) *Law & Contemporary Problems* 83, 93 (discussing this common example). The length of the shadow is the consequent of the relevant empirically derived causal law, rather than being part of the antecedent.

[19] Above n 4, text at n 13.

[20] *Ibid*, at bk III ch V s 3, ch VIII ss 1-4, ch X ss 1-3. It is often stated that, to be a cause, a condition must 'make a difference'. Eg Hart and Honoré, above n 3, at 29, 34-35. This is true, but two possible implications must be avoided, as Hart and Honoré generally recognise. *Ibid*, at 29, 112-13, 122-25; but see n 27 below. The first erroneous implication is that the caused situation must be different than the preexisting situation. In many cases, a condition causes the continuation of, rather than a change in, the preexisting situation—for example, the preservation of plant or animal life by the intake of food or water. In these (and all other) situations, the cause 'makes a difference' in relation to what would otherwise subsequently occur in its absence. The second erroneous implication is that the difference would not have occurred in the absence of the condition at issue. As is discussed in the text above, this is not true in situations involving causal overdetermination, in which the causal condition does not 'make a difference' by itself, but rather, as part of a group of causally relevant conditions.

[21] HLA Hart and AM Honoré, *Causation in the Law* (Oxford, Oxford University Press, 1959) 105-7.

sufficient for the occurrence of the consequence. The relevant notion of sufficiency is the instantiation of each condition in the antecedent of the relevant causal law.[22]

The necessary-condition ('but-for') test and the independently-sufficient-condition test, which usually are treated as distinct, alternative tests of causation,[23] are each simply corollaries of the NESS test. Rather than being the exclusive test of causation, as some have argued or assumed, the necessary-condition test works only as an inclusive test of causation, in situations in which (as is usually true) there was only one set of antecedent conditions that was or would have been sufficient for the occurrence of the consequence on the particular occasion, or, if there was more than one such set, the condition was necessary for the sufficiency of each of the sets. In such situations, the NESS test reduces down to the necessary-condition test. The independently-sufficient-condition test is similarly an inclusive rather than exclusive test, which works if the relevant necessary condition (eg, fire of a certain magnitude) in the fully instantiated antecedent of the relevant causal law is fully instantiated by the conduct or event at issue (eg, an actual fire of at least that magnitude). Implicit in the independently-sufficient-condition test is the requirement that the condition at issue be necessary for the sufficiency of the set of antecedent conditions. Without this requirement, totally irrelevant conditions could be treated as independently sufficient conditions merely by adding them to an already sufficient set of existing antecedent conditions.

The NESS test subsumes but is more inclusive than the necessary-condition test, the independently-sufficient condition test, or the combination of these two tests. For example, if fire of X magnitude is required to destroy a house, or water of X magnitude is required to overflow or burst a dam, or X drops of poison are required to kill a person, and each of three or more persons supplies one-half X of fire or water or poison, none of their individual contributions is either necessary or independently sufficient for the relevant injury, which, however, will occur if all the other necessary antecedent conditions in the relevant causal law have been instantiated. If we are limited to using the necessary-condition and independently-sufficient-condition tests, we must implausibly conclude that none of the individuals contributed to the relevant injury, which instead somehow mysteriously and spontaneously occurred. Under the NESS test, each individual's contribution is correctly found to be a cause, since it is necessary for the sufficiency of a set of actual antecedent conditions that includes only one of the other individuals' contributions. Alternatively,

---

[22] Wright, above n 6, at 1788-1807; Wright, above n 3, at 1018-42; Wright, *Once More*, above n 12, at 1101-31; Wright, *Legal Responsibility*, above n 1, at 1440-51.

[23] Eg, *Restatement Second*, above n 5, at § 432; *Draft Restatement Third*, above n 16, at §§ 26, 27.

each individual's contribution is necessary for the sufficiency of a set of actual antecedent conditions that is described as including contributions by others of at least one-half X, which is itself an instantiated actual condition.[24]

Contrary to what some have argued,[25] the NESS analysis in cases of causal overdetermination does not employ an unrealistic, counterfactual assumption that the existing conditions omitted from the description of the sufficient set of antecedent conditions did not actually exist. It rather ropes off the excluded actual conditions, without denying their existence, in order to determine whether the included, non-roped-off actual conditions were sufficient by themselves for the occurrence of the injury, by asking whether the included actual conditions constitute the complete instantiation of the antecedent of the relevant causal law.[26]

Similarly, the necessity aspect of the NESS test and its 'but-for' test reduction do not result, as is commonly assumed,[27] in a counterfactual analysis of hypothetical other worlds or nonexistent situations. The focus in the analysis of factual causation is (or should be) not on what might have happened if things had been different, but rather on what actually did happen and why. The necessity analysis simply involves a matching of the

---

[24] Wright, above n 6, at 1792-94; Wright, Once More, above n 12, at 1106-7; Wright, Legal Responsibility, above n 1, at 1442-45; *Draft Restatement Third*, above n 16, at § 27, comments f, g & i. Hart and Honoré do not consider this type of situation, but rather, apparently limit 'causally relevant conditions' under their version of the NESS test to necessary or independently sufficient conditions. See Hart and Honoré, above n 3, at 112-13, 123-24, 206-7, 235-53. Fischer cites cases involving unnecessary and insufficient conditions that supposedly are inconsistent with the NESS test. See Fischer, 'Insufficient Causes', above n 3, at 278-79, 286-88. However, Fischer once again confuses the causal issue with the liability issue. In the cases that he cites, the courts acknowledge causal contribution but deny liability because the contribution was not sufficiently material or perceptible or because the injury or harm would have occurred anyway as a result of nonliable conditions. See Fischer, Omission Cases, above n 3, at 1344-60; Wright, Once More, above n 12, at 1121 fn 172.

[25] Eg, Fischer, Omission Cases, above n 3, at 1359, 1362; Fischer, Insufficient Causes, above n 3, at 303, 307-8; Mark Kelman, 'The Necessary Myth of Objective Causation Judgments in Liberal Political Theory' (1987) 63 *Chicago-Kent Law Review* 579, 602-6.

[26] Wright, above n 3, at 1035-42.

[27] Eg, Tony Honoré, *Responsibility and Fault* (Oxford, Hart Publishing, 1999) 102-7; see Wright, above n 6, at 1803-7. Honoré's arguments focus on determining whether the condition at issue 'made a difference' in a but-for sense, although at one point he acknowledges that the possibility that the injury may have occurred anyway would not affect a NESS condition's causal status but may affect the injured person's claim. Honoré, above, at 104; cf Wright, Legal Responsibility, above n 1, at 1434-67 (discussing the 'no worse off' limitation on the extent of legal responsibility for tortiously caused consequences). I once assumed that the necessity aspect of the NESS test required a counterfactual analysis, in part because I assumed that the necessity analysis had to be undertaken when assessing singular instances of causation, rather than having previously been addressed during the elaboration of the relevant causal generalisation. See Wright, above n 6, at 1803-4. However, I emphasised that the 'counterfactual' analysis should proceed not by a conjectural exploration of what might have happened in the absence of the condition at issue, but rather should focus on what actually happened by fitting the existing conditions into the applicable causal generalisations. Wright, above n 6, at 1804-7.

condition at issue against the required conditions in the antecedent of the relevant causal law, to see if it actually is part of the antecedent of the fully instantiated causal law. One way to do this is to exclude or rope off the condition being tested to see if the remaining included actual conditions encompass all of the required conditions in the antecedent of the relevant causal law. The other way is simply to ask if the actual condition being tested is a required condition in the antecedent of the relevant fully instantiated causal law.[28] Note that one of these two equivalent *sufficiency* analyses must be and is undertaken, implicitly if not explicitly, whenever the but-for test is used.

Indeed, as I have previously noted,[29] the necessity aspect of the NESS test for singular instances of causation is a heuristic rather than an essential analytic element of the test. The necessity aspect has already been taken care of in the (proper) formulation of the relevant causal laws, which include in their antecedents only those conditions necessary for the sufficiency of the antecedent, as determined through experience and scientific investigation. Our judgments regarding singular instances of causation do and must rely on this acquired knowledge of causal laws, even if the acquired knowledge is tentatively induced from the single experience at issue—for example, the first time a child burns its hand in a fire or on a hot stove.[30]

Thus, the test for singular instances of causation could (and perhaps should) be stated as I initially stated it above, without any reference to necessity: a condition was a cause of some consequence if and only if it was part of the complete instantiation of the antecedent of a causal law that links the antecedent and the consequent.[31] In the hypotheticals involving three or more individuals who each supply one-half of the fire, water, or poison required as a necessary condition in the antecedent of the relevant causal law, anyone who contributes to the instantiation of that necessary condition in the antecedent is a cause of the consequent if all the other conditions in the antecedent are also instantiated. It does not matter that the relevant condition was more than minimally instantiated—that more than enough fire, water, or poison was duplicatively or redundantly supplied—unless the excess supply somehow resulted in the failure (the lack of instantiation) of some other necessary condition in the antecedent of the causal law. The necessity aspect of the NESS test for singular instances of causation is merely a heuristic to try to ensure (1) that causally irrelevant conditions (conditions that do not match a condition in the antecedent of the relevant causal law) are not treated as causes and (2) that

---

[28]   Wright, above n 3, at 1039–42.
[29]   Wright, Legal Responsibility, above n 1, at 1445 fn 67; Wright, above n 3, at 1042.
[30]   Wright, above n 3, at 1031–34.
[31]   Text at n 19.

we do not overlook preemptive causes, which prevent the antecedent of the relevant causal law from being fully instantiated.

The same analysis applies to reasons for action or inaction. Although a certain reason may not have been necessary or independently sufficient for some decision, it contributed to that decision if it was considered by the decision maker and it counted positively, rather than negatively or not at all, in favour of the decision.[32] Some theorists argue that volitional human actions, unlike physical events, are neither subject to nor explainable in terms of causal generalisations. Hart and Honoré acknowledge that generalisations apply to human action, but they deny repeatability in (what they assume to be) identical circumstances. They treat human actions as being 'induced' by provided reasons or information or 'occasioned' by provided opportunities rather than being caused, and as involving a 'causal connection' only in a metaphorical or 'near-causal' sense.[33] However, with human actions as with physical events, if *all* the relevant conditions (accumulated experience and knowledge, beliefs, goals, mood, and so forth) were the same, surely the decision or action would also be the same. To assert otherwise is to assert that human action is random or arbitrary. Human action is less regular and predictable than physical events because humans learn from prior experiences and new information, the range of relevant conditions is much broader, and the applicable causal generalisations are much more complex and less well understood.[34]

Understanding that sufficiency in causal analysis means (being part of) the complete instantiation of the antecedent of the relevant causal law is critical for distinguishing situations involving causal duplication from situations involving causal preemption. In the situation involving two fires, each sufficient to burn down a house if it reaches the house, suppose that one of the fires reaches the house and burns it down before the other fire arrives. Clearly, the first fire caused the destruction of the house; the second fire did not. Yet, empirically, the destruction of the house was guaranteed by the second fire, whether or not the first fire existed; this is why the but-for test (erroneously) fails to treat the first fire as a cause of

---

[32] Wright, above n 3, at 1037; see Fischer, Insufficient Causes, above n 3, at 286 fn 39 (citing two illustrative cases).

[33] Hart and Honoré, above n 3, at 22-23, 51-52, 55-57, 60-61; Honoré, above n 27, at 2-3, 96, 116-19.

[34] See generally Tom L Beauchamp and Alexander Rosenberg, *Hume and the Problem of Causation* (Oxford, Oxford University Press, 1981) 314-27; John Mackie, *The Cement of the Universe* (Oxford, Oxford University Press, 1974) 120-26; Michael Moore, 'Causation and the Excuses' (1985) 73 *California Law Review* 1091, 1112, 1124-27, 1132-37; Honoré, above n 27, at 117. Viewing human action as causally determined is not incompatible with free will, given the very complex and goal-directed nature of human decision-making. Conversely, the presence of a random or probabilistic element in human decision-making would not undermine the concept of causation or make it impossible to provide causal explanations of human actions. See Wright, above n 3, at 1028-31.

the destruction of the house. Some theorists sometimes assume that the guaranteed occurrence of the consequence is the sense of sufficiency employed in the NESS test or proper causal analysis.[35] If this were true, the second fire as well as the first should be treated as a cause of the destruction of the house, a second collapsed bridge further downstream as well as the first collapsed bridge should be treated as a cause of the delay of a ship travelling down a river, or a person's drinking a deadly but slow poison for which there is no antidote as well as being fatally shot immediately after drinking the poison should be treated as a cause of the person's death. But none of these conclusions would be correct. Although the relevant consequence may be guaranteed to occur, it is not guaranteed that it will occur as a result of the condition that gave rise to the guarantee; it may instead result from some other condition that preempts and frustrates the causal process associated with the condition that gave rise to the guarantee.

To be a cause, the condition at issue must be part of the complete instantiation of the antecedent of the relevant causal law (usually in its incompletely specified form as a causal generalisation). Only the first fire was part of the complete instantiation of the antecedent of the fire-destroys-house causal generalisation, which requires, among other things, that the fire reach the house while it is still standing (undestroyed). That necessary condition in the antecedent of the relevant causal law was instantiated for the first fire, but not for the second fire. Similarly, assuming that the ship went down the river as far as it could before having to stop, only the first downstream collapsed bridge was part of the complete instantiation of the river-blockage-stops-ship causal generalisation, which requires, among other things, that the ship reach the blockage and either physically run into it or be stopped by the captain when he sees the blockage. Those necessary conditions in the antecedent of the relevant causal laws were instantiated for the first collapsed bridge, but not for the second. The only way that the second collapsed bridge could be a cause of the ship's stopping is if the captain learned of it first and decided, based on that knowledge, to stop immediately rather than continuing down the river as far as the ship could go before stopping. The antecedent of the death-by-shot causal generalisation was fully instantiated, but the antecedent of the death-by-slow-acting-poison causal generalisation was not. The latter generalisation requires, among other things, that a certain amount of

---

[35] See, eg, Fischer, Insufficient Causes, above n 3, at 310; Stapleton, Perspectives, above n 11, at 83, fns 56-57, 84, fns 62-63. Even Hart and Honoré occasionally confuse these two issues. See Hart and Honoré, above n 3, at 239-40, 246-48, 250-51.

time elapse after the swallowing of the poison in order for the poison to cause death, but that necessary condition did not occur.[36]

Understanding that a condition was a cause of some consequence if and only if it was part of the complete instantiation of the antecedent of a causal law that links the antecedent and the consequent also enables one to understand the requirements for proper proof of causation and the methods that lawyers should and do employ to make persuasive arguments regarding causation in a particular situation. Lawyers argue competing causal stories, which are simply descriptions of the relevant causal generalisations. They build up a causal story by introducing particularistic evidence of the actual existence on the particular occasion of the necessary conditions in the antecedent of the relevant causal generalisation. The more complete their proof of the instantiation of all the conditions in the antecedent of the causal generalisation is, the greater is the ex post probability that their causal story is the correct one. They undermine a causal story by introducing evidence that one or more necessary conditions in the antecedent of the causal generalisation did not exist on the particular occasion. Conclusive proof of the nonexistence of even a single necessary condition reduces the ex post probability of the causal story to zero, regardless of how great its ex ante mathematical probability, based on its general frequency of occurrence, might have been.[37] As the court in *Day v Boston & Maine RR* stated:

> Quantitative [ex ante] probability, however, is only the greater chance. It is not proof, nor even probative evidence, of the proposition to be proved. That in one throw of the dice there is a quantitative probability, or greater chance, that a less number of spots than sixes will fall uppermost is no evidence whatever that in a given throw such was the actual result. Without something more, the actual result of the throw would still be utterly unknown. The slightest real [particularistic instantiation] evidence that sixes did in fact fall uppermost would outweigh all the probability otherwise.[38]

Such ex ante, frequency-based causal probabilities or, even worse, naked statistics unrelated to causal generalisations—for example, a 75% probability that my dog bit someone because I own 75% of the dogs in the

---

[36] Jane Stapleton agrees with this particular conclusion, but inconsistently argues in the similar desert-traveller hypothetical—in which A poisons the traveller's only water supply, B dumps the poisoned water out of the cask before the traveller drinks any of it, and the traveller dies of thirst in the desert—that A is a cause of the traveller's death, since the traveller was bound to die once the water was poisoned. See Stapleton, Perspectives, above n 11, at 83-84, criticised in Wright, Once More, above n 12, at 1115-18. For further discussion, see text following n 49.

[37] LJ Cohen, *The Probable and the Provable* (Oxford, Oxford University Press, 1977) 248-55.

[38] 52 A 771 (Maine 1902) 774. For a similar statement, which emphasises the need to induce a minimal belief in the proposition to be proved, see *Smith v Rapid Transit, Inc* 58 NE 2d 754 (Mass 1945).

area—cannot properly be used to establish actual causation in a particular situation. Instead, what is required is concrete, particularistic evidence of the actual instantiation of the consequent and all the necessary conditions in the antecedent of the relevant causal generalisation. Such particularistic evidence builds up, lowers, or zeroes the ex post probability that the purported causal story is true. When the ex post probability for one causal story is sufficiently great and the ex post probability for any competing causal story is sufficiently low, a belief, with varying degrees of strength depending on the weight of the evidence, is formed in the truth of the first causal story. Contrary to what is unreflectively assumed by a great many lawyers and courts, the civil standard of proof by a 'preponderance of the evidence', properly understood, does not simply require a mere 50+% 'more likely than not' 'balance of probability', even when the probabilities involved are ex post probabilities based on particularistic evidence of the instantiation of the relevant causal law. Instead, proof by a preponderance of the evidence requires (or should require) that the particularistic evidence of instantiation of the relevant causal law induce a minimal 'bare preponderance' belief in the truth of the particular causal story.[39]

My insistence on a clear understanding of the concept of causation and of what constitutes adequate proof of causation should not be confused with a position that I do not advocate: that liability should never be imposed in the absence of proof of actual causation. Although liability despite disproof of causation is, in my view, unjust and hence improper,[40] there are good reasons as a matter of justice to impose proportional or even full liability in some situations in which the defendant's wrongful conduct may have caused some or all of the plaintiff's injury, but it is impossible for the plaintiff to prove that such causation occurred. If liability is imposed in such cases, it is best conceived as liability for the actual injury based on 'second-best' causation doctrines, such as shifted burdens of proof or liability in proportion to the probability of causation, rather than (as I once argued) being liability for the imposition of risk, even if liability for the imposition of risk is limited to situations in which actual injury occurred.[41] As always, proper resolution of the normative liability issue is more likely if the uncertainty over actual causation is explicitly recognised and acknowledged.

The 'decision causation' cases discussed by Vaughan Black, in which resolution of the causal issue requires evaluation of what a person subsequently would have decided if the defendant had not behaved

---

[39] Wright, above n 3, at 1042-67.
[40] Wright, *Legal Responsibility*, above n 1, at 1430-31.
[41] See, eg, *Holtby v Brigham & Cowan (Hull) Ltd* [2000] 3 All ER 421 (CA); Wright, above n 6, at 1813-26; Wright, above n 3, at 1067-77.

tortiously,[42] often raise such policy issues. These cases, unlike the situations discussed above in which there was an actual decision and the issue is whether some prior condition contributed to that decision,[43] do require a hypothetical, counterfactual inquiry—an inquiry into what decision *would* have been made if the defendant had not behaved tortiously. Thus, while Black is correct in arguing that the causal issues in these cases are not necessarily more difficult to evaluate than the causal issues in other types of cases, which also can involve difficult, structurally embedded proof problems due to incomplete scientific knowledge about the causal processes involved, I believe he is incorrect in arguing that there is not a significant difference between decision-causation cases and other cases. The significant difference is the necessity of employing hypothetical, counterfactual analysis.

The most common decision-causation cases are those involving a defendant's tortious failure to provide a safeguard (device, information, or warning), in which, as we have noted, the courts view the dispositive causal issue as whether, if the safeguard had been provided, the person to whom the safeguard should have been provided would have decided to act (or not act) in a certain way, which would have prevented the injury that occurred. If he would have, the failure to provide the safeguard was a necessary condition for and hence a but-for (negative) cause of the injury. If he would not have, the failure to provide the safeguard was not a cause, but rather—as is discussed in part IV below—was preempted by the fact that there would have been no attempt to use the safeguard.[44] Courts reasonably could decide in these cases to shift the burden of proof on whether the safeguard would have been used to the defendant,[45] or to impose proportional liability based on the probability that the safeguard would have been used.

IV.   OVERDETERMINED NEGATIVE CAUSATION

As was discussed in part II above, a negative cause of some consequence X is a condition that contributes in a negative manner to the occurrence of X through causal process A by causing the failure of a distinct causal process B that, if it had occurred, would have prevented the occurrence of X by causing the failure of causal process A. A negative cause of X is an instantiation of a negative condition—the absence of a preventing

---

[42]   See Vaughan Black, 'Decision Causation: Pandora's Tool-Box' ch 12.
[43]   Text at nn 32-34.
[44]   Text at nn 8-9.
[45]   See Fischer, Omission Cases, above n 3, at 1355-56.

cause—in the completely instantiated antecedent of the causal generalisation for causal process A. This negative condition in causal process A is instantiated by the *failure* of causal process B, which occurs if one of more of the necessary positive conditions in causal process B was *not instantiated*.

If more than one condition in causal process B was not instantiated, the failure of causal process B to occur was overdetermined. To determine which of the non-instantiated conditions actually caused (rather than merely guaranteed) its failure,[46] we need to determine whether the multiple non-instantiated conditions had a duplicative causal effect or, instead, one or more of them preempted the potential causal effect of the others. However, we cannot do this in the same way that we determine duplication versus preemption for positive causal effects, by asking whether each of the conditions at issue was part of the complete instantiation of the antecedent of the relevant causal law. Instead, when determining which absent conditions had the negative causal effect of causing the failure or non-occurrence of a causal process rather than its successful completion, we must analyse the sequencing and possible interdependency of the necessary conditions in the antecedent of the relevant causal law for the failed causal process.[47]

Consider a situation in which there was sufficient time to brake to stop a car before it hit some object. The braking-stops-car causal process, if it occurs, is a positive preventing cause that prevents the successful completion of the moving-car-hits-object-in-path causal process. When the brake pedal is depressed and the car subsequently stops, we infer from those two facts alone, which are instantiations of the consequent and a single condition in the antecedent of the braking-stops-car causal generalisation, that all of the very many conditions in the antecedent of that generalisation and its underlying causal laws were instantiated.

If the brake pedal is not depressed, but the brake system was working properly, the failure to depress the brake, which is a necessary condition in the antecedent of the braking-stops-car causal generalisation, is a but-for cause of the non-occurrence of the braking-stops-car causal process. 'Non-occurrence' seems more appropriate than 'failure' here since the causal process was never initiated. Conversely, if the brake pedal is depressed and the car fails to slow and stop, the braking-stops-car causal

---

[46] See text at nn 35-36; text following n 49.

[47] Wright, Once More, above n 12, at 1128-31. Fischer's discussions of overdetermined negative causation fail to appreciate (1) the difference between guaranteeing a result and causing that result, (2) that the focus in negative causation is on the failure of the preventive causal process rather than on the successful complete instantiation of the unprevented causal process, and (3) that a different type of analysis (employing the same basic NESS concept of causation) is needed to determine what caused the failure rather than the success of a causal process. See Fischer, Insufficient Causes, above n 3, at 309-10.

process was initiated but was not completed; it failed. We infer that it failed as a result of something wrong with the braking system—that is, that there was at least one non-instantiated condition in the antecedent of the causal generalisation for the working of the braking system. If there was only one non-instantiated condition, its non-instantiation was a but-for cause of the failure of the braking system.

If there was more than one non-instantiated condition in the antecedent of the causal generalisation for the working of the braking system—for example, the lack of a bolt connecting the brake pedal to the lever rod between it and the master cylinder and the lack of sufficient hydraulic fluid in the master cylinder—the failure of the braking system was overdetermined. It was even more overdetermined if, as alleged in *Saunders*,[48] the driver did not attempt to use the brakes by (timely) depressing the brake pedal. Each of these non-instantiated conditions independently guarantees the non-occurrence or failure of the braking-stops-car causal process, but only the failure to attempt to use the brakes had an actual negative causal effect. The failure to attempt to use the brakes preempted the potential negative causal effect of the other non-instantiated conditions in the braking-stops-car causal process.

This conclusion is based on our knowledge of the sequence of events that must take place for the occurrence of the braking-stops-car causal process, which actually is a complex combination of a large number of more discrete causal processes, each of which is dependent for its occurrence on the occurrence of prior stages in the causal sequence. Some of the necessary events, in order of occurrence, are: (1) the driver's applying force to depress the brake pedal; (2) the depression of the brake pedal operating a lever to put pressure on the hydraulic brake fluid in the master cylinder; (3) the pressure in the brake fluid being transmitted through pipes and tubes to the brake cylinders; (4) the pressure in the brake cylinders pushing braking pads against the rotating brake drum or disc in the wheel assembly; and (5) the friction created by such contact slowing and stopping the rotation of the wheels. Each of these stages of the braking-stops-car causal process, which occur in sequence, is itself a causal process; each has its own set of necessary antecedent conditions, most related to the structure and integrity of the mechanical, hydraulic and electrical components of the various parts of the braking system.

The failure of any prior stage in the sequence of events prevents the causal process from proceeding any further in the sequence of dependent events. It thus preempts the potential negative causal effect of any non-instantiated conditions in subsequent stages, which would have caused the causal process to fail if it had proceeded that far. When the very first

---

[48] Above n 7.

event, the driver's depressing the brake pedal, does not occur, the causal process fails—actually never gets started—at that point in the causal sequence. The causal process does not get as far as stage (2), although if it had gotten that far, it would then have failed due to the missing bolt connecting the brake pedal to the lever, which would have preempted the potential negative causal effect of the insufficient brake fluid in the master cylinder, which in turn would have caused the causal process to fail at stage (3) if the causal process had proceeded that far.

A contrary conclusion is based on the erroneous idea, discussed above,[49] that a condition was a cause of some consequence merely because it guaranteed that the consequence would occur. Poisoning a person's only source of water guarantees that she will die, but not that she will die as a result of the poisoning of the water; an intervening event, such as the shooting of the person or the emptying of the water container, may occur and preempt the potential positive causal effect of death by poisoning. The collapse of a bridge on a river guarantees that a ship coming down the river will be delayed, but not that the delay will be caused by the collapse of the bridge; an intervening event, such as the ship's engine failing or the ship's running aground or encountering another collapsed bridge further upstream, may occur and preempt the potential positive causal effect of the collapse of the bridge further downstream. Similarly, a defect in the braking system, such as the missing bolt or the insufficient brake fluid, guarantees that the braking system will not work, but not that the defect will be a cause of the braking system's not working; an intervening event, the failure to attempt to use the brakes by pressing down on the brake pedal, may occur and preempt the potential negative causal effect of the defect in the braking system.

Duplicative as well as preemptive negative causation can occur. For example, if one mechanic put insufficient hydraulic brake fluid into the master cylinder for it to work and another failed to seal it properly so that whatever fluid was in it would leak out, their respective omissions, which negate required positive conditions for the occurrence of stage (3) of the braking-stops-car causal process, are duplicative negative causes of the failure of the braking system to work, due to the non-occurrence of stage (3), when the brake pedal is subsequently depressed. Hart and Honoré describe two similar situations:

> [S]uppose that two switches need to be turned off in order to avert a fire, and that X has a duty to turn off one, Y the other [but] neither does so and a fire which would have been averted had they both performed their duty breaks out . . . .. Suppose, again, that a house can be built and profitably sold only if X delivers bricks and Y mortar [but] both default in delivery so that the projected

---

[49] Text at nn 35-36.

house cannot be built and sold . . ... [L]awyers and ordinary people would agree in saying, in these cases of concurrent failure to intervene in a physical process or to provide opportunities for gain, that the omission of each is causally relevant to the ensuing harm and that each could in a proper case be held responsible for it.[50]

In each of these situations, the dual omissions that overdetermine the failure of the causal process at issue are assumed to occur in the same stage of that causal process, rather than in different stages of a sequenced process in which the occurrence of subsequent stages depends on the prior occurrence of the previous stages. Although the building of a house occurs in sequential, dependent stages, the bricks and mortar are used together simultaneously in the same stage in the same causal process of mortaring and laying bricks. The required use of one material is dependent on the simultaneous rather than the prior use of the other material. The absence of either material results in the failure of the house-building causal process at the brick-laying stage. The simultaneous absence of both overdetermines the failure of the brick-laying stage for the duration of their simultaneous absence; there is duplicative negative causation. If instead there was a simultaneous failure to deliver concrete for the foundation and lumber for the framing of the house, the failure to deliver the concrete, which results in the failure of the house-building causal process at the foundation-building stage, preempts the potential negative causal effect of the failure to deliver the lumber, which is not needed until the subsequent framing stage, the occurrence of which depends on the prior occurrence of the foundation-building stage.

The two-switches hypothetical is insufficiently described. Assume that the fire resulted from overheating of a wire in an electrical circuit because the electrical load on the circuit was too great, that each of the two switches independently controls a different operating appliance (a subcircuit) on the same circuit, and that both switches must be turned off to reduce the load on the main circuit to a safe, non-fire-generating level. Neither the operation of each switch nor its effect on the main circuit's load is dependent on the operation of the other switch. Instead, turning on each switch initiates a distinct positive causal process—the operation of the associated appliance with its particular load on the main circuit—that is not affected by the operation of the other switch. The failure to turn off each switch is a duplicative negative cause of the overloading of the main circuit and hence of the fire, for which the overloading of the main circuit is a necessary positive condition.

If the two switches control the same appliance, which operates and overloads the circuit as long as at least one of the switches is on, the

---

[50] Hart and Honoré, above n 3, at 128; see also at 236.

analysis is somewhat different but the conclusion is the same. If only one switch is on, it is a but-for positive cause of the operation of the appliance and of the fire. If both switches are on, they are duplicative independently sufficient positive causes of the operation of the appliance and of the fire (although only the first switch to be turned on *initiated* the operation of the appliance). As before, neither switch's operation affects the operation of the other switch or the effect of the other switch as a positive cause of the operation of the appliance. The only difference is that, in this scenario, turning one switch off will not have the effect of turning the appliance off unless the other switch also is off, but, as in the two-appliance scenario, it does not matter whether one is turned off before the other or if they are turned off simultaneously; not until they are both turned off will the appliance's operation (and the circuit overload) be terminated. Thus, the failure to turn off either switch is a duplicative negative cause of the circuit's being overloaded and the resulting fire.

V.   CONCLUSION

Debates over the meaning and role of causation in attributions of legal responsibility are hardly new. However, the debates have been much more widespread and urgent in recent years, as advances in science combined with mass production and distribution of products have created an expanding number of risks and harms, which, however, are often difficult to attribute to specific actors. In the current debates, as in past debates, considerable confusion—and sometimes bad legal results—have been generated by the failure of many courts, lawyers, and theorists to clearly distinguish the issue of factual causation from the issue of legal responsibility, for which a finding of factual causation (or at least the possibility of factual causation) remains a necessary but not sufficient prerequisite. Difficult normative issues of proper legal responsibility have gone unrecognised or been ignored by, on the one hand, judicial findings of 'no causation' (and thus no liability) when factual causation clearly existed in the particular situation and, on the other hand, judicial findings of 'causation' (and thus full liability) when only the probability or even mere possibility of factual causation could be established. The necessary first step in clear thinking about legal responsibility is to isolate and clarify the concept of factual causation and the requirements for establishing factual causation in particular situations. This chapter is an attempt to contribute to that understanding.

12

Decision Causation: Pandora's Tool-Box

VAUGHAN BLACK*

I. INTRODUCTION

A CHARACTERISTIC OF the recent doctrinal change in the law of causation has been a proliferation of new standards adopted, not as generally-available criteria, but only as tests geared to specific circumstances. Courts have not sought to replace the time-honoured approach that requires plaintiffs to prove sine qua non causation on a balance of probabilities. That test—appealingly straightforward and profoundly intuitive—is seen as virtually *defining* cause-in-fact, so that alternatives are but a sort of surrogate or constructive causation.[1] However, it is now widely agreed that 'the "but for" test is unworkable in some circumstances'[2] and should be supplemented by new analyses when those circumstances arise. The most elaborate version of this new attitude is what we might call the array approach. It is the notion that we need a tool-chest of tests for cause-in-fact, with judges selecting the right one for the job in any given case. In the words of Lord Hoffmann:

> There is... no uniform causal requirement for liability in tort. Instead, there are varying causal requirements, depending on the basis and purpose of liability.[3]

* Professor, Dalhousie Law School, Halifax. Many thanks to the participants in the conference at which this chapter was presented as a paper, and to David Cheifetz, Dennis Klimchuk and Stephanie Lane for comments on a draft.
[1] I am thinking of statements like Lord Scott's in *Barker v Corus (UK) Ltd* (2006) 2 WLR 1027 (HL) [*Barker*]. There, in describing the holding on causation in *Fairchild v Glenhaven Funeral Services* [2003] 1 AC 32 (HL) [*Fairchild*] he wrote, at [53], that the causative link had not been found but merely imposed. This suggests that he regards the but-for test, which was not satisfied in *Fairchild*, as the only true test for causation.
[2] *Athey v Leonati* [1996] 3 SCR 458 [*Athey*]. Canadian law lacks a workable definition of unworkable.
[3] *Kuwait Airways Corpn v Iraqi Airways Co (Nos 4 and 5)* [2002] 2 AC 883 (HL), [128]. He began to forge this link in *Environmental Agency v Empress Car Co (Abertillery)* [1999] 2 AC 22 (HL), 29 [*Abertillery*].

Of course there is a powerful counter-example to this proliferation of causal criteria. Richard Wright's necessary-element-of-a-sufficient-set approach in the previous chapter stands as an ambitious articulation of a unified theory of causation, one that would bring together both the traditional necessitation requirement and the various tests that judges have deployed to deal with the over-determination problem in cases of causal redundancy, where the but-for test famously flops.[4] In courts, however, the trend is toward splitting rather than lumping. Perhaps due to judicial reservations about Big Theory or conceptual elegance, the most common forensic response to situations where the application of but-for appears to lead to injustice has not been to grope toward some new general test but rather to retain the traditional standard while making ad hoc adjustments and additions. In the United States the *Third Restatement*[5] seeks to curtail this propagation of new causal tests, and the latest causation decision from the House of Lords may signal some attempt to inhibit further growth,[6] but in Canada judicial receptivity to additions to but-for causation appears to be alive and well.

The notion that we are best served by an assortment of tests for factual causation raises interesting questions. One of those is how many different tests for cause-in-fact could there possibly be? That is, apart from altering or reversing the burden-of-proof, it is far from clear how many distinct inquiries there could be that might qualify as investigations into causation. There are, of course, a variety of new labels in play—material contribution, substantial contribution, substantial factor, material cause, and so on—but it is not obvious how many distinct tests are denoted by these titles.

A second set of questions presented by the array approach asks which circumstances justify resort to one or another of these new causation standards. Here, there seem to be two variables. The first is the perceived need for either tougher or easier causal criteria depending on the need to either facilitate or restrict liability in a given area of legal regulation. Thus we have seen courts advocate easily-satisfied causal tests for environmental offences or manufacturers' liability because of the need to protect the environment or injured consumers.[7] Likewise we have seen the selection of defendant-favouring rules for physicians on the grounds that with doctors we can to some extent rely on their professional ethic to ensure that they do a good job, so we have correspondingly less need of civil liability.[8] The

---

[4]   R Wright, 'Causation in Tort Law' (1985) 73 *California Law Review* 1735.

[5]   *Restatement (Third) of Torts: Liability for Physical Harm (Proposed Final Draft)* (2005), especially §§ 26-27.

[6]   *Barker*, above n 1.

[7]   *Abertillery*, above n 3; *Hollis v Dow Corning Corpn* [1995] 4 SCR 634 [*Hollis*].

[8]   *Hollis*, above. In *Gregg v Scott* [2005] UKHL 2, [217] Baroness Hale deployed this argument against imposing a more easily satisfied causal standard on defendant doctors.

second variable has to do with the perceived unfairness of requiring plaintiffs to establish proof on the conventional standard in the face of systemic uncertainties, particularly ones associated with certain harms. Of course, the fact that a plaintiff in a given case faces a tough time proving causation is not of itself a reason for adopting some more easily satisfied standard. After all, the difficulty might arise because the facts make it clear that the wrong simply did not cause the harm in question, at least not according to any definition of causation we might imagine adopting. However, with certain types of injury—mesothelioma for instance, or the cancers of DES daughters—the difficulties of proof seem structural; they would arise in most or all cases involving that sort of harm. Moreover, perhaps because the defendants' carelessness in such cases has almost certainly harmed *someone*, even if not necessarily this plaintiff, the difficulties in satisfying the traditional criterion seem to be the sort of thing that should not be visited on plaintiffs.

The focus of this chapter is on one instance of the second variety of justification for opening up the new causal tool-box. I address the cluster of claims made in some judicial opinions and academic writing to the effect that counterfactual inquiries involving judgments about hypothetical decisions are unique, or at least are distinct from those inquiries which do not—so much so that they require special rules which operate as exceptions to the usual standard for factual causation. This is the problem of decision causation.[9]

In focusing on decisions in the counterfactual inquiry I am not, of course, referring to choices made by defendants that relate to or constitute the wrongful behaviour that allegedly occasioned the plaintiff's injury—for example, a decision to drive recklessly or breach a contract. Such decisions are not within the casual chain; they are the choices that constitute the initial fault. Rather, by 'decision causation' we mean the problem that arises when the speculation involved in the counterfactual inquiry into what would have happened had the defendant not violated the plaintiff's rights brings up an inquiry into what some later decision would have been.

There seem to be two distinct claims about the way in which decision causation differs from regular causation. One is that the two are discrete phenomena. A leading instance of this in Canada is found in an article by Denis Boivin.[10] Boivin addresses the situation where manufacturers neglect to advise consumers about risks accompanying some product—say, a pharmaceutical. He argues that such cases require a new approach to

---

[9] The coiners of this phrase appear to have been A Meisel and LD Kabnick, 'Informed Consent to Medical Treatment: An Analysis of Recent Legislation' (1980) 41 *University of Pittsburgh Law Review* 407, 439.

[10] 'Factual Causation in the Law of Manufacturer Failure to Warn' (1998) 30 *Ottawa Law Review* 47.

causation. The ground on which his argument rests involves dividing the causal inquiry into two parts. The first is injury causation—the assessment of whether the use of the product did result in damage to the plaintiff. Boivin describes the counterfactual exercise of investigating this question as 'scientific' and 'truly a factual inquiry'.[11] The second part of the analysis is decision causation—would the injured party have used the product anyway, even if warned? Boivin's description of the nature of this exploration is an excellent instance of regarding decision causation as radically distinct from non-decision causation:

> unlike injury causation, this element requires a counterfactual inquiry of a non-scientific nature. In essence, the fact finder must speculate about what might have been, if selected historical conditions had been different. It is a form of 'hypothetical causation,' particular to cases where a failure to provide information constitutes the basis of the cause of action.[12]

Later he writes that 'decision causation is counterfactual in nature and, as such, is fundamentally different from the causal inquiry involved in other tort actions'.[13] He further notes that what is special about such causal inquiries is that 'the plaintiff's will interposes itself between the defendant's conduct and the subsequent damage'.[14] A similar distinction appears in an article by Patricia Peppin.[15]

The second sort of claim about the unicity of decision causation does not mark it off as different in type from other counterfactual inquiries, but asserts only that we have less reason to be confident of our judgments about decision causation. There are numerous statements of this sort, relying on the assertion that people are capricious and unknowable, and that decisions they might make are unpredictable. For instance, in *Walker Estate v York Finch General Hospital*[16] the Supreme Court of Canada dealt with a case where the Red Cross was found not to have given adequate warnings to dissuade those in a high-risk-for-HIV category from giving blood. After an HIV-positive donation was made, Ms Walker was

---

[11]   *Ibid*, at 50.

[12]   *Ibid*, at 51 (citations omitted).

[13]   *Ibid*, at 75. Boivin claims, at 51, that support for a category difference between injury causation and decision causation can be found in RN Strassfeld, 'If …: Counterfactuals in the Law' (1992) 60 *George Washington Law Review* 339. I disagree. Strassfeld emphasises the difference between factual determinations and counterfactual ones, but he does not claim that distinction maps onto the division between injury causation and decision causation. Further, while Strassfeld does mention predictions about human behaviour as one sort of counterfactual inquiry, at 368, he does not claim it is importantly distinct from counterfactual inquiries implicating scientific knowledge. In fact, he calls attention to the structural similarities between such inquiries.

[14]   Boivin, above n 10, at 68-69.

[15]   'Drug/Vaccine Risks: Patient Decision-Making and Harm Reduction in the Pharmaceutical Company Duty to Warn' (1991) 70 *Canadian Bar Review* 473, 499-508.

[16]   [2001] 1 SCR 647 [*Walker Estate*].

subsequently infused with that blood, contracted AIDS and died. In the claim by her estate, the defendant maintained that causation had not been made out. It argued that even if it had provided an adequate warning, the donor in question would have given blood. The donor had been identified and there was reason to believe that even a stronger warning would not have dissuaded him from making the fatal donation. This raised a decision-causation issue, and in the course of addressing it the court noted that:

> In cases of negligent donor screening, it may be difficult or impossible to prove hypothetically what the donor would have done had he or she been properly screened by the C.R.C.S. The added element of donor conduct in these cases means that the but-for test could operate unfairly, highlighting the possibility of leaving legitimate plaintiffs uncompensated.[17]

Regardless of whether the claim about the unicity of decision causation rests on an assertion that it is essentially different from non-decision inquiry, or only on a claim about differing degrees of difficulty, the resulting argument is that requiring judges or juries to speculate about what decision some person would have made in some hypothetical situation requires them to undertake a particularly dicey exercise, one in whose answer we could have little reason to have confidence and which—in the more radical versions of the claims—should be regarded as virtually non-justiciable.[18]

Note that this assessment is one that must be made against the reality that many *non*-decision-causation cases present thorny problems of speculation. Consider a case where a polluter has exposed a plaintiff to some chemical agent and the latter has developed cancer. The causal inquiry would involve judgements about the intensity and duration of the plaintiff's contact with the allegedly-harmful agent, a judgement about the accuracy of the diagnosis of the cancer in question, a determination about whether the chemical is even capable of causing that condition in humans, and a conclusion about whether the plaintiff might have developed the disease anyway, even in the absence of exposure to the chemical. All of this could be obscured by a long latency period and fading memories. The judgement about whether the test for causation is satisfied in such circumstances would be difficult. However, it is not a decision-causation case. In short, many non-decision-causation cases raise difficult causation problems, so if the claim that decision-causation cases require special rules rests on an assertion that they are particularly hard to assess, then they must be pretty hard indeed.

---

[17] *Ibid*, at [88].
[18] A Twerski and N Cohen, 'Informed Decision Making and the Law of Torts: The Myth of Justiciable Causation' [1988] *University of Illinois Law Review* 607.

I suggest that we have reason for misgivings about both the claim that decision causation is different in type from non-decision causation and the assertion that we should have diminished confidence in our conclusions about it. Accordingly—since I accept the correctness of both the necessitation standard and the better-than-50 per cent burden of proof, at least as general rules, and think that departures from those standards are permitted only for convincing reasons—I regard with suspicion the notion that the mere fact that a case presents an issue of decision causation is, on its own, justification for any departure from the orthodox test. At the very least, courts need to be clearer than they have been about exactly what characteristic of decision causation justifies resorting to one of the new devices in the causal tool-box.

Before pursuing these suggestions, however, we need a somewhat more detailed account of what decision causation is, and also an account of those areas where decision causation has been advanced as justification for some special causation rule. It should be noted at this early stage that it is not the case that courts have used the phrase 'decision causation' every time they encounter a decision causation case as defined above. In fact, although the phrase has acquired some currency in the academic literature on causation, courts have not warmed to it. What judges *have* done, however, is to claim in a variety of different contexts that causal inquiries about hypothetical choices are distinct and oblige us to change our usual approach.

It should also be pointed out that the contexts in which courts have accorded extraordinary treatment to decision-causation cases do not appear to include all such cases. That is, some decision-causation cases have not been regarded as being special or as mandating any departure from the orthodox causation test. Indeed the fact that they entail speculations as to some hypothetical decision has sometimes gone unremarked and even unnoticed. Consider the following, from a decision of the Supreme Court of Canada.[19] A stop sign falls down and the relevant governmental authority neglects to replace it. A driver then fails to halt at the intersection, gets involved in an accident with someone else entering the intersection and suffers injury. The driver sues the government for failure to replace the sign. That claim would require the driver to show, among other things, that had there been a stop sign he would have stopped, thus avoiding the accident in question. The case was not regarded as presenting difficult issues of causation. However, it was clearly a decision-causation case.

---

[19]   *Parkland v Stetar* [1975] 2 SCR 884. For a stop-sign case in which the plaintiff failed to show he would have stopped anyway, see *Thomas v Baltimore & Ohio Railroad* 310 A 2d 186 (Md Ct Spec App 1973).

I make the following observations arising from this stop-sign case. First, speculations as to decisions in causal chains are far more frequent than judicial references to them; there are many unacknowledged decision-causation cases out there. In fact it may be that assertions that decision-causation problems are rarities are false. Perhaps most causal inquiries involve decision causation. By definition all claims for misrepresentation do; likewise cases where the defendant's fault is the failure to supply some safety device. Maybe rigorous scrutiny would reveal that it is the *non*-decision-causation cases that are the rare exceptions. Second, speculation as to some decisions is not at all troublesome and is far easier than in some non-decision-causation cases, such as the cancer example above. Drivers of cars nearly always halt at stop signs, or at least slow down enough that they can and do stop if other cars are about to enter the intersection. Requiring a plaintiff to prove that the car would have been brought to a stop had there been a sign at the intersection sets no difficult causal hurdle to surmount, especially when we recall that all he or she would be required to show is that it was more likely than not that, had the sign been there, he or she would have stopped.

This is not surprising in light of the more general fact that courts, understandably, are not famous for dealing consistently with counterfactuals. As Robert Strassfeld noted:

> Courts often fail to recognize that they are dealing with counterfactuals. When they do recognize the counterfactual nature of their inquiry, they fail to relate it to other counterfactual inquiries in the law. Lacking a general understanding of counterfactuals and their place in legal decisionmaking, courts' treatment of legal counterfactuals is ad hoc, localized, and inconsistent.[20]

Be that as it may, courts in decision-causation cases have frequently claimed that the fact that they must speculate as to some counterfactual decision is a unique feature of the case before them mandating some departure from the orthodox approach to causation.

A question that arises when delineating the decision-causation field is that of just who these hypothetical deciders are. The answer seems to be that they might be just about anyone. Many such decisions are ones that would have been made by one of the parties to the litigation. The hypothetical decider might be the plaintiff, as in the example of the under-informed patient or consumer. It could also be the defendant, as in the well-known beauty-contest case of *Chaplin v Hicks*.[21] The decider might also be some third party, someone unconnected to the claim and unavailable as a witness, or even someone whose identity is unknown.

---

[20] Strassfeld, above n 13, at 348.
[21] [1911] 2 KB 786 (CA) [*Chaplin*].

It is not quite the case, however, that the deciders can be just about anyone. They must be human beings, or at least human-directed entities such as corporations. Decisions made by computers or non-human animals do not count, at least on my survey of the cases. Obviously, the notion that they might count raises a philosophical question about whether entities other than humans can perform the activity we describe as 'making a decision'. For what it may be worth, despite the fact that my computer can beat me at chess every time, I doubt that anything done by a computer amounts to making a decision. Non-human animals present a tougher case, and there are cases aplenty where the counterfactual inquiry involves asking what some non-human animal would have done had the defendant behaved differently. Cases involving claims against owners of dogs which (decide to?) bite someone sometimes exhibit this feature. Such counterfactual inquiries would appear to present judges with formidable mental exercises: what would a bat decide? I do not address here the questions about whether creatures other than humans can have sufficient agency to be deciders. The common law is committed to the view that while non-human animals have behaviour, they do not have agency. Consistent with this commitment to a radical gulf between humans and non-humans, courts treat the question of the behaviour of non-human animals much like they treat the question of the behaviour of cancer-causing chemicals. Note that I am not suggesting that causal inquiries requiring speculation as to the likely actions of non-humans in hypothetical circumstances are not difficult, but only that courts have not regarded them as a species of decision causation or as otherwise constituting some discrete causal category.

II.   THE CASES

With that in hand, I will now survey the cases in which Canadian courts have found decision causation relevant to the selection of some alternative causation test. One area in which decision causation has become relevant concerns determinations about when to abandon the but-for test and find causation when the defendant can be shown to have done no more than to have augmented the risk of the occurrence of the type of injury the plaintiff has suffered. This is sometimes known as material-contribution or substantial-factor causation, but the term risk-augmentation causation is more accurate. Permitting the plaintiff to establish cause-in-fact on a risk-augmentation standard instead of on the necessitation basis is an approach that radically favours the plaintiff.

In the only decision of the Supreme Court of Canada to apply the risk-augmentation test, the justification for this radical departure from the traditional causal standard was decision causation. The case is *Walker*, mentioned above.[22] There the Supreme Court held that it was an error on the part of the trial judge to confine himself to the but-for test when addressing the question of whether the HIV-positive donor would have been dissuaded from giving blood had the defendant supplied a better warning. The Supreme Court found causation to be made out. It did so on the basis that an alternative causal standard was available in the circumstances of that case. Specifically, it held causation to be satisfied on a risk-augmentation basis; that is, that an adequate warning would at least have increased the chances that the donor would have been dissuaded, and that in the circumstances of this case that was sufficient. It justified resort to that standard by a decision-causation argument:

> In cases of negligent donor screening, it may be difficult or impossible to prove hypothetically what the donor would have done had he or she been properly screened by the [defendant]. The added element of donor conduct in these cases means that the but-for test could operate unfairly.[23]

Walker is a third-party decision-causation case where abandoning sine qua non as the operative causal criterion was justified by the plaintiff's supposed difficulties in proving on the more-likely-than-not standard that the defendant's fault was a necessary antecedent to a third party's decision to take a course of action that harmed the plaintiff.

It is important to note that the court in *Walker* did not claim that third-party decision-causation cases would invariably operate to make this lower causal threshold available. The Supreme Court in *Walker* did not say that decision-causation cases would always justify resorting to the risk-augmentation test, and it did not rule out the possibly that risk-augmentation causation might be available some future *non*-decision-causation case. Its decision in *Walker* was simply that one circumstance where this more readily satisfied causal standard, there described as material contribution, should be available was 'when there is the added element of donor misconduct'. That cannot possibly be the final word on the subject, and indeed an appeal currently before the Supreme Court of Canada is likely to shed further light on the issue.[24] Nevertheless, despite its provisional, ad hoc nature, *Walker* stands as a decision-causation case.

---

[22] Above n 16.

[23] *Ibid*, at [88]. There was an alternative holding in *Walker*, namely that but-for causation was in fact established.

[24] In fact in February 2007, just as this book was being readied for publication, the Supreme Court of Canada decided that case. In *Resurfice Corpn v Hanke* 2007 SCC 7 the court affirmed, at [28], that *Walker*, above n 16, was correct in holding that resort to the risk-augmentation test could be justified 'where it is impossible to prove what a particular person in the causal chain would have done had the defendant not committed a negligent act or omission.' Unfortunately the court's judgment in this case did not further clarify the relation between decision causation and this alternative test for cause-in-fact.

A second area where decision causation has become pertinent is with respect to probabilistic causation, or proportional liability. As a general rule, plaintiffs must prove causation on the balance of probabilities. Any occurrence that the plaintiff demonstrates was more likely than not (that is, greater than 50 per cent) caused by the defendant's wrong is taken to be proven and the plaintiff is recompensed for the full amount of the loss. Harms that cannot, on that 50 per cent-or-better standard, be shown to have been caused by the defendant's behaviour are taken not to have been caused by the defendant at all, and the plaintiff loses. An understandably attractive alternative is to abandon this practice of according crucial significance to the 50 per cent threshold and adopt proportional liability: a plaintiff who proves that it was, say, 20 per cent likely that her loss was caused (on the necessitation standard) by the defendant's conduct could receive an award of 20 per cent of the compensable value of the injury.

Proportional liability is not the general approach to causation, but courts in Canada and elsewhere occasionally employ it. There are two main areas where a proportional-causation exception to this all-or-nothing approach is permitted. The first, which is well established, is with respect to future losses, both hypothetical and otherwise—that is, losses that, if they occur, will occur or would have occurred after trial. The justification offered for this departure from the balance-of-probabilities approach is that it is unfair to plaintiffs to require them to show today, to a greater-than-50 per cent likelihood, that some future event will occur. As the House of Lords has noted:

> When the question is whether a certain thing is or is not true—whether a certain event did or did not happen—then the court must decide one way or the other. There is no question of chance or probability. Either it did or did not happen . . . You can prove that a past event happened, but you cannot prove that a future event will happen and I do not think that the law is so foolish as to suppose that you can. All that you can do is to evaluate the chance.[25]

The second exception to the all-or-nothing rule is loss of chance. Loss of chance designates those circumstances where uncertainty about the past will be dealt with on the simple-probabilities basis normally accorded only to future matters.[26] The situations in which loss-of-chance damages are available are not fully defined, either in Canada or elsewhere. However, one line of thinking in Canada is that they are available in third-party

---

[25] *Davies v Taylor* [1974] AC 207 (HL), 212-13 (Lord Reid), approved on this point in *Shrump v Koot* (1977) 18 OR (2d) 337 (CA). The recent decision in *Barker*, above n 1, may now constitute a third area in which proportional liability is available, at least in the UK.

[26] Academic support for a broad adoption of this approach appears to have originated with J King, 'Causation, Valuation, and Chance in Personal Injury Torts Involving Pre-exiting Conditions and Future Consequences' (1981) 90 *Yale Law Journal* 1353.

decision-causation cases. A leading case is the decision of the Saskatchewan Court of Appeal in *Henderson v Hagblom*,[27] where a man sued his former lawyer for negligent conduct of a trial he had lost. The court accepted the plaintiff's argument that his lawyer had fallen below a professional standard of care in the original hearing. To establish causation the plaintiff had to demonstrate that had his former lawyer performed competently, the result in the first trial would have been favourable. That depended on the court in the second trial constructing a counterfactual in which the lawyer in the initial trial performed proficiently, and then deciding whether that would have made a difference to the outcome in that trial. The court held that a proportional-liability approach to causation was justified because causation depended on the hypothetical decision of a third party, the judge in the initial trial. As a result:

> the issue fell within the sphere of quantification of damages dependent on the evaluation of the chance that the third party would have taken the action which would have enabled the loss to be avoided.[28]

The argument here seems to be that requiring proof of hypothetical decisions, or at least those by third parties, on a more-likely-than-not basis sets an unfairly high hurdle for plaintiffs. In that respect, it rests on the same sort of reasoning used to justify abandonment of the all-or-nothing approach to possible future harms. That is, just as we consider it unfair to require plaintiffs to show, on the balance of probabilities, that some future event will occur, we likewise think it unreasonable to require them to prove that some third party would have come to a certain decision.

Note again that although decision causation is offered as a reason for the adoption of an exceptional approach to causation, it is under-inclusive. It may be that the third-party decision-causation explanation is the predominant common identifier in those Canadian and English cases in which loss-of-chance claims have been recognised. However, there are plenty of third-party decision causation cases in which loss-of-chance damages are not awarded. In fact, the Supreme Court of Canada appears to have ruled

---

[27] (2003) 232 Sask R 81 (CA) [*Henderson*], leave to appeal refused [2004] 1 SCR ix. The Supreme Court of Canada noted the existence of loss-of-chance causation in *Athey*, above n 2, but left for another day the question of its availability.

[28] *Henderson*, above, at [203]. In *Folland v Reardon* (2005) 74 OR (3d) 688 [*Folland*] the Ontario Court of Appeal entertained a similar claim and decided against loss-of-chance. It agreed, at [73], that third-party decision causation might be a triggering factor for loss-of-chance causation in contract cases, but it rejected it in the claims of lawyer's negligence in conducting a trial. For more about *Folland* see below n 46. Note that in the UK decision-causation is not the sole criterion relied upon to justify resort to proportional liability: see *Barker*, above n 1.

out loss-of-chance in cases of physician or hospital negligence,[29] and many medical misadventure cases involve decision causation.

It should also be noted that a seminal English loss-of-chance decision, *Chaplin*,[30] justified the proportional-liability approach to causation by reference to the decision-causation factor, but there the decider would have been the defendant. The defendant's error was a failure to give notice to the plaintiff of her right to appear in the finals of a beauty contest. He defended on the grounds of lack of causation: even if he had lived up to his obligation the plaintiff would only have been among the finalists. She might not have won, and since fewer than half the finalists would win, the odds were that the plaintiff had lost nothing. The court rejected that argument, awarding damages based on a proportion of the value of the winning prize, justifying the award on the basis that the decision-causation aspect of the causal inquiry required a departure from the balance-of-probabilities standard.

A third area where a decision-causation argument has prevailed in Canada is in the well-known type of case that arises in the medical context when physicians have neglected to provide their patients with information about the material risks involved in some contemplated procedure—say, an operation or some course of pharmaceutical treatment. The patient then goes ahead with the procedure and the risk materialises. If the patient sues the doctor, the doctor might defend on the grounds that causation is not made out, claiming that even had he or she given the information the patient would have gone ahead with the procedure.

Canadian courts faced with cases of this sort have adverted to the difficulties in deciding what the patient would have elected to do had she been properly informed of the risks. In particular, they have pointed to concerns about plaintiff self-deception. Courts reason that, with the benefit of hindsight, plaintiffs might convince *themselves* that they would have chosen differently had they been adequately advised, even though in fact they would not have, and that as true believers such self-deceiving plaintiffs will be particularly convincing witnesses on the point. In response, Canadian courts, like those in some other jurisdictions, have amended the standard but-for test.[31] The but-for test would require an

---

[29]   *Laferrière v Lawson* [1991] 1 SCR 541; *St-Jean v Mercier* [2002] 1 SCR 491. The Supreme Court's bar to loss of chance in medical causation, and its apparent willingness to at least contemplate the notion of such claims in other areas of the law, are particularly interesting in light of the fact that in the US medical misadventure is about the only area where loss of chance has had much success.

[30]   Above n 21. The court seems to have erred in the calculations, but this is not uncommon in calculation of loss-of-chance damages: see L Noah, 'An Inventory of Mathematical Blunders in Applying the Loss-of-a-Chance Doctrine' (2005) 24 *The Review of Litigation* 369.

[31]   *Reibl v Hughes* [1980] 2 SCR 880; *Arndt v Smith* [1997] 2 SCR 539.

inquiry into what the plaintiff would have decided had he or she been properly advised. Canadian courts have held that what is instead required is an inquiry into what a reasonable person in the plaintiff's position would have elected to do. The form of that inquiry remains but-for, but to the extent that the reasonable person is a normative construct, this substitutes a normative, value-laden judgment for an individualised one.[32]

This rule is a contentious one and much has been written about it. In practice it favours defendant physicians—doctors who have failed in their duty to inform their patients. It has been rejected by some other courts.[33] My goal here is not to take sides in the debate about whether the exception is justified, but only to note that where the exception is in place it rests on a claim about the difficulties involved in assessing hypothetical decisions by plaintiffs. However, it is important to draw attention to four things. The first is that although the argument for a special rule is premised on difficulties in forming reliable[34] judgements about hypothetical decisions, the concern is not, as it was in the two previous types of decision causation, that it is unfair to plaintiffs to require them to prove what some decision would have been. Rather, the concern is that the defendant will be unable to disprove causation.

Second, it should be noted that although the problem is an evidentiary one—we would be more inclined than we should be to credit the testimony of a self-deceiving plaintiff as to the decisions he or she would have made—the judicial response is not an evidentiary one, such as an admonition to judges to be wary of crediting the testimony of plaintiffs on this issue. Rather, it is a substantive solution.

The third observation is that this special rule has not prevailed outside the doctor-patient context. Consider a case where careless advice is given about, say, the risks involved in some contemplated business venture. If the recipient proceeds with the scheme and suffers a loss, then, despite the fact that his claim in respect of that advice involves a decision inquiry that would present the problem of plaintiff hindsight, it has not attracted special rules. When the Supreme Court of Canada was urged to apply this doctor-specific rule against a non-doctor defendant it declined to do so. It viewed the evidentiary problem of the self-deceiving plaintiff as one that could be addressed without departure from orthodoxy: 'this concern can

---

[32] Stephen Waddams has advocated a different solution to this causal difficulty, namely proportional liability: S Waddams, 'The Valuation of Chances' (1998) 30 *Canadian Business Law Journal* 86.

[33] *March v Stramare* (1991) 171 CLR 507 (HCA); *Chappel v Hart* (1998) 195 CLR 232 (HCA); *Sidaway v Bethlem Royal Hospital Governors* [1985] AC 871 (HL).

[34] 'Reliable' is not quite the right word here, since verification is not an option. We will never know how the hypothetical decision would have been made. There is no later time at which the court's holding on the causation point will be proven wrong or right.

be adequately addressed at the trial level through cross-examination and through proper weighing by the trial judge of the relevant testimony'.[35]

The fourth point to note in connection with the special causation rule devised for claims against under-informing physicians is that some courts have augmented the special causation rule by providing a consolation prize for plaintiffs who fail to satisfy the altered, doctor-favouring causation test. They have been prepared to treat the plaintiff's undermined decision-making as a harm. *Lachambre v Nair*[36] is an instance of this. As a general proposition, impairing a person's autonomy—at least as that autonomy might be expressed through one's right to be informed with respect to some decision one must make—is not regarded as a harm in itself. Only the injuries to one's body, property and other cognisable interests are protected, insofar as those flow from the impaired decision-making capacity. Note that an under-informed plaintiff who *is* able to establish the causal link between the failure to supply adequate information and the subsequent injury—because he or she is able to prove that a different decision would have been made had accurate information been supplied—is given nothing for his or her abused dignity; only compensation for the physical harm. Yet his or her autonomy was undermined every bit as much as was the plaintiff's in *Lachambre*. Consistency would seem to require an award for both the infringed dignity and the physical injury that was demonstrated to flow from it. But that is not the result; the abused-autonomy award seems only available as a consolation prize.

It should be noted in passing that, in addition to the foregoing instances of courts justifying resort to special causation rules on some variation of a decision-causation argument, there are instances of academics doing the same. Boivin's article on manufacturers' liability for failure to warn, referenced above, is one instance of this. He argues that the decision-causation problem in that case should be resolved in favour of presuming causation in cases where the failure to warn was a material one.[37] A comparable claim is advanced by Margaret Hall, who argues for a relaxed causal standard where a defendant's negligence plays into a third-party's decision to commit an intentional tort.[38] There are examples in American scholarship as well,[39] but a full account of all instances where scholars

---

[35] *Hollis*, above n 7, at 675.

[36] (1989) 74 Sask R 87 (QB) [*Lachambre*]. For scholarly support of this approach see R Crisp, 'Medical Negligence, Assault, Informed Consent and Autonomy' (1990) 17 *Journal of Law & Society* 77; M Geistfeld, 'Scientific Uncertainty and Causation in Tort Law' (2001) 54 *Vanderbilt Law Review* 1001, 1017-21; N Levit, 'Ethereal Torts' (1992) 61 *George Washington Law Review* 136; T Honoré, 'Medical Non-Disclosure, Causation and Risk: *Chappel v Hart*' (1999) 7 *Torts Law Journal* 1.

[37] Boivin, above n 10, at 92-93.

[38] M Hall, 'Duty, Causation, and Third-Party Perpetrators: The *Bonnie Mooney* Case' (2005) 50 *McGill Law Journal* 597. For another example see Waddams, above n 32.

[39] Twerski and Cohen, above n 18.

have argued for special causation standards based, at least in part, on decision-causation arguments would lengthen this chapter unduly, so I have confined this exposition to situations where Canadian courts have accepted such arguments.

III.   ANALYSIS

What can we make of these claims about the unicity of decision causation and the departures from the orthodox causation test that rest on them? A few general observations can be ventured about judicial treatment of decision causation. The first is that although much has been made about the unique and special nature of the problem, the field is unsystematic in several ways. Some judgements about hypothetical decisions are thought to favour plaintiffs; some, defendants. Sometimes they are viewed as easily proven; more often as so difficult to predict as to be non-justiciable. Statements are made about the difficulties of decision causation in certain fields, notably health care, and in light of those statements extraordinary rules are adopted in those fields, but little effort is made to show why the problem is confined to those domains. Comparable problems in other areas are thought not to require special rules or, worse yet, are not even perceived as decision-causation cases. Claims are made about the special difficulty in coming to reliable conclusions about hypothetical decisions, but no empirical support is advanced to demonstrate that judges and juries are any worse at evaluating those cases than they are at non-decision-causation cases. And, assuming that the problem of decision causation does justify a special treatment, there is no consistency in what that approach might be. Sometimes it is deployed to justify resort to loss of chance, other times it supports use of the risk-augmentation standard, elsewhere still it is called upon to justify an objectivised version of the but-for test, and occasionally the undermined decisions are themselves elevated to the status of novel protected interests. The subject seems to cry out for one of two responses: either a rejection of all claims that there is anything special about decision causation cases that justifies a departure from the orthodox approach to cause-in-fact, or an embracing of the special nature of decision-causation cases accompanied by some effort to systemise the response to this problem.

   Of course in branding the field as inconsistent we should not be ungenerous. We should not underestimate the considerable difficulty in coming up with some consistently workable scheme for when a court might permissibly stray from but-for causation and pursue one of the new causation tests. Consider the struggles of the Law Lords in *Fairchild*[40] and *Barker*[41] they attempted to lay down workable rules for when deficiencies in scientific knowledge justify departures from the necessitation standard in the injury-causation inquiry. A possible resolution to the general problem of when but-for may be supplemented by other tests would be for appeal courts to simply tell trial judges that they might relax but-for when, in light of all the circumstances, which might include the decision-causation factor among others, it seems unfair to hold the plaintiff to the orthodox standard. However such an open-ended response is unlikely to satisfy the requirements of predictive certainty. Appeal courts are likely to have to struggle for some time with articulating general tests for when, and how, to permit departures from sine qua non. The decision-causation problem does seem to be one plausible variable in this endeavour, and we need not be too critical of the fact that courts have not fully worked out the pertinence of this factor. It is a fair criticism, however, that the various claims about decision causation are under-scrutinised and that the links between the various areas in which those claims have been accepted have not been adequately explored.

I noted at the outset that there are two sorts of argument about the unique nature of decision causation. One asserts that it is different in type from non-decision causation, and the other asserts only that there is a difference in our degree of justified confidence in the reliability of our conclusions. There is reason to question both of these. For the first, it simply seems false to claim that non-decision causation involves a factual decision while decision causation is *counter*factual. By definition, each requires *both* a factual determination *and* a construction of the most plausible counterfactual world, followed by a comparison of the two. That is, with injury causation we have to determine the facts: is the plaintiff really injured, or maybe just faking it?—*and* the counterfactual: had the defendant acted as he should have, would that injury have occurred in any event? Likewise with decision causation we have to determine the facts: what decision was made?—and the counterfactual: what decision would have been made had the decision maker been adequately informed or otherwise differently positioned? There simply is no distinction to be drawn between decision and non-decision causation with respect to the variable of counterfactuality.

As for the contention that injury causation is fundamentally distinct from decision causation because it is scientific, while decision causation is non-scientific, it is difficult to know quite what to make of that. The reference to science certainly cannot be intended to indicate any version of

---

[40]   Above n 1.
[41]   Above n 1.

the scientific method. Admittedly, when constructing the counterfactual world in so-called injury causation cases one is more likely to draw on *evidence* from the hard sciences (physics, chemistry) or perhaps from epidemiological studies or other public health data, than when construct-ing counterfactuals for decision-causation cases, where scientific evidence, if presented at all, would be more likely to be of the behavioural-science variety. Those different sources of evidence might go to the reliability of our judgements in those two types of decision,[42] but do not seem to make them different in essence.

The second type of claim about the distinct status of decision causation is an assertion that while it involves the same *type* of inquiry as other causal investigations, we are unjustified in having the degree of confidence in the conclusions we arrive at in decision-causation inquiries that we have in our conclusions in non-decision-causation inquiries. It is hard to know how to resolve such a claim. Strassfeld, in a useful article about the use of counterfactuals in law, took note of two distinct attitudes on the part of judges and legal scholars.[43] He labelled these counterfactual bravado and counterfactual dread. The former is an unfounded confidence in one's ability to make reliable counterfactual judgments. It emphasises that counterfactual thinking is the bread and butter of everyday cognition. We may be biologically selected to be good at it. Counterfactual dread is the opposite: the feeling that the speculative construction of the unreal alternative world which counterfactual thinking requires is a fanciful process that cannot be disciplined and—at least in the administration of justice—should be avoided if possible. It is important to note that Strassfeld did not claim that this distinction maps onto the one between non-decision causation and decision causation. Indeed the examples that he gives show that he thinks it does not.[44] He simply points out that judicial opinions are replete with instances of both counterfactual bravado and counterfactual dread. This suggests that if we are trying to evaluate whether decision-causation cases pose a greater reliability barrier than non-decision-causation cases, we probably cannot get very far by simply relying on judicial statements about them.

In evaluating claims that we are unjustified in feeling confident about our evaluation of decision-causation cases, we might simply look at instances of such inquiries. But it is hard to get very far doing so. Some decision-causation speculations are incontestably easier than some non-decision causation claims. The stop sign case is an instance of this. But

---

[42] That is, *if* we have more confidence in evidence from the hard sciences than we do in evidence from the social sciences.

[43] Strassfeld, above n 13, at 348-52.

[44] *Ibid*, at 351.

equally, some decision-causation inquiries—the beauty contest case for instance—are hard to call. There are easy and hard cases of both types.

Now of course the claim about decision-causation judgements being harder to make than non-decision-causation judgements need not rest on a claim that this is so in all instances. Recall here the distinction that law draws between past and future facts, and the consequences that distinction has for the standard of proof: the plaintiff must demonstrate the former[45] on a more-likely-than-not basis, while with the latter we apply simple probabilities. The most commonly offered justification for that rests on ease of proof and the unfairness of setting too high a hurdle in the face of an injured plaintiff. Future events—that is, the likelihood of their happening—are thought to be harder to prove than past ones, so we adopt a different causal standard for all such events. However, *some* future events—for instance, that the sun will come up tomorrow—would not be at all difficult to establish, at least on a more-likely-than-not basis. Equally many past events are the result of ongoing contestation and may never be resolved. Yet we might still agree that *on the whole* future events are harder to prove than past ones, sufficiently so as to justify the selection of some different causal standard for all such events. Perhaps the same can be said about decision-causation cases—namely that *in general* we would be unjustified in having the degree of confidence in them that we have in our judgments in non-decision-causation cases, and that fact calls out for some abandonment of the necessitation standard for causation. Even so, it is hard to assess whether this premise is true.

In speculating about whether it might be, it seems worth noting that judicial statements that human decisions are different from anything and everything else are made in an atmosphere characterised by the commitment to free will that permeates the common law. The law tends to be metaphysically libertarian—viewing (human) decisions as products of free will which stand outside the deterministic causal world within which the rest of nature functions. To say that we can predict a given human decision is in some sense disrespectfully to rank the decision maker as a predictable and less-than-fully-autonomous cipher. And the law resists this. In this context it is worth recalling the role that the doctrine of novus actus interveniens plays in the parallel doctrine of proximate cause. It operates to cut off the defendant's legal responsibility because of the intervention of some act of free will. It does so in circumstances where mere intervention of the natural world would not operate to cut off such responsibility or, if it would, we would endow the natural phenomenon with a metaphorical free will by labelling it an act of God.

---

[45]   Meaning before the trial.

It seems also worth drawing attention to a second phenomenon that may prompt judges conducting causal inquiries to treat human decisions as special. The first part of the counterfactual causal inquiry requires judges to search backward through a myriad of sine qua non causes of the harm until they light upon the one causal ancestor that will be regarded as the operative legal cause. Because judges are predisposed to focus on human action rather than other causes, their focus is on the defendant's misbehaviour. That is, in the face of a general causal profligacy, we initially search back in time, ignoring other physical elements that are necessary preconditions for the plaintiff's harm and ignoring general states of affairs, until we light upon the defendant's fault. It seems small wonder then that when we start searching *forward* in time in the counterfactual inquiry we are primed to regard human actions as distinct from other features of that hypothetical world.

However, both of the foregoing points—the allegiance to free will and the solution to causal proliferation—operate only as explanations for why judges would be psychologically disposed to treat decision causation as distinct, not as justifications for doing so. Perhaps these points should operate to make us suspicious of assertions that there is anything special about decision causation cases that requires special rules. At the least they might make us backtrack and question whether the classification 'decision' is itself the right one for our purposes. So far, this chapter has proceeded on the basis that, for instance, (1) a woman's decision whether to have an abortion in light of some special risk associated with her pregnancy, and (2) a driver's decision to stop at a stop sign, are both *decisions*. Yet arguably these two are not the same thing at all. One is a serious and life-wrenching deliberation that might involve seeking the views of medical experts, loved ones and religious advisors. The other may be more akin to an automatic reflex than a conscious process. And what about decisions made by corporations? It could be argued that we should not be using the same word—decision—to describe these disparate phenomena.

This in turn should remind us of the instability of the distinction between decision- and non-decision-causation cases. It is no accident that cases like the stop-sign case—which on a technical analysis would qualify as a decision-causation inquiry—are not identified by the judges as decision-causation cases. Consider a case where a factory pollutes the air above a city and a resident of the city breathes the air over a period of years and eventually contracts some lung disease. This seems to be a non-decision-causation case. Yet if the resident had not decided to breathe he or she would not have contracted the lung disease. Of course, despite the fact that breathing is to some extent under voluntary control, we do not generally regard breathing as a decision, and rightly so. However, one might conjure up some sort of spectrum of voluntariness, with breathing near one end, stopping at stop signs in the middle, and decisions about major life choices at the other end.

It may be that there are variables at stake here apart from that of relative confidence in our judgements about different types of counterfactuals. So far this chapter has proceeded as though confidence and reliability were the only things at stake, because that was the principal concern that courts have expressed about decision-causation cases. Are there other concerns?

There might be cases where courts fear that entertaining evidence about certain types of decisions brings the judicial system into disrepute—that is, if the decisions themselves were in some sense not respectable. Consider the beauty contest case, *Chaplin*. If the court had to resolve the causation issue in that case on the basis of the orthodox approach to causation then there would have to be a forensic replication of the decision in question. The judge would have to conjure up a counterfactual in which the plaintiff had been notified that she was among the finalists and had shown up to be judged. When one contemplates how things might proceed when the court reached the bathing suit portion of the trial one can well imagine judges casting about for some alternative approach. The solution reached in *Chaplin*—giving the plaintiff the portion of the value of winning the contest equivalent to her being one of a dozen finalists—might be seen as a way of avoiding having a judge assess whether she looked like a beauty contest winner or loser. It is worth recalling here that courts are in a perpetual legitimacy crisis and thus disposed if possible to avoid procedures that might tend to undermine their authority. There are examples in the law of otherwise relevant inquiries that are avoided because they are too distasteful or embarrassing to pursue publicly, and one might speculate that some instances of decision causation—in particular ones where courts rely on it as justifying a purely statistical, proportional approach to causation—could be explained on those grounds. However, it does not seem that this is a problem that would arise more than very occasionally. It seems unlikely, at least on its own, to amount to a justification for special causation rules.

What about decisions where there is a particular history of disregard or even abuse of decision-making autonomy? An example here might be choices about medical treatment, especially decisions by members of historically-subjugated groups, such as women or persons diagnosed with a mental illness. Arguably the medical profession's record of paternalism and undervaluation of patient autonomy might leave us today with a wish to treat decision-making by such persons as in need of special protection. When someone has violated that autonomy, as a doctor will have done if he or she fails to provide information about material risks, then there may be some reason, at least in judicial deliberations about civil liability, to vindicate that abused autonomy by treating that decision as special, regardless of what we might think about our ability to predict how it might have been made. The consolation-prize approach in *Lachambre* does this, and related concerns might motivate and explain other judicial claims that decision causation is special and merits distinctive treatment. Possibly such concerns might even operate to justify such special treatment.

However, it is not clear what such special treatment should be. Here the decision of the Ontario Court of Appeal in *Folland v Reardon*[46] is of interest. Like *Henderson*,[47] the case involved a claim against a lawyer who had been negligent in the conduct of a trial. It raised the same decision-causation issue: would competent conduct have produced a different result? As in *Henderson*, the plaintiff in *Folland* advocated loss-of-chance causation. But here the court rejected it. It did so partly on its judgement that although loss-of-chance was fine for a beauty-contest case like *Chaplin*, the result of a trial, even a hypothetical one, was more predictable: 'the outcome of a criminal trial is knowable in the sense that an informed, reasonable assessment can be made of what the outcome would be if the relevant evidence is known'.[48] But, although the distinction drawn by the court in *Folland* rested largely on predictability, it went somewhat beyond that. The court branded the beauty-contest outcome as dependant on chance, fate and fortune, as opposed to trials which 'are supposed to be decided on the proper application of known legal principles'.[49] Loss-of-chance causation was appropriate to evaluating the value of a lost lottery ticket, and the court in *Folland* did not want to place a hypothetical trial in that same category.

The treatment of decision causation in *Folland* is noteworthy for its explicit concern with the way in which selecting a given causation test to apply to a given hypothetical decision says something important about that decision and, in this case, by extension says something about the administration of justice.

I conclude, then, with a suggestion for further investigation. If claims about the unicity of decision causation rest entirely on the relative reliability of our speculations about hypothetical choices, as opposed to speculations about hypotheticals that do not involve choices, then we should be wary of them; it is far from clear that the special rules that rest on such claims stand on sound ground. There are explanations for why we might be psychologically disposed to treat decisions, including hypothetical ones, as singular, exceptional phenomena, but it is far from obvious that we are any worse at predicting the outcomes of decisions than we are at

---

[46] Above n 28.
[47] Above n 27.
[48] *Folland*, above n 28, at [90].
[49] *Ibid.*

predicting the ordinary, non-decision outcomes. However, there are decisions and then there are decisions, and those same explanations for why we might be inclined to see some classes of decisions as distinctive might both explain why judges have so often been inclined to treat them as exceptional and, more importantly, point the way to a more refined justification for why we might, at least on occasion, be right to do so.

13

Non-Delegable Duties and Vicarious Liability

ROBERT STEVENS*

I. INTRODUCTION

A disguised form of vicarious liability is imposed whenever the defendant is said to be under a 'non-delegable' duty, in the sense that he cannot acquit himself by exercising reasonable care in entrusting the work to a reputable contractor but must actually assure that it is done—and done carefully.[1]

THE PURPOSE OF this chapter is to doubt the widely-held view that non-delegable duties of care are a disguised form of vicarious liability.[2] If they are, non-delegable duties would offend the general rule that it is impossible to be vicariously liable for the unauthorised acts of independent contractors.[3] Consequently non-delegable duties would be a logical fraud.[4] This chapter's thesis is that the law is not so dishonest.

To state that a duty is 'non-delegable' is only to state its nature and not the reason for its existence. The same criticism might, of course, be levelled at the 'tort' of negligence. The key to understanding non-delegable duties is that there are several situations where the law imposes strict liability with disparate underlying rationales.[5] These are only a logical fraud if it is assumed that the common law of torts only imposes liability where the defendant is at fault.

---

* Barrister; University of Oxford.
[1] J Fleming, *The Law of Torts,* 9th edn (Sydney, LBC Information Services, 1998) 433. Cf JP Swanton 'Non-Delegable Duties: Liability for the Negligence of Independent Contractors' (1991) 4 *Journal of Contract Law* 183 and (1992) 5 *Journal of Contract Law* 26.
[2] See the New South Wales Civil Liability Act 2002 s 5Q; DA Ipp (Chairman), 'Review of the Law of Negligence: Final Report' (Australia 2002) [11.11].
[3] *Quarman v Burnett* (1840) 6 M & W 499, 151 ER 509 (Ex) [*Quarman*]; *671122 Ontario Ltd v Sagaz Industries Canada Inc* [2001] 2 SCR 983; *Sweeney v Boylan Nominees Pty Ltd* [2006] HCA 19.
[4] G Williams, 'Liability for Independent Contractors' [1956] *CLJ* 180.
[5] *KLB v British Columbia* [2003] 2 SCR 403, [31] (McLachlin CJ) [*KLB*].

The label 'non-delegable duty' is arguably a misnomer. Strictly speaking, all duties not to harm others are incapable of delegation.[6] However, if I merely owe a duty to take care, then if I select a competent contractor and provide appropriate supervision, then I have discharged my duty by doing so. A non-delegable duty cannot be discharged through the careful selection and supervision of someone else to carry out the task.

Sometimes the non-delegable duty approaches the absolute, a duty to achieve a particular result.[7] Sometimes the obligation is that reasonable care will be taken of the claimant. Where care is not taken, the defendant cannot escape liability by establishing that he or she personally is not at fault. When, why and to what extent liability will be imposed is not explained by describing a duty as non-delegable. However in each case, the defendant's liability is primary, not vicarious.

II. ATTRIBUTION

In order to make good the proposition that non-delegable duties are not examples of vicarious liability, it is first necessary to provide a preliminary account of when it is possible to be liable for the commission of a tort, although the words or actions which constitute the tort are not factually spoken or performed by the defendant.

Pollock claimed that he introduced the label of 'vicarious liability' into the common law.[8] This label accorded with his view that what is attributed is liability for the tort, not the words or actions themselves. This is now academic orthodoxy and vicarious liability is commonly described as a species of strict liability.[9] On this view, sometimes called the 'Servant's Tort' theory, one party is held liable for the torts of another despite not personally committing the tort. The most common form of vicarious liability is the liability of an employer for the torts committed by an employee in the course of employment. Whilst it may be an essential element of the tort committed by the employee that he or she was at fault, this is irrelevant so far as the liability of the employer is concerned.

However, it is an error to think that the only rules of attribution are those arising from an employment relationship. There are cases where one person's words or actions may be attributed to another outside of employment. If X authorises, ratifies, procures or conspires with Y for the commission of words or acts by Y, the commission of those words or acts by Y are attributed to X. If those words or acts would constitute a tort if

---

[6] *Cassidy v Ministry of Health* [1951] 2 KB 343 (CA) 363 (Denning LJ).

[7] Eg Provision and Use of Work Equipment Regulations 1998, reg 11.

[8] OW Holmes, *Holmes-Pollock Letters: The Correspondence of Mr Justice Holmes and Sir Frederick Pollock 1874-1932* vol I (Cambridge, Cambridge University Press, 1941) 233.

[9] Eg *Bernard v The Attorney General of Jamaica* [2004] UKPC 47, [21] (Lord Steyn).

committed by either of them acting independently, X and Y are jointly liable as principals for the same tort. These examples of attribution establish the necessary link between the actor and the person to whom the actions are attributed through the latter's participation in the action. It is unnecessary to show any employment relationship between X and Y. The fact that the party whose actions or words are authorised, ratified, procured or conspired with is an independent contractor does not prevent the attribution of those actions or words.

Cases of authorisation have most commonly occurred in relation to nuisance and defamation.[10] An example of an authorised public nuisance is *Ellis v Sheffield Gas Consumers Co.*[11] The defendant, without statutory authority, engaged a contractor to dig up a highway so that it could lay some gas pipes. The contractor left a heap of rubble on the pavement, over which the claimant tripped, injuring himself. The defendant was held liable on the basis that the digging up of the highway was a public nuisance which the defendant had authorised. The action as it had been authorised was attributed to the defendant who was held liable. That the party who dug up the road was an independent contractor was irrelevant.

It is in relation to the attribution of words that the question of authorisation most commonly arises. In relation to a statement it is orthodoxy that what is attributed is the statement and not the wrong. If I authorise a statement knowing it to be untrue I can be liable in deceit, regardless of whether the person who actually speaks is wholly innocent.[12] The elements of the tort of deceit, a misstatement and dishonesty, can both be attributed to me. Similarly, where the statement is defamatory, the attribution of the statement to the principal will mean that the principal has committed a tort because defamation is a tort of strict liability. In *Colonial Mutual Life Assurace Society Ltd v Producers and Citizens Co-Operative Assurance Co of Australia Ltd* a canvasser was engaged by an insurance company.[13] The canvasser did not have authority, either actual or ostensible, to conclude a contract on behalf of his principal but he did have authority, actual and ostensible, to 'speak, and in fact spoke, with the voice of the defendant'.[14] He was expressly prohibited from

---

[10] Eg *Egger v Viscount Chelmsford* [1965] 1 QB 248 (CA) [*Egger*].

[11] (1853) 2 El & Bl 767, 118 ER 955 (CA); cf *Holliday v National Telephone Co* [1899] 2 QB 392 (CA) [*Holliday*].

[12] *Cornfoot v Fowke* (1840) 6 M & W 358, 370, 372, 373-74, 151 ER 450 (Ex); *Ludgater v Love* (1881) 44 LT 694 (CA); *Gordon Hill Trust Ltd v Segall* [1941] 2 All ER 379 (CA) 390; *Egger*, above n 10, 261; *Sugar v Peat Marwick Ltd* (1988) 66 OR (2d) 766 (HCJ) 238-39. In *Armstrong v Strain* [1952] 1 KB 232 (CA) the principal knew that facts contained in a statement made by his agent were untrue but did not know that the statement had been made. As neither the principal nor agent were guilty of dishonesty the claim failed.

[13] [1931] 46 CLR 41 (HCA); cf *Colonial Mutual Life Assurance Society Ltd v Macdonald* [1931] AD 412.

[14] [1931] 46 CLR 41 (HCA), at 48 (Dixon J).

defaming any other insurance company. In breach of this prohibition, he defamed the plaintiff. The High Court of Australia held the principal liable even though the agent was an independent contractor.[15] It suffices that the words (or actions) are authorised, even if the commission of a tort is not.[16] The agent canvasser would also be liable.

It is sometimes possible to attribute an agent's statement to the principal where there is only apparent and not actual authority. There are two doctrinal bases for such attribution, which it is important to keep separate. First, a principal may hold an agent out as having authority to make statements on his or her behalf. If a third party relies on this holding out, the principal may be estopped from denying the agent's lack of authority. Second, a principal who creates the objective impression that an agent has authority to enter into contracts on his or her behalf will be bound by such agreements the agent enters into. This is part of the general rule that we are bound by the objective impression of agreement that we create, even if this impression is false. In many cases the principal will be bound on either basis by the words of the agent. The significance of the difference is that in order to rely upon estoppel, it is necessary to show reliance, which is not a necessary pre-condition of a contract. Where the claim is not contractual, for example in the case of defamatory statements, it will be necessary to establish reliance where the statement is unauthorised.

Where one person acts on behalf of another, but without authority, and that other subsequently ratifies and assents to the act done, he or she thereby becomes responsible for it, just as if he or she had authorised the act in advance.[17] In *Hilbery v Hatton* an agent bought a ship on behalf of the defendant from a party who had no title to it.[18] The agent lacked the defendant's authority, but the defendant subsequently ratified the purchase of the ship. The defendant was held liable for conversion. It is necessary that the ratifying party knows the nature of the act, but it is not necessary that he or she knows that it is wrongful. Again it is irrelevant that the agent was an independent contractor.

It is in relation to the liability of the management of companies that the attribution of acts that they have procured is of most importance. To procure is to take positive steps to induce or persuade. Unlike authorisation, in order to establish that an act has been procured it is unnecessary to show that it is carried out on the other's behalf. For example in *Wah Tat Bank Ltd v Chan* the managing director of a shipping company was

---

[15] Cf Fleming, above n 1, at 413-14.

[16] Cf PS Atiyah, *Vicarious Liability in the Law of Torts* (London, Butterworths, 1967) 300-1.

[17] *Wilson v Tumman* (1843) 6 Man & G 236, 242, 134 ER 879, 882 (CP) (Tindal CJ).

[18] (1864) 2 H & C 822, 159 ER 341 (Ex).

responsible for the company's policy of delivering goods without production of the necessary documentation by the consignee.[19] This amounted to conversion of the goods to which the claimant banks had good possessory title. The managing director was held liable jointly with his company for his procuring the commission of the tort, although the employees were acting on behalf of the company, not the director.

Where 'two persons... agree on common action, in the course of, and to further which, one of them commits a tort'[20] both are liable as joint tortfeasors. The most famous example of the application of this principle is *Brooke v Bool*.[21] The defendant let a shop to the claimant next door to the defendant's home. By arrangement, the defendant entered the shop to check that it was secured. A lodger in the defendant's house told him that he could smell gas coming from the shop and they both went to investigate. They both examined a gas pipe using a naked flame, the lodger examining the inaccessible upper half because the defendant was elderly. An explosion occurred as a result of the lodger examining the pipe. The plaintiff sued the defendant for the damage done because of the lodger's careless action. Several alternative grounds for the result were given, but it was accepted that as they had been engaged in a joint enterprise the actions of the lodger would be attributed to the landlord and they were held jointly liable. One advantage to the claimant from this rule of attribution is that it would be unnecessary to prove which of the flames of the two conspirators caused the explosion.[22] As the acts of each are attributed to them all, all are liable.

Outside cases of authorisation, ratification, procurement and conspiracy, the necessary link between the party acting or speaking, and the person to whom the words or actions are attributed may be established by a relationship of employment where the words or actions are within the course of employment. Here attribution takes place because the words or acts are within the scope of the relationship, not because of any participation in what was said or done.

There are other occasions where the necessary relationship for the purposes of attribution may be established where there is no contract of employment or any contract at all.[23] Where the owner of a motor car

---

[19] [1975] AC 507 (PC).
[20] *The Koursk* [1924] P 140 (CA) 155 (Scrutton LJ).
[21] [1928] 2 KB 578.
[22] Cf *Cook v Lewis* [1951] SCR 830.
[23] This is one reason why the view that vicarious liability is based upon a claim brought by the third party upon an implied contractual indemnity by the employer to the employee must be rejected; see J Neyers, 'A Theory of Vicarious Liability' (2005) 43 *Alberta Law Review* 287. Other objections include: (1) there is no indemnity from employer to employee, rather it is the employee who is required to indemnify the employer: *Lister v Romford Ice and Cold Storage Ltd* [1957] AC 555 (HL); (2) it offends privity of contract; (3) it would allow the employer to escape liability by excluding the indemnity; and (4) it cannot explain vicarious liability for malicious or prohibited torts.

entrusts the vehicle to another for the performance of a task for the owner, the owner of the car will be liable for torts committed during such use of the car.[24] The same principle has been applied to boats.[25]

A rule which was confined to motor cars or the use of chattels would be anomalous and have little to recommend it. In obiter dicta a majority of the House of Lords in *Launchbury v Morgans* rejected any such limited rule.[26] A more general principle could be formulated. Whenever one party carries out a task for the benefit of another and the beneficiary exercises control over the identity and conduct of the person carrying out the task, the conduct of the task is attributed to the beneficiary. Under this formulation, a contract of employment or the ownership of the chattel used are merely methods of demonstrating the requisite control. The recognition in England[27] and Canada[28] of the liability of a temporary employer who has no contract of employment with the employee but has the requisite degree of control supports this broad formulation. It is potentially misleading to use the language of 'agency' in this context. The rules of attribution of one person's wrongs or acts to another are not necessarily the same as the rules for determining when one person has the actual or ostensible authority to vary another's contractual or other obligations.

However, the majority of the High Court of Australia (with McHugh J in powerful dissent) in *Scott v Davis* rejected such a broad doctrine, confining vicarious liability to situations of employment, subject to an anomalous motor car exception.[29] In England and Canada, such a minimalist approach is becoming difficult to support.

Regardless of whether a broad or narrow approach to the nature of the relationship sufficient for the purposes of attribution is adopted, where the task is performed by an independent contractor, the beneficiary has not retained sufficient control over the conduct of the task for it to be attributed to him or her.[30]

The examples of non-delegable duties which are usually given are abnormal or extra-hazardous activities, private nuisance, public nuisance, breaches of various statutory duties, an employer's duty in respect of the safety of employees, a carrier's duty of seaworthines, occupiers' duties to

---

[24] *Ormrod v Crosville Motor Services Ltd* [1953] 1 WLR 409 (Devlin J), affd [1953] 1 WLR 1120 (CA).

[25] *'Thelma' (Owners) v University College School* [1953] 2 Lloyd's Rep 613.

[26] [1973] AC 127 (CA) 135 (Lord Wilberforce), 140 (Lord Pearson), 148 (Lord Salmon).

[27] *Viasystems (Tyneside) Ltd v Thermal Transfer(Northern) Ltd* [2005] All ER(D) 93 (CA).

[28] *Blackwater v Plint* [2005] 3 SCR 3.

[29] (2000) 204 CLR 333 (HCA).

[30] *Quarman*, above n 3.

visitors, bailees' duties to bailors, hospitals' duties to patients and (possibly) various other cases where there has been an assumption of responsibility by the defendant to the claimant.[31]

The view that these cases are properly seen as examples of disguised vicarious liability is closely related to the view that the general position in the common law is that there is no liability without fault. Where liability is imposed without fault, it is assumed that this is vicarious liability disguised. In order to show that this is not necessarily so, some consideration of when and why the law requires fault to be shown before a tort is actionable is necessary.

III.   FAULT

A tort is a species of wrong.[32] A wrong is a breach of a duty. A breach of a duty is an infringement of a right. Before a defendant can be characterised as a tortfeasor the anterior question of whether the claimant had a right against him or her must be answered.[33]

Cave J in *Allen v Flood*,[34] in a passage described by Hohfeld as 'unusually discriminating and instructive',[35] stated: 'The personal rights with which we are most familiar are: 1. Rights of reputation; 2. Rights of bodily safety and freedom; 3. Rights of property'.[36] Cave J is providing a list of classes of rights which are personal to us and which are exigible against the rest of the world. His list is not exhaustive.

Once it is accepted that the law of torts is concerned with the secondary obligations generated by the infringement of (real) primary rights, with correlative (real) duties imposed on others, it becomes apparent that there are constraints on when it is meaningful to speak of liability based upon a tort. Not all liabilities can be convincingly classified as based upon the breach of an anterior duty. My obligation to pay tax is not imposed because of the infringement of a right the state has against me that I will not earn income. Rather, my liability to pay tax is primary, triggered whenever my income passes a certain threshold.

Our (primary) rights good against everyone else are not absolute. All actions carry with them the risk of some harm to someone else. If my right

---

[31]   Atiyah, above n 16, at 350-73.

[32]   P Birks, 'The Concept of a Civil Wrong' in DG Owen (ed), *Philosophical Foundations of Tort Law* (Oxford, Clarendon Press, 1995) 29; cf OW Holmes, *The Common Law* (Boston, Little, Brown & Co, 1881) 144.

[33]   *Allen v Flood* [1898] AC 1 (HL) 28 (Cave J) [*Allen*]; A Goodhart, 'The foundation of tortious liability' (1938) 2 *MLR* 1.

[34]   *Allen*, above n 33.

[35]   WN Hohfeld, 'Rights and Jural Relations' in WW Cook (ed), *Fundamental Legal Conceptions* (New Haven and London, Yale University Press, 1919) 35-64.

[36]   *Allen*, above n 33, at 29.

to bodily safety was absolute, this would require a real correlative duty on all others that they refrain from all conduct which posed some risk of harm to me. If all persons had a right of such a kind it would entail that all of us were under a duty that we refrain from any conduct which exposed any other to the risk of harm. We would all, therefore, be under a duty to each other not to drive a car, not to manufacture anything and, indeed, not to get out of bed in the morning in case we harmed anyone else by so doing. All conduct carries some risk of harm to someone else, however unlikely. It should be apparent that such absolute rights would be unacceptable.[37] Consequently, whilst it would be possible to require all those who by their actions cause others harm to pay compensation, this could not be justified on the basis that they have committed a tort in relation to the person harmed. We all have no choice but to act somehow, even if it is just to roll over in bed.[38] This does not mean that such liability is impossible to contemplate, but merely that like our liability to pay tax it would not be based upon the breach of an anterior duty to refrain from acting in a certain way.

In determining the scope of our primary rights against everyone else, the law must compromise between everyone's interest in not being harmed and everyone's interest in liberty of action. As Lord Reid said in *Bolton v Stone*, 'In the crowded conditions of modern life even the most careful person cannot avoid creating some risks and accepting others'.[39]

This compromise does not always require proof of fault. If without permission I deliberately kiss another, destroy someone else's car, publish a statement about another which is defamatory, block the public highway or walk on another's land I am prima facie a tortfeasor. I am liable even if I am wholly without fault. If I reasonably but mistakenly believe that I have permission to kiss, that the car is mine, that the statement is true,[40] that I have statutory authorisation to block the road or that I have a right of way over the land I cross, I am still a wrongdoer. It is unnecessary to show the intention to cause harm, or commit a wrong. It suffices that I act with the intention of exercising a liberty which I do not have with respect to the claimant. So, it is sufficient to show that I intended to kiss, to smash, to publish, to block or to walk where I did. The law of torts does not allow us to take liberties.

When in acting the defendant lacked the intention in the above sense, the law generally requires that there will only be a breach of duty where the defendant has been negligent. However, this requirement of fault in cases

---

[37] S Perry, 'The Impossibility of General Strict Liability' (1988) 1 *Canadian Journal of Law & Jurisprudence* 143.

[38] Holmes, above n 32, at 95.

[39] [1951] AC 850 (HL) 867.

[40] Eg *E Hulton & Co v Jones* [1910] AC 20 (HL).

of unintentional conduct is not as all-pervasive in the common law as is generally assumed. Moreover, the exceptions are not necessarily disguised vicarious liability.

IV. NORMAL AND ABNORMAL RISKS

A. The 'rule in *Rylands v Fletcher*'

When lawyers do not understand the scope and rationale for a rule of law, instead of giving it a name which describes its meaning (like negligence, remoteness, causation, nuisance or privity) the rule is named after the case which gave birth to it. One example of this phenomenon is the 'rule in *Rylands v Fletcher*'.[41] Is it or any of its progeny best seen as vicarious liability disguised?

It is part of the bargain of being a member of a society that we must all absorb the costs of ordinary risks reasonably run. Of course there is no *real* agreement between everyone, but the metaphor of the bargain is useful for the purpose of exposition and allows us to see when it is, and is not, appropriate to require fault.

Automobiles are 'one of the background risks that must be borne as part of group living'.[42] When first introduced, automobiles were not one of the usual risks with which we each had to put up,[43] but this is no longer true today. I am at liberty to drive a car so long as I do so carefully, and the quid pro quo is that you are too. You may object that you loathe automobiles and would consider the world a better place if we all walked. However, individual members of society do not get to choose the risks they have to accept. This decision is made by the courts. If members of society were able to bargain ex ante behind a veil of ignorance, assuming that they are rational but with no knowledge of their own personal preferences, what reasonable risks would be accepted as normal to be borne by all of us? Like it or not, driving a car is normal. In ascertaining what is reasonable conduct, the courts take into account both the foreseeable risks of the claimant's conduct and its expected social value, but they do not simply aggregate these values in a utilitarian manner in order to maximise wealth, as some economists have suggested.[44]

---

[41] (1868) LR 3 HL 330.

[42] G Fletcher, 'Fairness and Utility in Tort Theory' 85 (1972) *Harvard Law Review* 537, 543.

[43] J Spencer, 'Motor Cars and the Rule in *Rylands v Fletcher*: A Chapter of Accidents in the History of Law and Motoring' [1983] *CLJ* 65.

[44] The most important work on this issue has been done by Richard Wright. See eg R Wright, 'The Standards of Care in Negligence Law' in Owen, above n 32; R Wright, 'Hand, Posner and the Myth of the "Hand Formula"' (2003) 4 *Theoretical Inquiries in Law* 145.

Of course, in the world as we find it risks are not reciprocal in the sense that we all engage in the same sort of activities. A majority of adults drive cars but some do not, and the extent of use differs. Although a tiny number of people fly aircraft, aeroplanes are an ordinary part of living in our society and we cannot justify a strict liability rule applicable to aircraft based upon the idea of reciprocity.[45] Behind a veil of ignorance it would be accepted that flying aircraft is normal, as are activities like making bottles of ginger beer, and that we must all accept the reasonable risks associated with such activities, whether we are involved in them ourselves or, indeed, whether we passionately oppose them.

The standard of care that all others are under to take care not to unintentionally injure my person or property is objective because I have the same right good against every other person.[46] A learner driver is held to the same standard of conduct as a competent driver.[47] A person who gets behind the wheel of a car for the first time is not morally responsible for failing to meet the standard the law imposes. She is not responsible for being a novice. Rather, the objective standard is the line the law has drawn where the claimant's right ends and the liberty of everyone, including the defendant, begins.[48]

Of course, what must be done in order to conform to this objective standard varies according to the circumstances. How a car may be driven on a motorway is different from the sort of conduct which is acceptable on a country lane. We cannot expect the blind to be able to see, although we can expect them to refrain from driving.

The compromise required between everyone's interest in liberty and everyone's interest in avoiding harm provides an explanation for the 'rule in *Rylands v Fletcher*'. The defendant, a textile manufacturer, constructed a reservoir on his land in order to provide water for steam engines in order to power his mills. Under the defendant's land were mining tunnels which, unknown to the defendant, connected with the claimant's mine. Reputable contractors were retained to perform the work. The water escaped, flooding and damaging the claimant's mining tunnels. The House of Lords held the defendant liable. The case has come to stand for the proposition that a defendant is strictly liable for damage caused by the 'non-natural' use of his or her land, where the damage results from the escape of

---

[45]   *Contra* Fletcher, above n 42, at 543. But see Civil Aviation Act 1982, s 76(2).

[46]   *Vaughan v Menlove* (1837) 3 Bing NC 468, 132 ER 490 (CP).

[47]   *Nettleship v Weston* [1971] 2 QB 691 (CA); cf *Guinness, Son & Co (Dublin) Ltd v The Freshfield (The Lady Gwendolen)* [1965] P 294 (CA).

[48]   N MacCormick, *Legal Right and Social Democracy: Essays in Legal and Political Philosophy* (Oxford, Clarendon Press, 1982) 218.

something which it could be reasonably foreseen would do such damage if it escaped. Liability is, and was, imposed even where the escape itself was wholly unforeseeable.

Rylands v Fletcher could have developed in England and Canada so as to be complementary with the requirement of negligence where the conduct complained of created 'normal' risks. This has occurred in the US.

If the defendant's conduct is abnormal it may be considered to be outside of the bargain that members of society would reach ex ante. I must accept the risks attached to your driving of your car, but I need not accept your need to keep lions in your back garden. Even if all reasonable care is taken to prevent the escape of a lion, the risk, however slight, of being mauled by a ferocious feline in the street is not one of the normal risks of group living which we must all be taken to have accepted, at least not in England or Canada.

In the original American *Restatement of the Law of Torts*, the 'rule in *Rylands v Fletcher*' was characterised as a special rule for ultra-hazardous activity.[49] A rule based solely upon the degree of risk the activity involves has few attractions. If I drive at 70 miles per hour the degree of care and attention which is required is higher than when driving at five miles per hour. Similarly the degree of care required when working with plutonium is rather different from that required when working with plasticine. Why should the mere fact that the risk run is very hazardous entail strict liability even where the decision to undertake the activity was reasonable and all reasonable care was taken in carrying it out?

The better rule, which was adopted in the *Restatement (Second)* and draft *Restatement (Third)*, is that the defendant must accept the risk of harm caused by 'abnormal' activity.[50] That an activity is ultra-hazardous may be good evidence that it is abnormal, but the two concepts are not co-extensive. Abnormality also fits more closely with the reasons given for the result in *Rylands v Fletcher* itself. Our membership of a society entails that we must bear the risks associated with normal activity. My having an Alsatian in my back garden may be more hazardous than your keeping lions within an ultra-secure pen next door, but it is the abnormality of your activity which means that you must bear the risk of all harm caused while I do not.

'Abnormal' is here used in a special sense and should not be confused with infrequently occurring. The manufacture of munitions for the purpose of a war with Nazi Germany, even if such an activity was a one-off occurrence or extremely hazardous, could not be said to be the creation of

---

[49] *Restatement of the Law of Torts* (1934) §519.
[50] *Restatement (Second) of the Law of Torts* (1965) §165; *Restatement (Third) of the Law of Torts: Liability for Physical Harm–Proposed Final Draft No 1* (2005) §20.

a risk which was not incident to living in England in 1942.[51] Members of a society have to put up with the reasonable risks incident to its defence. What is meant by 'abnormal' is that the risk run is one which is outside of the bargain of those risks which must be accepted as part of group living in our society. The reservoir in *Rylands v Fletcher* was constructed for the defendant's personal benefit, not anyone else's. At the time, such a reservoir was outside of the normal risks neighbours imposed upon one another. Seen in this way, the 'rule in *Rylands v Fletcher*' is not a separate tort at all, but rather one way in which a right can be infringed although the defendant has not acted intentionally or carelessly. Seen in this way, *Rylands v Fletcher* is not an example of disguised vicarious liability for the acts of the independent contractor. Rather the landowner was liable for his own conduct, and that which he authorised, which was outside of the normal risks acceptable as between neighbours.

In England, the rule in *Rylands v Fletcher* has been neutered so that it has become merely a species of private nuisance. It is now an anomalous rule associated with isolated escapes from land. It is so enfeebled that it would be better if it was put out of its misery.[52] One of the reasons for its emasculation in England may be that, however normatively attractive, requiring the determination of what is an 'abnormal' risk is considered too uncertain on which to base a rule which can be administered by a court. Despite this, other pockets of the abnormal risks rule persist. For example, in relation to dangerous animals, or animals with unusually dangerous characteristics, strict liability for damage caused is enshrined in legislation.[53] Similarly the strict liability of nuclear installations may be based upon the same principle. Although it would be preferable to generalise these individual pockets into a wider rule as has occurred in the US, it may be that this is no longer possible in England.

An alternative categorisation of *Rylands v Fletcher* is that it is a form of 'enterprise liability'.[54] This categorisation argues that a profit-making enterprise should bear all of the costs it creates, regardless of fault. Some have sought to justify 'enterprise liability' in economic terms. It is sometimes said that all of an enterprise's costs should be internalised to it, resulting in the price of its product or service accurately reflecting the costs involved. In a competitive market, those enterprises with the lowest costs will thrive, resulting in wealth maximisation. A moral argument in favour of 'enterprise liability' is that if an enterprise is profit-making, it should

---

[51]   *Read v Lyons* [1947] AC 156 (HL) [*Read*].
[52]   D Nolan, 'The Distinctiveness of *Rylands v Fletcher*' (2005) 121 *LQR* 421.
[53]   Animals Act 1972, s 2.
[54]   *Transco v Stockport Metropolitan Borough Council* [2004] 1 All ER 589 (HL) [*Transco*].

have to pay for all of the harm it causes on the basis that it should not be able to take the benefit of an activity without accepting all of the attendant burdens.

If the 'rule in *Rylands v Fletcher*' is an example of enterprise liability, it is anomalous. There is no general strict liability for harm caused by enterprises; the general rule is that the claimant must show negligence where the defendant's actions were unintentional. Support for the view that *Rylands v Fletcher* is anomalous can be obtained from the narrow, and seemingly arbitrary, limits within which the rule has been confined in England, for example the requirements that there must have been an escape from the defendant's land.

A third method of categorisation, which is of most relevance to the current discussion, is that *Rylands v Fletcher* should be (re-)interpreted as decided on the basis of vicarious liability for the extra-hazardous activity of independent contractors.[55] The engineers employed by the defendants had been careless in ascertaining whether the reservoir could bear the pressure of water. However, such an interpretation cannot be squared either with the reasoning in the case itself or with how the rule has subsequently been formulated.

There is some English and Canadian[56] authority supporting the view that there should be vicarious liability for the torts of independent contractors where the task undertaken is 'extra-hazardous'. If strict liability for abnormal or extra-hazardous activities is rejected, such a rule applicable to independent contractors appears anomalous and should also be rejected.[57]

In England the modern foundation for the proposition that an employer can be vicariously liable for an independent contractor in cases of extra-hazardous activity is the decision of the Court of Appeal in *Honeywill & Stein Ltd v Larkin Bros Ltd*.[58] A cinema company employed the defendants to install a sound system. With the company's permission, the defendants employed photographers to photograph the equipment for their own business purposes. The photographers used flashes which set fire to the theatre and the defendants were held to be liable for the damage. It was said that an employer could be liable for the 'extra-hazardous'[59] acts carried out by the independent contractor. At the time it was decided, 1934, this was a defensible position. Since the actions of the contractor were authorised by the defendants, they were attributed to it. If, as was

---

[55] *Dunne v North Western Gas Board* [1964] 2 QB 806 (CA) 831; cf *Burnie Port Authority v General Jones Pty Ltd* (1994) 179 CLR 520 (HCA).
[56] Eg *City of St John v Donald* [1926] SCR 371; *Savage v Wilby* [1954] SCR 376.
[57] Atiyah, above n 16, at ch 22.
[58] [1934] 1 KB 191 (CA) [*Honeywill*].
[59] *Ibid*, at 197 (Slesser LJ); cf 200.

then arguable, the law imposed strict liability for harm caused by such extra-hazardous activity, the result is correct. On this view, *Honeywill* is not a disguised form of vicarious liability. However, by 1947 a special rule of strict liability for 'extra-hazardous' activity had been rejected by the House of Lords, a rejection recently reaffirmed,[60] and the basis of the reasoning in *Honeywill* has been undermined. It seems insupportable that a defendant will be held strictly liable for the extra-hazardous activity of an independent contractor, when it would not be so liable if it carefully carried out the same activity itself. The liability for the authorised extra-hazardous or abnormal activities of an independent contractor ought to stand or fall with the choice as to whether there is strict liability generally for such activity.

B.   Australia

In Australia the rule in *Rylands v Fletcher* that limps on in England and Canada has been killed off. In a difficult case, the High Court of Australia in *Burnie Port Authority v General Jones Pty Ltd* refashioned the law by incorporating the rule in *Rylands v Fletcher* into the torts of negligence, nuisance and trespass.[61] The defendants had employed independent contractors to do welding work. They did this next to highly-flammable material, which caused a fire, destroying the building in which the claimant's frozen vegetables were stored. The court held that the defendants were liable in negligence for the breach of their 'non-delegable' duty. However, unless the duty was non-delegable because of the rule in *Rylands v Fletcher*, it is difficult to see the basis for this conclusion. In the earlier decision of *Stevens v Brodribb Sawmilling Co Pty Ltd* the High Court of Australia had rejected any vicarious liability for independent contractors in cases of extra-hazardous activity.[62] Although in *Kondis v State Transport Authority* Mason J had expressed a broader principle underlying some cases of 'non-delegable' duties, which is discussed below, he had expressly disclaimed any single principle underlying *all* cases which was capable of encompassing *Burnie*.[63]

In *Burnie* the majority held that a non-delegable duty arose where:

> One party to that relationship is a person who is in control of premises and who has taken advantage of that control to introduce thereon or to retain therein a dangerous substance or to undertake thereon a dangerous activity or to allow

---

[60]   *Read*, above n 51; *Transco*, above n 54; cf 'Civil Liability for Dangerous Things and Activities' (Law Com No 32).

[61]   Above n 55 [*Burnie*], at 551 (Mason CJ, Deane, Dawson, Toohey and Gaudron JJ).

[62]   (1986) 160 CLR 16 (HCA) [*Stevens*].

[63]   (1984) 154 CLR 672 (HCA) [*Kondis*].

another person to do one of those things. The other party to that relationship is a person, outside the premises and without control over what occurs therein, whose person or property is thereby exposed to a foreseeable risk of danger.[64]

Because this rule is confined to occupiers, it is capable of being squared with the court's earlier rejection of vicarious liability for the actions of independent contractors in the case of extra-hazardous activities in *Stevens*. However, the doctrinal basis for the rule established in *Burnie*, where there is no 'relationship' between the claimant and defendant except that which exists between persons generally, is unclear.

It is ironic that the two dissenters (Brennan and McHugh JJ, with McHugh J's dissent again being particularly powerful) who would have retained the strict liability of the rule in *Rylands v Fletcher* were not prepared to find the defendant liable on the basis of this principle or in negligence.[65] The majority, who opposed the retention of the strict liability of *Rylands v Fletcher* and insisted upon the generalisation of negligence principles, imposed strict liability. Although the rule in *Rylands v Fletcher* as it has developed in the Commonwealth is hedged with indefensible qualifications, the exceptional form of vicarious liability accepted in *Burnie* appears even more anomalous. It should be rejected.

C. Qualified Privilege

Although the reasoning adopted in *Honeywill* appears difficult to defend today, the result seems correct. The claimants were entrusting their premises to the defendants. That no trespass was committed was because of the licence to enter. The defendants' licence to use the theatre did not confer upon them the liberty to burn it down. The licence was implicitly qualified. Indeed, on this explanation the result should have been the same regardless of whether the work done was 'extra-hazardous'. In contrast, if the defendants had employed the same independent contractors to take photographs of the outside of the building from the street, and the negligence of the contractors had resulted in the building's destruction, the defendants should not have been liable. This was not the basis of the decision, however, and the principle has been applied where there is no pre-existing relationship between claimant and defendant.[66]

A privilege or licence is granted by a right-holder, who may expressly qualify it. If I entrust my watch to another on the basis that the borrower must pay for any damage suffered during its use, the borrower should be

---

[64] Above n 55, at 551.

[65] *Ibid*, at 567-81 (Brennan J), 584-95 (McHugh J).

[66] *Johnson v BJW Property Developments Ltd* [2002] 3 All ER 574 (QB) [*Johnson*], although this case may be seen as an example of the application of nuisance principles.

liable for such damage even if wholly without fault in causing it. In many cases it will be possible to infer a contractual promise by the borrower to pay for damage in return for the loan of the object. However, this is unnecessary and may be impossible if, for example, the borrower lacks contractual capacity. My claim can be based upon the infringement of the right to my watch, the privilege to use it having been expressly qualified. It is unnecessary for me to establish that there was a contract between us in order to show that the borrower's privilege to possess was limited.

One effect of the protection of a right may be to generate a privilege to act which would not otherwise exist. It will not always provide the defendant with an absolute privilege and excuse liability to pay damages for consequential losses. If an occupier of premises refuses on request to deliver up to their owner goods taken on to the occupier's land by a person other than the owner, the owner has a licence to enter the land and re-take them[67] but in so doing must pay for any damage he or she commits.[68] The licence is qualified.

Similarly a privilege or licence may be granted by statute but may not be absolute. Anyone who digs up the public highway, either personally or by authorising a contractor to do so on their behalf, commits a public nuisance. A public body may be granted a statutory privilege to dig up the road for the purposes of maintenance, or a private concern may be granted a privilege to lay cables or pipes. The privilege may be qualified so that the work cannot be stopped by those affected but compensation for the nuisance may still be payable. Alternatively, the privilege may be more extensive, so that damages are only payable if the work is carried out carelessly, whether by the defendant or an independent contractor working on his or her behalf.[69] Such cases of qualified privilege are, again, not vicarious liability in disguise.

The decision of the English Court of Appeal in *Alcock v Wraith*,[70] also commonly seen as an example of a non-delegable duty, is also best explained in the same way.[71] An independent contractor was employed by the defendant to replace the roofing slates of a terrace house with tiles. This was a difficult task because of the problem of creating a waterproof seal between the slates of the neighbouring property and the replacement tiles. The defendant was held liable for damage caused by the carelessness

---

[67] RVF Heuston and RA Buckley, *Salmond & Heuston on The Law of Torts*, 21st edn (London, Sweet & Maxwell, 1996) 573-74.

[68] *Anthony v Haney* (1832) 8 Bing 186, 193, 131 ER 372 (Tindal CJ).

[69] *Hardaker v Idle DC* [1896] 1 QB 335 (CA); *Penny v Wimbledon UDC* [1899] 2 QB 72 (CA); *Holliday*, above n 11; *Leichhardt Municipal Council v Montgomery* [2005] NSWCA 432; cf *Rowe v Herman* [1997] 1 WLR 1390 (CA).

[70] (1991) 59 Build LR 16 (CA); cf *Salsbury v Woodland* [1970] 1 QB 324 (CA).

[71] Cf A Dugdale (ed), *Clerk & Lindsell on Torts*, 18th edn (London, Sweet & Maxwell, 2001) [5.59].

of the contractor in working on the seal between the two properties. A homeowner has the privilege to carry out work on a wall or other division between his or her property and an adjoining property of which he or she is not the owner. This is an important privilege in a country dominated by terraced housing. Where that work involves a risk of damage to the adjoining property, the law requires the homeowner to pay for any damage caused by the work not being carried out with due care. The homeowner cannot escape liability by demonstrating that he took all care in selecting a reputable independent contractor. Again, this is not an example of disguised vicarious liability.

That the privilege may be qualified where it is conferred for the defendant's own benefit is further illustrated by the (in)famous case of *Vincent v Lake Erie Transportation Co*.[72] The defendant's crew had just finished unloading the defendant's ship at the claimants' dock when an unusually severe storm arose. The claimants terminated their permission to tie to the dock, but the crew lashed the ship to the dock during the storm. The ship repeatedly banged against the dock, causing $500 damage.

Prima facie the intentional lashing of the ship to the dock without permission was a trespass and it is irrelevant that the defendant and its crew were without fault in relation to the resultant damage. However, the threat of the storm to the ship created a situation of necessity, giving rise to a qualified privilege. It was factually impossible for the claimants to have sought an injunction restraining the use of the dock, but if there had been a judge at dockside, it would have been refused. Similarly, the claimants were not at liberty to exercise 'self help' and if they had untied the ship's cables from the dock this would have been the tort of conversion and they would have been liable for the loss of the ship.[73]

However, this privilege of using the dock was qualified and the Supreme Court of Minnesota held that the defendant was liable to pay for the damage caused by the ship.[74] Some commentators have sought to explain the result as based upon the defendant's unjust enrichment in saving its ship at the expense of the claimants' dock.[75] Although this may be an alternative analysis on some facts, it is unsatisfactory as a complete

---

[72]   124 NW 221 (Minn Sup Ct 1910) [*Vincent*]; cf *Romney Marsh v Trinity House* (1870) LR 5 Ex 204; *Whalley v Lancashire and Yorkshire Railway Co* (1884) 13 QBD 131 (CA); *Esso Petroleum Co Ltd v Southport Corp* [1956] AC 218 (HL).

[73]   *Ploof v Putnam* 71 A 188 (Vt Sup Ct 1908).

[74]   Cf *Burmah Oil v Lord Advocate* [1965] AC 75 (HL).

[75]   R Keeton, 'Conditional Fault in the Law of Torts' (1959) 72 *Harvard Law Review* 401, 411, 418; D Laycock, 'The Scope and Significance of Restitution' (1989) 67 *Texas Law Review* 1277, 1285-86; A Kull, 'Rationalizing Restitution' (1995) 83 *California Law Review* 1191; L Smith, 'Restitution: The Heart of Corrective Justice' (2001) 79 *Texas Law Review* 2115, 2146-48; E Weinrib, *The Idea of Private Law* (Cambridge, Mass, Harvard University Press, 1995) 196-203; D Friedmann, 'Restitution for Wrongs: The Measure of Recovery' (2001) 79 *Texas Law Review* 1879, 1888.

explanation. The court in *Vincent* awarded $500 as damages for loss; no attempt was made to calculate the gain the defendant made. It might be said that a claimant is only entitled to claim the gain made up to the extent that he or she has suffered loss. However, such a limitation would mean that where the loss suffered is greater than the value of the ship, he or she would not be able to recover in full. Further, if the ship had sunk despite its being lashed to the dock, the defendant would have made no gain from its conduct, but it should still be obliged to pay for the damage caused by tying up the ship. The better analysis is that the defendant had a privilege to tie its ship to the dock, but that this privilege was qualified and did not excuse it from having to pay for damage suffered as a result of its exercise.

V.   STATUTORY DUTIES

The degree of fault required to make a defendant's conduct tortious varies according to the type of right relied on by the claimant. Where the right arises from a statutory duty imposed upon another, the standard of duty imposed is one of statutory construction.[76] The standard adopted can be as varied as wit allows, but there are three principal options. The first is an absolute obligation to achieve a state of affairs. If the state of affairs is not achieved, liability is imposed regardless of whether the failure to achieve it is not for want of any care on the part of anyone. The liability in England of licensees of nuclear installations for injuries to person and damage to property because of nuclear matter or ionising radiation is (almost) of this kind.[77] There is one defence. Although the licensee will be liable even in a case of Act of God or terrorism, liability is not imposed where it is the result of 'hostile action in the course of armed conflict'. Second, the legislation may impose a duty to take care on the defendant personally. The common duty of care expected of occupiers towards their visitors under the English Occupiers Liability Act 1957 and under equivalent Canadian legislation[78] is an obvious example. In between an absolute duty and a duty to take care are a variety of possibilities. A third, and common, intermediate position is a duty that care will be taken of the plaintiff, as opposed to a personal duty on the defendant to take care. Many statutes impose a duty which is actionable in tort where the duty cannot be discharged by employing an apparently competent contractor to perform it. For example, under the English Highways Act 1980 a highway authority which maintains the highway at public expense is under an

---

[76] K Stanton, M Harris and P Skidmore, *Statutory Torts* (London, Sweet & Mawxell, 2003) 283-310.

[77] Nuclear Installations Act 1965, ss 7 and 12.

[78] Eg Ontario Occupiers' Liability Act RSO 1990 c O.2, s 3(1).

express positive duty to the public to maintain the highway.[79] In an action for damage for failure to maintain, the authority has a defence if it can show that it took such care as in all the circumstances was reasonably required to ensure that the highway was not dangerous to traffic.[80] However, this defence cannot be made out by showing that the highway authority had arranged for an apparently competent person to carry out or supervise the work.[81] The duty is one that care will be taken of users of the highway. A similar construction has been adopted in Canada in relation to the Crown's duty to maintain the highways.[82] However, it cannot be pretended that the relevant Canadian provision clearly imposed such a standard of duty actionable by anyone injured as a result of the carelessness of an independent contractor.[83] A possibly better way of reaching the result would have been to conclude that the statutory privilege conferred upon the Crown for the purposes of carrying out work upon the highway did not, on its true construction, extend to situations where the work was carried out carelessly.

Again, the liability imposed where the standard of statutory duty is higher than that merely to take care is not a disguised form of vicarious liability.

VI.   MISCELLANEOUS CASES

A.   Fire

The traditional common law rule is that where a claim is made for loss or damage arising from the spread of fire, an occupier will be liable if the fire was either negligently lit or negligently allowed to get out of control.[84] It does not matter whether it is the occupier or his or her independent contractor who is responsible.[85] Again, however, this is not an example of vicarious liability. Prior to the Fires Prevention (Metropolis) Act 1774, an occupier's liability was strict unless he or she could show that the escape was due to the act of a stranger or an Act of God.[86] Where the fire is lit or allowed to get out of control due to negligence the statute will not protect

---

[79]   Highway Act 1980, s 41(1).
[80]   *Ibid*, s 58(1).
[81]   *Ibid*, s 58(2).
[82]   *Lewis (Guardian ad litem of) v British Columbia* [1997] 3 SCR 1145.
[83]   The relevant provision was the British Columbia Ministry of Transportation and Highways Act RSBC 1979 c 280 s 48: 'The minister shall direct the construction, maintenance and repair of all government buildings, highways and public works in progress, or constructed or maintained at the expense of the Province, and which are under his control.'
[84]   As amended by the Fires Prevention (Metropolis) Act 1774.
[85]   *Black v Christchurch Finance Co Ltd* [1894] AC 48 (HL).
[86]   *Tuberville v Stampe* (1697) 1 Raym Ld 264, 91 ER 1072 (KB).

the occupier unless the fire was started by a stranger.[87] 'Stranger' for these purposes probably does not simply mean any person who is not a servant or an independent contractor. Therefore, if the fire is negligently started by a guest the occupier will be liable. Such liability is not best seen as an example of vicarious liability. Rather, it follows from the common law liability for fire as amended by legislation.

Although the rule in relation to fire is usually treated as related to the 'rule in *Rylands v Fletcher*', they can no longer be seen as the same rule. Whilst fires may escape, they are not non-natural, extra-hazardous or abnormal. In Australia, the special rule relating to fire was put out in *Burnie*.

B.   Private Nuisance

If, as the House of Lords has now twice told us, the rule in *Rylands v Fletcher* is an incidence of the law of private nuisance concerned with isolated escapes,[88] it would appear to follow that where a nuisance is created on the defendant's land the defendant will be liable even if he or she was not responsible for its creation. There is some support for such a proposition.[89] An occupier of land from which a nuisance emanates may be liable even where the source of harm was originally created by a trespasser[90] or an Act of God.[91] The law imposes a positive duty on occupiers to take steps to control a nuisance.[92] The rights of an occupier of land to its exclusive enjoyment carries with it attendant obligations. So, in *Goldman v Hargrave* a tall red gum tree on the defendant's land was struck by lightning and caught fire.[93] The defendant decided to let the fire burn itself out and five days later the fire spread to the claimant's land, causing extensive damage. The Privy Council held the defendant liable for the careless failure to realise that the fire needed to be put out.

It is therefore understandable that an occupier will be liable where a nuisance is created by an independent contractor. In *Matania v National Provincial Bank Ltd* the defendants employed independent contractors to

---

[87] *Balfour v Barty-King (Hyder & Sons (Builders) Ltd, Third Parties)* [1957] 1 QB 496 (CA) 504; *H&N Emanuel Ltd v Greater London Council* [1971] 2 All ER 835 (CA); *Johnson*, above n 66.

[88] *Cambridge Water Co v Eastern Counties Leather Plc* [1994] 2 AC 264 (HL); *Transco*, above n 54.

[89] *Spicer v Smee* [1946] 1 All ER 489 (KB); cf *Blake v Woolf* [1898] 2 QB 426 (QB).

[90] *Sedleigh-Denfield v O'Callaghan* [1940] AC 880 (HL) [*Sedleigh-Denfield*].

[91] *Goldman v Hargrave* [1967] 1 AC 645 (PC).

[92] *Sic utere tuo ut alienum non heads* (everyone must so use his own property so as not to injure his neighbours). See also *Pickard v Smith* (1861) 10 CB (NS) 470, 142 ER 535 (CP).

[93] Above n 91 [*Goldman*]; cf *Sedleigh-Denfield*, above n 90; *Leakey v National Trust* [1980] QB 485 (CA) [*Leakey*]; *Smith v Littlewoods* [1987] AC 241 (HL).

make alterations to their flat.[94] Dust and noise from the work constituted a nuisance to the claimant's flat above. The Court of Appeal held the defendants liable for the nuisance created by their contractors. Some have argued that liability should be confined to those cases where there is a 'special danger' of the nuisance.[95] Whatever the scope of liability, the better view is that this is not a form of vicarious liability but follows from the general rule that occupiers are liable for the unreasonable use of their land where this causes a nuisance.

C. Withdrawal of Support from Neighbouring Land

A line of nineteenth-century cases in nuisance lays down a rule of liability for the fault of independent contractors where there has been a withdrawal of support from land.[96] The principle has been applied to cover the work on party walls in terrace housing.[97] Atiyah interpreted these cases as being true examples of vicarious liability as it was once thought that there was no positive duty to provide support and that an occupier could not be liable for the excavations of a previous owner in undermining a neighbour's house.[98] This line of authority runs counter to the modern view that there can be liability in nuisance for failure to control a nuisance which starts on one's own land.[99] Again, the positive duty arises as part of the quid pro quo between neighbouring landowners. The English Court of Appeal has now concluded that there is a positive duty on landowners to provide support[100] and consequently the liability of an occupier for the acts of an independent contractor in removing support need not be seen as an example of vicarious liability but as part of this general rule.

D. Public Nuisance

In *Tarry v Ashton* a lamp attached to the defendant's public house overhung the highway.[101] The claimant, a barmaid from Dulwich, was injured when the lamp fell on to the pavement. The preceding August a gas fitter had repaired the lamp carelessly. The defendant was held under a

---

[94] [1936] 2 All ER 633 (CA).
[95] *Ibid*, at 646 (Slesser LJ); Fleming , above n 1, at 436; *Clerk & Lindsell*, above n 71, at [5-58].
[96] *Bower v Peate* (1876) 1 QBD 321 (QB); *Dalton v Angus* (1881) 6 App Cas 740 (HL).
[97] See *Johnson*, above n 66.
[98] *Greenwell v Low Beechburn Coal Co* [1897] 2 QB 165 (QB); *Bond v Norman* [1939] Ch 847.
[99] *Sedleigh-Denfield*, above n 90; *Goldman*, above n 91; *Leakey*, above n 93.
[100] *Holbeck Hall Hotel Ltd v Scarborough Borough Council* [2000] QB 836 (CA).
[101] (1876) 1 QBD 314 (QB) [*Tarry*].

duty to users of the highway to maintain his premises in good repair and was liable. Again, this is not an example of vicarious liability. The defendant's duty to users of the highway to maintain his premises was strict and not discharged by employing an apparently competent contractor. The scope of this duty is illustrated by *Salsbury v Woodland*.[102] The defendant employed a contractor to cut down a tree in his front garden near the highway. Due to the negligence of the contractor, the tree fell into some telephone wires. These fell into the highway, causing an accident in which the claimant was injured. No liability was imposed. No non-delegable duty is owed in relation to work done near the highway. Similarly, if a branch of a tree growing on the defendant's land overhangs the highway, he or she will not be liable if it falls and injures someone due to an undiscoverable latent defect. The defendant has neither done nor authorised anything to be done for which liability could attach.[103]

Those who take the benefit of signs or lamps which overhang the highway, thereby encroaching on to the public space, must accept the burden. The result in *Tarry* ought to be the same regardless of who was responsible for the defect in the fitting of the lamp.

VII.   CONTRACTUAL AND CONSENSUAL DUTIES

A.   Exigibility

The rights which we have which are good against the rest of the world are essentially negative. I can exclude you from my property, you may not touch me without consent and you may not harm my reputation. I cannot compel you to repair my car, cure my illness or speak well of me.

It is possible to create a right by making an undertaking to another. The core example is a right conferred by contract. Such rights are only exigible against the person making the undertaking. Contract is not, however, the only way of voluntarily creating duties.

One example of a voluntarily-created right exigible against only one person arises from bailment. My ownership of my car gives rise to a right good against you that you will not by your actions carelessly damage it. However, you are not under a positive obligation to take care that my car is not damaged by a third party. If I bail my car to you, you come under a voluntarily-assumed positive obligation that care is taken of my car. This

---

[102]   Above n 70.
[103]   *Noble v Harrison* [1926] 2 KB 332 (KB); cf *Wringe v Cohen* [1940] 1 KB 229 (KB).

right of the bailor is only exigible against the bailee. This right need not be contractual since the bailment may be gratuitous.[104]

It may be objected that the right of the bailor arises by operation of law, just like our right not to have our property carelessly damaged. Without the legal system it would not exist. However, this is trivial. Precisely the same could be said of contractual rights. The event which generates the right enforceable by law is the bailee's consent. This is not true of our rights to the things we own which are exigible against everyone else, regardless of their consent. Many other duties that care will be taken arise because they have been voluntarily created.

The law of torts, in particular liability for negligence, protects many voluntarily-created rights.[105] Doctors are entitled to walk passed the sick, but if you put up a sign saying 'Public Hospital' you assume a duty that care will be taken towards those who turn up expecting treatment.[106] The rights that we have which are good against the rest of the world entitle us to damages to the extent that our position has been worsened by the defendant's conduct. Voluntarily-assumed obligations commonly entitle us to be placed in the better position we would have been in if the defendant had taken care. Hospital emergency units are obliged not only not to make the position of patients worse than if they had never turned up but also to exercise positive care in their treatment. Where reasonable care would cure the patient, doctors are obliged to make the patient better off than he or she otherwise would be.[107] Similarly, an occupier assumes responsibility towards those invited on to his or her premises that they will be reasonably safe. If there is a hidden danger on the land, of which he or she ought to be aware, he or she must take care to remove it or warn of its existence, even if not responsible for its creation. Proof of reliance is unnecessary.

The 'tort of negligence' is a result of twisting together cases where the right arose from an undertaking by one party to another with cases where the right relied upon is exigible against the rest of the world.[108] One problem created by this twisting together is that the fault standard applicable to claims based upon rights good against everyone is not necessarily appropriate where the claim is based upon a voluntary relationship. Just as in the law of contract, the law has default rules for determining the appropriate standard of duty undertaken. Where the duty

---

[104] *Coggs v Bernard* (1703) 2 Raym Ld 909, 92 ER 107 (KB).

[105] Cf JH Beale, 'Gratuitous Undertakings' (1891-92) 5 *Harvard Law Review* 222; E Jenks, 'On Negligence and Deceit in the Law of Torts' (1910) 26 *LQR* 159, 162.

[106] *Barnett v Chelsea & Kensington Hospital Management Committee* [1969] 1 QB 428 (QB).

[107] J Stapleton, 'The Normal Expectancies Measure in Tort Damages' (1997) 113 *LQR* 257.

[108] D Ibbetson, '"The Law of Business Rome": Foundations of the Anglo-American Tort of Negligence' [1999] *Current Legal Problems* 74, 78.

has been voluntarily assumed by the defendant the law is, inevitably, less concerned with preserving his or her interest in liberty of action. It is therefore appropriate in many cases that the default rule should be a higher standard than it is in relation to duties which are not voluntarily assumed.

B.   Bailment

Where a bailee deputes his or her task of safe-keeping to an independent contractor, the bailee will be liable if the goods are lost through carelessness even though the bailee is not personally at fault.[109] In *BRS v Arthur v Crutchley* the Court of Appeal held that a warehouse is liable to the bailor of goods if they are stolen because of the carelessness of a night watchman supplied by an independent security firm. Where there is a contract between bailor and bailee this may be seen as arising under an implied term of the contract of bailment.[110] There is, however, an identical liability imposed upon a sub-bailee for reward where he or she is aware of the head bailment to the principal bailor. Today this duty could be seen as arising under the Contracts (Rights of Third Parties) Act 1999 but its historical provenance is independent of contract and arises from the law of bailment. Where the goods are lost, even where the bailment is gratuitous, the onus is on the bailee to show that the loss was not caused by the negligence or misconduct of his or her servants or anyone to whom the goods were entrusted.[111] The bailee's liability is primary, based upon the assumption of responsibility arising from the bailment, not vicarious.

C.   Employer's Duty to an Employee

The duty of an employer to an employee to provide a safe system of work is similarly non-delegable and voluntarily assumed.[112] In *McDermid v Nash Dredging and Reclamation Co Ltd* the claimant was employed as a deckhand by the defendants.[113] He was sent to work on a tug owned and operated by the parent company of the defendants and suffered serious injuries as a result of the negligence of the master of the ship. The House of Lords held that the employer has a non-delegable duty to provide a safe system of work. Although a system had been developed it was not in

---

[109]   *Morris v CW Martin & Sons Ltd* [1966] 1 QB 716 (CA); *Gilchrist Watt & Sanderson Pty Ltd v York Products Pty Ltd* [1970] 1 WLR 1262 (PC).

[110]   [1968] 1 All ER 811 (CA).

[111]   *Port Swettenham Authority v T W Wu & Co (M) Sdn Bhd* [1979] AC 580 (PC).

[112]   *Marshment v Borgstrom* [1942] SCR 374; *Ferraloro v Preston Timber Pty Ltd* (1982) 56 AJLR 872 (HCA).

[113]   [1987] AC 906 (HL) [*McDermid*].

operation at the time of the accident and the defendant was liable. That the employer's duty to provide a safe system of work is non-delegable is long established,[114] and *McDermid* is important only in that it demonstrates that the duty extends to the operation and not merely the establishment of the system.

Employer liability is traditionally seen as part of the tort of negligence.[115] However, this is apt to mislead. The right of an employee against his or her employer differs from, say, the rights we all have against the rest of the world not to be injured. First, the employer can be liable for non-feasance: he or she must positively act to create a safe system of work. Second, the employer can be liable despite the fact that neither he or she nor any of the employees are careless. Like the duty of a bailee, it is a duty that care is taken, not a duty to take care. As with a bailee, the employee has a right against the employer because of the voluntary assumption of responsibility. Unlike a bailee for no reward, an employee provides consideration by the promise and performance of work. The duty of the employer is therefore probably best seen as contractual. As Lord Rodger recently stated, 'in determining the content of any duty of care [that an employer owes an employee it is] necessary to have due regard to the relevant provisions of his contract with them, embodying these terms and conditions'.[116]

It might be objected that the duty to provide a safe system of work has not been expressly agreed to and is implied into all employment relationships. However, the same could be said of the uncontroversially contractual duty of a seller to supply goods of satisfactory quality which is implied into contracts of sale. Absent the contract, it would not exist.

Analysed in this way, the result in the House of Lords' decision in *Davie v New Merton Board Mills Ltd*[117] appears incorrect. An employee was injured at work by a defective tool. The defect was due to the negligence of the manufacturer and could not reasonably have been detected by the employer. The employer was held not liable. This decision appears anomalous not only in relation to other cases of an employer's liability to ensure his employee's safety but also in relation to the duties of those who rent tools. Under contracts to hire tools there is an implied term that the goods hired are of satisfactory quality. This is a strict obligation, and not one merely to ensure that due care and skill was exercised in making them.[118]

---

[114] *Wilson & Clyde Coal Ltd v English* [1938] AC 57 (HL).
[115] Eg *Davie v New Merton Board Mills Ltd* [1959] AC 604 (HL) 642 (Lord Reid).
[116] *Barber v Somerset County Council* [2004] UKHL 13.
[117] Above n 115 [*Davie*].
[118] Supply of Goods and Services Act 1982, s 9; cf *White v John Warwick* [1953] 1 WLR 1285 (CA).

It might be argued that *Davie* was not a case where the employer had delegated some part of the duty to be performed by another but rather where the negligence was that of a stranger. However, this is an unsatisfactory distinction.[119] An employer cannot escape liability for the failure to provide a safe system of work by showing that the party at fault was one with whom he or she had no contractual relationship. The result in *Davie* has now been reversed by statute.[120]

D.   Carriers

The position of employers may be compared with the obligation of a carrier to exercise due diligence to make a ship seaworthy.[121] If cargo is damaged because the ship is unseaworthy the carrier is liable even though the unseaworthiness is the result of carelessness by independent contractors. The carrier has not discharged his or her obligation merely by selecting apparently competent independent contractors.[122] This obligation is a 'statutory contractual obligation'[123] implied by the Carriage of Goods by Sea Act 1971 and is not an example of vicarious liability in tort.[124]

E.   Hospitals

More controversially, the better view is that the duty voluntarily assumed by a hospital to its patients is non-delegable. In England the position was authoritatively stated in *Cassidy v Ministry of Health* by Denning LJ:

> when hospital authorities undertake to treat a patient, and themselves select and appoint ... the professional men and women who are to give the treatment, then they are responsible for the negligence of those persons in failing to give proper treatment, no matter whether they are doctors, surgeons, nurses or anyone else.[125]

So, if a patient admitted to a hospital is cared for by a consultant who is not an employee of that hospital, and if that consultant is careless in his treatment of the patient, the patient should have a claim against the

---

[119]   See *Davie*, above n 115, at 625 (Viscount Simonds).
[120]   Employers' Liability (Defective Equipment) Act 1969.
[121]   Carriage of Goods by Sea Act 1971, Sch, Art iii(1).
[122]   *Riverstone Meat Co Pty Ltd v Lancashire Shipping Co Ltd* [1961] AC 807 (HL) [*Riverstone*]; cf *Leesh River Tea Co Ltd v British India Steam Navigation Co Ltd* [1966] 3 All ER 593 (CA).
[123]   *Riverstone*, above n 122, at 871 (Lord Keith of Avonholm).
[124]   Above n 121.
[125]   [1951] 2 KB 343 (CA) 362; See also *Gold v Essex County Council* [1942] 2 KB 293 (CA) (Lord Greene MR); *Roe v Minister of Health* [1954] 2 QB 66 (CA).

hospital. It does not matter that the consultant was apparently competent and was selected for the task without fault by any employee of the hospital. Nor should it matter whether the patient is treated privately under a contract or gratuitously by a public hospital. Like the duty of a bailee, the duty which has been voluntarily assumed is that care will be taken of the patient, not merely a duty to personally take care. It is, to that extent, strict.

Further, in principle, if the duty is one that care will be taken and reasonable care would have resulted in the patient having been cured, a patient who is admitted to a hospital who is not cured should have a claim. If it can be shown that this was the result of a 'system failure', this suffices. If a hospital has an inadequate system in place for the prevention of cross-infection[126] or an unreliable system for summoning expert assistance in an emergency,[127] the hospital is liable. This is not because the hospital has acted carelessly. Hospitals, like all corporate bodies, cannot *do* anything except through human agents in the real world. However, one of the reasons why it is a mistake to see non-delegable duties as a 'disguised form of vicarious liability'[128] is that liability is imposed even where it can be shown that the failure to achieve the result which care would achieve is not the fault of any individual. Attribution of anything other than the initial assumption of responsibility is unnecessary.

In Canada, in a divided decision, the Ontario Court of Appeal held in *Yepremian v Scarborough General Hospital* that hospitals are not liable for the negligence of physicians having hospital privileges or specialist status who are not also employees.[129] The majority, whilst assuming that the duty relied upon was voluntarily created, held that it was merely a duty to take care.

F. Occupiers

Until the passing of the English Occupiers Liability Act 1957, the duty of an occupier to visitors, at least to those who had provided consideration,[130] was a non-delegable duty that care would be taken. Consequently an occupier was liable to visitors for harm caused by the carelessness of

---

[126] *Vancouver General Hospital v McDaniel* (1934) 152 LT 56 (PC) 57.

[127] *Bull v Devon Area Health Authority* [1993] 4 Med LR 117.

[128] Fleming, above n 1, at 433.

[129] (1980) 28 OR (2d) 494 (CA) (Mackinnon ACJO, Arnup and Morden JJA, in the majority and Blair and Houlden JJA dissenting); cf *Osburn v Mohindra* (1980) 29 NBR (2d) 340 (QB); *Stewart v Noone* [1992] BCJ No 1017, 1992 CarswellBC 1881 (SC).

[130] Cf *Haseldine v C and A Daw & Son Ltd* [1941] 2 KB 343 (CA); *Woodward v Hastings Corporation* [1945] KB 174 (CA).

independent contractors.[131] In jurisdictions which have not amended the common law by statute, such as in parts of Australia and Canada, this remains the case.[132]

Today in England an occupier's duty to visitors is only to personally take care and he or she will be not liable for the carelessness of an independent contractor, so long as it was reasonable to entrust the work to the contractor and he or she has taken reasonable steps (if any) to be satisfied that the contractor was competent and that the work had been properly done.[133] The dominance of the view that the standard of care within a unitary tort of negligence is uniform, regardless of the nature of the right relied on, means that it is rarely questioned whether such a standard is appropriate or consistent with that applied in other cases of voluntarily-assumed obligations. If a spectator at a football match is injured by the collapse of a stand carelessly constructed by an apparently competent independent contractor, why should the standard of duty assumed by the occupier to a visitor be lower than that of a hospital to its patients?

The cutting back of the duty of occupiers by legislation potentially leads to incoherent results. This possibility was raised, but avoided, by the English Court of Appeal in *Maguire v Sefton Metropolitan Borough Council*.[134] The claimant suffered injury whilst using an exercise machine at the defendant's leisure centre. The machine was defective as a result of the carelessness of the supplier, an independent contractor. The claimant sought to argue that there was an implied term in his contract with the defendant that any machine was safe to use. Put another way, he argued for a duty that care would be taken of him, not that the defendant would take care. In relation to the duties of occupiers, such an implied term is excluded by the legislation, which limits the duty to one to take care.[135] The Court of Appeal, overturning the trial judge, held that the duty alleged was an occupancy duty within the statute and that no greater duty than that contained therein could be implied.

However, not all duties of occupiers are occupancy duties. A hospital which supplies food to patients is not performing an occupancy duty within the legislation. Can it be correct in principle that where a patient contracts a disease because an independent contractor has carelessly failed to clean the floors, he or she has no claim against the hospital, but that

---

[131]   *Francis v Cockerell* (1870) LR 5 QB 501 (Ex); *Maclenan v Segar* [1917] 2 KB 325 (KB); *Thomson v Cremin* [1953] 2 All ER 1185 (HL); cf *Green v Fibreglass Ltd* [1958] 2 QB 245.

[132]   *Voli v Inglewood Shire Council* (1963) 110 CLR 74 (HCA); *Brown v B& F Theatres Ltd* [1947] SCR 486; cf *Australian Safeway Stores Pty Ltd v Zaluzna* (1987) 162 CLR 479 (HCA); L Klar, *Tort Law*, 3rd edn (Toronto, Thomson Carswell, 2003) 539.

[133]   Occupiers Liability Act 1957, s 2(4)(b).

[134]   [2006] EWCA Civ 316.

[135]   Occupiers Liability Act 1957, s 5(1).

where the illness results from meals carelessly prepared by another independent contractor, the hospital will be liable?

G.   Landlords

In *Northern Sandblasting Pty Ltd v Harris* a four-to-three majority of the High Court of Australia found a landlord liable where a tenant's child electrocuted herself.[136] There were two possible causes of the electrocution: defective wiring that pre-dated the tenancy and the carelessness of an independent contractor after the tenancy had been granted. Two of the justices in the majority based their conclusion that the landlord was liable on the careless failure to inspect the premises before granting the lease. By contrast, Toohey and McHugh JJ found the landlord liable on the basis that he had assumed a non-delegable duty that the work in relation to the premises would be performed with reasonable care. The Supreme Court of Canada found a similar non-delegable duty where a lodger was asphyxiated by inhaling gas from a defective stove in the room he rented.[137]

In England, the Defective Premises Act 1972 excludes the position adopted by Toohey and McHugh JJ, stipulating that the landlord 'owes a duty to take such care as is reasonable in all the circumstances'.[138] The employment of a reputable contractor would discharge this duty.

H.   Assumed Duties Generally?

The most important question which needs to be addressed is whether the cases of bailment, employment, carriage, hospitals, occupiers and landlords are examples of a more general rule. Where the defendant has voluntarily assumed responsibility for the defendant's care, will he or she be liable where the claimant suffers loss because of a lack of care, even though the defendant personally was careful? Over 20 years ago Mason J in the High Court of Australia thought that such a general principle was discernible:

> In these situations the special duty arises because the person on whom it is imposed has undertaken the care, supervision or control of the person or property of another or is so placed in relation to that person or his property as to assume a particular responsibility for his or its safety, in circumstances where the person affected might reasonably expect that due care will be exercised.[139]

---

[136] (1997) 71 AJLR 1428 (HCA); see TK Feng, 'Landlord's Liability' (1998) 114 *LQR* 193.

[137] *Carriss v Buxton* [1958] SCR 441.

[138] Defective Premises Act 1972, s 4(1).

[139] *Kondis*, above n 62, at 687.

At a minimum, where the relationship between the parties is contractual, it is defensible that the default standard of duty owed is higher than a mere personal duty to take care. In the context of the sale of goods, the default standard for the seller's duty in relation to the condition of the goods sold is strict: they are to be of satisfactory quality. If in the context of the provision of a service, such as hospital care, the standard is non-delegable. So the gap between the default standard for contracts for the supply of goods and services is less pronounced.

The difference between adopting an expanded notion of vicarious liability and relying upon a primary duty that care will be taken which has been voluntarily assumed is illustrated by the different approaches to claims for the effects of abuse brought by children taken into care. Such claims have come before the ultimate appellate courts of Canada, Australia and England in recent years. Although not identical, for present purposes the facts of these cases can be treated together. A child is abused by a teacher whilst at school. The teacher's conduct is clearly intentional wrongdoing which is prohibited by his or her employer.

First, can there be vicarious liability for this tort by an employee? Unlike the cases so far discussed, the difficulty with explaining liability on such a basis is not that the requisite relationship for the purposes of attribution is missing. Rather, on a traditional approach child abuse is not conduct within the scope of the relationship. Under the traditional Salmond test, words or actions are within the course of employment if they are either (a) a wrongful act authorised or (b) a wrongful or unauthorised mode of doing an authorised act.[140] Although this test is open-textured, and the first limb is otiose, it is unarguable that child abuse comes within either category. Teachers are employed to care for children, not to abuse them. It is the very opposite of what they have been authorised to do. Applying this test, a majority of the High Court of Australia in *New South Wales v Lepore*[141] refused to hold the defendant vicariously liable for the teacher's abuse. The English Court of Appeal had earlier reached the same conclusion applying the same test, although it was to be overturned.[142]

Second, has the school assumed a non-delegable duty to the child? McHugh J in *Lepore* (yet again in powerful dissent) argued that the duty assumed by a school authority to pupils was voluntarily assumed and non-delegable. Not only could he rely upon the examples of employment and bailment discussed above by way of analogy, there was High Court of Australia authority assuming that this was correct as between a school authority and a child.[143] The school authorities could therefore be held

---

[140]   Heuston and Buckley, above n 67, at 443.
[141]   (2004) 212 CLR 511 (HCA) [*Lepore*].
[142]   *Trotman v Yorkshire County Council* [1999] LGR 584 (CA).
[143]   *The Commonwealth v Introvigne* (1982) 150 CLR 258 (HCA).

primarily liable. The majority disagreed, arguing that the non-delegable duty assumed should only extend to the failure of a delegatee to act with care, and not to intentional wrongdoing.[144] This is indefensible. Liability for the breach of a primary duty cannot be avoided by showing that the breach was gross. It is as if a seller of canned soup could escape liability for its defective quality if it could be shown that it had been deliberately poisoned by the manufacturer. If the duty assumed is a duty that care will be taken, this is breached where the child is abused. This does not mean that the duty assumed is absolute. A child who falls over in the playground does not necessarily have a claim. However, liability for deliberate abuse follows a fortiori from liability for want of care. Only if non-delegable duties are seen as a 'disguised' form of vicarious liability does it make sense to refuse the claim on the basis that the wrongdoing was intentional. This was the majority's assumption.[145]

While the majority of the High Court of Australia reached the wrong result for many of the right reasons, the Supreme Court of Canada in *Bazley v Curry* reached the right result for the wrong reasons.[146] The claim was against a non-profit organisation operated for the treatment and care of emotionally-troubled children. Although appropriate checks were carried out, a paedophile was employed who abused children in the organisation's care. Before the Supreme Court of Canada, the case was solely presented on the basis of vicarious liability for the wrongs of the employee. No argument based on the existence of a non-delegable duty seems to have been considered. The court abandoned the traditional Salmond test, substituting the test of whether the wrong was sufficiently closely related to what the employee had been employed to do.[147] Here, because the enterprise 'created or materially enhanced'[148] the risk of abuse, it was held to be appropriate to impose liability.

This reasoning is unsatisfactory. First, vicarious liability cannot be explained in terms of an enterprise being required to internalise the risks of the activity it creates.[149] If we seek to explain vicarious liability in such terms, there is no justification for confining liability to *torts* by *employees*. If the law was that an enterprise ought to bear all of the costs associated with its activities, these limitations on when it is possible to hold the defendant liable make no sense. Vicarious liability is better seen as a species of more general rules of attribution, rather than as an inadequate proxy for enterprise liability. Second, on the facts of *Bazley*, it stretches

---

[144] *Lepore*, above n 141, at [31] (Gleeson CJ), [264]-[266] (Gummow and Hayne JJ).

[145] *Ibid*, at [257] (Gummow and Hayne JJ), [289]-[296] (Kirby J).

[146] [1999] 2 SCR 534 [*Bazley*].

[147] *Ibid*, at [40] (McLachlin J).

[148] *Ibid*, at [39] (McLachlin J)

[149] Cf *Hollis v Vabu Pty Ltd* (2001) 207 CLR 21 (HCA) [42] (Gleeson CJ, Gaudron, Gummow, Kirby and Hayne JJ) [*Hollis*].

credulity to suggest that running a non-profit residential care home for emotionally troubled children *increases* the risk of children being abused. The case was not analogous to that of a manufacturer imposing non-reciprocal risks upon bystanders for its own gain by putting a product into the market.

In contrast, in the subsequent case of *EDG v Hammer* the Supreme Court of Canada was confronted with the argument that a non-delegable duty was owed, this time in relation to the sexual assault committed by a school's janitor on a student.[150] The court treated the issue as determined by the relevant legislation. As it imposed no such duty, no non-delegable duty arose. The possibility of non-delegable duties arising for other reasons was not considered.

The uncertainty introduced by *Bazley* is illustrated by its companion case, *Jacobi v Griffiths*.[151] The court split four-to-three in finding no vicarious liability where an employee of a children's club, who had been encouraged to establish a rapport with the children, abused his position and assaulted the two plaintiffs. *Bazley* and *Jacobi* can be distinguished. *Bazley* involved residential care, which *Jacobi*, like *Lepore*, did not. In *Jacobi*, unlike *Bazley*, the abuse had taken place outside of club hours and off-site. However it is difficult to see how they can be distinguished on the basis of the test for vicarious liability the court employed. By running a club for children, the employer did, in the sense used in *Bazley*, 'materially increase the risk' that those children would be abused by a member of their staff. It may be said that the risk was lower in *Jacobi* than in *Bazley* but this is incapable of assessment or formulation as a rule. The dissent was delivered by McLachlin J, who had delivered the judgment of the court in *Bazley*.

By contrast, if the claims in *Bazley* and *Jacobi* had been seen as based upon voluntarily assumed duties that care would be taken of the children, the difference in result is readily explicable. The scope of the duty undertaken must be ascertained.[152] What was the club in *Jacobi* undertaking to do? There was an undertaking that care would be taken of the children at the club, but they are not assuming a duty to care for the child once he or she goes home.

In England, the House of Lords followed the Canadian lead and abandoned the traditional Salmond test in *Lister v Hesley Hall Ltd*.[153] In the analysis there was a similarly unfortunate failure to distinguish between vicarious liability based on the attribution of the abuse to the

---

[150] [2003] 2 SCR 459.
[151] [1999] 2 SCR 570 [*Jacobi*]. See also *KLB*, above n 5.
[152] *Ellis v Wallsend DC* (1989) 17 NSWLR 553 (CA) 604 (Samuels JA).
[153] [2002] 1 AC 215 (HL) [*Lister*].

employer and liability based upon the failure to comply with a voluntarily assumed obligation. Lord Hobhouse, in terms similar to those used by McHugh J in *Lepore*, stated:

> The liability of the employer derives from the voluntary assumption of the relationship towards the plaintiff and the duties that arise from that relationship and their choosing to entrust the performance of those duties to their servant.[154]

This is correct, but it supports the existence of a non-delegable duty, not the imposition of vicarious liability. The leading speech was given by Lord Steyn, with whom Lords Hutton and Hobhouse agreed, who described the judgments of the Supreme Court of Canada as the 'starting point' and adopted the 'close connection' test.[155]

It may be doubted whether *Lister* is consistent with the earlier decision of the House of Lords in *The Ocean Frost*.[156] The Vice President of a company, authorised to negotiate the sale of a ship belonging to the company, purported to enter into a simultaneous agreement to take the ship back on a charter containing unusual terms. The Vice President falsely represented that he had authority to enter into the charter. Whether the statement could be attributed to the company is determined by whether the director had actual or ostensible authority to make it. Whether the company should be vicariously liable for its Vice President's deceit should be determined by whether he was acting in the course of his employment. Lord Keith regarded these two tests as 'meaning one and the same thing'.[157] Consequently, the employer could not be vicariously liable for fraudulent statements made by an employee acting without actual or ostensible authority. Yet under the 'close connection' test the conclusion ought to be that by entrusting the Vice President with the negotiations as it did, the defendant company had materially increased the risk of the fraud which took place. Unless there are separate rules for deceit and other forms of deliberate wrongdoing, *Lister* and *The Ocean Frost* are difficult to reconcile,[158] save on the basis that liability in *Lister* was not truly vicarious at all.

---

[154] *Ibid*, at [55].

[155] *Ibid*, at [70] (Lord Millett).

[156] *Armagas Ltd v Mundogas SA (The Ocean Frost)* [1986] AC 717 (HL); cf *Credit Lyonnais Bank Nederland NV v Export Credit Guarantee Department* [2000] 1 AC 486 (HL).

[157] *The Ocean Frost*, above n 156, at 781; cf *Lloyd v Grace Smith & Co* [1912] AC 716 (HL) 736 (Lord Macnaghten) [*Lloyd*]; *Navarro v Moregrand Ltd* [1951] 2 TLR 674 (CA) 680 (Denning LJ); F Reynolds, *Bowstead and Reynolds on Agency*, 18th edn (London, Sweet & Maxwell Ltd, 2006) 422;

[158] The better view of related cases such as *Lloyd*, above n 157 and *Briess v Woolley* [1954] AC 333 (HL) is that they are based upon primary and not vicarious liability: see R Stevens, 'Why do Agents "Drop Out"?' [2005] *Lloyd's Maritime and Commercial Law Quarterly* 101.

The difference between expanding vicarious liability and recognising primary liability based upon non-delegable duties is not simply one of form. They lead to different results in real situations. Liability may be both narrower and wider. If a stranger gains access to school premises and abuses a child, there is no possibility of the school being vicariously liable for his or her actions. If his or her presence is a result of a system failure for which it is impossible to hold any individual to blame, the school cannot be liable on this basis. If there was a contract between parents and school, it may be possible to find the school liable for beach of a contractual undertaking that care would be taken of the child. In a school where no consideration has been provided, this is not possible. However, in principle, the child has a right exigible against the school arising from its assumption of responsibility that positive steps will be taken to ensure his or her safety. If such steps have not been taken, liability should be imposed, regardless of the absence of liability of any natural person in the real world whose actions can be attributed to the school. Liability may be wider if the non-delegable duty analysis is adopted.

The expansion of vicarious liability distorts the rules of attribution in cases where no non-delegable duty could be relied on. Such expansion is now evident in England. In *Mattis v Pollock* the claimant fell into an argument with an unlicensed nightclub bouncer called Cranston.[159] The bouncer was hit by the claimant and others, and then left for home where he armed himself with a knife. He returned to the vicinity of the club, ran towards the group he believed had humiliated him, and stabbed the claimant in the back. The Court of Appeal found the club vicariously liable on the basis that there was a close connection between the force he was employed, and encouraged, to use as a bouncer and the violent attack. Similarly, in the decision of the Privy Council in *Bernard v Attorney General of Jamaica* a policeman tried to obtain the use of a public telephone from the claimant.[160] When the claimant refused to give up the receiver, an altercation ensued. The policeman announced that he was a policeman and shot the claimant at point blank range. The Crown as his employer was held vicariously liable. There was no assumption of responsibility by the defendant to the claimant upon which a non-delegable duty could have been founded in either case. It is doubtful whether in either case the traditional Salmond test could have been satisfied.

Within any system of law a set of rules for the attribution of one person's words or acts to another are essential. At one extreme, attribution could be limited to those acts which are expressly authorised. At the other, whenever one person carries out a task on another's behalf all words or actions

---

[159]   [2003] 1 WLR 2158 (CA); cf *Daniels v Whetstone Entertainment Ltd* [1962] 2 Lloyd's Rep 1 (CA);
[160]   Above n 9.

could be attributed. The common law does not adopt either extreme approach. There is no demonstrably correct intermediate position. An analogy may be drawn with the rules of a game. How many players should a football team contain? Five? Eight? Eleven? Twenty? There are different ways in which rational rules can be formulated. At the margin, what is of greater importance than the detail of the rules themselves is that the rules of attribution are settled, certain and consistent. Many rules are of this kind. The detail as to what counts as 'offside' in the game of football is of less importance than that the rule is settled, certain and consistent. It is difficult to claim that these qualities are now found in the rules of attribution in England and Canada.

I. A Radical Thought and a Doubt

If it is correct that there are several situations where the default rule is that a gratuitous assumption of responsibility gives rise to a non-delegable duty that care will be taken, what should the position be if the standard undertaken is made express? In principle, the standard required should be that stipulated. If, therefore, a bailee makes it clear that he or she is only undertaking to exercise a minimal level of care, he or she should not be held to any higher standard. If by contrast the undertaking is to guarantee a result, and then if all care is exercised but that result is not reached, a claim for consequential loss should be available. It might be objected that such a radical conclusion would circumvent the requirement of consideration in contract. However, this is not necessarily so. The rights generated by a gratuitous undertaking are of a different order from contractual undertakings. For example, the availability of specific remedies, the defences applicable, the certainty with which the promise must be evidenced and whether proof of loss consequent on breach is necessary may all be different.

In any event, the scope of the duty assumed will always be a matter of construction. This is illustrated by *A v Ministry of Defence*.[161] The UK Ministry of Defence made arrangements for service personnel and their families stationed in Germany who required medical services to receive care in local hospitals. The claimant was born disabled as a result of the carelessness of a German obstetrician who was in charge of his birth, his mother's care at the German hospital having been arranged by the Ministry. The child claimed against the Ministry, alleging a non-delegable duty to provide medical care. The Court of Appeal correctly rejected this claim. The duty assumed was only to arrange for treatment, not to provide it. No claim for the careless treatment was therefore possible. This may be

---

[161] [2005] QB 183 (CA) [A].

contrasted with the earlier decision of the same court in *Rogers v Night Riders*.[162] There the claimant's mother telephoned the defendants and requested a minicab to take the claimant to the railway station. The minicabs were owned and maintained by the drivers who were independent contractors. During the course of the journey, a car door flew open, resulting in injuries to the claimant. The driver could not subsequently be traced. The Court of Appeal held the defendants liable on the basis that they had held themselves out to be operating a car hire firm, and that the duty they assumed was non-delegable. However, the correct interpretation of the relationship is that a minicab service is merely a clearing centre, promising to arrange for an independent contractor to carry the passenger. Minicab firms do not promise to provide the carriage, anymore than the Ministry of Defence in *A* was undertaking to provide care.

If a right is generated by a voluntary assumption of responsibility, it should not arise if it is made objectively apparent that no duty is being assumed. Rights truly based upon an implicit undertaking can be disclaimed, as demonstrated by the House of Lords' decision in *Hedley Byrne v Heller*.[163] Where the right relied upon is independent of an assumption of responsibility, a disclaimer per se should be of no effect. If drivers place large neon signs on the roof of their cars stating that they accept no responsibility towards those they carelessly crash into, this will not avail them against their victims, even those who have read the notice.

This ability to disclaim is, however, controlled by legislation for the protection of the vulnerable.[164] Even absent such legislation, it must be doubtful whether a school could escape liability to the children in its care by making it apparent to them that no duty was assumed. However, in principle it would be possible to disclaim liability by making this apparent to a parent or guardian. A parent or guardian may well be in breach of his or her duty of care to the child by allowing the child to attend such a school. The positive duties parents and guardians owe their children cannot be disclaimed at all. Just because some positive duties arise from an assumption of responsibility, we should not conclude that all do so.

VIII.   CONCLUSION

The central thesis of this chapter is a conservative one. It is possible for the scope of vicarious liability to be greatly expanded. The distinction between contracts of service and contracts for services is not only used to determine the scope of vicarious liability but is also important for tax purposes and

---

[162] [1984] RTR 324 (CA).
[163] [1964] AC 465 (HL).
[164] Eg Unfair Contract Terms Act 1977, s 2(1).

the application of employment rights protection. It can be argued that to have three quite different issues determined by the same criterion is inappropriate. Who it is appropriate to classify as an employee for one purpose may be inappropriate for another.[165]

Unless the rule is to become that we can be vicariously liable for the acts of anyone with whom we contract, some definition of the requisite relationship for purposes of attribution is required. There are situations where the requisite relationship is not present, and the label 'independent contractor' has commonly been used to describe them. If the argument suggested here is rejected, it will become necessary to define the category of independent contractors for whose actions it is possible to be vicariously liable.[166] Perhaps those outside this category should be called 'very independent contractors'?

The most defensible approach both in relation to vicarious liability and non-delegable duties has been consistently adopted by McHugh J in the High Court of Australia. The failure by others to keep separate the issues of whether there is vicarious liability or the breach of a non-delegable duty has led to incoherence being introduced into both.

The search for a single factor which links all of the cases commonly grouped together as non-delegable duties is a mistake. For example, the extra-hazardous activity cases cannot be explained on the basis of an assumption of responsibility. The fact that a concept such as an 'assumption of responsibility' is not a universal solvent, capable of explaining all of the cases, should not cause us to conclude that it is a fraud incapable of explaining any case.[167] Attempts to deem there to have been an assumption of responsibility, when as a matter of observable fact there has not,[168] result in the concept becoming discredited. If, for example, we attempt to explain the positive obligation of a landowner to provide support for a neighbour's land on the basis of an implied undertaking to do so, the undertaking is clearly fictional, and we are driven back to asking why the law implies such an undertaking in the face of the facts. Duties which arise independently of an assumption of responsibility cannot be disclaimed. So, neither the reservoir builder in *Rylands v Fletcher* nor the employer of the welder in *Burnie* could have escaped liability by telling the neighbour beforehand that it accepted no responsibility for the work undertaken. It is important to recognise the diversity of rationales which justify non-delegable duties.

---

[165] Cf *Hollis*, above n 149.

[166] For an attempt at defining those independent contractors who are not sufficiently independent see Atiyah, above n 16, at 340-46.

[167] Cf K Barker, 'Unreliable Assumptions in the Modern Law of Negligence' (1993) 109 *LQR* 461.

[168] Cf *White v Jones* [1995] 2 AC 207 (HL) (Lord Goff).

Hostility to non-delegable duties springs from a one-size-fits-all approach to fault. The dominance of the view that the common law is resistant to the imposition of liability where the defendant has not been negligent has led to non-delegable duties being treated as an inexplicable rag-bag of cases, somehow related to vicarious liability. Consequently, most textbooks include them as an embarrassing coda to vicarious liability. The twisting together of claims based upon different sorts of rights, and their treatment together within a single uber-tort of negligence, has misled us into thinking that a uniform standard of care is always applicable. Similarly, outside of negligence, cases imposing strict liability such as *Rylands v Fletcher* are dismissed as anomalous and are subject to arbitrary restrictions. If our rules for the attribution of words and acts are not to be distorted, it is important to realise that the common law's approach to fault is explicably more diverse than is sometimes realised.

Non-delegable duties are not the cuckoos in the nest. The swollen 'tort' of negligence is.

14

Juridical Foundations of Common Law Non-Delegable Duties

I. INTRODUCTION

WHILE JUDGES IN most common law jurisdictions seem content to recognise, and even occasionally invoke, the device of non-delegable duty in order to resolve certain difficult cases, they nonetheless seem reluctant—perhaps even unable—to propound a clear theoretical account of the nature and scope of such duties. The absence of any such account has been noted with regret by judges and jurists alike.[1] So it is that we remain in juridical darkness. For despite a fairly sizeable number of well-settled instances in which non-delegable duties have been imposed in the past, most present-day discussions of non-delegable duties continue to refer to the conceptual uncertainty behind which such duties seem to be veiled.

It is sometimes said that the non-delegable duty is a relatively rare species. But even if this were true—which arguably it is not—it would not necessarily follow that any attempt to theorise such duties would be an academic exercise in both the literal and the pejorative senses. At least in so

---

* Reader in Law, University of Manchester. I am grateful to Peter Cane, Francesco Giglio, Paula Giliker, Jason Neyers, Anthony Ogus, Stephen Waddams and Christian Witting for their helpful comments on an earlier version of this chapter. I am also indebted to Harold Luntz and David Cheifetz for alerting me, respectively, to some useful Australian and Canadian materials.
[1] See, eg, *New South Wales v Lepore* (2003) 212 CLR 511 (HCA) [5] (Gleeson CJ): 'The ambit of duties that are regarded as non-delegable has never been defined, and the extent of potential tort liability involved is uncertain' [*Lepore*]. In similar vein, see *ibid*, [246] (Gummow and Hayne JJ); *Salsbury v Woodland* [1970] 1 QB 324 (CA) 331 (Widgery LJ); *KLB v British Columbia* [2003] 2 SCR 403, [31] (McLachlin CJ) [*KLB*]; S Deakin *et al*, *Markesinis and Deakin's Tort Law* (Oxford, OUP, 2003) 597; G Williams, 'Liability for Independent Contractors' [1956] *CLJ* 180, 193; E McKendrick, 'Vicarious Liability and Independent Contractors—A Re-examination' (1990) 53 *MLR* 770, 772; J Wangmann, 'Liability for Institutional Child Sexual Assault: Where Does *Lepore* Leave Australia?' (2004) 28 *Melbourne University Law Review* 169, 178.

far as such duties may provide the only means by which a relatively deep-pocketed employer may be held liable for the torts of a comparatively impecunious contractor, they represent an important species of liability. Indeed, non-delegable duties are increasingly called upon to plug the gaps left by the vicarious liability doctrine, a doctrine which applies only in those (dwindling) instances in which there is a formal employee-employer relationship.[2] Furthermore, any serious attempt to theorise vicarious liability will probably be contingent to some extent in distinguishing an employer's vicarious liability from his or her primary liability for breach of non-delegable duty arising from the wrongs of his or her servants or contractors.[3] Finally, continuing to place emphasis upon the employee/contractor distinction is likely to have important practical implications for employers and contractors alike spanning matters of insurance, statutory employment rights and taxation categories.

The need to distinguish non-delegable duty from vicarious liability is plain given the way in which the two doctrines have become remarkably intertwined in recent years.[4] The point of departure, then, for theorising about non-delegable duties is a rigorous examination of the confusion between the two doctrines. Only once we identify the central juristic features of non-delegable duties can we proceed to elaborate a comprehensive normative and explanatory account of such duties that makes clear not only their juridical foundations but also their distinctiveness.

---

[2] As Ewan McKendrick has noted, many modern working arrangements 'depart radically from the standard employment relationship': McKendrick, above n 1, at 770. At the same time, however, the uncertainty surrounding the rationale for non-delegable duties has perhaps contributed to an artificial stretching of the doctrine of vicarious liability, especially in sexual abuse cases.

[3] See especially the theory of vicarious liability based on an employer's 'implied promise in the contract of employment to indemnify the employee in the conduct of the employer's business': J Neyers, 'A Theory of Vicarious Liability' (2005) *Alberta L Rev* 289, 301. Note that this theory is at loggerheads with the House of Lords' decision in *Lister v Romford Ice & Cold Storage Co* [1957] AC 555 (HL) and that it fails to account for *Lister v Hesley Hall* [2002] 1 AC 215 (HL) [*Lister*], *Bazley v Curry* [1999] 2 SCR 534 [*Bazley*] and *Jacobi v Griffiths* [1999] 2 SCR 570 [*Jacobi*] for as Neyers admits at 302, '[l]egal liability for ... intentional torts [other than those arising from a 'situation of friction'] would be excluded since it can hardly seem rational that an employer would indemnify unrelated frolics and wrongs'.

[4] Confusion can be traced not just to decided cases (which are the primary focus here), but also to leading academics such as John Fleming who once proclaimed non-delegable duty to be a 'disguised form of vicarious liability': J Fleming, *The Law of Torts* (Sydney, LBC Information Services, 1998) 433. How such a profound mistake could ever be made, when non-delegable duties can exist in two-party cases (such as *General Cleaning Contractors Ltd v Christmas* [1953] AC 180 (PC)) while vicarious liability necessarily requires the involvement of three parties, is hard to fathom. For further analysis on this point, see C Witting, 'Breach of the Non-Delegable Duty: Defending Limited Strict Liability in Tort' (2006) 29 *University of New South Wales Law Journal* 33

II. THE NON-DELEGABLE DUTY/VICARIOUS LIABILITY RELATIONSHIP: SOME RED HERRINGS

There are three main aspects to the confusion between non-delegable duties and vicarious liability. Thus, before examining what I consider to be the essential characteristics for non-delegable duty, I want to identify and discard these three juristic red herrings. Only once I have done this can I aspire to provide a compelling normative and explanatory theory of non-delegable duties that eliminates the present confusion with vicarious liability. In particular, I want, first, to expose the fact that the courts and tort law jurists often put forward the same inadequate justifications for both non-delegable duties and vicarious liability. Second, I shall attempt to unpick the juridical obfuscation that derives from three particular cases decided by the English superior courts. Finally, I want to expose and eliminate the confusing language that has sometimes been deployed by the appellate courts in order to describe the two doctrines. This is because there are cases of non-delegable duty in which the language used to justify the duty is more in tune with vicarious liability, while there are also cases of vicarious liability in which the language used seems more germane to non-delegable duty.

A. Two Misleading Rationales

One frequently invoked justification for both vicarious liability and the imposition of non-delegable duty is the need to provide compensation for the innocent tort victim from a defendant who is assumed, either because of insurance coverage or personal wealth, to be able to guarantee the payment of adequate damages.[5] In *Bazley v Curry*, for example, the court expressly approved the view of Bruce Feldthusen that '[o]ne of the most important social goals served by vicarious liability is victim compensation … [since it] improves the chances that the victim can recover the judgment from a solvent defendant'.[6] And thinking similarly, Glanville Williams once

---

[5] See, eg, *Limpus v London General Omnibus Company* (1862) 158 ER 993, 998 (Willes J); *Soblusky v Egan* (1960) 103 CLR 215 (HCA) (Dixon CJ, Kitto and Windeyer JJ); *Rose v Plenty* [1976] 1 WLR 141 (CA) 148 (Scarman LJ); *Bazley*, above n 3, at [30] (McLachlin J); *Lepore*, above n 1, at [242] (Gummow and Hayne JJ).

[6] Above n 3, at [30] quoting B Feldthusen, 'Vicarious Liability for Sexual Torts' in NJ Mullany & AM Linden (eds), *Torts Tomorrow: A Tribute to John Fleming* (Sydney, LBC Information Services, 1998). See also Fleming, above n 4, at 410: '[the master] is a more promising source of recompense than his servant'.

wrote of a significant English case[7] that it served to ensure 'that the employer of the contractor is liable for [that contractor] where the contractor is insolvent'.[8]

Yet the supposition that non-delegable duty and vicarious liability will both guarantee the claimant a deep-pocketed defendant to sue can be questioned on two counts. First, even though the point may generally be true,[9] it is not universally the case that an employer will possess sufficient wealth or insurance to ensure proper damages. In both *Bazley v Curry*[10] and *Jacobi v Griffiths*,[11] for example, the defendant was a charitable non-profit organisation. And while the charities in those cases did in fact have the necessary finances, they nonetheless help illustrate the point that it may be a matter of chance whether the defendant can pay the award.[12] Second, the deep-pockets argument also rests on a flawed assumption that an independent contractor is unlikely to be able to cover the award of damages. It may well be, for example, that in the field of construction work, the contractor will be wealthier than the person or firm that engages him.

Even in cases where the employer does have the requisite deep pockets, one might still invoke Atiyah's observation that simply focusing on the claimant's need for compensation does not answer the crucial question, 'why should the employer out of all the other wealthy people in the world be singled out for liability?'[13] Certainly, any answer resting on the assumption that an employer will be better placed than either an employee or contractor to spread the loss through the usual price increase mechanism runs into obvious problems in the case of employers with charitable status; for they are unlikely to have any customers. In short, the claimant's need for compensation is as much a non-universal justification for the imposition of non-delegable duty as it is for the imposition of vicarious liability.

Deterrence is a second inadequate rationale sometimes advanced in relation to both non-delegable duty and vicarious liability cases. In both instances, at least where the harm resulted from the commission of an

---

[7] *Honeywill & Stein v Larkin Bros* [1934] 1 KB 191 (CA).

[8] Williams, above n 1, at 187.

[9] As Flannigan notes, '[g]enerally speaking, an employer will be richer ... than the workers he employs, whether they are servants or independent contractors': R Flannigan, 'Enterprise Control: The Servant-Independent Contractor Distinction' (1987) 37 *University of Toronto Law Journal* 25, 28.

[10] Above, n 3.

[11] *Ibid.*

[12] In *Lepore*, above n 1, at [36] Gleeson CJ stated that, '[i]t would be wrong to assume that the persons or entities potentially subject to [a non-delegable duty] ... have 'deep pockets', or could obtain, at reasonable rates, insurance cover to indemnify them in respect of the consequences of criminal acts of their employees or independent contractors'.

[13] PS Atiyah, *Vicarious Liability in the Law of Torts* (London, Butterworths, 1967) 22.

intentional tort, the truth seems to be that the prospect of the employer being held liable appears to be of nugatory effect. Presumably, employers normally only select their employees with reasonable care. Indeed, the employer's genuine and reasonable mistake in engaging the 'wrong person' will only come to light once the latter's criminal proclivities are revealed while working for the defendant. So how, in such circumstances, could one conceivably be deterred from employing potential criminals? Their criminality will always have been, at the relevant time, unknown and unknowable to an employer.[14] In *New South Wales v Lepore*, Gleeson CJ noted and expatiated upon this point:

> [I]f deterrence of criminal behaviour is regarded as a reason for imposing tortious liability upon innocent parties, three things need to be remembered. First, the problem only arises where there has been no ... failure [by the employer] to exercise reasonable care to prevent foreseeable criminal behaviour on the part of the employee. Secondly, it is primarily the function of the criminal law, and the criminal justice system, to deal with matters of crime and punishment.... Thirdly, by hypothesis, the sanctions provided by the criminal law have failed to deter the employee who has committed the crime.[15]

Furthermore, as Gummow and Hayne JJ noted in that case: '[i]f the criminal law will not deter the wrongdoer there seems little deterrent value in holding the employer of the offender liable in damages for the assault committed'.[16] Of course, it might be countered that the prospect of the employer being held liable might encourage him to take greater measures to eliminate opportunities for an employee or contractor to engage in criminal acts such as sexual assaults in the first place. But such measures—eg, internal discipline—would be most unlikely to deter a committed paedophile for whom certain jobs and institutional settings appear attractive *precisely because* they offer greater opportunities for paedophile activities than in any ordinary walks of life.[17] The same would seem to go for those who take jobs in shops in order to 'skim' credit card details for future fraudulent uses,[18] and presumably also for other kinds of job that present particular criminal opportunities. As such, even severe informal

---

[14] For further insights into the misguided invocation of deterrence vis-à-vis an employer in relation to vicarious liability, see Neyers, above n 3, at 293-96.

[15] Above n 1, at [36].

[16] *Ibid*, at [219].

[17] See, eg, Department of Health, *Learning the Lessons: The Government's Response to 'Lost in Care: The Report of the Tribunal of Inquiry into the abuse of Children in Care in the Former county Council Areas of Gwynedd and Clwyd since 1974'* <www.publications.doh.gov.uk/pdfs/lostincare.pdf>. And for a similar experience in Australia, see Senate Community Affairs References Committee, *Inquiry into Children in Institutional Care* <www.aph.gov.au/senate/committee/clac_ctte/inst_care/index.htm>.

[18] For details of the various ways in which 'skimming' can occur, see <http://www.paynetsystems.com/blog/2005/03/application-frauds-in-credit-card.html.>

sanctions imposed by an employer are unlikely to deter the criminal employee if the general criminal law will not.

We might conclude, then, that any *general* theory of non-delegable duty (or vicarious liability for that matter) cannot sensibly be founded arguments about deterrence or deep pockets,[19] and any such thinking ought to be rejected.

B. Three Problematic Cases

There are three particular cases that are especially difficult to explain in the context of the present endeavour to disentangle non-delegable duty from vicarious liability. They are, *McDermid v Nash Dredging and Reclamation Co Ltd*,[20] *Morris v CW Martin & Sons Ltd*[21] and *Lloyd v Grace, Smith & Co*.[22]

In *McDermid*, the House of Lords held the defendants liable on the basis of a non-delegable duty to *ensure the proper operation* of a safe system of work even though the defendants had no control over that system of work.[23] It was this absence of control that led Ewan McKendrick to remark that 'the effect was as if vicarious liability had been imposed for the tort of an independent contractor [who had injured the claimant]'.[24] Certainly, the decision tends to conceal the distinction between non-delegable duty and vicarious liability by appearing to impose a form of strict liability upon the employer who is made to pay for harm he was not at fault in causing or in failing to control. And for anyone that accepts that an employer's duty to his or her employees is a sub-branch of the (fault-based) law of negligence,[25] this presents an ostensible problem. However, the fact that the case *appears* to impose strict liability need not

---

[19] As McLachlin CJ pointed out on behalf of the majority in the Supreme Court of Canada in *KLB*, above n 1, at [20]: 'liability in the context of an employer/independent contractor relationship will not generally satisfy these two policy goals. Compensation will not be fair where the organisation fixed with responsibility for the tort is too remote from the tortfeasor for the latter to be acting on behalf of it... [And there will be] no deterrent effect where the tortfeasor is too independent for the organisation to be able to take any measures to prevent such conduct'.

[20] [1987] AC 906 (HL).

[21] [1966] 1 QB 716 (CA) [*Morris*].

[22] [1912] AC 716 (HL) [*Lloyd*].

[23] Lord Brandon stated that, '[f]or the failure of Captain Sas to operate the system of work he had devised, the defendants, as the plaintiff's employers, are personally, not vicariously, liable to him': Above n 20, at 919.

[24] McKendrick, above n 1, at 773-74.

[25] One scholar has argued boldly that breach of non-delegable duty is an independent tort with no real connection to the law of negligence: see Witting, above n 4. But for a rejection of this account, and for a contrary explanation, see J Murphy: 'The Liability Bases of Common Law Non-Delegable Duties – A Reply to Christian Witting' (2007) 30 *University of New South Wales Law Journal* (forthcoming).

trouble us. It can be argued simply that the presence of the risk of a serious form of harm coupled with the vulnerability of the claimant served to push the required standard of care to the point where there was in effect no dividing line between strict and fault based liability. *Nettleship v Weston*, a classic negligence case, presented comparable features in that there was risk of a driving mishap (which would tend to augment the magnitude of harm) while the passenger was at risk from a learner driver (which would tend to elevate the likelihood of harm).[26] And as Peter Birks once observed, commenting on the case: 'the reality of the common law of negligence is that it imposes what is in effect strict liability for bad practice. ... It sets an objective standard ... but does not ask whether the particular defendant was in fact worthy of reproach'.[27]

The second case that tends to blur the respective domains of non-delegable duty and vicarious liability is *Morris v CW Martin & Sons Ltd*. In that case, the claimant sent her mink stole to be cleaned by a local furrier. With the consent of the claimant, the furrier delivered the stole to the defendant cleaners to be cleaned by them. The fur was then stolen by the very employee who had been given the task of cleaning it. The Court of Appeal unanimously held the defendant liable to the claimant in respect of the theft of the fur. What is interesting, however, is that there were two distinct routes by which this decision was reached. Lord Denning MR held that the defendants, being sub-bailees for reward, owed the claimant the non-delegable duty of a bailee for reward to take care of the fur. He said:

> If the master is under a duty to use care to keep goods safely and protect them from theft and depredation he cannot get rid of his responsibility by delegating his duty to another. If he entrusts that duty to his servant, he is answerable for the way in which the servant conducts himself... [n]o matter whether the servant be negligent, fraudulent or dishonest.[28]

By contrast, Diplock LJ favoured holding the defendants liable on the basis of vicarious liability: 'What he [the thieving employee] was doing, albeit dishonestly, he was doing in the scope or course of his employment... [Thus] [t]he defendants as his masters are responsible for his tortious act'.[29] The judgment of Salmon LJ seemed to support both approaches. At one point he said: 'the defendants are liable for what amounted to ... conversion by their servant in the course of his employment'.[30] Yet elsewhere he observed that a bailee for reward is liable in respect of a theft by those 'deputed by him to discharge some part of *his duty* of taking

---

[26] [1971] 2 QB 691 (CA).

[27] PBH Birks, 'The Concept of a Civil Wrong' in D Owen (ed), *Philosophical Foundations of Tort Law*' (Oxford, OUP, 1995).

[28] Above n 21, at 725.

[29] *Ibid*, at 737.

[30] *Ibid*, at 739.

reasonable care'.[31] The question then arises as to which of the two approaches should be taken to be the majority approach. The key clearly lies in the judgment of Salmon LJ. And the opening paragraph of his judgment seems to provide a useful clue since he began by observing that the bailor-bailee relationship 'imposes a common law duty upon the bailee (a) to take reasonable care to keep the goods safe, and (b) not to do any intentional act inconsistent with the bailor's rights in the goods'.[32] He then asserted what he saw to be the critical issue in the case. '*The real question in this case* turns upon whether *the defendants were in breach* of either of these duties because of the theft of the fur by their servant'.[33] Two things thus emerge. First, that Salmon LJ saw the existence of a duty arising from the bailment as central to the case; and secondly, that the servant's conversion of the fur triggered the defendants' personal (not vicarious) liability. For this reason, it is submitted that we ought really to understand *Morris* as a case of personal liability. Certainly, that was the impression left upon the author of the headnote of the case which records that '[t]he defendants, being sub-bailees for reward, owed the plaintiff, the owner of the fur, the duties of a bailee for reward to take reasonable care of the fur [so] the plaintiff could sue the defendants direct'.[34] On the other hand, their Lordships were unanimous in *Lister v Hesley Hall* in treating *Morris* as though it were an authority on vicarious liability.[35] I shall return to the dubious way in which this was done later.

The third problematic case is *Lloyd v Grace, Smith and Co*. There, the defendant solicitors were held liable when their managing clerk fraudulently conveyed real property to himself rather than in accordance with the client's instructions. The case has again been interpreted by superior courts around the Commonwealth as one involving vicarious liability.[36] Yet the preferable interpretation would again seem to be one of personal liability

---

[31] *Ibid*, at 740-41(emphasis added). For the argument that it should not matter whether the task is deputed to a servant or an independent contractor for these purposes, see Weir, *Tort Law* (Oxford, OUP, 2002) 102.

[32] *Morris*, above n 21, at 738 (emphasis added).

[33] *Ibid*.

[34] *Ibid*, at 716. This is an interpretation for which some support appears in *Lepore*, above n 1. Gummow and Hayne JJ opined that '[i]n *Morris*, there had been a bailment of goods. It was for the employer to demonstrate that its inability to return them in good order was not due to fault on its part': *Lepore* above n 1, at [236]. Gaudron J noted that the case could 'be explained on the basis of a personal or non-delegable duty resulting in direct rather than vicarious liability': *Lepore* above n 1, at [112].

[35] Above n 3, at [19], [46], [52], [58]-[59] and [75]. For further Privy Council and (obiter) House of Lords interpretations of *Morris* as a case of vicarious liability, see *Port Swettenham Authority v T W Wu & Co (M) Sdn Bhd* [1979] AC 580 (PC) and *Photo Production Ltd v Securicor Transport Ltd* [1980] AC 827 (HL), respectively.

[36] See *Lister*, above n 3, at [17], [36], [52] and [57]; *Bazley*, above n 3, at [20]; *Jacobi*, above n 3, at [53].

based on non-delegable duty. In a roughly contemporaneous note, Frederick Pollock stressed the personal nature of the duty: 'the relation of a solicitor and client is a personal relation' such that, although 'the solicitor may delegate office work ... the client is entitled to have his business supervised, where it is not actually conducted, by the solicitor whom he employs'.[37]

It is easy to see why Pollock should analyse the case in those terms. For while Earl Loreburn opined that it was 'a breach by the defendant's agent of a contract made by him as defendant's agent to apply diligence and honesty in carrying through a business within his delegated powers and entrusted to him in that capacity',[38] Lord Macnaghten insisted that the employer, having put the employee in the place of the employer to do a certain class of acts, must answer for the way in which that agent has conducted himself.[39] Picking up on these dicta, several of the judges in *Lepore* thought that *Lloyd* might better be understood as a case of non-delegable duty.[40]

All in all, there is little to be gained by treating *Morris* and *Lloyd* as vicarious liability cases. Furthermore, although the House of Lords regarded them as vicarious liability cases in *Lister*, it based its interpretation, not on the traditional course of employment test, but upon the close connection test propounded by McLachlin J in *Bazley*. Equally, although the cases were also regarded as turning on vicarious liability in *Photo Production v Securicor Transport Ltd*[41] and *Port Swettenham Authority v T W Wu & Co (M) Sdn Bhd*,[42] the first of these cases can be disregarded on the basis that their Lordships were speaking obiter, and the latter—if only from an English perspective—on the basis that the case is not technically an English one. As such, the way is still open, at least in England, to follow the approaches suggested by a number of the judges in *Lepore* including Gaudron J who advised that: 'there is no advantage and considerable disadvantage in holding a person vicariously liable in circumstances in which he or she is directly liable ... as was the case in *Lloyd v Grace, Smith & Co* and, also, in *Morris v CW Martin & Sons Ltd*'.[43]

---

[37] (1913) 29 *LQR* 10, 10.
[38] *Lloyd*, above n 22, at 724.
[39] *Ibid*, at 733.
[40] *Lepore*, above n 1, at [110] (Gaudron J); at [235] (Gummow and Hayne JJ).
[41] Above, n 35.
[42] *Ibid*.
[43] *Lepore*, above n 1, at [127].

C. Judicial Confusion

The third problem with the existing authorities on non-delegable duties and vicarious liability is that, sometimes, the judicial language used to explain the one form of liability more closely resembles the language one would expect to find in the context of the other. Such misuses of language are doubly unhelpful: they misguide us in our search for a theory of non-delegable duty, and they create the misleading impression of a greater degree of synthesis between non-delegable duty and vicarious liability than actually exists. Take, for example, Lord Hobhouse's explanation of vicarious liability in cases where the employee has committed a criminal assault. He began by saying that '[t]he liability of employers derives from *their voluntary assumption of the relationship to the plaintiff*';[44] then elaborated thus:

> [W]here the defendant has assumed a relationship to the plaintiff which carries with it a specific duty towards the plaintiff, the defendant is vicariously liable in tort if his servant, to whom the performance of that duty has been entrusted, breaches that duty.[45]

In the same case, Lord Millett made a similar point in very similar language;[46] while in *Mattis v Pollock*, which involved a violent nightclub doorman attacking a patron of the nightclub in the street, Seymour J (at first instance) said 'I take the view ... that vicarious liability depends upon the *employer owing a duty* to the victim the performance of which he has elected to entrust to an employee who then commits the wrongdoing in question'.[47] In each case, the judicial language resonates with the use of concepts more appositely associated with non-delegable duty. Emphasis is placed upon the defendant's personal 'duty' or 'responsibility' and upon the act of 'delegating' or 'entrusting' that duty or responsibility. Yet in each case, also, the individual judges purported to hold the defendant liable on the basis of vicarious liability.

The converse mistake is evident in the language used in *Lloyd*. And noticing this confusion, Gaudron J remarked in *Lepore* that:

> Although the decision in *Lloyd v Grace, Smith & Co* is explicable on the basis of the solicitors' 'personal obligation' ... the language used [by] ... Earl Loreburn, Lord Macnaghten and Lord Shaw of Dunfermline, is the language of liability or legal responsibility [for] an agent acting in the course of his or her employment.[48]

---

[44]   *Lister*, above n 3, at [55] (emphasis added).
[45]   *Ibid*, at [57] (emphasis added).
[46]   *Ibid*, at [82]-[83].
[47]   [2002] EWHC 2177, [74], decision reversed at [2003] 1 WLR 2158 (CA) (emphasis added).
[48]   *Lepore*, above n 1, at [111].

There was confusion, too, in *Lepore* itself, where, although most of the judges in that case sought strenuously to keep their analyses of vicarious liability and non-delegable duty apart on the grounds that they were seen as distinct forms of liability, Gummow and Hayne JJ claimed, most surprisingly, that a '[non-delegable] duty to ensure that reasonable care is taken ... can be seen to be a species of vicarious responsibility'.[49]

These various dicta clearly reveal the extent of the modern confusion concerning the relationship between vicarious liability and non-delegable duty. It is almost as if the historical point of imposing an non-delegable duty in *Wilsons and Clyde Coal Co v English*[50]—namely, to circumvent the shortcomings of vicarious liability caused by the doctrine of common employment—had been totally forgotten.[51] Furthermore, Gummow and Hayne JJ seem to overlook the equally obvious point that while vicarious liability cannot be imposed in relation to the torts of independent contractors, primary liability may exist in such cases. In short, they ignored both an important practical and an important historical separation between the two doctrines.[52] For this reason, their speech (in this regard), and the other dicta quoted in this section ought to be seen as judicial aberrations.

III. THE JURIDICAL FOUNDATIONS OF NON-DELEGABLE DUTIES

Having exposed and discarded the three main sources of confusion as to the relationship between non-delegable duties and vicarious liability, I shall now endeavour to identify what seems to be the essential characteristics of non-delegable duty. In this respect I shall be concerned with *all* non-delegable duties, and not merely those that that have arisen in the employment-of-workers context. My aim, after all, is to establish the foundations for a general theory of non-delegable duties.

In elaborating such a theory, I am conscious of two concerns: that any such theory must supply *both* a compelling normative justification for non-delegable duties *and* a satisfactory explanation of *the bulk* of the existing case law. Any theory that fails to do the latter is self-evidently an

---

[49] *Ibid*, [257]. This is a clear echo of Fleming's view that an employer's non-delegable duty was a 'disguised form of vicarious liability': *Fleming*, above n 4, at 433.

[50] [1938] AC 57 (HL).

[51] Until the Law Reform (Personal Injuries) Act 1948, any employer who was sued by a first employee on the basis of the employer's vicarious liability for the tort of a second employee (causing loss or harm to the first employee) could successfully raise a complete defence known as 'common employment'. As such, the personal duty of an employer—in the form of a non-delegable duty—was strenuously kept separate from liability under the vicarious liability doctrine.

[52] This is not to suggest, however, that the two doctrines are never available simultaneously.

inadequate theory since, as Cane puts it, 'there must come a point where gaps between the *explanandum* and the *explanans* cast doubt on the value of the explanation'.[53]

A. Two Competing Features?

Any detailed study of the non-delegable duty case law will reveal two main characteristics that seem popular among Commonwealth judges. These are: first, that the defendant's enterprise carried with it a substantial risk; and second, that the defendant assumed a particular responsibility towards the claimant. As will be seen, these justifications seemed to emerge quite independently of one another in the classic non-delegable duty cases. Accordingly, they tend to create the impression that they are alternative theoretical bases for the imposition of such a duty. Indeed, the fact that they have been presented by the courts as independent rationales for non-delegable duties without *explicitly* stating a preference for either, is no doubt a further contributory factor to the ongoing uncertainty about the essential juridical features of non-delegable duties. In this section, however, I shall contend that both features can in fact be collapsed into one central concern: the assumption of responsibility. More particularly, I shall argue that the creation of a substantial risk carries with it a necessary assumption (or imputation) of responsibility, and that they therefore represent not rival bases for non-delegable duties, but rather two different stages of the inquiry (risk creation preceding the assumption of responsibility).

Before considering these key features, however, it is useful to make two prefatory observations. The first is that the language of risk and of assumed responsibility also features in the leading modern cases on vicarious liability where they are often joined, in cases involving an intentional tort on the part of the employee, by a third concern—the vulnerability of the claimant.[54] While the relevance of these considerations to vicarious liability cannot be denied, it is nonetheless true that although this constitutes a genuine overlap between vicarious liability and non-delegable duty in the limited sense that 'risk' and 'an assumption of responsibility' may just as well be invoked to ground both forms of liability, it by no means follows that they are closely linked juristic concepts any more than, say, liability under the fault-based narrow rule in

---

[53] P Cane, 'The Anatomy of Private Law Theory: A 25th Anniversary Essay' (2005) 25 *OJLS* 203, 207. For essentially the same point, see E Weinrib, 'Understanding Tort Law' (1989) 23 *Valparaiso University Law Review* 485, 490: 'Because we know, however inarticulately or provisionally, what tort law is even before we confront the question [what is tort law?], we can insist that the response be true to that knowledge'.

[54] See *Bazley*, above n 3, at [58] (McLachlin J); *Jacobi*, above n 3, at [19] (McLachlin J) and [37] (Binnie J); *Lister*, above n 3, at [54] (Lord Hobhouse) and [83] (Lord Millett).

Donoghue v Stevenson and strict liability under the Consumer Protection Act 1987 are necessarily juridically linked by virtue of the fact that both may ground actions based on defective products.

Second, I need to say a word or two about the role of vulnerability since, although more commonly asserted to be an independent policy basis for vicarious liability,[55] it has also occasionally been invoked as a possible ground for the imposition of a non-delegable duty. In *Lepore*, for example, Gleeson CJ opined that, 'in cases where the care of children, or other vulnerable people, is involved, it is difficult to see what kind of relationship would not give rise to a non-delegable duty of care'.[56] However, although vulnerability is presented here as a freestanding basis on which to ground non-delegable duty, it is submitted that it comprises no more than the inverse of abnormal risk. Noting this connection, McHugh J pointed out in *Lepore* that, '[i]n each case the duty arises because the school authority has control of the pupil whose *immaturity is likely to lead to harm* unless [care is taken]'.[57] In other words, McHugh J, as well as a number of other judges,[58] correctly identified that enterprise risk and vulnerability are frequently no more than opposite sides of the same coin.

(i) Risk

In the earliest reported cases, the creation of risk seemed to be the driving force behind the imposition of non-delegable duties. In *Pickard v Smith*—the very first reported non-delegable duty case—the defendant was the occupier of a refreshment room and coal cellar on a railway platform.[59] The trap door to the cellar was the cause of an accident after it had been left open by a coal merchant delivering coal. Williams J held that, '[t]he act of opening it was the act of the employer, though done through the agency of the coal-merchant; and the defendant, having thereby caused danger, was bound to take reasonable means to prevent mischief... and the fact of his having intrusted it to a person who also neglected it, furnishes no excuse'.[60] Fifteen years later, risk was again seen as central to the imposition of non-delegable duty in both *Bower v Peate*[61] and *Tarry v*

---

[55] See, eg, *Bazley*, above n 3, at [41] (McLachlin J); *Lister*, above n 3, at [83] (Lord Millett).

[56] *Lepore*, above n 1, at [36]. To like effect in the same case, see Gaudron J at [125].

[57] *Lepore*, above n 1, at [139] (emphasis added).

[58] See, eg, *Lister*, above n 3, at [83] (Lord Millett); *Lepore*, above n 1, at [327] (Kirby J); *Richards v Victoria* [1969] VR 136 (SC) 139-40 (Winneke CJ).

[59] (1861) 10 CB (NS) 470, 142 ER 535.

[60] *Ibid*, at 539.

[61] '[A] man who orders a work to be executed, from which, in the natural course of things, injurious consequences to his neighbour must be expected is bound to see to the doing of that which is necessary to prevent the mischief, and cannot relieve himself of his responsibility by employing some one else': (1876) 1 QBD 321, 326 (Cockburn CJ).

Ashton.[62] And the emphasis on sub-contractors performing 'work necessarily attended with risk' received the endorsement of the House of Lords in the early years of the next decade.[63]

By the first half of the 20th century, however, the tenor of the judgments had changed so that the idea of 'exceptional' or 'abnormal' risk seemed to have replaced the bare requirement of 'risk', 'danger' or 'peril'. Thus, in *Honeywill & Stein v Larkin Bros* Slesser LJ averred that the key to liability was something with a "dangerous character, which imposes on the ultimate employers an obligation to take special precautions, and they cannot delegate this obligation by having the work carried out by independent contractors'.[64] And in *Home Office v Dorset Yacht* the duty owed by the borstal officers was seen to be grounded in the 'manifest and obvious risk' to others' property.[65] Yet, notwithstanding the established case law that seemed to emphasise risk-creation, the middle of the 20th century saw a second justificatory premise begin to gain prominence in non-delegable duty cases. This was the assumption of responsibility.

We can really only speculate as to why this occurred, given that the focus on the risk criterion was not totally eclipsed.[66] The relevant cases are themselves silent on why an assumption of responsibility should be preferred; but at least three possible reasons for selecting a different rationale can be suggested. First, it may have been an eagerness to keep non-delegable duties notionally separate from vicarious liability that accounted for the change in approach. The idea that, what we now call 'enterprise risk' might be invoked as a rationale for vicarious liability can be traced to at least the early 19th century in England.[67] But it seems not to

---

[62] 'A person who puts up or continues a lamp in that position, puts the public safety in peril, and it is his duty to keep it in such a state as not to be dangerous; and he cannot get rid of the liability for not having kept it by saying he paid a proper person to put it in repair': (1876) 1 QBD 314, 320 (Lush J).

[63] *Dalton v Angus* (1881) 6 App Cas 740, 831 (Lord Watson).

[64] [1934] 1 KB 191 (CA) 199 (Slesser LJ on behalf of the court).

[65] [1970] AC 1004 (HL) 1035 (Lord Morris) [*Dorset Yacht*].

[66] See, eg, *Darling v AG* [1950] 2 All ER 793 (Durham Assizes) for a mid-20th century case in which the creation of unnecessary danger was treated as the central premise for a non-delegable duty. See also, *Dorset Yacht*, above n 65.

[67] There are signs of it in Lord Brougham's speech in *Duncan v Finlater* (1839) Cl & F 894, 910; 7 ER 934, 940 ('by employing him, I set the whole thing in motion…[thus] I am responsible for the consequences'). But this approach was implicitly doubted the following year by Parke B in *Quarman v Burnett* (1840) 6 M & W 509, 151 ER 509. For its emergence as a prominent explanation of vicarious liability in the USA, see HJ Laski, 'The Basis of Vicarious Liability' (1916) 26 *Yale Law Journal* 105, 109-11. And for even earlier academic support in England, see Frederick Pollock's essay, 'Employer's Liability' in F Pollock, *Essays in Jurisprudence and Ethics* (London, Macmillan, 1882) esp 122-25.

have been until the 20th Century that it became a *popular* justification for imposing vicarious (as opposed to personal) liability; especially in North America.[68]

A second possible explanation as to why the English judiciary began increasingly to focus upon assumptions of responsibility may inhere in the decision of the House of Lords in *Read v Lyons* in which their Lordships attempted to quash the notion that English law applied any special rule of strict liability to ultra-hazardous activities.[69] Finally, there may simply have been an unarticulated recognition by some judges of the fact that, by itself, risk creation—even abnormal risk creation—was a poor premise upon which to ground a doctrine of non-delegable duty. After all, the normative significance of risk creation cannot logically be confined to either non-delegable duty cases or, for that matter, those turning on vicarious liability. It might equally well be invoked in *any negligence case* on the basis that high risks to potential claimants are more foreseeable than remote ones (hence grounding the ordinary duty of care),[70] or because the creation of risk might be taken to be indicative of breach of duty,[71] or because the creation of risk possesses causative significance.[72]

(ii) Assumption of Responsibility

There is appellate authority in both England and Australia for the proposition that non-delegable duty may be imposed on the basis of an assumption of responsibility on the part of the defendant. In the English Court of Appeal decision in *Gold v Essex County Council* Greene MR said:

---

[68] For mid-20th century examples see *Gotreaux v Gary* 94 So 2d 293 (La SC 1957) and *Jones v Morgan* 96 So 2d 109 (1st Cir 1957). Enterprise risk still features prominently in Commonwealth jurisdictions: see eg, *Jacobi*, above n 3, at [67] (Binnie J); *Lister*, above n 3, at [65] (Lord Millett); *Dubai Aluminium v Salaam* [2003] 2 AC 366 (HL) [21] (Lord Nicholls); *Bazley*, above n 3, at [31] (McLachlin J). However, for a trenchant but compelling attack on the use of enterprise liability as a sufficient justification for the imposition of vicarious liability, see Neyers, above n 3, at 297-300.

[69] [1947] AC 156 (HL). Something very like that has, however, re-emerged. In *Transco Plc v Stockport MBC* [2004] 2 AC 1 (HL), a case concerning the rule in *Rylands v Fletcher*, Lord Bingham stated at [11] that the rule would only operate in the presence of an 'exceptionally high risk of danger or mischief' and Lord Hoffmann suggested at [49] the need for an 'exceptional risk'.

[70] Another reason for the decline in popularity of the risk criterion may well be captured in Weinrib's point that 'all doing involves some risk that someone else will suffer' so naturally '[t]ort law cannot forbid the creation of risk without thereby forbidding action itself': Weinrib, above n 53, at 518.

[71] See *Bolton v Stone* [1951] AC 850 (HL).

[72] See, eg, Epstein's idea that D should be treated as causatively responsible for loss to C if D created a sufficiently dangerous condition in his 'paradigm of dangerous conditions' account of causation: R Epstein, 'A Theory of Strict Liability' (1973) 2 *Journal of Legal Studies* 151, 179. See also *Barker v Saint Gobain Pipelines plc* [2006] 2 WLR 1027 (HL) [48] per Lord Hoffmann.

the extent of the obligation which one person *assumes towards another* is to be inferred from the circumstances of the case. Once this is discovered, it follows of necessity that the person accused of a breach of the obligation cannot escape liability because he has employed another person, whether servant or agent, to discharge it on his behalf.[73]

The approach encapsulated in this dictum has proved itself to be popular ever since.[74] And adopting essentially the same tack, Mason J famously said in the Australian case of *Kondis v State Transport Authority* that 'the special [non-delegable] duty arises because the person on whom it is imposed has undertaken the care, supervision or control of the person or his property as to assume a particular responsibility for his or its safety'.[75]

Judging from its wide acceptance and abundant citation with approval in *Lepore*,[76] it is probably fair to describe this dictum as being the classic statement on non-delegable duties in that jurisdiction.[77] At the very least, the assumption of responsibility approach now seems *implicitly* to be the preferred test in both jurisdictions. But this all begs two important questions for any coherent theory of non-delegable duty. The first is whether the assumption of responsibility approach can be reconciled with the risk-based reasoning that so dominated the early cases. The second is whether an assumption of responsibility is, by itself, a sufficient criterion to ground non-delegable duties.

Before we can answer either question however, it is important to clarify what is meant by an 'assumption of responsibility', since such language is apt to mislead in this context insofar as it suggests an element of voluntariness on the part of the defendant which is clearly absent in most non-delegable duty cases and which, in any event, is more the language of contract than of tort.[78] The truth is that 'assumed responsibilities' in non-delegable duty cases are more commonly imputed by the courts than voluntarily undertaken by defendants. Recognising this, Stephen Waddams

---

[73]   [1942] 2 KB 293 (CA) 301-02 (emphasis added).

[74]   See, eg, *Cassidy v Ministry of Health* [1951] 2 KB 343 (CA) [*Cassidy*]; *Carmarthenshire County Council v Lewis* [1955] AC 549 (HL); *Rogers v Night Riders* [1983] RTR 324 (CA); *Esso Petroleum Co v Hall Russell & Co Ltd* [1989] AC 643 (HL).

[75]   (1984) 154 CLR 672 (HCA) 677.

[76]   See, eg, *Lepore*, above n 1, at [99]-[105] (Gaudron J), [154]-[166] (McHugh J), and [259] (Gummow and Hayne JJ). See also its acceptance in *Burnie Port Authority v General Jones Pty Ltd* (1994) 179 CLR 520 (HCA) 551 (Mason CJ, Deane, Dawson, Toohey and Gaudron JJ) [*Burnie Port Authority*].

[77]   Mason J's dictum did not come out of the blue. It was simply a development of what he had said in another High Court case: *The Commonwealth v Introvigne* (1982) 150 CLR 258 (HCA) 271 [*Introvigne*]. As such, *Kondis* and *Lepore* merely entrenched the 'assumption of responsibility' approach.

[78]   For a particularly acute attack on the language of 'assumption of responsibility', see K Barker, 'Unreliable Assumptions in the Modern Law of Negligence' (1993) 109 *LQR* 461.

has identified 'imputed guarantee'[79] as a central juristic feature of non-delegable duties. Yet while the notion of 'imputation' is, of course, consistent with the general idea that duties in tort are imposed rather than voluntarily assumed, the composite term 'imputed guarantee' is objectionable in that it fails to account for non-delegable duty cases that genuinely feature a voluntary assumption of responsibility.[80] Furthermore, while the notion of 'imputation' may suggest a tortious obligation, the term 'guarantee' is more akin to contract—especially business contracts for the sale of goods—than it is to tort.[81] But all of this can ultimately be viewed as academic since the argument about the right label is essentially semantic rather than substantive. Certainly, it is notable that the courts have managed for years, in the context of negligent misstatements and the associated case law, along the lines of equally fictitious 'assumptions' of responsibility without producing a body of case law that defies rationalisation.[82] And to insist on the language of tort rather than the language of contract is to presume a divide between the two that is far from clear or perfect.[83] Take, for example, the offer and acceptance cases of *Storer v Manchester City Council*[84] and *Byrne v Van Tienhoven*[85] in which contractual obligations were imposed without being voluntarily assumed. Given this blurring of the contract/tort divide, what appears more appropriate than the quest for the perfect label, is the pragmatic approach of Lord Steyn in another 'assumption of responsibility' case, *Williams v Natural Life Health Foods Ltd*. In his view, '[t]he touchstone of liability is not the state of mind of the defendant'; rather, '[t]he primary focus must be on things ... done by the defendant'.[86] Once this is grasped, it matters little whether we talk of imputed responsibilities, imputed guarantees or assumed responsibilities for none of these terms accurately captures the

---

[79] See S Waddams, *Dimensions of Private Law: Categories and Concepts in Anglo-American Legal Reasoning* (Cambridge, CUP, 2003) 104.

[80] Not only do the cases of *Lloyd* and *Morris* fall into this category, so too do others expressly decided on the basis of non-delegable duty: see, eg, *Rogers v Night Riders*, above n 74.

[81] Waddams himself presents this very point in terms of a resemblance between non-delegable duties and such contracts: above n 79, at 97-104.

[82] See C Witting, 'Duty of Care – An Analytical Approach' (2005) 25 *OJLS* 33.

[83] Waddams' broader enterprise in *Dimensions*, above n 79, establishes this very point particularly well. For further blurring of the contract/tort divide see J Murphy, 'Expectation Losses, Negligent Omissions and the Tortious Duty of Care' [1996] 55 *CLJ* 43.

[84] [1974] 1 WLR 1403 (CA) [*Storer*]. According to Lord Denning MR at 1408: 'In contracts you do not look into the actual intent in a man's mind. You look at what he said and did'.

[85] (1879-80) LR 5 CPD 344. According to Lindley J at 345, the offeror had '*impliedly assented* to treat an answer duly posted as a sufficient acceptance' notwithstanding his attempted revocation.

[86] [1998] 1 WLR 830 (HL) 835. This is almost an exact echo of Lord Denning's words in *Storer*, above n 84. See also *Phelps v Hillingdon LBC* [2001] 2 AC 619 (HL).

essence of all the case law. On the other hand, by favouring the 'assumption of responsibility' label, the present analysis at least remains faithful to the language of the courts in the leading non-delegable duty cases (even if what the courts frequently do strays beyond the language they use to describe what they do).

With Lord Steyn's approach in mind, we can return to our first question about whether the rival risk-based and assumption of responsibility tests can be reconciled. And here reconciliation becomes relatively straightforward: the creation of an exceptional risk can be invoked to justify the imputation to the defendant of an 'assumed' responsibility if the defendant does not voluntarily undertake such a duty. There are many examples of courts recognising the interrelation between the production of an abnormal risk and the imputation of responsibility. For example, in *Dalton v Angus*, Lord Blackburn spoke of '[a] person causing something to be done, the doing of which casts on him a duty'[87] while Lord Watson was more explicit in stating that 'in cases where the work [done] is necessarily attended with risk, [the defendant] cannot free himself from liability by binding the contractor to take effectual precautions'.[88] In the USA, too, as Blomquist records: 'in *Pendergrass v Lovelace*,[89] [it was] held that a landowner was not immune from tort liability in negligence just because the pesticide spraying [causing damage to a neighbour] was conducted by an independent contractor'.[90] Rather, '*because* the work was inherently dangerous ... the defendant landowner was deemed to have assumed full responsibility'.[91] Similarly, focusing instead on the vulnerability side of the vulnerability/risk equation, five members of the High Court of Australia in *Burnie Port Authority v General Jones Pty Ltd* thought that the kinds of relationship giving rise to non-delegable duties involved one person being so placed in relation to another as 'to assume a particular responsibility for [that other's] safety *because of* the other's special dependence or vulnerability'.[92]

But reconciling the abnormal risk and assumed responsibility cases only takes us so far. It reveals that an assumption/imputation of responsibility is

---

[87]   Above, n 63, at 820.

[88]   *Ibid*, at 831.

[89]   262 P.2d 231 (NM SC 1953).

[90]   RF Blomquist, 'Applying Pesticides: Reconceptualizing Liability to Neighbors for Crop, Livestock and Personal Damages from Agricultural Chemical Drift' (1995) 48 *Oklahoma Law Review* 393, 398.

[91]   *Ibid*.

[92]   Above, n 76, at 550 (Mason CJ, Deane, Dawson, Toohey, and Gaudron JJ). This is also what underpinned the original promulgation of the criterion of 'assumed responsibility' in the speeches of Lords Reid, Morris and Devlin in *Hedley Byrne & Co v Heller & Partners Ltd* [1964] AC 465 (HL) 486, 503 and 528-29 respectively.

often (though not always[93]) contingent upon the creation of an abnormal risk; and that the responsibility thus arising is deemed (because of the degree of risk) to be non-delegable. At this point, however, our second question arises: 'Is the assumption of responsibility both a *necessary* and *sufficient* precondition of non-delegable duties?'

To answer this question we must first recall that the assumption of responsibility criterion also functions, however inadequately,[94] to ground an 'ordinary' duty of care in negligence cases—especially those falling within what is nowadays dubbed the 'extended *Hedley Byrne*' category. It therefore follows that if the 'special', non-delegable duty is to be distinguished from the 'ordinary' duty of care, some further criterion must be found to be working in tandem with an assumption of responsibility so as to ground such a 'special' duty. It is no good arguing that where the assumption of responsibility is imputed on the basis of an *abnormal* risk there will be adequate grounds to justify the imposition of a non-delegable duty. This is because, despite some support for the idea,[95] it does no more than restore the early 20th century approach of treating 'especial risk' as the key element in non-delegable duty cases. As such, it fails to explain the decisions in both *Morris* and *Lloyd* where there was no especial danger in either entrusting a stole to a cleaner, or in relying on a firm of solicitors honestly to perform a conveyance.

B. A Second Precondition: Affirmative Duty

I indicated earlier that any theory of non-delegable duties must possess explanatory as well as normative force. As such, it must, at the very least, be able to account for the bulk of the relevant case law by revealing the juridical lowest common denominator in such cases. And so far as supplying a cogent explanation of the existing categories of non-delegable duties is concerned, we must turn to other types of non-delegable duty case than merely those involving contractors in order to discover the second key ingredient. In considering them, it will be noted that our first essential characteristic of assumed responsibility—whether overtly in evidence, or merely implicit in the existence of risk or vulnerability—is present in each case.

As Gaudron J stated in *Lepore*:

[93] For example, there was no especial danger or vulnerability to theft in entrusting the mink stole to the bailee for reward in *Morris*.

[94] See Barker, above n 78.

[95] *Lepore*, above n 1, at [328] (Kirby J). For criticism of the 'extra-hazardous risk' standard, see Williams, above n 1, at 192.

certain relationships have been identified as giving rise to duties which have been described as 'non-delegable' or 'personal', including master and servant (in relation to the provision of a safe system of work), adjoining owners of land (in relation to work threatening support or common walls), hospital and patient and, relevantly for these appeals, education authority and pupil. The relationships [all involve] ... a person being so placed in relation to another as 'to assume a particular responsibility for [that other's] safety' because of the latter's 'special dependence or vulnerability'.[96]

Examples of each of these four kinds of case can readily be found. *Wilsons and Clyde Coal Co v English* is a clear authority on the duty to provide a safe place of work. Yet a further point, not always made, in connection with that case can be invoked here: namely, that the duty adumbrated there was affirmative in nature.[97] It constitutes one of the few exceptions to the general rule that tort law does not generally recognise positive duties to act for another's benefit.[98] The same is true of the duty as between neighbours to ensure reasonable care and skill are deployed in works affecting a party wall. As Lord Blackburn said in *Hughes v Percival*:

the duty went so far as to *require him to see* that reasonable skill and care were exercised in those operations... [Such that] [i]f such a duty were cast upon the defendant he could not get rid of responsibility by delegating the performance of it to third parties.[99]

The positive nature of non-delegable duties is equally apparent in cases where the defendant has undertaken to provide medical or nursing care to the claimant,[100] or, analogously, where the defendant has undertaken to

---

[96] *Lepore*, above n 1, at [100]. Pre-echoing most of these categories, and adding that of prisons/prisoners, Lord Hobhouse in *Lister*, above n 3, opined (at [54]-[55]): 'the employer, *by reason of assuming a relationship to the plaintiff*, owes to the plaintiff *duties which are more extensive* than those owed by the public at large... the classes of persons or institutions that are in this type of special relationship to another human being include schools, prisons [and] hospitals'.

[97] Lord Wright opined that the employer's personal duty 'is fulfilled by *the exercise* of due care and skill. But it is not fulfilled by entrusting its fulfillment to employees, even though selected with due care and skill': [1938] AC 57 (HL) 78. For an American equivalent see *Shimp v New Jersey Bell Telephone Co* 368 A 2d 408 (NJ SC 1976).

[98] As Basil Markesinis has observed, 'English common law (more so than American common law) still reflects ... the values of an era in which private selfishness was elevated to the rank of public virtue': B Markesinis, 'Negligence, Nuisance and Duties of Affirmative Action' (1989) 105 *LQR* 104, 112.

[99] (1888) 8 App Cas 443, 446 (emphasis added).

[100] In *Cassidy*, above n 74, Lord Denning said at 360: 'In my opinion, authorities who run a hospital ... are under the self same duty as the humblest doctor; *whenever they accept a patient for treatment*, they must use reasonable care and skill to cure him of his ailment' (emphasis added). Likewise, see *Barrett v Ministry of Defence* [1995] 3 All ER 87 (CA) (no general duty to protect a serviceman from the effects of his own idiotic drunkenness; but a duty exists to follow through with care once D had begun to provide assistance to him).

provide care for children.[101] Even beyond the categories identified by Gaudron J, there are clear affirmative duties in non-delegable duty cases where the defendant has assumed responsibility to control either a dangerous person[102] or a dangerous thing;[103] and where the defendant has assumed responsibility to take care of the claimant's goods[104] or legal affairs.[105]

The only judge to notice this facet in *Lepore*, despite the thoroughgoing analysis of such duties in that case, was Gaudron J:

> There is another feature of the duty arising out of the particular relationships that have been identified as giving rise to a non-delegable duty of care which should be stressed. It is that the relevant duty can be *expressed positively and not merely in terms of a duty to refrain from doing something* that involves a foreseeable risk of injury.[106]

Equally, in the leading Canadian authority on non-delegable duty, a majority agreed that 'a common law duty does not usually demand compliance with a specific obligation. It is only when an act is undertaken by a party that a general duty arises to perform the act with reasonable care'.[107] Similarly, in their account of the law on affirmative duties in the USA, the current editors of one leading English textbook remark:

> In all of the American States certain relationships (between the victim and the eventual defendant) are viewed as sufficient to give rise to general duty of protection that is broad enough to include protection against ... the crimes and intentional torts of others. This ... most frequently invoked of the exceptions to the no-duty-to-act rule [applies to] ... a school, its pupils; a jail, its prisoners; a hospital, its patients, an employer, its employees".[108]

---

[101] For example, in *Introvigne*, above n 77, at [10] it was noted by the majority that '[t]he circumstances of the case required *positive action to discharge the duty* to take reasonable steps to protect the pupils' (emphasis added). The presence of nonfeasance was reiterated in *Lepore*, above n 1, at [31] per Gleeson CJ.

[102] See *Dorset Yacht*, above n 65.

[103] See *Burnie Port Authority*, above n 76. In England, it seems the dangerous thing must be in a position to be 'sparked off' and must thus pose an imminent threat: *Smith v Littlewoods* [1987] AC 241 (HL) 273-74 per Lord Goff.

[104] *Morris*, above n 21, at 725: the defendant's duty, according to Lord Denning MR was a positive one 'to use due care to keep goods safely and protect them from theft and depredation'.

[105] *Lloyd*, above n 22. Gleeson CJ in *Lepore*, above n 1, at [52] considered the duty there to be affirmative by virtue of the fiduciary relationship.

[106] *Lepore*, above n 1, at [104] (emphasis added).

[107] *Lewis v British Colombia* [1997] 3 SCR 1145, [17] (Cory J on behalf of the majority).

[108] Deakin *et al*, above n 1, at 247. For further academic notice of the positive nature of these duties, see McKendrick, above n 1, at 777 and Witting, above n 4.

Thus, two crucial elements common to each of the major cases on non-delegable duties transpire: first, an assumption of responsibility (generously conceived); and secondly, an 'assumed responsibility' that corresponds to an affirmative duty to act.[109] These features not only explain the overwhelming majority of the cases garnered from around the Commonwealth,[110] they also supply a clear theoretical basis upon which future non-delegable duties may be based.[111] They also make good sense. The fact that X assumes a responsibility is a good reason both to describe the duty as personal to X, and to continue to hold X responsible for its fulfilment notwithstanding any attempt to delegate it to a third party, however carefully chosen.

IV. CONCLUSION

I have considered the leading Commonwealth decisions in an attempt to discern the essential juridical characteristics of non-delegable duties. Two have emerged: the assumption of responsibility (which, admittedly, is often imputed rather than voluntarily assumed), and the presence of an affirmative duty. There is also weighty judicial support for this account of non-delegable duty in *Lepore* where Gaudron J, after identifying the requirement of an assumption of responsibility, went on:

> There is another feature of ... a non-delegable duty of care which should be stressed. It is that the relevant duty can be expressed positively and not merely in terms of a duty to refrain from doing something that involves a foreseeable risk of injury... *Once the relevant duty is stated in those terms it is readily understandable that the duty should be described as non-delegable.*[112]

This understanding of non-delegable duties links not just the old leading cases with the new ones, but also all the major Commonwealth cases decided at appellate level. It provides, in short, a solid anchoring for the

[109] It could be argued that affirmative duties always arise where there is an assumed responsibility, hence making my second precondition redundant. But this is not so. There are numerous examples of advice cases – see, eg, *Chaudhry v Prabhakar* [1989] 1 WLR 29 (CA) – in which the duty has been held to be one *not to* mislead rather than one *to do* X or Y.

[110] One exception is *Aiken v Stewart-Wrightson* [1995] 1 WLR 1281 (CA) in which there was an assumed duty, positive in nature but it was held not to be non-delegable. But this is a peculiar, mere first instance decision premised largely on an unwillingness to follow the very exceptional non-delegable duty case of *Cynat Products v Landbuild* [1984] 3 All ER 513 (QB).

[111] One might seek, in line with Ernest Weinrib ('The Case for a Duty to Rescue' (1980) 90 *Yale Law Journal* 247, 254 *et seq*) to complicate the analysis by sub-dividing the cases into the categories of 'true nonfeasance' and 'pseudo-nonfeasance'. But while so doing helps to elaborate a distinction between nonfeasance and misfeasance, it serves no obvious purpose in the present context where all that is contended is that D was under a positive duty to act in a particular way in each of the cases considered.

[112] *Lepore*, above n 1, at [104] (emphasis added).

juridical foundations of non-delegable duties and a platform for the principled expansion of non-delegable duty categories. But even beyond this, as is evident from the italicised words in the excerpt from Gaudron J's judgment, there is something satisfying about the fact that non-delegable duties display these features (quite apart from the fact that they posses normative and explanatory significance). This is their ethical quality.[113] Because a non-delegable duty will arises out of something the defendant has done (or had done) to place the claimant at risk, or heighten his or her vulnerability, it seems fitting and proper that the resulting non-delegable duty should be seen as *belonging to the defendant personally* and one which requires *him or her* to do something positive to ensure that the risk created does not materialise, or that the vulnerability heightened does not get wrongfully exploited.

---

[113] See generally P Cane, *The Anatomy of Tort Law* (Oxford, Hart, 1997).

15

Perish Vicarious Liability?

DAVID R WINGFIELD[*]

I. INTRODUCTION

THIS CHAPTER MAKES a radical suggestion: let us remove vicarious liability from the lexicon of the law. By this I do not mean that we remove from the law the ability to make persons other than the direct tortfeasor liable for the harm caused—though some would welcome such a limitation. Rather, I mean simply that we stop using the words 'vicarious liability' to describe the type of liability that is imposed on this person and describe the nature of the liability by what it really is: strict liability.

Now, ordinarily a word or two out of the thousands of words that lawyers use to describe legal relations would not seem to be of such significance that it would be worth the effort to debate whether they should be kept or discarded. Yet in this case it does matter. Our philosophy of law is based on the correct application of certain terms of legal art to the mass of events raised by parties so as to bring order to the chaos of the facts and determine the parties' rights, duties and liabilities. Terms of art serve as a kind of short hand, defining and describing a person's rights and obligations in particular circumstances.[1] Vicarious liability is one of these terms.

Vicarious liability lies at the juncture of fault and no-fault liability. The person who wrongfully commits an act causing harm is understood to be liable because the injury is his 'fault' and the person who is held jointly responsible to pay the damages without proof of personal wrongdoing is seen as having 'no fault' liability. The direct tortfeasor is liable because it is his wrongful act (or occasionally omission) that has caused the harm for which liability is imposed whereas the person who is vicariously liable is lawfully responsible to pay for the harm even though he did not personally cause the harm, indeed the harm may have been something he tried to

* Partner, WeirFoulds LLP.
[1] One of the best works on the use of legal language is WN Hohfeld, *Fundamental Legal Conceptions* (New Haven, Yale University Press, 1919).

prevent. The direct tortfeasor is thus liable because of the close spatial and temporal relationship between his wrongful act and the harmful consequence and the person vicariously liable is liable despite not having committed any wrongful act at all. For this reason, lawyers and judges define vicarious liability by reference to the relationship between the person who is directly liable and the one who is (or on whom it is sought to make) indirectly liable.[2] Where this relationship possesses certain requisite elements, which the substantive law of each jurisdiction defines, the liability of one person is added to that of another—hence the adjective 'vicarious'.

Though the concept has been around for a very long time—since before the Great War in its modern form[3]—lawyers and judges have a great deal of difficulty agreeing on when it is appropriate to impose liability on a person other than the direct tortfeasor. Indeed, when one looks at the number of judges from the trial to the ultimate appellate courts in common law jurisdictions who look at the same facts but disagree on the legal consequences for the person on whom vicarious liability is sought to be imposed, one is drawn to conclude that judges treat vicarious liability like Justice Stewart's description of pornography: 'But I know it when I see it.'[4] As one judge put it in a recent decision:

> A legal notion that began in Roman law, in concepts of responsibility for the actions of slaves and animals, which is still replete with the language of servitude and talk of 'servants' and 'masters,' and which has only lately accepted the language of 'employment,' is obviously in need of more than verbal repair and re-expression.[5]

As a result, 'vicarious liability' has ceased to be useful as a term of art to explain why liability is imposed on a person who did not commit a wrongful act. For this reason it is safe to say that the extent of a person's risk of vicarious liability from harm caused by someone with whom he has a relationship is potentially limitless and thus for all practicable purposes unknowable before it is imposed.

The words we use to define the obligations people owe and the duties they assume as members of society also serve to describe the moral principles that sustain these obligations and duties. The words 'vicarious liability' are tied to the Salmond test which places the master's moral obligation to pay for the harm caused by his servant in the master's voluntary assumption of such

---

[2]   *671122 Ontario Limited v Sagaz Industries Canada Inc* [2001] 2 SCR 983, [25].

[3]   JW Salmond, *The Law of Torts*, 1st edn (London, Stevens and Haynes, 1907) 84. See also *Lloyd v Grace, Smith & Co* [1912] AC 716 (HL) [*Lloyd v Grace, Smith & Co*]. As explained in *Salmond & Heuston*, the doctrine has its roots in mediaeval law and was refined in the Victorian era, *Salmond and Heuston on the Law of Torts*, 21st edn (London, Sweet & Maxwell, 1996) §21.1.

[4]   *Jacobellis v Ohio* 378 US 184, 197 (1964).

[5]   *Sweeney v Boylan Nominees Pty Limited* [2006] HCA 19, [37] [*Sweeney*] (Kirby J dissenting) (internal footnotes omitted).

liability as expressed in his contract with his servant. The moral basis of tort law, however, lies in the citizen's obligation to be just or, to a lesser extent, in society's utilitarian calculus. Though the recent reformulations of the Salmond test by the Supreme Court of Canada and the House of Lords try to situate the employer's vicarious obligation within the general moral realm of tort law, these courts, along with the High Court of Australia, still apply the doctrine as if it is based on the terms of the employer's contract with the employee. Thus, in practice, the law still situates vicarious liability in the moral realm of the employer's voluntary assumption of liability even though the language these courts use to describe this liability is based on a different, and broader, moral notion. This is what leads to the incoherent and often confused application of the doctrine. In order to bring coherence to the doctrine of vicarious liability, then, the legal profession needs to find an authentic tort law basis for what vicarious liability is trying to do. To do this the doctrine of vicarious liability must be situated within the moral framework of tort law generally, which will not happen until the mental baggage of voluntary acceptance is left behind.

II. VICARIOUS LIABILITY WAS ONCE A CONTRACTUAL DOCTRINE

The classic statement of the elements comprising vicarious liability is the so-called Salmond test, from the first edition of *Salmond on Torts*.[6] This test, which was adapted from *Barwick v English Joint Stock Bank*,[7] requires that before vicarious liability can be imposed a relationship of 'master and servant' must exist between the defendant and the person committing the wrong complained of and that the servant, in committing the wrong, must have been acting in the course of his employment.[8] A servant is deemed to be acting in the course of his employment if his act is either (i) a wrongful act authorised by the master; or (ii) a wrongful and unauthorised mode of doing some act authorised by the master.[9]

As *Barwick* makes clear, however, vicarious liability was originally rooted in contractual principles.[10] In this case, the court of Exchequer

---

[6] Above n 3.

[7] *Barwick v English Joint Stock Bank* (1867) LR 2 Ex 259, 266 [*Barwick*], explained and restated in *Lloyd v Grace, Smith & Co*, above n 3.

[8] *Salmond and Heuston*, above n 3, at 434.

[9] *Ibid*, at 443.

[10] Professor Neyers argues that *because* vicarious liability is rooted in contract principles the extent to which a person is vicariously liable should be limited by his contractual liability. See, JW Neyers, 'A Theory of Vicarious Liability' (2005) 43 *Alberta Law Review* 287. In contrast, this chapter argues that because the doctrine is now part of tort law and is universally treated as such it should be developed in accordance with the moral principles that comprise tort law.

Chamber[11] had to decide whether a bank was liable for the fraudulent misrepresentation of its manager. Writing for the court, Willes J held that the bank was liable. He held that the liability for the act of an agent in the course of the principal's business does not depend on the type of wrong, stating that 'no sensible distinction can be drawn between the case of fraud and any other wrong'.[12] Rather, this liability arises because the principal has 'put the agent in his place to do that class of acts' and must therefore be responsible for 'the manner in which the agent has conducted himself in doing the business which it was the act of his master to place him in'.[13] The moral justification for the liability described in *Barwick* (it was not at that time known as vicarious liability) was, accordingly, the master's voluntary assumption of liability as found in his contract with his servant.

It is not surprising that mid-Victorian courts described vicarious liability in these terms. The year 1867 was the near high water mark of the law's emphasis on agreement as the 'touch-stone of liability' and the legal profession's belief that liability should arise only out of obligations voluntarily assumed.[14] As the great Sir George Jessel said:

> [I]f there is one thing more than another which public policy requires, it is that men of full age and competent understanding shall have the utmost liberty of contracting and that their contracts, when entered into freely and voluntarily, shall be held sacred and shall be enforced by courts of justice.[15]

At this time, tort law did not exist in anything resembling its modern form, being more of a 'rag-bag of disparate actions'.[16] Instead, contract law, and, more accurately, the bargain theory of contracts, was doctrinally supreme.[17] After all, *Donoghue v Stevenson*,[18] which permitted the law of negligence to break free of contract law, lay 65 years into the future. Therefore, although *Barwick* contains a reasonably expansive view of what constitutes a principal's authorisation for the purpose of determining his liability, the theory underlying the decision was still contractual: that it is just to hold the principal liable only for those obligations he had voluntary assumed as part of his contract with the agent. The court's job was to interpret the limits of

---

[11]   The Exchequer Chamber was, at that time, the court to which appeals were taken from the three common law courts of Queen's Bench, Common Pleas and Exchequer. Exchequer Chamber was established by 11 Geo IV & Will IV, c 70 and its judges came from the common law courts other than the one from which the appeal was taken. *Barwick* was decided by a court comprised of Willes, Blackburn, Keating, Mellor, Montague Smith and Lush JJ.

[12]   *Barwick*, above n 7, at 265.

[13]   *Ibid*, at 266.

[14]   John PS McLaren, 'The Convergence of Tort and Contract: A Return to a More Venerable Wisdom?' (1989) 68 *Canadian Bar Review* 30, 53.

[15]   *Printing and Numerical Registering Co v Sampson* (1875) LR 19 Eq 464, 465.

[16]   McLaren, above n 14, at 46.

[17]   PS Atiyah, *The Rise and Fall of Freedom of Contract*, 1st edn (Oxford, Clarendon Press, 1979).

[18]   *Donoghue v Stevenson* [1932] AC 562 (HL).

this contract. The contract could be stretched, as it was in *Barwick* and subsequent cases, but it could not be ignored entirely, for to ignore the contract would be to replace the principal's voluntary assumption of liability with something else entirely, which, to Victorian eyes, would be unjust. For this reason, acts committed by the agent that could not have been part of the risks assumed by the principal on the most generous reading of the terms of his contract with his agent, could not form the basis of any liability he owed. Third parties dealing with the agent were bound by this agreement too, should they seek recourse against the principal.

This theory was consistent with the rest of the nineteenth century law of obligations, as we now call it. The 'freedom and sanctity of contract were the necessary instruments of *laissez faire,* and it was the function of the courts to foster the one and to vindicate the other'.[19] In the absence of a contract, a consumer could not sue for injury caused by a defective product.[20] In the absence of a contract, a person could not sue for economic losses caused by his reasonable reliance on the words or acts of another.[21] Parties were prevented from conferring by their bargain rights or liabilities on others.[22] And, reversing this logic, where a contract existed, the parties' rights were governed by their bargain and not by any broader duties found in tort law,[23] except where the defendant had a special calling, like a doctor.[24] The principle of ultra vires meant that many bodies were legally incapacitated from using their property for purposes not comprehended by their constituting documents, such as paying tort liability.[25] Even the rise of fault-based tort liability in place of strict liability was animated by these individualistic notions.[26]

In short, 19th century law reflected, as it always does, the social and economic forces that animated society at the time. Those forces gave private rights as defined by property and exchange relations a status in the law not

---

[19] *Cheshire and Fifoot's Law of Contract*, 8th edn (London, Butterworths, 1972) 19.

[20] *Winterbottom v Wright* (1842) 10 M & W 109, 152 ER 402 (Exch).

[21] *Derry v Peek* (1889) 14 App Cas 337 (HL).

[22] *Tweddle v Atkinson* (1861) 1 B & S 393, 212 ER 762 (QB). See also, WR Anson, *Principles of the English Law of Contract and of Agency in its Relation to Contract*, 14th edn (Oxford, Clarendon Press, 1917) 272-73.

[23] See McLaren, above n 14, at 51 and *Tai Hing Cotton Mill Ltd v Liu Chong Hing Bank Ltd* [1986] AC 80 (PC) 107. This principle was finally put to rest in Canada by *Central Trust Co v Rafuse* [1988] 2 SCR 147 and in England by *Henderson v Merrett Syndicate Ltd* [1995] 2 AC 145 (HL).

[24] *Fish v Kapur* [1948] 2 All ER 176 (KB).

[25] David R Wingfield, *The Short Life and Long After Life of Charitable Immunity in the Common Law* (2003) 82 *Canadian Bar Review* 315, 327.

[26] Richard A Epstein, 'A Theory of Strict Liability' (1973) 2 *Journal of Legal Studies* 151. As explained by Epstein, in an action in trespass the lack of fault was an *excuse* to avoid what would otherwise have been strict liability; fault was not a condition to the imposition of such liability. As was stated in *Weaver v Ward* (1616) 179 Hobart 135, 80 ER 284 (KB) 284: 'No man may be excused of a trespass...except it may be judged entirely without his fault.'

seen before or since. Understandably, the principles of vicarious liability developed by the courts in the nineteenth century reflected these broader social and economic forces too. Thus, the moral justification for imposing vicarious liability was the same as the moral foundations of the rest of nineteenth century law: that as a general matter it was morally sound to impose liability on people only when they voluntary assumed the risk that led to the liability and this assumption of risk had to be found either in property rights or contractual relations. Since the only contract that existed between the master and the person injured was the contract between the master and servant himself, it was only natural that the terms of this contract provided the only morally sound basis to impose liability on the master.

III.   CONTRACT PRINCIPLES DO NOT EXPLAIN OR JUSTIFY THE IMPOSITION OF VICARIOUS LIABILITY IN ALL CIRCUMSTANCES

The Salmond test provides a morally sound basis for the imposition of strict liability in some circumstances. The employer's voluntary acceptance of such liability under the terms of his contract with his servant is morally sound because voluntary acceptance accords with our understanding of free will and is consistent with other values underlying the common law. Therefore, it is easy to justify the imposition of strict liability on a person who assumes such liability. That is why vicarious liability—and in particular the Salmond test—is uncontroversial in the run of the mill cases where it is applied.

Where vicarious liability is controversial, however, is when it is used to attribute responsibility to a person who did not and indeed could not rationally be taken to have voluntarily assumed liability for the harm that someone is trying to attribute to him. This problem arises whenever vicarious liability is sought to be imposed on a person for harm caused by the intentionally wrongful—and especially criminal—acts of another. Since people ordinarily do not voluntarily assume responsibility for someone else's deliberately wrongful acts, it is seen in many quarters as morally unjust to make a person strictly liable to pay compensation for the harm caused in such circumstances. Nevertheless, since it is not altogether uncommon for employees to cause harm by their deliberate, and sometimes criminal acts, courts, as a matter of policy as much as principle, have extended vicarious liability to ensure that people harmed by these acts can recover from the employer. In doing so, the logic of the Salmond test has expanded past its breaking point and, as a result, in those jurisdictions where vicarious liability has been applied to make the master liable for the servant's intentionally wrongful acts, the test has been replaced or modified. The highest courts of Canada, the United Kingdom have, respectively, replaced and modified the test, whereas the High Court of Australia has, in effect, chosen to retain the test in its original form. Those courts that have changed the test have made vicarious liability a truly tortious doctrine; that court which has retained the test has kept vicarious liability a contractual doctrine.

The first high court to tackle the Salmond test head on was the Supreme Court of Canada in *Bazley v Curry.*[27] In this case, the Supreme Court in effect jettisoned the Salmond test and replaced it with the concept of 'enterprise risk'. Enterprise risk, which perhaps can more accurately be described as enterprise liability, was originally proposed by Professor Atiyah in 1967 as offering a better explanation (and by inference a better test) for determining when the imposition of vicarious liability is appropriate.[28] As explained by the Supreme Court, where the enterprise of which the personal tortfeasor is a part has 'materially increased' the risk of certain harm the enterprise may be liable to pay compensation when this harm has materialised.[29] Whether the enterprise is liable, though, depends on policy considerations which the court described as the fair and efficient compensation for wrong and deterrence.[30] To determine whether policy supports the imposition of vicarious liability where the enterprise has materially increased the risk of the harm, the trial court is required to investigate the employee's 'specific duties' and to determine whether they gave rise to 'special opportunities' for wrongdoing.[31]

In *Bazley*, the Supreme Court unanimously agreed that the defendant (a residential care facility) was liable for the criminal acts of its employee (who committed sexual assault on the children in the care of the facility) because those acts took place on the defendant's premises and were committed by an employee who was authorised to have contact with the children in the defendant's care. But in *Jacobi v Griffiths* ,[32] a companion decision released along with *Bazley*, the Court did not accept that a charitable organisation that provided recreational activities to children was liable for the criminal sexual assaults committed by one of its employees.

In *Jacobi*, the organisation's employee met the children whom he later raped when he was working for the organisation but he abused the children at his home outside working hours. The Court could not agree on whether there was not a 'strong enough' connection between the employee's acts and the employer's enterprise to permit vicarious liability to be imposed. Five judges held that vicarious liability should not be imposed and four held that it should be. One factor the majority relied upon in

---

[27] *Bazley v Curry* [1999] 2 SCR 534 [*Bazley*]. La Forest J also dealt with the doctrine in his dissent in *London Drugs v Kuehne & Nagel International* [1992] 3 SCR 299, 334 *et seq.* Justice La Forest's analysis provided the foundation of then Justice McLachlin's analysis in *Bazley* at [28].
[28] Atiyah, above n 17.
[29] *Bazley*, above n 27, at [46].
[30] *Ibid.*
[31] *Ibid.*
[32] *Jacobi v Griffiths* [1999] 2 SCR 570.

denying vicarious liability was the fact that because the defendant was a charitable organisation, it could not pass on the costs of any vicarious liability to the users of its charitable missions and thus it could not be said that the policy of efficient compensation would be met in this circumstance.[33] This factor, however, was effectively disavowed by the whole court in *Doe v Bennett*.[34]

In a number of subsequent cases the Supreme Court of Canada fleshed out the factors that would permit a court to find the existence of a sufficiently strong connection between the employer and employee (hence the risk created by the employer's enterprise) and the wrongful act. The most that can be said of these factors, however, is that the Court *rejected* the view that a mere opportunity the employer provided the employee to commit the tortious act is a sufficiently strong connection to found a case for vicarious liability.[35]

The Supreme Court of Canada has also considered whether the principles for imposing vicarious liability they had developed in *Bazley* and *Jacobi* apply in the context of commercial relationships. In *671122 Ontario Ltd v Sagaz Industries*,[36] the Supreme Court of Canada held that these principles were of general application but confirmed that vicarious liability is generally only appropriate in employer-employee relationships, and not relationships arising by way of independent contracts. Thus, although the Supreme Court now uses the test of 'enterprise risk' to define the circumstances when it is appropriate to impose vicarious liability, it has retained the Salmond test at least to the extent of requiring, usually, an employer-employee relationship before the enterprise risk test can be imposed.

In *Lister and Others v Hesley Hall Ltd*,[37] the House of Lords chose to modify the Salmond test. Like the Supreme Court of Canada in *Bazley v Curry*, the House of Lords in *Lister* had to consider the doctrine of vicarious liability in the context of a sexual assault on boys by an employee of a school. With varying degrees of enthusiasm, their Lordships held that the Salmond test could embrace an employer's liability for an employee's intentional wrongdoing, even if it is criminal.

Lord Steyn, with whom Lord Hutton agreed,[38] accepted that although the Salmond test does not 'cope ideally' with cases of intentional wrongdoing it is at root a 'practical test' which serves to demark the dividing line between

---

[33]   *Ibid*, at [71].
[34]   *John Doe v Bennett* [2004] 1 SCR 436 [*Bennett*].
[35]   *KLB v British Columbia* [2003] 2 SCR 403; *HL v Canada (Attorney General)* [2005] 1 SCR 401; *G (ED) v Hammer* [2003] 2 SCR 459; *EB v Order of Oblates of Mary Immaculate in the Province of British Columbia* [2005] 3 SCR 45 [*Oblates*].
[36]   *671122 Ontario Ltd v Sagaz Industries* [2001] SCR 983.
[37]   *Lister and Others v Hesley Hall Ltd* [2002] 1 AC 215 (HL) [*Lister*].
[38]   *Ibid*, at [52].

cases where it is or is not just to impose vicarious liability.[39] According to Lord Steyn, the second branch of the Salmond test encompasses intentionally wrongful acts so long as they are 'connected' to the acts the employer authorised the employee to perform.[40] Lord Clyde's speech largely duplicates Lord Steyn's reasoning with the additional emphasis that whether the act complained of is garden variety negligence or a criminal sexual assault makes no difference to the principle of vicarious liability which is concerned with a broad understanding of scope of employment.[41] Lord Hobhouse held that the second branch of the Salmond test was a convenient rule of thumb but that it did not 'represent the fundamental criterion' and therefore he rejected it (and the Supreme Court of Canada's approach from *Bazley v Curry* too).[42] Instead, his Lordship held that to impose vicarious liability a court must compare the duties owed by the employee to the plaintiff, on the one hand, and to his employer, on the other.[43] By way of contrast, Lord Millett accepted the Supreme Court of Canada's analysis that vicarious liability is at its root a loss distribution device. His Lordship held that an employer is liable for the employee's tort—even if it is a deliberate one—if the risk of the tort is one which experience shows is inherent in the nature of the employer's activities.[44]

Thus, the majority of their Lordships used a narrower test for vicarious liability than did the Supreme Court of Canada. Yet, in comparison to how the Supreme Court applied its test in *Jacobi* and in subsequent cases,[45] the House of Lords applied its formulation more generously to find liability on a school in circumstances where the Supreme Court might very well have denied it.

In a parallel to the Supreme Court of Canada, shortly after deciding *Lister*, the House of Lords addressed vicarious liability in a commercial case as well. In *Dubai Aluminium Company Ltd v Salaam*[46] their Lordship's confirmed that vicarious liability applies to deliberately wrongful acts which would never have been authorised by the defendant. In that case liability was imposed on a partnership of solicitors for the wrongful act of assisting a fraud committed by one of the partners. Their Lordships each agreed that vicarious liability is not based on whether the tortfeasor had actual or apparent authority to do as he did when committing the tort, but rather on whether the wrongful act was so closely connected to the affairs

---

[39] *Ibid*, at [20].
[40] *Ibid*.
[41] *Ibid*, at [48], [50].
[42] *Ibid*, at [60].
[43] *Ibid*.
[44] *Ibid*, at [65]. His Lordship used the word 'business' not activities.
[45] See the cases referred to in n 35.
[46] *Dubai Aluminium Company Ltd v Salaam* [2003] 2 AC 366 (HL).

of the person sought to be vicariously liable that the act could be regarded as the act of the latter person. As Lord Nicholls said:

> [T]he wrongful conduct must be so closely connected with acts the partner or employee was authorised to do that, for the purpose of liability of the firm or the employer to third parties, the wrongful conduct *may fairly and properly be regarded* as done by the partner while acting in the ordinary course of the firm's business or the employee's employment.[47]

Interestingly, this gloss on the Salmond test harkens back to the old 'master's tort' theory which was rejected by *dicta* in the House of Lords over forty years before.[48] Under this theory, the servant's *act* is attributed to the master, rather than the servant's *tort*. The master himself is thus seen as having committed the wrongful act through his servant. This theory, which actually has much to commend it, has been criticised because it deems as a fact that which did not in fact occur (the master's tort) and thus induces artificiality into the analysis of vicarious liability.[49]

In their analysis of the issue the High Court of Australia took a different tack from both the Supreme Court of Canada and the House of Lords. In a case that considered both vicarious liability and non-delegable duty, the High Court held, in *New South Wales v Lepore* that in the absence of fault, a school authority would not be liable for the intentional criminal conduct of an employee.[50] The High Court came to its conclusion after a detailed analysis of the reasoning of the Supreme Court of Canada in *Bazley* and the House of Lords in *Lister* (and their progeny). Though six justices agreed on the outcome of the appeals, their reasons for doing so varied greatly.

On the issue of vicarious liability, two judgments were favourably disposed to the approach taken by the House of Lords and the Supreme Court of Canada, but they nevertheless rejected liability for intentional misconduct unless the conduct could be considered to have taken place in the course of the employee's employment, thus applying the Salmond test in effect.[51] The joint judgment of Gummow and Hayne JJ expressly relied on the Salmond test and rejected the imposition of vicarious liability for intentional misconduct.[52] One judgment accepted that the Salmond test did not permit the imposition of vicarious liability for intentional misconduct but permitted an argument based on estoppel.[53] The remaining judgment

---

[47]   *Ibid*, at [21] (emphasis in original). See also, the discussions at [23] (Lord Nicholls) and at [107] (Lord Millett).

[48]   *Staveley Iron & Chemical Co v Jones* [1956] AC 627 (HL) [*Staveley Iron*]; *Imperial Chemical Industries Ltd Shatwell* [1965] AC 656 (HL).

[49]   Atiyah, above n 17, at 6.

[50]   *New South Wales v Lepore; Samin v Queensland; Rich v Queensland* [2003] 212 CLR 511 (HCA).

[51]   *Ibid*, at [39], [85] (Gleeson CJ); [316] (Kirby J).

[52]   *Ibid*, at [240-42] (Gummow and Hayne JJ).

[53]   *Ibid*, at [132] (Gaudron J).

accepted that the Salmond test generally applies and does not permit the imposition of vicarious liability for intentional wrongdoing but rejected the test in cases where harm was intentionally caused to children in the care of educational establishments.[54]

On the issue of non-delegable duty, the judges agreed that where such a duty exists it cannot be delegated to a third party so as to eliminate the liability owed by the first party. The majority of the judges also agreed that there was no absolute duty on a school to avoid harm to the students—that fault, in other words, was still an element of liability for breach of a school's duty to its students. Since the sexual assaults committed by the teachers in the cases before the court were not caused by the fault of the schools, there was no liability on the school boards for breaching any duty of care they owed their students.

In summary, the High Court of Australia held as follows. First, that since fault was not an element of the vicarious liability of the employer it was unjust to make employers liable for *all* of their employee's wrongful acts. The court defined the employee's duties for which the employer was strictly liable, however, in such a way that vicarious liability was generally not possible for intentional torts. Second, that since fault is an element of the direct liability of the employer for breach of non-delegable duty, where no fault is found, no direct liability is possible.

To complete the Commonwealth parallelism, the High Court too followed a case in which vicarious liability was considered in relation to child sex abuse case with a case in which the doctrine was considered in the commercial context. In *Sweeney v Bowlan Nominees Pty Ltd* the plaintiff was injured at a convenience store when a refrigerator door she opened fell on her.[55] The store was found not liable because it had taken reasonable steps to have the door repaired by engaging a repair company. The repair company in turn had engaged the repairman as an independent contractor. The company was found to be vicariously liable at trial, despite not having been served with notice of the proceedings. On appeal, the company was found not liable because the repairman was an independent contractor and that decision was upheld by the High Court.

The majority of the High Court held that despite some controversy over the historical development and limits of the doctrine of vicarious liability, certain basic propositions could be identified as being central to this body of law. The first proposition the court identified was that the law distinguishes between employees (for whose conduct the employer will generally be vicariously liable) and independent contractors (for whose

---

[54] *Ibid*, at [342], [350] (Callinan J).
[55] *Sweeney*, above n 5 (Gleeson CJ, Gummow, Hayne, Heydon and Crennan JJ), (Kirby J dissenting).

conduct the person engaging the contractor will generally not be vicariously liable). The second proposition was that the law places prime importance on whether the wrong was committed by the employee in the course of his employment. Significantly, the court rejected (as had the Supreme Court of Canada) the contention that if the second person's actions were intended to benefit the first or were undertaken to advance some purpose being pursued by the first person, then, on that basis alone, should be vicariously liable for the conduct of the second.[56] For these reasons, the court concluded that the company that was engaged by the convenience store to repair the refrigerator door and which in turn engaged the repairman to effect the repairs was not liable for the plaintiff's injuries when the refrigerator door fell on her. Thus, the plaintiff had to bear the costs of the injury she suffered.

When one looks at the body of recent law on the doctrine of vicarious liability from the Supreme Court of Canada, the House of Lords, and the High Court of Australia, it appears that the Salmond test reigns supreme, despite the fact that two of these courts (the Supreme Court of Canada and the House of Lords) now use different language to analyse the imposition of vicarious liability. In all these jurisdictions, the fact that the tortfeasor was an independent contractor will be determinative in precluding the imposition of vicarious liability on the person who was directly engaged to perform the service and who sub-contracted the performance to the tortfeasor. Where the tort is deliberately wrongful, tort liability depends on the enterprise's role in creating the risk that materialised in harm, except that duties the enterprise authorised the wrong-doing employee to perform may limit or negate this liability entirely, which is an application of the Salmond test in substance. Thus, even though the Salmond test is no longer regarded by any of the senior Commonwealth courts as providing a sufficient basis for determining the existence or limits of vicarious liability, at root all of the Commonwealth's most senior judges[57] seem to apply this test in substance even when discounting the test in theory. How can this be sound? Well, in short, it is not. To understand why it is not, however, we need to go back to basics, to the moral foundations of tort law.

IV.   TORT PRINCIPLES DO EXPLAIN AND JUSTIFY THE IMPOSITION OF VICARIOUS LIABILITY IN ALL CIRCUMSTANCES

Tort law provides the legal foundation for shifting the monetary consequences of an event causing harm from the person who suffers the harm to

---

[56]   *Ibid*, at [12], [13].
[57]   By the time *Oblates*, above n 35 was decided there were five new judges on the Supreme Court of Canada.

someone else. Since the law cannot restore lost limbs or remove the psychological trauma of an injury or reverse any other physical damage, it can deal with these things only by ordering that someone pay a sum of money in compensation. There is more to tort law's remedies than this, of course. A court can also grant orders compelling or restraining certain behaviour and can punish wrongdoers with special types of damages (punitive) or with monetary remedies calculated by reference to the defendant's gain and not the plaintiff's loss (waiver of tort). But these types of orders are rare. An action in damages as compensation for loss is the mark of a tort.[58] When these damages are awarded, the court is shifting the economic consequences of harm from the person who suffers it to someone else. Tort law tells us when this should occur. It tells us how and why responsibility for harm is attributed to one person rather than another, or to no one.

Tort law attributes responsibility by 'defining the conduct giving rise to liability and also the occurrences for which one will be responsible', sometimes casting the net broadly, and other times, quite narrowly.[59] For example, sometimes the court will impose liability where there is a substantial possibility that the defendant caused the plaintiff's loss, but no proof that the defendant actually did so.[60] In other cases, the law will deny liability even when it is clear that the defendant caused the plaintiff's loss and that such loss was foreseeable.[61] And in still other cases tort law will *exempt* the wrongdoer but attribute responsibility for the wrongful act to another.[62] Moreover, as any textbook on tort law demonstrates, there are also many types of wrongs for which tort law attributes responsibility but which are not based on the defendant's intentional or negligent breach of duty—strict liability, in other words.[63] Tort law permits liability to be imposed on the owner for harm caused due to the condition of his property, such as in *Rylands v Fletcher*,[64] on occupiers for dangerous conditions,[65] and for trespass,[66] amongst others. And of course, tort law imposes vicarious liability.

---

[58] *Salmond and Heuston*, above n 3, at §2.1.

[59] Lord Hoffmann, 'Causation' (2005) 121 *LQR* 592, 595.

[60] *Fairchild v Glenhaven Funeral Services Ltd* [2003] AC 32 (HL) [*Fairchild*].

[61] Eg pure economic loss, see *Murphy v Brentwood District Council* [1991] 1 AC 398 (HL) [*Murphy*].

[62] *Williams v Natural Life Health Foods Ltd* [1998] 1 WLR 830 (HL). See also Stephen Todd, 'Assuming Responsibility for Torts' (2003) 119 *LQR* 199.

[63] Lord Hoffmann, above n 59, at 597.

[64] *Fletcher v Rylands* (1865) 3 H & C 774, 159 ER 737 (Ex Div), revd (1866), LR 1 Ex. 265, affd (*sub nom. Rylands v Fletcher*) LR 3 HL 330.

[65] *Indermaur v Dames* (1866) LR 1 CP 274; *McErlean v Sarel* (1987) 61 OR (2d) 396 (CA).

[66] *Salmond and Heuston*, above n 3, at ch 5.

In all cases, though, responsibility is only attributed to a person who has caused the complained of harm or risk of harm.[67] Causation is the indispensable element of every species of tort liability. Nevertheless, because the historical connections that tie events together are potentially limitless—as the story of Mrs O'Leary's cow causing the Great Chicago fire attests—the law has to make a decision about where in the chain of events that leads to a harmful occurrence responsibility for the occurrence is to be attributed.[68] This decision, as Hart and Honoré explained almost fifty years ago, is a legal not a factual one:

> Usually in discussion of the law and occasionally in morals, to say that someone is responsible for some harm means that in accordance with legal rules or moral principles it is at least permissible, if not mandatory, to blame or punish or exact compensation from him. In this use the expression 'responsible for' does not refer to a factual connection between the person held responsible and the harm but simply to his liability under the rules to be blamed, punished or made to pay.[69]

Our law does not simply make the person who has some historical connection to the injured person and who is more economically capable of absorbing the monetary consequences of a loss do so, or make society at large do so by requiring the state to pay—though, some advocate this approach.[70] Instead, our law, reflecting the principles of liberal individualism around which our society is—still barely—based,[71] restricts the ability of an injured person to seek compensation from another person to those circumstances where the second person is morally bound to pay. As stated by the Supreme Court of Canada in a recent case, 'the law of negligence not only considers the plaintiff's loss, but explains why it is just and fair to impose the cost of that loss on the particular defendant before the court'.[72] To put this another way, the legal rules defining causation in tort thus reflect a moral calculation.

---

[67] *Barker v Corus* [2006] 2 WLR 1027 (HL) [17], [31], [35-36], [49] (Lord Hoffmann); [61-62] (Lord Scott); [113] (Lord Walker); [126] (Baroness Hale) [*Barker*].

[68] Lord Hoffmann, above n 59, at 597.

[69] HLA Hart and AM Honoré, *Causation in the Law*, 2nd edn (Oxford, Clarendon Press, 1985) 65. The first edition was published in 1959.

[70] Stephen D Sugarman, 'Doing Away with Tort Law' (1985) 73 *California Law Review* 555; Marc A Franklin, 'Replacing the Negligence Lottery: Compensation and Selective Reimbursement' (1967) 53 *Virginia Law Review* 774. See also the examples cited in L Klar, *Tort Law*, 3d edn (Toronto, Thomson-Carswell, 2003) 19.

[71] CB Macpherson, *The Political Theory of Possessive Individualism: Hobbes to Locke* (Oxford, Clarendon Press, 1962).

[72] *Childs v Desormeaux* (2006) 266 DLR (4th) 257 (SCC) [25] [*Childs*].

The 'but for test',[73] the test of 'material contribution to harm',[74] and the test of 'material contribution to the risk of harm'[75] each locate, as a matter of law, the causal link between a person injured by some unnatural occurrence and another person's actions or omissions at different historical points. In each case, though, the attribution of responsibility based on these tests is understood as being required due to our views of free will, the way in which the natural world operates and theory of justice which follow from these views.[76] For the same reason, the law does not attribute to a person all the direct physical consequences that flow from his wrongful acts, although it once did.[77] Rather, only those consequences that were reasonably foreseeable are attributed to him[78] or, where he contributed to the risk of harm, only his proportionate share of the contribution to the risk is attributed to him.[79] It is regarded as unjust to impose liability on a person who could not objectively be expected to have appreciated that his conduct could lead to such liability[80] or whose conduct did not create the harm, but only a proportion of the risk that the harm would occur.[81]

Those cases, like the ones with which this chapter began from the Supreme Court of Canada, the House of Lords and the Australian High Court, almost always analyse the imposition of strict liability by contrasting such liability with fault-based liability. This, naturally, makes it seem as if the two species of liability are found under different *genera*. Yet, both species of liability actually belong to the same *genus*, which Honoré describes as 'outcome-responsibility' and thus share a common moral foundation.[82] Indeed, were that not so, the law could not impose tort liability on people whose personal characteristics made it impossible for them to meet the objective standard of behaviour against which negligent conduct is measured.[83]

Modern tort law reflects two moral principles; or, perhaps it is more accurate to say that two competing moral principles are reflected in

---

[73] *Snell v Farrell* [1990] 2 SCR 311.

[74] *Athey v Leonati* [1996] 3 SCR 458; *Fairchild*, above n 60.

[75] *Barker*, above n 67.

[76] Lord Steyn, 'Perspectives of Corrective and Distributive Justice' (2002) 37 *Irish Jurist* 1. Lord Steyn's article is derived from Aristotle's notions of corrective and distributive justice, see WD Ross (tr), *Nicomachean Ethics*, (Oxford, Clarendon Press, 1908).

[77] *Polemis & Furniss Withy & Co, Re,* [1921] 3 KB 560 (CA) [*Re Polemis*].

[78] *Overseas Tankship (UK) v Morts Dock & Engineering Co (The Wagon Mound)* [1961] AC 388 (PC) 422 [*The Wagon Mound (No 1)*].

[79] *Barker*, above n 67.

[80] Tony Honoré, 'Responsibility and Luck' (1988) 104 *LQR* 530, 531.

[81] *Barker*, above n 67.

[82] Honoré, above n 80. One reason why strict and fault based liability are seen as belonging to different worlds is because most strict liability torts are off-shoots of the old action of trespass, whereas negligence is an off-shoot of action on the case. See *Salmond and Heuston*, above n 3, at ch 1, §§1.1-1.2.

[83] Honoré, above n 80, at 546. Epstein, above n 26, at 153.

modern tort law. One principle, and by far the strongest, is the principle of justice.[84] This principle, whose leading modern proponent is John Rawls, holds that each person is entitled to an equal right to the most extensive basic liberty compatible with a similar liberty for others.[85] Under this principle, all individuals in society have the right to roughly the same degree of security from risk.[86] As a corollary, each person is subjected to suffering harm, without compensation, from 'background risks'.[87] These are risks that are shared equally by all arising from our shared membership in society. Based on this principle, no one may unreasonably create additional risks to others without the concomitant obligation to pay compensation to persons harmed by that risk.[88] As explained by Lord Steyn:

> The primary aim of tort law is the pursuit of corrective justice. It requires somebody who has harmed another without justification to indemnify the other. There is, however, another perspective, namely considerations of distributive justice. It concentrates on the place of the plaintiff and defendant in society.[89]

Though the common law has developed many different formulations for describing the legal standard for the imposition of liability in tort,[90] in reality, however, in every case where the court finds that the defendant breached a duty of care he owed the plaintiff the court is expressing an opinion on whether the defendant unreasonably created the risk that materialised in harm to the plaintiff and hence whether the imposition of liability is morally justified.[91]

---

[84]   See, eg, one of the seminal articles in this area, G Calabresi and AD Melamed, 'Property Rules, Liability Rules, and Inalienability: One View of the Cathedral' (1972) 85 *Harvard Law Review* 1089, 1102-5.

[85]   This is, of course, the liberty principle of Rawls' theory of distributive justice: J Rawls, *A Theory of Justice*, (Cambridge, Massachusetts, Harvard University Press, 1971) 24.

[86]   George P Fletcher, 'Fairness and Utility in Tort Theory' (1972) 85 *Harvard Law Review* 537.

[87]   *Ibid*, at 543.

[88]   *Ibid*, at 541-43.

[89]   Lord Steyn, above n 76, at 5. See also the judgment of Crennan J in *Harriton v Stephens* [2006] HCA 15, [274].

[90]   In negligence they include: *Donoghue v Stevenson*, above n 18; *Anns v Merton London Borough Council* [1978] AC 728 (HL), as modified by *Murphy*, above n 61 and *Caparo Industries plc v Dickman*, [1990] 2 AC 605 (HL); *Barker*, above n 67; *Kamloops (City of) v Nielsen* [1984] 2 SCR 2; *Odhavji Estate v Woodhouse* [2003] 3 SCR 263; *Council of the Shire of Sutherland v Heyman* (1985) 157 CLR 424 (HCA); *Sullivan v Moody* (2001) 207 CLR 562 (HCA); *South Pacific Manufacturing Co Ltd v New Zealand Security Consultants & Investigations Ltd* [1992] 2 NZLR 282 (CA).

[91]   Fletcher, above n 86, at 557. Accordingly, the significance of *Barker*, above lies more in their Lordship's decision to allocate liability based on the proportionate contribution of each defendant to the risk that the plaintiff would suffer the harm he did than it does to their decision to describe the basis of this liability as being the defendants' contribution to the risk instead of describing it as contribution to the harm itself.

When a court analyses the duty of care it is therefore really expressing an opinion on whether the risk from an activity that is historically related to the harm a person suffered is something that the person who suffers the harm needs to bear as part of membership in a liberal society or is something that the person who engaged in the activity creating the risk needs to bear. This principle lies at the core of the Supreme Court of Canada's analysis in *Childs v Desormeaux*, for example, where the court said:

> The law does not impose a duty to eliminate risk. It accepts that competent people have the right to engage in risky activities. Conversely, it permits third parties witnessing risk to decide not to become rescuers or otherwise intervene. It is only when these third parties have a special relationship to the person in danger or a material role in the creation or management of the risk that the law may impinge on autonomy.[92]

The House of Lords has also applied this principle in case where a number of defendants each caused or materially contributed to the risk that a harmful even would occur, as it did. In *Barker*,[93] their Lordships held that all defendants were liable, but ordered them to pay the plaintiff damages in proportion to the contribution they made to the relevant risk that the plaintiff would be harmed.

In *Nova Mink Ltd v Trans-Can Airlines*,[94] to use an opposite example, an airline was found not liable for having caused injury to minks on a farm by virtue of the noise created when the airplanes flew overhead. Since it is to be expected that in a modern society commonly used transportation will generate noise that all must be expected to bear, the defendant's conduct was excused. Likewise, in *Childs*[95] a person was found not to be liable for an automobile accident that was caused by person who got drunk at his party before driving away. The court found that the defendant did not create or materially contribute to the risk that materialised in the harm to the plaintiff.

Some risks cannot ever be imposed on others, though, no matter how careful and responsible the defendant's conduct might have been. When dealing with these types of risks the defendant cannot argue that his conduct was objectively reasonable because the risk he created is unreasonable *as a matter of law*. This is the province of strict liability torts. In these cases the plaintiff does not have to prove that the defendant acted with intent to harm or that his actions fell below an objective standard of behaviour. Instead, the materialisation of the harm from the unlawful risk is all that matters. *Rylands v Fletcher*,[96] for example, is based on the concept that adjoining

---

[92] *Childs*, above n 72.
[93] *Barker*, above n 67.
[94] *Nova Mink Ltd v Trans-Can Airlines* [1951] 2 DLR 241 (NSSC).
[95] *Childs*, above n 72.
[96] Above n 64.

landowners owe one another mutual duties not to allow dangerous things to escape from their respective lands.[97] If dangerous things do escape the defendant is liable because he is not, as a matter of law, allowed to impose this risk on his neighbour. What is dangerous, of course, is a matter of the court's opinion, which is informed by the facts of the case. As has been pointed out, if the landowner in *Rylands v Fletcher* had built his pond in an area where storing water to run mills was common and the water flooded the lands of people who were engaged in the same activity, rather than building his pond in an area where mining was common and in which his water flooded a mine, the court might not have found any liability.[98] Nevertheless, once the court is of the opinion that the condition which led to harm was dangerous, liability follows as a matter of law.

Whether the risks for which an injured person seeks compensation are risks that he must bear because of his membership in society, or are risks that someone else must bear because they were unreasonably imposed on the victim, does not depend on whether the tortfeasor's act is characterised as negligent or intentional or his liability is fault or non-fault based. Whatever view one takes of the facts—on which reasonable people may differ—it is the law that determines whether the risk is one that is to be borne by the person who suffered harm as a result of it or who has some historical connection with introducing it. The principle of justice requires that in all cases the loss be shifted from the one who suffered it to the one whose activity unreasonably caused it—whatever the historical connection between his acts and the resulting harm may happen to be. Indeed, it is precisely this moral principle that led the House of Lords to adopt risk apportionment in *Barker*.[99]

There is a second—and weaker—moral theory that underlies modern tort law, however. This theory is derived, not from the social contract, but from utilitarianism.[100] Utilitarianism lurks behind the ideas of efficient loss distribution and deterrence, both of which are accepted as purposes of tort liability.[101] Under a utilitarian calculus the law must distribute the burdens of risk-creating behaviour causing harm in a manner that expands social welfare over all. Sometimes this means that the victim must be denied an effective remedy in order to contribute to the common welfare; at other times, and for the same reason, it means that liability must be imposed on a defendant. Many of the arguments for reforming or replacing tort law with some form of socially-guaranteed compensation for harm are based

---

[97]   Cf *Read v J Lyons & Co* [1947] AC 156 (HL) 173-74 (Lord MacMillan).
[98]   Fletcher, above n 86, at 545.
[99]   *Barker*, above n 67.
[100]   Whose leading exponents are Jeremy Bentham and John Stuart Mill.
[101]   For the theory of efficient loss distribution, see Richard A Posner, 'A Theory of Negligence' (1972) 1 *Journal of Legal Studies* 29. For deterrence as a purpose of tort law, see Lord Steyn, above n 76, 3.

on utilitarian principles.[102] These arguments are that tort law, as presently conceived, fails to provide the optimal utilitarian results it is supposed to do, and therefore should be reformed so that it does.

Lord Denning's judgment in *Miller v Jackson* is perhaps the most well-known (and colourful) example of the court's denying an effective remedy for a tort based on a naked utilitarian analysis of social benefit of the harm versus the private benefit of the remedy.[103] The plaintiff in this case had built a house near a long-standing cricket pitch and later complained of the number of balls that were hit into his garden. He was denied an injunction because had the court granted the injunction it would have reduced the net social welfare of the village. It did not matter that the plaintiff's injury was foreseeable and caused by the repetitive and deliberate actions of others. What mattered is that the villager's benefits from the cricket pitch outweighed the harm suffered by the home-owner from cricketing.

Efficient loss distribution is morally justified only on utilitarian principles: the party who is better placed to bear the burden of an injury-producing activity does so. This was the principle Justice Learned Hand used in *United States v Carroll Towing Co* to determine whether a duty of care was owed by the owner of barge to keep an attendent on board while the barge was moored.[104] Justice Hand held that whether a duty was owed depends on three variables, 'if the the probability be called P; the injury, L; and the burden, B; liability depends upon whether B is less than L mulitplied by P: ie, whether B is [less than] PL'.[105] Deterrence too is morally justified only on utilitarian principles: punish one person today to prevent greater harm to others tomorrow.

The moral basis, then, for imposing liability in tort for fault-based and non fault-based harm is closer than one might think just from reading judicial decisions on strict liability torts.[106] When the basis of the defendant's liability is his fault, a court asks if the plaintiff's injury was caused by the negligence of the defendant. When the basis of the defendant's liability is not due to his fault, a court asks if the plaintiff's injury was caused by the defendant's activity. The difference between the two is found in the difference between locating the cause of the injury in one place (negligent conduct) versus another place (harmful activity). It is the moral principles that underlie modern tort law that explain why the law chooses to locate the cause of the plaintiff's harm and thus the legal liability of the defendant in his negligence in some cases or in his activity in others.

---

[102] Sugarman, above n 70; Franklin, above n 70.
[103] *Miller v Jackson* [1977] QB 966 (CA).
[104] *United States v Carroll Towing Co* 159 F 2d 169 (2nd Cir 1947).
[105] *Ibid*, at 173.
[106] See, eg, Lord Steyn's speech in *McFarlane v Tayside Health Board* [2000] 2 AC 59 (HL) 82.

Once it is accepted that the same moral principles underlie *both* fault-based and non-fault based (or strict liability) torts, then it can be readily appreciated that there is no need to justify the imposition of liability on a person who is found vicariously liable by reference to the tort of the person who is directly at fault. After all, it is hard to imagine an injury to which tort law provides a remedy and that is not based on some human action, or inaction, that brought into being a chain of events leading to the victim's harm. Indeed, in most cases of corporate tort liability no effort is made to analyse the corporation's liability by reference to the tort of the person who is directly at fault. For example, in one of the most famous tort cases of all, the *Wagon Mound No 1*, there is no discussion of whether the corporate defendant's liability followed from the acts of its employees even though all of the damage caused in that case was a direct result of the poor decisions made by a number of individual people. The court had to determine which legal entity was liable and for what damage. It was able to make this decision without any regard to how or why individual people acted as they did.

What matters, then, to tort law is determining when a natural or corporate person is to be held strictly liable for harm that is historically connected to him rather than to be held liable only for conduct that falls below a general standard to which all are subject. In other words, when does the law state that the risk of harm created by a person is *per se* unreasonable such that that person can be made strictly liable for the harm that materialises from this risk versus when does the law state that the risk of harm is not *per se* unreasonable such that liability can be imposed on a person only when he is personally at fault? The answer Professor Atiyah gave forty years ago in the case of people organised through a corporation or like enterprise was that the person is to be held liable when the activity he is engaged in inherently creates the risk that materialised into the plaintiff's harm.[107] This is the answer Lord Millett Steyn gave in *Lister* too.

This is still the correct answer. But because Professor Atiyah did not situate his answer in the general moral realm of tort law, and in particular demonstrate how the moral justification for vicarious liability is the same as the moral justification for strict liabilty in tort, this answer is paid only lip-service by the legal profession. Following the moral basis for imposing tort liability generally, the relevant inquiries for the imposition of vicarious liability, then, are these: whether the risk of the harm suffered by the victim is inherent in the enterprise's activities?; whether it is unreasonable for the enterprise to impose this risk on other members of society?; and whether society is better off by making the enterprise bear the costs of any harm

---

[107]   Atiyah, above n 17, at 28.

that materialises from this risk, or whether society is better off by making the victim bear the harm himself or herself?

V. UNFORTUNATELY COURTS STILL LOOK TO CONTRACT PRINCIPLES TO JUSTIFY THE IMPOSITION OF VICARIOUS LIABILITY

Both the Supreme Court of Canada and the House of Lords (but not the High Court of Australia) have tried to position vicarious liability squarely within the moral foundations of modern tort law generally. In *Bazley*, the Supreme Court of Canada held that the principle of justice requires 'that the person who introduces a risk incurs a duty to those who may be injured' and that this principle 'lies at the heart of tort law'.[108] The Court, quoting from Chief Justice Cardozo's famous decision, *Palsgraf v Long Island Railroad Co*,[109] held as follows:

'[t]he risk reasonably to be perceived defines the duty to be obeyed, and risk imparts relation; it is risk to another or to others within the range of apprehension.' This principle of fairness applies to the employment enterprise and hence to the issue of vicarious liability.[110]

The Court went on to explain that because the employer puts in the community an enterprise which carries with it certain risks, when those risks materialise into harm it is fair that the person or organisation that created the enterprise and hence created the risk should bear the loss.[111] This reasoning is, of course, at the core of the justice principle forming one of the moral foundations of tort law. This principle requires people who create a risk that is found, as a matter of law, to be unreasonable, to pay for the resulting harm, either fully or, following *Baker*, in proportion to the risk that they create. Although the court described this principle as a matter of policy, not morality, nothing turns on this nomenclature. This is, in fact, a moral principle.

In *Lister*, the majority of their Lordships said much the same thing. Lord Millett said that vicarious liability is 'based on the more general idea that a person who employs another for his own ends inevitably creates a risk that the employee will commit a legal wrong. ... He is liable only if the risk is one which experience shows in inherent in the nature of the business.'[112] Lord Steyn and Lord Clyde also based their analyses on whether the

---

[108] *Bazley*, above n 27, at [30].
[109] *Palsgraf v Long Island Railroad Co* 162 NE 99 (NYCA 1928) 100.
[110] *Bazley*, above n 27, at [30].
[111] *Ibid*, at [31].
[112] *Lister*, above n 37, at [65] (Lord Millett).

employer undertook the risk-creating activity (in that case, caring for children), though using the language of duty instead of risk.[113]

The Supreme Court of Canada in *Bazley* also justified vicarious liability on the grounds of deterrence. Again, although deterrence was described as a policy, it is in fact an aspect of utilitarian morality, and is used as such by the Supreme Court in its analysis. As stated by the court:

> Beyond the narrow band of employer conduct that attracts direct liability in negligence lies a vast area where imaginative and efficient administration and supervision can reduce the risk that the employer has introduced into the community. Holding the employer vicariously liable for the wrongs of its employee may encourage the employer to take such steps, and hence, reduce the risk of future harm.[114]

Had the Supreme Court of Canada or their Lordships left the analysis here, this chapter would not have been necessary. But they did not. Instead, when these courts go to apply vicarious liability they still situate the employer's liability in his *contract with his employee*, thus reintroducing the very concept that the courts say they are trying to avoid. For instance, in *Bazley*, the Supreme Court held that:

> [T]here must be a strong connection between what the employer was asking the employee to do (the risk created by the employer's enterprise) and the wrongful act. It must be possible to say that the employer significantly increased the risk of the harm by putting the employee in his or her position and requiring him to perform assigned tasks.[115]

And later, the Court held that 'the test for vicarious liability ... should focus on whether the employer's enterprise and empowerment of the employee materially increased the risk of the ... harm'.[116]

We can see this clearly in a recent decision of the Supreme Court of Canada, *EB v Order of Oblates of Mary Immaculate in the Province of British Columbia*.[117] The order of Oblates ran a school in a secluded area staffed by 16 to 20 adults and populated by 150 or so students. Martin Saxey was one of the Oblates' employees. They hired him shortly after he was released from prison. He had been convicted of manslaughter. Saxey was hired to work in the school's bakery and to perform odd jobs around

---

[113] *Ibid*, at [20], (Lord Steyn) ('It becomes possible to consider the question of vicarious liability on the basis that the employer undertook to care for the boys through the services of the warden...'); and at [50] (Lord Clyde) ('His general duty was to look after and to care for, among others, the appellants. That function was one which the respondents had delegated to him.').

[114] *Bazley*, above n 27, at [33].

[115] *Bazley*, above n 27, at [42].

[116] *Ibid*, at [46].

[117] Above n 35.

the school. At some point, Saxey lured one of the children who resided at the school to his room, located on school property, where he raped the child. He did this for several years.

The trial judge, applying the *Bazley* test, held that the operational characteristic of the school created risks for its students and thus found the Oblates vicariously liable for Saxey's torts. The Court of Appeal for British Columbia, also applying the *Bazley* test, disagreed. They found the Oblates not vicariously liable. The Supreme Court of Canada, also applying the *Bazley* test, agreed with the results reached by the Court of Appeal, though for slightly different reasons.

Speaking for a majority of the Supreme Court, Binnie J held that the trial judge's mistake lay in not putting adequate weight on the 'school-created features of the relationship between *this* claimant and *this* wrongdoing employee and the contribution of the [Oblates'] enterprise to enabling the wrongdoer Saxey to do what he did in *this* case'.[118] In considering the nature of the contribution of the employer's enterprise to the harm caused, Binnie J held that the court must examine the 'job-created power and the nature of the employee's duties as a fundamental component of determining if a particular enterprise increased the risk of *the employee's* wrongdoing in relation to the claimant'.[119] Applying these principles to the facts, Binnie J held that because Saxey's job did not put him in a position of power, trust or intimacy with the children at the school, the connection between his duties and his rapes were insufficiently 'strong' to make the Oblates liable to pay the plaintiff's damages.[120] Binnie J's language of 'job created power', then, is just a different verbal formulation for the Salmond test's 'scope of employment', which in turn is merely the terms of the contract writ large. Since the Oblates did not contract with Saxey to have any contact with the children at the school, reasoned Binnie J, the Oblate's should not be liable for the improper contact Saxey in fact had with them.

As Binnie J's analysis in *EB* demonstrates, locating the employer's liability in his employment contract with the employee provides an inadequate moral foundation for the imposition of liability because the particularity at which one defines the scope of employment defines the liability. What would have happened had Saxey's duties included, say, instructing students how to work in the kitchen? What would have happened had the plaintiff not been one of the students he instructed? What would have happened had Saxey negligently caused a fire which injured some children? What would have happened had Saxey deliberately caused the fire? What would have happened had a teacher, occupying a position of power, trust and intimacy with the students, gone into the

---

[118] *Oblates*, above n 35, at [4].
[119] *Ibid*, at [29].
[120] *Ibid*, at [51].

kitchen and negligently caused a fire which injured some children? What would have happened had the teacher deliberately set fire to school property injuring some children?

Each of these acts is wrongful, some of them because of negligence and others because of wrongful intent. But which of them is a result of 'job created power', to use Binnie J's language, and which ones not? There is no way of knowing. It all depends on whether the 'job created power' or the more familiar 'scope of employment' is defined in a broad and generous manner or given a pinched and narrow construction.

Likewise, in *Lister*, their Lordships looked to the employment relationship to answer the question of whether the employer was vicariously liable. Lord Steyn held that there had to be a 'close connection' between the terms of the employee's employment and his torts.[121] Lord Hobhouse held that the correct approach is to 'ask what was the duty of the servant towards the plaintiff which was broken by the servant and what was the contractual duty of the servant towards his employer'.[122] Lord Millett held that 'what is critical is that attention should be directed to the closeness of the connection between the employee's duties and his wrongdoing... .'[123]

So, despite how the Commonwealth courts try to position vicarious liability, it is clear that they all still use the terms of the master's contract with his servant as the touchstone for the imposition of such liability—directly so in the case of the High Court of Australia and indirectly so in the case of the Supreme Court of Canada and the House of Lords. To put this another way; however the scope of employment is defined, the courts still situate the moral basis for the employer's liability in his voluntary acceptance of liability. Indeed, the Supreme Court of Canada's analysis in *EB* and the High Court of Australia's analysis in *Lepore*, and even the House of Lords' analysis in *Lister*, are each examples of courts' attempting to locate the employer's liability in his voluntary acceptance of liability based on the terms of his employment relationship with his faithless or criminally-minded employee. Each of these cases and their progeny are enquiries into whether the misconduct that led to the harm is of a nature and type that the employer would or should have accepted as part of his natural activities. Had a different question been posed—did the harm for which compensation is sought arise out of the risk created by the employer's enterprise, say?—there should not have been any doubt about the liability in any of these cases.

Common experience now, sadly, teaches us that schools attract paedophiles. Paedophiles try to hide their proclivities and criminal activities. The risk of misconduct by paedophiles, or sexual misconduct by teachers

---

[121]   *Lister*, above n 37, at [20].
[122]   *Ibid*, at [60].
[123]   *Ibid*, at [70].

generally, is a risk that is, beyond question, inherent in the operation of schools. Such liability should have been found in all cases as a matter of course. Indeed, where the enterprise's liability is not a product of criminal or other immoral behaviour, there is no question but that the employer is liable for all the risks that are inherent in its activities, such as a trucking company's liability for the stupid act of one of its employees while in possession of the employer's trucks.[124] So why is this not accepted universally? Why, in other words, do the courts—at least in Canada and England—not have the courage of their convictions and just ask: what risks are inherent in this enterprise and are there any reasons why the enterprise and those who use its services should not bear them? It is, simply, because the habits of the judicial mindset treat vicarious liability as an aspect of voluntary acceptance of liability even when the expressed basis for the doctrine is to be found elsewhere.

VI. CONCLUSION: IN ORDER TO CHANGE OUR CONTRACTUAL MINDSET WE NEED TO USE TORTIOUS WORDS

The common law—which for this purpose includes equity too—does not develop evenly and coherently across all fronts and at the same time. The law develops in fits and starts and in many different ways, as befits a system of practical law which responds to the needs of litigants pursuing their private rights. Sometimes, as with *Donoghue v Stevenson*, the law takes a sudden shift in a new direction. At other times, old verities—such as the principle that a tortfeasor is liable for all the direct consequences of his act[125]—are chipped away bit by bit until the principle itself is finally rejected and replaced by another one.[126] Occasionally the law gets ahead of itself—such as when the House of Lords permitted liability in tort for pure economic loss[127]—and then retreats.[128] And, rarely, an entire body of case law gets re-organised around a new principle, shifting the legal landscape in its wake, as has happened with the development of the law of restitution based on the unjust enrichment principle.[129]

In this process some concepts retain a hold on the legal imagination long after they have in fact been supplanted by the law's evolution.[130] This is

---

[124] *Walker v Ritchie* (2005) 197 OAC 81 (CA).

[125] *Re Polemis*, above n 77.

[126] *The Wagon Mound (No 1)*, above n 78.

[127] *Junior Books Ltd v Veitchi Co* [1983] 1 AC 520 (HL).

[128] As the House of Lords did in *Murphy*, above n 61 when it denied that liability is available in tort for economic loss unless the plaintiff or his property is physically injured.

[129] R Goff and G Jones, *The Law of Restitution*, 6th edn (London, Sweet & Maxwell, 2002) ch 1.

[130] Charitable Immunity is one such example. See, Wingfield, above n 25 and *Bennett*, above n 34.

what has happened with vicarious liability. Even though they have changed the terms of reference—like the Supreme Court of Canada did in *Bazley* or the House of Lords did in *Lister*—by adding a 'connection' element to the wrongful act and the terms of the employer's relationship to the employee, modern courts still locate vicarious liability in the employer's contractual relationship with the employee. Thus, although vicarious liability is accepted as part of tort law, courts use a different (and non-tortious) moral principle to attribute responsibility in cases where a person is sought to be made vicarious liable than they do in every other area of tort law. The basis of vicarious liability is really contractual, not tortious. Scratch the surface of *Bazley* or *Lister* and their progeny and you find that this is so.

Accordingly, in order to move past the idea that a third party's ability to recover for harm he suffered arising out of a risk that a person has unreasonably introduced is dependent on the employer's contract with his wrong-doing employee, we need to move past the language we use to describe, define and analyse such liability. In short, we need simply to describe this liability by what it is—strict liability. We need, therefore, to ask whether justice or utility demands that the person whose activity introduced into society the risk that materialised into the harm ought, for that reason alone, to be liable for the damages caused by that harm or whether he should be liable only if he was negligent. Asked in this way, it would seem easy to conclude that harm materialising from those risks which are inherent in the activities society supports or promotes (eg business activities, charitable activities) ought to be borne, by the activity, and those who benefit from it, and not the person who was harmed by it. This accords with our moral understanding and is consistent with what the courts usually do—and, one suspects, would always do, if they were not tied up into verbal knots over the language of vicarious liability.

16

Comparative Perspectives on Vicarious Liability: Defining the Scope of Employment

PAULA GILIKER*

I. INTRODUCTION

VICARIOUS LIABILITY HAS traditionally been defined as 'a liability imposed by the law upon a person as a result of (1) a tortious act or omission by another, (2) some relationship between the actual tortfeasor and the defendant whom it is sought to make liable, and (3) some connection between the tortious act or omission and that relationship'.[1] This three-fold definition forms the basis of liability not only in common law, but also other civil law jurisdictions.[2] Article 1384(5) of the French *Code civil* provides that '[m]asters and employers [are liable] for the damage caused by their servants and employees in the functions for which they have been employed'.[3] Similarly German law at § 831(1) BGB states that '[a] person who employs another to do any work is bound to compensate for any damage which the other unlawfully causes to a third

---

* Reader in Comparative Law, University of Bristol.

[1] PS Atiyah, *Vicarious Liability in the Law of Torts* (London, Butterworths, 1967) 3.

[2] Indeed the concept of liability for another may be traced back to Roman law where the head of the family (the *paterfamilias*) was personally answerable for the delicts of his child or slave. See R Zimmermann, *The Law of Obligations: Roman Foundations of the Civilian Tradition* (Oxford, Clarendon Press, 1996) 1118 ff. Although the common law development is usually attributed to early medieval ideas of identification of a master through the acts of their servants, Zimmermann finds some influence of Roman law. David Johnstone (see 'Limiting liability: Roman and the Civil Law Tradition' (1995) 70 *Chicago-Kent Law Review* 1515, 1528-32) argues, however, that the idea of a functional limit on employers' liability was developed by Roman jurists only in the case of contractual agency and was introduced into delict by subsequent commentators such as Pothier in his *Traité des Obligations* (Paris, Chez Debure, 1768). The common law development of this notion equally seems to derive from around 1800: see Lord Kenyon's judgments in *Ellis v Turner* (1800) 8 TR 531, 101 ER 1529 and *Laugher v Pointer* (1826) 5 B & C 547, 108 ER 204.

[3] 'Les maîtres et les commettants, du dommage causé par leurs domestiques et préposés dans les fonctions auxquelles ils les ont employés'.

party in the performance of his work'.[4] The requirements of a tort, a specific relationship (usually employment),[5] and that the tort takes place in the course of employment thus form a common frame of analysis. This is reflected in recent proposals for unified European models of 'liability for the acts of other' which, despite certain differences, identify this framework as the 'common core' of European legal systems.[6]

Yet these well-established principles belie the controversial nature of vicarious liability in a system of tort. Why should a person find him or herself liable for a wrong committed by another in circumstances where no fault can be attributed to him or her? How does one balance the need of an innocent tort victim for compensation against the promotion of business enterprise in a market economy? The apparent unfairness of the imposition of such a burden on a faultless employer led the drafters of the German BGB to impose a presumption of liability rebuttable by evidence of care (*Exkuplationsbeweis*):

> The duty to compensate does not arise if the employer has exercised necessary care in the selection of the employee; and, where he has to supply apparatus or equipment or to supervise the work, has also exercised ordinary care as regards such supply or supervision, or if the damage would have arisen notwithstanding the exercise of such care.[7]

It would also seem that the French provision was initially read as based on an assumption of fault by the employer for his or her negligent choice or supervision of employee.[8] Indeed, the original draft of the Code allowed

---

[4] 'Wer einen anderen zu einer Verrichtung bestellt, ist zum Ersatz des Schadens verpflichtet, den der andere in Ausführung der Verrichtung einem Dritten widerrechtlich zufügt'.

[5] I am focusing on employment relationships, but vicarious liability does extend beyond such relationships to include, for example, liability of partners for each other. French law adopts a particularly broad view of relationships which extends to family and friends where one person supervises, directs and controls the other: see, for example, where an electoral candidate was held liable for one of his supporters getting in a fight with a supporter of another candidate which led to the other's death (Crim 20 May 1976,(Gaz Pal 1976.2.545 note YM, RTDC 1976.786 obs G Durry)).

[6] See Art 6:102 of the *Principles of European Tort Law* (Wien, Springer, 2005): 'A person is liable for damage caused by his auxiliaries acting within the scope of their functions provided that they violated the required standard of conduct'. See also Art 3:201, Study Group on a European Civil Code, *Principles of European Law* (2004) (<http://www.sgecc.net>): '(1) A person who employs or similarly engages another, is accountable for the causation of legally relevant damage suffered by a third person when the person employed or engaged (a) caused the damage in the course of employment or engagement, and (b) caused the damage intentionally or negligently, or is otherwise accountable for the causation of the damage' (date accessed: 21 August 2006).

[7] § 831(1): 'Die Ersatzpflicht tritt nicht ein, wenn der Geschäftsherr bei der Auswahl der bestellten Person und, sofern er Vorrichtungen oder Gerätschaften zu beschaffen oder die Ausführung der Verrichtung zu leiten hat, bei der Beschaffung oder der Leitung die im Verkehr erforderliche Sorgfalt beobachtet oder wenn der Schaden auch bei Anwendung dieser Sorgfalt entstanden sein würde'.

[8] J Carbonnier, *Droit Civil 4, Les Obligations*, 22nd edn (Paris, Presses Universitaires de France, 2000) no 243.

the employer a due diligence defence, although this was subsequently rejected, seemingly on the basis that the employer should bear the consequences of employing a person who causes harm to another.[9] In contrast to German law, Article 1384(5) soon came to be interpreted as a rule of strict liability due to concerns as to the solvency of employees.

The movement from fault to strict liability, notably in the context of employers, thus crosses legal systems. In the face of strong lobbying from trade, industry and agriculture, and the fault-based reasoning of the pandectists,[10] German law was initially reluctant to impose liability without fault on employers, but this attitude has changed. Far from its original conservatism, the courts have construed § 831 of the BGB contrary to the interests of employers and relied heavily on the stricter provisions relating to contractual liability.[11] Zimmermann has remarked that '§ 831 BGB has turned out to be a major source of embarrassment ... the rather extravagant encroachment of contractual remedies in the law of delict, for instance ... is based largely on the desire to make available, for the benefit of the injured party, the stricter rule of § 278 BGB'.[12] The circumvention in practice of § 831 BGB and the wide acceptance of the need for vicarious liability demonstrates the status of vicarious liability as a necessary concept in any industrially advanced state.

This chapter will examine how the limitation of the 'scope of employment' has been used to identify the extent of the burden placed on the employer. No system imposes vicarious liability without restriction. It is confined to certain relationships where one party has committed a tort against another. The causal link between the tortious act and the employment provides a means by which the scope of the doctrine can be judged. A narrow interpretation suggests limited support for no fault liability, whilst the broader the doctrine, the greater the burden on the innocent employer. It is submitted that the recent expansion of vicarious liability in common and civil law systems, notably in the context of intentional torts, requires

---

[9]   JG Locre, *La Législation Civile Commerciale et Criminelle de la France* (Paris, Treuttel et Würtz , 1827) vol 13, 25.

[10]   See HH Seiler 'Die deliktische Gehilfenhaftung in historischer Sicht' (1967) *Juristenzeitung* 525.

[11]   See § 278 BGB. [Responsibility for persons employed in performing obligation]: 'A debtor is responsible for the fault of his legal representative and of persons whom he employs in performing his obligation, to the same extent as for his own fault. The provision of § 276(2) does not apply'. Note also the development of *Organisationsverschulden* (duty to organise one's enterprise) under § 823(1) and §31 BGB (liability of association for the damage to third parties by executive committee, member of the executive committee or another constitutionally destined representative). Special rules also exist for public servants under §839 [Liability for breach of official duty] and under § 34 sub 1, GG.

[12]   Zimmermann, above n 2, at 1125-26. See also BS Markesinis, *The German Law of Obligations Vol II The Law of Tort: A Comparative Introduction*, 3rd edn (Oxford, Clarendon, 1997) 686-90.

justification in that it represents a further movement away from fault-based reasoning and the principles of corrective justice. This chapter will seek to identify the reasons for this movement and what guidance exists for the future development of this fundamental doctrine of the law of tort.

II. SCOPE OF EMPLOYMENT

Whether one uses the term 'course of employment', '*les fonctions aux-quelles ils les ont employés*', or '*in Ausführing der Verrichtung*', this criterion lies at the heart of the modern development of vicarious liability and has troubled the highest common and civil law courts in recent years. The French Supreme Court struggled for 30 years to find an acceptable approach to this question, whilst it has arisen in England, Canada and Australia more recently.[13] Each jurisdiction faced the same question—when should an innocent party be held liable for the tortious acts of another? This question becomes even more difficult when the innocent party is to be held liable for intentional wrongs of another, which usually amount to criminal offences. Whilst it may be acceptable for an employer to find him- or herself liable for negligent conduct of the employee—an obvious risk of employing any human being—it is far more difficult to justify rendering the employer liable for intentional misconduct, which harms the reputation of the employer as well as the claimant. Such conduct does not generally benefit the employer, and the employee is well aware of this. To reallocate responsibility by means of vicarious liability in such circumstances would seem to mark a significant move away from the idea of fault-based liability.

It becomes, in this context, very difficult *not* to address the question of justification for such a broad view of vicarious liability. In extending liability far beyond any concept of authority (be it express or implied), the courts raise two fundamental questions. First, how far common and civil law systems have been prepared to extend vicarious liability to include acts contrary to the employer's interests, and secondly, what justification or rationale can be found for such an extension? These questions are not distinct. It is far easier to justify a broad principle of vicarious liability if a strong rationale for recovery can be identified. Equally, the weaker or more questionable the justification, the more we may find liability without fault difficult to accept. It will be suggested that problems arise not by virtue of a wide or narrow doctrine of vicarious liability, but by a failure of the courts to provide a clear rationale for recovery. Such an absence creates a

---

[13] See *Lister v Hesley Hall Ltd* [2002] 1 AC 215 (HL) [*Lister*] (England and Wales); *Bazley v Curry* [1999] 2 SCR 534 and *Jacobi v Griffiths* [1999] 2 SCR 570 (Canada); and *New South Wales v Lepore* (2003) 212 CLR 511 (HCA) [*Lepore*] (Australia) respectively.

vacuum in which participants in the legal process will inevitably question the application and the legitimacy of the rules in question.

III. DECIPHERING THE 'SCOPE OF EMPLOYMENT': THE COMMON LAW APPROACH

The recent decisions of the English House of Lords,[14] and Canadian Supreme Court,[15] which favour a test of 'close connection' to determine scope of employment, may differ in their treatment of this test, but there is agreement that intentional torts, as serious as child abuse, may nevertheless fall within the course of an employee's employment.[16] This is far removed from the astonishment expressed by Butler-Sloss LJ in 1999, who found sexual assault 'to be far removed from an unauthorised mode of carrying out a teacher's duties on behalf of his employer. Rather it is a negation of the duty of the council to look after children for whom it was responsible'.[17] Such a bold step away from the traditional Salmond test, which focused on 'a wrongful and unauthorised mode of doing some act authorised by the master',[18] suggests a greater willingness to rely on strict liability to ensure compensation for victims, but inevitably leads one to question the basis on which such an extension would arise.

The English House of Lords in *Lister v Hesley Hall Ltd* found this question difficult to answer.[19] There was agreement in favour of developing the law in line with Salmond's subsequent comment that 'a master . . . is liable even for acts which he has not authorised, provided they are so *connected* with acts which he has authorised, that they may rightly be regarded as modes—although improper modes—of doing them'. Reference was made to the application of this test by the Supreme Court of Canada in *Bazley v Curry*[20] and *Jacobi v Griffiths*,[21] although the reasoning of the Canadian courts was rejected. In the words of Lord Hobhouse, 'I do not believe that it is appropriate to follow the lead given by the Supreme Court

---

[14] See *Lister*, above.

[15] See *Bazley v Curry* and *Jacobi v Griffiths*, above n 13.

[16]   Contrast, however, the division in the High Court of Australia in *Lepore*, above n 13.

[17] *Trotman v North Yorkshire County Council* [1999] LGR 584 (CA) 591. Cf 'il avait commis une faute volontaire, contraire par essence à son emploi': Cass Ass plén 15 November 1985 D 1986.81, JCP 1986 II 20568.

[18] *Salmond & Heuston on the Law of Torts*, 21st edn (London, Sweet and Maxwell, 1996) 443: 'A master is not responsible for a wrongful act done by his servant unless it is done in the course of his employment. It is deemed to be so done if it is either (1) a wrongful act authorised by his master, or (2) a wrongful and unauthorised mode of doing some act authorised by the master'.

[19] *Lister*, above n 13.

[20] Above n 13.

[21] Above n 13, both noted by P Cane 'Vicarious Liability for Sexual Abuse' (2000) 116 *LQR* 21.

of Canada ... The judgments contain a useful and impressive discussion of the social and economic reasons for having a principle of vicarious liability as part of the law of tort which extends to embrace acts of child abuse. But an exposition of the policy reasons for a rule (or even a description) is not the same as defining the criteria for its application'.[22] In rejecting the policy objectives of a fair allocation of risk and deterrence, their Lordships were happy to divorce the test stated in *Bazley* from its underlying rationale. This is worrying in terms of legal theory in that one might question the ability of a legal system to transplant a test without its underlying reasoning, but also presupposes an alternative English approach which states the test for course of employment with a greater degree of clarity and definition. Identifying a test of 'close connection', it is submitted, is not enough. The question remains how this test will operate in practice.

One can, in fact, identify four separate approaches in *Lister*. These do overlap to a certain extent, but represent different perceptions of the basis for vicarious liability in this case and how it may be justified. A close connection exists:

(i)   Where it would be fair and just to hold the employers vicariously liable (Lord Steyn)[23]

(ii) Where the employer has assumed a relationship with the claimant which imposes specific duties in tort upon the employer. The employee is the person to whom the employer has entrusted the performance of that duty (Lord Hobhouse).

(iii) Where the employer's objectives cannot be achieved without a serious risk of the employee committing the kind of wrong which he has in fact committed. The employer is liable only if the risk is one which experience shows is inherent in the nature of the business (Lord Millett)

(iv) Where, looking the matters in the round, the wrongful act can be seen as ways of carrying out the work the employer has authorised (Lord Clyde).

This variety of approaches has given rise to a number of problems. First, they are inconsistent. A concept of 'assumption of responsibility' in which an employer establishes direct liability towards the victim may be distinguished from liability imposed on an innocent party either because it is fair and just or in response to an inherent risk. Second, despite the best efforts of their Lordships to avoid the policy framework of the Supreme Court of Canada, these approaches, with perhaps the exclusion of the pragmatic test of Lord Clyde, do encapsulate policy objectives. Third, it is far from clear which approach a subsequent court should apply.

---

[22]   *Lister*, above n 13, at [60].
[23]   Lord Hutton agreed with Lord Steyn.

The last point may be illustrated first. The courts have valiantly sought to apply *Lister* and reconcile the different approaches of the House of Lords. Whilst the earliest case focused on Lord Hobhouse's test,[24] later cases moved towards an amalgam of the Steyn/Millett/Clyde approach. In *Dubai Aluminium Co Ltd v Salaam*,[25] therefore, Lord Nicholls, in the context of a partnership, found that:

> Perhaps the best general answer is that the wrongful conduct must be so closely connected with acts the partner or employee was authorised to do that, for the purpose of the liability of the firm or the employer to third parties, the wrongful conduct *may fairly and properly be regarded* as done by the partner while acting in the ordinary course of the firm's business or the employee's employment.[26]

His Lordship restated this test more recently in *Majrowski v Guy's and St Thomas's NHS Trust* , approving the imposition of vicarious liability for breaches of statutory duty giving rise to civil liability.[27] Nevertheless, his Lordship did acknowledge in *Dubai Aluminium* the limitations of a 'close connection' test. Whilst focusing attention in the right direction, concern was raised that 'it affords no guidance on the type or degree of connection which will normally be regarded as sufficiently close'.[28] Yet, in the absence of any other guidance, the courts have continued to rely on the test, but in an increasingly broad fashion. For Lord Steyn in *Bernard v Attorney General of Jamaica*, therefore, the correct approach must be to examine the closeness of the connection between the employment and tort and, looking at the matter in the round, consider whether it was just and reasonable to hold the employers vicariously liability.[29] In so doing, his Lordship accepted that the risk created by the employer in entrusting a task to another would be a relevant factor. Auld LJ in the Court of Appeal and Lord Nicholls in the House of Lords in *Majrowski* equally favour a composite test, which combines the guidance in *Lister* and *Dubai* to reach a decision by which it is just and reasonable to find an employer

---

[24] See *Balfron Trustees Ltd v Peterson* [2001] IRLR 758 (HC).

[25] [2003] 2 AC 366 (HL) [*Dubai Aluminium*].

[26] *Ibid*, at [23]. Italics in text. Approved by Lord Carswell in *Brown v Robinson* [2004] UKPC 56 (PC), who adds at paragraph 11: 'The risk which may have been created by such acts on the employer's part as arming his employees is a relevant consideration, as it may form a strong policy reason underlying the legal rule . . .'. and Lord Nicholls himself in *Attorney General of the British Virgin Islands v Hartwell* [2004] 1 WLR 1273 (PC) 1278: 'The applicable test is whether PC Laurent's wrongful use of the gun was so closely connected with acts he was authorised to do that, for the purposes of liability of the Government as his employer, his wrongful use may fairly and properly be regarded as made by him while acting in the ordinary course of his employment as a police officer': see *Lister*, above n 13, at [28], [69], and *Dubai Aluminium*, above n 25, at [23].

[27] [2006] 3 WLR 125 (HL) [10] (employer vicariously liable for harassment of employee by his manager under s 3, Protection from Harassment Act 1997).

[28] *Dubai Aluminium*, above n 25, at [25].

[29] [2005] IRLR 398 (PC) [*Bernard*].

vicariously liable.[30] In the words of Auld LJ, '[t]he criteria of "close connection" and "reasonably incidental risk" are the means in this context by which the justice and reasonableness of imposing vicarious, that is, absolute, liability are determined'.[31]

The resultant test is therefore flexible, reminiscent of the 'fair, just and reasonableness' test used in novel 'duty of care' situations.[32] It is clear that policy factors such as risk will be relevant, although it will not, it would seem, be the sole factor to be considered. Lord Steyn in *Bernard* stresses that the terms 'fair and just' do not amount to vague notions of justice between man and man and are not infinitely extendable.[33] Much will, therefore, depend on the circumstances of each case. One must, however, question in the absence of precedent or the ability to reason by analogy to what extent the 'fair and just' test may achieve at least the equivalent level of certainty given to the duty of care test. Without such guidance, there would seem to be limited assistance for the courts.

Therefore, despite the intention of the House of Lords to avoid overt reference to policy concerns, the imposition of liability on the employer for intentional torts has inevitably led to the consideration of matters of social policy. Two fundamentally divergent forms of analysis may be found in *Lister*: that of finding the innocent employer liable for the tortious acts of his or her employees, and that of finding an employer personally liable for a wrongful performance of a duty owed to the victim when performance has been entrusted to an employee. Each will raise questions of policy. The first approach accepts that vicarious liability on an employer can be justified, but requires the courts to consider questions of risk/benefit, social risk or even simply availability of means. The latter comes closer to the notion of fault or corrective justice. By recognising a duty that the employer has assumed towards the victim, the employer becomes identified with the employee's fault. This does not, however, remove the question of policy which must determine when, and why, an employer should be deemed to have assumed a duty towards a victim.[34] If, by analogy to

---

[30] *Majrowski v Guy's and St Thomas's NHS Trust* [2005] QB 848 (CA).

[31] *Ibid*, at 861. Lord Nicholls in the House of Lords openly acknowledges at paragraph 9 that fairness requires that those responsible for risk-creating activities should bear the cost of any resulting injury. It is interesting to note certain similarities between his judgment and that of La Forest J in *London Drugs Ltd v Kuehne & Nagel International Ltd* [1992] 3 SCR 299 (both influenced by the policy concerns identified by Fleming in his classic text: JG Fleming, *The Law of Torts*, 9th edn (NSW, LBC Information Services, 1998)).

[32] See *Caparo Industries Plc v Dickman* [1990] 2 AC 605 (HL).

[33] Above n 29, at [23].

[34] If we classify such a duty as non-delegable, a useful comparison may be found in the development of duties personal to the employer to circumvent the doctrine of common employment: *Wilsons & Clyde Coal Co Ltd v English* [1938] AC 57 (HL).

Morris v Martin,[35] liability is to be confined to circumstances where vulnerable people are entrusted into the care of organisations, which operate by means of individually employed carers, then we have a narrow extension to the concept of vicarious liability, which arguably has its justification in increasing standards of care in such organisations, which will usually be of a public nature.[36] If the doctrine has a wider remit, there is little guidance when (and why) such a duty will arise. It is submitted that the trend in the subsequent decisions of the courts has been to eschew such a narrow interpretation in favour of a broader notion of vicarious liability.

This leaves us with a principle based on 'fairness and justice'. The great advantage of broad principle in the common law is that it can disguise divergent policy ideas under an apparent consensus. The different views amongst common law judges are ably demonstrated by the High Court of Australia in *New South Wales v Lepore*, which, in a similar context to *Lister*, favoured the 'close connection' test ((Gleeson CJ and Kirby J), the Salmond test of authority (Gummow and Hayne JJ), the idea of non-delegable duty on the State to take reasonable care to prevent harm to pupils (McHugh J dissenting) and even an argument based on estoppel (Gaudron J).[37]

If, however, the real question is one of policy, not form, then it is submitted that the focus of the common law should be on the policy rationale underlying vicarious liability as a means of understanding its scope and justification. This becomes increasingly important where the courts are moving to vague tests of 'close connection' and what is 'fair and just' where some guidance as to the content of these tests will be demanded by members of the legal community.

IV. A FRESH PERSPECTIVE: LIABILITY FOR THE ACTS OF OTHERS IN CIVIL LAW

In view of the inability of the common law world to reach agreement on the basis for vicarious liability, justification must be sought elsewhere. Civil law has long developed concepts of vicarious liability and the development of these principles from the 18th century onwards demonstrate a comparable response to growing industrialisation and political change. Whilst

---

[35] *Morris v C W Martin & Sons Ltd* [1966] 1 QB 716 (CA) (valuable coat entrusted to the care of cleaners) [*Morris v Martin*].

[36] Compare the high level of liability placed on French public institutions. Hesley Hall Ltd was a private organisation, but operating on behalf of local authorities which sent children with emotional and behavioural difficulties to the home.

[37] Above n 13 (sexual abuse by schoolteachers). Comment N McBride 'Vicarious liability in England and Australia' (2003) 62 *CLJ* 255; J Wangmann 'Liability for Institutional Child Sexual Assault: Where Does *Lepore* Leave Australia?' (2004) 28 *Melbourne University Law Review* 169.

German law still sought in the 1900s to protect its business community and small-scale farmers, the French *Code civil des Français* of 1804 recognised in Article 1384 liability for the acts of others, resting notably on the employer:

> (1) A person is liable not only for the damages he causes by his own act, but also for that which is caused by the acts of persons for whom he is responsible, or by things which are in his custody.

> (5) Masters and employers [are liable] for the damage caused by their servants and employees in the functions for which they have been employed.[38]

By the end of the 19th century, the courts had adopted a 'victim-centred' approach which sought to apply Article 1384(5) as widely as possible to ensure victim compensation. The employer was seen as the '*garant*'/ 'guarantor' of the employee, providing the victim with a solvent defendant from whom to recover compensation. As a '*garant*', the guarantor could naturally seek an indemnity from the debtor (the employee), but the primary goal was to ensure that the victim's needs were met. These early cases also demonstrate a very broad interpretation of the requirement that the tort must be committed 'in the functions for which they have been employed'. In a case of 1946,[39] for example, Favreau was employed by Alexis as an 'aide-chauffeur' for his garage. On the day in question, Favreau had been instructed to take a lorry for repairs and then return it to the garage. For this purpose, he was given the key to the garage. Favreau, however, decided to hire out the lorry for 250FF to take a group of people to a local dance. An accident occurred in which one of the passengers was killed and Favreau was convicted of manslaughter. The *Chambre criminelle* found the employer liable. It was an '*abus de fonction*', but the victim had believed that the driver was acting for the employer at the time and was acting within his general driving function.[40]

The development of French law is instructive in a number of ways. First, the courts have openly debated the test for 'scope of employment' and how it should be applied in response to contemporary needs. Second, French law bears a greater resemblance to the common law than its German counterpart, which has a very different structure and relies heavily on contract law to impose strict liability. Third, the rationale for liability has

---

[38] Art 1384(5) CcF. This is more remarkable in view of the late industrialisation of France due to the upheaval of the revolution, although by 1848 France could be recognised as an industrial power.

[39] Cass crim 18 October 1946 S 1947 1.39.

[40] It should be noted that vicarious liability may also arise in the French criminal courts where the victim may make a claim for compensation as a '*partie civile*' (the French treat the commission of a criminal offence as a civil fault and permit a claim for compensation in the criminal court): see J Bell, S Boyron and S Whittaker, *Principles of French Law* (Oxford, Oxford University Press, 1998) 359.

been seen as a question which cannot be avoided. If an extension of liability is desired, then it must be seen as representing a preference for one particular argument over another. The law is not seen to exist in a theoretical vacuum. Finally, French law highlights the difficulties and cost of finding consensus and the ongoing controversy of having a no-fault principle at the heart of a system of corrective justice.

A.   The Concept of 'Abus de Fonction'

It is unsurprising that French law, in common with other modern systems, has had to face the question whether the misconduct of the employee will take him or her outside the course of employment. This is characterised in France as a question of '*abus de fonction*', requiring a distinction to be drawn between a 'détournement' (diversion) from one's task rather than 'dépassement' (exceeding) one's tasks.[41] From the 1950s until 1988, the civil and criminal chambers of the *Cour de cassation* were divided as to the correct approach to be taken.[42]

Whilst the *Chambre criminelle* continued the liberal approach of the past, the *Chambre civile*, notably the second chamber, favoured a more restrictive approach. On four occasions, the *Chambres réunies,* and *Assemblée plénière* supported the civil chamber's narrow approach and rejected liability where the injury arose due to the employee acting to his own personal ends.[43]

The first two decisions in 1960 and 1977 concerned misuse of vehicles provided for employment. In the 1960 decision, an agricultural worker had 'borrowed' his employer's van in his absence and later crashed through a shop window. The court found this act to be 'à des fins personnelles, au mépris des ordres et à l'insu de son commettant'.[44] It was independent of the job he was employed to do, which only gave him the opportunity to take the van. The decision of the *Assemblée plénière* in 1977 is more controversial. Here, the negligent driver had been employed to drive the delivery van in which his friends were injured (and one killed) due to his negligent driving on a Saturday night. He was told to garage the car at

---

[41]   Trav Assoc H Capitant (Paris, LGDJ, 1977) 79.

[42]   See Civ (2) 1 July 1954 D 1954.628, requiring causal link between functions of employee and tortious act.

[43]   Ch réun 9 March 1960 D 1960.329 note R Savatier, JCP 1960 II 11559 note R Rodière, Gaz Pal 1960.1.313; Ass plén 10 June 1977 D 1977.465 note C Larroumet, JCP 1977 II 18730 concl P Gulphe, Def 1977.1517 note JL Aubert, RTDC 1977.74 obs G Durry; Cass Ass plén, 17 June 1983 JCP 1983 II 20120 concl PA Sadon, note F Chabas, D 1984.134 note D Denis, RTDC 1983.749 obs G Durry. Ass plén 17 November 1985 D 1986.81 note JL Aubert, JCP 1986 II 20568 note G Viney, RTDC 1986.128 obs J Huet.

[44]   '[F]or his own personal benefit, in contempt of his orders and without the knowledge of his employer' (my translation).

home, but forbidden to use the van outside work. Nevertheless, the court found that using a car 'sans autorisation, à des fins personnelles' took him outside the course of his employment.

Nevertheless, the 1960 and 1977 decisions did little to change the practice of the *Chambre criminelle*. The divergence continued; the criminal chamber confining the 1977 decision to the wrongful use of vehicle.[45] Whilst the *loi Badinter* of 1985[46] rendered liability for the act of another less important in this context,[47] this did little to resolve the issue in other contexts.

The 1983 decision of the *Assemblée plénière* raised a slightly different situation: a lorry driver legitimately driving his lorry but trying to steal petrol destined for a client. He suspected that he was being followed and therefore dumped the fuel in a quarry which led to environmental pollution. At the time he was supposed to be working for the employer. Again, we see a strict line:

> *le préposé, qui agissant, sans autorisation, à des fins étrangères à ses attributions, s'est placé hors des fonctions auxquelles il était employé.*[48]

This is repeated in the later decision of 1985 where an employee had deliberately set fire to the factory he was employed to protect, supposedly to highlight insufficient security measures![49] These decisions send a clear message that merely giving an employee the opportunity to commit a tort would not suffice.

One may note at this stage that French law adopted a similar, if not slightly more restrictive, approach to the common law. In common with the English cases of *Whatman v Pearson*[50] and *Storey v Ashton*,[51] the question in both systems seems to revolve around whether the employee is 'on a frolic of his own',[52] or, 'à des fins personnelles'. *Photo Production Ltd v Securicor Transport Ltd*[53]—recognising vicarious liability where a

---

[45] See comments of Larroumet D 1977.466. Note the practice of chambre criminelle: Crim 18 July 1978 Bull crim No 237, p 627 and contrast its approach otherwise in Crim 18 June 1979 Bull crim no 212, D 1980 IR 36 obs Larroumet. Comment T Hassler D 1980 chron 125.

[46] *Loi* 5 July 1985, no 85-677 (statute imposing a form of strict liability for traffic accidents).

[47] Compare the comments of Lord Denning MR in *Rose v Plenty* [1976] 1 WLR 141 (CA) 145 on the impact of compulsory vehicle insurance under the Road Traffic Act 1972 (UK).

[48] Cass Ass plén, 17 June 1983 D 1984 Jur 134 note D Denis, JCP 1983 II 20120. 'the employee, who is acting, without authorisation to his own ends, has placed himself outside the scope of his employment' (my translation).

[49] Ass plén 17 November 1985 D 1986.81 note JL Aubert, JCP 1986 II 20568 note G Viney.

[50] (1868) LR 3 CP 422.

[51] (1869) LR 4 QB 476.

[52] Baron Parke in *Joel v Morison* (1834) 6 C&P 501, 503; 127 ER 1338.

[53] [1980] AC 827 (HL).

security guard had deliberately started a small fire in a factory he was employed to protect[54]—suggests a broader approach to that adopted in the 1985 case.[55] It is perhaps unsurprising that *Photo Productions* and *Morris v Martin* were used by the House of Lords in *Lister v Hesley Hall Ltd*[56] to justify the extension of liability.[57] The *Assemblée plénière* decision of 17 November 1985 has been criticised as threatening to undermine the security firm's contractual obligations to his client in such circumstances.[58]

In 1988, the *Assemblée plénière* finally gave way. In its decision of 19 May 1988,[59] the court found an insurance company liable for its employee, M Héro, who had defrauded Mme Guyot while advising her at her home. Mme Guyot had believed that M Héro was acting on behalf of the company, which had authorised M Héro to accept funds. Although he was clearly acting to his own ends and without authorisation, he was not found to be acting '*hors des fonctions*'.

This clearly involves a modification of the formula stated above. Liability for the acts of others will now lie unless the act of the employee is:

– Without authorisation/Sans autorisation,
– For his or her own ends/à des fins étrangères à ses attributions
– Outside the normal duties of his or her job/hors de ses fonctions

The test in future would thus concentrate on whether the job provides '*l'occasion et les moyens de sa faute*'. The employee will be acting within his of her functions if the employment provides the occasion or time and place of the tort (for example, it takes place during the working day),[60] and the means by which the tort is committed (eg, the victim is knocked over by a car that the employee is told to drive). The court will also look at more subjective factors, such as whether the employee was acting in the employer's interest—what was the purpose and aim of the tort? Was the tort foreseeable and preventable by the employer? Was the victim unaware that the employee was acting on his or her own behalf?[61]

---

[54] On the basis of *Morris v Martin*, above n 35, at 739.

[55] Although it was alternatively decided on the basis of breach of contract by Securicor itself: see Lord Wilberforce at 846. Lords Keith and Scarman expressed agreement with Lord Wilberforce.

[56] Above n 13.

[57] See Lord Steyn, [22]; Clyde [46]; Hobhouse [57]; Millett [76].

[58] F Terré, P Simler and Y Lequette, *Droit Civil: Les Obligations*, 9th edn (Paris, Dalloz, 2005) 835, Y Lambert-Faivre 'L'abus de fonctions' D 1986 chron 143.

[59] D 1988.513 note C Larroumet, Gaz Pal 1988.2.640 concl M Dorwling-Carter, Def 1988.1097 note JL Aubert, RTDC 1989.89 obs P Jourdain. Followed by Crim 4 January 1996 JCP 1996 IV 1028.

[60] Here there is a rebuttable presumption that it is in the course of employment. The classic example of a tort outside the course of employment is that of a murder outside working hours for personal reasons: see Terré , above n 58, at 834.

[61] Carbonnier, above n 8, at 243.

As Terré recognises, by focusing on whether the job gave the opportunity and means for the tort, the court adopted the traditional position of the *Chambre criminelle* and its primary concern for the welfare of victims above that of the economic interests of the business community.[62] Such a development, at first glance surprising in view of the gradual movement of the *Chambre criminelle* towards acceptance of the 1985 decision of the *Assemblée plénière*,[63] reflects a recognition of the increased role of no fault liability in French law.[64] Interpreting broadly the wording of Article 1384(1), the courts have recently shown themselves willing not only to impose liability on defined groups of people—employers and parents—but on anyone who has the power to organise, manage and control another in the absence of *force majeure*, act of a third party, or fault of the victim.[65] Equally, the courts have demonstrated a willingness to increase the burden on parents under Article 1384(4) for damage resulting from their children's acts.[66] The influence of public law also cannot be ignored—a separate system of law in France with its own court structure. It is well established that a state employee will not be held personally responsible if he or she commits a *'faute de service'*.[67] The State alone will be liable. This is interpreted generously and the private law courts have been reluctant in recent years to accept a disparity between private and public law liability. As Carbonnier pertinently asks, what difference may be found between such employees and those working for large private enterprises?[68] Post-1993, the courts have moved to protect the employee from liability, save in the case of *faute personnelle* when the employee exceeds the scope of his or her employment.[69] Fabre-Magnan has questioned whether in so doing, the

---

[62] Terré, above n 58, at 835.

[63] See Cass crim 15 May 1986 Gaz Pal 1986.2.682; 22 January 1987 Bull crim No 37, p91; 10 November 1987 D 1988 IR 23.

[64] It may also owe something to its context: the fraudster had acted without authorisation on a frolic of his own and, without more, the employer could escape liability.

[65] See l'arrêt Blieck—liability imposed on a day centre for mentally handicapped people when one of their members had started a fire in a forest: Ass plén 29 March 1991 D 1991.324 note C Larroumet, chr G Viney p157, JCP 1991 II 21673, concl H Dontenwille, note J Ghestin. This has been extended towards sporting organisations which organise, manage and control the activities of their members in competition: Cass (2) civ 22 May 1995 JCP 1995 II 22550 note J Mouly, JCP I 3893 no 5 obs G Viney, RTDC 1995.899 obs P Jourdain; 3 February 2000 JCP 2000 II 10316 note J Mouly.

[66] See l'arrêt Füllenwarth Ass plén 9 May 1984 D 1984.525 concl J Cabannes, note F Chabas, JCP 1984 II 20255 note N Dejean de La Bâtie (liability where the child's act was the direct cause of the damage) and l'arrêt Bertrand (JCP 1997 II 22848 concl R Kessous, note G Viney, D 1997.265 note P Jourdain (strict liability in absence of *force majeure* or fault by the victim)).

[67] See M Paillet, Juris Classeur Administratif: Fasc. 818: Faute de service. See T confl, 30 July 1873, Pelletier: Rec CE, p 117; DP 1874, 3, p 5, concl. David; GAJA, n 2. This signifies that the victim will almost always be assured of compensation from the administration.

[68] Above n 8, at no 246.

[69] See L'arrêt Rochas (Cass com 12 October 1993 D 1994.124 note G Viney, JCP 1995 II 22493 note F Chabas, Def 1994.812 obs J-L Aubert, RTDC 1994.111 obs P Jourdain)

courts have in fact reduced the rights of victims by removing the possibility of targeting the employee should it be impossible to pursue the employer.[70]

Yet, such a test still leaves room for uncertainty. Tensions continue between the contrasting goals of ensuring compensation for victims, protecting employees and not placing too great a burden on employers. Whilst the *Assemblée plénière* decision of 19 May 1988 represents not simply a new formula, but an acceptance of the principle of vicarious liability as a means of responding to the risks arising from misconduct of employees, this has not prevented subsequent courts refusing liability where the victim has reason to believe that the employee is acting outside the scope of his or her employment.[71] Nor has it discouraged academic writers from suggesting new means for determining the notion of *abus de fonction*.[72] Nevertheless, in reaching such a broad rule of vicarious liability, one can identify an acceptance that the value placed by society in ensuring the victim compensation for acts indirectly linked to the employer should outweigh the concerns of corrective justice. It is this policy-based step which is important.

V.   FINDING A RATIONALE FOR VICARIOUS LIABILITY

Consideration of recent case law strongly indicates that one can waste much time fine-tuning a formula, often to little avail. The term 'close connection' provides a vehicle, not an explanation, for vicarious liability. This is acceptable provided it is clear what the term is a vehicle for. The two tests—the common law 'close connection' test and the more unwieldy French test of 'acting outside the functions for which he was employed, without authorisation and for his own ends'—give little indication how the doctrine should operate in practice. The answer must ultimately lie on how far a legal system is prepared to impose on the employer the burden of dealing with employee-created risks. This raises questions of a socio-political nature. As Fleming noted, 'the modern doctrine of vicarious liability cannot parade as a deduction from legalistic premises, but should be frankly recognised as having its basis in a combination of policy considerations'.[73]

---

followed by Ass plén 25 February 2000 JCP 2000 II 10295 rapp Kessous, note M Billiau, JCP 2000 I 241 obs G Viney, D 2000.673 note Ph Brun (L'arrêt Costedoat). Cf CE 30 July 1873 (L'affaire Pelletier).

[70]   M Fabre-Magnan, *Les Obligations* (Paris, Presses Universitaires de France, 2004) no 327.

[71]   See Civ (2) 22 May 2003 Bull civ 2003 II N° 156 p 132, Banque et droit 2003.76 no 91.

[72]   See N Molfessis, Dr Soc 2004.31, 'Vie professionnelle, vie personnelle et responsabilité des commettants du fait de leurs préposés'; J Julien, *La Responsabilité Civile du Fait d'Autrui: Ruptures et Continuités* (Aix-en-Provence, Presses Universitaires d'Aix Marseille, 2001).

[73]   Fleming, above n 31, at 410.

It is therefore unsurprising that vicarious liability is seen in all the systems surveyed as controversial. In raising fundamental questions of risk distribution and compensation burdens for which there is no obvious societal consensus, it is likely to meet a variety of responses depending on the dominant policy of the time. One must therefore deal with some care with earlier precedents, decided at a time in which a particular form of social policy was dominant. The use and structure of insurance may equally not be ignored. In France, liability insurance for any accidental damage caused to another person or another person's property is widespread, for example *assurance responsabilité civile* is commonly part of a comprehensive home policy. Insurance thus forms a backdrop to any extension of civil liability and the *Code des assurances* expressly states that the insurer must cover the losses and damage 'caused by persons for whom the insured is legally liable pursuant to Article 1384 of the Civil Code, regardless of the nature and seriousness of such persons' faults'.[74] Recognition of the role played by insurance, a widened burden on the State for the acts of their employees and those for whom they are responsible, and a willingness to talk openly in terms of social risk have led to a generous system of liability for the acts of others. The 2000 *Costedoat* decision would appear to mark a shift away from the view of employer as mere guarantor. Here, the court firmly rejected the previous rule that an employer could seek an indemnity from his employee. Although this has long been limited by legislation,[75] the decision confirmed that, provided the employee is acting in the course of his or her employment, the employer now takes full responsibility for his or her actions.[76] The employee is now only personally liable in the case of *faute personnelle*.[77]

The experience of French law also highlights the difficulties of finding agreement on the scope of vicarious liability. Although the leading cases appear to focus on the exact wording of the test formulated by the

---

[74] Article L121-2 of *Code des assurances*. These terms are treated as having the status of 'd'ordre public' and so cannot be modified by agreement.

[75] See Article 36(3) of *loi* 13 July 1930 (now L 121-12(3), *Code des assurances*: 'Notwithstanding the above provisions, the insurer shall have no recourse against the children, descendants, ascendants, relations in direct line, officials, employees, workers or servants and in general any person normally living in the insured's home, except in the case of 'malveillance' committed by one of such persons'. 'Malveillance' is defined by insurance law as an intentional act committed against the insured, that is, an act intended to harm the insured: Cass ass plén 13 November 1987: Bull ass plén No 5.

[76] Ass plén 25 February 2000 JCP 2000 II 10295 rapp Kessous, note M Billiau, JCP 2000 I 241 obs G Viney, D 2000.673 note Ph Brun (L'arrêt Costedoat). This follows l'arrêt Rochas (Com 12 October 1993 D 1994.124 note G Viney, JCP 1995 note F Chabas, Def 1994.812 obs J-L Aubert, RTDC 1994.111 obs P Jourdain).

[77] That is, if the employee deliberately commits a criminal act, even under the orders of his employer, he remains liable: l'arrêt Cousin: Bull Ass plén 14 December 2001 No 2 JCP 2002 II 10026 note M Billiau, I 124 No 7 par G Viney, D 2002.Somm 1317 obs D Mazeaud, RTDC 2002.109 obs P Jourdain.

Assemblée plénière, in reality the decision in 1988 represented a change of policy and a recognition of the use of strict liability in the late twentieth century to ensure compensation for victims on the basis of a broad notion of risk. On this basis, if you profit from another's actions, you must accept the risks associated with these actions (*théorie du risque/profit*). In taking responsibility for such conduct, it is expected that the employer will be covered by third party insurance. This would suggest a broad reading of the requirement that the employee is acting in the course of his or her employment. The view of the employer as mere guarantor for the employee's tort, while still preferred by some,[78] has been weakened by case law which has severely limited the ability of the employer to receive an indemnity from his or her employees.

Nevertheless, French law has clearly not avoided the problems experienced by the common law in finding a satisfactory explanation for vicarious liability. One can still identify differing views as to the basis for liability. While recent case law demonstrates a general movement towards greater acceptance of social risk as the basis for a broader rule of liability,[79] commentators have also identified limitations. Risk-based reasoning may take the form of *risque/profit*,[80] *risque/enterprise*[81] or *risque/autorité*;[82] each having its own meaning and justification. Risk additionally cannot explain all cases of vicarious liability in French law, for example, where, under the broad definition of the *commettant/préposé* relationship, liability is imposed for the acts of family members and friends.[83] Malaurie and Aynès also express doubts how such a theory is consistent with the traditional right of an employer for indemnification, although the movement by recent case law to confine this right makes the theory easier to argue.[84] More important questions derive from the structure of vicarious liability itself. If risk is the sole justification, why should it be confined to harm caused by the torts of employees?[85] Logically, any action which harms another could be regarded as a risk of employment. The French courts have not gone so far. The risk undertaken remains that arising from a tort with a causal connection to the employment. The 'tort' requirement

---

[78] F Bénac-Schmidt and C Larroumet, *Responsabilité du Fait d'Autrui*, 2nd edn (Paris, Rép civ Dalloz, 1990).

[79] G Viney and P Jourdain, *Les Conditions de la Responsabilité*, 3rd edn (Paris, LGDJ, 2006) no 791-1. See also Viney D 1994.124 (note below Cass com 12 October 1993).

[80] Liability arises because the employer profits from the activities of the employee.

[81] Liability arises because the employee's activities represent one of the risks of the enterprise.

[82] Liability arises because the employer exercises authority over the employee.

[83] Carbonnier, above n 8, at no 247.

[84] P Malaurie, L Aynès and P Stoffel-Munck, *Les Obligations* (Paris, Defrénois, 2003) 158.

[85] This is no longer required in relation to parental liability: see l'arrêt Füllenwarth, above n 66.

ensures that there is still some incentive for the employee to take care to avoid accidents even if in practice he or she is unlikely to be sued personally.

These weaknesses would also apply to English law. Here, risk, as a general theory, has received considerable support and has in recent years been relied upon by Lord Millett in *Lister* and *Dubai* and Lord Nicholls in *Dubai* and *Majrowski* as an explanation for recovery without any sense that this might be controversial. Noticeably, however, the courts have steered clear of more complicated interpretations of risk, in particular the economic concept of enterprise risk favoured by the North American courts. The House of Lords in *Lister* rejected the arguments of economic efficiency and risk-minimalisation, stated so clearly by McLachlin J in *Bazley v Curry*[86] and applied in subsequent case law,[87] in favour of a broad concept of social justice. Yet the vagueness of a loose concept of risk cannot be ignored. Whilst it cannot be denied that all forms of economic activity have risks attached and that loss distribution may have desirable effects, if, as seen in French law, risk is taken to represent a guiding principle, it must be limited by some notion of balance. If seen simply as 'the most convenient and efficient way of ensuring that persons injured in the course of business enterprises do not go uncompensated',[88] it must nevertheless be given some content beyond what is just and equitable.

Opposition to risk-based reasoning continues to be argued in France. Chabas, for example, has maintained the opposition of Mazeaud to this explanation of French law.[89] The requirement of a tort by the employee and the ability (albeit now limited) of the employer to seek an indemnity from the employee supports, in his view, a continuation of the traditional

---

[86]   Above n 13, at 557: 'The policy purposes underlying the imposition of vicarious liability on employers are served only where the wrong is so connected with the employment that it can be said that the employer has introduced the risk of the wrong (and is thereby fairly and usefully charged with its management and minimisation). The question in each case is whether there is a connection or nexus between the employment enterprise and that wrong that justifies imposition of vicarious liability on the employer for the wrong, in terms of fair allocation of the consequences of the risk and/or deterrence'.

[87]   See *Jacobi v Griffiths*, above n 13 and, notably, McLachlin CJ in *KLB v British Columbia* [2003] 2 SCR 403, [19]-[20] (majority refuse to extend vicarious liability to the relationship between government and foster parents for assaults of children in their care), and *John Doe v Bennett* [2004] 1 SCR 436, [20]-[1] (Episcopal corporation vicariously liable for sexual assaults of priest on children in his parishes). Note also *EB v Order of the Oblates of Mary Immaculate* [2005] 3 SCR 45, [38]-[40] (Binnie J) (mere opportunity insufficient when sexual assaults by odd job man living in quarters on school grounds off-limits to students).

[88]   Atiyah, above n 1, at 26.

[89]   See H, L and J Mazeaud and F Chabas, *Leçons de Droit Civil t 2, vol 1, Obligations: Théorie Générale*, 9th edn (Paris, Montchestien, 1998) by F Chabas, Nos 483-84.

view by which the law identifies the employer with the employee's fault.[90] The employer is liable because of his or her close link with the employee— *qui facit per alium facit per se* (who brings something about through another does it himself).[91] The identification of employer with employee thus represents a closer link with individual responsibility, and still finds favour with certain civil and common law commentators. Ernest Weinrib in *The Idea of Private Law* argues that the ideas of *respondeat superior* and *qui facit per alium facit per se* can still be seen to be within a concept of corrective justice: '*respondeat superior* fits into corrective justice only if the employer can, in some sense, be regarded as a doer of the harm. Corrective justice requires us to think that the employee at fault is so closely connected with the employer that responsibility for the former's acts can be imputed to the latter'.[92]

A connection may clearly be drawn between the idea of identification of employer/employee with the common law concept of non-delegable duties. Here the argument is that the employer assumes a specific duty to the victim, whose performance is entrusted to the employee.[93] In *Lister*, therefore, the boys were entrusted into the care of Hesley Hall Ltd, and, in the words of Lord Hobhouse, '[t]he liability of the employers derives from their voluntary assumption of the relationship towards the plaintiff and the duties that arise from that relationship and their choosing to entrust the performance of those duties to their servant'.[94] This is the language of non-delegable duties, not vicarious liability, justified by the attribution of fault of one to another. Despite the obvious confusion of vicarious/primary liability,[95] his Lordship's aim is to place direct responsibility at the feet of Hesley Hall and thereby justify the extension of liability imposed by the case. Such a specific duty focuses on the relationship of the parties, be it carer/child or teacher/pupil, and does not lend itself to a general rule. Each duty will require its own justification, based on particular rules of social policy.

Both systems additionally find assistance in the idea of legitimate reliance placed by the victim on the employee (using the doctrines of

---

[90] *Ibid*, at no 470. Liability is founded on the assimilation by law of the fault of the *préposé* with that of the *commettant*. See also F Bertrand 'Les Aspects nouveaux de la notion de préposé et de l'idée de représentation dans l'article 1384 al 5 nouveau du Code civil, étude critique de jurisprudence' (th Aix, 1935).

[91] 'La faute demeure donc le fondement de la responsabilité du commettant: la faute du préposé est, pour la victime, la propre faute du commettant': Mazeaud, above n 89, at no 484.

[92] E Weinrib, *The Idea of Private Law* (Cambridge, Harvard University Press, 1995) 186. 'Fault, consisting in either intentional or negligent harm, is the organising principle of the common law': *Ibid*, at 184.

[93] See Lord Hobhouse *Lister*, above n 13, at [57].

[94] *Ibid*, at [55].

[95] See my comments in 'Rough Justice in an Unjust World' (2002) 65 *MLR* 269.

apparence/ostensible authority). On this basis, justice requires that the employer meets (or the French would say, guarantees)[96] the liability of parties the victim legitimately believes to be acting on behalf of the employer. Owing much to the law of agency, the aim is to ensure that the trust of the victim is not undermined. Whilst arising generally in the context of fraud,[97] it provides a reason for imposing liability based not on the conduct of the employer, but on the victim's perception of the employer/employee relationship. Thus, where the victim is aware that the employee is acting outside his or her authority, the employer should not be liable.[98] Such a 'victim-centred' approach has received considerable support in France as a relevant factor to be considered in applying the three-fold test of liability. It will not explain liability where the victim has no prior relationship with the employee, but is recognised as useful in 'ensur[ing] reasonable protection for the victims whilst encouraging them to be vigilant and making it possible to thwart possible collusions with the dishonest employee'.[99]

VI. CONCLUSION

What conclusions may we draw from these arguments? No system adheres to one particular theory. Such obfuscation results from the difficulties, present in all legal systems, in finding consensus as to the motivation behind vicarious liability. This doctrine does not rest easily in a system of fault-based liability and clearly represents an ongoing debate between personal responsibility and social risk inherent in the law of tort. In light of the differing views as to the merits of vicarious liability, it is perhaps understandable why courts have tried to avoid dealing with difficult questions, such as the underlying basis for the scope of employment test. It is far easier to find support for a doctrine which may be explained on a number of contradictory bases than find agreement on one dominant theory, particularly if it is contrary to the notion of corrective justice.

Yet recent case law extending the notion of 'scope of employment' must lead us to question the continuing validity of the courts' unwillingness to address such issues. A more generous interpretation of the scope of employment signifies the imposition of a greater burden on employers and

[96] See C Larroumet D 1984.173 and 1988.513.

[97] See, in English law, *Lloyd v Grace, Smith & Co* [1912] AC 716 (HL), *Uxbridge Permanent Benefit Building Society v Pickard* [1939] 2 KB 248 (CA) and *Noel v Poland* [2001] 2 BCLC 645 (QB), and, in French law, see Ass plén 19 May 1988 D 1988.513 note C Larroumet.

[98] See *Armagas v Mundogas (The Ocean Frost)* [1986] AC 717 (HL) and Cass (2) 7 July 1993 (4 cases) Bull civ II No 249, Resp civ et assur 1993, comm 330, JCP 1993 IV 2325.

[99] G Viney JCP 1993 I 3727 no 24 (my translation).

their insurers and this cannot go unacknowledged. Equally, if one wishes for predictability in a legal system in the interest of settlements, vague phrases, be it 'close connection' or '*dans les fonctions auxquelles ils les ont employés*', do little to guide future litigants and their advisers. The content and rationale of these labels thus becomes important. It is suggested that the time has come to make some key choices.

It is submitted that to continue to develop the law without further guidance is likely to lead to confusion and incoherence. My examination of French law suggests that while consensus on one single justification will be difficult to achieve, a gradual acceptance of the primacy of risk-reasoning has allowed the system to embrace a wider system of liability in the full knowledge of the burdens which will result. Thirty years of debate has led to a position with which all might not agree, but guidance may be found. Five years after *Lister*, English law is still left with some key questions: is the duty non-delegable or not? What role does, and should, the doctrine of risk play? How far should employers and their insurers respond to the added burden of no-fault liability? Why should they be liable for criminal acts against their interests and which they would clearly condemn? To fail to confront these questions is to ignore the inherently controversial nature of strict liability in a system of individual responsibility and to leave the doctrine without any clear guiding principle. It is to be hoped that the English courts will follow the lead of the Canadian courts in seeking a policy-based framework for analysis. Such a move would be courageous and force the courts away from the safety of imprecision, but, it is argued, is vital if this doctrine is to continue to develop in a coherent way.

17

What is a Loss?

ANDREW TETTENBORN*

I. INTRODUCTION

A S ANY MEMBER of the defendants' bar will happily confirm, a plaintiff who proves a tort or breach of contract[1] is only half-way, if that, to a damages award. The defendant can—and in the majority of cases will—put her to proof of loss and damage in addition. If she cannot jump this fence, then (leaving aside punitive damages, nominal awards and other pathological cases) she has failed.

However, all this skates over a disconcerting question: just what do we *mean* when we say that a plaintiff whose rights have been infringed has nevertheless suffered no loss? Or, if you prefer to put the query positively, what is the law referring to when it talks about 'loss'?

II. TRADITIONAL IDEAS: MONEY, LOSS AND OTHER

Ask a common lawyer to define 'loss' in the context of damages law, and his or her answer, it is suggested, would be on something like these lines. The lawyer would have to admit that the concept he or she had in mind was diffuse rather than precisely delineated, with a relatively hard centre shading off into an increasingly uncertain and ill-defined penumbra.[2]

The core idea of 'loss' is relatively uncontroversial. In so far as the wrong causes a direct and measurable pecuniary effect on the plaintiff, then on any account she has suffered a loss. The paradigm case is thus the net expenditure (or deprivation) of cash; it embraces such obvious instances as the plaintiff compelled to spend large sums on medical bills or

---

* Bracton Professor of Law in the University of Exeter, England.
[1] This is, of course, a torts collection arising from a torts conference. Nevertheless, it is suggested that the same issues arise in contracts and torts as regards the definition of 'loss', and hence I make no apology for referring to both here.
[2] An object lesson, in fact, in the idea of definition popularised in HLA Hart, 'Positivism and the Separation of Law and Morals' (1958) 71 *Harvard Law Review* 593.

car repairs, duped into paying more for an asset than it is worth, or forced to buy in an expensive market something the defendant ought to have provided her with but did not. In addition, hot on the heels of actual expenditure come some very close, and virtually indistinguishable, relatives. If the expenditure of money counts as loss, then by parity of reasoning the same must apply to the failure to receive money one would otherwise have got (lost earnings or profits), and in addition the prospect of having to disburse it in the future (prospective medical expenses). Also, and very importantly, the logic must also extend to loss of the *potential* to obtain money. It is this that allows us—as we invariably do—to assimilate balance sheet deficiencies to cash losses. Suppose a chattel is wrongfully damaged or destroyed, or professional malpractice or other negligence devalues some asset owned by the plaintiff. There may not necessarily be a cash shortfall, since the asset may not in the event be replaced or repaired at all. Nevertheless, there is the next best thing: after all, non-cash assets, as any accountant will confirm, can without too much violence be regarded as interchangeable with the amount of cash that someone would give for them.

Outside these certainties, there are a few other cases which are apparently controversial but to which (it is suggested) similar reasoning can be convincingly applied. One such occurs when the plaintiff is saddled as a result of the defendant's wrong with an enforceable liability to a third party. At least if there is no serious likelihood that she will not in fact discharge this liability,[3] an effect of this sort is rightly treated in the same way as a cash loss.[4] Another such situation occurs when we shift our attention from marginal to other kinds of costs, such as overhead or maintenance expenses. Suppose, for example, that botched building work, or a neighbour's carelessness, deprives a plaintiff of the use of her house for a few weeks; during this time she stays gratis with friends but still has to pay outgoings on an unusable home.[5] Or imagine the fairly common situation where a city bus is damaged and off the road, but the city

---

[3] If there is such a doubt, matters are less certain, and acute problems of the definition of 'loss' arise. This matter is dealt with below.

[4] The classic case arises in contract, eg, where A sells B defective goods which B sells to C, thus becoming liable to C (see *Randall v Raper* (1858) EB & E 84, 120 ER 438 and cf *Hydrocarbons Great Britain Ltd v Cammell Laird Shipbuilders Ltd* (1993) 53 BLR 84 (CA)). But it can also appear in tort: for example, where A damages B's car and B hires a replacement from C on credit but has not paid the bill (see *Giles v Thompson* [1994] 1 AC 142 (HL)).

[5] As in *Bella Casa Ltd v Vinestone Ltd* [2006] Build LR 72 (QB) [*Bella Casa*]. See too *Calabar Properties Ltd v Stitcher* [1984] 1 WLR 287 (CA), where it seems such a claim would have succeeded but for the fact that the plaintiff had also elected to claim for expenditure on another property, and to award both sums would overcompensate it.

substitutes a spare vehicle it keeps against such eventualities.[6] True, in neither case is the plaintiff absolutely worse off by one cent: the costs would have been incurred anyway, and hence the plaintiff's bank-balance is technically undepleted. Nevertheless, a claim for the upkeep cost of the uninhabitable house or the damaged bus is entirely plausible. The expenditure itself may have been constant, but what it has been spent on has not: it has been involuntarily transmuted from an investment in something the plaintiff wanted to a charge levied on her for maintaining what has become—at least for the time being—a white elephant.[7]

Stopping here for a moment, this instinctive concentration on cash deficiency and its analogies is not particularly surprising. Damages being calibrated in cash, it is naturally easier to relate them to cashlike effects than to others. Moreover, the traditional connotations of the word 'loss' reinforce this instinct. When we say someone has suffered a loss, we instinctively contemplate her being worse off in some factual, verifiable sense[8]—something entirely straightforward where she can point to a balance-sheet deficiency or something like it, but much less so when she cannot do this and has to allege some more abstract affectation or deprivation.[9] But it is not simply a matter of psychology or instinct. There is a further, more subtle, intellectual factor at work. To say a plaintiff must prove not only wrong but loss logically implies the conceptual possibility of *injuria absque damno*—a plaintiff wronged but unharmed—which in turn necessarily implies that *damnum* must be something different from *injuria*.[10] Now, since nearly all entitlements plaintiffs seek to vindicate,

---

[6] As in *Birmingham Corporation v Sowsbery* [1970] RTR 84 (QB) [*Sowsbery*]. See too the identical *Edmonton (City) v Haberstock* (1982) 40 AR 167 (QB), and compare the shipping case of *The Marpessa* [1907] AC 241 (HL).

[7] Cf *The Susquehanna* [1926] AC 655 (HL) allowing interest on the capital tied up in a disabled ship. As Lord Sumner put it at 664, 'the loss of user for the time of repair, in effect, made the [ship's] then capital value infructuous for the time being'. And see *The West Wales* (1932) 43 Ll L L Rep 504 (HL) (wages of crew of disabled ship).

[8] A straightforward example is the (rarely attempted) definition of 'loss' approved by Stephenson LJ in *Forster v Outred & Co* [1982] 1 WLR 86 (CA) 95: loss is 'any detriment, liability or loss capable of assessment in money terms and it includes liabilities which may arise on a contingency, particularly a contingency over which the plaintiff has no control; things like loss of earning capacity, loss of a chance or bargain, loss of profit, losses incurred from onerous provisions or covenants in leases'.

[9] There is also another linguistic point here. French-style civil law jurisdictions oblige defendants not to cause others to suffer such things as *préjudice* (Art 1457 CCQ) or *dommage* (Art 1382 C Civ). These terms patently refer to something different from the fact of the wrong, but in addition cover pecuniary loss and nonpecuniary affectation without discrimination. Unfortunately English has no real equivalent to them. 'Loss' has inescapably pecuniary overtones: 'damage' wavers uncertainly between tangible loss and the more nebulous idea that the plaintiff has simply been deprived of something she was entitled to.

[10] Cf J Raz, *The Morality of Freedom*, (Oxford, Oxford University Press, 1986) 165-92 and S Perry, 'Harm, History, and Counterfactuals' (2003) 40 *San Diego Law Review* 1283, 1307-8, both making the point that there is a difference between the infringement of an interest (*injuria*) and harm (*damnum*).

whether in contract or tort, are actually non-cash benefits—bodily integrity, carefully-provided services, delivery of goods, etc—it follows that in so far as the effect of a wrong can be expressed in terms of some resulting monetary transaction or balance sheet deficiency, segregating wrong done from damage caused is correspondingly easy. By contrast, where this is not the case this distinction is acutely difficult to draw. When, and how far, does it make sense to say that a plaintiff has suffered a loss if, albeit wronged, she cannot say she is poorer in terms of cash or other assets than she would otherwise have been?

It is thus these cases—the cases outside the penumbra that cannot be assimilated to cash losses—that form the nub of the problem inherent in trying to explain the idea of loss, and deciding just how abstract a conception of it is acceptable for the purposes of damages law. In effect this question splits into one main issue and a couple of sub-issues. The main issue (a) concerns whether there is any relevant loss at all. The sub-issues are (b) what happens where there is a wrong and a prima facie loss, but something happens which prevents its effects being felt by the plaintiff; and (c) what happens when a wrong has a clear effect, but that effect is felt by someone other than the plaintiff.

A.   Is There any Relevant Loss at All?

Assuming the defendant is liable for a tort or breach of contract, but that there is no cash loss or anything that can be regarded as equivalent to it, what else can be regarded as a loss? This difficulty of principle arises in all sorts of cases: what appears below is a representative sample.

First, there is what can be summed up as the problem of incommensurables:[11] that is, effects on the plaintiff in respect of which there is no conceivable direct translation into money.[12] An obvious instance is pain, suffering and loss of amenity in personal injury suits; however, we will leave this aside, since damages of this sort should arguably be recognised as *sui generis*,[13] and there are plenty of other examples more to the point. For

---

[11]   Note that here I am taking it as accepted that incommensurables may be valued in some way. I am not concerned with the problem of how to value them, which is a major topic in its own right: see, eg, M Radin, 'Compensation and Commensurability' (1993) 43 *Duke Law Journal* 56 and Cass R Sunstein, 'Incommensurability and Valuation in Law' (1994) 92 *Michigan Law Review* 779.

[12]   More formally, where it cannot be said that a plaintiff who receives damages for a wrong is better off, or worse off, or neither of these, than she was before: J Raz, above n 10, at 325.

[13]   Particularly in Canada since decisions such as *Andrews v Grand Toy Alberta Ltd* [1978] 2 SCR 229, *Arnold v Teno* [1978] 2 SCR 287 and *Thornton v Trustees of School District No 2* [1978] 2 SCR 267, which by introducing a 'functional' element effectively put nonpecuniaries in personal injury suits on a rather different footing from other damages.

a more instructive case, take a situation arising out of some wrong not actionable per se,[14] but where it is accepted that a plaintiff can nevertheless claim damages for non-material loss (ie, distress, vexation, mental suffering or whatever else lawyers choose to call it). Breach of a contract to provide fun or excitement, or to save the plaintiff from disturbance, is one obvious instance.[15] Other instances include wrongful damage to, or destruction of, property held for pleasure or amenity rather than profit,[16] and (a bit less obviously) some forms of tortious fraud.[17] When a court makes a non-pecuniary award in such a scenario, just what 'loss' is it compensating? One's first instinct is to regard the answer as obvious: the plaintiff has suffered a discrete form of damage over and above the breach, in the same way as a plaintiff who can show more orthodox evil consequences, such as a broken leg or $1,000 in lost profits, and it is this she is being made good for.[18] But this is problematical. A plaintiff complaining that her leg is broken, or that she is poorer by $1,000, is emphatically expected to prove this factual affectation: no proof, no damages. On the other hand, to get general non-pecuniary damages she is not normally required to demonstrate actual distress or anything like it: there is little, if any, evidence of defendants being allowed to reduce their exposure by alleging that she is either unusually phlegmatic, or indeed not really unhappy at all.[19] But if so, it follows that the 'loss' supposedly associated with nonmaterial claims is actually artificial. What the courts are actually doing is giving damages on no basis other than the simple fact that the plaintiff's rights have been

---

[14] Ie excluding torts like libel, assault or false imprisonment, where substantial (and not merely nominal) damages are admittedly available merely on proof of the wrong itself.

[15] Eg, *Jarvis v Swan's Tours Ltd* [1973] QB 233 (CA); *Hamilton-Jones v David & Snape* [2004] 1 WLR 924 (Ch) [*Hamilton-Jones*]. American courts tend to take the same view: see, eg, *Jankowski v Mazzotta* 152 NW 2d 49 (Mich CA 1967) and E A Farnsworth, *Contracts*, 3rd edn (New York, Aspen, 2004) § 12.17. Canadian courts can be more generous, apparently requiring merely that the distress be foreseeable on *Hadley v Baxendale* criteria: see *Fidler v Sun Life Assurance Co of Canada* 2006 SCC 30, and cf *Turczinski Estate v Dupont Heating & Air Conditioning Ltd* (2004) 246 DLR (4th) 95 (Ont CA). But this does not affect the point in the text.

[16] Eg, household knicknacks (*Carlisle v RUC Chief Constable* [1988] NI 307 (CA)); a stamp collection (cf the Australian decision in *Graham v Voigt* (1989) 89 ACTR 11 (CA)); or a pet animal (see the American decision of *Brown v Crocker* 139 So 2d 779 (La CA 1962)).

[17] Eg, *Saunders v Edwards* [1987] 1 WLR 1116 (CA) (fraud as to the amenity of an apartment); and see the colourful *Beaulne v Ricketts* (1979) 96 DLR (3d) 550 (Alta SC) (plaintiff duped into bigamous marriage).

[18] An attitude not limited to common lawyers. French writers, for example, regard such claims as being based on a form of *dommage*: they merely christen it *dommage* mora. See, eg, P Malaurie and L Aynès, *Droit Civil—Les Obligations* (Paris, Cujas, 1994) § 247.

[19] Though there is the odd maverick decision: see, eg, *Cringle v Northern Union Insurance Co* (1981) 124 DLR (3d) 22 (BCSC) [*Cringle*], which did refuse such damages partly on the ground of no proved actual distress.

infringed;[20] and if this is true, then the distinction between *damnum* and *injuria* which forms the whole basis of the requirement of loss has effectively vanished. Indeed, sometimes the judges have come close to admitting as much, and saying that in cases like this we are simply giving damages for breach alone. In the well-known but difficult case of *Ruxley Electronics Ltd v Forsyth*, for example, the House of Lords was faced with a problem where swimming-pool constructors had broken their contract by disobeying instructions (they built the pool a few inches too shallow), but where this had caused no appreciable loss, nor even inconvenience, to their homeowner client.[21] The House declined to limit the client to nominal damages, but equally did not base its award on any notional 'distress' or 'vexation' allegedly suffered by him. Instead it simply upheld the judge's award of a moderate sum to reflect the simple fact that the householder had not got that which he had had a right to have.[22]

Incommensurables are not the only area where it is awkward to construct a workable theory of what counts as a loss. For another, take the use or provision by the plaintiff of abstract resources that do not easily transfer onto a balance sheet. Suppose, for example, that the only alleged loss consists of services rendered by the plaintiff. An accountant, for example, is deceived (or negligently advised) into providing professional services to a third party who disappears without paying.[23] Now add a further assumption: there is no allegation of income forgone or other opportunity costs (ie the plaintiff was under-employed at the time, or otherwise cannot show that, had she not been misled, she would have been doing other work for which she would have been paid). Although it seems self-evident that the plaintiff should recover a figure based on the reasonable value of the services provided,[24] just what kind of loss she is claiming

---

[20]   Compare a similar point made in relation to general damages for personal injury in L Jaffe, 'Damages for Personal Injury: The Impact of Insurance' (1953) 18 *Law & Contemporary Problems* 219, 224: it does not make sense to regard such damages as actually making good anything at all.

[21]   [1996] AC 344 (HL).

[22]   See in particular the opinion of Lord Mustill, *ibid*, at 359-61. Compare the more recent decision of the House of Lords in *Rees v Darlington Memorial Hospital NHS Trust* [2004] 1 AC 309 (HL), that the victim of a failed sterilisation should get a conventional award. As Lord Bingham put it in *Rees*, at [8], such an award, while it 'would not be, and would not be intended to be, compensatory', should explicitly exist to 'afford some measure of recognition of the wrong done'.

[23]   Another more technical example is where a company is caused by a defendant's negligence to issue shares in itself, for instance in the course of a takeover. In one sense the shares may have value which the company has lost, but on the other hand the shares cost the company nothing to issue beyond administrative and printing costs. See *Pilmer v Duke Group Ltd* (1991) 180 ALR 249 (HC) and the thoughtful F Oditah, 'Takeovers, Share Exchanges and the Meaning of Loss' (1996) 112 *LQR* 424.

[24]   Such English authority as there is suggests that there is: see *Smith Kline & French Laboratories Ltd v Long* [1989] 1 WLR 1 (CA) (plaintiffs deceived into manufacturing and supplying pharmaceuticals at a discount: damages based on ultimate value of goods supplied,

to have compensated is obscure. One could of course say that the expenditure of time and trouble itself was a form of 'loss' within the meaning of the law: but this, to say the least, rather stretches the meaning of loss,[25] and savours of an arbitrary solution.

Moreover, this problem can also arise—and in more acute form—the other way round; that is, in the case of wrongful deprivation of services with no measurable end-product. Admittedly, sometimes there is not too much difficulty here: if a diner pays $50 for an upmarket meal but receives the $20 *table d'hôte*, there is a loss of at least something of tangible value. But this escape is not always available. For example, suppose a trucking company, having agreed to transport the plaintiff's goods in high-security trucks, carries them in ordinary vehicles; in the event all arrive safely and on time. It has been suggested, with apparent plausibility, that the plaintiff here has suffered a loss, measured by the difference between the value of the service actually received and the value of secure transportation.[26] But again this is conceptually difficult.[27] The only way we can say she has suffered a loss is to characterise her non-receipt of what she was entitled to as a loss in and of itself:[28] but if we do that, then we again in effect collapse the distinction between wrong and loss, and make nonsense of the idea that there can be a wrong that causes no loss.

Claims for the loss of use of property provide a further conundrum.[29] A plaintiff wrongfully deprived of the use of a house, car or ship can obviously obtain the cost of hiring a replacement (if she does) or lost profits (if she cannot). But what if neither applies? If we ask whether there is still a loss here, there is simply no obvious answer. On the one hand we can argue that, just as the ownership of property has value, so also does its use. If so, then just as a plaintiff can recover the hypothetical sale value of a destroyed car even though she would not in fact have sold it (she might

---

not marginal costs of manufacturing them (which were negligible). And cf *AG v Shillibeer* (1849) 4 Exch 606, 154 ER 1356 and *Portman Building Society v Bevan Ashford* [2000] PNLR 344 (CA) [*Portman*] (time of in-house professionals recoverable as consequential damages when incurred as result of wrong).

[25] Particularly since in other cases courts have denied that expenditure of time, without more, is a loss: see, eg, *Pearson v Sanders Witherspoon* [2000] PNLR 110 (CA) [*Pearson*] (referred to below n 44).

[26] In *White Arrow Express Ltd v Lamey's Distribution Ltd* (1995) 15 *Trading Law* 69; (1995) Times, 21 July (CA), the English Court of Appeal regarded this as arguable, though the claim failed for lack of adequate particularisation. Compare the labour relations case of *National Coal Board v Galley* [1958] 1 WLR 16 (CA) (miner paid to work six days works five: damages of the value of one day's work). See too C Hawes, 'Damages for Defective Goods' (2005) 121 *LQR* 389.

[27] Compare the old (and notorious) Louisiana decision in *City of New Orleans v Firemen's Charitable Association* 9 So 486 (La SC 1891), robustly denying that there is any loss in this type of situation.

[28] As suggested in H Beale, 'Damages for Poor Service' (1996) 112 *LQR* 205.

[29] Other than those for actual costs of upkeep, etc, referred to above.

have intended to give it away or, like the late Keith Moon of The Who, drive it into a swimming pool and leave it there), she ought to recover the would-be use value of a disabled or detained chattel whether or not she would in fact have hired it out.[30] However, one can detect a whiff of unreality here: however logical the parallel with destroyed goods, it sounds odd to characterise as a 'loss' the inability to use what one could not, or would not, have profited from anyway. Not surprisingly, the jurisprudence has reflected this indeterminacy, and is best described as erratic. It is possible to find cases rejecting use claims entirely;[31] allowing them on a rough-and-ready basis on the unstated assumption that it seems perverse to allow the defendant to escape scot-free;[32] allowing them on the basis of some notional distress or inconvenience;[33] allowing them for depreciating assets but not others;[34] ducking the loss issue entirely by reclassifying them as claims for unjust enrichment;[35] and so on.

A variant on loss of use claims, raising similar difficulties, is a claim against a defendant who has gained some advantage from infringing some other right of the plaintiff without causing the latter any immediate harm. Typical are cases where he has trespassed on (or under) otherwise unproductive land to use it for mining, transport or storage,[36] built on his own land in breach of a restrictive covenant,[37] or broken an agreement to concede an exclusive right to publish a song.[38] Above-nominal awards

---

[30] The amount might be a reasonable hire charge, as in cases such as *Strand Electric Co Ltd v Brisford Entertainments Ltd* [1952] 2 QB 246 (CA) (see too the American decision in *KLM v United Technologies Corp* 610 F 2d 1052 (2nd Cir 1979) 1056. Or it might be some more exotic measure such as interest on the notional capital value: compare the shipping cases of *The Marpessa*, above n 6 and *The Chekiang* [1926] AC 637 (HL). Amortization is another possibility: *Nauru Local Gov't Council v NZ Seamen's Union* [1986] 1 NZLR 466 (HC) [*Nauru Local Gov't Council*].

[31] As in the decision of the US Supreme Court in *The Conqueror*, 166 US 110 (1897) (no damages for loss of opportunity to use pleasure yacht).

[32] Eg, *The Greta Holme* [1897] AC 596 (HL); see also *The Mediana* [1900] AC 113 (HL) (where, however, the measure of damages, if available at all, was agreed).

[33] As in cases allowing fairly arbitrary weekly sums for loss of use of a car: see Tettenborn *et al, Law of Damages* (London, Butterworths, 2003) § 14.83.

[34] *Bella Casa*, above n 5.

[35] See Lord Nicholls in *AG v Blake* [2001] 1 AC 268 (HL) 278 [*Blake*]. Similarly Morden JA in *Ronald Elwyn Lister Ltd v Dayton Tire Canada Ltd* (1985) 52 OR (2d) 88 (CA) regarded hire charge awards as not really compensatory at all. But this simply moves the problem elsewhere: if the defendant has not in fact gained financially from the goods, is not his supposed profit just as artificial as the plaintiff's alleged loss?

[36] Eg, *Martin v Porter* (1839) 5 M & W 351, 151 ER 149; *Whitwham v Westminster Brymbo Coal Co* [1896] 2 Ch 538 (CA); *Jaggard v Sawyer* [1995] 1 WLR 269 (CA); *Roberts v Rodney DC* [2001] 2 NZLR 402 (CA). Damages for mesne profits against an overstaying tenant are similar: *Ministry of Defence v Ashman* (1993) 66 P & CR 105 (CA).

[37] As in the well-known *Wrotham Park Estates Ltd v Parkside Homes Ltd* [1974] 1 WLR 798 (Ch). See too the similar Canadian decision in *Arbutus Park Estates Ltd v Fuller* [1977] 1 WWR 729 (BCSC).

[38] See, eg, *Experience Hendrix LLC v PPX Enterprises Ltd* [2003] 1 All ER (Comm) 830 (CA).

(normally based on a reasonable wayleave, royalty or buyout price) are commonplace here;[39] their legal basis more problematical. Although it can be argued that such awards have nothing to do with loss at all,[40] they can quite plausibly be regarded as compensatory: if the right to use property has a value, why not the right to exclude others from using it (or from using it in a particular way)?[41] Once again, it all depends on what one means by 'loss': is the effective nullification of the plaintiff's right enough, or must it manifest itself in the form of some further effect on her?

One more instance is worth mentioning here: that of what can be called 'management resource' claims. Suppose a wrong to the plaintiff means that well-paid executives employed by the plaintiff have to be redeployed to deal with its effects.[42] Suppose also that, whether because of superb corporate organisation, unusually efficient (or under-employed) management, or some other reason, the plaintiff cannot prove profits foregone. Does any claim lie, as it undoubtedly would have had the plaintiff paid to draft in temporary staff *ad hoc*? Once again, a logical case can be made either way. On one argument, this is really the same as rent and rates continuing payable on a house rendered uninhabitable, the only relevant difference being that the diverted resource is human and not material.[43] On the other hand, it could equally be argued that this is really just a clever attempt to create a loss where there is none in reality, and hence there should be no liability. Courts once again have split, English judges largely taking the latter view [44] (except, perhaps ironically, for in-house lawyers and similar professionals),[45] while American courts have been generally more plaintiff-friendly.[46]

---

[39] See the cases referred to above n 36.

[40] They have, for instance, been regarded as essentially unjust enrichment claims, on the basis that the defendant has profited from doing what he should not have done, but the plaintiff is not one cent worse off as a result. See particularly A Burrows, *The Law of Restitution*, 2nd edn (London, Butterworths, 2002) 471-72 and Lord Nicholls's comments in *Blake*, above n 35, at 283. Some American authority had earlier taken a similar view: eg, *Edwards v Lee's Administrator* 96 SW 2d 1028 (Ky CA 1936).

[41] See Tettenborn *et al*, above n 33, at § 2.77; J Edelman, *Gain-based damages: Contract, Tort, Equity and Intellectual Property* (Oxford, Hart, 2002) ch 3.

[42] For example, serious property damage or professional malpractice causing major business disruption.

[43] Ie, even if the management would have been paid anyway, they are now being paid to clear up the mess created by the defendant and not to do what the plaintiff really wanted them to do.

[44] See *Pearson*, above n 25, at 131-32; *Admiral Management Services Ltd v Para-Protect Europe Ltd* [2002] 1 WLR 2722 (HC) 2737; and *Standard Chartered Bank Ltd v Pakistan National Shipping Corporation (Assessment of Damages)* [2001] 1 All ER (Comm) 822 (CA).

[45] See, eg, *Henderson v Merthyr Tydfil UDC* [1900] 1 QB 434 (DC); *Portman*, above n 24. Indeed, it seems the lawyer himself can sue if he or she is the plaintiff: *Stockler v Fourways Estates Ltd* (unreported, QB, 31 July 1985).

[46] See, eg, *Convoy Co v Sperry-Rand Corp* 672 F 2d 781 (9th Cir 1982) 785 (issue is 'not whether Convoy would have paid the supervisors' salaries if the defendant had not breached

B.   Loss and its Impact on the Plaintiff

The previous section dealt with one possible meaning of a defendant's plea of 'no loss': namely, that no-one has suffered anything that qualifies as a loss at all. But now suppose a variation: the defendant admits a loss (for example, damage to property or depreciation of some asset), but pleads instead *that it did not impact on the plaintiff.* Imagine, for example, that the plaintiff's car is tortiously damaged and off the road for a month: however, her father picks up the repair bill, and she herself borrows a friend's car while her own is being repaired. Again, suppose her surveyor's negligence causes her to buy a lease on an apartment with serious defects, but these problems are then corrected by the lessor under the terms of the lease at no charge to her:[47] or that a defendant damages property belonging to her, whereupon she has it repaired on credit but then goes bankrupt, with the result that the repairs will never have to be paid for.[48] And, of course, the so-called collateral source rule in personal injury embodies the same issue. A plaintiff is disabled from working, but receives a pension or surrogate pay from some source or other:[49] or her injuries necessitate her being cared for, but such care is provided by a third party,[50] or by the defendant himself,[51] and so on.

Is there a loss here? Most lawyers instinctively say the answer is 'No'. To them, as to an accountant, it is self-evident that 'loss' means net loss: the plaintiff cannot, so to speak, take the plums but leave the duff. Thus if damages are awarded which discount matters mitigating the effect of the wrong on the plaintiff, this can only be by way of anomaly or exception—a proposition frequently expressed in judicial statements, especially in commercial contexts.[52] Unfortunately, real life is rather less straightforward, and the argument is by no means all one way.

---

the contract, but whether the breach deprived Convoy of the services it paid for'). See too *Dunn Appraisal Co v Honeywell Information Systems Inc* 687 F 2d 877 (6th Cir 1982). Canadian courts predominantly seem to accept this view: eg, *Lay's Transport Ltd v Meadow Lake Consumer's Co-operative Assn Ltd* (1982) 20 Sask R 8 (QB), *Yukon Helicopters Ltd v Zoochkan* (1994) 96 Man R (2d) 306 (QB).

[47]   As in *Gardner v Marsh & Parsons* [1997] 1 WLR 489 (CA).

[48]   As in the old Admiralty case of *The Endeavour* (1890) 6 Asp MLC 511 (CA) [*The Endeavour*].

[49]   Ie, the rule encapsulated in *Parry v Cleaver* [1970] AC 1 (HL).

[50]   As in *Cunningham v Harrison* [1973] QB 942 (CA).

[51]   See *Hunt v Severs* [1994] 2 AC 350 (HL) [*Hunt*].

[52]   As Lord Haldane stated in *British Westinghouse Electric & Manufacturing Co Ltd v Underground Electric Railways Co Ltd* [1912] AC 673 (HL) 681: 'I think the principle which applies here is that which makes it right for the jury or arbitrator to look at what actually happened, and to balance loss and gain'. [*British Westinghouse*]. See too *British Transport Commission v Gourley* [1956] AC 185 (HL) 202-03 (Earl Jowitt), 213 (Lord Reid); *Hodgson v Trapp* [1989] 1 AC 807 (HL) 819 (Lord Bridge); *Hunt*, above n 51, at 357 (Lord Bridge); *Dimond v Lovell* [2002] 1 AC 384 (HL) 399 (Lord Hoffmann) [*Dimond*].

To begin with, if we accept that loss does not necessarily mean financial impoverishment, then the argument from net loss loses much of its force: we can no longer regard it as a logical necessity that damages must be reduced merely because the financial effects on the plaintiff have been reduced, or even eliminated. Furthermore, it is in any case not self-evident that, when we talk about a plaintiff suffering loss, the phrase 'suffering loss' must be synonymous with 'feeling the ultimate effect of a wrong'. There may be good reasons in some cases for saying that it is, especially in a business context: after all most businesses, by their nature, are simply concerned with the bottom line at the year end. But there is nothing logically incoherent in separating a loss from its effects. A plaintiff, it is suggested, can quite plausibly say, 'I have suffered a loss, but its effects on me have been mitigated by some other factor.'[53] Yet again, there is the point summed up in the venerable phrase *res inter alios acta*. In so far as some transaction between the plaintiff and a third party—an insurance arrangement, charitable gift, third party recovery, or whatever—reduces the impact of the wrong on her personally, it is an instinctively plausible argument that this is no business of the defendant.[54] It does not alter the fact that he has damnified the plaintiff, and should not necessarily go to negative his duty to compensate her.

In short, here too the definition of loss is disconcertingly indeterminate: and, once again, the authorities show it. In many commercial and similar situations, the orthodox view prevails almost without question: loss means net or ultimate loss, and where something happens to reduce or eliminate the effect of the wrong on the plaintiff, her recovery is docked accordingly.[55] So if a seller fails to provide promised machinery to an industrialist and the latter purchases something more profitable, the extra profit reduces any damages[56] Likewise, if an adviser's negligence lands a buyer with a house that is saddled with a mortgage, or is apparently subject to landslip, then a later release of the mortgage, or lessening of the danger of collapse, once again reduces recovery.[57] Again, suppose a plaintiff's car is damaged and off the road and she hires another one on credit: if for some reason the credit agreement is unenforceable against her, she recovers

---

[53] Cf Perry, above n 10, at 1304 arguing that the idea of 'harm' does not necessarily involve a netting-out of all detriments and benefits.

[54] Eg, *Burdis v Livsey* [2003] QB 36 (CA) [91] (Aldous LJ); *Hamilton-Jones*, above n 15, at 943 (Neuberger J).

[55] Statements are legion: besides *British Westinghouse*, above n 52, see *Maredelanto Cia Naviera SA v Bergbau-Handel GmbH* (*The Mihalis Angelos*) [1971] 1 QB 164 (CA) 195 (Lord Denning MR); *Kennedy v van Emden* [1996] PNLR 409 (CA) 414 (Nourse LJ: compensation makes good 'real, not hypothetical, loss').

[56] *British Westinghouse*, above n 52.

[57] See *Gregory v Shepherds* [2000] PNLR 769 (CA) and *McKinnon v e surv Ltd* [2003] Lloyd's Rep PN 174 (HC).

nothing for loss of use on the basis that she has suffered nothing.[58] Yet again, if a plaintiff is misled into buying a moribund business, recovery is reduced by any tax advantage thus gained.[59] And so on and so forth. But, on the other hand, there are major exceptions. For example, where goods are damaged or destroyed, the owner is considered as suffering a loss even though not she but someone else actually stands to lose, for example because the goods are at the risk of a buyer who has agreed to, and does, pay the full price.[60] Again, if a defendant's wrong damages a building, but by the time the damage becomes apparent the building has been sold by the plaintiff to someone else for full value, it seems the plaintiff can recover the costs of repair even though she will not have to incur them: the loss is, as it were, crystallised by the damage itself.[61] Yet again, a plaintiff (or rather her trustee in bankruptcy) can apparently sue for the costs incurred in repairing damaged property even if because of the bankruptcy those costs will never in fact be paid.[62] Furthermore, events which are relatively remote from the defendant's wrong can also be disregarded,[63] as are events that can reasonably be said to result from the plaintiff's own exertions or business decisions.[64] And finally, apart from these cases there is always the collateral source rule and its ramifications; the disregard of insurance and benevolent payments, etc.

C. The Wrong Directly Impacts on Someone other than the Plaintiff

A variant on the 'no impact on the plaintiff' argument can also arise in a slightly different situation. This is where (as above) the plaintiff herself does not feel the effect of the defendant's wrong, but the reason for this is that, under some pre-existing relationship, she is in effect standing in for someone else who does. It is certainly possible to find statements that, as logic would suggest, the plaintiff has suffered no loss and hence recovers no damages.[65] Nevertheless, in a number of situations it is regarded as

---

[58] *Dimond*, above n 52.

[59] *Levison v Farin* [1978] 2 All ER 1129 (QB).

[60] *The Charlotte* [1908] P 206 (CA).

[61] See *St Martins Property Corporation v Sir Robert McAlpine Ltd* [1994] 1 AC 85 (HL) and *Alfred McAlpine Ltd v Panatown Ltd* [2001] 1 AC 518 (HL) [*Alfred McAlpine*]. In the former case this was put as an exception to the principle that a plaintiff could recover only if she had suffered loss: but Lord Griffiths there thought that the seller would have suffered a loss within the meaning of the law. In the latter case it seems that Lord Griffiths's view was largely accepted.

[62] *The Endeavour*, above n 48.

[63] Eg, *Hussey v Eels* [1990] 2 QB 227 (CA).

[64] Eg, *Jewelowski v Propp* [1944] KB 510 (KB); *Great Future International Ltd v Sealand Housing Corporation* [2002] All ER (D) 28 (Ch).

[65] Eg, *Albacruz (Cargo Owners) v Albazero (Owners) (The Albazero)* [1977] AC 774 (HL) 845 ('the general rule of English law that a party to a contract apart from nominal

possible to separate loss from consequences, and to ignore the lack of effect on the plaintiff herself. Assume, for example, that the plaintiff contracts to buy goods as an agent, but that the contract provides that she, as well as the principal, can sue under it. If the seller fails to deliver, it seems that she can not only sue but recover substantial damages: the fact that the real loss is borne by the principal is disregarded.[66] A similar situation is where a defendant's wrong causes loss to a trust, or to those who stand to benefit from a deceased's estate. A simple example is where the value of the trust estate is diminished as a result of some legal malpractice or other wrong. Here too a similar analysis applies: the trustee or executrix can in general[67] recover substantial damages despite the fact that she personally is no worse off.[68] Yet again, at least to some extent a bailee is permitted to sue for damages for loss or damage to goods entrusted to her even though she is not out-of-pocket at all.[69]

A related situation is where there is some other, less formal, pre-existing relation between the plaintiff and some third party which has the effect of insulating the plaintiff from the risk of loss. For example, suppose a bank lends against security which has been negligently overvalued. Suppose further, however, that in fact the loan is syndicated, so that whereas the bank is technically the lender it is entitled to be indemnified for most of its loss by the other participants; or, alternatively, that all the funds are actually provided, and the entire risk taken, not by the bank but by its holding company. In both these cases the bank is, it seems, entitled to recover in full though itself none the poorer.[70]

---

damages, can only recover for its breach such actual loss as he has himself sustained' (Lord Diplock); *Woodar Investment Development Ltd v Wimpey Construction (UK) Ltd* [1980] 1 WLR 277 (HL) 283 (Lord Wilberforce).

[66] There is very little authority in England: but see *Joseph v Knox* (1813) 3 Camp 320, 170 ER 1397, and see the undisclosed agency case of *Allen v O'Hearn* [1937] AC 213 (PC) 218 (though these are doubted in W Bowstead and F Reynolds, *Agency*, 17th edn (London, Sweet & Maxwell, 2001) § 9-010). The Restatement allows substantial recovery here: see *Restatement (Second) of the Law of Agency* (1958) § 364 cmt k.

[67] Though not always: *Welburn v Dibb Lupton Broomhead* [2003] PNLR 28 (CA) (debtor, trustee for creditors under insolvency arrangement of right of action, cannot recover substantial damages).

[68] See *Chappell v Somers & Blake* [2004] 3 WLR 1233 (Ch) (malpractice) [*Chappell*]; *Malkins Nominees Ltd v Société Financière Mirelis SA* [2004] All ER (D) 336 (Ch) (conversion).

[69] See, eg, *Hepburn v Tomlinson (Hauliers) Ltd* [1966] AC 451 (HL).

[70] See *Interallianz Finance AG v Independent Insurance Co Ltd* (unreported, QB, 18 December 1997) (syndication); *Legal & General Mortgage Services Ltd v Underwoods* [1997] PNLR 567 (QB) (money from holding company).

III.   THE LOGIC OF LOSS

So far this chapter has been more concerned with questions than with answers. I have argued that there is only one situation where the concept of 'loss' is relatively uncontroversial: namely where the plaintiff (a) is clearly worse off in her own right in money or money's worth as a result of the defendant's wrong, and (b) has not had that shortfall reduced or made good as a result of some other event. Outside these cases, the idea of 'loss' is pretty indeterminate. There is no coherent or watertight way to define it: and the courts' decisions reflect this fact. They vary in no particularly logical way between taking an overall balance sheet or asset view, and defining loss in a more abstract way.

Where do we go from here?

One possible solution is to abandon the attempt to make sense of the notion of 'loss', and to accept that the question 'has the plaintiff suffered a loss?' actually hides a determination made on other grounds. This idea has a certain plausibility, at least in some areas. One such is the collateral source rule, disregarding such matters as insurance recoveries or charitable or benevolent gifts. Although some of the older cases regarded the question of what benefits fell to be disregarded as a doctrinal matter of analysis of damages law, invoking such ideas as *res inter alios acta*,[71] close connection or remoteness,[72] this approach is largely discredited today. The modern tendency when discussing disregards of this sort is overwhelmingly to talk in terms of public policy and social desirability.[73] Similarly, in a number of cases where substantial recovery has been allowed despite the lack of any measurable effect on the plaintiff's wealth, one suspects that the result has been reached with one eye on producing a just and convenient result. For instance, in the case of trustees and personal representatives it is pretty clear that the courts were troubled by the anomaly of the defendant otherwise escaping scot-free, and that they in effect accepted the necessity of creating a *de facto* right of action for the benefit of the trust beneficiaries or heirs.[74] In similar vein, given the strict economic loss rule denying a cause of action for damage to property in anyone other than the owner of that property,[75] it is not surprising that the courts allowed the owner to sue without enquiring too closely where the real loss lay. The

---

[71]   Eg, *Shearman v Folland* [1950] 2 KB 43 (CA) 45.

[72]   See, eg, *Bradburn v Gt Western Ry Co* (1874) LR 10 Ex 1 and *Redpath v Belfast & Co Down Ry Co* [1947] NI 167 (KB) where the collateral sources disregard of insurance payments and private charity was put partly on this basis.

[73]   See, eg, *Hunt*, above n 51, at 358 (Lord Bridge); *Dimond*, above n 52, at 399 (Lord Hoffmann).

[74]   See above n 62.

[75]   Epitomised in the *Leigh and Suillivan Ltd v Aliakmon Shipping Co Ltd (The Aliakmon)* [1986] AC 785 (HL) and the Privy Council (originally Australian) decision in *Candlewood Navigation Corporation Ltd v Mitsui OSK Lines Ltd (The Mineral Transporter)* [1986] AC 1

same goes for damage to buildings subsequently sold: it is pretty clear that the buyer could not sue, and hence if the person who owned the building at the time of the damage could not recover, then the defendant's liability would have disappeared into a kind of 'legal black hole'.[76] Elsewhere, for example in cases such as *Ruxley v Forsyth*,[77] the case of the slightly-too-shallow swimming pool, there is clear evidence that the courts simply thought that there should be some sort of compensation for a plaintiff deprived of her entitlement even in the absence of anything separate that might, on an orthodox entitlement, be regarded as a 'loss'.[78]

A second possibility is to retain the idea of 'loss', but to abandon any attempt closely to define the concept. Instead one should return to the general principle that damages exist, in so far as money can do it, to return a plaintiff as near as possible to her unwronged position, and leave it up to the judge in a particular case to take a broad view as to what award will do this.

On the other hand, solutions such as these are somewhat unsatisfying. It is true that in some situations, like the collateral source rule in personal injury law, may indeed be based on fairly naked considerations of policy rather than any sophisticated idea of what 'loss' means. But in many cases the issue of whether the plaintiff has actually been prejudiced, or lost something, as a result of a wrong done to her does seem the logically prior one: in other words, our feeling as to whether there ought to be substantial damages depends on whether we think the plaintiff is in some way worse off, and not vice versa. For example, compare two cases concerned with deprivation of property. One is *Brandeis Goldschmidt Ltd v Western Transport Ltd*,[79] where the defendant temporarily but wrongfully detained a quantity of raw copper belonging to the plaintiff; the other, already mentioned, is *Birmingham Corpn v Sowsbery*,[80] where a damaged city bus was replaced by a spare vehicle kept by the plaintiffs. In the first case, this being a commodity where possession as such was of no value (indeed, the plaintiff was saved the trouble of storing it), the Court of Appeal not surprisingly said he had nothing to complain of and declined anything more than a nominal award. However, in the second case Geoffrey Lane J

(PC). Canadian courts are slightly less ferocious in this respect (eg, *CNR v Norsk Pacific SN Co* [1992] 1 SCR 1021) but still largely, together with American courts, follow the economic loss rule in this respect.

[76] A term coined by Lord Stewart in the Scottish case of *GUS Property Management Ltd v Littlewoods Mail Order Stores Ltd*, 1982 SC(HL) 157, 166: see too *Alfred McAlpine*, above n 61, at 528, 548 (Lords Clyde and Goff).

[77] Above n 21.

[78] As stated by Lord Mustill, *Ruxley*, above, at 360: 'The law must cater for those occasions where the value of the promise to the promisee exceeds the financial enhancement of his position which full performance will secure'.

[79] [1981] QB 864 (CA) [*Brandeis*].

[80] Above n 6, 84.

equally predictably gave substantial damages, and declined to accept the defendant's plea that the plaintiff had suffered no loss since no marginal costs had been incurred. In situations such as these, the issue cannot be sidestepped or reduced to one of judicial impressionism: and in the cases concerned it was rightly regarded as turning on whether the plaintiff had suffered anything that could be called a 'loss' or 'prejudice' as a result of the defendant's wrong.

IV.   A NEW APPROACH TO THE PROBLEM OF LOSS

Thus far we have looked at possible ways of defining loss for the purposes of damages law, and pointed out that finding a workable description is, to say the least, remarkably difficult. Why should this be? The answer, it is suggested, is that by looking for an acceptable definition of the idea of 'loss' *in abstracto* we have been approaching the problem from the wrong end. In particular, we have been assuming that 'loss' is an objectively observable juridical phenomenon like, say, breach of contract. Breach of contract is a black-and-white concept. A defendant has either broken his contract or he has not. Given the facts, plus an adequate idea of the parties' obligations and any relevant rules of law, we can on principle always tell whether or not a breach has occurred. Now, in attempting to define 'loss', we have been tacitly assuming that it works in the same way: a wronged plaintiff either has suffered it or she has not, and to decide whether she has all we need is an effective definition to enable us to recognise it when we see it. But it is submitted that this assumption is wrong. The idea of 'loss', unlike breach of contract, is essentially indeterminate: it contains large normative and evaluative elements as well as factual ones. If we need an analogy, it is suggested that a more apposite one is with a concept such as causation rather than with breach of contract. In that context we have long since given up arguing, bluntly if speciously, that the defendant's wrong either did or did not cause the plaintiff's injuries, and that to answer this question all we have to do is unearth an effective definition of causation. Instead, we recognise that there are some straight-forward cases where causation (or the lack of it) is clear; but that, as soon as we get beyond these trivial cases, the question of whether a given wrong caused a given harm cannot be answered in stark 'yes / no' terms.[81] A wrongdoer disables a plaintiff's leg: a later accident means the same leg has to be amputated. A defendant negligently leaves a can of rat-poison on a ledge where children can reach it: heat from a stove causes the can to explode and burn a passing child. For the purposes of the law, is the loss of

---

[81]   The literature is vast: but the process is usefully summarised in R Wright, 'Causation in Tort Law' 73 *California Law Review* (1985) 1735, 1738.

use of the leg after the second accident, or the injury to the child, 'caused' by the tortfeasor's fault? The answer can only be 'It depends on how you look at it: in one sense there is causation, but in another there is not.'[82] Exactly the same reasoning, it is suggested, applies to the idea of 'loss'. Of course there are the easy cases, for example where there is an obvious financial impoverishment flowing directly from the wrong. But faced with the more awkward problem of a tort victim with an undepleted pocket-book and unchanged balance-sheet, or a plaintiff whose prejudice is offset by subsequent events or underwritten by some third party. The answer to the question 'has she suffered a loss?' can equally only be 'in one sense, yes, but in another, no'.

How, then, should we approach the issue of 'loss'? The key to the problem, it is suggested, is that, just as causation questions effectively reduce to issues, not of fact, but of attribution—when it makes sense to attribute the plaintiff's damage to the defendant's wrong or to some other event or state of affairs—questions of 'loss' really boil down to issues of valuation. Given that some legally-protected interest of the plaintiff has been infringed or nullified by the defendant's wrong, what (if anything) is the proper money value for the court to put on the interest concerned for compensation purposes?[83] Now, if this analysis is right, the issue of 'loss or no loss' becomes subtly reformulated. The real question is now whether the valuation of the interest infringed is, in the circumstances, positive or nil. If positive there is a loss: if nil, there is not.

In referring to 'valuation' in this context, a preliminary point is in order. It should be pointed out that the word 'valuation' is being used here in a slightly specialised context. It is not simply a matter of putting a notional value on the plaintiff's right immediately before infringement. Admittedly the exercise is sometimes limited to this: thus in a simple case of conversion or destruction of a commercial chattel, the value of the chattel in the plaintiff's hands immediately before the wrong is likely to be the relevant figure for any damage computation; and again, in a loss of use claim it may be permissible to take some notional value of the abstract right to

---

[82] Straightforward descriptions of this reasoning can be found in J Stapleton, 'Legal cause: Cause-in-Fact and the Scope of Liability for Consequences' (2001) 54 *Vanderbilt Law Review* 941 and J Stapleton, 'Cause-in-Fact and the Scope of Liability for Consequences' (2003) 119 *LQR* 388.

[83] The author himself touched on the same point in an earlier article: see A Tettenborn, 'Non-Pecuniary Loss: the Right Answer but Bad Reasoning?' (2003) 2 *Journal of Obligations & Remedies* 94. See too Bell's comment: 'Tort compensation, unlike insurance payouts, represents society's valuation of the plaintiff's loss'. (P Bell, 'Analyzing tort law: the flawed promise of neocontract' (1990) 74 *Minnesota Law Review* 1177, 1236), and also the argument in J Goldberg, 'Harm, Injury, and Proximate Cause' (2003) 40 *San Diego Law Review* 1315, 1330-32.

possession and use, and award damages on that basis.[84] But on principle, the exercise is a wider one; namely, valuing the interest infringed from the point of view of the plaintiff, and with regard to the particular consequences of its infringement as regards her, such as consequential injury or expense.[85] Thus the 'valuation' of a broken leg will depend on how serious, painful, etc, the resulting fracture is, together with the amount of any lost earnings or other expenses caused by the injury. Again, in many commercial cases the valuation of the interest involved—the right not to be deceived or misadvised on commercial matters, to have a contract kept, or whatever—is likely to be the amount of any money or similar losses.

With this point out of the way, we can now turn to defending this valuation approach. Although at first sight it may seem a somewhat counter-intuitive way of approaching the problem of 'loss', on closer inspection it has a number of distinct attractions, together with the ability to explain a number of phenomena that otherwise cause difficulty.

Its first advantage is that it neatly encapsulates an important point about the nature of damage awards. The traditional formulation of the damages rule—that the right to recover damages for a wrong is the right to be compensated for the losses suffered as a result of that wrong—on a closer look turns out to be a deceptive oversimplification.[86] The overwhelming majority of torts and other wrongs involve the infringement of non-cash interests. This is obvious in the case of personal injury, or torts to dignitary or emotional interests. In these situations, the plaintiff complains that she has been deprived of a sound leg, or bodily integrity, or unsmirched reputation, and in giving damages the law is simply doing the best it can to put a cash value on the infringed interest.[87] But exactly the same reasoning applies to other kinds of wrong. A plaintiff, for instance, is wrongfully denied the use of her house or car; or for that matter a cargo of soya beans belonging to her is negligently destroyed. Her actual complaint—the ground on which she claims damages—is not that she has suffered some financial loss, but that she does not have a house to live in, a car to drive,

---

[84] Such as a standard rate of interest on capital tied up in the chattel (eg, *The Marpessa*, above n 6) or a figure for capital amortisation (eg, *Nauru Local Government Council*, above n 30).

[85] To put the matter more precisely, the legally protected interest of the plaintiff which falls to be valued may include not only her interest in not suffering the wrong, but also her interest in not being consequentially harmed by it.

[86] Compare the acute observation in Perry, above n 10, at 1311: the idea that damages exist to put the plaintiff back in her non-wronged position only 'states a first approximation of such an understanding, for there are exceptions'.

[87] On which there is a largish literature. See, eg, Sunstein, above n 11; R Epstein, 'Are Values Incommensurable, or is Utility the Ruler of the World?' (1995) *Utah Law Review* 683; M Geistfeld, 'Putting a Price on Pain and Suffering' (1995) 83 *California Law Review* 773.

or any soya beans.[88] Of course, in very large numbers of such cases the prejudice suffered by the plaintiff will in fact be a straightforward financial loss—lost earnings or profits, the costs of renting another house or buying some more soya beans, and so on. But these 'losses' are relevant, not to the legal harm she is suing for, but to the valuation of it and its proper and just translation into the language of damages—ie money.[89]

Second, a valuation analysis conveniently explains why the pocketbook deficiency of $1,000, or its equivalent,[90] is a special (and easy) case. The point is not so much that the $1,000 demonstrates that the plaintiff has suffered a loss—we have seen that this can mean anything or nothing—but rather that it provides a conclusive way of valuing the interest the plaintiff has been wrongfully deprived of. The intrinsic value to the plaintiff of having a contract kept, or of her property not being trespassed on, is to say the least uncertain: but once she proves a resulting loss of $1,000 the problem, to that extent, goes away. The $1,000 loss, as it were, cements an otherwise indeterminate figure. Conversely, the absence of a cash deficiency is significant, not so much because it shows that the plaintiff has somehow failed to demonstrate a loss, as because the valuation of the relevant interest is now going to be much more difficult. A proper figure may actually be zero (imagine a plaintiff who can show nothing except the unavailability to her of a car she never drove anyway):[91] or it may be substantial (as in the case of a trespass involving a gross invasion of privacy,[92] or a bus company claiming the maintenance and depreciation on a spare bus while another is incapacitated).[93] But whatever it is, its reckoning is unlikely to be as straightforward.

Third, if we take the approach advocated here we find we can explain a number of distinctions that are puzzling when viewed against the background of a simple 'loss—no loss' theory. For example, take loss of use claims where there are no actual financial costs (such as the expenses of hiring a substitute). As pointed out above, trying to pinpoint just what counts as a loss can be particularly frustrating here: on the other hand, a valuation viewpoint can make many of the difficulties disappear. Where a

---

[88] While this proposition is almost universally true, there are occasional exceptions to it. For example, where a defendant steals $100 in cash from the plaintiff or wrongfully causes her bank balance to be depleted by $1,000, the prejudice is directly to a cash interest. But these are relatively untypical foundations for litigation, and do not affect the point in the text.

[89] Cf *Perry*, above n 10, at 1311, dealing with the problem of the house tortiously destroyed moments before it would have been incinerated from natural causes: a limitation on the plaintiff's right to recover full value reflects no conceptual necessity, but is simply 'a reasonable view of what justice requires between the parties to say that [the defendant] does not have to pay for the house'.

[90] See text accompanying nn 3-6.

[91] Cf *Alexander v Rolls-Royce Motor Cars Ltd* [1996] RTR 95 (CA).

[92] As in *Jolliffe v Willmett & Co* [1971] 1 All ER 478 (QB).

[93] See above n 5.

commercial plaintiff (or a non-profit or public corporation) is deprived of the use of a chattel used in its operations but cannot show a direct marginal balance-sheet effect,[94] what matters is not so much some abstract determination that there is a 'loss', but that a valuation of the interest infringed in terms of use value, depreciation or interest on capital, together with any wasted maintenance expenses, is simply more convincing than any other in a business context. Now contrast the situation where a plaintiff's complaint is merely that she has been temporarily deprived of some item of stock, which she had no immediate intention to use and which if anything would have cost her money to store. Here it is difficult to justify anything other than a nil valuation (and award).[95] And it is not difficult to think of other examples where similar reasoning is appropriate—for instance, a claim by a corporation for the temporary deprivation of some item of non-commercial property (such as a picture decorating the CEO's office).

Indeed, this analysis may well help to throw light on further possible distinctions. For instance, it may well be right to treat commercial or organisational plaintiffs in a different way from others in this context, on the basis that the valuation of the use of their assets ought to vary according to the use to which they are put. Hence where an individual is deprived of the use of a car, or a picture, there is much to be said for the practice of making at least a modest award in respect of that deprivation:[96] again, not because of some factitious 'loss' or 'distress', but because the aesthetic or other advantage to be gained must be able to be valued at something more than nil, however difficult or imprecise the valuation may be.[97]

Fourth, the interest-valuing approach also conveniently makes sense of the related issue of what can be called 'exclusivity' cases:[98] that is, cases involving the plaintiff's right to exclude others from using her assets or to prevent certain uses of the defendant's own property. Examples include situations where the defendant trespasses on the plaintiff's land, or infringes a restrictive covenant affecting his own, but does so without apparently damnifying the defendant. The possibility of award of substantial damages in such cases is well-accepted. But, as observed above, explaining the basis of such damages, or what loss they are meant to

---

[94]   See the cases discussed in nn 29-35, above.

[95]   Cf *Brandeis*, above n 79.

[96]   As is the practice in England, where a glance at the annual volumes of *Current Law* reveals numerous cases of awards of between £50 and £100 per week, over and above any proved loss, to those deprived of the use of a car.

[97]   But again, this must be open to qualification. For instance, if the property was not actually used by the plaintiff —a picture in store, for example, or a little-used spare car—then that lack of use could well dictate a nil valuation and hence nominal or no damages.

[98]   See text accompanying n 41.

represent, is awkward. Attempting to analyse these awards as based on unjust enrichment is also problematical, since if they are it is difficult to see why the defendant is not liable for the whole profit actually made, rather than (as is the general rule) a reasonable rent, wayleave or buyout price.[99] However, once abandon the idea of 'loss' as the touchstone for damages, and the matter neatly falls into place. The plaintiff's right to exclude the defendant from using her property (or his own, in the case of the restrictive covenant) has been wrongfully set at nought: the question therefore is simply one of putting a value on that right. And the obvious answer for valuation purposes (indeed, arguably the only plausible one) is the amount for which that right could have been disposed of in the market—ie the reasonable rent, or whatever. In fact the analysis becomes similar to that obtaining in the case of straightforward theft or destruction of a physical asset: the plaintiff is entitled to the value of the interest destroyed (ie the value of the goods), without the need to argue what further effects there may have been on her.

Fifth, there are the cases where the plaintiff is suing in what is in effect a representative capacity.[100] As has been pointed out earlier, these are particularly difficult: for while the desirability of allowing the plaintiff to sue is clear, this is extremely difficult to defend on principle if damages are necessarily linked to some concept of 'loss'. To say the trustee-plaintiff has suffered a loss in the same way as a plaintiff who is absolute owner is palpably untrue; and to say that she is deemed to have suffered a loss is simply question-begging.[101] But a looser idea of valuation can easily take this kind of situation in its stride. The plaintiff has suffered an infringement of her own rights, for example her right not to have some chattel she (legally) owns damaged, or her right as trustee to have professional services performed properly. In these circumstances, it is suggested, there is nothing illogical in valuing that right as it stands, without reference to her relationship with the beneficiaries (who will of course have the right to any recovery she may make). And a similar argument can apply to the bailee complaining of loss or damage to chattels. Although it would be possible (and not logically incoherent) to limit the bailee to the value of her interest, there is equally nothing illogical in allowing the bailee to disregard the bailment and value her interest, as it were, at face value.

---

[99] See Edelman, above n 41, at ch 3; Tettenborn *et al*, above n 33, at § 2.77. There is also the further problem that any gain made by the defendant may also be just as difficult to quantify in a financial sense as any loss suffered by the plaintiff.

[100] See text accompanying n 62, above.

[101] Thus it is noteworthy that in *Chappell*, above n 68, where just this point arose, Neuberger J rather skated over the question of loss, fastening instead on the claimant's title to sue and the undesirability of allowing the defendants (there, negligent solicitors) to escape scot-free.

Sixth, it is suggested that the theory advanced here may be able to make better sense of at least some of the rules about when matters going to reduce loss are, and are not, in account. This is important, since if one takes the view that the victim of a wrong is entitled to recover some uniquely definable form of loss, then loss *must* mean net loss. If the prejudice the plaintiff wants to be compensated for is cash loss, by parity of reasoning cash gain (or other matters going to reduce the cash loss) must be in account to reduce the plaintiff's recovery. If the essence of the plaintiff's complaint is the wrongful destruction of a chattel, the provision of a replacement from whatever source—commercial, insurance-based or charitable—must be credited: and so on. There is no logical room for the collateral source rule or any other disregard—such disregards can only be defended (if at all) as anomalous or policy-based exceptions.[102] On the other hand, this problem largely disappears if we adopt the idea of valuation suggested here. To begin with, the valuation process is itself flexible: while it is consistent with a 'net loss' rule, it is equally reconcilable with one or more disregards or other adjustments. Thus if an insured car is destroyed, or a person is injured and loses income but receives a pension or insurance payout, then whatever the situation as regards 'loss', there is nothing illogical about saying that the value of the plaintiff's interest interfered with was the market worth of the car or her ability to earn, and that the insurance receipt is irrelevant.

More importantly, this approach not only accommodates disregards, but also may have something to say about when gains may, or ought not to, be taken into account. In the case mentioned above of destruction of a chattel, where generally speaking the collateral source rule applies, it can be argued that the nub of the plaintiff's complaint is that she has been deprived of the chattel in question: again, it can equally be argued that the plaintiff disabled from working is really complaining about the loss of earning *capacity*.[103] Now, the chattel, or the loss of earning capacity, is capable of being valued on its own: it is therefore entirely plausible simply to take that value as the measure of recovery available for its deprivation, unless it is felt that there are strong policy reasons to the contrary. On the other hand, there are other cases, notably claims by purely commercial plaintiffs, where this is a good deal less plausible, even on a valuation theory. Take, for example, the situation in the *British Westinghouse* case:[104] a defendant in breach of contract fails to deliver a profit-earning machine, whereupon the

---

[102]   See D Fellman, 'Note: Unreason in the Law of Damages: the Collateral Source Rule' (1964) 77 *Harvard Law Review* 741; and generally J Fleming, 'The Collateral Source Rule and Loss Allocation in Tort Law' (1966) 54 *California Law Review* 1478.

[103]   Cf H Street, *Principles of the Law of Damages*, (London, Sweet & Maxwell, 1962) 44–55; H Luntz, *Assessment of Damages for Personal Injury and Death*, 4th edn (Sydney, Butterworths, 2002) ch 5, suggesting use of this terminology.

[104]   *British Westinghouse*, above n 52.

(commercial) plaintiff purchases a replacement which in the event is cheaper to run and thus more profitable. Here the plaintiff's right to delivery is best regarded as not being a right to a machine *tout simple*, but rather to a machine *for use in her business*. If so, then it is suggested that her right is most plausibly valued by reference to its impact on the (cash) profitability of that business. If this is right, then there is every reason to take an overall figure and thus deduct the increased profitability of the replacement. Again, similar reasoning applies to many other commercial cases, such as those involving professional malpractice. For example, imagine that as a result of a lawyer's negligence the plaintiff buys a house encumbered with a mortgage, but the mortgage is later discharged without cost to her:[105] or that auditors' negligence causes a bank to continue to employ a dishonest trader who causes it grievous loss, but not before that trader has in other transactions added considerably to the bank's profits.[106] Here the interest infringed is best regarded as the right to receive competent advice for the purpose of protecting the plaintiff's financial interests. If this is so, by parity of reasoning, the valuation to be placed on that interest should be the overall impact, taking gains as well as losses into account.

Seventh, and perhaps most interestingly, a valuation approach may be able to make easier some vexed issues relating to non-pecuniary losses. Generally speaking, on the traditional view there are two difficulties with non-pecuniary claims: when they ought to lie, and (as pointed out above)[107] just what 'loss' they purport to compensate. In fact, both problems largely vanish if we abandon the idea that there is some discrete kind of 'loss' called 'mental suffering', 'distress' or similar which the plaintiff is seeking to recover. Instead, on the valuation approach the exercise is one of looking to the interest which the plaintiff complains has been infringed, and then seeking the proper way of valuing it.[108] In so far as that interest is an essentially commercial one, then it is suggested that, in valuing it, there is no reason to take into account anything other than commercial factors, or any reason to give damages over and above the commercial valuation concerned[109]—businessmen are in business for money, and money alone. But if there is something more than a commercial interest involved—something personal or aesthetic—then there is no reason why this should not form part of the valuation exercise. We have already observed that this is a highly plausible justification for awards such

---

[105] See *Gregory v Shepherds*, above n 57.

[106] As in *Barings Plc (In Liquidation) v Coopers & Lybrand (Issues Re Liability)* [2003] PNLR 34 (HC).

[107] See text accompanying nn 18-20.

[108] As the author has argued elsewhere: see Tettenborn, above n 83.

[109] As English law pretty consistently does: eg, *Hayes v James & Charles Dodd* [1990] 2 All ER 815 (CA) and *Johnson v Gore Wood & Co* [2002] 2 AC 1 (HL).

as those made to individuals for loss of the use of something like a car: but the matter goes further than this, and may affect the law of damages as a whole. One example is professional malpractice cases, where instead of the traditional criteria—whether non-pecuniary loss was foreseeable, or whether the contract with the service provider somehow included in its objects freedom from distress—which are, to say the least, problematical, it may be better to ask whether or not the plaintiff's interest involves simply commercial matters. If it does, then the valuation should reflect this fact, but if there are other matters then it should range wider.[110] But one can take it even further than that. The decision in *Ruxley v Forsyth* is a case in point.[111] There, it will be remembered, the House of Lords countenanced an award to a householder who had had a swimming-pool built slightly too shallow, despite the lack of any overt ill-effects on the householder or his property. Despite the understandable feeling of the House that it was clearly appropriate for some award to be made here (a suggestion that seems intuitively plausible), this result is remarkably problematical on the orthodox 'loss' analysis. There was no loss whatever in money or money's worth to the householder, and furthermore, even if there were evidence of distress or disappointment, the case did not come within the traditional area where such awards were available. On the other hand, if we take the interest approach there is once again little, if any, difficulty. The interest here, that of having the work correctly done, existed for non-commercial purposes: it had clearly been infringed, and there seems no objection to taking this into account when valuing it.

So far, so good. At this point, however, it might be objected that the approach advocated in this section, for all its theoretical attractiveness, involves a quite unacceptable degree of uncertainty. After all, the valuation of admitted incommensurables like pain and suffering is already notoriously vague; and if we insist on abandoning the concrete idea of 'loss' and reducing all damages to the more imprecise question of putting a pecuniary value on non-pecuniary prejudice, are we not simply extending that difficulty elsewhere?

Oddly enough, it is suggested that we are doing no such thing. In fact it is suggested that a re-characterisation of damages law on the lines suggested above is actually compatible with a great deal of precision when it comes to making actual awards. Return for a moment to the analogy of causation described above.[112] We may have admitted that the process of ascribing causation is a potentially fluid doctrine of attribution, rather than an all-or-nothing factual question: but this has not made the answering of

---

[110] As in *Heywood v Wellers* [1976] QB 446 (CA) or *Hamilton-Jones*, above n 15, at 943.
[111] Above n 21.
[112] See text accompanying nn 81-82, above.

causation questions simply a free-for-all, or an exercise in judicial impreci-sion. On the contrary, most causation questions in practice remain rela-tively easy to answer, and as for the difficult ones the attribution approach makes them, if anything, easier to deal with, since at least we are applying a defensible theory rather than looking for theoretical precision that is not there. It is suggested that exactly the same is likely to be true when it comes to quantifying recovery—or, if you prefer it, looking for the true 'loss' suffered. On the theory advanced in this chapter, the straightforward cases—actual pecuniary loss, destruction of easily-valued chattels, loss of commercial profits, and so on—will remain as straightforward as they ever were. It is difficult to think of any just or plausible valuation of the interest other than the amount of the loss or the value of the chattel concerned.[113] It follows that whether we talk about valuing the plaintiff's interest, or about determining the 'loss' she has suffered, the answer will be much the same. Outside this area there will of course remain the difficult areas: liability in the absence of balance-sheet loss, losses really suffered by third parties, collateral source problems, and so on. But if anything these questions will be easier to deal with against a background of a coherent theory of valuation rather than a vacuous one of loss. They are certainly unlikely to be any more difficult.

V. CONCLUSION

So far I have made three suggestions. The first is that for the purposes of fashioning a logical law of damages, the idea that there is some unitary concept of 'loss' waiting out there for the finding is unhelpful and ultimately unworkable. Second, I have argued that, for this reason, the traditional idea that damages exist to compensate 'loss' is also unhelpful. Finally, I have suggested that the best way forward is to abandon the idea of 'loss' as a touchstone for damages and instead to look to the interest of the plaintiff that has been infringed, and then undertake a valuation of that interest.

It must be noted, however, that this is merely a starting-point, and there are a number of limitations to it.

First, the theory of damages advanced here is aimed predominantly at providing a workable intellectual framework, rather than necessarily providing clear answers to every concrete case. The process of valuation is an inherently imprecise one: while in some cases (such as commercial claims based on proved money losses) it is pretty clear whet the result will

---

[113] A point made in Goldberg, above n 83, at 1331: 'For cases in which it is nearly possible to restore the status quo ante, historical worsening might set the appropriate measure of damages'.

be, elsewhere there will inevitably be much judicial leeway. Apart from the fact that valuing personal or aesthetic interests must be an arbitrary exercise, it leaves a number of other points of principle open. For example, as regards loss of use claims by commercial plaintiffs who have not suffered financial loss it suggests that such claims are permissible (in the sense of not being illogical): but it does not rule out a decision that in at least some cases the proper valuation should be nil. Again, while this theory suggests a broad approach to the question whether gains, or other matters going to reduce the effect of a loss on the plaintiff, ought to go to reduce recovery, it does not necessarily dictate the result in particular instances.

Second, just as it has always been accepted that the traditional loss-based view of damages is subject to exceptions and anomalies—policy-based or otherwise—the approach adopted here may also be subject to justifiable exceptions. An obvious example, touched on above, is the collateral source rule: whatever valuation reasoning might tell us, there may be good social reasons for either extending it (for instance, so as not encourage the prudent from insuring against loss) or restricting it (for example, to save taxpayers from having to pay out social security to those already compensated elsewhere). There are others too. For example, take the case of claims for management time spent in order to clear up the effects of a defendant's wrong. Logically it is difficult to separate claims of this sort from claims for the maintenance costs of other assets wrongfully damaged or diverted: the only difference is that the resource concerned happens to be human rather than inanimate. But other matters may indicate a different result. If, for example, an employer cannot generally claim in tort for the salary paid to a tortiously-injured employee,[114] then arguably the same result should follow for claims for diversion as for injury.

Nevertheless, despite these difficulties, it is suggested that the theory of damages advanced here does provide a useful starting-point, and one that is more coherent and logical than the traditional one. If it causes courts and others to think properly about what damages are about, rather than wasting their time on intractable problems like trying to define the indefinable, it will not have been in vain.

---

[114] See *Metropolitan Police Receiver v Croydon Corporation* [1957] 2 QB 154 (CA); and in Canada the earlier *R v CPR* [1947] SCR 185 (though the actio per quod may sometimes fill the gap: see *Genereux v Peterson, Howell & Heather (Canada) Ltd* [1973] 2 OR 558 (CA)). Although in French law such actions are commonplace, oddly enough Québec also applies the common law rule here: *R v Sylvain* [1965] SCR 164.

18

The Changing Face of the Gist of Negligence

KUMARALINGAM AMIRTHALINGAM[*]

I. INTRODUCTION

ALMOST TWENTY YEARS ago, Jane Stapleton published an article entitled 'The Gist of Negligence' in which she argued that it was incumbent on courts to isolate and identify the 'damage' that was the minimum required for an actionable claim in negligence.[1] That article was written in the context of pure economic loss and loss of chance, and raised issues that are ever-more pertinent today. Damage—the gist of negligence—was in its early days confined to property and personal injury.[2] As medical and scientific knowledge progressed in the 19th century, courts began to recognise that psychiatric injury could qualify as actionable damage, but were reluctant to do so for fear of both unmeritorious and speculative, albeit legitimate, claims.[3] Eventually psychiatric injury was recognised as actionable damage and an entire jurisprudence of nervous shock developed.

By the mid-20th century, economic interests came to be protected under the tort of negligence, and claims for pure economic loss were recognised.[4] This development spawned another distinct subset of negligence. In both the cases of nervous shock and pure economic loss, the general principles of negligence, in particular the duty concept, were modified to accommodate these new categories of actionable damage. The late 20th century saw another change taking place with greater emphasis on human rights, dignity and autonomy. This has brought forth a new generation of

[*] LLB (Hons), PhD (Australian National University); Associate Professor and Director, International Programmes, Faculty of Law, National University of Singapore.
[1] J Stapleton, 'The Gist of Negligence' (1988) *LQR* 213, 389.
[2] See generally the progressive views on protected interests expressed almost a hundred years ago by R Pound, 'Interests of Personality' (1915) 28 *Harvard Law Review* 343, 445.
[3] See DH Parry, 'Nervous Shock as a Cause of Action in Tort' (1925) 41 *LQR* 297.
[4] First recognised in *Hedley Byrne & Co v Heller & Partners Ltd* [1964] AC 465 (HL).

actionable damage claiming legitimacy within negligence; and the first five years of the 21st century saw the House of Lords dealing with negligence claims for exposure to increased risk,[5] loss of chance,[6] violation of individual autonomy[7] and deprivation of educational opportunity.[8] This time, instead of turning to the over-worked concept of duty, courts focused on the principles governing the concept of causation to deal with these new categories of damage.

This chapter argues that the law of causation, as developed by the House of Lords and the High Court of Australia, offers a sufficiently flexible and normative framework for courts to balance principle and pragmatism in dealing with these emerging categories of damage. Much of the controversy surrounding causation may be alleviated if courts focused instead on the gist of negligence and were more receptive to novel categories of actionable damage, as the tort of negligence evolves to meet 21st century interests which are increasingly characterised by less tangible rights and expectations. Whether this leads to an unjustified expansion of negligence liability is something that needs to be closely watched.

II.   THE CHANGING FACE OF THE GIST OF NEGLIGENCE

Tort law has evidenced two clear trends in recent years. One is the increasing emphasis on individual interests that extend beyond physical integrity and lend themselves to rights-based arguments.[9] The House of Lords has in the last two years heard rights-based appeals on nuisance,[10] privacy,[11] negligence[12] and misfeasance in public office;[13] and the Singapore High Court has recognised a new common law tort of harassment.[14] The second trend is the increasing significance of the concept of vulnerability and how that is viewed as being central to tort claims.[15] Tort law is thus

---

[5]   See, eg, *Barker v Corus* [2006] 2 WLR 1027 [*Barker*].

[6]   See, eg, *Gregg v Scott* [2005] 2 AC 176 (HL) [*Gregg*].

[7]   See, eg, *Chester v Afshar* [2005] 1 AC 134 (HL) [*Chester*].

[8]   See, eg, *Phelps v Hillingdon London Borough Council* [2001] 2 AC 619 (HL) [*Phelps*].

[9]   See N Jansen, 'Duties and Rights in Negligence: A Comparative and Historical Perspective on the European Law of Extracontractual Liability' (2004) 24 *OJLS* 443, who argues that negligence should be rights-based, rather than duty-based.

[10]   *Marcic v Thames Water Utilities Ltd* [2004] 2 AC 42 (HL).

[11]   *Wainwright v Home Office* [2004] 2 AC 406 (HL).

[12]   *Chester*, above n 7.

[13]   *Watkins v The Secretary of State of the Home Department & Ors* [2006] 2 WLR 807 (HL).

[14]   *Malcomson v Naresh Kumar Mehta* [2001] 4 SLR 4 (HC). The English Court of Appeal had earlier developed the common law along similar lines to protect against harassment and invasion of privacy (see *Khorasandjian v Bush* [1993] QB 727 (CA)), but that decision was overruled by the House of Lords in *Hunter v Canary Wharf Ltd* [1997] AC 655 (HL).

[15]   The Australian High Court, since the demise of proximity as the determinant of duty of care in negligence, has often emphasised the need to protect the vulnerable claimant. See

operating in a climate that is very conscious of broader personal interest and the need to protect vulnerable claimants, particularly when the defendant is especially powerful.

Courts may choose to develop a plethora of new torts to address these new trends or, bearing in mind the tort of negligence's 'staggering march' over disparate torts in the previous century,[16] may choose to pre-empt a repeat of history and allow negligence to embrace these new areas. Unless a principled approach can be found to carry the tort of negligence into these new vistas, there will always be a danger of the emergence of a 'compensation culture' as a result of rights-based arguments,[17] or the risk of over-reliance on arbitrary policy and philosophical arguments in striking a balance between plaintiffs and defendants in tort law.[18]

The recent trilogy of House of Lords causation decisions—*Fairchild v Glenhaven Funeral Services*,[19] *Chester v Afshar*[20] and *Gregg v Scott*[21]— represent three emerging categories of damage that should be treated as meeting the threshold requirement for the gist of negligence, namely increased/industrial risk, individual autonomy/rights/choice and loss of chance. A fourth category, which will not be analysed in this chapter is the education cases, represented by the line of authorities following *Phelps v Hillingdon London Borough Council*,[22] where the gist of negligence may be classified as loss of educational opportunity.

A. Increased/Industrial Risk

Fairchild was by any standards a seminal decision on the law of causation in the common law. Its real significance, however, is its status as the

---

especially, *Crimmins v Stevedoring Industry Finance Committee* (1999) 200 CLR 1 (HCA); *Perre v Apand Pty Ltd* (1999) 198 CLR 180 (HCA).

[16] T Weir, 'The Staggering March of Negligence' in P Cane and J Stapleton (eds), *The Law of Obligations: Essays in Celebration of John Fleming* (Oxford, Clarendon Press, 1998).

[17] C Harlow, 'Damages and Human Rights' [2004] *New Zealand Law Review* 429.

[18] B Markesinis, 'Plaintiff's Tort Law or Defendant's Tort Law? Is the House of Lords Moving Towards a Synthesis?' (2001) 9 *Torts Law Journal* 167. See especially, the recent decisions on wrongful birth and wrongful life, that have split the House of Lords and the High Court of Australia: *McFarlane v Tayside Health Board* [2000] 2 AC 59 (HL); *Parkinson v St James and Seacroft University Hospital NHS Trust* [2002] QB 266 (CA); *Rees v Darlington Memorial Hospital NHS Trust* [2004] 1 AC 360 (HL); *Cattanach v Melchior* (2003) 215 CLR 1 (HCA); *Harriton v Stephens* [2006] HCA 15.

[19] [2003] 1 AC 32 (HL) [*Fairchild*].

[20] Above n 7.

[21] Above n 6.

[22] [2001] 2 AC 619 (HL). See *DN (By his Father and Litigation Friend RN) v London Borough of Greenwich* [2005] 1 FCR 112; *Devon County Council v Stuart Clarke* [2005] 1 FCR 752; *Adams v Bracknell Forest Borough Council* [2005] 1 AC 76; *Skipper v Calderdale Metropolitan Borough Council, The Governors of Crossley Health School* [2006] EWCA Civ 238.

catalyst of a series of cases, which have the potential of introducing novel categories of damage to the gist of negligence.[23] The claimants in the *Fairchild* litigation were victims of asbestos exposure and dependants of victims who had died as a result of contracting mesothelioma. While existing scientific knowledge is in no doubt that the disease is caused by exposure to asbestos, the precise aetiology of the disease is as yet unknown. It is not clear, unlike with asbestosis, whether accumulation of asbestos fibres in a person's system increases the risk of contracting the disease. In *Fairchild*, the victim had worked for several employers and had been exposed to asbestos at each employment. It was therefore impossible to prove which exposure caused the disease, and hence it was impossible for the claimants to discharge the burden of proof with respect to causation.

Instead of focusing on the gist of negligence, the House of Lords focused on causation and, after an extensive review of the law, revived the formerly discredited approach in *McGhee v National Coal Board*.[24] In *McGhee*, the claimant had been exposed to coal dust at work and alleged that the defendant was negligent in failing to provide shower facilities, thereby prolonging the exposure of the claimants to the dust as they returned home after work. The gist of negligence in *McGhee* was really either a loss of chance or industrial risk; the pursuer's expert witness testified as much, 'No one could say that [the showers] would prevent that man developing the condition. It would be likely to reduce the chances.'[25] Nevertheless, Lord Wilberforce, having rejected 'increased risk' as the gist of negligence,[26] held that in some cases where actual proof of causation was impossible, proof of a material increase in risk was sufficient to hold the defendant liable, unless the defendant could prove that the injury was not caused by his or her negligence.[27]

The *Fairchild* court approved the *McGhee* approach and held that in exceptional cases, ordinary principles governing causation should be relaxed to allow deserving claimants to be compensated. The difficulty with this is that causation, which is the lynchpin of liability in negligence, risks being thrown into the abyss of intuition and policy. When does the *Fairchild* relaxation apply? Or to paraphrase Professor Stapleton,[28] 'When

---

[23] Witness the developments in *Chester*, above n 7, *Gregg*, above n 6, and *Barker*, above n 5.

[24] [1973] 1 WLR 1 (HL) [*McGhee*]. *McGhee* was effectively neutered in *Wilsher v Essex Area Health Authority* [1988] AC 1074 (HL) [*Wilsher*]. See earlier development of this line of authority in *Bonnington Castings Ltd v Wardlaw* [1956] AC 613 (HL); *Nicholson v Atlas Steel Foundry and Engineering Co Ltd* [1957] 1 WLR 613 (HL).

[25] Quoted in *Fairchild*, above n 19, at 50 (Lord Bingham of Cornhill).

[26] *McGhee*, above n 24, at 6.

[27] *Ibid.*

[28] J Stapleton, 'Lords a'Leaping Evidentiary Gaps' (2002) 10 *Torts Law Journal* 276.

can judges play leap frog in the playground of legal principles and evidentiary rules?' Some guidance was offered by the Lords, the broad parameters of which are that the claimant's injury must clearly be within the scope of foreseeable harm and be the very injury that the duty was designed to prevent; that the defendant's conduct must have theoretically increased the risk of the injury; and that it was inherently impossible for the claimant to prove the causal connection between the defendant's negligence and the claimant's injury.

While the *Fairchild* analysis of causation provides further jurisprudential support for a highly normative approach to causation,[29] it would have been better if the case had been analysed squarely as one about liability for industrial (or unacceptable) risk.[30] Its failure to do so has cast a shadow on the scope of *Fairchild's* application, even though Lord Hoffmann has recently rejected that there is anything mysterious about causation or the application of *Fairchild*. In his Blackstone Lecture delivered on 14 May 2005 at Pembroke College, Oxford, Lord Hoffmann reviewed the law of causation as applied in *Fairchild*, *Chester* and *Gregg*, and ended with this confident conclusion:

> There is nothing special or mysterious about the law of causation. One decides, as a matter of law, what causal connection the law requires and one then decides, as a question of fact, whether the claimant has satisfied the requirements of the law. There is, in my opinion, nothing more to be said.[31]

In the House of Lords' most recent asbestos decision of *Barker v Corus*,[32] Lord Hoffmann reopened the *Fairchild* debate. His Lordship rejected the conventional understanding of *Fairchild* as having accepted *McGhee* as authority for the proposition that a material increase in risk was to be

---

[29] The House of Lords has preferred a purposive approach to causation supplemented by consideration of whether attributing causal responsibility would be fair, just and reasonable. See, *Environment Agency (formerly National Rivers Authority) v Empress Car Co (Abertillery) Ltd* [1999] 2 AC 22 (HL); *Kuwait Airways Corporation v Iraqi Airways Co (Nos 4 and 5)* [2002] 2 AC 883 (HL). The Australian High Court has adopted a similar normative approach in the form of the common sense approach to causation: *March v E & MH Stramare Pty Ltd* (1991) 171 CLR 506 (HCA); *Bennett v Minister of Community Welfare* (1992) 176 CLR 408 (HCA); *Chappel v Hart* (1998) 195 CLR 232 (HCA) [*Chappel*].

[30] The term 'unacceptable risk' is used to denote a class of risks, negligent exposure to which is itself sufficient to ground an action in negligence. These risks can be divided into two classes: the first defined by the nature of the risk and the second by the scope of the duty. The former category includes those risks which a court can fairly hold to be one that is so unjustified as to be unacceptable, for example, the risk of preventable death at work. The second includes those risks, which are the very raison d'être of the duty, for example, loss of chance in the *Gregg* or *Kitchen* type of cases (see text surrounding nn 79-81).

[31] Lord Hoffmann, 'Causation' (2005) 121 *LQR* 592, 603. Interestingly, in *Barker*, above n 5, at [11], Lord Hoffmann, in analysing *Fairchild*, stated, 'On the other hand, no one thought that the formulations in *Fairchild* were the last word on the scope of the exception.' For a recent academic review of the three decisions, see S Green, 'Coherence of Medical Negligence Cases: A Game of Doctors and Purses' (2006) 14 *Medical Law Review* 1.

[32] Above n 5.

treated as materially contributing to the injury, ie, that it established the necessary causal connection between the defendant's negligence and the claimant's injury.[33] Instead, Lord Hoffmann held that the increased risk was itself the gist of negligence and that it was a fiction to hold that the actual injury in such cases was proved to have been caused by the defendant.[34] Lord Rodger of Earlsferry, who disagreed with Lord Hoffmann's analysis, did not mince his words when he declared that such a view was 'not so much reinterpreting as rewriting the key decisions in *McGhee* ... and *Fairchild*'.[35]

Nevertheless, there was majority support in *Barker* for the proposition that the 'increased risk' in the *Fairchild*-type asbestos cases is sufficient to qualify as the gist of negligence. This squarely raised the question as to whether loss of chance should also be treated as the gist of negligence, and Lord Hoffmann seemed to suggest that it should. His Lordship then went on to justify the decision in *Gregg* on the policy ground that allowing loss of chance in *Gregg* would have extended such claims to all areas of medical negligence.

> Although the House, by a majority, answered [the loss of chance] question in the negative, it was not on the ground that there was some conceptual objection to treating the diminution in the chances of a favourable outcome or (putting the same thing in a different way) the increase in the risk of an unfavourable outcome as actionable damage. The reason was that the adoption of such a rule in *Gregg v Scott* would in effect have extended the *Fairchild* exception to all cases of medical negligence, if not beyond, and would have been inconsistent with *Wilsher*, in which the negligent doctor had increased the chances of the baby suffering RLF (or reduced his chances of escaping it).[36]

One issue in *Barker* was whether *Fairchild* could apply to a situation where the claimant, who had been exposed to asbestos by the defendant, had also been exposed to asbestos while working for himself, ie, a situation where part of the exposure was non-tortious and due to the claimant himself. The second, and more critical, issue was whether liability in such cases should be several or in solidium. The majority preferred to impose proportionate liability, holding the defendant liable only to the extent of his contribution to the risk.[37] Lord Rodger argued that the majority had adopted the 'increased risk as the gist of negligence' approach in order to justify several

---

[33] *Barker*, above n 5, at [33] (Lord Hoffmann).
[34] *Ibid*, at [31].
[35] *Ibid*, at [71].
[36] *Ibid*, at [39].
[37] See generally, A Porat and A Stein, 'Indeterminate Causation and Apportionment of Damages: An Essay on *Holtby, Allen*, and *Fairchild*' (2003) 23 *OJLS* 667.

liability and attacked what he viewed as a wholly inappropriate exercise of a policy choice by the court of favouring defendants over claimants in such cases. He stated:

> Of course, it may seem hard if a defendant is held liable in solidum even though all that can be shown is that he made a material contribution to the risk that the victim would develop mesothelioma. But it is also hard—and settled law—that a defendant is held liable in solidum even though all that can be shown is that he made a material, say 5%, contribution to the claimant's indivisible injury. That is a form of rough justice which the law has not hitherto sought to smooth, preferring instead, as a matter of policy, to place the risk of the insolvency of a wrongdoer or his insurer on the other wrongdoers and their insurers. Now the House is deciding that, in this particular enclave of the law, the risk of the insolvency of a wrongdoer or his insurer is to bypass the other wrongdoers and their insurers and to be shouldered entirely by the innocent claimant. As a result, claimants will often end up with only a small proportion of the damages which would normally be payable for their loss. *The desirability of the courts, rather than Parliament, throwing this lifeline to wrongdoers and their insurers at the expense of claimants is not obvious to me.*[38]

The majority's preference for proportionate liability seems odd, when they had stressed that liability was not based on the mere loss of chance or increased risk, even though that was the gist of negligence in such cases; rather, it was based on the actual injury that was suffered. 'Although the *Fairchild* exception treats the risk of contracting mesothelioma as the damage, it applies only when the disease has actually been contracted.'[39] The majority opinion seems to have been delivered with a forked tongue, and, as Lord Rodger pointed out, is anti-claimant. A claimant who proves all the elements of negligence in such a case cannot claim anything unless the risk fully materialises. However, once the risk fully materialises, the claimant is only entitled to recover a proportion of his or her loss from the defendant; in cases of multiple defendants, the risk of the insolvent defendant is transferred to the claimant rather than to the other defendants.[40] A better approach would have been to hold the defendant wholly

---

[38] *Barker*, above n 5, at [90] (emphasis added).

[39] *Barker*, above n 5, at [48] (Lord Hoffmann).

[40] The intuitive injustice in this has been recognised by the Lord Chancellor of the United Kingdom who has proposed to amend the Compensation Bill to impose joint and several liability to ensure that the risk of impecunious defendants is not carried by the claimants. The Secretary of State for the Department of Work and Pensions, John Hutton directly referred to *Barker* and stated, 'I have seen first hand the devastating effect this disease can have on individuals and their families—it can lie dormant for years then kill quickly. The consequences of the *Barker* judgment would have made it much more difficult for sufferers and their families to get the compensation they deserve, so I am pleased to announce today that we are going to take action to make claims easier.' See, <http://www.gnn.gov.uk/environment/detail.asp?ReleaseID=209056&NewsAreaID=2&NavigatedFromDepartment=True> (date accessed: 10 July 2006).

liable, subject to any reduction on the ground of contributory negligence. This places the burden of the claimant's own contribution on the claimant but leaves the risk of insolvency of other potential defendants on the defendants.

While the majority's identification of 'increased risk' as the gist of negligence is a welcome development, *Barker* is an unsatisfactory decision in that it does not explain why 'increased risk' should qualify as the gist of negligence. It may open a new can of worms, as the distinction between types of 'increased risk' or 'loss of chance' that are compensable will be left to trial courts to work out without any guidance in terms of principle. *Clough v First Choice Holidays and Flights Ltd*,[41] decided four months before *Barker*, involved a claimant who, while on holiday at a resort, slipped from a wall separating two swimming pools and broke his neck. It was accepted that the defendant had been negligent in failing to use non-slip paint on the wall, but the claim failed on causation. On appeal, it was argued that the trial judge had incorrectly applied the *Fairchild* line of authorities on material contribution and increased risk.

The Court of Appeal's interpretation of *Fairchild* was certainly not that of the majority in *Barker*, and the President of the Queen's Bench Division, who gave the leading judgment, referred expressly to Lord Rodger's views in *Fairchild*. The President, in upholding the trial judge's finding on causation and increased risk, stated: 'In short, the risk represented by the absence of non-slip paint was just that, an increased risk which in his judgment, as a matter of fact, did not cause or materially contribute to the appellant's accident.' This reasoning may well be challenged under the novel approach adopted by the majority in *Barker*. Another Court of Appeal decision, *Rothwell v Chemical & Insulating Co Ltd*,[42] handed down around the same time as *Clough*, concerned asbestos exposure and may also be challenged under *Barker*, as the majority in *Rothwell* rejected the argument that increased risk could constitute actionable damage.

Rothwell involved several claimants, each of whom had been negligently exposed to asbestos by his employer. Five of the claimants had developed pleural plaques,[43] which put the claimant at risk of contracting an asbestos related disease and which had caused the claimants to suffer anxiety at this fate. The majority (Lord Phillips CJ and Longmore LJ) held that none of these three heads—the pleural plaques, the risk of contracting an asbestos-related disease and the anxiety—could independently constitute the gist of

---

[41]   [2006] EWCA Civ 15.

[42]   [2006] EWCA Civ 27 [*Rothwell*].

[43]   Pleural plaques are caused by a thickening of localised areas on the pleura, which is a membrane that helps the movement of lungs in the course of respiration. It is generally accepted that pleural plaques are themselves benign and do not increase the risk of lung cancer.

negligence. The pleural plaques were held to be too insignificant a physical injury, thereby not passing the *de minimis* requirement. The risk or chance of contracting a disease was held not to be damage sufficient to constitute the gist of negligence. The anxiety was held to fall outside the established principles governing nervous shock.

The trial judge took the view that by combining these three elements, a claimant could demonstrate that there was sufficient damage to constitute the gist of negligence. The majority overturned the trial judgment, and in the process, several other first instance decisions,[44] and held that there was 'no legal precedent in this country, beyond first instance decisions, for aggregating three heads of claim which, individually, could not found a cause of action, so as to constitute sufficient damage to give rise to a legal claim'.[45] The dissenting judge, Smith LJ accepted that while the pleural plaques themselves might be *de minimis*, the gist of negligence had to be viewed in terms of its whole effect on the claimant: 'The sum of the very minor physical damage and the much more serious damage comprising the risks amounts to material, actionable, damage.'[46]

If, according to *Barker*, 'increased risk' is to be recognised as the gist of negligence, the nature of this new gist of negligence needs to be clearly defined to avoid fanciful or speculative claims being made. One way is to limit this new category to its facts, ie increased risk of mesothelioma as a result of asbestos exposure at the work place. This seems arbitrary. Perhaps, it could be broadened to employment risks; again this is arbitrary because there are many employment risks that should not be actionable. A better approach would be to take the view that only 'unacceptable risks' should qualify as the gist of negligence. This provides a normative framework for courts to determine what sort of risks should be classed as unacceptable, and incrementally develop the law. Courts have long recognised that there are certain employment risks where it would clearly be unconscionable to allow causation arguments to defeat the claim.[47]

---

[44] *Church v Ministry of Defence* (unreported, Peter Pain J, 23 February 1984); *Sykes v Ministry of Defence* (unreported, Otton J, 19 March 1984); *Patterson v Ministry of Defence* (unreported, Simon Brown J, 29 July 1986).

[45] *Rothwell*, above n 42, at [68].

[46] *Ibid*, at [135].

[47] The clearest examples involve cases where the employee is violently robbed while carrying out tasks for the employer, which carry a real risk of exposure to such violence. The Australian decision of *Chomentowski v Red Garter Restaurant Pty Ltd* (1970) 92 WN (NSW) 1070 [*Chomentowski*], where an employee was violently assaulted by a robber while depositing his employer's restaurant takings for the day, is a vivid illustration of this. Mason JA stated, 'The injury which the plaintiff sustained, although occasioned by deliberate human intervention, was the outcome of the very risk against which it was the duty of the defendants to safeguard the plaintiff as their employee. If, as was the case, it was the existence of that risk of injury which called for the exercise of care and the taking of precautions by the defendants, then the defendants' failure to take care may properly be regarded as the cause of the injury which occurred when the risk became an actuality' (*Chomentowski*, above n 47, at 1086).

Negligently exposing workers to a potentially fatal disease is an unacceptable risk by any measure, and it would almost certainly be so if tried by a jury. As Smith LJ noted in *Rothwell*:

> I ... venture to suggest that most people on the Clapham omnibus would consider that workmen who have been put in the position of these claimants have suffered real harm. I do not think that they would regard these consequences of asbestos exposure as trivial and undeserving of compensation.[48]

B. Medical Risk and Patient Autonomy

Another area where the failure to identify the gist of negligence resulted in courts distorting the principles of causation is the medical duty to inform. The two leading authorities in this area are the decision of the House of Lords in *Chester* and that of the High Court of Australia in *Chappel v Hart*.[49] The facts of the two cases are similar. The claimants underwent surgery and suffered injury due to the materialisation of inherent risks. In both cases, there was no negligence in the performance of the surgeries, but in both cases, the defendants had breached their respective duties to warn about the inherent risk. In *Chester*, the surgery was to the spine and the claimant was left paralysed, while in *Chappel*, the surgery was to the throat and the claimant was left with a severely diminished vocal capacity. The only material difference between the two cases was that in *Chappel*, the claimant alleged that had she been warned of the risk she would have sought a better surgeon, whereas in *Chester*, the claimant merely said that she would have deferred the surgery.[50] In both cases, the claimants had no choice but to eventually undergo precisely the same type of surgery, as there was no other remedy for their ailments.

On the face of it, neither claimant could prove that she would have avoided the risk. In both cases, that very risk would have had to be faced and therefore it could not be said that the defendant's negligence in failing to warn had caused the plaintiff to suffer the injury. Nevertheless, in both cases, the respective courts, by 3-2 majorities, found in favour of the claimant. In *Chappel*, Gaudron J focused on the common sense test of causation and held that the injury that occurred was precisely that which was within the scope of the risk.[51] This, in a way collapses the causation

---

[48]   *Rothwell*, above n 42, at [144] (Smith LJ).

[49]   Above n 29. The leading Canadian authority in this area is *Arndt v Smith* [1994] 8 WWR 568 (BCCA), which takes a different approach to causation in these cases by preferring an objective patient test. See the commentary of this decision by Tony Honoré, 'Causation and Disclosure of Medical Risks' (1998) 114 *LQR* 52.

[50]   This theoretically put the *Chappel* claimant in a slightly better position, as acknowledged by the majority in *Chester*, but it was held that this difference was ultimately irrelevant.

[51]   *Chappel*, above n 29, at [8] (Gaudron J), relying on *Betts v Whittingslowe* (1945) 71 CLR 637 (HCA) where Dixon J stated at 649, 'breach of duty coupled with an accident of the

and remoteness inquiries into a composite one of 'causal responsibility'.[52] Kirby J and Gummow J focused on the significance of the purpose of the doctor's duty to inform,[53] as developed in *Rogers v Whitaker*,[54] which was to protect the right of the patient to make fully informed decisions about his or her body. That right deserved to be protected by the law of negligence. The dissenting judges, McHugh J and Hayne J, adopted a narrow approach to causation, holding that since the claimant would in any case have been exposed to the same risk of injury, it could not be said that the defendant had caused the injury or even increased the risk of injury.[55]

A majority in *Chester* agreed with the majority decision in *Chappel*. Lord Steyn held that this type of case warranted a *Fairchild* style relaxation of the rules of causation.[56] Lord Hope delivered a powerful rights-based opinion in *Chester*, holding that causation was satisfied on policy grounds alone:

> I start with the proposition that the law which imposed the duty to warn on the doctor has at its heart the right of the patient to make an informed choice as to whether and if so when and by whom, to be operated on. ... The function of the law is to enable rights to be vindicated and to provide remedies when duties have been breached. Unless this is done the duty is a hollow one, stripped of all practical force and devoid of all content. It will have lost its ability to protect the patient and thus fulfil the only purpose which brought it into existence.[57]

It is apparent that the gist of negligence in such cases is not the actual physical injury, which simply goes to the quantification of the damage, but it is really the patient's right or autonomy,[58] or the risk to which the patient is subjected. While there is no increase in risk, one can say that this risk, as was the case in *Fairchild/Barker*, is one that the ordinary person would

---

kind that might thereby be caused is enough to justify an inference, in the absence of any sufficient reason to the contrary, that in fact the accident did occur owing to the act or omission amounting to the breach'.

[52] McHugh J, in his dissenting argument (*Chappel*, above n 29, at [24]) recognised this development: 'As a natural consequence of the rejection of the 'but for' test as the sole determinant of causation, the Court has refused to regard the concept of remoteness of damage as the appropriate mechanism for determining the extent to which policy considerations should limit the consequences of causation-in-fact.'

[53] *Chappel* above n 29, at [65] (Gummow J), [95] (Kirby J).

[54] (1992) 175 CLR 479 (HCA).

[55] *Chappel*, above n 29, at [42] (McHugh J), [146] (Hayne J).

[56] *Chester*, above n 7, at [23]. See also, Lord Walker of Gestingthorpe, [101].

[57] *Chester* above n 7, at [86]-[87]. See also, Lord Steyn [18], Lord Walker of Gestingthorpe [92].

[58] This argument on patient autonomy and medical negligence has been pursued elsewhere in a series of notes: K Amirthalingam, 'Causation and the Gist of Negligence' (2005) 64 *CLJ* 32; K Amirthalingam, 'Loss of Chance—Lost Cause or Remote Possibility?' (2003) 62 *CLJ* 253; K Amirthalingam, 'Medical Non-Disclosure, Causation and Autonomy' (2002) 118 *LQR* 540; K Amirthalingam, 'A New Dawn for Patient's Rights?' (2001) 117 *LQR* 532.

describe as an unacceptable one—a risk which should result in remedy. As Lord Steyn put it in *Chester*, 'the decision announced by the House today reflects the reasonable expectation of the public in contemporary society'.[59] Just as it is unacceptable for an employer to expose an employee to a potentially fatal risk, once the significance of individual rights and patient autonomy is given due regard, it is equally unacceptable for a doctor to expose a patient to an inherent risk of surgery, without properly informing the patient.

Chester and *Chappel* have enlarged the scope of causation to bridge the gap between the negligent failure to inform and the physical injury of the patient, despite the doctrinal difficulties that this approach entails. The common law's leading expert on causation, Tony Honoré has justified *Chappel* on the ground that the defendant had been negligent in failing to inform and that he had in effect caused the harm by non-negligently operating on her: 'Morally he was responsible for the outcome of what he did.'[60]

This holistic approach has been implicitly approved by the Court of Appeal in its application of *Fairchild* to another industrial risk situation, this time not exposure to asbestos but damage due to the use of vibrating tools. In *Transco Plc v Griggs*,[61] the claimant suffered injury to his hands due to the use of vibrating tools. The exact injury that the claimant suffered was in dispute as was whether the injury could have been caused by the use of non-negligent vibrating tools. The Court of Appeal upheld the trial judge's finding of liability and held that this type of case came within the *Fairchild* extension of causation. Hale LJ, in delivering the leading judgment, stated:

> Here we have a global breach of duty in relation to protecting employees from vibration induced disease. ... In any event even if the but for test could not be satisfied, there can be little doubt that the employer's failure to have a proper system for detecting and preventing vibration induced diseases materially increased the risk of an employee sustaining such a disease. ... *it would be·an unjust legal system which did not hold the employer responsible for what had happened.*[62]

C. Loss of Chance

The final category to be considered is the controversial loss of chance. A distinction must be drawn between loss of chance as actionable damage

---

[59] *Chester,* above n 7, at [25].

[60] T Honoré, 'Medical Non-Disclosure, Causation and Risk: *Chappel v Hart*' (1999) 7 *Torts Law Journal* 1, 8.

[61] [2003] EWCA Civ 564.

[62] *Ibid,* at [32], [35] (emphasis added).

and loss of chance as a measure of damages. The latter is not controversial, as damage forming the gist of negligence has been proved on the balance of probabilities, and assessment of future damage always involves speculation and weighing up of probable outcomes.[63] It is the former, where all that the claimant can prove is that the defendant has caused him or her to lose a less than even chance either of avoiding a negative outcome or of gaining a positive outcome, that is at issue. The conventional view in England has been that loss of chance is not recoverable in negligence, subject to some exceptions.[64] However, the majority opinion in *Barker* may have turned that around so that loss of chance is recognised as damage that constitutes the gist of negligence, subject to some exceptions, cases like *Gregg* apparently being one of them.

Most of the academic writers have focused on the theoretical nature of loss of chance and developed sophisticated arguments for and against recovery. Distinctions between statistical and personal chances, past and future hypothetical facts, deterministic and indeterministic cases abound in the literature on this subject.[65] These theoretical analyses are intellectually stimulating, but they risk overshadowing the simple—and now uncontroversial—fact that causal responsibility in negligence is less about science and logic than it is about fairness and justice. More importantly, the analysis should not be at the abstract level of whether every type of loss of chance case, *mutatis mutandis*, should be compensable in negligence. The question has to be far more nuanced and focused on particular categories where loss of chance ought to be compensable in negligence.

---

[63] See, *Mallet v McMonagle* [1970] AC 166 (HL) [176] [*Mallet*] (Lord Diplock): 'In determining what did happen in the past a court decides on the balance of probabilities. Anything that is more probable than not it treats as certain. But in assessing damages which depend upon its view as to what will happen in the future or would have happened in the future if something had not happened in the past, the court must make an estimate as to what are the chances that a particular thing will or would have happened and reflect those chances, whether they are more or less than even, in the amount of damages which it awards.' See also, *Malec v JC Hutton Pty Ltd* (1990) 169 CLR 638 (HCA).

[64] For Canada, see *Laferrière v Lawson* [1991] 1 SCR 541, which rejected loss of chance claims in medical negligence. H Luntz, 'Loss of Chance' in I Freckelton and D Mendelson (eds), *Causation in Law and Medicine* (Aldershot, Ashgate Publishing Ltd, 2002) 152, 180 has argued that, as that decision was based on Quebec civil law, it did not preclude loss of chance being recognised under the Canadian common law.

[65] MA Meldrum, 'Loss of a Chance in Medical Malpractice Litigation: Expanding Liability of Health Professionals Versus Providing Justice to Those Who Have Lost' (2001) 9 *Journal of Law and Medicine* 200; B Smith, 'Loss of a Chance' (1999) 29 *Victoria University of Wellington Law Review* 225; D Hamer, '"Chance Would be a Fine Thing": Proof of Causation and Quantum in an Unpredictable World' (1999) 23 *Melbourne University Law Review* 557; M Stauch, 'Causation, Risk, and Loss of Chance in Medical Negligence' (1997) 17 *OJLS* 205; H Reece, 'Losses of Chances in the Law' (1996) 59 *Modern Law Review* 188; T Hill, 'A Lost Chance for Compensation in the Tort of Negligence by the House of Lords' (1991) 54 *MLR* 511; J Stapleton, above n 1, at 389; JH King, 'Causation, Valuation and Chance in Personal Injury Torts Involving Preexisting Conditions and Future Consequences' (1981) 90 *Yale Law Journal* 1353.

English case law suggests two clear categories,[66] and it is argued that the *Gregg* type case should be added to these two categories. The High Court of Australia has not pronounced on this issue yet,[67] but several State Courts have accepted loss of chance claims in medical negligence.[68]

The first case where loss of chance was recognised as compensable loss is *Chaplin v Hicks*, which involved a breach of contract that deprived the claimant of the opportunity of participating in a beauty contest, and thereby the chance of winning the contest.[69] Almost half a century later, the English Court of Appeal, in *Kitchen v Royal Air Force Association*,[70] without referring to *Chaplin*, applied a loss of chance approach to a negligence action. The claimant's husband had died of electrocution, allegedly due to the negligence of the electricity company. The claimant's solicitors negligently allowed the action to lapse and the claimant sued the solicitors. The Court of Appeal held that the solicitor had indeed been negligent and had caused the claimant to lose the opportunity to press her claim in court. It was recognised that, in this case, all the claimant could show was that she had lost an opportunity to recover her losses; she could not show that in all probability she would have won had her claim been litigated. As Lord Evershed MR argued:

> In my judgment, what the court has to do (assuming that the plaintiff has established negligence) in such a case as the present, is to determine what the plaintiff has by that negligence lost. The question is, has the plaintiff lost some right of value, some chose in action of reality and substance? In such a case, it may be that its value is not easy to determine, but it is the duty of the court to determine that value as best it can.[71]

Kitchen is an example of one bright line of cases where courts have recognised that loss of chance is clearly the gist of negligence — these are cases involving solicitors who have negligently deprived the claimants of the opportunity to pursue their claims.[72] There are two other related

---

[66]   See below text surrounding nn 73, 74.

[67]   Apart from inconclusive obiter comments in *Naxakis v Western General Hospital* (1999) 197 CLR 269 (HCA) and *Chappel*, above n 29.

[68]   Recent appellate decisions include, *Carney v Newton* [2006] TASSC 4; *State of New South Wales v Burton* [2006] NSWCA 12; *Rufo v Hoskings* (2004) 61 NSWLR 678 (CA), *Mouratidis v Brown* [2002] FCAFC 330; *Gavalas v Singh* (2001) 3 VR 404 (CA). For a review of earlier first instance decisions see, H Luntz, above n 64, at 188-190; MA Meldrum, 'Loss of a Chance in Medical Malpractice Litigation: Expanding Liability of Health Professionals Versus Providing Justice to Those Who Have Lost' (2001) 9 *Journal of Law and Medicine* 200, 206-7.

[69]   [1911] 2 KB 786 (CA).

[70]   [1958] 1 WLR 563 (CA) [*Kitchen*].

[71]   *Ibid*, at 575.

[72]   *Mount v Barker Austin* [1998] PNLR 494 (CA); *Sharif v Garret & Co* [2002] 1 WLR 3118 (CA); *Sharpe (By his Mother and Litigation Friend Christine Cunningham) v Addison (Trading as Addison Lister)* [2003] EWCA Civ 1189; *Dixon v Clement Jones Solicitors (A Firm)* [2004] EWCA Civ 1005.

categories where loss of chance has been recognised. One includes cases involving negligent professional advice resulting in lost economic opportunity that is contingent on the hypothetical conduct of a third party,[73] and the other involves professional advice and lost employment opportunities.[74]

What all of these cases have in common is that the purpose of the duty in question was either to protect the claimant from being deprived of economic opportunity or to provide the claimant with an opportunity to recover losses. Following the House of Lords' decisions in *Fairchild* and *Chester*, with the renewed emphasis on the purposive approach to causation, it seemed logical that the claimant in *Gregg* should have succeeded.[75] The claimant had non-Hodgkin's lymphoma, which was not diagnosed by the defendant general practitioner, who failed to refer him to a specialist. As a result, the claimant's chance of recovery was further diminished. Because his chance of survival at the time of his initial consultation was assessed at 42%, it could not be found on a balance of probabilities that, had the defendant not been negligent, it was more likely than not that that he would have survived. One of the arguments advanced in the House of Lords was for loss of chance to be treated as the gist of negligence.[76]

By a 3-2 majority, the House of Lords dismissed the appeal and confirmed that loss of chance was not actionable in medical negligence.[77]

---

[73] *Allied Maples Group Ltd v Simmons & Simmons (a firm)* (1995) 1 WLR 1602 (CA); *Ogilvy v Mather Ltd v Rubinstein Callingham Polden & Gale* [1999] EWCA Civ 1896; *Channon v Lindley Johnstone (A Firm)* [2002] Lloyd's Law Rep PN 342 (CA); *Williams & Ors v Glyn & Co* [2003] All ER (D) 124 (CA); *Coudert Brothers v Norman Bay Ltd (formerly Illingworth Morris Ltd)* [2004] EWCA Civ 215 [*Coudert Brother*]; *Talisman Property Co (UK) Ltd v Norton Rose* [2005] EWHC 85 (Ch).

[74] *Spring v Guardian Assurance plc* [1995] 2 AC 196 (HL); *Cox v Sun Alliance Life Ltd* [2001] IRLR 448 (CA); *Singh v Royal Life Insurance Ltd* (unreported, Aylen QC, 6 November 2000). An emerging category is the education cases, where the gist of negligence is the lost opportunities due to a deprived education, although the courts have so far tried to rationalise these claim as personal injury claims. See, *Phelps*, above n 8, and cases listed above n 22.

[75] All three judges in *Coudert Brothers*, above n 73 expressed their disquiet at the Court of Appeal's decision to deny liability in *Gregg*, above n 6, with Laws LJ expressing this comment on *Gregg* (*Coudert Brothers*, [68]): 'But I am driven to an unhappy sense that the common law has lost its way. If a man's chance of a cure from a potentially fatal cancer has been reduced by another's negligence from 42% to 25%, would not a reasonable jury say that he had been grievously hurt by the negligence?'

[76] The other argument was that the defendant's negligence had caused an injury, which was the enlargement of the tumour, and the loss that flowed was thus consequential on the physical injury. This was an attempt to circumvent the gist of negligence argument by casting the loss of chance within the realm of quantification. Cf *Mallett*, above n 63.

[77] The majority consisted of Lords Hoffmann and Phillips of Worth Matravers and Baroness Hale of Richmond. The minority was constituted by Lords Nicholls of Birkenhead and Hope of Craighead.

Baroness Hale referred to *Kitchen* and posed a penetrating question by comparing the approach to loss of chance claims against doctors vis-à-vis such claims against lawyers:

> So why should my solicitor be liable for negligently depriving me of the chance of winning my action, even if I never had a better than evens chance of success, when my doctor is not liable for negligently depriving me of the chance of getting better, even if I never had a better than evens chance of getting better? Is this another example of the law being kinder to the medical profession than to other professionals?[78]

Baroness Hale then distinguished the two, largely on the basis that one involved economic loss and the other personal injury, and took the view that personal injuries were better compensated on an all or nothing approach rather than on a loss of chance approach, as that could cut both ways. Under the loss of chance approach, defendant doctors could argue for a reduction in damages in cases where the claimant could only show a 60% chance of recovery, which traditionally would have given the claimant full recovery on the balance of probabilities approach to causation. The majority was clearly concerned with the potential for an unjustified extension of medical liability if loss of chance claims were allowed. One policy consideration that did not persuade the majority, but found favour with Lord Nicholls was that failure to recognise loss of chance claims would diminish the deterrent effect of negligence on medical practitioners, as they could be as negligent as they liked with respect to patients who had a less than even chance of a successful outcome.[79]

The general practitioner of today is more often than not a gate keeper, whose principal role is to make a diagnosis and refer the patient to the relevant specialist for treatment. In cases of potentially serious illness or disease, a patient goes to the general practitioner in order to be referred to the appropriate specialist who is trained to treat the particular problem. The sole purpose of the general practitioner's duty in such cases is to provide the patient with the opportunity of a timely referral to the appropriate specialist. Nobody expects the local general practitioner to cure a patient of cancer or to prevent the likelihood or consequences of an imminent heart attack.[80] This is exactly why solicitors are held liable for

---

[78] *Gregg,* above n 6, at [218].

[79] *Gregg,* above n 6, at [43] Lord Nichols, referring to Dore J in *Herskovits v Group Health Cooperative of Puget Sound* 664 P 2d 474 (Wash Sup Ct 1983) 477. See also, Luntz, above n 64, at 183.

[80] *Breeze v Ahmad* [2005] EWCA Civ 223 was just such a situation. The claimant's husband had complained of serious chest pains and went to the defendant general practitioner, who without carrying out a physical examination, told the deceased to go home and take some painkillers. The trial judge described the defendant's negligence as gross. However, the claim failed as the trial judge was not persuaded that, on the balance of probabilities, timely referral would have allowed the deceased to have survived the fatal heart attack a

negligently depriving their clients of their day in court. The solicitor's duty is not to provide the client with guaranteed success, but to provide the client with an opportunity to test his or her claim in court, just as the general medical practitioner's duty is to allow his or her patient to have an opportunity of being appropriately treated by a specialist.

Gregg, analysed in this way, is a classic illustration of a category of cases where denial of recovery on the basis of causation destroys the very *raison d'être* of the duty, bringing it precisely within the *Fairchild/Chester* reasoning on causation. Medical loss of chance claims should be limited to this type of 'diagnostic medical negligence', where the misdiagnosis deprives the patient of the opportunity for potentially successful treatment. By focusing on the gist of negligence rather than on policy-based relaxation of causation, better control over the categories of recovery for loss of chance is retained.[81] On this analysis, loss of chance claims need not be extended to other areas of medical negligence, where the gist of negligence remains the physical injury and not the chance. Cases like *Wilsher v Essex Area Health Authority*[82] can thus be distinguished on principle.

III.   CONCLUSION AND THE FUTURE OF NEGLIGENCE

A normative approach to determining both the gist of negligence and the extent of recovery is essential. The purposive approach of the House of Lords and the common sense plus 'scope of risk' approach of the High Court of Australia have gone a long way to addressing this issue. The only refinement that is required, and which has been recognised in *Barker*, is the reorientation of the gist of negligence. Instead of focusing on the causal connection between the negligent conduct and the ultimate physical injury, in some cases, the focus should be shifted to the intermediate harm—whether it is exposure to risk (*Fairchild/Barker*), or loss of chance (*Gregg*) or loss of rights (*Chester*).

This reinterpretation inevitably raises new problems of quantification of loss, as *Barker* and *Chester* clearly demonstrate. Should the claimant be compensated for the full extent of the injury that resulted as a consequence of the increased risk or loss of right or the lost chance? Or should the claimant be compensated for the value of the right or chance? While this is

---

month later. The Court of Appeal allowed the appeal on the ground that there were procedural errors with the evidence and remitted the case for trial on causation. No argument on the basis of loss of chance was advanced.

[81] Cf J Stapleton, 'Loss of a Chance' (2005) 68 *MLR* 996, 1002 n38, who accepts Baroness Hale's argument in *Gregg* that allowing loss of chance claims would inevitably result in such claims cutting across other fields.

[82] *Wilsher*, above n 24.

an important practical question, the difficulty of quantification should not detract from the substantial question of whether the tort of negligence should evolve to address 21st century concerns which are framed in the language of rights and expectations. The recent trend of cases suggests a greater judicial willingness to protect certain rights and expectations, infringement of which has the potential to, and in most cases does, result in physical harm or death.

The difficulties of quantification may be met at two levels. First, there should be less emphasis on the *Wagon Mound* reasonable foreseeability test as the control device for remoteness of damage,[83] and courts should instead base the scope of liability on an ex post reasonable recoverability test. Second, courts should use this opportunity to extend the remedies for negligence beyond mere compensation and consider innovative solutions, including the use of equitable or public law remedies. The nervous shock cases underscore part of the first argument that the *Wagon Mound* reasonable foreseeability test may be more apt to the duty question rather than the remoteness question.[84] Because courts were preoccupied with the actual gist of negligence, ie, nervous shock, they naturally determined the scope of duty on the basis of foreseeability of nervous shock. In the uncontroversial physical injury cases, foreseeability of the type of damage is deferred to the remoteness stage, when in fact it should be considered at the scope of duty stage.

The weakness of reasonable foreseeability as a sensible test for the scope of liability (as opposed to the scope of duty) is evident from the fact that the law insists that the defendant take the victim as he or she is.[85] The strongest support for a reasonable recoverability argument is the survival of the eggshell skull principle following the *Wagon Mound*.[86] In these cases, defendants are held liable for damage that is not reasonably foreseeable, but clearly should be reasonably recoverable. It would be manifestly unfair for the innocent claimant to be denied the full extent of his or her loss due to his or her personal susceptibility, despite the fact that

---

[83] *Overseas Tankship (UK), Ltd v Morts Dock & Engineering Co, Ltd (The Wagon Mound (No 1))* [1961] 1 AC 388 (PC) [*Wagon Mound*].

[84] Viscount Simonds in *Wagon Mound*, above, at 426 alluded to the 'shadowy line' between culpability and compensation, and based his conclusion on liability on the nervous shock cases: 'We have come back to the plain common sense stated by Lord Russell of Killowen in *Bourhill v Young*. As Denning LJ said in *King v Phillips*: "there can be no doubt since *Bourhill v Young* that the test of *liability for shock* is foreseeability of *injury by shock*". Their Lordships substitute the word "fire" for "shock" and endorse this statement of the law.'

[85] If a defendant runs over a pedestrian, it is not relevant to the reasonable foreseeability inquiry whether the victim is a vagrant or a multi-billionaire; the defendant simply takes the consequences.

[86] *Smith v Leech Brain* [1962] 2 QB 405 (QB); *Stephenson v Waite Tileman Ltd* [1973] 1 NZLR 152 (CA); *Robinson v Post Office* [1974] 1 WLR 1176 (CA); *Page v Smith* [1996] 1 AC 155 (HL) [*Page*].

such injury was not reasonable foreseeable by the defendant. Even apart from the eggshell skull cases, courts have stretched the concept of reasonable foreseeability to accommodate sympathetic cases;[87] and in some instances, have completely abandoned the need for reasonable foreseeability of injury.[88]

Focusing on reasonable recovery also gives courts greater scope to enhance the deterrent role of negligence. This is particularly relevant in cases like *Chester*, *Gregg* and *Barker*. Allowing compensation, whether full or proportionate, in such cases may expose the defendant to paying for more than his or her actual contribution to the risk or even the ultimate damage. However, this may be justified on the ground of deterrence; emphasising the deterrent role of negligence will pave the way for a more caring and responsible society in a changing world where risks to personal integrity and security are on the rise.

Alternatively, courts could import equitable or public law remedies into the tort of negligence and give the tort a far more valuable role to play in this era where our personal rights are especially vulnerable. Where the defendant is a large corporation or a public authority, remedies such as injunctions or declarations may be more effective than compensation, and would be an effective means of deterring risky or unjustified conduct. There are indirect examples, such as *Shimp v New Jersey Bell Telephone Co*,[89] where the court held that where 'an employer is under a common law duty to act, a court of equity may enforce an employee's rights by ordering the employer to eliminate any preventable hazardous condition which the court finds to exist'.[90]

The 21st century is imposing new demands on the law of negligence with social norms and community expectations being shaped by very different forces from those that shaped the earlier eras. Globalisation, the knowledge revolution, and the renewed emphasis on human rights have attached significant value to intangible interests such as information,[91] expectation, educational opportunity, autonomy, and rights. There are exciting choices to be made at this point in the development of the tort of negligence. What interests should it cover? What degree of connection is required between

---

[87] For example in *Nader v Urban Transit Authority of NSW* (1985) 2 NSWLR 501 (CA), a child suffered a minor laceration to his head as he fell from a bus. He subsequently developed bizarre psychiatric symptoms and was diagnosed with an extremely rare disorder known as 'Ganser Syndrome', which the Court of Appeal found to be reasonably foreseeable, despite the trial judge's finding that the condition was extremely rare and complex as well as little understood by the medical profession itself.

[88] For example, *Page* above n 86.

[89] A 2d 408 (NJ SC 1976). See N McBride, 'Duties of Care—Do They Really Exist?' (2004) 24 *OJLS* 417, 427-29.

[90] *Ibid*, at 521.

[91] See, D McLeod, 'Regulating Damage on the Internet: A Tortious Approach?' (2001) 27 *Monash University Law Review* 344.

the defendant's conduct and the claimant's loss? Who should bear the burden of risky enterprise? What remedies can the tort of negligence provide? Is it a tort that needs to be wound back, or is it a tort that is only now about to live up to its true potential of fostering a caring, responsible society?

Linden JA, one of the greatest champions of *Donoghue v Stevenson*[92] and the law of negligence, has long argued for an expanded role for negligence, not merely as a means of providing compensation but as a means of regulating conduct and empowering the vulnerable.[93] These recent rights-based cases suggest that his vision of negligence may be a step closer to reality:

> For me *D & S* (or at least its spirit) plays a role in the law not unlike the role that the Bible plays for Christians, or the Torah plays for Jews, or the Koran for Moslems. It inspires those noble thoughts and deeds of which we need more in the modern world, not less. It challenges us to dream of a beautiful world where people care about one another, feel responsible for one another, and even—dare I say it—love one another.[94]

The birthright of the tort of negligence is its commitment to protecting the vulnerable, and in that pursuit, adapting itself to reflect societal changes and to meet new challenges. *Donoghue* was its golden moment, as the tort of negligence rose to address the risks of mass manufacture and distribution brought about by the industrial revolution.[95] We are now in the era of rights and expectations, and once again the tort of negligence is rising to the challenge. Courts and 'tortophobic' academics should not attempt to choke off the natural evolution of this tort.

---

[92] [1932] AC 562 (HL).

[93] AM Linden, 'Tort Law as Ombudsman' (1973) 51 *Canadian Bar Review* 155; AM Linden, 'Torts Tomorrow—Empowering the Injured' in NJ Mullany and AM Linden, *Torts Tomorrow: A Tribute to John Fleming* (Sydney, NSW, LBC Information Services, 1998) 321.

[94] AM Linden, 'Viva *Donoghue v Stevenson*!' in PT Burns and SJ Lyons, *Donoghue v Stevenson and the Modern Law of Negligence* (Vancouver, The Continuing Legal Education Society of British Columbia, 1991) 228.

[95] Lord Atkin was strongly of the view that the law should accord with the changing times and community expectation: 'It is a proposition which I venture to say no one in Scotland or England who was not a lawyer would for one moment doubt. It will be an advantage to make it clear that the law in this matter, as in most others, is in accordance with sound common sense' (*Donoghue v Stevenson* [1932] 1 AC 562 (HL) 599).

19

Tort Law in Practice: Appearance and Reality in Reforming Periodical Payments of Damages

RICHARD LEWIS*

I. INTRODUCTION

THIS CHAPTER IS distinct from almost all the others in this book and is part of a different tradition in tort scholarship. This is because it is founded on experience of the practical operation of the tort system and because it refers to empirical work which describes how that system operates. The other chapters are not as directly concerned with who actually pays and in what manner for personal injury—the most important type of tort claim as far as most practitioners are concerned. The conference for which this chapter was prepared exposed a gulf between the views of such practitioners and the particular academic discourse which predominated in the papers presented at the event. This gulf was brilliantly highlighted in a devastating after-dinner speech by Justice Ian Binnie of the Supreme Court of Canada. This chapter attempts to bridge the divide by setting a particular 'emerging issue in tort law' in its wider economic and political context, and reflecting on both its academic and its practical implications. It also outlines the basis for comparative work by noting legislation in Canada which is similar to that in the UK which forms the focus for this study.

This chapter deals with the recently renewed attack upon paying damages for personal injury in the form of a lump sum as opposed to periodically. Almost twenty years ago the concept of a structured settlement was imported from North America and first used in the UK in order

* Professor of Law, Cardiff Law School, Cardiff University. For their comments and assistance I am indebted to various Cardiff colleagues and to John Rousseau of the McKellar Group.

to provide continuing lifetime payments for seriously injured claimants.[1] However, the idea was slow to develop. Proposals for a structure were easily defeated if either of the parties objected. To counter this, legislation has now removed the veto: taking into account the needs of the claimant, a judge can make a periodical payments order even if it is against the wishes of either or even both of the parties. The court must consider making such an order in any case involving future financial loss. The lump sum award is thus under attack.

I will look at the impact of this reform on the settlement system and the bargaining power of the parties. The relationship between the new legislative regime and the existing approach to structured settlements is examined. Looking at the wider context, my analysis reveals that in this reform there was an inadequate assessment of the economic and financial factors which affect the payment of damages. In particular, the cost to liability insurers of changing the form of payment was under-estimated. Although having the greatest effect on insurers, the reform is in fact driven by government concern about the impact of lump sum awards upon National Health Service budgets in clinical negligence cases. Deferring the full payment of damages to later years is politically attractive, and gives the state an interest in how damages are paid. This interest was insufficiently acknowledged in the justifications provided for the reform, so that it appears to have been enacted for one set of reasons but in fact was enacted for another. This chapter therefore emphasises that there are sharp differences between the surface appearance of the legislation and the realities of tort law in practice.

II. THE FIRST JUDICIALLY APPROVED STRUCTURE

Traditionally damages for personal injury in the UK were always paid by means of a lump sum, and never a pension. It did not matter that the compensation was for losses that might be suffered in the future: both the monthly wage that the accident victim may have lost, and the continuing costs of care that would have to be met, were compensated by one large payment. In recent years this once-and-for-all lump sum system has been subject to increasing criticism. In particular, it results in much uncertainty and imposes upon a claimant an enormous responsibility for safeguarding the future. Inflation and the vagaries of the returns on investment of the lump sum can result in rapid erosion of the compensation. As a result, a new form of payment via a structured settlement has made limited inroads

---

[1] R Lewis, *Structured Settlements: The Law and Practice* (London, Sweet & Maxwell, 1993) and I Goldrein and M de Haas (eds), *Structured Settlements: A Practical Guide*, 2nd edn (London, Butterworths, 1997).

into the use of lump sums. In effect, such a settlement usually converts the traditional lump sum into a series of payments derived from an annuity and these continue to be made no matter how long the claimant lives. In addition, these payments can be protected against price inflation and are free of tax.

These attractions of periodical payments were clearly illustrated in 1989 by the first judicially approved structure for a UK resident. *Kelly v Dawes* arose out of a tragic road accident which took place three years earlier. Catherine Kelly was then a 22-year-old nurse, and was a passenger in a car driven by her husband, Andrew, a stonemason.[2] Not far from their home they were involved in a road accident caused entirely by the negligence of the driver of the other vehicle. Both drivers were killed. Catherine lost the husband she had recently married, and suffered catastrophic injuries herself. The judge described the effect upon her as follows:

> She was transformed from a lively young woman . . . into a bedridden invalid with grossly impaired neurological functions, almost totally unaware of her surroundings, totally dependent on skilled nursing care and the devoted atten-tion of her loving parents and family. Her condition will not improve for the rest of her life, in respect of which her life expectancy has been reduced to some 20 years. That figure is the product of a compromise medical view between doctors whose best guesses are on either side of the figure agreed.[3]

In seeking damages on her behalf, Catherine's father was keen to ensure that she would be looked after in a private nursing home for the rest of her life. Any money that might accrue to her estate upon her death was not an important consideration. Instead the major concern was that, given her uncertain life expectancy, the damages should be managed in order to ensure that, if she lived longer than the projected period, there would continue to be money to pay for her care. The best means of achieving this proved to be via a structure.

The settlement provided for most of Catherine's damages to be used to purchase an annuity from a life insurance company. The damages could be used in this way because there remained additional capital to provide a contingency fund for unexpected events. This reserve fund derived from the equity in Catherine's home, and from the estate she inherited from her husband, including the damages for his fatal accident. The annuity purchased with the damages was for an 'impaired life'. This meant that it provided a substantially higher annual return than a standard policy because the life insurer believed that the accident had reduced Catherine's life expectancy and the payments would therefore be made over a shorter

---

[2] (1990) Times, 27 September (QB) [*Kelly*].
[3] Transcript of the judgment of Potter J reproduced in Lewis, above n 1, at app 4, [2].

period of time. In fact, for rating purposes the life office treated her as thirty-five years older than she actually was.

The major benefits of structuring the award were clearly revealed: the index-linked instalment payments were free of tax, and to last either for the rest of Catherine's life or for ten years, whichever proved longer. They would therefore ensure that she could continue to be kept at a private nursing home even if she lived beyond her projected span of years. Based on certain assumptions, the monies from a lump sum settlement invested in the conventional portfolio of fixed interest stocks and blue-chip shares would have been exhausted within twelve years, whereas the monthly payments under a structure would continue to be made. In addition, Catherine's father would not be subject to the stress of having to invest and be responsible for a lump sum greater than most people would encounter in their lifetime. Nor would the cost of obtaining investment advice have to be met. The financial advantages of the structure and the peace of mind it gave to the concerned relatives were clearly shown.

Ten years after the settlement Catherine's father spoke about his decision to seek periodical payments. He said:

> I wanted the certainty of knowing that money would be available for the rest of Cathy's life. Looking back, the medical experts' view on her life expectation ranged from 5–10 years to 10–20 years. Physically, Cathy is in better shape now and if they come back today, they would say that she could live another 20–30 years from now. They got it wrong . . .. I have absolute peace of mind in knowing that, even if I am no longer here, there will still be money available for Cathy's needs for the rest of her life.[4]

III.   THE NEED TO IMPOSE PERIODICAL PAYMENTS

Since *Kelly* there have been over 1,500 seriously-injured people who have received part of their compensation in the form of periodical payments.[5] However, further expansion of structured settlements has been hindered in several ways. One difficulty has been the refusal by many lawyers to give proper consideration to the merits of the alternative form of payment, even though they might be liable for failing to do so.[6] Their reluctance to investigate structures has partly been attributed to the innate conservatism

---

[4] I Goldrein, M de Haas and J Frenkel, *Personal Injury Major Claims Handling: Cost Effective Case Management* (London, Butterworths, 2000) [17.168].

[5] I estimate this figure on the basis of various statistics supplied over the years by the major intermediaries in the field. It sharply contrasts with the higher figures for various years reported by the Compensation Recovery Unit. Based on my own empirical work at the Compensation Recovery Unit, its figures are the result of clerical error and inaccurate coding.

[6] R Lewis, 'A Lawyer's Duty to Consider a Structured Settlement' (1993) 9 *Professional Negligence* 126.

of the legal profession,[7] together with ignorance or misconception of what might be involved. Sometimes structures have been raised as a possibility only at a late stage in the proceedings, by which time the claimant and his or her advisors have become used to the idea of receiving a lump sum and are suspicious of the change in approach. As a result, in practice, structures have been examined only in a minority of the cases in which they could have been sought. For example, in 2001-02 the National Health Service (NHS) paid over 500 claims in excess of £100,000 and yet less than ten per cent involved a structured settlement.[8]

The overall result has been that, largely through inertia, the lump sum has retained its dominance. A major factor in this has been the ability of either of the parties to object and thereby defeat with ease any proposed settlement based on periodical payments.[9] It is this veto which is directly attacked by the new legislation. After lengthy consultation,[10] the parties' veto was removed by the Courts Act 2003 with effect from 2005.[11] Taking into account the needs of the claimant, a judge can make a periodical payments order (PPO) even if it is against the wishes of both parties. If a personal injury case comes to court and involves future pecuniary loss, the judge has no choice but to consider making a PPO. An order can be made even if not requested or wanted by the parties or where they envisaged an alternative award. The cases affected will usually be those involving serious

---

[7]   W Norris, 'Structured Settlements: Past and Future Developments' (paper delivered to the Legal Wales Conference, September 2003) (cited with author's permission). Similarly Lord Steyn could think of no substantial argument against judicial imposition of periodical payments other than 'the distaste of personal injury lawyers for change to a familiar system' in *Wells v Wells* [1999] AC 345 (HL) 384.

[8]   Lord Chancellor's Department, 'Courts Bill: Regulatory Impact Assessment' (November 2002) table 1.

[9]   The need for the consent of both parties was affirmed as early as *Burke v Tower Hamlets* (1989) Times, 10 August (QB). The point was reinforced by *R v Liverpool Health Authority et al ex p Hopley* [2002] Lloyd's Rep Medical 494 (HC), discussed in R Lewis, 'Clinical Negligence and the NHS Refusal to Structure Settlements With Profit' (2003) 19 *Professional Negligence* 297.

[10]   Lord Chancellor's Department, 'Damages for Future Loss' (Consultation Paper CP 01/02, March 2002) and its 'Analyses of the Responses' (CP(R) 01/02, November 2002). The Department addressed this issue more briefly in its previous paper, 'The Discount Rate and Alternatives to Lump Sum Payments' (Consultation Paper CP 3/00, March 2000). See also the Clinical Disputes Forum Discussion Paper, 'Lump Sum Damages and Periodical Payments' (2000) and the report summarising the responses (April 2002). With structures in their infancy in 1994, the Law Commission considered it premature to give judges the power to impose periodical payments in 'Structured Settlements and Interim and Provisional Damages' (Law Com No 224, 1994) [3.37] et seq. In a limited form periodical payments were recommended by Lord Pearson, 'Report of the Royal Commission on Civil Liability and Compensation for Personal Injury' (Cmnd 7054, 1978) vol 1, [573] [Pearson Report]. Earlier, reviewable periodical payments had been canvassed by the Law Commission, Working Paper No 41 (1971) but the response was so critical that the proposal was abandoned in its final report, 'Personal Injury Litigation: Assessment of Damages' (Law Com No 56, 1973).

[11]   The changes were made by ss 100 and 101 of the Courts Act 2003 which amended the Damages Act 1996.

injury where claims for future earnings or the cost of care are made. Although relatively few in number, these are much more likely to come before a court and to be in the public eye. They are also where the claimant is likely to be in the most need and in the greatest danger of being under-compensated.[12] Although the court's power to make a PPO is limited, the threat of its use affects the bargaining position of the parties in most major cases.

IV.   LIMITS ON THE POWER TO IMPOSE PERIODICAL PAYMENTS

The power to make a PPO is limited in three particular respects. First, the power cannot be exercised in respect of damages for past pecuniary or non-pecuniary loss unless the parties agree. This means that only a minority of all claims in tort are in danger of having an order imposed because over 90 per cent involve only these two heads of damage and have no element of future loss.[13] The typical claim is for a very small sum of money[14] and it will continue to be disposed of by means of a lump sum. The preponderance of these small claims in the system is reflected in the fact that non-pecuniary loss accounts for about two-thirds of the overall amount of damages awarded and past financial loss accounts for about a further quarter.[15] However, these percentages change considerably in serious injury cases when future loss becomes much more important. For example, it has been estimated that, on average, 83 per cent of a claim exceeding £250,000 against the NHS comprises future loss.[16] In addition, it must be emphasised that these few serious injury cases are responsible for a substantial amount of the overall total of damages awarded: in 2002

---

[12] For example, it is likely that certain claimants will be substantially under-compensated for loss of earnings. R Lewis, R McNabb, H Robinson and V Wass, 'Court Awards of Damages for Loss of Future Earnings: An Empirical Study and an Alternative Method of Calculation' (2002) 29 *Journal of Law & Society* 406 and [2002] *Journal of Personal Injury Law* 151 and, by the same authors, 'Loss of Earnings Following Personal Injury: Do the Courts Adequately Compensate Injured Parties?' (2003) 113 *Economic Journal* F568.

[13] Future pecuniary loss was found in only 7.5 per cent of cases, and comprised only 8.3 per cent of the total damages paid in tort. See the Pearson Report, above n 10, vol 2, at [44] and table 107.

[14] £2,500 was the median figure in the survey of 81,000 cases receiving legal aid and closed in 1996-97 in P Pleasence, *Personal Injury Litigation in Practice* (London, Legal Aid Board Research Unit, 1998) 40, fig 3.17. In 70 per cent of successful cases the damages were less than £5,000, although the overall average was £11,000. P Fenn and N Rickman, 'Costs of Low Value Liability Claims 1997-2002' report average damages of only £3,000 for employers liability accident claims, although this study of almost 100,000 cases related only to claims for less than £15,000. See <http://www.dca.gov.uk/majrep/claims/elclaims.htm> (date accessed: 17 July 2006).

[15] As found by the Pearson Report, above n 10, vol 2, at table 107.

[16] Lord Chancellor's Department, above n 8, at table 3. However, in table 8 the Association of British Insurers estimated that only 46 per cent of the value of claims between £100,000 and £250,000 comprised future loss.

insurers estimated that although only 1 per cent of cases resulted in a payment of £100,000 or more, they accounted for 32 per cent of the total compensation received by claimants.[17] It is in cases involving this level of damages, albeit a minority of all claims, where the new rules will have the greatest effect.

Second, a PPO can only be made if the continuity of payment is 'reasonably secure'.[18] Legislation prescribes that the payments will be secure if either they are to be made by a government or health service body,[19] or if they are protected by a compensation scheme which guarantees payment in the event of an insurer's insolvency.[20] In effect, this means that orders can be made in the overwhelming majority of personal injury claims. One exception is that the Motor Insurers Bureau is not covered, but it has already been able to demonstrate successfully to a court that it is sufficiently secure for a PPO to be made in cases in which it is involved.[21] Those against whom questions of security will be raised include Lloyd's syndicates, the medical defence organisations, offshore insurance companies, and private self-insured defendants. Even in these cases, a PPO can still be made and the security requirement met if the payments are arranged via the purchase of an annuity from a life insurer which is covered by the scheme guaranteeing payment in the event of insolvency.

The third and final limitation on the power to impose periodical payments is the most important in practice. The power can only be exercised if the case comes to court. Even though cases of serious injury are more likely to come before a judge, it remains the case that only a minority of them do so.[22] Therefore, if neither party wants periodical payments to be considered, they can achieve their aim by settling privately for a lump sum. No matter what the court might have considered to be the needs of the claimant, the parties will get their wish for a lump sum deal if they keep their negotiations behind closed doors and avoid judicial involvement.

---

[17] Lord Chancellor's Department, above n 8, at table 1.

[18] Damages Act 1996, s 2(3) as amended by the Courts Act 2003, s 100.

[19] As specified in the Damages (Government and Heath Service Bodies) Order 2005, SI 2005/474.

[20] Financial Services and Markets Act 2000, s 213, discussed in detail in Annex C of Department for Constitutional Affairs, 'Guidance on Periodical Payments' (April 2005). Also acceptable are Ministerial guarantees under the Damages Act 1996, s 6.

[21] *Thacker v Steeples and the MIB* (QB 16 May 2005;Lawtell Quantum AM 0900821) and *Daniels v Edge and the MIB* (2005) 15 *Personal Injury Focus* 23 (QB).

[22] Before being set down for trial 98 per cent of cases are settled and many more are concluded before any hearing takes place: Pearson Report, above n 10, vol 2, at table 12. Similarly Pleasence, above n 14, at 12 reveals that only five out of the 762 'ordinary' cases with costs of less than £5,000 went to trial. However, a much larger percentage of serious injury cases end up in court. In cases involving very substantial awards of damages ten per cent of payments were found to be the result of formal court orders by P Cornes, *Coping with Catastrophic Injury* (Edinburgh, Rehabilitation Studies Unit, 1993) 20.

V. EXERCISE OF THE COURT'S DISCRETION TO AWARD PERIODICAL PAYMENTS

As noted, in any case involving future pecuniary loss the court must consider making a PPO. Whether it imposes such an order lies within its discretion and depends upon the particular facts of the case. The legislation offers only limited guidance about what might affect this decision. The most important consideration is the claimant's needs.[23] Only in a Practice Direction is the court referred to the secondary issue of whether either of the parties prefers a lump sum and their reasons for doing so.

The emphasis on the claimant's needs is novel: it is not to be found in earlier legislation dealing with damages. Need never affects compensation for lost earnings or pain and suffering, for example, although it is implicit in any assessment of housing or nursing care costs. Need is notoriously difficult to define,[24] but focusing on it can produce a different perspective on an award. It contrasts with the usual objective in tort of returning the claimant to the pre-accident position. In particular, need requires a more detailed analysis of the claimant's future than the tort system has previously attempted.

Apart from need, the court must also have regard to the nature of any financial advice received by the claimant. This advice will rarely be that of the claimant's own solicitor, because legislation prevents financial advice being given by those who are not authorised.[25] Instead the court will require the opinion of an independent financial advisor. This will have to be sought early in the proceedings because, as soon as is reasonably practicable, the court is required to give the parties a preliminary indication of which form of payment it considers the more appropriate.[26] Financial intermediaries will therefore have an even more important part to play than they did in the past with structured settlements, for then they were often involved only at a late stage. The projections of these experts concerning the extent that the lump sum will be eroded compared to the constant value of the periodical payments will be crucial in determining the form of the award, and their opinion will now be given at an early stage in the proceedings.

The court must also consider 'the scale of the annual payments taking into account any deduction for contributory negligence'.[27] One area of

---

[23]   Civil Procedure Rules 1998, r 41.7 as amended by SI 2004/3129.

[24]   For the most recent assessment of the difficulties involved see M Tibble, 'Review of Existing Research on the Extra Costs of Disability' (Department of Work and Pensions, Working Paper no 21, 2005).

[25]   Financial Services and Markets Act 2000, Sch 6.

[26]   Civil Procedure Rules 1998, r 41.6. See J Stone and A Sands, 'Periodical Payments: The Need for a Pragmatic Approach' (2005) 15 *Personal Injury Focus* 18.

[27]   CPR Practice Direction 41B, 1(1).

uncertainty is the level of damages below which it might not be worthwhile to move towards a periodic award because its size may not merit the time and trouble involved. Under the old rules the court had to be satisfied that a structured settlement had been considered by the parties in any case involving damages for future loss of £500,000 or more.[28] However, for a periodical payment under the new rules Ministers concluded that the size of an award should not be the determining factor. Perhaps they had in mind the experience of the US, where structured settlements have become commonplace even at damages levels below £100,000. Instead of setting a damages threshold, therefore, the government has left the court to assess only whether arranging the award in a new form might involve disproportionate effort.[29] Although in theory any award of future loss could therefore be paid periodically, in practice a PPO will be less appropriate for certain types of claim. For example, although there is nothing to prevent a court imposing an order no matter what the age of the claimant, the objection of an elderly person to being paid periodically might be expected to have more force given the shorter duration of the payments.[30]

Another factor affecting the level at which a PPO may be made and the extent they will be used is that, in most serious injury cases, the claimant should be left with a contingency lump sum fund to meet unexpected needs. It is essential that this element of flexibility exists to safeguard the future, even though it is not mentioned in the legislation. There are fears that judges will not take it into account sufficiently.[31] Capital may be needed not only to buy and adapt accommodation, but also to care for the claimant, for example in the event of the unexpected death or divorce of his or her carer spouse. Capital might also be needed if, as expected, care costs outpace price inflation. For structured settlements in the past, on average, only about half of the award was used to arrange the periodic payments. The remainder was accounted for by interim payments, the capital needed to discharge debts and pay for immediate purchases, and the contingency fund.[32] Will judges take a similar approach?

---

[28] Former RSC Practice Direction 21[6.4]. The practice of the NHS was to consider a structure in any case having a minimum value of £250,000.

[29] Department for Constitutional Affairs, 'Guidance on Periodical Payments' (April 2005) [9]. See <http://www.dca.gov.uk/pubs/pps-guidance-final.pdf> (date accessed: 17 July 2006).

[30] The life expectancy of the claimant is mentioned as a factor in Explanatory Note 356 to the Courts Act 2003, but is not referred to elsewhere.

[31] N Leech, 'New Rules Could Prove Damaging' (2005) 10 *Legal & Medical* 25 and A Sands, 'Periodical Payments—the Development of a Pragmatic Approach' (2006) 74 *Medico-Legal Journal* 69. See also the Master of the Court of Protection, D Lush, 'Damages for Personal Injury: Why Some Claimants Prefer a Conventional Lump Sum to Periodical Payments' (2005) 1 *London Law Review* 187, 191.

[32] Lewis, above n 1, at [9]-[66] et seq where the factors affecting the size of the contingency fund are examined in detail.

One area of concern with regard to when an order may be made is whether the award of damages is to be reduced for contributory negligence. This may not become apparent until a late stage in the proceedings, and yet it could be crucial in influencing the financial adviser as to the form of the award. If there is to be a reduction in damages, a PPO may not then be enough to pay the cost of the claimant's immediate nursing needs. It might then be thought better to award a lump sum. Although that payment is more likely to be exhausted earlier if not within the tax shelter provided by periodical payments, it may be preferable for this to occur and for the claimant's actual needs to be met for only a short time, rather than leaving a permanently inadequate source of funds to offer insufficient protection against needs which have yet to occur.

VI.   A CHANGE TO THE METHOD FOR ASSESSING DAMAGES

Where periodical payments are thought appropriate, the court is required to make a fundamental change in the way that it calculates damages: instead of a 'top-down' approach it must adopt a 'bottom-up' approach,[33] thereby focusing more precisely upon the claimant's needs.

The more familiar top-down approach begins only after arriving at the traditional lump sum. It then calculates the income stream which can be derived from that capital, and this can be used to assess whether it will meet the claimant's annual needs. This top-down approach does not avoid the most serious criticisms made of lump sums: the need to forecast how long the payments will be required, and the rate of return, after taxation and inflation, which could be obtained from investment of the lump sum. In particular, the claimant's life expectancy is usually an element in estimating how long the payments will be required. It is usually only *after* the lump sum has been calculated using these traditional methods that it is used in a structured settlement to transfer from the claimant to an insurer the risk of the claimant living beyond his or her estimated life expectancy. This is usually achieved by the liability insurer using the lump sum to purchase annuities from a life office to provide a stream of payments for as long as the claimant actually lives. Structures, therefore, usually involve only changing the form of payment after the parties have gone through the traditional approach and, as a result, they retain many of the disadvantages of the lump sum.

By contrast, for a PPO the new legislation requires a bottom-up approach. Unlike top-down, this does not require the lump sum to be calculated at all. Instead, irrespective of the capital cost, the court assesses the periodical payments the claimant needs for the future and orders that

---

[33] *Ibid*, at [9]-[10] et seq.

they be index-linked and paid for the duration of the loss, this often being the claimant's lifetime. Unlike under the traditional form of payment, it is the defendant who is burdened with both the risk of the investment return and the longevity of the claimant.

Overall a complex budget for life may be needed, and there is great pressure to 'get it right'.[34] Detailed planning of the claimant's future is encouraged by allowing the payments to increase in steps, or even decrease.[35] However, these variations in payment can only take place if the court specifies in the original order the precise dates for the changes to take effect. The court is encouraged to plan for a variety of factors including those affecting earnings (the claimant ceasing to work, or gaining a promotional increase in pay) and affecting care (loss of the existing gratuitous carers, or changes in the medical condition).

The crucial difference from previous practice is that the court is not concerned with the lump sum cost of providing for these needs. Nor does it have to speculate for how long there will still be such need. Clairvoyant estimates of how long the claimant will live, for example, are made redundant. In addition, there is no need to speculate about the returns possible upon investment of a lump sum. There is no place for the 'Ogden Tables'.[36] Multipliers and discount rates are otiose: no multiplier is required to reflect the period of years of the loss in order to convert it into an immediate capital amount, and no discount rate is needed to convert the future stream of financial losses into a capital sum representing present day values. It is the defendant who must now assume liability over time for these risks.

VII.   THE IMPACT ON THE BARGAINING POWER OF THE PARTIES

It would be a mistake to assume that because new legislation has been passed it will necessarily be used in the way intended by the drafters. The legal rules provide a framework for bargaining between the parties, and the results can be very different from the picture of litigation envisaged by the black-letter lawyer. Within the shadow of the new rules it is likely that a number of claimants will try to take advantage of the removal of the defendant's veto: they will threaten to take the case to court and burden the defendant with a PPO involving uncertain liabilities unless there is agreement to a higher lump sum than previously was on offer. Exactly the

---

[34] Law Commission, 'Structured Settlements and Interim and Provisional Damages' (Consultation Paper No 125, 1992) [3.19].

[35] CPR Practice Direction 41B [2.2].

[36] Government Actuary's Department, *Actuarial Tables For Use In Personal Injury And Fatal Accident Cases*, 5th edn (London, The Stationery Office, 2004).

same tactic has been used to extract a larger lump sum when the power to award provisional damages has been in issue.

Somewhat less successfully, insurers may also use the threat of periodical payments to bargain harder with a claimant who is set on receiving a lump sum, or worried about whether the court's assessment of needs will correspond to his or her own. Can a judge be trusted to leave enough of a contingency lump sum fund to provide for unexpected events? Claimants may also be concerned that even an index-linked settlement may not be enough to pay for their future care costs. Because of these worries bargains will be struck to settle out of court. The experience of other countries is that these deals have undermined the power to make periodic awards to such an extent that 'lump-sum settlements have like termites reduced the [periodical payments] rent system to but a hollow shell'.[37] Because negotiations between the parties will water down the effect of the reform we can expect lump sums to be commonly used even in the majority of serious injury cases involving future financial losses. But the possibility of imposing a PPO substantially influences the bargaining position of the parties, and it is in that sense that all serious injury cases are affected.

The move towards imposing an uncertain liability upon defendants is likely to strengthen the claimant's hand more than that of the defendant. However, it is important to consider the effect of the changes upon the mechanics of making a deal. In particular, for costs purposes, how is it to be determined whether offers to settle made by either of the parties are reasonable when one of them is based on the traditional lump sum and the other is based partly on an assessment of the claimant's annual needs? In complex cases there could be a mixture of approaches depending upon different care regimes and earnings losses. How is the court to assess the reasonableness of the rejection of a periodical payments offer if it is not based on its capital value but on wider social and family reasons? Although the Civil Procedure Rules specify that costs consequences follow if the court judgment is not 'more advantageous' than the other party's offer, the Rules do not specify what may constitute an advantage in the context of periodical payments.[38] As a result there is scope here for clever tactics from skilled litigators.[39] It remains to be seen whether the broad discretion given

---

[37] JG Fleming, 'Damages: Capital or Rent?' (1969) 19 *University of Toronto Law Journal* 295, 299.

[38] Civil Procedure (Amendment No 3) Rules 2004, SI 2004/3129 inserting the new r 36.2A.

[39] Association of Personal Injury Lawyers (APIL), 'Periodical Payments and Part 36: A Response' (14 April 2004) fears that the uncertainty introduced makes it difficult for lawyers to advise their clients, and claimants will be unfairly disadvantaged. The Master of the Court of Protection notes that the reasons for resisting lump sums could be 'not simply financial but extend across a much broader range of considerations—medical, social and personal—and more holistic insofar as they treat the claimant as a member of a family rather than in isolation'.: Lush, above n 31, at 203.

to the court as to costs will be further used to encourage litigants to negotiate on a periodical payments basis. The attitude and training of the judiciary will be crucial in determining the long-term success of the new provisions.

VIII. WHY COSTS FOR INSURERS WILL INCREASE

Although insurers are faced with a variety of technical and administrative problems as a result of the new legislation, their main concern is the increased cost of settlements. Insurers will have to pay substantially more to fund a PPO than a traditional lump sum, and the government failed to anticipate this. The regulatory impact assessment for the legislation argued that the reforms 'would not materially increase the value of claims',[40] even suggesting that liability insurers might save four per cent by purchasing annuities rather than using lump sums. This is far from the case, and the suggestion that there were savings to be made came as a shock to those with knowledge of the compensation industry: it was based upon 'spurious assumptions'.[41] The policy implications of the reforms must be looked at afresh.

To understand why the regulatory impact assessment was so very wide of the mark we must consider how most compensators will provide for their liability to make index-linked payments for an uncertain time and for an unknown total cost. Liability insurers will almost always fund PPOs by purchasing annuities from a life insurer. A possible alternative method open to large composite insurers is to self-fund the payments by using the facilities of their own life offices, but there is little enthusiasm for this, and in the past it was almost never done for structured settlements. Unlike insurers, public bodies such as NHS trusts are able to self-fund the payments from their own resources because they are able to satisfy the security requirement in the legislation. However, most other defendants will be forced into the annuity market to fund PPOs. This could prove difficult and very expensive for them because there are only a small number of suitable financial products available and only at a high cost.

There are two main reasons for this difficulty and expense. First, there is little competition in the market to provide annuities for tort claimants. This has the effect of making quotations less keen than, for example, in the US where there are at least 15 annuity providers. By contrast, in the UK at the end of 2003 there was a real danger that there would be no life insurers involved at all. This would have completely undermined the planned

---

[40] Lord Chancellor's Department, above n 8, at [25].

[41] N Leech, 'The Good, the Bad, and the Imposition!' (paper made available to the Legal Wales Conference, September 2003) (cited with author's permission).

reforms. Fortunately, a couple of new providers have now emerged but the market remains fragile.[42] Life insurers are deterred because few such annuities are sought, the market being of almost no significance compared to that for annuities for retirement pensions. There is a marked contrast with the £6 billion a year spent on structured settlements in the US. Another discouraging factor is the particular difficulty of underwriting annuities for the 'impaired lives' of many of the injured claimants. When there is only limited experience of the effect of injury on life expectancy, underwriting becomes far more an art than a science, and a miscalculated gamble can prove costly. As a result the market is limited, premiums have fluctuated widely, and the cost of annuities is high. Yet it remains of crucial importance to the future of PPOs, and the government has been urged to intervene to stabilise matters.[43]

The second factor which drives up the cost of annuities is linking them to increases in the Retail Prices Index (RPI). This results in regulatory restrictions being imposed upon the providers. Life insurers are required by the Financial Services Authority to meet their solvency requirements by providing assets which closely match their liabilities. In practice this means that to fund RPI annuities they have to purchase index-linked gilts issued by the government. These are expensive to buy, the market for them being dominated by pension funds anxious to meet their own statutory obligations to obtain matching funds for their index-linked returns. In addition, the government has made too few of these gilts available to the market.[44] Because of the high demand and the limited provision the yields have been very low. In turn, this means that the RPI annuity rates offered by providers are poor value. Where the top-down approach is used to arrange a settlement these rates make it difficult to ensure that the periodical payments derived from the traditional lump sum will meet all of the claimant's needs. With bottom-up arrangements under a PPO, defendants can now be forced to make RPI linked periodical payments whatever the cost. If they do not self-fund, they will be forced to purchase annuities in this limited market.

The overall result for liability insurers is that it will be much more expensive to purchase annuities to fund the payments under a PPO than to

---

[42] The volatile life market was analysed in Lewis, above n 1, at ch 11. For the recent history of providers see A Ritchie et al, *Kemp & Kemp: Personal Injury Law, Practice and Procedure* (London, Sweet & Maxwell, 2005) vol 1, 22-061.

[43] For example, APIL have asked that relevant discussion between the Department of Trade and the Department for Constitutional Affairs be given higher priority: APIL, 'Periodical Payments: An Assessment of Concerns and Solutions' (March 2004).

[44] Gilts are bonds issued by the UK government. Indexed linked gilts were first issued in 1981 and the last but one was issued in 2002 with a final date for redemption in 2035. Government was repeatedly urged by insurers, APIL and others to issue more gilts, and it eventually complied in September 2005 when it made available a new issue with a maturity date of 2055. The issue was immediately over-subscribed.

hand over the traditional lump sum. Anecdotal evidence suggests that the cost of these settlements has increased by as much as a quarter or even a third, and insurance reserves have been revised accordingly.[45] One barrister has suggested that the PPO regime:

> is going to cost insurers, both directly and indirectly, a lot more money and expense to service these damages. I do not believe that they have, as yet, appreciated the extent of their troubles.[46]

One case that was settled privately on an RPI basis illustrates this. If settlement had been based upon the traditional lump sum the multiplier would have been 29. However, funding RPI periodical payments in effect increased the capital sum needed to purchase the annuities such that the corresponding multiplier rose to 45. The cost of future financial loss therefore rose by 55 per cent.[47]

IX. THE POLITICAL REASONS FOR THE REFORM

As we have seen, there are strong arguments to support the more widespread use of periodical payments. Many of these focus upon the needs of claimants and the desirability of providing compensation equivalent to that which has been lost. On the surface the government can be seen to be supporting a fairer system which helps ensure that compensation meets needs and is used for the purposes for which it was awarded. These are the *only* reasons for the reform listed by the Department for Constitutional Affairs in the guidance it provides.[48] But if we look at the organisations that gave the most support to the new legislation we get a different picture of the reasons why it was passed.

The Association of Personal Injury Lawyers is a claimant lawyers' organisation, very active in test-case litigation and in lobbying the government. Although generally in support of periodical payments as a means to ensure full compensation of victims, it opposed the imposition of PPOs against claimants' wishes unless there were exceptional circumstances.[49] Not surprisingly, insurers, together with the defence organisation, the

---

[45] M Hardman, 'Periodical Payments: A Defendant Lawyer's Perspective' (paper presented to a conference at the Institute of Actuaries, March 2005). The paper can be accessed at <http://www.actuaries.org.uk/Display_Page.cgi?url=/damages/seminar20050307.html> (date accessed: 17 July 2006).

[46] R De Wilde, 'Periodical Payments—A Journey into the Unknown' [2005] *Journal of Personal Injury Law* 320, 325.

[47] Details of this case must remain confidential. It must be remembered that the increase would not apply to the lump sum element of the damages which should form a contingency fund and which would be a substantial element in most settlements.

[48] 'Guidance on Periodical Payments' (April 2005) [6]-[8].

[49] APIL, 'Response to the Lord Chancellor's Consultation Paper' (May 2002)

Forum of Insurance Lawyers, were not in favour of the reform. Nor was change sought by the intermediaries who arrange structured settlements. Frenkel Topping, the innovative firm responsible for arranging the great majority of such deals, has been influential in previous reforms. But it opposed PPOs on the ground that they would unduly interfere with the consensual approach. In total, only a bare majority (57 per cent) of respondents to the Lord Chancellor's consultation paper gave an unqualified welcome to imposition.

Instead the catalysts for the reform lay within the government itself. Although the legislation was the prime responsibility of the Lord Chancellor's Department, it had no enthusiasm to make the change urgently. However, both the Treasury and the Department of Health were keen supporters of immediate action, and they were the driving forces behind the sudden implementation of the enabling legislation. Parliamentary time was found by inserting the relevant provisions, rather anomalously, into a bill dealing with criminal law and administration. Claimants' interests were very much secondary to those involving public finance and the demands of the NHS. Far from being what they appear on the surface, the reforms in fact were politically driven.

The political and economic advantages to the government of periodical payments are as follows. In contrast to the problems faced by liability insurers, the government bodies such as the Ministry of Defence and especially the NHS will make immediate gains. This is because their budgets will no longer be denuded by the loss of large capital sums paid as damages.[50] Their cash-flow will be improved because they can self-fund the periodical payments and they are not required to enter the expensive annuity market. It was forecast that in the first year of the new regime the NHS could save as much as £245 million out of the £330 million it would otherwise have to pay for the larger claims.[51] This cash-flow saving will continue at a diminishing rate for 24 years until the accumulated liabilities reach, and thereafter outgrow, what would have been the capital sums needed to dispose of the claims entirely. That is, at that time not only will the good times come to an end and have to be paid for, but also there will be a real and increasing additional cost to the public purse. This cost may

---

[50] In 2001-02 the MOD paid out £81million in compensation according to the National Audit Office, 'Ministry of Defence: Compensation Claims' (HC 957 2002-03). By contrast, in the same year the NHS paid out more than five times as much, amounting to £446 million according to the Department of Health, 'Making Amends: A Consultation Paper Setting out Proposals for Reforming the Approach to Clinical Negligence in the NHS' (2003) table, 60. For wider statistical analysis see R Lewis, A Morris, and K Oliphant, 'Tort Personal Injury Claim Statistics: Is there a Compensation Culture in the UK?' (2006) 14 *Torts Law Journal* 158 and [2006] *Journal of Personal Injury Law* 87.

[51] Lord Chancellor's Department, above n 8, at table 14. This is based on converting into periodical payments 80 per cent of all awards over £250,000 and 40 per cent of all awards between £100,000 and £250,000.

be relatively small in relation to the entire NHS budget, but government finances should beware of these contingent liabilities, especially in the light of current concern about whether we should be paying more to fund future pensions in general. In the past, damages awards have had dramatic effects upon individual heath care budgets: major capital expenditure has been deferred and even wards have closed. At present, health trusts in England are running at a deficit which soon could reach a billion pounds.[52] It is not therefore surprising to find that the NHS has welcomed the new regime, and is much more likely than liability insurers to take advantage of it by forcing claimants to accept periodical payments. For many years it has self-funded all its structured settlements, and it now self-funds all its PPOs. It refuses to buy annuities from outside providers. The savings in cash-flow are too good to miss.

Although the reforms were driven by the NHS, it is important to note that clinical negligence comprises only a minority of claims even if the focus is confined to serious injuries. Liability insurers remain the predominant paymasters. The NHS was responsible for only 11 per cent of all personal injury claims resulting in an award of over £100,000 in 2001-02. For claims of this size in that year liability insurers paid out over £2.26 billion, almost six times as much as the NHS's £0.4 billion.[53] This statistic reveals how the emphasis has been misplaced, and how in this reform the NHS tail is wagging the insurance dog. In the great majority of cases it will be liability insurers and premium payers who will have to bear the increased costs resulting from the reforms, whilst in only the minority of cases, in the short-term, it will be the taxpayer who benefits.

This is only one of several areas in which changes have been made which result in an increase in tort damages but also transfer costs from the public to the private sphere. Insurers have recently been made to bear the cost of the removal of legal aid and the introduction of conditional fees. They now pay the claimant's costs, including the solicitor's success fee and the insurance premium against the possibility of losing. Insurers also have been required to pay for the cost of providing social security benefits to accident victims and, more recently, for the cost of their NHS treatment.[54] As a

---

[52] G Jones, 'NHS told to cut costs as Hewitt confirms spending squeeze' *The Daily Telegraph* (London 18 January 2006), and 'NHS on critical list as cash crisis spirals' *The Times* (London 26 January 2006). Up to fifty trusts were said to have lost control of their finances. Those in most difficulty revealed they had closed beds, wards or entire hospitals. Others had cancelled operations and cut staff levels. However, in the last three years the overall expenditure on the NHS has grown rapidly from £65 billion in 2002-03 to £87 billion in 2005-06.

[53] Lord Chancellor's Department, above n 8.

[54] For recovery of social security and NHS treatment costs see R Lewis, *Deducting Benefits From Damages For Personal Injury* (Oxford, Oxford University Press, 1999) and R Lewis, 'Recovery of NHS Accident Costs: Tort as a Vehicle for Raising Public Funds' (1999) 62 *MLR* 903. Recovery has been extended by Part III of the Heath and Social Care

result of the present reforms they now must bear the brunt of further savings in public expenditure. Of course, the transfer results in a 'stealth tax' which all premium payers and, ultimately, society at large must pay. Tort law, whether made by judges or Parliament, has always been influenced by politics in the wider sense,[55] and this is especially apparent in the recent and continuing struggles that are taking place over damages law.

X.   CANADIAN COMPARISONS

Given the conference for which this chapter was originally prepared, it is appropriate to outline a Canadian context within which comparative work could be done in this area. Although structured settlements in Canada pre-date those in the UK, they have generated little academic interest.[56] Following empirical research in both countries, I compared the two regimes in an article published some years ago,[57] but present Canadian academic texts devote little, if any, space to the subject. This is in spite of continuing legislative efforts in Canadian provinces to introduce an element of compulsion into the previously consensual periodical payment regimes. Reflecting on these legislative changes, Frank McKellar, the leading structured settlement intermediary, has recently concluded that there has been 'a steady regulatory drive towards mandatory court-ordered structured settlements'.[58] Here is a major area of tort law in which 'emerging issues' comparable to those in the UK arise, yet which has not been subject to academic scrutiny.

There are six provinces in which there is legislation which enables courts to impose PPOs against the wishes of at least one of the parties. These are Ontario, Manitoba, British Columbia, Nova Scotia, Quebec and, most recently, Alberta.[59] One basis for making such an award is where the plaintiff requests that damages be increased to allow for the income tax that must be paid when the compensation is invested. The legislation then allows defendants to apply for an award of periodical payments, and the court may order such payment even if opposed by the plaintiff. The

---

(Community Health Standards) Act 2003. Hypothecation, in theory, then returns the money collected for the cost of treatment to the appropriate specific hospital trust or other NHS budget.

[55] R Lewis, 'Lobbying and the Damages Act 1996: "Whispering in Appropriate Ears"' (1997) 60 *MLR* 230.

[56] The notable exception is JP Weir, *Structured Settlements* (Toronto, Carswell, 1984).

[57] R Lewis, 'Structured Settlements of Damages Awards in Britain and Canada' (1993) 42 *ICLQ* 780.

[58] P Chisholm, 'Province has Plans for New Compulsory Structures' *Law Times* (Aurora 12 December 2005).

[59] For Alberta see the Insurance Act RSA 2000 c I-3, s 650.2, under which no regulations have been made, and the Justice Statutes Amendment Act SA 2004 c 11, s 3, amending the Judicature Act RSA 2000 c J-2 and in force from 30 June 2006.

justification for this is that periodical payments are free of tax, and this obviates the need for damages to be grossed-up. In the UK the claimant does not seek such additional monies because the discount rate, in theory at least, already makes allowance for the tax that will be collected from the income that arises on investment of the damages.

The limits on the use of PPOs vary in each province. The Quebec Civil Code makes the most limited provision: periodical payments can only be imposed in cases involving minors.[60] Manitoba[61] and Nova Scotia[62] make the widest provision, enabling courts to exercise the power in any claim for personal injury or death. An Ontario statute confines the power to cases in which a tax gross-up is sought.[63] This is further limited in British Columbia by applying only to claims arising from the use of a motor vehicle, although the power can also be exercised in any motor vehicle case even if no gross-up is sought, provided that the pecuniary loss is at least $100,000.[64] Regulations under a second statute in Ontario[65] similarly make special provision for motor vehicle accidents irrespective of gross-up by allowing a PPO if any two of the following four conditions are satisfied: the award is for more than $100,000, the plaintiff is aged under 18, the plaintiff has no other means to fund future care, and the plaintiff is not likely to manage the award in a prudent manner.

Except in Manitoba and Nova Scotia, the power of the court to order a PPO is expressly prohibited if it is against the 'best interests of the plaintiff'. Generally this is interpreted as giving the court a wide discretion. In British Columbia the effect has been that, subject to notable exceptions, the court usually defers to the wishes of the plaintiff.[66] The factors applied by the various Canadian courts could prove instructive for any practitioner or judge in the UK trying to interpret the new powers to impose PPOs.

There are obvious differences in the scope of the Canadian and UK legislation, but let us focus here upon the justifications for the statutes. The tax gross-up which distinguishes the regimes in the two countries has

---

[60]   Civil Code of Quebec SQ 1991 c 64, art 1616.

[61]   Court of Queen's Bench Act CCSM c C280, s 88 as applied in *Lusignan v Concordia Hospital* (1997) 117 Man R (2d) 241 (QB).

[62]   Automobile Insurance Reform Act SNS 2003 c 1, s 26 which, despite its title, is not confined to motor accidents and was based on the Manitoba legislation. See also the Nova Scotia Barristers Society, 'Information Paper on the Use of Court Ordered Structured Settlement in Nova Scotia' (2002). See <http://www.nsbs.ns.ca/notices/struc_set_discus.htm> (date accessed: 17 July 2006) and the Law Reform Commission of Nova Scotia, 'Court-ordered Structured Settlements for Personal injury Damage Awards' (2004).

[63]   Courts of Justice Act RSO 1990 c 43, s 116, as applied in the medical malpractice case of *Chesher v Monaghan* (2000) 48 OR (3d) 451 (CA).

[64]   Insurance (Motor Vehicle) Act RSBC 1996 c 231, s 55.

[65]   OReg 461/96, s 6, enacted under the Insurance Act RSO 1990 c I.8.

[66]   Contrast *Abraham v Abbinante* (1998) 55 BCLR (3d) 150 (SC) and *Lee v Dawson* (2003) 17 BCLR (4th) 80 (SC) with the order made in *O'Brien v Anderson* (2001) 91 BCLR (3d) 137 (SC).

already been discussed. Apart from this factor it may appear on the surface that the legislation in both countries has been concerned primarily with protecting claimants. However, this chapter has exposed the limitations of such a perspective as far as the UK is concerned. Should a similar reservation be made concerning the Canadian position? On the surface there is a case for doing so because, in practice, many Canadian defendants find structures attractive propositions. But can we trace any concern about escalating medical costs and the benefits that might accrue to the state from the use of PPOs—factors which have so influenced developments in the UK? There is at least some evidence of these factors being relevant in Canada. In 2005 an Access to Justice Bill in Ontario proposed that for medical malpractice cases alone courts should be forced to use periodical payments to compensate for the cost of future care.[67] By making this change the Ministry of Health and Long-term Care hoped to save over $12 million a year.[68] Although the Bill failed, the subject is still under review. Overall, however, we remain unsure of the influences upon, and the effect of, the PPO legislation in the Canadian provinces. It is an 'emerging issue' in need of further comment and analysis.

XI.   CONCLUSIONS

In the UK, how important is the new judicial power to award damages in a form other than that sought by the parties? A former President of APIL has called it 'perhaps the most important development ever relating to the law of damages'.[69] Similarly, insurers have described it as:

> the most fundamental change in 150 years in the quantification of bodily injury claims involving continuing losses. The changes will affect not only the level of damages awarded but will also require a new approach to the quantification of claims.[70]

It is true that the reform undermines the traditional approach to damages, first by requiring bottom-up assessments which focus upon claimants' annual needs, and second by guaranteeing that these needs will be satisfied no matter how long the claimant actually lives and whatever the level of

[67] Bill 14, Access to Justice Act, 2006, 2d Sess, 38th Parl, Ontario. The bill received first reading 27 October 2005 and carried second reading 11 April 2006.

[68] Ontario Trial Lawyers Association, 'Submissions on Taxation and Payment of Personal Injury Awards' (2004). See <http://www.otla.com/Content.asp?page=news> (date accessed: 17 July 2006).

[69] C Ettinger, 'Compensating for Future Loss' (2005) 155 *New Law Journal* 525. His views are repeated by his successor as APIL President, A Gore, in APIL, 'Annual Report' (2005) 5.

[70] London International Insurance and Reinsurance Market Association, *Third UK Bodily Injury Awards Study* (London, International Underwriting Association of London, 2003) 83.

price inflation. These needs are to be met irrespective of the resulting lump sum cost. In addition, the parties must give early consideration to the form in which the damages are to be paid. A change is thus being sought not only in legal method, but also in the culture of personal injury practitioners.

However, the effect of the legislation may be less profound and certainly much harder to see if it is hidden in the settlement system, and predominantly results only in insurers paying higher lump sums than otherwise would be the case. There is every incentive for insurers to settle privately in this way in order to avoid the cost and difficulty of arranging the annuity payments usually required to satisfy a PPO. The legislation failed to anticipate the problems insurers have in accommodating the new regime within their wider financial world. Because of the difficulties insurers will be keen to maintain the traditional form of settlement. Even if this proves to be the case, it can still be argued that the reform is important because all serious injury cases are affected by the threat of imposition of a PPO, whether or not they eventually come to court. The potential exercise of the power generally strengthens the claimant's hand and affects the bargains that are struck in the tort system.

In one way or another, therefore, the changes will result in many seriously injured claimants obtaining more money at the expense of insurance companies. But also to benefit from the legislation is one group of defendants—government departments and public bodies, especially the NHS. Unlike insurers, they can self-fund the periodical payments and thereby retain within their budgets the capital sums they would otherwise have to pay. They can avoid paying for today's liabilities until tomorrow. This effect upon public expenditure was not among the main reasons put forward for the reform. However, in exposing the true costs and benefits of the legislation, this chapter has revealed a political dimension which could easily be overlooked by the casual observer.

In spite of their importance, these changes have been implemented without apparent detection by academics. Tort scholarship is very partial. It is extraordinary how much attention is focused upon issues of liability as opposed to the quantum of damages. Practitioners are bemused by the pre-occupation of academics with the rules on fault: they are aware that liability is infrequently challenged by insurers—being raised as a preliminary issue in only about 20 per cent of their cases[71] – whereas the amount of compensation is almost always open to some negotiation. This chapter

---

[71] T Goriely, R Moorhead and P Abrams, *More Civil Justice? The Impact of the Woolf Reforms on Pre-Action Behaviour* (London, The Law Society and the Civil Justice Council, 2002) 103. However, liability was more readily denied in another survey conducted by APIL, 'Potential Impact of the Threshold Limit for Personal Injury Cases within the Small Claims Court being raised to £5000' (2005).

goes a little way towards redressing the imbalance in tort scholarship. The traditional tort textbook can leave the reader with a very misleading impression about how the compensation system operates in cases of personal injury.[72] In practice, the system is transformed into something which has but a limited relationship to the theoretical picture portrayed. But it is not only the experience of practice which throws down a challenge to tort scholars: it is also changes to the basic rules themselves. These new rules undermine the tradition of awarding damages in a once-and-for-all lump sum, and expose the fragility of the conventional claim that the aim in tort is to return the claimant, in so far as possible, to the position enjoyed before the accident. As such they raise fundamental questions concerning the rationale and future direction of the law of tort. Who really pays, how much, and in what manner, are questions that will not go away.[73]

---

[72]   R Lewis, 'Insurance and the Tort System' (2005) 25 *Legal Studies* 85.

[73]   Cf PS Atiyah, 'No Fault Compensation: A Question that will not Go Away' (1980) 54 *Tulane Law Review* 271.

20

The Structure of the Intentional Torts

KEN OLIPHANT[*]

I. INTRODUCTION

THE QUESTION THAT prompted this chapter is: why has the common law no general principle of liability for intentional harm like those which one finds in the civilian codes?[1] Even the American theory of prima facie tort is not truly equivalent because it acts as a residual category of liability—'a tort of last resort'[2]—rather than a foundational principle. Yet in the crucial formative period of modern tort law—the years following the abolition of the forms of action in England[3]—a general principle of liability for intentional (or 'malicious') harm did in fact seem set to emerge. But the idea never came to fruition, and we are left with a ragbag collection of specific torts about which very little 'general part' analysis is possible.[4]

The answer I shall endeavour to advance in this chapter is explanatory rather than justificatory. I shall not claim that the common law's approach to intentional injury is better than the civil law's, or vice versa. And my

---

[*] City Solicitors' Educational Trust Reader in Tort, School of Law, University of Bristol.

[1] I am thinking primarily of the general liability for fault under art 1382 of the French *Code civil* (C civ), which implicitly covers intention as well as negligence, and the three basic tort liability provisions of the German Bürgerliches Gesetzbuch (BGB)—§ 823 I, § 823 II and § 826—of which the last merits special mention as it applies only to intentional, not negligent, injury and is unconstrained by any set of protected set of protected interests such as limits the scope of the general liability for fault under § 823 I, but imposes an additional requirement of bad faith.

[2] K Vandevelde, 'The Modern Prima Facie Tort Doctrine' (1990/91) 79 *Kentucky Law Journal* 519, 537.

[3] A process initiated by the Common Law Procedure Act 1852 (UK) and completed by the Judicature Acts 1873-1875 (UK). I shall concentrate on the English common law not only because that is the system with which I am most familiar, but also because English law of that period had a crucial influence on developments elsewhere in the common law world.

[4] Cf P Cane, 'General and Special Tort Law: Uses (and Abuses) of Theory' in this collection.

explanation will be primarily historical, though not perhaps the historical explanation that might be expected. I shall not argue, as might be anticipated, that the modern pattern of intentional torts was dictated by the ancient forms of action, a historical residue, arising by accident rather than reasoned choice, demonstrating the truth of Maitland's famous dictum: 'The forms of action we have buried, but they still rule us from their graves'.[5] My interpretation is rather different. In a nutshell, it is that the abolition of the forms of action created a conceptual space in which the substantive grounds of tortious liability might be addressed for the first time in a systematic and analytical fashion. One sees this, for example, in the debates that emerged about fault and strict liability.[6] But one also sees it in contemporaneous debates, both academic and judicial, about the recognition of general liabilities for both negligence *and* intentional injury, the latter often described as 'malicious', a term with numerous different shades of meaning. These are debates with which I suppose that most tort lawyers are at least vaguely familiar, largely because of the famous discussions of malice and motive in the House of Lords decision in *Bradford v Pickles* in 1895.[7] But it is not so widely appreciated quite how close the English common law, and through it the law of other Commonwealth jurisdictions, came to recognising a general liability for intentional injury. Ultimately, however, despite both academic and judicial support for a general liability for intentional (or malicious) injury, the courts rejected that approach, opting in effect for an approach based on different standards of liability for different protected interests, with specific defences tailored to each. But that was a reasoned decision, based on cogent considerations, not simply the unreflective perpetuation of old pockets of liability.

In this chapter, I shall first explain briefly what I mean by the term 'intentional torts', emphasising their diversity, and identifying a number of particular factors which prevent us from rationalising them as simple instantiations of a general liability for intentional injury. Then, in the central section, I shall trace the development of the idea of a general liability for intentional ('malicious') wrongdoing, first in the early English tort treatises, then in the case law, before considering its rejection by the House of Lords in a series of landmark cases in the 1890s.

---

[5] FW Maitland, *The Forms of Action at Common Law: A Course of Lectures*, AH Chaytor and WJ Whittaker (eds) (Cambridge, Cambridge University Press, 1936) 1.

[6] See especially: *Rylands v Fletcher* (1866) LR 1 Exch 265, (1868) LR 3 HL 330; *Readhead v Midland Railway Co* (1867) LR 2 QB 412 (QB), (1869) LR 4 QB 379 (Ex Ch); *Holmes v Mather* (1875) LR 10 Exch 261. My own interpretation of this history may be found in K Oliphant, '*Rylands v Fletcher* and the Emergence of Enterprise Liability' in H Koziol and BC Steininger (eds), *European Tort Law 2004* (Vienna, Springer, 2005).

[7] *Mayor of Bradford v Pickles* [1895] AC 587 (HL) [*Bradford v Pickles*].

II. THE INTENTIONAL TORTS

A. Meaning of 'Intentional Tort'

I do not wish to stipulate any formal definition of 'intentional tort', but merely to indicate the bounds of my inquiry. A survey of the literature suggests that the term has most often been employed as if its meaning were self-evident, and that there has been little rigorous analysis of which torts are included and which are not. In *The Common Law*,[8] writing of 'intentional wrongs', Holmes listed deceit, libel and slander, malicious prosecution and conspiracy as the chief actions in which fraud, malice and intent were 'necessary elements'.[9] He did not include trespass, which then lay for unintentional as well as intended wrongs.[10] For Pollock, however, trespass to the person (assault, battery and false imprisonment) fell into the class of wrongs—'personal wrongs'—which were generally 'wilful or wanton'; this included the actions on Holmes's list as well.[11] But Pollock's focus seems to have been on whether the act in question was intended to cause *harm*,[12] a somewhat narrower test than whether intention was a necessary element in the cause of action.

It is Holmes who is credited[13] with developing the tripartite classification of torts according to standards of liability—intention, negligence and strict liability—adopted in the American Law Institute's *Restatements of the Law of Torts*,[14] though nowhere in *The Common Law* or in his earlier writings does Holmes propose a classificatory scheme in quite those terms,[15] far less adopt it as a framework for his own analysis, though it certainly reflects distinctions to be found in his work.[16] The Restatements themselves offer no definition of intentional tort. They separate off their treatment of deceit and interference with business from the volume on intentional harms with which they commence, and they (dubiously) include

---

[8] OW Holmes, *The Common Law* (Boston, Little, Brown & Co, 1881).

[9] *Ibid*, at 132.

[10] *Ibid*, at 80.

[11] F Pollock, *The Law of Torts: A Treatise on the Principles of Obligations Arising from Civil Wrongs in the Common Law* (London, Stevens and Sons, 1887) 7-8. Pollock's personal wrongs also included seduction and the enticing away of servants, which Holmes may have considered too insignificant to warrant his attention, while his chapter on Wrongs of Fraud and Malice includes intentional wrongs of an *impersonal* nature, eg malicious interference with contract.

[12] Pollock, above, at 8 and 19.

[13] See, eg, by JG Fleming, *The Law of Torts*, 9th edn (Sydney, Law Book Co, 1998) 18.

[14] *Restatement of the Law of Torts* (1939); *Restatement (Second) of the Law of Torts* (1979).

[15] Cf OW Holmes, 'The Theory of Torts' (1873) 7 *American Law Review* 652, 653, where Holmes had, in effect, identified the following three standards of liability: subjective culpability (including but not limited to wilful injury), objective culpability, and strict liability.

[16] See, eg, above n 8, at 145-46.

amongst the latter trespass to land and chattels, and conversion.[17] In the second *Restatement*, a general liability for intentional injury is added almost as an afterthought.[18] In the third *Restatement*, which is being drafted in stages, it appears that the tripartite classification according to standards of liability has been abandoned, with a harm-based classification substituted in its place.[19]

The scheme of the *Restatements* was famously adopted by Fleming in his great text.[20] For him, an intentional tort is one in which the liability is based on 'an intent to interfere with the plaintiff's interests'.[21] But his heading 'intentional wrongs' (not explicitly limited, as in the *Restatements*, to harm to persons, land and chattels) makes even more striking the dubious exclusions (amongst them, deceit and unlawful interference with business). Like the *Restatements*, Fleming treats trespass to land and goods, and conversion, as intentional wrongs.

For present purposes, I am prepared to adopt the wider test, derived from Holmes, of whether intention is a necessary element of the cause of action rather than requiring an intent to harm (Pollock) or at least to interfere with the plaintiff's interests (Fleming). To me, it is immaterial whether the intention relates to damage as such (as is generally the case), or to actionable interference not amounting to damage (as with trespass to the person and procuring breach of contract), or even to some essential circumstance (as with deceit)[22]. I should also add that I am, as yet, drawing no distinction between malice and intention, nor between direct intention (*dolus directus*) and indirect intention (*dolus eventualis*), nor even between intention and recklessness, and that I am treating knowledge of relevant circumstances as equivalent (for present purposes) to intention as to consequences.

Applying this expansive test, I would categorise the following torts as intentional: trespass to the person (assault, battery and false imprisonment); intentional interference with the person (under what in English law is known as The Rule in *Wilkinson v Downton*)[23]; intentional interference with economic interests, whether by procuring a breach of contract,

---

[17]   See, eg, *Restatement (Second)*, above n 14, at §158 (intentional trespass to land), §217 (trespass to chattel) and §223 (conversion).

[18]   *Restatement (Second)*, above n 14, at §870.

[19]   The current draft of the *Restatement (Third) of the Law of Torts: Liability for Physical Harm (Proposed Final Draft)* (2005) is to be followed by one on liability for economic loss <http://www.ali.org> (date accessed: 25 July 2006).

[20]   Fleming, above n 13, at 18.

[21]   *Ibid.*

[22]   The defendant must be shown to have known of, or at least been reckless as to, the falsity of his representation, but needed not have intended to cause any loss: *Derry v Peek* (1889) 14 App Cas 337 (HL) 374 (Lord Herschell).

[23]   [1897] 2 QB 57 (QB).

intimidation, conspiracy or otherwise ('the economic torts'); deceit, injurious falsehood, malicious prosecution, and misfeasance in public office. This is not meant to be an exclusive list. I do not include torts which may be committed intentionally, but need not—for example, nuisance, even where it involves intentional interference with another's use or enjoyment of land.[24] Nor do I include defamation, though malice was indeed once required, because (at least in English law) the tort no longer requires any intention to defame,[25] nor even to publish the material in question.[26] For reasons to be explored below, I would also omit trespass to land and goods, and conversion.

B.   The Lack of General Principle in the Intentional Torts

Just to elaborate such a list is to illuminate the ragbag character of the intentional torts, but perhaps I need to do a little more to make out my claim that there is no underlying general principle which unites these diverse causes of action. I shall do so by pointing to four features of the current law which, to me, prevent us from thinking in terms of a generalised common law liability for intentional wrongdoing.

First there is the actionability per se (ie without proof of damage) of the trespass torts.[27] For the other intentional torts, it is necessary for the plaintiff to show some damage or other loss consequent on the defendant's actions.[28] Even in the area of interference with the person, there is a lack of a common approach because the rule in *Wilkinson v Downton* requires loss—precisely what loss is perhaps questionable[29]—whereas assault, battery and false imprisonment do not.

Second, there is the curious exclusion of the property torts from those requiring proof of intention. In trespass to land, for example, the entry

---

[24]   Contrary to the approach of the *Restatement (Second)*, above n 14, at §870 cmt e.

[25]   *Cassidy v Daily Mirror Newspapers Ltd* [1929] 2 KB 331 (CA).

[26]   *Slipper v BBC* [1991] 1 QB 283 (CA).

[27]   See, eg, *Letang v Cooper* [1965] 1 QB 232 (CA) 240 (Lord Denning MR) (battery) [*Letang*].

[28]   See, eg, *Sefton v Tophams Ltd* [1965] Ch 1140 (CA) (procuring breach of contract), overruled on different grounds at [1967] 1 AC 50 (HL); *Lonrho Ltd v Shell Petroleum Co Ltd* [1982] AC 173 (HL) 188 (Lord Diplock) (conspiracy); *Derry v Peek*, above n 22, at 343 (Lord Halsbury) (deceit); *Savile v Roberts* (1698) 1 Ld Raym 374, 378; 91 ER 1147, 1150 (KB) (Holt CJ) (malicious prosecution). The House of Lords has recently rejected an argument that an exception is to be allowed, in the tort of misfeasance in public office, where the officer maliciously interferes with the plaintiff's constitutional right: *Watkins v Secretary of State for the Home Department* [2006] 2 WLR 807 (HL), reversing [2005] QB 883 (CA).

[29]   Whether mental distress not amounting to a recognised psychiatric condition is actionable was left open by the House of Lords in *Wainwright v Home Office* [2004] 2 AC 406 (HL). In Canada, cf *Guay v Sun Publishing Co* [1953] 2 SCR 216, 238 (Estey J).

does not have to be intentional, but merely negligent,[30] and one commits the tort even if one honestly and reasonably believes that the land in question is one's own.[31] Broadly the same approach applies in the torts of trespass to goods and conversion.[32] These causes of action ought not, at least in English law, be included amongst the intentional torts.[33] They are distinguishable in this regard from trespass to the person, where the contact must at least be intentional, even if the defendant's mistake as to justifying circumstances (eg consent) is immaterial.[34] The property torts require *voluntary* action, but not intention. In effect, they are torts of strict liability.[35] English law does not recognise any tortious liability specifically for intentional interference with another's property.

Third, in the case of the economic torts, the requirement of intent to injure is supplemented by a requirement of unlawfulness that does not apply elsewhere in the intentional torts.[36] The defendant must be shown to have intentionally procured the violation of the claimant's contractual right[37]—sometimes even a non-contractual right will do[38]—or to have used unlawful means with the intention of causing injury to trade or business.[39]

---

[30]   *League against Cruel Sports Ltd v Scott* [1968] QB 240 (QB).

[31]   *Basely v Clarkson* (1681) 3 Lev 37, 83 ER 565 [*Basely*].

[32]   See, eg, *Fowler v Hollins* (1875) LR 7 HL 757 (innocent conversion); *National Coal Board v JE Evans & Co (Cardiff) Ltd* [1951] 2 KB 861(CA) (accepting negligent trespass to goods might give rise to liability).

[33]   See further: P Cane, *The Anatomy of Tort Law* (Oxford, Hart Publishing, 1997) 32-33.

[34]   There was a very interesting discussion on trespass and fault on the Obligations Discussion Group list. See threads entitled 'Can Trespass to land be committed without fault (other than in Canada)?' and 'Innocent intentional trespass', 22-28 February 2006, archived at <http://www.ucc.ie/law/odg/home.htm> (date accessed: 25 July 2006). As a matter of English law, I would dispute Richard Wright's claim that, '[i]f I slap at a fly on a leg under the table, mistakenly thinking it is my leg, I have committed a battery, no matter how reasonable my mistake' <http://www.ucc.ie/law/odg/messages/060222c.htm>. Trespass to the person requires an intention to batter, etc, another person, and hence knowledge that the body part one is touching is someone else's. It is thus different from trespass to land and goods, where English authority is clear, and appears to match the law in other common law jurisdictions: the defendant's honest belief that the property belongs to him is immaterial (see *Basely*, above n 31). It also appears that one does not commit battery in English law if one believes that the thing to which one is applying force is a chattel, rather than a person. Cf the criminal law case of *R v Pembliton* (1874) LR 2 CCR 119: defendant throwing stone at people he had been fighting, but missing and hitting a window; not liable for malicious damage. Of course, if one intends to batter another person, mistake of identity is no defence; nor, in trespass to goods, is mistake as to the nature of chattel in question. It appears that if one deliberately drives over a cardboard box, one is liable for trespass to the goods in the box (but not battery if the box contains a small child).

[35]   *Marfani & Co Ltd v Midland Bank Ltd* [1968] 1 WLR 956 (CA) 970-71 (CA) (Diplock LJ) (conversion).

[36]   See text accompanying nn 111-12 below.

[37]   *Lumley v Gye* (1853) 2 El & Bl 216, 118 ER 749 (QB).

[38]   See, eg, *Prudential Assurance Co Ltd v Lorenz* (1971) 11 KIR 78 (Ch Div) (inducing breach of agent's duty to account to his principal). Cf *Metall and Rohstoff AG v Donaldson Lufkin & Jenrette Inc* [1990] 1 QB 391 (CA) (no tort of inducing a breach of trust).

[39]   *Merkur Island Shipping Corporation v Laughton* [1983] 2 AC 570 (HL).

There is no comparable restriction of liability for, say, intentional interference with the person—certainly not under *Wilkinson v Downton*, nor even (I believe) in trespass to the person. Admittedly, the various forms of trespass to the person are *coincidentally* crimes as well, but it is not necessary to establish the criminal liability to establish the tort.[40] In fact, a finding of criminal liability can *preclude* any action in tort, at least under English law, provided the defendant has paid the stipulated penalty.[41]

Finally, there is apparently no consistency of approach to what may be termed the 'mens rea' element of the intentional torts.[42] An initial question—scarcely ever addressed—is the meaning of 'intention' itself: does it extend to consequences foreseen but not desired? The answer seems to be, Yes: as a general rule[43]—but not in the 'unlawful means' economic torts, where inflicting harm must be the defendant's object or purpose.[44] In the anomalous tort of conspiracy to injure, but not in 'unlawful means' conspiracy,[45] injuring the plaintiff must even be the defendant's predominant purpose, not merely the side-effect (even the inevitable side effect) of his or her conduct.[46] Then there is recklessness, which in some contexts is treated as equivalent to intention,[47] while in others this is denied.[48] Whether in English law recklessness amounts to 'intent' for the purposes of trespass to the person has yet to be decided. Additionally, in some cases the mens rea is described as 'malice', and the question arises whether this requires hostility or ill-will towards the claimant,[49] or just a knowing (or maybe foreseen) infringement of the plaintiff's rights.[50] Improper exercise of a power or privilege may also amount to malice, even if there is no

---

[40] *Halford v Brookes (No 3)* [1992] PIQR P175 (QB).

[41] Offences Against the Person Act 1861 (UK), s 45. The provision applies to assault and battery but not false imprisonment: s 44.

[42] Cf P Cane, 'Mens Rea in Tort Law' (2000) 20 *OJLS* 533.

[43] *Restatement (Second)*, above n 14, at §8A. For further analysis, see J Finnis, 'Intention in Tort Law', in DG Owen (ed), *Philosophical Foundations of Tort Law* (Oxford, Clarendon Press, 1995).

[44] *Douglas v Hello! Ltd (No 3)* [2006] QB 125 (CA).

[45] *Lonrho plc v Fayed* [1992] 1 AC 448 (HL).

[46] *Crofter Hand Woven Harris Tweed Co Ltd v Veitch* [1942] AC 435 (HL (Sc)), followed in *Canada Cement LaFarge Ltd v British Columbia Lightweight Aggregate Ltd* [1983] 1 SCR 452 [*Canada Cement*].

[47] See, eg, *Derry v Peek*, above n 22 (deceit); *Three Rivers District Council v Governor and Company of the Bank of England* [2003] 2 AC 1 (HL) [*Three Rivers*] (misfeasance in public office); *Emerald Construction Co Ltd v Lowthian* [1966] 1 WLR 691 (CA) (procuring breach of contract), not followed in *Mainstream Properties Ltd v Young* [2005] IRLR 964 (CA) (set down for hearing in the House of Lords in March 2006).

[48] See, eg, *Douglas v Hello! Ltd*, above n 44 (unlawful interference with business, unlawful means conspiracy). The House of Lords has granted leave to appeal: [2005] 1 WLR 3732.

[49] In some torts, this is sufficient but not necessary. See, eg, *Three Rivers*, above n 47 ('targeted malice' in misfeasance in public office).

[50] *Bromage v Prosser* (1824) 1 Car & P 475, 107 ER 1051 [*Bromage*].

hostility towards or intent to injure the plaintiff.[51] Again, it is clear that 'malice' does not have the same meaning in all the specific torts of which it is an element. Finally, there is the 'reference point' of the required intent: must the defendant intend harm or just to infringe the plaintiff's rights?[52] Even a brief survey like this shows that the 'intentional torts' are far from expressing a coherent theory of liability for intentional injury. Indeed, the Court of Appeal has recently rejected an attempt to equate the mental element in different intentional torts on the basis that they perform very different functions.[53]

III.   A GENERAL LIABILITY FOR INTENTIONAL INJURY?

The old system of the forms of action obstructed methodical thinking about tort law's rational basis.[54] What we think of as tort gradually emerged from the twin concepts of trespass and case—the latter an especially diverse category. The scope of these two basic actions was determined by a distinction between direct and indirect injury that strikes lawyers today as utterly irrelevant, and has been largely discarded. Discussion of fault was at best rudimentary, and more usually entirely nonexistent. Though negligence was from very early on identified as *a* basis of liability in case, the nature of the fault requirement in trespass, if any, was obscure until almost a century following the abolition of the forms of action.[55] It was this reform that first created the space necessary for the principled consideration of the bases of tort liability. In fact, the decades following the Common Law Procedure Act 1852 (UK) were considered a 'classical period' for the English common law, which saw for the first time '[t]he really scientific treatment of principles'.[56] One of the fruits was, of course, the recognition of a general liability for negligence, finally confirmed in English law by *Donoghue v Stevenson*[57] (though Lord Atkin's neighbour principle was foreshadowed in the nineteenth century by Brett MR in *Heaven v Pender*).[58] But what is less known is that the idea of a general liability for intentional injury also attracted influential support amongst contemporary treatise writers. What is more, the issue was not of merely academic interest, and for some considerable time it seemed that a

---

[51]   See, eg, *Three Rivers*, above n 47 ('untargeted malice' in misfeasance in public office).

[52]   As in battery: *Wilson v Pringle* [1987] QB 237 (CA).

[53]   *Douglas v Hello! Ltd*, above n 44, at [222].

[54]   For the emergence of modern tort law from the old writ system, see M Lunney and K Oliphant, *Tort Law: Text and Materials* (Oxford, Oxford University Press, 2003) 1-18 and references cited therein.

[55]   In English law, it was only resolved in *Letang*, above n 27.

[56]   Pollock, above n 11, at vii. See also Holmes, above n 8, at 78.

[57]   [1932] AC 562 (HL).

[58]   (1883) 11 QBD 503 (CA) 509.

general liability for intentional harm was poised to emerge under the label of 'malice', here bearing no necessary connotation of hostility or ill-will.

A.   The Early Tort Treatises

The first English treatise to attempt a treatment of tort law as such was Charles Addison's *Torts* published in 1860.[59] Little more than an indexed catalogue of causes of action, the book gave the strong impression that tort law was an only tenuously-linked collection of rather disparate rules. In fact, it was on having to review an American abridgement of Addison's work that Oliver Wendell Holmes was famously moved to write that '[t]orts is not a proper subject for a law book'.[60] (Obviously he later changed his mind, otherwise we would not now have the great essays on tort in *The Common Law*). Yet even the notoriously unsystematic Addison felt able to formulate a general principle of liability for intentional harm: 'Every malicious act is wrongful in itself in the eye of the law, and if it causes hurt or damage to another, it is a tort, and may be made the foundation of an action'.[61] It is fair to observe that Addison's formulation of the general proposition seems not to have affected the chaotic organisation of subsequent chapters of his book to any discernable extent at all.

Almost a quarter of a century passed before the first edition of *the great* early tort law text: Sir Frederick Pollock's *Law of Torts* in 1887.[62] Like Addison, Pollock thought that, with the abolition of the forms of action, it was possible to identify 'a general proposition of English law that it is a wrong to do wilful harm to one's neighbour without lawful justification'.[63] And in a draft Civil Wrongs Act that he prepared for the government of India in the 1880s, the first basis of liability is expressed in the following general clause: 'Everyone commits a wrong who harms another... by an

---

[59] CG Addison, *Wrongs and their Remedies, Being a Treatise on The Law of Torts* (London, V and R Stevens and Sons, 1860).

[60] Book Notice, 'The Law of Torts By CG Addison, Esq' (1871) 5 *America Law Review* 340, 341.

[61] This proposition first appears in a new chapter, 'The Law of Torts', inserted in the second edition: CG Addison, *Wrongs and their Remedies, Being a Treatise on The Law of Torts*, 2nd edn (London: V and R Stevens, Sons, and Haynes, 1864) 23. Pollock has been accorded the accolade of being the first treatise writer to posit a general theory of intentional tort (K Vandevelde, 'A History of Prima Facie Tort: The Origins of a General Theory of Intentional Tort' (1990) 19 *Hofstra Law Review* 447, 471), but Addison beat him to it by more than 20 years.

[62] Pollock, above n 11.

[63] *Ibid*, at 21. It is striking to see a 'neighbour principle' being pressed into service in respect of intentional injury.

act intended to cause harm'.[64] Such a broad principle of liability required a broad defence, which for Pollock arose in respect of 'any act done for a lawful purpose and in a lawful manner in the exercise of ordinary rights'.[65] As with Addison, however, but perhaps more surprisingly, Pollock failed to follow through on this general conception of liability for intentional injury, and there is no chapter of his great work which deals with the intentional torts as such. Instead, we get a list of specific wrongs—personal wrongs, defamation, wrongs of fraud and malice, wrongs to possession and property, etc—in which the defendant's intention may or may not be relevant. By contrast, almost fifty years before *Donoghue v Stevenson*, Pollock was able to treat negligence as an independent wrong meriting a separate chapter on its own.[66]

The idea of a general liability for intentional injury also took hold amongst other writers, on both sides of the Atlantic. Bishop, for example, included amongst his 'foundation principles' that 'he who means the injury is answerable in damages for what he inflicts, should it be of a sort and degree whereof the law takes cognizance'.[67]

Holmes's position was more subtle.[68] In *The Common Law*, his view seems to have been that mature legal systems should attach little special significance to the intentional infliction of injury. He considered that the early law's focus on intentional wrongs, and its use of the vocabulary of morals and blameworthiness, had been displaced by an emphasis on external standards of conduct,[69] with liability based on the defendant's knowledge of facts which would make a prudent man perceive danger, and warranted the description of his conduct as malicious, intentional or negligence.[70] Everyone thus had 'a fair chance to avoid doing the harm before he is held responsible for it'.[71] In the mature law, it appears, *actual* intent was generally irrelevant, except that, 'if intent to cause a certain harm is shown, there is no need to prove knowledge of facts which made it likely that harm would follow'.[72]

---

[64] Draft Civil Wrongs Act, cl 8. The draft, which was never implemented, was printed as an appendix to F Pollock, *The Law of Torts: A Treatise on the Principles of Obligations Arising From Civil Wrongs in the Common Law*, 2nd edn (London, Stevens and Sons, 1890).

[65] Draft Civil Wrongs Act, above n 64, at cl 22.

[66] Above n 11, at ch 11.

[67] JW Bishop, *Commentaries on the Non-Contract Law and especially as to Common Affairs not of Contract or the Everyday Rights and Torts* (Chicago, TH Flood & Co, 1889) 8.

[68] See further: K Vandevelde, above n 61, at 457-62 and 473-76.

[69] Above n 8, at 161-62.

[70] *Ibid*, at 146-47. Cf OW Holmes, 'The Path of Law' (1897) 10 *Harvard Law Review* 457, 471: 'commonly malice, intent, and negligence mean only that the danger was manifest to a greater or less degree...'.

[71] Above n 8, at 144.

[72] *Ibid*, at 159.

In his famous article of 1894, 'Privilege, Malice, and Intent',[73] Holmes maintained this general theory of tortious responsibility, but sought at the same time to show how it was consistent with the view that malice might make a man liable for an act that was otherwise lawful.[74] Building on and refining another observation he had made in *The Common Law*—that 'the law... allows certain harms to be inflicted irrespective of the moral condition of him who inflicts them'[75]—Holmes now admitted that the 'privilege' to commit such harms might not necessarily be absolute, but might be a qualified privilege negated by proof of actual malice.[76] This, he considered, remained consistent with his general theory, because 'the external standard applied for the purpose of seeing whether the defendant had notice of the probable consequences of his act, has little or nothing to do with the question of privilege'.[77] Thus, though Holmes cited the 'the commonplace, that the intentional infliction of temporal damage... is actionable if done without just cause',[78] he notably refrained from endorsing it as such, and his interest in it was as the basis for his theory of 'just cause' or 'privilege', explaining those cases where the defendant was *not* liable for intended harm, rather than as new ground of liability. Nevertheless, the result of his recognition that privilege might be qualified was that malice made unlawful what the defendant otherwise would have had a right or privilege to do. Holmes was subsequently to give judicial recognition to a prima facie liability for intentional injury,[79] based on the same reasoning as in 'Privilege, Malice, and Intent', and so laid the foundation for the doctrine of prima facie tort in the United States.[80]

The line-up of writers behind the idea of a general (prima facie) liability for intentional injury was thus pretty impressive, including Pollock, Holmes and Bishop, to say nothing of the much-maligned Addison. But it would be idle to pretend that this view attracted unanimous support in the early treatises, even if it provoked little explicit opposition. The principle had no place in the conceptual schemes advanced in the same period by Underhill (1871), for whom the cardinal rule of torts was *sic utere tuo ut*

---

[73]   OW Holmes, 'Privilege, Malice, and Intent' (1894) 8 *Harvard Law Review* 1
[74]   *Ibid*, at 5.
[75]   Above n 8, at 145.
[76]   Above n 73, at 6–7.
[77]   *Ibid*, at 6.
[78]   *Ibid*, at 2–3 citing *Walker v Cronin* 107 Mass 555 (Sup Jud Ct 1871) 562 and *Mogul Steamship Co v McGregor* (1889) 23 QBD 598 (CA) 613 & 619 (Bowen LJ) [*Mogul Steamship*]. See text accompanying n 97 below.
[79]   See *Aikens v State of Wisconsin* 195 US 194, 204 (1904) [*Aikens*] and text accompanying n 100 below.
[80]   See further: Vandevelde, above n 2; Vandevelde, above n 61; C Witting, 'Of Principle and Prima Facie Tort' (1999) 25 *Monash University Law Review* 295; and *Restatement (Second)*, above n 14, at §870.

alienum non laedas,[81] and Cooley (1879), whose classification of torts was based on the rights or interests affected, rather than the nature of the defendant's conduct.[82] To Cooley, whether or not the defendant acted with an 'evil motive' was in general unimportant.[83] Clerk and Lindsell (1889) also identified the defendant's invasion of the plaintiff's right as the main common characteristic of torts, but explicitly denied the possibility of laying down any general principle to which all tort law could be referred.[84] Though it was also possible to speak of 'three classes of tort',[85] in which wilful injury was put alongside negligence and strict liability, there was no general liability for intentional injury, as opposed to specific torts where intention might be required. In general, '[a]n act which does not amount to a legal injury cannot be actionable because it is done with a bad intent'.[86] This conception of a law of *torts* (plural), rather than tort (singular), was later particularly associated with Salmond.[87]

Despite the doubters, however, the number and prestige of the authors supporting a general liability for intentional injury were such that it can be no surprise to see the idea taken up judicially as well, albeit in terms of 'malice' rather than 'intention'.

B.   Liability for Malice in 19th-century Tort Cases

By the mid-nineteenth century, malice was established as *an element* of a number of specific torts, though not considered an independent ground of liability. Misfeasance in public office,[88] malicious falsehood,[89] and malicious prosecution,[90] for example, all required proof of malice. And in the contemporary law of libel and slander, and into the twentieth century, liability rested on the defendant's *malicious* publication of defamatory

---

[81]   A Underhill, *A Summary of the Law of Torts, or Wrongs Independent of Contract* (London, Butterworths, 1873) 4-5.

[82]   TM Cooley, *A Treatise on the Law of Torts, or the Wrongs which arise Independent of Contract* (Chicago, Callaghan, 1879).

[83]   Cooley, above, at 688.

[84]   JF Clerk and WHB Lindsell, *The Law of Torts* (London, Sweet & Maxwell, 1889) 3. See also: TA Street, *The Foundations of Legal Liability: A Presentation of the Theory and Development of the Common Law, Vol 1: Theory and Principles of Tort* (Northport NY, E Thompson Co, 1906) xxv-xxvi.

[85]   Clerk and Lindsell, above, at 5.

[86]   *Ibid*, at 18 (quoting *Stevenson v Newnham* (1853) 13 CB 285, 297, 138 ER 1208, 1213 per curiam).

[87]   J Salmond, *The Law of Torts: A Treatise on the English Law of Liability for Civil Injuries* (London, Stevens & Haynes, 1907).

[88]   *Tozer v Child* (1857) 7 E&B 377, 119 ER 1286.

[89]   *White v Mellin* [1895] AC 154 (HL).

[90]   *Hicks v Faulkner* (1881) LR 8 QBD 167.

material,[91] though the law's reliance on progressively stronger presumptions of malice eventually robbed this requirement of its substance, and—in England—paved the way for the openly strict liability of the modern law.[92] In the sphere of economic interests too, malice appeared crucial. In his classic formulation of the underlying principle in *Lumley v Gye*, Erle J seemingly gave malice a central role: 'He who maliciously procures a damage to another by violation of his right ought to be made to indemnify'.[93]

In most of these contexts, malice came to denote something broader than simply hostility or ill-will towards the plaintiff or another person. 'Malice in law', inferred from the defendant's intentional interference with the plaintiff's rights, was distinguished from 'malice in fact'.[94] Subsequently, it was suggested that liability might arise even where there was no violation of the plaintiff's pre-existing rights but only malicious interference with an expectation. In 1875, for example, the Divisional Court lead by Blackburn J was prepared to assume that malicious interference with a contract so as to make it less profitable to perform might be tortious.[95]

Judges also began to formulate general principles of liability for intentional acts, rather than restricting their analysis to specific torts. In 1882, Lord Blackburn stated: 'if [the defendant], without excuse or justification, did what he knew or ought to have known was calculated to injure the plaintiff, he must (at least civilly) be responsible for the consequences'.[96] Later the same decade, when the *Mogul Steamship* case was in the Court of Appeal, Bowen LJ cited Blackburn in support of the following proposition:

> [I]ntentionally to do that which is calculated in the ordinary course of events to damage, and which does, in fact, damage another in that other person's property or trade, is actionable if done without just cause or excuse. Such intentional action when done without just cause or excuse is what the law calls a malicious wrong.[97]

A few years later, Bowen stated the principle in even wider terms, not limited to interference with property or trade, in a case involving construction of a statute. 'At Common Law', he said, drawing out a contrast with

---

[91] See especially: *Bromage*, above n 50 and *Capital and Counties Bank v Henty & Sons* (1882) 7 App Cas 741 (HL) [*Capital and Counties Bank*].

[92] See P Mitchell, *The Making of the Modern Law of Defamation* (Oxford, Hart Publishing, 2005) 101-17.

[93] Above n 87, at 233.

[94] *Bromage*, above n 50, at 255 (Bayley J).

[95] *Cattle v Stockton Waterworks Co* (1875) LR 10 QB 453, 458.

[96] *Capital and Counties Bank*, above n 91, at 772. The case was one of libel, and it may be noted that, despite the generality of the quoted dictum, Blackburn, at 780, considered it to be insufficient for the plaintiff to charge a malicious motive and a calumnious tendency if he did not show that there was a libel.

[97] *Mogul Steamship*, above n 78, at 613.

the legislation, 'there was a cause of action whenever one person did damage to another wilfully and intentionally, and without just cause or excuse'.[98]

Holmes himself was subsequently to rely on the earlier of these dicta, not just in his extra-judicial writings,[99] but also in the United States Supreme Court, paraphrasing Bowen's idea as follows: 'prima facie, the intentional infliction of temporal damages is a cause of action, which ... requires a justification if the defendant is to escape'.[100] From this arose the doctrine of prima facie tort.[101]

C. The Rejection of Liability for Malicious Injury per se

Despite these statements, the English common law never came to recognise a general liability for intentional or malicious wrongdoing. Any possible move in that direction was decisively blocked by a series of decisions in the 1890s, first and foremost in the sphere of economic interests, but also in connection with rights over property. Contemporaneous developments relating to intentional interference with the person make an instructive contrast.

(i)   Interference with Economic Interests

Lumley v Gye paved the way for the common law's recognition of liability for the intentional interference with economic interests.[102] But that great case was premised upon the (alleged)[103] violation of the plaintiff's contractual right following the defendant's inducement of the contract debtor's non-performance. The question that remained to be resolved in the last decade of the 19th century was whether liability could arise for malicious injury even where there was no procurement of an actionable wrong, nor any recourse to unlawful means.

The issue first came before the House of Lords in the *Mogul Steamship* case in 1892.[104] A shipowners' trading association wanted to secure the export trade in China tea at remunerative freight rates, and offered incentives to shippers who dealt exclusively with the association, while threatening their agents with dismissal if they acted in the interests of

---

[98]   *Skinner & Co v Shew & Co* [1893] 1 Ch 413 (CA) 422.

[99]   See above n 73.

[100]   *Aikens*, above n 79.

[101]   See authority cited above n 80.

[102]   Above n 37.

[103]   It was never proved, and the plaintiff in fact lost at the subsequent trial. See generally S Waddams, 'Joanna Wagner and the Rival Opera Houses' (2001) 117 *LQR* 431.

[104]   *Mogul Steamship Co Ltd v McGregor, Gow & Co* [1892] AC 25 (HL) [*Mogul Steamship*].

competing shipowners. The plaintiffs, shipowners excluded from the association, attempted to secure cargoes in China but a number of association vessels underbid them and caused a general reduction in freight rates. The plaintiffs' vessels ultimately succeeded in obtaining cargoes, but at very low and un-remunerative rates. They sued. The claim was put on a number of bases—conspiracy and deprivation of trade by wrongful means amongst them—but our interest now is on the argument that seeking to deprive a rival of his trade or to prevent him carrying it out was *in itself* illegitimate.[105] The House of Lords rejected the claim, holding (as the head-note puts it) that 'since the acts of the defendants were done with the lawful object of protecting and extending their trade and increasing their profits, and since they had not employed any unlawful means, the plaintiffs had no cause of action'.[106] But there was a crucial ambiguity in the decision. Did the House of Lords accept the proposition stated by Bowen in the Court of Appeal—set out above[107]—but, like him, find that the defendants' own commercial motives gave them just cause?[108] (Bowen thought so, because he reiterated the proposition *the year after* the House of Lords' decision)[109]. Or did the House of Lords reject that broad proposition on the basis that liability required a finding of unlawful combination or the use of unlawful means.[110]

The issue was not authoritatively addressed until the decision of the House of Lords shortly afterwards in *Allen v Flood*.[111] The case arose out of a 'demarcation' dispute between ironworkers and shipwrights working in the London docks. The ironworkers learned that two shipwrights who had been engaged on their vessel had previously done ironwork on a different vessel. The ironworkers' trade union representative informed the dock manager that his members would not return to work the next day if the shipwrights were allowed to continue, and the dock manager terminated the shipwrights' employment. They brought an action for damages against the union representative, arguing that he had unlawfully interfered with their trade and means of livelihood, and that, even if otherwise lawful, his acts were made unlawful by his malicious intention to injure the

---

[105]   *Ibid*, at 30.

[106]   *Ibid*, at 26.

[107]   Text accompanying n 97.

[108]   Cf Lord Morris's observation that '[i]t is not illegal for a trader to aim at driving a competitor out of trade, provided the motive be his own gain by appropriation of the trade, and the means he uses be lawful weapons': *Mogul Steamship*, above n 104, at 49. See also 56-57 (Lord Field).

[109]   Text accompanying above n 98.

[110]   As is suggested by a number of passages in the opinions: see, eg, *Mogul Steamship*, above n 105, at 41-42 (Lord Watson); 49 (Lord Bramwell). Lord Hannen, at 59, expressly withheld his opinion on the case where the defendants had a malicious intent, namely, to injure the plaintiffs, rather than the sole object of benefiting themselves.

[111]   [1898] AC 1 (HL).

shipwrights. The House of Lords rejected the claim by a majority of 6-3. They ruled, first, that as the shipwrights had been engaged by the day, on terms that they might be discharged at any time, the defendant had not procured any violation of their contractual rights; second, a lawful act did not become unlawful merely because done with a bad motive. Lord Herschell expressly rejected as 'far too wide' Bowen's well-known dictum in the *Mogul Steamship* case, and explained that 'everything depends on the nature of the act, and whether it is wrongful or not'.[112]

Though this conclusion was presented as the outcome of a 'legal' analysis, it is clear that ulterior considerations played a significant part. The majority Law Lords were alarmed at the 'very grave consequences'[113] that might result if the law was declared to be what the plaintiffs argued it was. Ultimately, said Lord Macnaghten, '[m]uch more harm than good would be done'.[114] In fact, a number of interlinked concerns may be identified in the opinions, overlapping to some extent those that were highlighted in *Mogul Steamship*. First, recognition of a liability for intentional injury—or 'interference'—would make competition, whether in trade or between rival groups of workers, prima facie unlawful. As Lord James observed: 'Competition represents 'interference', and yet it is in the interest of the community that it should exist'.[115] And this applied equally to competition in labour.[116]

Second, neither judge nor jury was suited to the task of setting the bounds of 'fair' competition, whether in trade or in the workplace. In the *Mogul Steamship* case, Lord Watson had declared:

> I cannot for a moment suppose that it is the proper function of English Courts of Law to fix the lowest prices at which traders can sell or hire, for the purpose of protecting or extending their business, without committing a legal wrong which will subject them in damages.[117]

Again, the same reasoning could be applied to matters of labour: it was no more the function of the Law Lords to express an opinion on the policy of trade unions.[118]

Third, if liability were to turn on malice or fairness, this would inevitably lead to uncertainty and inconsistency, especially if these questions were determined by jury. In such matters, there was 'room for infinite differences of opinion', and all would turn on 'the fluctuating opinions of

---

[112] *Ibid*, at 139-40. See also 151 (Lord Macnaghten); 171 (Lord Davey).

[113] *Ibid*, at 179 (Lord James).

[114] *Ibid*, at 152-53.

[115] *Ibid*, at 179.

[116] See, *ibid*, at 164 (Lord Shand) ('competition in labour... is in all essentials analogous to competition in trade').

[117] *Mogul Steamship*, above n 104.

[118] *Allen v Flood*, above n 111, at 129 (Lord Herschell).

the tribunal before whom the case may chance to come'.[119] There would be 'intolerable' inquisitions, with a 'probability of injustice being done by juries in a class of cases in which there would be ample room for speculation and wide scope for prejudice'.[120] Summing up such concerns, Lord Herschell declared:

> I can imagine no greater danger to the community than that a jury should be at liberty to impose the penalty of paying damages for acts which are otherwise lawful, because they choose, without any legal definition of the term, to say that they are malicious. No one would know what his rights were. The result would be to put all our actions at the mercy of a particular tribunal whose view of their propriety might differ from our own.[121]

Finally, the proposed liability ran counter to the Law Lords' wider liberal concerns: 'individual liberty', said Lord Herschell, 'is never in greater danger than when a tribunal is urged to restrict liberty of action because the manner in which it has been exercised in a particular instance may be distasteful'.[122] However, such arguments could be invoked on either side of the debate,[123] and are susceptible to numerous below-the-surface readings. In *Allen v Flood*, the House of Lords ostensibly ruled that the freedoms available to trade competitors should be equally available to workers,[124] but a cynic might suggest that the decision was more than a little influenced by the perceived desirability of protecting *the employer's* unfettered right to discharge his workers at will, with which the worker's right to withdraw his labour was logically linked.[125]

Allen v Flood underpins the modern Anglo-Commonwealth law of tortious interference with economic interests.[126] The view which has largely prevailed is that liability will arise without independent unlawfulness only in the tort of conspiracy to injury, and not otherwise, though there was sufficient uncertainty about the precise *ratio decidendi* in the last of the turn-of-the-century trilogy of great economic tort cases in the House

---

[119] *Ibid*, at 119 (Lord Herschell).
[120] *Ibid*, at 153 (Lord Macnaghten).
[121] *Ibid*, at 118.
[122] *Ibid*, at 142 (Lord Herschell).
[123] Cf *ibid*, at 72-73 and 90 (Lord Halsbury LC).
[124] *Ibid*, at 141. See also 98-99 (Lord Watson); 166 (Lord Shand).
[125] Cf *ibid*, at 172 (Lord Davey).
[126] See especially: *Sanders v Snell* (1998) 196 CLR 329 (HCA) (Australia); *Perrault v Gauthier* (1898) 28 SCR 241 (Canada); *Emms v Brad Lovett Ltd* [1973] 1 NZLR 282 (Sup Ct) (New Zealand). On conspiracy to injure, see *McKernan v Fraser* (1931) 46 CLR 343 (HCA) (Australia); *Canada Cement*, above n 46 (Canada); *Pete's Towing Services Ltd v Northern Road Transport, etc, Union of Workers* [1970] NZLR 32 (SC) (New Zealand). It may be noted that even the anomalous, and now defunct, Australian doctrine of *Beaudesert Shire Council v Smith* (1969) 120 CLR 145 (HCA) is consistent with the *Allen v Flood* requirement of unlawful means.

of Lords, *Quinn v Leathem*,[127] to encourage Lord Denning's at least temporarily successful attempt to create a liability for interference with contractual relations falling short of breach where the interference was direct and deliberate but no unlawful means were employed.[128] Despite considerable criticism of Lord Denning's extension of the relevant principles,[129] the Court of Appeal has treated it as binding,[130] though the House of Lords will shortly have the opportunity to settle the matter.[131]

By contrast, *Allen v Flood* never took hold in the United States. There, the earlier—inconsistent and overruled—decision of the Court of Appeal in *Temperton v Russell*[132] seems to have had more effect, forming the basis of a jurisprudence on tortious interference with prospective economic advantage.[133] This may in turn be associated with the development of a common law liability for *unfair* (rather than unlawful) competition.[134] There is thus a marked contrast with the Anglo-Commonwealth common law. It has been observed, however, that unfair competition does not describe a single tort but rather 'a general category into which a number of new torts may be placed when recognized by the courts'.[135] This is still a way short of the generalised liability for unfair competition recognised in France under art 1382 CC,[136] and that for harm caused intentionally and in bad faith under § 826 BGB.[137]

(ii)   Interference with Land

In the middle of the debate about intentional interference with trade, the issue of malice surfaced elsewhere in the law of tort. The law of private nuisance has long resembled a chequer board of black and white squares denoting ways in which one can use one's land despite knowing it will interfere with the use and enjoyment of land of one's neighbour,[138] and

---

[127] [1901] AC 495 (HL).

[128] *Torquay Hotel Co Ltd v Cousins* [1969] 2 Ch 106 (CA). Lord Denning relied in part, at 138, on a dictum of Lord Macnaghten in *Quinn v Leathem*, above n 127, 510.

[129] See, eg, H Carty, *An Analysis of the Economic Torts* (Oxford, Oxford University Press, 2001) 54-55; A Grubb (ed), *The Law of Torts* (London, Butterworths, 2002) §§ 27.37-38; T Weir, *Economic Torts* (Oxford, Oxford University Pres, 1997) 37-38.

[130] *OBG Ltd v Allan* [2005] QB 762 (CA) [45] (Peter Gibson LJ); [117] (Carnwath LJ).

[131] See *OBG Ltd v Allan* [2005] 1 WLR 2847 (HL) (grant of leave to appeal).

[132] [1893] 1 QB 715 (CA).

[133] See, eg, WP Keeton *et al*, *Prosser & Keeton on Torts*, 5th edn (St Paul, West Publishing, 1984) 1005. See also *Restatement (Second)*, above n 14, at §766B.

[134] *Tuttle v Buck* 119 NW 946 (Minn SC 1909). Cf *Restatement (Second)*, above n 14, at §768.

[135] Keeton, above n 133, at 1015.

[136] See generally, V Palmer, 'Comparative Study (From a Common Law Perspective) of the French Action for Wrongful Interference with Contract' (1992) 40 *American Journal of Comparative Law* 297.

[137] For a comparative overview, see Weir, above n 130, at ch 4.

[138] See, the examples given in Holmes, above n 8, at 145.

ways in which one cannot. In recent times, the principle of unreasonable user has made increasing inroads on these segregated compartments,[139] but it has yet to take over the entire field. So, even in modern English law, one can safely excavate one's land despite knowing that one's neighbour's building will consequently fall down, unless it has been there for 20 years;[140] one can freely drain one's land even though this will likely cause the neighbour's land to subside;[141] and one can equally well interfere with other aspects of the neighbour's use and enjoyment of land that are capable of being acquired as an easement, but have not been so acquired.[142]

In *Mayor of Bradford v Pickles*, the House of Lords ruled that these 'rights' were not forfeited by the presence of a malicious intent.[143] The facts of the case are too well-known to require a full restatement here. In summary, the House of Lords ruled that the defendant landowner was entitled to extract or divert water percolating under his land, no matter that this would disrupt the supply of water to the inhabitants of Bradford. His right to do so was absolute, and therefore not affected by the motivation with which he acted, namely, to force Bradford Corporation to buy him out at a price he considered satisfactory. The Corporation, conversely, had no right to the flow of water from under his land. Implicitly, the House of Lords rejected the proposition formulated in the *Mogul Steamship* case by Bowen LJ, upon whose judgment the plaintiffs relied.[144] Some of the dicta, however, go further than was necessary for the decision, and cannot be supported in the light of subsequent authority, amongst them Lord Watson's statement—adopted by the head-note writer as the *ratio decidendi*—that '[n]o use of property, which would be legal if due to a proper motive, can become illegal because it is prompted by a motive which is improper or even malicious'.[145]

The decision was an acknowledged influence on members of the House of Lords in the case of *Allen v Flood* just two years later, in which it was considered to be authority in connection with not just rights over property, but rights in general.[146] It demonstrates that the concern with the clear designation of the reciprocal rights and duties of potential rivals, so as to provide a certain legal framework within which they can conduct their ongoing affairs, was not unique to the spheres of trade and labour

---

[139] See, eg, the treatment of natural nuisances following *Goldman v Hargrave* [1967] 1 AC 645 (PC) and *Leakey v National Trust* [1980] QB 485 (CA).

[140] *Dalton v Angus* (1881) 6 App Cas 740 (HL).

[141] *Langbrook Properties v Surrey County Council* [1970] 1 WLR 161 (Ch Div).

[142] See, eg, *Webb v Bird* (1862) 13 CBNS 841 (obstruction of the passage of air).

[143] *Bradford v Pickles*, above n 7.

[144] See *ibid*, at 591.

[145] *Ibid*, at 598 (Lord Watson). Cf *Hollywood Silver Fox Farm Ltd v Emmett* [1936] 2 KB 468.

[146] See *Allen v Flood*, above n 111, at 124 (Lord Herschell); 167-68 (Lord Shand).

relations. Also very much to the fore are the same liberal impulses which were later so strongly evident in *Allen v Flood*.[147]

(iii)   Interference with the Person

In 1897, in *Wilkinson v Downton*, the English High Court was presented with an opportunity to consider a general principle of liability for intentional injury to the person.[148] In fact, the opportunity coincided precisely in point of time with the House of Lords' hearings in *Allen v Flood*.[149] In March-April 1897, Wright J, who was assigned to hear the action, was one of the judges specially summoned to the Lords to hear a reprise of the arguments in the case and, subsequently, to express an opinion on them. He argued against the imposition of liability on the facts: it was no tort wilfully to procure persons to refuse to make or renew contracts with the plaintiff in the way of his trade or employment, thereby directly causing damage, and the defendant did not become liable for doing with malicious motive, spite or ill-will that which he might lawfully do without such a motive.[150] This opinion went against that of the judge at first instance, the majority of the Court of Appeal, and six of the eight judges summoned to attend the hearing—only Mathew J reached the same conclusion—but (as we have seen) it was the view that prevailed in the Lords, by a 6-3 majority.

In the period between hearing the arguments in *Allen v Flood* and delivering his opinion, Wright heard and gave judgment in *Wilkinson v Downton*. He accepted that liability for intentionally causing physical harm could arise even if the case did not fall within any pre-existing category of liability, and recognised a new cause of action where '[t]he defendant has... wilfully done an act calculated to cause physical harm to the plaintiff—that is to say, to infringe her legal right to personal safety, and has in fact thereby caused physical harm to her..., there being no justification alleged for the act'.[151] 'This wilful injuria', he explained, 'is in law malicious, although no malicious purpose to cause the harm which was caused nor any motive of spite is imputed to the defendant'.[152] He cited no authority for these propositions, but the terminology must by then have been very familiar to his legal audience. His judgment is dated 8 May

---

[147] See further: M Taggart, *Private Property and Abuse of Rights in Victorian England: The Story of Edward Pickles and the Bradford Water Supply* (Oxford, Oxford University Press, 2002) 158-65.

[148] Above n 23. See further: M Lunney, 'Practical Joking and its Penalty: *Wilkinson v Downton* in Context' (2002) 10 *Tort Law Review* 168.

[149] Above n 111.

[150] *Allen v Flood*, above n 111, at 62-67.

[151] *Wilkinson v Downton*, above n 23, at 58-59.

[152] *Ibid*, at 59.

1897, almost a month before he gave his opinion to the House of Lords in *Allen v Flood* (on 3 June). It is instructive to compare the two. His conclusion in the latter case was that 'malicious motive, as distinguished from the wilful violation of a known right…, is not of itself in conjunction with damage enough in general to constitute a cause of action where no legal right is infringed'.[153] It is plain that he was talking of malice in fact, not malice in law. He made no mention at all of *Wilkinson v Downton*, though his judgment was so recent that the ink could scarcely have dried. Nevertheless, it is plausible to suggest that he must have taken care to formulate the cause of action in *Wilkinson* as involving an infringement of the plaintiff's legal right to personal safety, therefore involving malice in law, so as to make plain its consistency with what he was going to argue in *Allen v Flood*.

While Wright J's proposition in *Wilkinson v Downton* was evidently expressed in general terms, it was not an attempt at generalisation in the same way as Blackburn J's judgment in *Rylands v Fletcher*[154] or Lord Atkins' in *Donoghue v Stevenson*.[155] Far from using his judgment to identify the principle underlying a disparate set of decided cases, Wright in fact cited no case authority for his proposition at all. He was not seeking to reconceptualise a hitherto misunderstood area of law, but merely to fashion a remedy on the facts. His principle was a fall-back to which he resorted because no specific cause of action would do. It should therefore come as no surprise that *Wilkinson v Downton* should denote a residual category of liability that is invoked only occasionally[156]—meant to fill in between, rather than displacing the ancient forms of trespass to the person.

Though *Wilkinson v Downton* may appear at first glance to embody a different (pro-generalisation) judicial philosophy from that apparent in *Allen v Flood* and *Bradford v Pickles*, it actually points up the tenacity of the old trespass forms, and prompts reflection on the reasons why they have survived in such rude health. This is too large a topic to embark upon here. Suffice it to say, for now, that I consider the two primary considerations to have been, first, the actionability per se of the various forms of trespass to the person, which gives them a role in protecting rights to bodily autonomy to which torts requiring proof of injury cannot aspire, and, second, the delicate balance that has been achieved—through the defences available—between those rights and various competing concerns that have merited the law's recognition. The courts have understandably been reluctant—in all the areas we have discussed in this chapter—to cast

---

[153] *Allen v Flood*, above n 111, at 66.
[154] Above n 6.
[155] Above n 57.
[156] See, eg, *Janvier v Sweeney* [1919] 2 KB 316 (CA); *Khorasandjian v Bush* [1993] QB 727 (CA). See further: Lunney, above n 148.

away a set of established, relatively certain rules in favour of a new general liability reined in by a broad and as yet undefined defence of just cause.

IV.   CONCLUSION

Should we regard the law's failure to adopt a general theory of liability for intentional injury as a deficiency? Is it true that, to adapt Wedderburn's phrase, the intentional torts have 'lacked their Lord Atkin'[157]—a judge with the imagination to envisage a general principle uniting the disparate causes of action in which proof of the defendant's intention to injure is required? I believe that the answer must be in the negative. The rejection of the general liability cannot be attributed to a lack of judicial imagination or daring, or to the unreflective continuation of patterns of thought inherited from the era of the forms of action. In fact, it was a reasoned decision taken for cogent reasons, leading to an approach which—while not necessarily preferable to that adopted in civilian jurisdictions—is certainly no less valid.

Lest it be considered that these reflections are insufficiently current for a collection of essays on 'emerging issues' in tort law, reflect on the following. It was the historical events that I have considered that established the principal contours of the modern law of liability for intentional injury in the common law—certainly in Anglo-Commonwealth law, and to some extent in the United States as well, though the law there has run a rather different course. But those contours cannot be regarded as immutably fixed. From time to time they are contested. In the near future, the House of Lords will consider a challenge to the broad proposition from *Allen v Flood*, namely, that interference with contracts is not actionable unless the defendant procures a breach of the plaintiff's contract or otherwise resorts to unlawful means.[158] Two other cases going to the Lords raise the meaning of 'intention' in the economic torts, and one issue that has already been raised is whether there is a case for uniformity of definition across the law of tort as a whole.[159] And, outside the courts, learned jurists assemble the skeleton of a common European tort law, employing the technique of the general liability clause, and thereby presupposing a prima facie liability for intentional injury.[160] Whatever

---

[157] KW Wedderburn, 'Rocking the Torts' (1983) 46 *MLR* 224, 229.

[158] Text accompanying above n 131.

[159] See above nn 47-48 and 53.

[160] See European Group on Tort Law, *Principles of European Tort Law: Text and Commentary* (Vienna, Springer, 2005), also available online at <http://civil.udg.es/tort/Principles/index.htm> (date accessed: 15 July 2006); Study Group on a European Civil Code, 'Tort Law (final)' <http://www.sgecc.net/media/downloads/text_of_articles_final.doc> (date accessed: 15 July 2006). For a common lawyer's arguments against the retention of the

one's position on such a principle, whether recognised judicially or by law reform, the debate must surely be informed by an understanding of how the common law got to where it is, and the factors that shaped its development.

specific intentional torts, and effectively in favour of a generalised liability for fault, see D Howarth, 'A Future for the Intentional Torts', in P Birks (ed), *The Classification of Obligations* (Oxford, Oxford University Press, 1997).

21

The Role of Intention in the Tort in Wilkinson v Downton

DENISE RÉAUME*

I. INTRODUCTION

THE LATEST TURN in the career of the odd, but lovable cause of action often referred to somewhat mysteriously as 'the tort in *Wilkinson v Downton*'[1] comes in the House of Lords decision in *Wainwright v Home Office*.[2] The enduring charm of this cause of action lies in the cryptic nature of the description of the tort in *Wilkinson* itself, which creates plenty of room for debate about exactly what the criteria for liability are. Yet more often than not since then, courts following it have repeated its central passages verbatim, like a magic spell. Little effort seems to have been taken to analyse closely the criteria for liability and fit it into the larger landscape of tort law. At least this has been so until *Wainwright*.

But *Wainwright* threatens to take all the mystery out of *Wilkinson*. Lord Hoffmann's decision for the court takes the rather striking view that *Wilkinson* was really grounded in negligence and not a separate cause of action at all.[3] He suggests that generations of judges adjudicating these cases have all this time been 'speaking negligence' without realising it. This analysis strikes me as anachronistic—it imputes a modern sensibility about and understanding of the tort of negligence to a judge operating at the dawn of the development of negligence as we now know it. This seems wrong to me. If there is a thought that cannot sensibly be attributed to Wright J in 1897, it is that the defendant deserved to be held liable simply

* Faculty of Law, University of Toronto. I am grateful to Jean Thomas for being an excellent sounding board and research assistant.

[1] [1897] 2 QB 57 [*Wilkinson*]. As the term 'nervous shock' has become increasingly antiquated, the original label, 'intentional infliction of nervous shock', has fallen out of favour, but a clear alternative has not yet emerged. Courts oscillate between intentional infliction of mental distress, emotional distress, and mental suffering. I will use the slightly more concise 'intentional infliction of distress'.
[2] [2004] 2 AC 406 [*Wainwright*].
[3] *Ibid*, at 425.

because he created an unreasonable risk of foreseeably causing physical injury to the plaintiff through the mechanism of the shock inflicted by the tall tale of her husband's injury. More importantly, by converting these cases into proto-negligence cases, Lord Hoffmann overlooks most of what is interesting in the reasoning in the case law over the years. The judges have been struggling to articulate a cause of action; I just don't think that they have been struggling to articulate negligence.

I aim to support this claim through a careful reading of the early cases, starting with the English cases, and then crossing the Atlantic to survey the Canadian scene. There has been more activity in this area in Canada than in the UK, providing more material to work with. Because the English case law is so sparse, Lord Hoffmann's revisionist account of *Wilkinson* is not an impossible account of English law. If we add in the Canadian cases, the picture is more complicated. One has to work harder to rewrite the larger body of law as simply exemplifying the negligence principle at work.

I will argue that the cases as a whole defy the very modern structure that Lord Hoffmann's decision implies. Over the course of the twentieth century, negligence emerged as the dominant principle in tort. In the process, negligence law was transformed from something like a patchwork quilt of instinctive judgements about whether the defendant did something wrong, whether he or she owed a duty to the plaintiff in particular, and whether the damage suffered was recoverable, into an increasingly integrated principle of liability in which these three elements were linked to one another through the idea of risk and the attendant notion of foreseeable consequences.[4] Instead of three independent questions determining liability, the law approached the adoption of a single principle dictating an answer to each of the three questions.[5] Lord Hoffmann's judgment exemplifies this structure in two ways.

First, he reinterprets the early intentional infliction of distress cases simply as cases in which the defendant created an unreasonable risk of *injury through nervous shock*, and which could therefore be covered by the negligence principle once the novelty of physical injury inflicted through impact on the senses rather than physical contact wore off. On this interpretation, judges simply came gradually to realise that injury through nervous shock is sometimes a foreseeable result of behaviour. I will refer to this as the subsumption argument—the argument that *Wilkinson v Downton* can now simply be subsumed into the law of negligence.

---

[4]   *Donoghue v Stevenson* [1932] AC 562 (HL) inaugurated this trend.

[5]   Arguably, integration was never fully complete; latest trends show a retreat from the reasonable foreseeability principle as a general principle, in favour of a more *ad hoc* adjustment of the basis of liability to the facts of specific cases. See, eg, the recent judgments of the Supreme Court of Canada in *Cooper v Hobart* [2001] 3 SCR 537; *Odhavji Estate v Woodhouse* [2003] 3 SCR 263; *Childs v Desormeaux* 2006 SCC 18.

Further, he suggests that, if intention is to play a role in a cause of action building on *Wilkinson*, we must be precise about exactly what the intended consequence is and define the limits of liability by reference to those very consequences.[6] On this view, if injury through nervous shock is to be compensated and the tort is to be grounded in intention, the defendant must therefore have intended to cause injury through nervous shock. This extends the ambition of integrated liability principles into the area of intention. If liability for negligence is grounded in each aspect of the tort's connection to reasonable foresight, liability for intentional behaviour should be grounded in intention with respect to all key ingredients in the tort. It is this impulse that leads Lord Hoffmann to note that, once negligence foreseeably causing injury through nervous shock is recognised as a valid cause of action, ratcheting up the level of fault to intention adds nothing to the basis for liability. Since it will be easier for a plaintiff to prove unreasonable risk of injury through nervous shock than intention to inflict such injury, no plaintiff will bother trying to establish the latter except insofar as it may increase the damage award. Thus, intention is redundant unless it pushes the boundaries of the tort in another way, such as grounding liability for a lesser harm than nervous shock-induced injury. Perhaps, Lord Hoffman says, leaving the matter open for future decision, one may be liable for intentionally causing 'mere' distress;[7] normally distress is too intangible and insignificant a harm to warrant legal protection, but it may be appropriate to compensate it if it is intentionally inflicted, in a strict sense of intention.[8]

In this way Lord Hoffmann's decision attempts to reinterpret the history and chart the future of this area of law in keeping with contemporary understandings of the structure of a cause of action in tort. However, the cases grounded in *Wilkinson* cannot be fitted so easily into what I will call this integrated structure. They are messier. It may be, at the end of the day, that it makes sense to allow their complexity to be superseded by the simple elegance of the modern structure, but we should first at least try to understand the logic of these cases on their own terms in order to be sure that we are not losing anything in the translation.

---

[6] *Wainwright*, above n 2, at 426.

[7] *Ibid.*

[8] It remains to be seen whether courts will pass through this door. In *Wong Tai Wai David v The Hong Kong SAR Government* (2004) CACV 19/2003, the Hong Kong Court of Appeal, on a motion to strike, held it to be an open question whether a claim for distress absent injury is available. By contrast, Field J in *C v D* [2006] EWHC 166 (QB) [101], denied recovery for a specific incident causing only distress, not psychiatric illness, saying, 'Lord Hoffmann was not definitively promulgating a new basis of tortious liability for "mere distress,"' but rather had reserved his position. It seems that only the House of Lords can recognise the new cause of action. The contrast with Wright J's boldness in *Wilkinson* is striking. I am grateful to Rick Glofcheski for bringing these cases to my attention.

II.   RECONSTRUCTING THE ORIGINAL UNDERSTANDING OF THE TORT IN *WILKINSON V DOWNTON*

Wilkinson v Downton dealt with a practical joke that went terribly wrong. The defendant told the plaintiff that her husband had been seriously injured in an accident, apparently hoping to send her on a wild goose chase to collect him. The shock of the news caused the plaintiff to become seriously ill, and it was the consequences of this illness for which she sued.

Wright J first considered whether the plaintiff's recovery for her illness could be covered by an action in fraud. But he held it would be an extension of the doctrine in *Pasley v Freeman*[9] to hold someone liable for nervous shock-induced injury flowing from such a lie, an extension he felt unable to approve. The sticking point is that fraud requires inducing someone to *act* in some detrimental way. Telling someone a shocking lie such that she suffers illness does not require that she act on the information in order to suffer harm.

Deprived of fraud as the specific basis for allowing recovery, Wright J based liability on a finding that the defendant has '*wilfully* done an act *calculated* to cause *physical harm* to the plaintiff—that is to say, to infringe her legal right to personal safety, and has in fact thereby caused physical harm to her'.[10] Since done without justification, it is actionable. Thus, although not treated as a species of fraud, the falseness of the report undercuts the defendant's ability to claim justification. Wright J treats the wilful *injuria* as malicious in law 'although no malicious purpose to cause the harm which was caused nor any motive of spite is imputed to the defendant'.[11] This treats the protected interest as the interest in personal safety, and locates the wrongfulness of the defendant's behaviour not in the deceit—or at least, not exclusively in the deceit—but in wilfully doing something calculated to cause *physical* harm. This is consistent with the description of the action as 'on the case'. The description of the wrongful conduct has two parts. First, the action must be wilful. This could simply mean 'voluntary', rather than accidental, as argued by John Irvine.[12] By itself, however, this would not distinguish this action from many negligence cases in which the defendant's action is also deliberate, even though he may not appreciate the risk it imposes. It would arguably also not make sense of

---

[9]   (1789) 3 TR 51, 100 ER 450 (KB).

[10]   *Wilkinson*, above n 1, at 58-59 (emphasis added). My analysis of this puzzling passage is largely in accordance with that of Mark Lunney, 'Practical Joking and its Penalty: Wilkinson v. Downton in Context' (2002) 10 *Tort Law Review* 168, which draws much more carefully on historical materials to reconstruct the influences on Wright J's thinking.

[11]   *Wilkinson*, above n 1, at 59.

[12]   See his annotation of *Timmermans v Buelow* (1984) 38 CCLT 136, at 139.

Wright J's emphasis on the element of wilfulness at play. This suggests that we look for a richer account of the wilfulness of the defendant's behaviour needed to ground liability.

Second, and more difficult to sort out, is what is meant by 'calculated to cause physical harm'. The denial of malicious motive seems to rule out any kind of attribution to the defendant of a *desire* to cause physical harm. The intention to cause harm is imputed. The defendant's act was 'so calculated to produce some effect of the kind which was produced that an intention to produce it ought to be imputed'.[13] Such a statement could not fail 'to produce grave effects under the circumstances'.[14] So the intention to produce 'grave effects' or 'some effect of the kind that was produced' can be imputed because it was a highly likely result. He notes that it is no defence that the effects were more serious than anticipated. However, Wright J was also at pains to point out that the plaintiff was of ordinary constitution, not predisposed to delicacy in any way. This seems to indicate that he is not relying on the thin skull doctrine, but rather on the ordinary principle that the full extent of damage may be recovered as long as the type is recoverable. As is well known, this distinction between type and extent of damage for purposes of determining remoteness in negligence is a slippery one. Its incorporation into the analysis in *Wilkinson* has given judges a great deal of leeway in deciding what is actionable.

Wilkinson was decided in the shadow of *Victorian Railways Commissioners v Coultas*,[15] a decision of the Privy Council denying recovery in negligence to a woman who suffered injury through nervous shock as a result of narrowly escaping a collision with a train because the injury was 'too remote'. *Coultas* is a classic example of negligence causing injury through nervous shock. The defendant opened a gate for the plaintiff's carriage to cross the railway tracks, not realising that a train was approaching. The creation of risk was inadvertent, but if a collision had occurred, there would have been liability for the resulting physical injuries. Yet the Privy Council denied relief because the injury was induced through the fear of collision. As a lowly justice of the Court of Queen's Bench, Wright J could hardly ignore the authority of *Coultas*. His effort to distinguish the case started a running debate about the relationship between negligence and the tort in *Wilkinson v Downton*. It is this debate that Lord Hoffmann claims is now over. But is it?

It is interesting to note first that Wright J was not entirely satisfied, despite its higher authority, that *Coultas* was good law. He catalogued the cases that had already cast doubt on its authority.[16] Yet he did not simply

---

[13] *Wilkinson*, above n 1, at 59.
[14] *Ibid.*
[15] (1888) 13 AC 222.
[16] *Wilkinson*, above n 1, at 60.

throw in his lot with these cases, declare his disagreement with the Privy Council, and find for Mrs Wilkinson on this basis. Instead, he relied on two aspects of the facts in *Wilkinson* to distinguish the case: 'there was not in that case [*Coultas*] any element of wilful wrong; nor perhaps was the illness so direct and natural a consequence of the defendant's conduct as it is in this case'.[17] It is his use of the element of wilfulness here that makes Irvine's interpretation questionable. If wilful simply means that the act in issue was deliberate, this ingredient does not distinguish *Wilkinson* and *Coultas*. Just as the defendant in *Wilkinson* deliberately told the plaintiff a false story about injury to her husband, so the defendant in *Coultas* deliberately opened the gate for the plaintiff's carriage. So there must be more to wilfulness than a deliberate act.

Lord Hoffmann, in *Wainwright*, treats the references to wilfulness or intention in *Wilkinson* as disingenuous. That is, he thinks that Wright J wanted to find the defendant liable whether he acted intentionally or negligently, but he could not come right out and ground liability in negligence because of *Coultas*. So he developed a standard as close to negligence as possible without actually being negligence; it certainly was not a genuine intent standard, according to Lord Hoffmann.[18] There are two problems with this analysis. First, if Wright J had merely wanted to distinguish *Coultas* somehow, he could simply have relied on his claim that the injury was more direct in this case than in *Coultas*, reading *Coultas* as simply drawing the remoteness line on its facts, rather than deciding that this type of damage is unrecoverable in negligence as a matter of principle. That may not persuade everyone, but directness is a more-or-less concept and reasonable people can disagree about how direct a consequence must be in order to be proximate. But Wright J does not put all his eggs in this basket. He leads off by distinguishing *Coultas* on the grounds that it did not involve *wilful* wrong. Second, Wright J noted that he himself had, just months earlier, decided a case clearly involving negligence causing nervous shock-induced injury *against* the plaintiff. This would seem to indicate a view that recovery for nervous shock injury is not to be had in negligence and thus militates against the claim that he was trying to sneak a negligence-based cause of action in by the back door.

Thus, it seems to me that to accept Lord Hoffmann's interpretation of the case, we must attribute a very un-Victorian level of disingenuousness to Wright J. Similarly, the next English case to arise, *Janvier v Sweeney*,[19] is a bit mysterious on Lord Hoffmann's analysis. In *Janvier*, in an effort to force the plaintiff to help the defendant acquire certain letters in the possession of the plaintiff's employer, the defendant, a private investigator,

---

[17] *Ibid.*
[18] *Wainwright*, above n 2, at 425.
[19] [1919] 2 KB 316 (CA) [*Janvier*].

pretended to be from Scotland Yard and told the plaintiff that she was wanted by the police because she corresponded with a German spy. The reference to the German spy was a reference to the plaintiff's German fiancé, who was interned because of the war. The plaintiff claimed to have suffered nervous shock-induced injury as a result of being so accused.

The reasoning in *Janvier* is more ambiguous, and thus provides some support for Lord Hoffmann's interpretation. For example, Bankes LJ claimed that no new rule of law was created in *Wilkinson*; it simply extended the principle of remoteness perhaps further than had been done in the past.[20] Bankes LJ also cited the approval of *Wilkinson* in *Dulieu v White & Sons*,[21] a negligence case that clearly contradicts *Coultas*.[22] Thus, Lord Hoffmann is right to point out that, by the time *Janvier* was decided in 1919, the proposition that nervous shock-induced injury was recoverable in negligence was gaining support. Yet, though the authority of *Coultas* was clearly in decline by this time, it is misleading to say that the *Janvier* court simply subsumes the tort in *Wilkinson* into negligence.[23]

To begin with, *Dulieu* itself implicitly treats *Wilkinson* as a tort apart. Kennedy J limited liability for negligence causing injury through nervous shock to situations of fear for the plaintiff's own personal safety.[24] On this analysis, Mrs Wilkinson should have lost in negligence. Yet *Dulieu* cites *Wilkinson* with approval, so it must be the fact that the behaviour in that case went beyond negligence in some way that justifies allowing the plaintiff to recover for a shock arising out of supposed threat or injury to someone else.

Further, though the judges in *Janvier* drew on the negligence case law, they did not describe the wrongfulness of the defendant's behaviour in terms of the creation of an unreasonable risk of injury through nervous shock, as a modern negligence analysis would require. Bankes LJ said:

> Barker [the defendant's employee] went to this house and deliberately threatened the plaintiff in order to induce or compel her to commit a gross breach of the duty she owed to her employer. It is no longer contended that this was not a wrongful act which would amount to an actionable wrong if damage which the law recognised can be shown to have flowed directly from that act.[25]

This treats the defendant's behaviour as wrongful, leaving the only issue to be whether this kind of damage is recoverable. But what does 'wrongful'

---

[20] *Ibid*, at 321.

[21] [1901] 2 KB 669 (CA) [*Dulieu*].

[22] In this he is followed by Duke LJ, above n 19, at 327.

[23] Janvier, Lord Hoffmann says, 'was entitled to succeed whether the detectives intended to cause her injury or were merely negligent as to the consequences of their threats'. *Wainwright*, above n 2, at 424.

[24] *Dulieu*, above n 21, at 357.

[25] *Janvier*, above n 19, at 321.

mean? Nothing about the analysis suggests that its wrongfulness lies in the foreseeability of its resulting in nervous shock-induced injury *per se*. Yet the negligence analysis that Lord Hoffmann ultimately validates was the one stated most crisply by Denning LJ: 'the test of liability for shock is foreseeability *of injury by shock*'.[26]

Lord Hoffmann's analysis makes even less sense of the reasons of Duke LJ, who described *Janvier* as a 'stronger case' than *Wilkinson* because in the latter:

> there was no intention to commit a wrongful act; the defendant merely intended to play a practical joke upon the plaintiff. In the present case there was an intention to terrify the plaintiff for the purpose of attaining an unlawful object.[27]

Oddly, Lord Hoffmann treats this passage as acknowledging that there was only negligence, not intention, in *Wilkinson*.[28] But this misses the point. Lord Hoffmann thinks there was only negligence in *Wilkinson* because there was no intention *to cause injury through nervous shock*. But in this regard, *Janvier* is not 'a stronger case'; it is no more plausible to think that the defendant in *Janvier* intended to cause nervous shock injury than that the jokester in *Wilkinson* did. Indeed, one might argue that *Janvier* is a weaker case on this measure since an intention to cause nervous shock injury would be at odds with the defendant's objective. Presumably, the defendant wanted a cowed, but functioning, accomplice. So Sweeney's behaviour is worse than Downton's, but not in being more aimed at producing nervous shock injury. Duke LJ locates the object of the intention in 'committing a wrongful act', which indicates that some form of intention is in fact significant to him, but that the wrongfulness lies elsewhere than in the foreseeable production of the actual result of physical harm.

Finally, interpreting references to wilfulness or intention as code for negligence in these cases seems implausible on the facts. At least this is the case if we adopt the contemporary conception of negligence, as Lord Hoffmann does. Can we really say that there is a 'substantial risk'[29] that telling someone her husband has been injured or that she is in trouble with the law will result in physical injury resulting from shock? Of course, such a result is possible, just as a cricket ball that has been hit over a fence once may be hit over again. But does the prospect of nervous shock-induced injury really cross the threshold required by the notion of substantial risk? Most commentators discussing these cases have agreed with Lord Hoffmann that these judges cannot have meant to ground liability in the

---

[26]   *King v Phillips* [1953] 1 QB 429 (CA), 441 (emphasis added).
[27]   *Janvier*, above n 19, at 326.
[28]   *Wainwright*, above n 2, at 424.
[29]   *Bolton v Stone* [1951] AC 850 (HL).

intention to cause nervous shock injury because that is a wholly implausible construction of the facts. But they have also assumed that the actual injury—physical injury arising out of the shock—was not reasonably foreseeable.[30] If it had been, we might expect the language of intention and wilfulness to have fallen away at a much earlier stage once the negligence cases involving injury through nervous shock were firmly entrenched. But, as we will see from the Canadian cases, it does not. So, to adopt Lord Hoffmann's analysis, we must assume that the judges in the early cases conspired to use the concept of intention disingenuously when the operative fault standard was negligence, and that later judges carried forward this terminological convention, when it was clearly no longer necessary, for reasons best known to themselves.

There must be a better explanation of the reasoning in these early cases; Lord Hoffmann's reading loses too much of the colour of the reasons. The judgments reveal that, while no one believed that the defendants had intended to cause nervous shock-induced injury, some form of intention was important to the judges. In *Wilkinson*, there is a constant focus on the fact that the defendant's story was deliberately false. In this respect his behaviour was intentional; it is not as though he honestly thought the plaintiff's husband had been injured and that the plaintiff would want to have this vital information (such a case *would* be a true negligence case). He also could not help but know—a fault standard going beyond negligence and entering into the realm of imputed intention—that such a story would be harmful, in some loose sense, to the plaintiff. He cannot have thought that she would be amused. By contrast, the defendant in *Coultas* opened a gate not realising that the train was coming. His action was intentional, but his subjective intention was to do something beneficial, even though his action was in fact unreasonably risky.

So Downton did something that was wilfully wrong in a loose sense of wrong, ie, one not tied to the foreseeability of a specific harmful consequence—injury through nervous shock. If we ask whether the defendant ought to have made the statement, the answer is clearly no, for several reasons; if we ask whether the defendant in *Coultas* ought to have opened the gate, the answer is yes, unless there was a foreseeable risk of harm. That is, the only basis for declaring the action wrongful in *Coultas* is its tendency to cause physical harm; in *Wilkinson* the action is wrong for other reasons.

There are two possible readings of *Wilkinson* in this regard, a less and a more stringent one. One might read the defendant's behaviour as wrong not only because it fraudulently induced the plaintiff to spend money, but also because his intentionally false representation could not help but cause

---

[30] See, eg, Irvine, above n 12, at 140.

distress. I will call this the broad *Wilkinson* test. It is the interpretation ultimately advanced by Fleming, but rejected by Hale LJ in *Wong v Parkside Health NHS Trust*.[31] The other interpretation—the narrow *Wilkinson* test—is that his behaviour was wrong because it carried a high likelihood that the bad news would cause some kind of physical response—fainting or racing of the heart, perhaps—even if not actual physical injury. This is to read the reference to 'grave consequences' as a requirement that some kind of physical response to the news is the relevant upshot, while the idea that such a consequence be 'calculated' implies such a level of likelihood that it is fair to impute intention to the defendant. The plausibility of both of these interpretations is increased by Lunney's discovery that, when delivering judgment, Wright J may have used the phrase 'physical pain' rather than 'physical harm' in describing what the defendant must have calculated, although it is 'harm' that appears in the reported version of the case.[32] 'Physical pain' would easily cover the usual sorts of physical response to severe stress, and can even be stretched to include severe distress.

On either interpretation, there is a gap between the intention that grounds the wrongfulness of the conduct and the ultimate consequences for which liability is imposed—one can be liable for actual physical injury through shock for intentionally making a false statement intended to cause distress, or for saying or doing something imputably intended to provoke a milder physical reaction. I claim it is this intention to behave wrongfully by intentionally making false statements designed to do some harm that justifies imposing liability even for unforeseeable consequences in Wright J's mind. This mismatch of sorts between the quality of the act that makes it wrong and the description of the consequences to which liability extends gives intention some role to play in grounding liability. Absent this, Lord Hoffmann is right that the advent of liability in negligence swallows up cases involving intention of any sort, unless the scope of liability is expanded in some other way, such as extending to a previously recognised form of harm.

That the defendant behaved intentionally wrongly in this loose sense is even clearer in *Janvier*, making sense of its treatment as a 'stronger case' than *Wilkinson*. The judges repeatedly emphasised that the defendant deliberately falsely represented himself as a member of Scotland Yard, falsely said the plaintiff was wanted by the police, intending that she should be terrified, and did all this in order to blackmail her. The conduct is multiply wrong, in a layperson's sense, but not because of its tendency to cause nervous shock-induced injury *per se*. Likewise, Bankes LJ refers to

---

[31] [2001] EWCA Civ 1721, [11] [*Wong*].
[32] Lunney, above n 10, at 181-82. As Lunney notices, the difference in wording encapsulates the struggle to fit *Wilkinson* into the larger landscape of tort law.

the defendant's behaviour not specifically as negligent, but generically as 'a wrongful act'.[33] The only descriptions of its wrongful nature have to do with its deliberately threatening quality and unlawful objective. He also adopts from *Dulieu* the following general principle: 'terror wrongfully induced and inducing physical mischief gives a cause of action'.[34] There is no precise analysis of what constitutes *wrongfully* inducing terror, so the judgment has something of a question begging quality. The concrete determination that behaviour is wrongful is announced by the judges on a case by case basis, rather than deduced from a theory. But it is clear that wrongfulness is not analysed in terms of the reasonable foreseeability of causing injury through nervous shock. Even the above quotation treats the quality of wrongfulness as separate from the causal fact of physical 'mischief' ultimately resulting.

Lord Hoffmann overlooks this interpretation because he is firmly entrenched in the integrated conception of tort liability. He has forgotten that there was a time when the elements of a cause of action, even negligence, were treated as independent of one another. Indeed, even *Dulieu* exemplifies the older structure more closely than it does the integrated structure. Because the case involved the careless operation of a horse-drawn van, it was easy to conclude that the defendant had behaved negligently without a sustained analysis of what the likely risks were and to whom. There is an interesting debate about whether the duty of care argument was strengthened because the plaintiff was inside a building rather than on the street—the suggestion was that perhaps other users of the street have accepted the risk of run-away vans and are therefore not owed a duty of care. This discussion turns contemporary sensibilities about duty of care upside down. Finally, the discussion of recovery for injury through nervous shock *per se* is couched in terms of the directness of the causal connection between the collision and the plaintiff's reaction,[35] not the foreseeability of that consequence.

For some reason, after *Janvier*, the tort in *Wilkinson* went out of fashion in England, and further development of the concept of intention involved was arrested until recently.[36] The case law on negligence causing nervous shock-induced injury developed over the years, but none of these cases involve the kind of wilful wrongdoing identified as the core of the tort in *Wilkinson* and *Janvier*. As liability for negligently caused nervous shock

---

[33] *Janvier*, above n 19, at 321.
[34] *Ibid*, at 322.
[35] *Dulieu*, above n 21, at 358.
[36] Recent developments in England have been largely channeled through debates over the existence of an action for harassment, now overtaken by the enactment of the Protection from Harassment Act 1997. For an overview of these cases, see Hale LJ's judgment in *Wong*, above n 31, at [18]-[30]. The legislative intervention has removed from the common law many of the sorts of fact situations frequently litigated in Canada.

injury crystallised, no one seems to have thought to apply that principle to a *Wilkinson*-like case. This, in itself, might be thought to cast doubt on Lord Hoffmann's revisionist history of the tort, unless *Wilkinson* and *Janvier* had the kind of deterrent effect judges usually can only dream about.

Indeed, most striking in this regard is the decision in *Wong*.[37] Hale LJ interprets *Wilkinson* very narrowly—liability only when one can impute to the defendant an intention to cause injury through nervous shock, *per se*—and finds intention not present on the facts.[38] This is unsurprising, since these cases rarely, if ever, exhibit such a high degree of fault. But this is exactly the approach that should be overtaken by a negligence analysis, according to Lord Hoffmann. If a defendant intends to inflict injury through nervous shock, he or she certainly takes an unreasonable risk of causing it, and therefore behaves negligently. Yet even though, obviously, one can create an unreasonable risk of nervous shock injury without intending it, Hale LJ does not even advert to whether the action might be grounded in the reasonable foreseeability that the campaign of harassment in issue would cause such injury.

In any event, the tort in *Wilkinson* was quickly transplanted to Canadian soil and has responded to local conditions. Its development here confirms my skepticism about reinterpreting *Wilkinson* as a negligence case. Although the English courts may not have had much opportunity to rethink the distinctiveness of the tort in *Wilkinson* until recently, Canadian courts have used the tort often without anyone ever suggesting that the intention nonsense could just be abandoned in favour of a straightforward negligence analysis. So, again, either these judges and lawyers are all terribly confused, or there is something in the instinctive sense of the underpinnings of this cause of action that is not captured by Lord Hoffmann's analysis.

III.   THE CANADIAN SEQUEL

A.   The Leap Across the Pond

The first Canadian case was a very close variation on the facts in *Wilkinson*. The defendant in *Bielitski v Obadiak* again made up a very nasty story—this time that a young man had committed suicide by hanging himself from a tree.[39] The plaintiff was the young man's mother, who, upon hearing this news, fell seriously ill. The twist in *Bielitski* was that the

---

[37]   Above n 31.
[38]   *Ibid*, at [12]-[13].
[39]   (1922) 65 DLR 627 (Sask CA).

defendant had not conveyed this story directly to the plaintiff. Instead he told a third party, and the story passed through two others before reaching the mother. Accepting the authority of *Wilkinson*, much of the discussion in the case was about whether the indirectness in the plaintiff's ultimate receipt of the information should block her claim.[40] The majority thought not, though there was a dissent on the point.[41] The court's analysis of the cause of action fits the parameters outlined above. Lamont JA broke the matter down into two issues: 'Did the defendant wilfully spread a false report; and if so, did his act cause and was it intended to cause the plaintiff's physical suffering'.[42] The first question focuses on the deliberate falsehood to establish wrongfulness. Lamont JA also followed Wright J in distinguishing *Coultas* as lacking 'any element of wilful wrong'.[43]

The majority dealt very quickly with the 'calculated to cause physical harm' element of the tort. Lamont JA simply says that the defendant's conduct would 'in all probability, cause her not only mental anguish but physical pain'.[44] Similarly, Turgeon JA asks rhetorically whether, such news having reached the mother, 'is it at all unlikely that it should affect her injuriously?'[45] The use of imprecise language such as 'pain' rather than 'harm' or 'injury', 'affect her injuriously' rather than 'cause nervous shock' allows the judges to avoid directly confronting the fact that the defendant did not intend the consequences to be anywhere near as serious as they were. Indeed, the judgments straddle exactly the ambiguity identified in *Wilkinson*. We might interpret them to base liability on wilfully making a false report, plus imputed intention to cause some kind of physical reaction, however minor. Or one might go further and read them as requiring merely intent to cause emotional distress.[46] Either way, the case is hard to reconcile with negligence. I would argue that it is no more reasonably foreseeable that a woman will suffer the extreme effects designated by the label 'nervous shock' as a result of hearing that her son had committed suicide, than that she will do so from hearing that her husband has been injured.[47]

---

[40] *Ibid*, at 631.
[41] *Ibid*, at 628 (Haultain CJS)
[42] *Ibid*, at 631.
[43] *Ibid*, at 632.
[44] *Ibid*, at 631.
[45] *Ibid*, at 635.
[46] Irvine, above n 12.
[47] *Bielitski* was followed by *Purdy v Woznesensky* [1937] 2 WWR 116 (Sask CA), essentially a case of negligence causing nervous shock. The defendant attacked the plaintiff's husband in the plaintiff's presence. By this time, mothers had been allowed recovery in negligence for physical injury resulting from witnessing a negligently caused injury to a child. It is hard to see why a brutal attack on one's husband would be any different. The *Purdy* facts exemplify intentional conduct that is swallowed up by negligence law as long as negligent conduct of a similar sort is sufficient to ground liability.

B.   The Rahemtulla Test: Intentional Infliction of Distress Canadian-Style

Litigation in this area picked up steam in the 1980s and 1990s. The typical context shifted from the kinds of discrete acts or statements characterising the early cases to recurring conduct often within an employment relationship. Indeed, many of the cases involve a claim both for unjust dismissal and tort damages. The cases that succeed in tort are also clear cases of unjust dismissal, but from the earliest of these cases, *Rahemtulla v Vanfed Credit Union*,[48] the courts have held that the plaintiff's claim for damages for physical illness through shock or other kinds of stress cannot simply be folded into the unjust dismissal action. As McLachlin J noted in *Rahemtulla*,[49] the resulting illness does not flow from the breach of contract—the failure to give proper notice—but rather from the treatment of the plaintiff either in being fired or induced to leave.[50]

Two significant departures from the early English cases are notable in the Canadian case law. First, *Rahemtulla* introduced an element from American jurisprudence—that the defendant's behaviour must be extreme, flagrant, or outrageous.[51] The idea is introduced as something of an afterthought,[52] but it has stuck and is now routinely listed as the first element in the test for liability. Second, Fleming's approach, claiming that the tort requires only that the defendant intend to frighten, alarm, or terrify the plaintiff—in other words, cause distress—has enjoyed significant influence.[53] This, of course, is the liability-expanding formulation that was rejected in *Wong*.[54]

The Canadian test that emerges from the cases[55] has three elements:

---

[48]   [1984] 3 WWR 296 (BCSC) [*Rahemtulla*].

[49]   *Ibid*, at [41].

[50]   See also *Prinzo v Baycrest Centre for Geriatric Care* (2002) 60 OR (3d) 474 (CA) [34]-[39] [*Prinzo*].

[51]   *Rahemtulla*, above n 48, at [52].

[52]   The defendant apparently sought to add an additional, more stringent element to the test for liability. McLachlin J quickly found the defendant's behaviour to be outrageous, as was that of defendants in other *Wilkinson*-like cases. *Rahemtulla*, above n 48, at [53].

[53]   See especially, *Timmermans v Buelow* (1984) 38 CCLT 136 (Ont SC) [*Timmermans*] and *Clark v The Queen* [1994] 3 FC 323 (TD) [*Clark*]. Both cases have been routinely cited. See, eg, *Bogden v Purolator* (1996) 182 AR 216 (QB) [*Bogden*]; *Campbell v Wellfund Audio-Visual* (1995) 14 CCEL (2d) 240 (BCSC) [*Campbell*]; *Smith v Alwarid* [1996] YJ No 139 (YSC) (QL) [*Smith*].

[54]   Above n 31.

[55]   The significant Canadian cases include *Timmermans v Buelow*, above n 53, *Boothman v The Queen* [1993] 3 FC 381 (TD) [*Boothman*]; *Clark*, above n 53; *Campbell*, above n 53; *Nolan v Toronto (Metropolitan) Police Force* [1996] OJ No 1764 (Gen Div) (QL) [*Nolan*]; *Bogden*, above n 53; *Smith*, above n 53; *Prinzo*, above n 50; *Haggarty v McCullogh* (2002) 309 AR 315 (Prov Ct) [*Haggarty*]; *Zorn-Smith v Bank of Montreal* [2003] OTC 1060 (SCJ) [*Zorn-Smith*]; *Downham v Lennox and Addington (County)* [2005] OJ No 5227 (SCJ) (QL).

1. Conduct that is outrageous, extreme, or flagrant;
2. Conduct calculated to produce some effect of the kind produced;
3. Actual harm in the form of visible and provable illness.

In quintessential Canadian fashion, the test blends American and English elements: the first from American law,[56] the second and third taken directly from *Wilkinson*. The three elements are easy to list; it is harder to glean their exact meaning. The judgments seem almost to have been crafted with a view to carefully maintaining ambiguity.

For example, McLachlin J in *Rahemtulla* begins by reformulating the 'intention' requirement in *Wilkinson* as follows:

> The law has long recognised as tortious the uttering of false words or threats with the *knowledge* that they are likely to cause, and which actually cause, nervous shock and physical injury.[57]

She then says the defendant's accusation of theft was made with a 'reckless disregard'[58] for whether or not shock would ensue. Knowledge of likely adverse consequences is here quickly watered down to recklessness, which is more in keeping with imputed intention. Furthermore, the initial formulation seems to require knowledge of the likelihood of shock *and* physical injury. 'Physical injury' is open to different interpretations. The narrowest—intention to cause physical illness through shock—would be subject to Lord Hoffmann's subsumption argument. More generous would be an interpretation following the narrow *Wilkinson* test, requiring only that there be a high likelihood that some physical response would result.

To compound the ambiguity, McLachlin J introduces the outrageousness requirement, then finds it satisfied because:

> the proper conduct of [the defendant's] affairs does not require that it be given the right to make reckless and very possibly untruthful accusations as to the employee's honesty which will foreseeably inflict shock and mental suffering.[59]

Note that the discussion of outrageousness is part of the discussion of the quality of intention necessary to establish liability. Thus, it seems that outrageousness is meant as another description of the kind of intentional wrongdoing required to ground liability. But now this 'reckless' conduct is said to *foreseeably* inflict shock *and mental suffering*. If we take seriously the characterisation of the conduct as reckless, foreseeability of the result is redundant; reckless conduct is behaviour so likely to cause injury that intention to cause it can be imputed. This goes beyond requiring merely

---

[56] *Restatement (Second) of Torts* (1965) § 46.
[57] *Rahemtulla*, above n 48, at [48].
[58] *Ibid*, at [50].
[59] *Ibid*, at [55].

that injury be foreseeable. More significant is that the relevant consequences are now described as shock and 'mental suffering'. If mental
suffering is meant as synonymous with physical illness suffered as a result
of shock, we have not moved away from our initial interpretation, but
have only given this aspect of the tort a new label—'outrageous conduct'.
If, however, the reference to mental suffering signals that intention to cause
distress is what constitutes outrageous conduct, the decision shades into
the broad *Wilkinson* test, that is, the Fleming approach.

The ambiguity is maintained by the discussion of the second element—
whether the conduct is calculated to produce some effect of the kind
produced. As we have seen, the vagueness of this formulation allows
ambiguity about just what must be 'calculated'—the actual effect in all its
seriousness, or merely some physical effect? This is complicated still further
by the separation of the 'calculated' element of the *Wilkinson* test from the
idea of recklessness or outrageousness built into the first element of the
Rahemtulla test. Given that, at this first stage, McLachlin J has found that
the defendant behaved recklessly in provoking shock and at least mental
suffering, it is difficult to see what further work is left to be done by the
requirement that his conduct be calculated to produce some effect of the
kind that was produced. If the second element describes a lower degree of
fault than the first element, it is redundant; if higher, it becomes the
effective test, rendering the first element redundant. In fact, McLachlin J's
description of the 'calculated' element seems essentially to repeat the
'outrageousness' element, offering further support for saying that it is
distress that must be calculated/intended, now with the adjective 'profound' attached: 'It was *clearly foreseeable* that the accusations of theft
which the defendant made against the plaintiff would cause her *profound
distress*'.[60]

C.   Recent Developments

Since *Rahemtulla*, it has become increasingly clear that the Canadian cases
are coalescing around the Fleming approach: liability requires only that an
intention to cause severe emotional distress is properly imputed to the
defendant. There are two points to note here: distress, not illness or
physical injury, is the relevant consequence, and intention to produce it can
be imputed from the high likelihood of the outcome.[61] Catzman J in

---

[60]   *Ibid*, at [56] (emphasis added).
[61]   One outlier in this respect is *Drizis v Restaurants Inc* [1996] OJ No 5021 [26]-[28]
(Gen Div) (QL) [*Drizis*]; liability was rejected because the defendant was not motivated by the
desire to cause distress.

Timmermans[62] clearly drew on Fleming, and most of the later cases followed along.[63] The employment cases tend to shift their language from fright and alarm, terms that suggest a discrete event, to the more general idea of intending to harass or cause emotional distress.[64]

The Canadian cases have also been consistent in requiring actual illness or physical manifestations of severe stress to complete the cause of action. Two of the cases, *Boothman*[65] and *Clark*,[66] have been explicit that foreseeability of such injury is not necessary. This is significant, of course, because Lord Hoffmann's subsumption argument would require that the kind of harm captured by the traditional label 'nervous shock' be foreseeable to be recoverable. The Canadian version of the tort in *Wilkinson v Downton* gives it a role in modern law by imposing liability for unforeseeable physical illness or harm, provided there is outrageous conduct and/or imputed intention to cause severe emotional distress. No Canadian case so far has been willing to take up Lord Hoffmann's suggestion that liability might be extended to distress falling short of illness based on a finding of subjective intention to inflict such distress,[67] even though several cases would satisfy such a stringent test.

Note also that, although some of the recent cases might well have been decided on negligence grounds, there has been little discussion of negligence as a possible basis for liability. This is despite the oblique suggestion in *Rahemtulla* that:

the general principles governing liability for negligence set forth in *Anns v Merton London Borough Council...* may well in the end reduce the importance of categorical distinctions such as those between intentional and negligent torts.[68]

---

[62] Above, n 53.

[63] See *Clark, Campbell* and *Bogden*, above n 53; *Nolan*, above n 55.

[64] *Boothman*, above n 55, at 391 goes further, adopting the widest test offered by Irvine—mere reasonable foreseeability that the conduct will cause fear or emotional upset. Noël J quotes a passage from Irvine's annotation of *Timmermans*, apparently thinking he is quoting from Catzman J's judgment. This extension is unnecessary to the decision; the defendant intended to cause a mental breakdown, which would clearly fit the narrower formulation of the test.

[65] Above n 55.

[66] Above n 53.

[67] An apparent exception is *Haggarty*, above n 55. Although the plaintiff had not proven actual psychiatric injury, the judge declared, at [29], that the offending behaviour 'clearly constituted the act of an intentional infliction of mental suffering' because it caused damage to the plaintiff's 'pride and dignity' for which the perpetrator could be liable in tort. The tendency, in employment cases, for this analysis to be carried out under the rubric of aggravated damages can make it difficult to separate the contract from the tort issues. The Ontario Court of Appeal recently offered some guidance on this question in *Prinzo*, above n 50, at [63]. Further, the insistence in *Prinzo*, at [62], on proof of physical illness would seem to implicitly overrule this aspect of *Haggarty*.

[68] Above n 48, at [58] (citations omitted).

Given that the latest cases have tended to involve ongoing conduct rather than a single 'shocking' event, one can sometimes argue that the defendant's behaviour gave rise to an unreasonable risk of the kinds of manifestations in physical illness that can accompany severe stress. For example, when fellow employees conduct a sustained campaign of harassment evidently designed to hound someone out of her job, as in *Clark*, or a manager constantly berates and belittles an employee, as in *Boothman* or possibly *Smith v Alwarid*,[69] one might say that the level of stress imposed foreseeably gives rise to depression and other stress-related illnesses. In *Clark*, the applicability of the negligence principle is considered in addition to intentional infliction of distress, although the discussion of negligence is somewhat sketchy; the feasibility of subsuming the former in the latter is not mentioned.[70] It is even more striking that, although *Clark* is much cited, rarely is its negligence analysis followed.[71]

The general eschewal of the negligence principle suggests a desire to preserve the freedom to impose liability for consequences that are not, strictly speaking, foreseeable. If the *Rahemtulla* test is wider in this remoteness respect than negligence, there is no need to work through the consequences of a shift to negligence, and this would explain why judges usually do not bother. Lawyers and judges alike seem to have understood instinctively that, in these cases, it is easier on the facts to satisfy a test of imputed intention to cause distress than to establish that the full consequences of the defendant's conduct were foreseeable.

One puzzling aspect of the cases is that no clarification has emerged of the relationship between the first element of the *Rahemtulla* test—the outrageousness element—and the second—the imputed intention to cause serious distress.[72] If what makes conduct outrageous is its tendency to provoke distress, the second element is redundant. Yet judges continue to lay out the two elements separately. The cases are not closely reasoned, so it is difficult to be confident of any particular account. I suggest, however, that the outrageousness requirement can be preserved as an independent

---

[69]   Above n 53. It is hard to place *Smith* on this issue. The judge does consider negligence and holds in the alternative that the defendant committed negligent infliction of mental distress; however, this is based on a finding of recklessness rather than mere negligence, suggesting that Hudson J assumes, at [72], that 'intention' for purposes of intentional infliction of distress requires a subjective intention to cause some kind of harm. Nor is there any sustained analysis of whether the actual harm suffered was foreseeable. The best interpretation of the case may be that, in effect, liability is imposed for recklessness in imposing serious distress, which is to say imputed intention to do so. This brings the case into line with most of the rest of the Canadian cases, rather than grounding it in negligence.

[70]   *Clark*, above n 53.

[71]   Other cases may use the adjective 'foreseeable' to refer to some aspect of the situation, but do not conduct a careful negligence analysis.

[72]   Either the two elements are listed separately and declared satisfied or not, as the case may be, or, as in *Zorn-Smith*, above n 55, at [169], the two elements seem to be collapsed together, though without acknowledgment or discussion.

element of the tort if read in light of the idea teased out of *Wilkinson* that what it takes to trigger liability is intentional wrongdoing in some looser sense than creating a risk of causing a particular type of harm. It is not hard to find this in the cases; they almost all involve a wrongful act or motivation of this kind that is fully intentional in the strictest sense.[73] In *Rahemtulla*, the defendant knowingly made a quite possibly false accusation of dishonesty; in *Timmermans*,[74] the defendant's bullying was aimed at evicting the plaintiff from his apartment in full knowledge that the eviction was unlawful; in *Nolan*,[75] the defendant police officers not only unlawfully detained the plaintiff, but subjected him to racist comments designed to belittle and humiliate him; the employment-related cases involve abusive co-workers or managers behaving aggressively and punitively, mostly to hound into quitting someone against whom no legitimate complaint could be made. The high-water mark in the employment cases is perhaps *Campbell*, in which the defendant employer tried to pressure the plaintiff into supporting the employer's knowingly false assertion that another employee had been fired for cause, and ultimately fired him when he refused.[76] The echoes of *Janvier* are unmistakable.

This is all behaviour 'calculated' to cause distress, but it seems wrongful or unjustified independently of its tendency to produce this result. It may be significant that deceit is a frequent theme in the cases; apart from this we may identify highhandedness about the defendant's behaviour that can only be described as contemptuous of the plaintiff. The outrageousness element can be seen as a stab at describing generically the kind of 'bad' behaviour that grounds liability and justifies extending damages beyond foreseeable consequences. It incorporates a seriousness threshold; not just any kind of misconduct will count. It is significant, I think, that the line in the cases seems to be drawn exactly between merely brusque, even harsh, managerial style, and contemptuous treatment.[77] This insight might usefully be connected, as a starting point, to the old-fashioned notion of malice. The instinct is that trying to cause harm of some sort without any

---

[73] An interesting possible exception to this pattern is *Zorn-Smith, ibid*—the plaintiff recovered for intentional infliction of distress despite the absence of the kind of abusiveness typical elsewhere. The defendant's wrongdoing seemed to consist in knowingly exploiting the plaintiff's hardworking nature to the point of causing her to 'burn out'.

[74] Above n 53.

[75] Above n 55.

[76] Above n 53.

[77] The height of the threshold is demonstrated, though not clearly explained, in *McGeady v Saskatchewan Wheat Pool* (1998) 174 Sask R 110 (QB). The court found sufficient bad faith to allow extension of the notice period for which damages are recoverable under *Wallace v United Grain Growers Ltd* [1997] 3 SCR 701, but no outrageousness. See also *Drizis*, above n 61, and *Kalaman v Singer Valve Co* (1997) 38 BCLR (3d) 331 (CA) in which the court opined at [76], that 'something more than emotional distress over loss of employment or unreasonable and insensitive conduct of the employer preceding dismissal is required to found a claim for damages for mental distress'.

sort of justification shows such disrespect that one cannot insist on confining liability to those consequences that are foreseeable. In the early cases like *Wilkinson*, the defendant may not have been trying to cause injury through nervous shock, but he was trying to do some harm without any justification. It is a short step to include cases, such as *Rahemtulla*, in which the defendant may not have exhibited actual malice, but could not help but know that his reckless accusation would be profoundly insulting, and had no justification for proceeding so hurtfully.

Elsewhere I have argued that the requirement of outrageousness marks the kind of behaviour that constitutes a violation of dignity.[78] This might be regarded as a general way of explaining the wrongfulness of behaviour that triggers liability for intentional infliction of distress, and might help explain why liability extends to unforeseeable consequences. When liability is grounded in unreasonable risk of physical injury, it is unfair to impose liability for unforeseeable consequences because it would not provide potential defendants with a fair opportunity to avoid liability. But one can always avoid the kind of wilful wrongdoing connoted by 'outrageous, extreme, or flagrant' conduct simply by not behaving deliberately outrageously.

Though we lack consensus around the precise contours of the test and its rationale, it is clear that the Canadian cases cannot be subsumed into negligence. They rely on a standard of fault that is, in some respects, more stringent than that of negligence, but tie this to a more generous remoteness standard, extending recovery beyond the injuries that are foreseeable. If this package makes sense, there is still a role for the tort in *Wilkinson v Downton* to play in modern law.[79]

---

[78] See Denise G Réaume, 'Indignities: Making a Place for Dignity in Modern Legal Thought' (2002) 28 *Queen's Law Journal* 61. The connection between this kind of outrageous conduct and the violation of dignity was made explicitly by the trial judge in *Haggarty*, above n 55, at [29].

[79] As Rick Glofcheski pointed out to me, the recent English case of *Bici v Ministry of Defence* [2004] EWHC 786 (QB) identifies another possible role for *Wilkinson*. While *Wilkinson* was rejected in favour of negligent infliction of psychiatric injury, in part based on *Wainwright*, Elias J suggested that there may be cases in which a plaintiff cannot succeed in negligence because the defendant owed no duty of care to him or her, but in which *Wilkinson* can fill the gap. The suggestion points up the fact that modern negligence law may not be as integrated as Lord Hoffmann gives it credit for. It makes no sense to think that Elias J refers to duty of care being denied because the plaintiff is not a foreseeable victim of harm; *Wilkinson* fact situations are invariably ones in which the plaintiff is the defendant's deliberate target. He must be referring to the kind of case in which a duty is denied *even though* the plaintiff is a foreseeable victim of emotionally induced physical illness and duty is denied for reasons extraneous to the nature of the risk. The recent tendency of courts to invoke duty of care in this manner arguably interrupts the project of developing an integrated doctrine of liability for negligence.

IV. CONCLUSION: FUTURE PROSPECTS

The intervention into this debate of the House of Lords in *Wainwright* makes it opportune to revisit and develop a deeper account of the Canadian case law on the tort in *Wilkinson v Downton*. Most of the Canadian judgments are trial judgments; the trend is clear, but the reasoning is sketchy. Although the House of Lords did not consider Canadian or other Commonwealth cases, it may well be that Canadian courts will not feel as comfortable ignoring their Lordships. Litigation is growing in this area in Canada,[80] and *Wainwright* is bound to be cited to Canadian courts in future. Without a clear sense of how Canadian law has developed differently, it might be tempting to adopt the elegantly simple subsumption argument.

That would, as we have seen, narrow the scope of liability; allowing *Wilkinson* to 'disappear beneath the surface of the law of negligence',[81] and would confine recovery to those cases in which mentally induced physical illness is a foreseeable result of the defendant's behaviour. This would require courts to be much clearer about how the type/extent distinction should play out in this context for foreseeability purposes. Some of the cases involve serious mental health problems triggered by the defendant's abusive behaviour, their effects lingering for years. A negligence analysis will require courts to decide how much of this was foreseeable as a result of a sometimes short campaign of harassment. Undoubtedly, some situations in which plaintiffs have succeeded in the past will fall afoul of a foreseeability requirement. This change would also bring to the forefront the appropriate role of the thin skull principle in these cases. Although Wright J was at pains in *Wilkinson* to disavow reliance on this principle, it is arguable that many cases do involve plaintiffs who are antecedently vulnerable to the effects of psychological stress. It has long been appreciated that the thin skull principle fits uneasily within the negligence principle. This tension will be exacerbated by introducing negligence into cases involving physical illness through emotional stress.

On the other hand, Lord Hoffmann's approach might spur Canadian courts to take the step they have not yet been willing to take—imposing liability for intentionally caused distress falling short of illness. As we have seen, the Canadian courts already express the intention requirement in the tort in *Wilkinson* largely in terms of imputed intention to cause distress. But they have refused to budge from the traditional requirement that the

---

[80] The tort both supplements contract actions in the employment area and provides a means of circumventing the problems of the human rights code process. For a survey of the debate about the respective roles of courts and human rights tribunals, see Gillian Demeyere, 'Common Law Actions for Sexual Harassment: The Jurisdiction Question Revisited' (2003) 28 *Queen's Law Journal* 637.

[81] *Wainwright*, above n 2, at 425.

plaintiff prove 'visible and provable illness'. As I have argued elsewhere, our courts already have adequate reason to make this move,[82] but a push from the House of Lords may help them do it.

Of course, Lord Hoffmann expressed the view that, if liability for 'mere' distress were to be allowed, the defendant must have 'have acted in a way which he *knew* to be unjustifiable and either intended to cause harm or at least acted without caring whether he caused harm or not'.[83] Imputed intention will not do. My suspicion is that if courts move in this direction, this distinction between actual knowledge and imputed intention will not stand for long; if it does, the action will be confined to a tiny handful of cases. Proving subjective knowledge is notoriously difficult, as adjudicators have discovered in legal context after legal context. It is hard to see why it is not sufficient that the defendant behaved so highhandedly that serious distress was virtually bound to ensue. Perhaps the experience that the Canadian courts have enjoyed in this area will enable others to forego the experiment with requiring proof of actual knowledge. A tort based on imputed intention would expand liability somewhat, and also virtually guarantee that the sort of nervous shock victims who have traditionally recovered under *Wilkinson v Downton* will receive some compensation for intentionally inflicted distress even though they may be denied full recovery for the resulting physical illness under a negligence analysis.

It seems unlikely, however, that Canadian courts will abandon the language of outrage. A move to encompass damages for distress falling short of physical illness may well continue to be informed by the characterisation of the defendant's behaviour as outrageous. To do so would address Lord Hoffmann's concern to prevent the courts being flooded with distress cases. Outrageousness may be especially useful in this regard if it is interpreted as separate from the likelihood of causing serious distress—that is, if it flags a separate aspect of the wrongfulness of the defendant's conduct. Indeed, one might argue that the seeds of this turn are already present in Lord Hoffmann's judgment. After all, he argues that a genuine intention standard would involve knowledge that one's conduct is *unjustified* and intended to cause harm. This description covers the facts of both *Wilkinson* and *Janvier*, and sounds to me like a starting point for identifying behaviour as 'outrageous'.

Even if the Canadian courts resist the pull of negligence thinking, we might expect that they will be prodded to revisit the remoteness dimension to the cause of action in *Wilkinson*. That there are good reasons for not confining liability to damages for foreseeable harm in this context does not mean there need be no remoteness-like control on the extent of liability. If

---

[82]   Réaume, above n 78.
[83]   *Wainwright*, above n 2, at 426 (emphasis added).

the number of cases involving lengthy periods of disability purportedly caused by intentionally abusive treatment of one sort of another grows, this issue will come to the fore.

Finally, it is worth noting that the elegant simplicity of the subsumption argument has yet to take firm hold in English law. In *C v D*,[84] the plaintiff sued his school headmaster for several acts cumulatively amounting to sexual abuse. Some incidents involving physical contact were dealt with as battery. But there were two incidents not involving touching—the defendant videotaped boys, including the plaintiff, naked in the school showers; on another occasion, as the plaintiff was lying down in the school infirmary feeling unwell, the defendant pulled his pants down and stared at his genitals. Curiously, even though the case was heard after *Wainwright*, counsel for the plaintiff declined to argue for liability for these incidents in negligence, relying, rather, on *Wilkinson*.[85]

If the subsumption argument were taken seriously, the concession that negligence was not applicable should have foreclosed consideration of *Wilkinson*. Yet Field J dutifully quoted from *Wainwright*, including the passage calling for *Wilkinson* to be subsumed into negligence, and then blithely considered the applicability of the tort in *Wilkinson*. He found for the plaintiff in respect of the second of the two incidents,[86] not acknowledging the contradiction with *Wainwright*. Even more interesting is that the *Wilkinson* analysis conforms to the pattern I have identified in that its starting point is a quality of wrongness of the defendant's action that is independent of its tendency to cause mentally induced injury. Field J described the defendant's behaviour as 'a gross invasion of [the plaintiff's] personal integrity'[87] under conditions of vulnerability. Confusingly, he then declared that the defendant was 'reckless' as to whether his behaviour would cause psychiatric illness, seemingly based on the judgment that, although psychiatric illness was not highly likely, it was foreseeable. This seems to collapse the analysis into negligence, yet there is no careful analysis of the foreseeability of psychiatric illness in this case, and given that Field J has narrowed his analysis to this one incident, it is not clear

---

[84]   Above n 8.

[85]   Counsel argued breach of duty to look out for the safety and welfare of the plaintiff, and in the alternative, under *Wilkinson*. It is unclear what sort of duty he meant—perhaps fiduciary duty—but Field J recognised only duties in negligence and battery. *Wilkinson*, above, at [89]. This cursory discussion of the duty issue is obliquely criticised by the English Court of Appeal in *A v Iorworth Hoare, H v Suffolk County Council, X and Y v London Borough of Wandsworth* [2006] EWCA Civ 395, [134], the Court distinguishing *C v D* precisely because 'the breadth of the potential duty of care was not explored as widely in that case as it was before us'. I am grateful to Alan McKenna for bringing this case to my attention.

[86]   Field J held that the videotaping incident caused only distress. *Wilkinson*, above, at [101].

[87]   Above n 8, at [98].

that it is plausible to hold psychiatric illness to be the likely upshot of a single incident of ogling. One is left wondering if the gross impropriety of the defendant's behaviour has not smoothed the way for this conclusion, which is to say that the spirit of *Wilkinson* is still very much alive.[88]

---

[88]   However, note that in *A v Iorworth Hoare*, above n 85, the Court of Appeal declined to allow the parties to make new submissions on the basis of the tort in *Wilkinson* in light of *C v D*, saying, 'It seems preferable for the law to develop along conventional modern lines rather than through recourse to this obscure tort, whose jurisprudential basis remains unclear'.

22

Where Principle Meets Pragmatism: Tort Law in Post-Colonial Hong Kong

RICK GLOFCHESKI*

I. INTRODUCTION

TORT LAW IN Hong Kong is not widely known for its distinctiveness. Nor has the judiciary been thought to be particularly activist. Although it would not be entirely fair to say that Hong Kong case law has not had an impact in the past, those leading case law authorities that have enjoyed wide readership and application, in particular in the area of the duty and standard of care in negligence,[1] were cases heard in earlier days under colonial rule. They were cases decided by the Privy Council, which by virtue of its status was bound to attract attention in common law courts around the world.

Yet the conditions are now present for a change in the way that Hong Kong's jurisprudence is perceived. A picture is beginning to emerge of a more robust, reform-minded judiciary, spurred in part by the break from colonial ties, and the introduction of a constitution that rings eloquently of high ideals in terms of judicial independence, equality of persons and basic rights and freedoms.[2] Although the administration has indicated little

---

* Associate Professor, Faculty of Law, University of Hong Kong.

[1] *Edward Wong Finance Company Ltd v Johnson, Stokes & Master* [1984] AC 296 (PC) (standard of care); *Ng Chun-pui v Lee Chuen-tat* [1988] 2 HKLR 425 (PC) (*res ipsa loquitur*); see also *Tai Hing Cotton Mill v Liu Chong Bank* [1986] AC 80 (PC) (duty of care); *Yuen Kun Yeu v A-G of Hong Kong* [1988] AC 175 (PC) (duty of care); *Cheng Yuen v The Royal Hong Kong Golf Club* [1997] 11 HKLRD 1132 (PC) (master/servant relationship).

[2] The Basic Law of the Hong Kong Special Administrative Region of the People's Republic of China, enacted by the National Peoples' Congress in March 1990 took effect in Hong Kong on 1 July 1997. Sometimes referred to as Hong Kong's mini-constitution, it provides a legal framework for post-handover Hong Kong, and entrenches fundamental rights and freedoms.

interest in statutory reforms,[3] the judiciary has shown signs of a willingness to re-examine established principles and introduce reforms in the content of the common law, suited to changing local needs and demands.

This chapter will outline the nature and characteristics of Hong Kong tort law, and will make an argument for its emerging distinctiveness, and its potential as a relevant source of law for other jurisdictions. It will do so with reference to the tort actions most commonly litigated in Hong Kong, in particular, the negligence-based tort actions. General trends will be identified and analysed, with a focus on those tort actions where the newly established Court of Final Appeal, and to a lesser extent, the lower courts, have fashioned new and distinct tort law principles.

II.   THE COMMON LAW IN HONG KONG

In order to appreciate the current picture in Hong Kong tort law, or, for that matter, the law generally, it will be helpful to have an understanding of Hong Kong's recent constitutional history. While the transfer of sovereignty from Britain to China in 1997 is well known, or at least unlikely to have completely faded from memory, the precise status of the English common law in the post-colonial era is not. Although the controversy that pre-occupied some academics[4] and was expected to dog the courts[5] in the

---

[3] This is not so much a reflection of the current administration as it is the historical position. There has been little statutory intervention in tort law, recent exceptions being the three discrimination ordinances passed into law shortly before the 1997 transfer of sovereignty. These provide a tort law remedy for relevant discriminatory acts: the Sex Discrimination Ordinance (Cap 480), the Disability Discrimination Ordinance (Cap 487), and the Family Status Discrimination Ordinance (Cap 527). A plethora of Law Reform Commission Reports dating to the late-1990s, each containing a significant tort law dimension, continues to gather dust, with little prospect for implementation: 'Civil Liability for Unsafe Products' (1998), 'Stalking' (2000), 'Regulation of Debt Collection Practices' (2002), 'Civil Liability for Invasion of Privacy' (2004), and 'Privacy and Media Intrusion' (2004), all available at <http://www.hkreform.gov.hk/reports/index.htm> (date accessed: 28 June 2006). Moreover, there has not, in Hong Kong, been any suggestion that a wholesale review of accident compensation law is in order, as has happened in recent years in Australia and the United Kingdom.

[4] For an early analysis anticipating some of the concerns, see D Chang, 'Towards a Jurisprudence of a Third Kind: One Country, Two Systems' (1988) 20 *Journal of International Law, Case Western Reserve*, 99. Regarding the binding effect of House of Lords and Privy Council decisions, see P Wesley-Smith, 'The Common Law of England in the Special Administrative Region' in Raymond Wacks (ed), *Hong Kong, China and 1997: Essays in Legal Theory* (Hong Kong, Hong Kong University Press, 1993) 5-40. For the argument that the common law which was in force at midnight on 30 June 1997 is the common law in the Special Administrative Region, see P Wesley-Smith, 'The Content of the Common Law in Hong Kong' in Raymond Wacks (ed) *The New Legal Order in Hong Kong* (Hong Kong, Hong Kong University Press, 1999) 9-39. See also Y Ghai, 'The Continuity of Laws and Legal Rights and Obligations in the SAR' (1997) 27 *Hong Kong Law Journal* 136; and A Chen, 'Hong Kong's Legal System after the 1997 Handover' (2001) 35 *Kobe University Law Review* 49.

immediate post-1997 period has given way to practicalities and all but dissipated, a few facts are in need of clarification.

As a relatively small jurisdiction that does not generate a huge volume of tort case law—and therefore lacks a full complement of precedents to guide the courts in the myriad fact patterns that emerge in the context of tort law—it is not surprising that the Hong Kong courts have generally followed the lead of the House of Lords in determining the content of tort law. Indeed, there can be little doubt that prior to 1 July 1997, they were obliged to do so, except in so far as such law was shown to be inapplicable to local circumstances.[6] Perhaps for this reason Hong Kong courts have never been known for their activism. They have rarely strayed from English authorities, and have all but shunned the common law as it has developed elsewhere in Asia. The practice has been to accept on its terms the tort law as developed in England, and so it is that, until recently, there has never been a serious judicial pronouncement in Hong Kong tort law that has deviated from the official position in the House of Lords or Privy Council.

With the 1997 change of sovereignty, the way was cleared for Hong Kong to develop the law without strict adherence to English precedents, in a way that was conducive to local needs and the expectations of Hong Kong's citizens. Although Article 8 of the Basic Law continues the application of the common law, Article 84 expressly authorises the court to refer to precedents of other common law jurisdictions. Certainly, the Court of Final Appeal, the court that replaced the Privy Council as the court of final adjudication,[7] is no longer bound by House of Lords decisions in developing the common law of Hong Kong.[8]

---

[5] See in particular *HKSAR v Ma Wai-kwan* [1997] 2 HKC 315 (CA).

[6] See s 3(1) of the Application of English Law Ordinance (Cap 88, Laws of Hong Kong), repealed in 1997. Hong Kong courts adopted a strict approach to this provision. English common law would be rejected only if its application would cause injustice or oppression: P Wesley-Smith, *An Introduction to the Hong Kong Legal System*, 3rd edn (Hong Kong, Hong Kong University Press, 1998) 43.

[7] The court comprises permanent judges from Hong Kong, as well as a panel of non-permanent judges, some of whom have held high judicial office or practiced in Hong Kong, and some of whom are foreign judges who have neither held office nor lived in Hong Kong but who sit or have sat on courts of unlimited jurisdiction in other common law jurisdictions: Hong Kong Court of Final Appeal Ordinance 1997 (Cap 484) s 12 (3). See also Art 82 of the Basic Law. The current panel of foreign judges consists of Sir Anthony Mason, Lord Cooke of Thorndon, Lord Hoffmann, Sir Gerard Brennan, Sir Thomas Eichelbaum, Lord Millett, Lord Woolf, Lord Scott and Sir Ivor Richardson. See Hong Kong Judiciary website <http://www.judiciary.gov.hk/en/organization/judges.htm> (date accessed: 26 June 2006).

[8] See, eg, *Tang Siu Man v HKSAR (No 2)* [1998] 1 HKLRD 350 (CFA) 368, where the Court of Final Appeal rejected as inapplicable to Hong Kong the relevant House of Lords authority on a trial judge's directions to the jury regarding the admissibility of good character evidence in a criminal trial; and see the dicta of Nazareth NPJ in *Bank of East Asia Ltd v Tsien Wui Marble Factory Ltd* [2000] 1 HKLRD 268 (CFA). However, not all members of the

III.   NEGLIGENCE

It has long been accepted that when applying the reasonable person standard in Hong Kong, it is the reasonable Hong Kong person that is contemplated, but does this imply a different standard than would be applied, for instance, in England, the jurisdiction from which many of Hong Kong's precedents are taken?

The risk of injury by accident is an accepted fact of life in Hong Kong. This is in part a consequence of Hong Kong's limited space, extremely high population density and the close proximity in which Hong Kong's citizens conduct their various activities. On the streets and roads, congestion is amongst the worst in the world, whether of pedestrians or motor vehicles, resulting in countless accidents. On development sites, the construction of high-rise office and residential towers squeezed into tight plots of land with little room for manoeuvre frequently gives rise to accidents, endangering the workers and others on or near the site. Moreover, urban density contributes to the risk of epidemics, as witnessed in the 2003 episode of Severe Acute Respiratory Disease (SARS), where Hong Kong experienced the worst of the SARS impact.[9] In addition to this must be considered the influx of illegal migrant workers, principally from China, who fall into a legal grey area, and who are often poorly-trained and who are themselves prepared to take risks in the pursuit of an income more generous than that available in China, increases the risk of injury by accident.[10]

It is probably fair to say that Hong Kong is a risk-prone society. Its crowded conditions and hurried pace are conducive to its citizens taking chances in activities as routine as driving a car or crossing the street. A culture of risk-taking has evolved, in which even the government appears to have turned a blind eye. Characteristic examples include: the ubiquitous elderly citizen pushing a handcart down a busy thoroughfare; the motor-cyclist weaving through traffic while ignoring lane markings and traffic rules in order to reach the head of the queue; and the ad hoc and illegal mass pedestrianisation of roadways as a result of overflow from crowded

---

Court are so adventurous: 'Nor is it for this Court to impose what it considers to be the best solution or a solution better than that laid down by the House of Lords'. See *Bank of East Asia*, above, at 325 (Ching PJ).

[9] Litigation has recently been commenced by twelve Hospital Authority workers and a supermarket worker against their employers. One patient and the widow of a deceased patient have also commenced actions against hospitals. See P Moy, 'SARS-affected workers file first group writ for damages' *South China Morning Post* (Hong Kong, 15 February 15) C5; and P Moy, 'SARS widow sues Baptist Hospital for Damages' *South China Morning Post* (Hong Kong, 11 February 2006) C3.

[10] In 2005 alone 19,273 prosecutions were instituted against illegal migrant workers: Immigration Department website <http://www.immd.gov.hk/ehtml/facts_4.htm> (date accessed: 15 November 2006). The actual number of illegal migrant workers is of course likely to be much higher.

sidewalks in some of the busier parts of Hong Kong. All of these are common occurrences in Hong Kong, and all of them create great risks to the persons involved, risks that must be obvious to them. Risk-taking on such a scale is not as common in other developed societies. A question naturally arises: if a majority of people are willing to take the risk, does it become reasonable to do so? If the laws of a place are to reflect the social norms and expectations of that place, it might be reasonable to expect that the standards applied in Hong Kong are different than elsewhere.

Of course, the reasonable person is not to be mistaken for the 'average person'. Although the judge deciding a case is sure to be influenced by what most people do, and although common practice is important evidence of what is reasonable, popular habits can sometimes be misleading as an indicator of the standard of reasonable care. As stated by Roberts CJ in an early seat belt case, in determining the reasonable person standard:

> we are not talking about what the average man actually does. We are prepared to accept the submission of counsel that many drivers and passengers in Hong Kong do not fasten seat belts, even when these are fitted in the vehicles in which they are traveling. We are concerned with what, as a matter of prudence, the average man ought to do.[11]

Reasonableness is ultimately for the judge to decide, and if the majority of people have developed risky habits, the common practice may be rejected as the reasonable person standard.

What is reasonable in Hong Kong may not be so elsewhere, including England—the source of many of the precedents cited by Hong Kong judges. It is a matter of debate as to whether different standards of care prevail between Hong Kong and other common law jurisdictions, but given the vastly different geographic and demographic conditions that exist in Hong Kong, and given the hurried pace for which Hong Kong is famous, it is at least arguable that the reasonable person in Hong Kong will take greater risks than his or her counterparts elsewhere. Judicial acceptance of this fact can perhaps be inferred from the case law concerning motor vehicle accidents involving pedestrians where, fortunately for the pedestrians, it is, as a general rule, the (insured) drivers[12] who bear the legal responsibility for pedestrian adventurers on the streets of Hong Kong.[13]

---

[11] *Ho Wing Cheung v Liu Siu Fun & Another* [1980] HKLR 300 (CA) 304.

[12] Third party liability insurance is compulsory in Hong Kong: Motor Vehicles Insurance (Third Party Risks) Ordinance (Cap 272), s 4.

[13] See eg *Lee Hon Cheung v Chan Tang Kai Lin & Another* [1995] 3 HKC 640 (HC): a driver approaching a studded pedestrian crossing is under a higher degree of care and was held liable even where the pedestrian was crossing outside, although adjacent to, the pedestrian crossing. Moreover, a driver is not exonerated merely because the pedestrian crosses in disregard of the red light. In such circumstances, a driver is not entitled to a lower standard of care, and is not entitled to disregard the presence of pedestrians (*Cheung Bing Kai*

Despite, or perhaps because of the culture of risk-taking, Hong Kong courts have generally held firm in exacting high standards of defendants in their activities, perhaps in recognition of the risks taken by adventurous plaintiffs. There is no suggestion of a standard of the reasonable Hong Kong risk-taker, unless perhaps he or she is the plaintiff.

One development worthy of note is the tendency of courts in recent years to adopt a more objectively-based analysis in the determination of the standard of reasonable care. In particular, Hong Kong courts have signalled a move away from the application of an indeterminate reasonable person standard to one that more explicitly takes into account cost-benefit analysis, weighing risks against the cost to eliminate or reduce the risk. Cost-benefit analysis has been regularly applied in Hong Kong, in particular in cases involving employers' breach of duty to employees. In *Wong Wai Ming v Hospital Authority*,[14] a case involving an attack by a psychiatrically unbalanced person against a nurse working as a receptionist at a psychiatric clinic, the Hospital Authority was found negligent in not providing a physical barrier between its staff at the reception counter and the public area. In finding a breach of duty, Cheung J said:

> It is the duty of an employer, in considering whether some precaution should be taken against a foreseeable risk, to weigh, on the one hand, the magnitude of the risk, the likelihood of an accident happening and the possible seriousness of the consequences if an accident does happen, and on the other hand, the difficulty and expense and any other disadvantage of taking the precaution.[15]

Similarly, in the Court of Appeal decision in *Wong Kit Chun v Wishing Long Hong*,[16] a personal assistant was killed as a result of poor lighting while accompanying his employer on an early morning mountain trek in China. Unlike others on the trek, he had not been provided with a torch. In reaching the conclusion that the employer was in breach of his duty, Woo JA said:

> The standard of care is always imposed on an hypothetical ordinary employer of reasonable prudence and competence . . . Factors in determining the standard of

---

v Tsui Kam Hung (2001) HCPI 116 of 2000). A similar judicial attitude is applied to passengers on public transportation: where a bus passenger stood up before the bus had come to a stop, and fell and suffered injury when the bus suddenly halted, the driver was negligent, and the passenger not contributorily negligent (*Ip Yin Fun v The Kowloon Motor Bus Co* (1933) Ltd (1987) HCA 1624 of 1986). Pedestrianisation of roadways is a common enough occurrence, but a measure of the court's approach can be seen from the recent case of *Yeung Yuk Yiu v Cheung Tung Ho* (2006) HCPI 573 of 2004, in which a driver was found to be in breach of the duty of care owed to pedestrians walking on the pavement, one of whom suddenly stepped onto the roadway, into the path of the defendant's approaching car. In that case, the plaintiff was found to be 2/3 contributorily negligent.

14   [2000] 4 HKC 330 (CFI), affd [2001] 3 HKLRD 209 (CA).
15   *Ibid*, at 334.
16   [2000] 4 HKC 748 (CA), affd [2001] 3 HKLRD 100 (CFA).

care include magnitude of the risk, likelihood of the occurrence of the risk, and the cost required to reduce or extinguish such risk. The torch only cost RMB 18 each. It is difficult to justify saying that . . . the deceased had to walk on the path under shared illumination or no illumination.[17]

The cost-benefit approach to the standard of care in negligence is now deeply-entrenched, and has in recent years been applied beyond the duty of care owed by employers to employees, to a broad range of negligence activities,[18] reflecting not so much any theoretical construct of justice but more likely judicial pragmatism, in which, in all cases in which cost-benefit analysis is referred to, the (normally) insured defendant is found liable.

IV. WORKERS AND TORT LAW

If, as stated by Brennan CJ, the issues that arise in litigation broadly reflect contemporary social concerns,[19] then one can infer that occupational safety is a major concern in Hong Kong. In particular this is so on construction sites, where contractors are notorious for the haste with which projects are completed and corners cut, typically at the expense of workers' safety. Such cases dominate the reported and unreported decisions, and contribute to the development of legal principles in three tort actions: negligence, occupiers' liability and breach of statutory duty. There is evidence of an instrumentalist approach—tort law rules developed and interpreted to address the culture of risk that prevails in construction and industry.

A. Employers' Duty of Care

The tendency of courts to have regard to the risk-taking habits of its citizens, and the utilisation of cost-benefit analysis in determining liability in negligence, has already been noted. So too in the workplace the courts have achieved a high level of sophistication in setting the standard of care that applies to employers.

---

[17] *Ibid*, at 756-57.

[18] A cost-benefit analysis was applied in the case of an incompetent golfer whose wayward shot injured his caddy (*Chau Fung-Yee v Lee Chi-Ming* [2000] 2 HKLRD 690 (HC) (though the caddy was found 1/3 contributorily negligent); to a flat-owner who employed workmen to install a window, which crashed to the ground, injuring the plaintiff (*Wong Sau Chun v Ho Kam Chiu* (2000) HCPI 872 of 1996); and to a school, whose negligently maintained spring door crushed a student's finger (*Wong Shek Hung v Pentecostal Lam Hon Kwong School* (2001) DCPI 48 of 2000).

[19] Brennan CJ, 'Foreword' in NJ Mullany (ed) *Torts in the Nineties* (North Ryde, NSW, LBC Information Services, 1997).

In a recent case concerning a flight attendant injured when opening a drawer from a bar cart containing drinks, the Court of Final Appeal laid down with unusual precision a number of principles applicable to the determination of the employer's duty of care,[20] imposing some degree of order and guidance in this frequently litigated tort action. While acknowledging the four-fold nature of the duty, the court asserted that this is essentially a single duty of care in negligence. The court observed that the practice of judges and academics alike is to speak in open-ended terms of the matters that 'system of work' includes, and that there was no known attempt to provide anything like an exhaustive list. Although the court doubted whether any such attempt could ever be successful, it went on to provide an analysis worthy of text book adoption. A system of work must be instituted even where the work consists of a regular and uniform kind.[21] Regard must be had to the fact that some workers have to function 'in circumstances in which the dangers are obscured by repetition',[22] and under considerable pressure.[23] An employer must always have in mind 'not only the careful man, but also the man who is inattentive to such a degree as can normally be expected'.[24] Although a heavy onus lays upon a plaintiff who seeks to have condemned as unsafe a system which has been used for a long time, there was 'no warrant for insisting that a complaint against the employer's system can never be established unless the plaintiff manages to propose an acceptable alternative system'. It is relevant to see if the plaintiff can propose an alternative system, but the failure to do so does not preclude the court from finding the employer in breach of its duty. Moreover, the absence of any previous accident, although relevant, is not conclusive.[25]

B. Occupiers' Liability

The negligence-based tort of occupiers' liability is alive and well in Hong Kong, and has been interpreted creatively by the judiciary in its effort to ensure a remedy for injured workers. Cases concerning work site accidents in Hong Kong reveal a surprising judicial robustness in interpreting the law in such a way as to include a wide range of persons as occupiers. This tendency results from a judicial recognition of the inadequacies and

---

[20] *Cathay Pacific Airways Limited v Wong Sau Lai* [2006] 810 HKCU 1 (CFA).

[21] Citing CT Walton, *Charlesworth and Percy on Negligence*, 10th edn (London, Sweet & Maxwell, 2001) [10]-[64].

[22] Citing *General Cleaning Contractors Ltd v Christmas* [1953] AC 180 (HL) 190.

[23] In the same vein, 'there can be liability where the injured employee had to do things in a hurry even though there would have been none otherwise'.

[24] Citing *Smith v National Coal Board* [1967] 1 WLR 871 (HL) 873.

[25] On this analysis, the finding of liability by the courts below was affirmed (plaintiff 50% contributorily negligent).

uncertainties in those areas of the law pertaining to workers' safety. Moreover, the Hong Kong work site is often organised in such a way as to result in unclear legal relationships. Labourers and workers with basic skills are often designated by employers in the written contract as independent contractors in order to avoid the legal responsibilities that follow from an employer/employee relationship.[26] The situation is exacerbated by three other trends, each of them more generalized and experienced worldwide: the increasing modularity of the workforce, in which workers find themselves without an employer (in the traditional sense) against whom compensation can be sought; the trend toward outsourcing, in which employers achieve operational efficiencies but avoid common law obligations to workers by passing the burden to entities often less capable of ensuring worker safety and protection; and as has already been mentioned, the influx of illegal migrant workers, often poorly-trained, who may fall outside the law's protection, and who in any case are more willing to take risks. These phenomena require fresh judicial solutions. Occupiers' liability law can provide a means for the court to find a defendant who, although not the employer, is in a duty relationship with the worker, and is capable of paying.

There is a discernible tendency in Hong Kong toward expanding the reach of the Occupiers' Liability Ordinance[27] to apply to work site injuries that arise not so much from a state of the premises but from activities, including the system of work. And so an occupier who was not the employer was found liable under the Ordinance for injuries to a scaffolding worker caused by the absence of safety harnesses.[28] By framing what appear to be 'activity duties' as 'occupier duties', the range of potential defendants is widened.

In cases where it is not otherwise clear whether the plaintiff is an employee, protected by the common law and the high standards it imposes on employers, or where it is not otherwise clear who is the plaintiff's employer, the occupiers' liability regime can provide a remedy, so long as the plaintiff/worker can show that he or she was permitted to be there (an easy test to satisfy), and so long as he or she can point to a defendant— usually a contractor or contractors on the site, ideally with deep pockets who can be shown to be an occupier of the site, or of the equipment comprising the injury-causing hazard. In this area, judicial creativity is taxed but rises to the occasion.

The requirements for being deemed an occupier have been relaxed. Control over the premises is the primary condition required by the

---

[26] A practice documented as long ago as 1970s by J Rear in 'Self-employment in the Building Industry' (1972) 2 *Hong Kong Law Journal* 150.

[27] Occupiers' Liability Ordinance (Cap 314).

[28] *Wong Kwok Tung v Tsang Hin Ping* [2000] 59 HKCU 1 (HC).

common law in order to find a defendant to be an occupier.[29] In Hong Kong this requirement has been found satisfied on the basis of the defendant/contractor's permission to use the site or the defective equipment in question. This development actually predates the 1997 handover. A flooring subcontractor, not the deceased's employer, and not the owner of the defective hoist that caused the accident, but who had the right, with other subcontractors, to use the hoist, was found to be an occupier for the purposes of liability under the Ordinance.[30] In another case, the plaintiff construction worker's fingers were cut off while operating a shearing machine that had an unguarded blade. The defendant was not the principal contractor of the site, nor the owner of the shearing machine, but as a subsidiary of the site-owner, was permitted by its parent company to have access to the site and to use the machine. Although the identity of the plaintiff's employer was unclear, while on the site the plaintiff took instructions from the defendant. On the basis of its permission to use the machine, the first defendant was found to be an occupier of the machine.[31] Finally, in yet another case, scaffolding installed by contractors some years earlier for renovation purposes adjacent to the defendant's residential building had not been dismantled and had fallen into disrepair. The defendants, incorporated owners of the building,[32] were held responsible as occupiers for injuries to a workman who decided to go on the scaffolding in order to investigate a water leak. It was held that, having failed to take steps to remove the scaffolding, the incorporated owners became occupiers for the purposes of the Ordinance, in effect by default. They had acquired control even though they did little or nothing to exercise it.[33]

All of these cases demonstrate that the concept of occupier on the Hong Kong work site is not a static thing. The purposive approach taken by the court is actuated by the looseness of the arrangements which continues to prevail on the Hong Kong work site and which will often leave the worker without an effective remedy. This approach widens the field of entities that can be liable for a worker's injuries. The degree of control required for a finding of occupier is minimal. The criteria for occupier status have become almost indistinguishable with that required for visitor status.

---

[29] *Wheat v Lacon & Co Ltd* [1966] AC 552 (HL).

[30] *Cheung Hung Yuk v Chiu Chai* [1990] HKLY 514 (HC).

[31] *Wong Chi Shing v Argos Engineering & Heavy Industries Co Ltd* [1993] 1 HKC 598 (HC); similarly, see *Ma Hui Tung Kuk v Cheong Hing Ha Kee Construction Co Ltd* [1992] 2 HKC 391 (HC).

[32] 'Incorporated owners' is the legal entity consisting of the owners of the individual flats in a residential building. Each of the owners can be made liable for a judgment against the incorporated owners: see *Aberdeen Winner Investments Company Limited v Incorporated Owners of Albert House* [2004] 3 HKLRD 910, and the Building Management Ordinance (Cap 344) ss 7, 8 and 17.

[33] *Ta Xuong v Incorporated Owners of Sun Hing Building* [1997] 4 HKC 171 (CFI).

Permission to use the site or to use the piece of equipment seems to be sufficient, where the court is so minded, to constitute control for the purpose of imposing liability as occupier. And this result can follow despite the fact that the defendant is only one of many with that permission.

C. Breach of Statutory Duty

The tort action for breach of statutory duty has not been abolished in Hong Kong, and continues to provide a sure-fire remedy for workers whenever it can be called upon. In common with most of the developed world, the Hong Kong Special Administrative Region is a highly regulated society. Through legislation, both primary and subsidiary, the government makes rules and sets standards regarding the conduct of the many important risk-creating activities necessary to the functioning of a large and complex urban community. This regulatory regime is criminal or quasi-criminal in nature in that a contravention of the provisions is normally punishable by fine, with the possibility of imprisonment for the most serious offences. The threat of a penalty is meant to encourage compliance with the legislation, although it is not always effective in doing so.

As in England, the primary issue is whether a cause of action was intended by the legislature despite the legislation being silent on the subject. Outside of the field of industrial safety, the Hong Kong case law is befuddled by a range of often contradictory presumptions that more often than not lead to a finding of no liability.

In the field of industrial safety, however, the courts in Hong Kong will readily infer a legislative intention to create a civil cause of action for damages, a tradition that dates back as far as the 19th century, to cases such as *Groves v Lord Wimborne*.[34] The courts have been willing to do so in open contradiction with, and normally without any discussion of or even reference to, the principles in the cases concerned with inferring the intention of the legislature. A pro-active judiciary has developed a long tradition of safeguarding the interest of workers' safety through the breach of statutory duty action, in tacit acknowledgement of both the shortcomings of Hong Kong's on-site monitoring and enforcement regimes, and the idiosyncrasies of its statutory employees' compensation scheme.

It is true that industrial safety legislation benefits a specific class, but the cases in which a cause of action has been inferred invariably concern

---

[34] [1898] 2 QB 402 (CA). This is not to say that the action is confined to cases of industrial injury. For example, a breach of statutory duty action was successfully pursued by a foreign domestic helper to recover excessive fees charged in violation of the relevant regulations by the employment agency that placed her: *Estinah v Golden Hand Indonesian Employment Agency* [2001] 754 HKCU 1 (CFI).

legislation that provides penalties, sometimes hefty fines with the possibility of imprisonment, and which are normally in the form of subsidiary legislation. Moreover, other common law remedies are normally available, including negligence and often, occupiers' liability. Industrial safety legislation quite simply represents an exception to the courts' normally circumspect approach in determining the question of legislative intention to create a cause of action for breach of statutory duty. It is almost always pleaded as a cause of action in industrial injury cases, whether as the primary or alternative cause of action, and invariably succeeds.

V.   LIABILITY FOR THE WRONGS OF OTHERS

Hong Kong courts have in recent years developed rules that extend liability beyond the immediate tortfeasor, developing traditional doctrines and devising new ones as the reach of liability is extended. This has occurred on a number of fronts, signalling a judicial intention that sounds in wider notions of enterprise responsibility.

A.   Property Management Companies

A prominent example is in the field of cases concerning property management. In Hong Kong, almost the entirety of the population lives in multiple-ownership buildings managed by property management companies. A duty of care in negligence is routinely imposed on property management companies for damage or theft caused by a third party, without reference to any contractual obligations, and without the establishment of separate proximity factors. Only a 'high degree of foreseeability' of the theft or burglary is required for a duty of care to be owed, ensuring that private property, in this shared public context, is protected.

In *David James Howells v On Kui Development Co Ltd*,[35] the plaintiffs' flat was burgled during their absence from Hong Kong. At the time of the burglary, renovation work on the building was being carried out, and involved the erection of a scaffold, which facilitated the burglars' intrusion into the flat. The court rejected the argument that for liability to attach, the plaintiffs had to show a special relationship between the property managers and burglars, akin to the relationship between the Home Office and the borstal boys in *Home Office v Dorset Yacht Co Ltd*.[36] The court held that it was sufficient for a duty of care if there is a high degree of foreseeability that the damage will occur.

---

[35]   [1987] HKDCLR 47.
[36]   [1970] AC 1004 (HL).

In *Always Win Ltd v Autofit Ltd (Citybase Property Management Ltd, Third Party)*,[37] the defendant car repairers stored the plaintiff's car in its landlord's secured car park. Although the defendant locked the car doors and activated the anti-theft device, the car was stolen by unknown persons. Cheung J said that the only exception to the general rule of no liability for the acts of third parties was where there was a high degree of foreseeability that damage would occur as a result of the act or omission of the defendant. In that case, the court found such a high degree of foreseeability, in view of the large number of automobile thefts that had recently occurred at that car park, and found both the defendant car repairers and the landlord/owner of the car park under a duty of care to the plaintiff.[38]

Of course, the determination of the question of a sufficiently high degree of foreseeability will depend very much on the judge's view of the facts. In *Luk Ka-yin v Hang Yik Property Management Ltd*,[39] the property management company was found not to owe a duty of care in regard to the theft of a car belonging to one of the tenants, because in the circumstances, there was no high degree of foreseeability of theft. The risk of theft was no different than if the car had been parked on the street.

B. Liability of Principal for Agent's Torts

There would appear to be no general principle imposing liability on a principal for the torts of an agent. This seems to follow from the law's development confining vicarious liability to the employer/employee and car owner/driver situations. After all, servants are, in some respects, agents of their employers, yet the vicarious liability principle has been confined in the cases to the master/servant context. It has not been extended to agents generally. Negligent car drivers acting under the authority of the owner

---

[37] [1995] 2 HKC 48 (HC).

[38] To similar effect, see: *Reebok Trading (Far East) Ltd v Pokfulam Property Management Ltd* [1994] 3 HKC 1 (HC) (defendant property management company found to owe a duty of care to a tenant for the theft (by unknown persons) of his car, on the basis of the high degree of foreseeability that damage might occur (there had been four such thefts in the previous year)); *Ng Ka-ho v Kanic Property Management Ltd* (2001) DCCJ 17055 of 2000 (defendant property management company was found to be under a duty of care to the plaintiff who parked his car there under a contractual arrangement with the owner of the car parks, on the simple basis that 'it is reasonably foreseeable that loss or damage might occur to the plaintiff's property'). In all of the property management cases, the question of whether there was a breach of the duty of care owed is determined in the usual way, having regard to the adequacy of the precautions taken by the property management company in light of the degree of risk of theft in the circumstances of that case. The plaintiff does not always succeed.

[39] (1995) DCCJ 11374 of 1994.

may be a specific example of liability for an agent's torts,[40] but there is no generally recognised principle of vicarious liability for the torts of an agent.

One may well ask, is the vicarious liability principle restricted to the context of driving cars? From the dicta of Lord Wilberforce in *Morgans v Launchbury*,[41] it would seem not. Vicarious liability attached to the use of horse-drawn carriages in an era that pre-dated the invention of motor vehicles. According to Lord Wilberforce, the principle applies to chattels generally.[42]

An employer's independent contractor can, in some circumstances, be an agent, but more often than not, is a principal in his own right. In any event, no general principle of vicarious liability for the torts of independent contractors has been developed. Yet, there has recently been some indication in Hong Kong of the emergence of a principle of liability for the torts of an agent.

According to the general law of agency, if an agent is authorised by the principal to perform a tortious act, liability should attach to the principal. Such an agent is acting within the scope of his or her authority, and so his or her act binds the principal. The same result would seem to follow where the principal subsequently ratifies the tortious conduct of an agent. Moreover, it has been held that where the agent is authorised to represent and speak for the principal, but the agent does so in a tortious (eg libellous) way, liability may attach to the principal.[43] Finally, it has been held that a principal is liable for the fraud of his or her agent acting within the scope of his or her authority, whether the fraud is committed for the

---

[40] See, eg, *Kwong Kwok Kin v Observatory Watch & Jewellery Co Ltd* [1987] 3 HKC 138 (CA). Indeed, it has been held that a defendant who has entrusted the car to another need not be the owner, in order for vicarious liability to attach. It is enough if the driver is driving in a genuine representative capacity as agent for and on behalf of the principal, whether or not the owner, for vicarious liability to attach: *So Wing Kwong v Cheng Chi Kwong* [1999] 3 HKLRD 689 (CFI) (defendant, who had borrowed the car, and entrusted it to a restaurant valet service, held vicariously liable for plaintiff's injuries). Moreover, the court held that the car owner's retention of the right to control the car was not a condition for vicarious liability to attach, or if it was, then a sufficient right to control is retained in the context of such a delegation to the driver. As Longley DJ said at 692: 'I am not satisfied that the retention of a right to control beyond that implicit in the delegation of a task or duty to an agent is a necessary element before vicarious liability can be established... . In other words, control is simply an alternative basis for vicarious liability'.

[41] [1973] AC 127 (HL) 135.

[42] *Ibid*, at 135. This view is to be contrasted with that of the majority of the High Court of Australia in *Scott v Davis* (2000) 204 CLR 333 (HCA), a case concerning the loan of a private airplane. The majority declined to extend the principle beyond the motor vehicle category. Gleeson CJ and McHugh J would have done so, although Gleeson CJ found no vicarious liability on the facts because the owner was not in the plane at the time of the accident, and was therefore not in a position to exert any control over the manner in which the pilot was flying the plane.

[43] *Colonial Mutual Life Assurance v Producers Assurance Co* (1931) 46 CLR 41 (HCA).

benefit of the principal or not.[44] In such cases, the agent's conduct is really the conduct of the principal, in whose representative capacity the agent is acting. To this extent, the liability is more properly characterised as personal rather than vicarious. However, the end result is very much like that in vicarious liability.

The problem of over-zealous debt collectors acting on behalf of creditors is endemic in Hong Kong. Indeed, a consultation paper on the topic was issued not long ago by the Law Reform Commission of Hong Kong.[45] Should a creditor be liable for the torts committed by a debt collector when attempting to collect a debt from a recalcitrant debtor?

In *Wong Wai Hing v Hui Wei Lee*[46] employees of a debt collection agency appointed by the defendant were found to have committed various assaults in the course of their attempts to collect debts apparently owed by the plaintiffs to the defendant. The plaintiffs sued the defendant for the assaults committed by the debt collectors. The trial judge found the defendant not liable for the assaults of the debt collector, as the defendant had not authorised such behaviour. On appeal, the Court of Appeal held otherwise. In the court's view, the defendant having asked the debt collection agency to represent her in the collection of the debt, the debt collection agency was her agent:

> The agent and its staff were representing the defendant when the plaintiffs were approached and spoken to . . .[The agent's staff] were doing that which the defendant had asked them to do, namely, to use colloquial terms, make such a nuisance of themselves that the plaintiff would pay the agent, who would receive the money on behalf of the defendant. In a general sense that was the task that they were engaged to do.[47]

Under this theory, liability is narrower than in vicarious liability. Liability would not extend to unauthorised modes of performing authorised acts. A principal is liable only for authorised acts, that is, those within the express or implied terms of the agency, including those, in the words of the court, that are 'so intimately representative of the principal that the principal

---

[44] See *Lloyd v Grace, Smith & Co* [1912] AC 716 (HL) where the solicitor's firm was held liable for the fraud perpetrated on a client by the firm's conveyancing clerk.

[45] See The Law Reform Commission of Hong Kong, 'The Regulation of Debt Collection Practices' (2000) <http://www.hkreform.gov.hk/en/publications/debt.htm> (date accessed: 28 June 2006).

[46] [2001] 1 HKLRD 736 (CA).

[47] *Ibid*, at 756-57. The result is all the more remarkable given that the defendant's contract with the debt collection agency permitted only lawful means of debt collection. The Court of Appeal viewed this contractual term not as limiting the 'sphere of agency' but only the mode in which the acts could be done. This part of the analysis comes perilously close to the principle that applies to employee/employer vicarious liability, leaving little distinction between the two forms of liability.

cannot be divorced from them'.[48] Assuming this narrower scope, there can be no doubt that the implications for agents generally are potentially very great, going far beyond the principles described in earlier case authorities.

C.   Employers' Vicarious Liability for the Torts of Employees

According to traditional doctrine, two requirements are necessary for vicarious liability, a master/servant relationship and a tort committed in the course of employment. Hong Kong courts have shown a tendency to interpret each of these conditions in innovative ways that tend to expand the scope of liability.

In keeping with developments elsewhere in the common law world, courts in Hong Kong are inclined toward a more flexible, pragmatic approach in characterising the relationship as one of master/servant as opposed to employer/independent contractor. Such an approach is becoming increasingly necessary, given the trend, not only in Hong Kong but worldwide, toward informal employment relationships. One may well ask why, in this changing economic environment, an injured plaintiff should be deprived of an action against the tortfeasor's employer simply because of internal employment arrangements put in place by the employer.

The court will look into the substance of the relationship, taking into consideration the peculiarities of the work and the realities of the workplace. The court will even disregard apparent 'agreements' between the worker and the employer, purporting to designate the relationship as one of independent contractor,[49] in order to prevent crafty employers from disregarding their general tort law obligations.

More interestingly, the Court of Final Appeal has recently extended the 'close connection' principle in *Lister v Hesley Hall*[50] far beyond what was required by that case, or, it is argued, what was intended by that case. The

---

[48]   The extension of liability to a principal for the torts of an agent, whether deliberately or negligently committed, poses special problems, and is justifiably restricted to narrower conditions than in the master/servant context. An accident that occurs when a servant negligently drives a vehicle while on a debt collection assignment will give rise to vicarious liability because the servant is acting in the course of the employment. An accident arising from an agent's negligent driving while on a similar mission should not give rise to the principal's liability. The agent is an independent contractor, whose driving ability is not subject to the training or control of the principal, and whose vehicle is not insured by the principal. The development of vicarious liability for the torts of an agent should proceed cautiously and incrementally, and within the limits imposed by the Court of Appeal in *Wong Wai Hing*.

[49]   *Lam Sik v Sen International Ventures Corp (HK) Ltd* [1994] 3 HKC 405 (Dist Ct). See also n 25 above and accompanying text.

[50]   [2002] 1 AC 215 (HL). In summary, the close connection principle requires that the employee's tort be so closely connected with the employment that it would be fair and just to

Hong Kong case, which included Lord Cooke of Thorndon on the panel, has the potential to have far-reaching consequences throughout the common law world.

In *Ming An Insurance Co (HK) Ltd v Ritz-Carlton Ltd*,[51] the plaintiffs were injured in an accident caused by the negligent driving of the defendant hotel's employee, who drove one of the hotel's courtesy cars in order to obtain some food for dinner. The employee was employed as a doorman, with occasional responsibilities as a car jockey to park cars for the hotel's customers, and to move the hotel's courtesy cars to make room for others. He was not otherwise employed or authorised to drive cars. In the lower courts his driving of the vehicle for the purpose of obtaining food was held to be outside of the course of his employment. The Court of Appeal agreed with the trial judge that the traditional Salmond formula, that would include within the course of employment 'a wrongful and unauthorised mode of doing some act authorised by the master',[52] was not satisfied, and in addition, with reference to the decision in *Lister v Hesley Hall*, found that the act in question was not sufficiently connected with the employment.

Despite the obvious poor fit with *Lister v Hesley Hall*, and for that matter *Bazley v Curry*,[53] on which the decision in *Lister* was based, the Court of Final Appeal unanimously found vicarious liability on the close connection principle propounded in *Lister v Hesley Hall*.

Bokhary PJ, giving the lead judgment (separate judgments were given by Litton NPJ and Mortimer NPJ), did not think that in most cases the close connection test was likely to lead to results different than under the traditional Salmond test.[54] He was of the view that the basic test for vicarious liability has never varied according to the type of tort, and noted that the judgments in *Lister v Hesley Hall*, although concerned with sexual assault, involved a consideration of negligence cases.

Moreover, he also noted that none of the judges in *Lister v Hesley Hall* confined their reasoning to cases of intentional wrongdoing, and that Lord Clyde expressly stated that the same approach should apply to negligence torts. To Bokhary PJ the close connection criterion was 'inherently just and fair for all cases of tort committed by an employee while engaged in an act not authorised by his employer ... the concept is a simple one which ought

---

hold the employer vicariously liable. In *Lister*, sexual assaults committed by a warden in charge of a home for boys with behavioural difficulties were found to be sufficiently connected to the employment.

[51] [2002] 1 HKLRD 844 (CFA) [*Ming An*].

[52] J Salmond, *The Law of Torts* (Steven and Haynes, London, 1907) 83.

[53] [1999] 2 SCR 534. I say 'poor fit' in the text since both cases concerned sexual assault against young persons in the charge of the employee.

[54] *Ming An*, above n 48, at 851-52.

not to be complicated by reading other requirements into it'.[55] He endorsed the approach of McLachlin J in *Bazley v Curry*, paraphrasing that 'the courts should openly confront the question of whether liability should lie against the employer, rather than obscuring the decision beneath semantic discussions of "scope of employment" and "mode of conduct"'.[56]

Bokhary PJ accepted that car jockeys were not authorised to drive limousines for the purpose of collecting food. However, he noted that car jockeys were authorised to drive limousines, albeit for a different purpose, and that in doing so they would occasionally be required to drive on the very road on which the accident took place. He also stressed that limousines were sometimes used for collecting food, albeit driven by licensed chauffeurs in the defendant's employ. He pointed out that the collecting of food for hotel staff served the hotel's purpose, in that it was in the interest of the hotel that staff be fed. For these reasons, Bokhary PJ was satisfied that the tort 'was so closely connected with [the] employment that it would be fair and just to hold the hotel company vicariously liable'.[57]

Although it is encouraging to see a more open approach to the question of the imposition of vicarious liability, Bokhary PJ's judgment is not without problems of its own. As with the judgments in *Lister v Hesley Hall*, it prompts the question whether the new test is really any more practical in setting the boundaries for vicarious liability. McLachlin J's test in *Bazley v Curry*, on which the decision in *Lister v Hesley Hall* relied, was proffered only in the context of intentional torts, and then only when precedent did not clearly settle the matter.[58] It is noteworthy that in deciding to impose vicarious liability, Bokhary PJ made no reference to the extensive line of precedent cases, in particular the frolic line of cases, preferring to reason according to the generalities of the new principle. Under his approach, judges are invited to 'openly confront' the question of vicarious liability on the basis of what justice and fairness requires, but with little guidance as to the criteria on which the assessment of close connection and justice and fairness should be based. It is an assessment that judges will have to make on a case-by-case basis, assessing the factual matrix according to their own perceptions of what is just and fair. However, it is submitted, something more precise is required than is provided by the *Lister v Hesley Hall* principle, if the new test is to apply to employee torts generally, and is to improve on the traditional approach.

---

[55]   *Ibid*, at 854.

[56]   *Ibid*.

[57]   *Ibid*, at 856. In addition, Bokhary PJ mentioned at 856, but 'did not consider important' the facts that the second defendant was in uniform when the accident happened, that it happened during work hours, and that he had set out from his place of employment.

[58]   *Bazley v Curry*, above n 51, at 559.

Certainly, something more precise is required, unless the current distribution of rights and responsibilities is to be significantly altered.

Treating the judgments as a whole, *Ming An* greatly expands the scope of employers' vicarious liability in its unmitigated search for deep pockets.[59] The law of vicarious liability in Hong Kong has been profoundly changed.[60]

VI.   INTENTIONAL TORTS

Trespassory tort actions in Hong Kong are encumbered by the same technicalities as apply in the English law. A difference is that they are buttressed by both a Bill of Rights,[61] which provides an independent tort action for abuses by the state (usually the police), and by the Basic Law,[62] which sounds in eloquent language in protecting individual freedoms and rights. There have been no independent developments in the area of trespassory torts against the person in Hong Kong that distinguish this area of the law from that in England. The same can be said for trespass against property, with one caveat; trespass to airspace may require a different rule in Hong Kong, where invasions of airspace occurring on construction sites by developers impinging on neighbouring land are routinely tolerated. Crowded conditions and over-development of property sites means there is little room for manoeuvre, making intrusions to airspace inevitable whenever development takes place. The rule of actionability per se in England[63] has been quietly supplanted for practical reasons by a rule tolerating such invasions.

Similarly, there have been no significant departures from English law in the area of economic torts.

However, the intentional tort action that takes its name from the case of *Wilkinson v Downton*[64] is worthy of a few observations, if only because of

---

[59] This despite the fact that even if the Court of Final Appeal did not find vicarious liability, the pedestrians would be paid by the limousine owner's insurers. The appeal was, in effect, a fight between two insurance companies.

[60] The preceding passage borrows from the arguments raised in R Glofcheski, 'A Frolic in the Law of Tort: Expanding the Scope of Employers' Liability' (2004) 12 *Tort Law Review* 18, 33-34.

[61] Bill of Rights Ordinance (Cap 383), enacted in 1991.

[62] See above n 2.

[63] See, eg, *Anchor Brewhouse Developments Ltd v Berkley House* [1987] 38 BLR 82 (Ch D).

[64] [1897] 2 QB 57 (QB). The court in *Wilkinson v Downton* recognised a cause of action in circumstances falling short of trespass. The harm (in that case psychiatric) did not result from a direct application of force (a requirement in a trespass action) but from a false story told by the defendant, and was not (in the usual sense of the term) 'intended'. The court found it sufficient for a cause of action that the defendant's conduct was wilfully calculated to cause harm of the sort that occurred such that the necessary intention should be imputed to him.

the impression left by Lord Hoffmann in *Wainwright v Home Office*[65] that the action has no leading role to play in the future of tort law. This is certainly not the law and practice in Hong Kong. The problem with Lord Hoffmann's thesis— namely, that negligence law can fill any gaps in the law regarding indirectly caused harm[66]—is that the negligence action is itself riddled with difficulties. A duty of care may well be difficult to prove, especially in actions against the state, and the damages, often in the form of mental injury, may well be found to be too remote according to negligence law formulations. This has led Hong Kong courts to pay rather more than lip service to the action in *Wilkinson v Downton*. The action has been raised successfully against abusive debt collectors,[67] and against the police,[68] and has been applied by the Court of Appeal in the post-*Wainwright* era in circumstances where a duty of care, in that case to a citizen under suspicion and investigation by the police, may very well have been difficult to prove.[69] These applications represent a pragmatic if tacit acknowledgement that the tort of negligence is not a panacea, and that there may be scope for a more generalised principle of liability for intentionally caused harms.

VII.   DEFAMATION

An assessment of recent developments in Hong Kong tort law and their implications for the wider common law world cannot be complete without reference to the tort of defamation. In *Cheng v Tse Wai-chun*,[70] Lord Nicholls, sitting as a non-permanent judge of the Court of Final Appeal, gave a judgment that resonates of greater freedoms in the area of speech, and in the process re-wrote the law concerning the fair comment defence in defamation.[71] After setting out the objective, 'outer limits' of the defence,[72]

---

[65]   [2004] 2 AC 406 (HL).

[66]   That is, negligence law in conjunction with the Protection from Harassment Act 1997 (UK). There is no such legislation in Hong Kong.

[67]   *Wong Kwai-fun v Li Fung* [1994] 1 HKC 549 (HC).

[68]   *Tso Yung v Cheng Yeung Hing* (2003) HCPI 1509 of 2000 (CFI). The plaintiff alleged that the police had wrongly threatened to prosecute her for obstructing justice, in order to pressure her to withdraw charges she intended to lay against an adversary. She alleged that she suffered psychiatric injury as a result of the police conduct. The court found insufficient intention on the part of the police to satisfy the requirements in *Wilkinson v Downton*, and dismissed her action. The case is currently on appeal to the Court of Appeal.

[69]   *Wong Tai Wai v Hong Kong Special Administrative Region* (2004) CACV 19 of 2003 (CA).

[70]   [2000] 3 HKLRD 418 (CFA).

[71]   For a fuller account of the significance of the decision, both for Hong Kong and the greater common law world, see J Cottrell, 'Fair Comment, Judges and Politics in Hong Kong' (2003) 27 *Melbourne University Law Review* 33.

[72]   These are: the comment must be on a matter of public interest; the statement must be recognisable as comment, as opposed to an imputation of fact; the comment must be based on

Lord Nicholls proceeded to explain the true meaning of malice, which if proved by the plaintiff has the effect of defeating the defence. In a clear departure from authority, Lord Nicholls said that it matters not whether the defendant was actuated by other motives, such as spite or ill-will, in making the statement. Under his formulation, malice can only be proved if the defendant did not honestly believe the truth of his comment. In reaching this conclusion Lord Nicholls shifted the balance between free speech and protection of reputation decidedly in favour of the former, at a time when basic rights and freedoms were the cause of considerable anxiety in post-handover Hong Kong. The decision, although not the final word on the subject, and far from being clear of complications,[73] has implications for the wider common law, and has already been cited in numerous English decisions and accepted as applicable in most of them.[74]

The law of defamation is in a state of transition, and the House of Lords hinted at this in its landmark decision in *Reynolds v Times Newspapers Ltd*, where the possibility of a wider freedom of speech for the media was contemplated in the context of the defence of qualified privilege.[75] In that case the House of Lords was concerned with reportage on political matters, but the Court of First Instance in Hong Kong recently applied Lord Nicholls' reasoning to newspaper reportage concerned with the mundane issue of the quality of service of a hair dressing salon.[76] In Hong Kong at least, with its post-1997 anxiety about rights and freedoms, the trend is clearly in favour of lifting the traditional restrictions imposed by the law of defamation on free speech.

VIII. CONCLUSION

The common law has planted roots in diverse places, and in each place it develops according to established principles but with regard to local conditions. In Hong Kong, with its peculiar and ambiguous political landscape, conditions are ripe for the development of tort law principles appropriate to these conditions. The courts, only recently de-linked from United Kingdom authority, have signalled a willingness to push the limits of previously accepted doctrine to new boundaries. This is particularly evident in the body of case law concerned with workers' safety, but is

---

facts which are true or are protected by privilege; the comment must indicate the facts on which it is based; and the comment must be one which could have been made by an honest person, however prejudiced he might be, and however exaggerated or obstinate his views.

[73] See, eg, T Weir, *A Casebook on Tort*, 10th edn (London, Sweet & Maxwell, 2004) 562.

[74] See, eg, *Branson v Bower* [2002] QB 737 (QB) (discussed by Weir, above) and more recently *Lowe v Associated Newspapers Ltd* [2006] 3 All ER 357 (QB).

[75] [2001] 2 AC 127 (HL).

[76] *Cutting de Heart v Sun News Ltd* [2005] 3 HKLRD 133 (CFI).

evident throughout tort law. As an emerging democracy there is a sense of urgency for the courts to get it right, and the trend is very much in favour of entrenching protections, be they of personal safety, or of basic rights such as free speech. This sense of urgency derives from circumstances that extend beyond merely local phenomena to more global trends taking place, particularly in the workplace. Established principles are very much under the microscope, not only with a view to ensuring that they meet local needs and conditions, but that they are right on their own terms. Although these developments are not without complications, and it may be too early to justify any optimistic assessment, this new-found spirit of judicial independence and adventurousness can only augur well for Hong Kong and may very well provide lessons for the rest of the common law world.

Epilogue

THE ARTICLES IN this book were presented as papers at a conference hosted at the University of Western Ontario on June 9-10, 2006. At the conference dinner, Stephen Todd of the University of Canterbury and the University of Nottingham was presented with the John G. Fleming Award for his contributions to the law of tort. His acceptance speech was highlighted by his singing of the song below, with the new lyrics he had written for the occasion. The song brought the house down and was followed by waves of applause.

TORT LAW

(To the tune of 'Go West' by the Village People[1])
   Together, we will sing a song
   Concerning a new civil wrong
   Our plaintiff, Mrs Donoghue
   In Paisley with her friend so true
   Wellmeadow café they did meet
   And ordered there a special treat
   Ice cream with finest ginger ale
   But added was a well brewed snail
   'No more', cried Mrs Donoghue
   'No more, I'm starting feeling blue
   No more, I think it's poisoned juice
   No more, and now my bowels are loose'
   She gasped and screamed and sobbed and groaned

---

[1] Written by Jacques Morali, Henri Belolo and Victor Willis. Released as a single and as Track 2 on 'Go West' (Casablanca US 1979), re-released on compact disc (Polygram US 1996). The song is included in several collections of the Village People's music, including the compact disc '20th Century Masters: The Millennium Collection: The Best of Village People' (Universal US 2001). The song was a bigger hit when covered by the Pet Shop Boys on a compact disc single (US 1993) and as Track 12 on 'Very' (Parlophone UK 1993). For more on the proper citation of popular music in legal writing, see V Black and D Fraser, 'Cites for Sore Ears (A Paper Moon)' (1993) 16 *Dalhousie Law Journal* 217.

She howled and yelled and wailed and moaned
She sicked, and then she sicked some more
Fell down, gurgling on the floor
And so she brought a claim at law
'Gainst brewer of the ginger beer
A tort she said it ought to be
In case of such calamity
An action in the courts was planned
Lord Atkin took a noble stand
'There should be liability
If maker is not neighbourly'
And so the manufacturer
Must pay for snails mixed in the beer
He must endeavour to ensure
That bugs don't make his drinks impure
Lord A, his eye on Mrs D
Rewarded her most handsomely
Two hundred pounds awarded so
Our May, her winnings she could blow[2]
Tort law

---

[2] Of course, the case went to the House of Lords on the preliminary question of whether Mrs Donoghue's claim was well-founded in law. Geoffrey Lewis cites Lord Normand, who as Solicitor-General for Scotland had argued the appeal for the defender, as stating that the defender died soon after the House of Lords decided the point, that the pursuer did not move to have the defender's executor added as a party, and that there were no further proceedings: G Lewis, *Lord Atkin* (Oxford, Hart Publishing Ltd, 1999) 52-53. In RVF Heuston and RA Buckley, *Salmond and Heuston on the Law of Torts*, 21st edn (London, Sweet & Maxwell Ltd, 1996) 297, n 37, we are told that the pursuer compromised the action for £200. See also the discussion by A Rodger, 'Mrs Donoghue and Alfenus Varus' [1988] *Current Legal Problems* 1, 9, who concludes that Mrs Donoghue was exceedingly poor and that if she really did recover the £200 then the settlement must have seemed like riches indeed.

Index

References to footnotes only have the letter 'n' following the page reference.

SA

346.
03
EME

500116826X